MACROECONOMICS

Theory • Policy • Application

A. Nag

Published by
ATLANTIC
PUBLISHERS & DISTRIBUTORS (P) LTD
7/22, Ansari Road, Darya Ganj, New Delhi-110002
Phones : +91-11-40775252, 40775214, 23273880, 23275880
Fax : +91-11-23285873
Web : www.atlanticbooks.com
E-mail : orders@atlanticbooks.com

Printed & bound in India by Atlantic Print Services

Dedicated to

My Father Late R.M. Nag
Who unfailingly cherished
the cause of education

Preface

In the market, there are many books on macroeconomics which have different objectives, approaches, and coverage of subject matter or content. Some are written for general reading in macroeconomics; some are meant as reference books; and some are designed as textbooks. Those proposed as textbooks also have different degrees of suitability or success in terms of approach, coverage of syllabus, development of theories, policies, and also applications.

Approach of the Present Book

The present book has been designed keeping in mind some of the limitations of the existing Indian books available in the market. It has been designed as a textbook for B.A. (Hons.) in Economics and B.Com. (Hons.). A condensed course (mentioned later) within the complete book would be equally suitable for B.A. (Pass), B.Com. (Pass), and MBA programmes. Since the book follows UGC syllabus or curriculum, all universities/colleges following UGC curriculum will find it appropriate as a textbook.

Development of the Text

In a book on economics, particularly macroeconomics, development or sequence of the topics is very important. The chapters (and sections and sub-sections) covering certain topics should be developed in a logical and sequential pattern for clear and easy understanding of the subject matter by the students. When the students read a particular chapter, it requires their understanding and knowledge of the previous chapter(s). Therefore, logical development of the text is essential.

Structure of the Book

The book has been structured keeping in mind the approach and logical development of the text. The book has been developed in 8 parts including 25 chapters, each dealing with a distinct area of macroeconomics. In Part I, in addition to introducing the subject matter of macroeconomics, basic concepts in macroeconomics have been explained (Chapter 1). These concepts help understanding of macroeconomic analysis undertaken in later parts and chapters. Part I (Chapter 2) also deals with classical theory and Keynesian economics which provide the foundation of macroeconomic thought and analysis.

Part II is devoted to national income determination and related aggregates—starting point for detailed macroeconomic analysis. These include concept and measurement of national income

(Chapter 3), consumption function analysis (Chapter 4), and investment decisions (Chapter 5). These also include the Keynesian theory of income determination—the basic and the extended models including the government sector and the foreign sector (Chapters, 6, 7, and 8).

In addition to the three basic macroeconomic variables—national income, aggregate consumption, and investment—key macroeconomic issues relate to aggregate demand, aggregate supply, economic fluctuations or business cycles, inflation and income distribution, poverty, and unemployment. The concepts, theories, and policies related to these have been analysed in Part-III (Chapters 9, 10, and 11) and Part-IV (Chapters 12 and 13). In Chapter 9, production function, aggregate demand, aggregate supply, and market equilibrium have been discussed. Income distribution, inequality, and poverty, with special reference to India, have been analysed in Chapter 10. Unemployment (Meaning, Measurement, Impact) has also been discussed with special reference to India in Chapter 11. Business cycles and anti-cyclical or stabilisation policies and measures have been separately discussed in Chapter 12 in two parts (A and B) to give necessary focus to the issues. Inflation—causes and control—has been analysed in Chapter 13.

In Part V of the book, the monetary sector or system and the real sector of the economy have been introduced. The monetary system has been covered through two Chapters (14 and 15). In Chapter 14, economic definition of 'money' and demand for and supply of money have been discussed including the quantity theory of money and the Cambridge equation. Chapter 15 deals with the monetary and credit system—commercial and central banking. Chapter 16 deals with a very important topic in macroeconomics—integration of the monetary and real sectors through IS-LM analysis for simultaneous determination of income and the rate of interest. Chapter 17 continues with the IS-LM analysis including the government sector and the foreign sector.

All these analyses lead to macroeconomic ratios and policies (Part-VI). Twelve important macroeconomic ratios including behavioural ratios, production structure ratios, and factor income ratios (distributive shares) have been explained in Chapter 18. Three types of macroeconomic policies—more commonly known monetary policy and fiscal policy, and, also physical policy—have been elaborately discussed in terms of their roles, effectiveness, and limitations in macroeconomic management (Chapters 19, 20, and 21). This also includes a comparative analysis of the roles of monetary and fiscal policies as anti-cyclical measures or instruments.

Analysis of macroeconomic thoughts, theories, and models undertaken so far has been essentially for a closed economy (except in Chapters 8 and 17). But, most of the modern economies are open with important international linkages through the foreign sector. International economics, foreign trade, and balance of payments have been discussed in Chapter 23 (Part-VIII). The foreign sector relates to external or international environment. In recent times, environmental factors are coming more into reckoning. Keeping this in view, macroeconomic environment, environmental economics, and interaction between macroeconomic environment and the business sector have been discussed in a separate chapter (Chapter 22).

Economic growth is the final objective of all countries and governments. Macroeconomic theories, models, and policy implementations should lead to economic growth with stability. Economic growth—meaning, theories, and models—and economic planning have been analysed in two separate parts (A and B) in Chapter 24.

In every field of study, new developments take place from time to time which either validate the old or existing thoughts or theories or give new perspectives or directions to the subject. The same is also true of macroeconomics. Developments in post-Keynesian macroeconomics have been many and varied. Major developments in macroeconomic thought including monetarism, supply side economics, and rational expectations theory have been discussed in Chapter 25 (Part-VIII).

At the end of the book, a glossary of Economic Terms—mini dictionary of economic terminologies—has been given for ready reference.

Condensed Course

B.A. (Pass), B.Com. (Pass), and MBA students need not go through the entire text. A condensed course is prescribed for them. These students may refer to Chapters 1, 3, 4, 5, 6, 10, 11, 12, 13, 14, 15, 19, 20, 23, and 24.

Distinctive Features of the Book

Distinctive features of the book, in comparison to the existing books in the market, are:

1. Separate analysis of macroeconomic ratios—a very important subject in macroeconomics (Chapter 18).
2. Separate analysis of physical policy (Chapter 21).
3. Separate analysis of macroeconomic environment and business—interrelations and interactions (Chapter 22).
4. Plenty of examples/illustrations from the Indian economy—this differentiates the book from foreign books which lack the Indian context.
5. Analysis of subjects (in chapters) is lucid (student friendly), precise, and focused, avoiding unnecessary elaborations/repetitions.
6. Macroeconomic database and sources—a new feature in the book mentioning sources and forms of official statistics for various macroeconomic variables or indicators (like income, consumption, price level, etc.). For any important macroeconomic data or information, these sources can be immediately consulted by the students.

Pedagogy

The text has been amply supported by appropriate pedagogical features.

In every chapter, the text is followed by review questions to test comprehension of the topics—theories, models, applications—by the students. Suggested reading mentioned at the end of the chapters is for supplementing the text with additional information.

In addition to these regular features, real life examples (mostly with reference to the Indian economy), problem solving, and applications have been incorporated wherever relevant or felt necessary. Applications are quantitative or algebraic solutions of the theoretical models.

A special pedagogical feature of the book is 'Macroeconomics: Knowledge Test (QUIZ)' given at the end of the text. Sixty two quizzes have been worked out to test the knowledge of the students in different fields of macroeconomics. At the end of the problems/quizzes, right answers or solutions have been provided so that knowledge of the students in macroeconomics is enriched.

Any suggestion for improvement of the book is welcome.

A. Nag

Contents

PART–I

INTRODUCTION AND OVERVIEW

This part is devoted to introduction to macroeconomics. The introduction includes discussion on the nature and importance of the study of macroeconomics also with reference to business management. The difference between macroeconomics and microeconomics has been explained. Some important macroeconomic concepts have been illustrated which would facilitate understanding of the subject matter of macroeconomics. Important stages in the development of macroeconomics over many decades and over three centuries, have also been discussed. All these have been covered in Chapter 1 in two parts (A and B). Chapter 2 deals with classical theory and Keynesian economics. Classical economics and Keynesian economics play key roles in the development of macroeconomics. One can even say that these are the foundations of the subject matter of macroeconomics. Therefore, an understanding of these two schools of thought is considered important in the beginning itself.

Chapter 1

Macroeconomics: Introduction and Concepts

A. INTRODUCTION AND SCOPE

WHAT IS ECONOMICS?

We start with the origin or meaning and significance of economics before we turn to macroeconomics.

The term 'economics' comes from two Greek words *oikon* and *nomos*; these two words together mean laws of households. This shows the significance or usefulness of economics to households, families, and, in general, to all human beings. But, economics is much more than this. This involves, in addition to households, firms and government and their decision making. These will be more clear if we go through the definitions of economics.

Economists have given different definitions of economics to explain its role and utility in the economy and society. We shall discuss here two basic definitions to understand its significance and scope. The first definition was given by Adam Smith—known as the father of economics—Karl Marx and others. The second definition came from the writings of neoclassical economists led by Lionel Robbins.

According to Adam Smith (1776), Karl Marx and others, economics is a social science which deals with human behaviour relating to production, exchange and consumption of goods and services (wealth).[1] The emphasis or focus was on *human behaviour, production* and *consumption.* The second definition, a distilled thought emerged in Lionel Robbins's book *An Essay on the Nature and Significance of Economic Science* (1932). According to this definition, economics is the analysis of universal type of problems of allocation of resources, which are given and versatile, among ends which are many and varied. The focus was on *allocation of resources* and *needs or ends*. The two definitions together explain the meaning and nature of economics including its different facets and implications.

Economics is concerned with production of goods and services; it involves allocation of resources both by firms and the government, resources are given or limited; consumer behaviour is involved; consumers create needs or demand which is varied in nature; this finally leads to consumption of goods and services; this brings in the market where goods are exchanged or bought and sold at different prices; over a period of time, growth of the market and economy is also involved.

1. Adam Smith's famous book is titled as *The Wealth of Nations*, published in 1776.

All these can be stated in another way/form in terms of six questions relating to decisions which economics answers or is intended to answer. The decision searching questions are:

1. **Production Decisions:** How much of different goods to produce? Who (firms) to produce what? What method or technique (labour-intensive or capital-intensive) to be used to produce these goods?
2. **Resource Allocation Decisions:** How are different resources (land, labour, capital and organisation or entrepreneurship) to be allocated to production of different goods and services? Who will decide the allocation of scarce resources—the firms or the government or both together?
3. **Exchange (including Price) Decisions:** Which goods to be exchanged (for money, i.e., sold) where (markets)? To whom (consumers) these goods are to be sold? What prices are to be charged for different goods?
4. **Consumption (Consumer) Decisions:** How much of different goods and services to be consumed? How to choose among the alternatives? What should be the right prices to be paid for different goods?
5. **Regulatory (Government) Decisions:** What role the government should play in allocation of scarce and non-renewable resources? How should the government regulate industry and trade? How should the government simultaneously promote industry, business and trade for growth and development of the country and benefit of society?
6. **Growth Decisions:** How to grow over time? What should be the growth policy? What should be the strategy in terms of balanced growth and unbalanced growth?

The above questions give a clear perspective of the various issues and situations economics has to address or deal with. Resources—land, labour, capital and organisation or entrepreneurship[2]—are always limited or scarce. In fact, *scarcity* is a fundamental phenomenon in economics or economic analysis. Because of scarcity of resources, allocation of those among different uses or alternatives is a matter of major decision-making problem for both firms and the government. This also implies choice among alternatives and 'opportunity cost'—the cost of foregoing an alternative choice. Because of this, everything that is scarce has a price, and, price governs or equalises demand and supply. Given the cost factor, price also determines profitability of a firm.

Scarcity also applies to consumer choice or decision or decision making. Consumers have limited resources, i.e., income to spend on various goods and services. If a consumer chooses to spend money (income) on particular goods and services, he (she) has to forego some other goods and services. So, there is a trade-off and scarcity always indicates or involves a trade-off. Also, given an income level, when a consumer spends more on consumption, less of his (her) income is kept for savings. Savings is required for the uncertain future.

Uncertainty is another important factor in decision making and economic analysis. Planning by firms for the future involves uncertainty. Uncertainty and risk go together. Risk and uncertainty are concomitant with business and profit (or loss). Government's planning for the economy also involves planning for an uncertain future. Uncertainty lies in various environmental factors which are not under control of either firms or the government.

WHAT IS MACROECONOMICS?

'Macro' is the concept of the aggregate. Macroeconomics, therefore, is the study of the aggregates; or rather, the study of economic phenomena at aggregate levels.

2. These are actually called the four factors of production.

Macroeconomics, then, deals with aggregate economic activity. It attempts to describe and explain the working of the economic system as a whole. It deals with variables such as total income of a country or a nation, total volume of output, consumption levels, savings and investment, employment levels and the general price level.

Macroeconomics provides answers to questions such as: what determines the level of output in the country? What are the factors which govern fluctuations in income or output? How are the general price level and changes in it determined? What are the functional relationships between consumption and income? What is the income generation process?

WHY MACROECONOMICS?

The answers to these questions are of great importance to students of economic and business management and corporate decision makers, planners and policy makers; to students primarily for learning the fundamentals of the macroeconomic system and policy makers as information on and guide to the functioning of the economy.

The concepts and estimates of national income or gross national product (GNP), for example, provide economists with a very useful tool to analyse the performance of an economy. An analysis of the composition of GNP also furnishes information about the size of the contribution of each sector of the economy to the GNP. Similarly, the national income and product estimates and aggregate investment or capital formation data give information about a nation's total earnings or income generation and growth during any given period of time.

Macroeconomics deals with some of the most difficult and challenging issues: unemployment, inflation, taxes, balanced and unbalanced budgets, role of the government in the economy, etc. It focusses attention on problems of growth and distribution of national income. Because of its focus on the distributional aspect of national income, study of macroeconomics also throws light on material well-being or economic welfare of the community or nation.

Study of macroeconomics or macroeconomic analysis is useful from both theoretical and practical points of view. On the theoretical side, macroeconomic analysis can help resolve some of the controversial theoretical issues such as the issue of neutrality of money—whether a change in the supply of money affects only the price level leaving the real variables, such as GNP, employment and interest rate unaffected, or whether it affects real variables also.

From the practical or policy point of view, macroeconomic analysis tells us how the various macroeconomic variables like GNP, total employment, general price level, wage rate, consumption, savings and investment levels, interest rate, etc., will be affected by a given change in government's spending or tax policy, the central bank's monetary policy, foreign exchange rate, labour supply, labour productivity, etc. When any one or more of these events occur, the macroeconomic model can be used to predict the quantitative impact of these events on the variable concerned.

MACROECONOMICS AND MICROECONOMICS

In contrast to macroeconomics that deals with aggregates, microeconomics is concerned with studies of economic variables or phenomena at disaggregated levels, i.e., at the level of individual unit. Microeconomics—'economics in the small'—studies the economic actions of individuals and firms.

Microeconomic theories are concerned with partial equilibrium analysis of consumer behaviour and firm's price-output determination under different market conditions and allocation of given economic resources to particular uses. Macroeconomic theory, on the other hand, employs general equilibrium analysis to study the determination of aggregate price, employment and output levels and fluctuations in these aggregate magnitudes.

For example, a microeconomist takes up the problem of determination of profit-maximising output of a firm for his study. He is interested in finding out what particular level of output out of the many possible options a firm must produce to maximise its total profit function or what particular factor combination a firm should use to produce a given quantity of output to minimise its total cost. Microeconomic theory helps him to find out the equilibrium of the firm at the point of optimum factor ratio. Similarly, microeconomics is concerned with the study of the manner in which an individual consumer allocates his given income among many goods and services available to him to maximise his total satisfaction or utility. Assuming the economy's total output or income as given, it attempts to analyse how total employment and income are distributed among individual firms and industries.

In contrast, for macroeconomics, aggregate output or income and related aggregates are important variables, whose size and changes in the size it aims to explain. Similarly, with regard to prices, while microeconomics regards relative prices of goods and services variable treating the general price level as given, macroeconomics studies the variability of the general price level, which is built on the prices in individual markets, by treating the relative prices as given.

MACROECONOMICS AND BUSINESS MANAGEMENT

It should be evident by now that the relationship between macroeconomics and microeconomics is more intimate than it may appear at first sight. The closeness of the relationship may be more clearly seen between macroeconomic variables or indicators and micro level business decisions or corporate management.

Managerial economics lays down the basic laws or principles of business or corporate behaviour in terms of cost concepts, laws of production and conditions of profit maximisation under various market conditions. In taking certain business decisions on the basis of the concepts, laws or methods laid down by managerial economics, the corporate manager should understand the prevailing economic environment and would normally take or would like to take decisions in conformity with various elements of the environment. It is this environment which macroeconomics provides in the form of various indicators and policy measures.

In planning certain production level and sales or before taking certain investment decisions on capacity or output expansion and growth, the corporate manager would like to know about the economic or business climate in the country. And, the best indicator of the state of the economy is national income, which is also the 'most macro of the macroeconomic concepts'. A growth or decline in national income or related aggregates as shown by macroeconomic analysis is taken as the most immediate and most authentic index of economic fluctuations. Other useful macroeconomic indicators are money supply, savings and investment levels, consumption levels, trade balance or balance of payments.

Besides macroeconomic indicators, the fiscal and monetary system including the interest rate and the tax structure, and the various monetary and fiscal policies have important bearing on business decisions at any point of time. A study of macroeconomics gives a clear understanding of the fundamentals of the fiscal and monetary systems; it tells how a change in the interest rate influences propensities to save and invest, and how changes in the rates and composition of taxes affect the spending habits of the individual and the community. All these are of direct relevance to corporate decision-making.

Another set of macroeconomic policy measures are the regulatory or physical controls like price controls, wage legislations, restrictive trade practices act, etc., which have a direct impact on corporate functioning. Any corporate management has to operate under the constraints and directives of these controls, and corporate policies and strategies have to be accordingly formulated. The corporate decision maker has to acquaint himself with the government's thinking on these controls which emanates from his close study of these measures and controls.

We have discussed above the various aspects of macroeconomic indicators and policy measures which have a bearing on corporate decision-making; these also demonstrate the relevance of the study of macroeconomic principles to business management and the link between macroeconomics and management studies.

DEVELOPMENT OF MACROECONOMICS

We now discuss the development, or rather evolution, of the subject matter of macroeconomics. This gives an idea of how macroeconomic theory has developed over more than three centuries into its present state. Development of macroeconomics can be broadly divided into four major stages. These stages have different roles or degrees of significance in the process of development of macroeconomic thought and analysis. The four stages are:

1. Classical macroeconomics
2. Neoclassical macroeconomics
3. Keynesian macroeconomics
4. Post-Keynesian macroeconomics

Macroeconomic analysis started with the physiocrats. The famous physiocratic economic table (*Tableau Economique*, 1758) was concerned with allocation of resources and the size of the net national product. The physiocrats introduced a fundamental concept of macroeconomic theory, namely that production creates income which constitutes the source from which the circular flow of aggregate income and expenditure is maintained in the economy.

Before we move to classical macroeconomics, we would make a mention of Adam Smith and his landmark book *An Enquiry into the Nature and Causes of Wealth of Nations* (1776) commonly or popularly known the *Wealth of Nations*. The origin of economics as a separate subject or discipline is often attributed to Adam Smith and *Wealth of Nations*. This is why he is sometimes called the 'father of economics'. Adam Smith defined economics as 'the science of wealth'. According to Adam Smith, economic growth (growth of national wealth) of a country depends on division of labour and specialisation.

CLASSICAL MACROECONOMICS[3]

Before Keynesian economics, classical economics of the classical school dominated economic thought and analysis. The classical economists did not develop any specific macroeconomic theory; their economic thoughts are contained in certain postulates regarding the economy and its functioning. The major postulates of classical economics are:

(a) Market forces of demand and supply should be allowed to operate freely.

(b) If this happens, there will be neither over-production nor under-production at the aggregate or macroeconomic level.

3. The term 'classical economics' does not refer to the economic thought of any one writer. It has to be comprehended, or rather distilled, from the writings of many economists. The leading members of this group of economists were David Ricardo (1772-1823), J.S. Mill (1773-1836) and J.B. Say (1767-1832).

(c) The economy will always be in full employment in the long-run; unemployment, if any, will be a short-term phenomenon.
(d) Because of neither over-production nor under-production and full employment, the economy will always be in equilibrium in the long-run.

Classical economics, assuming full employment, was primarily microeconomic theory concerned with the analysis of allocation of resources between different competing uses and determination of relative prices. But, it may not be correct to say that there was no classical macroeconomic theory concerned with the analysis of aggregate output, employment and general price level. The classicists had their own views on the theory of general price level distinguished from the theory of relative prices. In the classical economics, the quantity theory of money, the theory of growth and discussion about cyclical fluctuations—subjects which are important in modern macroeconomic theory—occupied significant place.

NEOCLASSICAL MACROECONOMICS

Led by Alfred Marshall, the neoclassical economists implicitly made the conclusions derived from Say's Law of Markets a premise of their analysis of value and distribution. Although Marshall's chief concern was with the explanation of determination of the commodity and factor relative prices, nevertheless he also discussed the relationship between the general price level (P), the quantity of money in circulation (M), the fraction of money which people hold in cash (K), and the amount of real output. He formulated the famous Cambridge or cash-balances equation of exchange of the quantity theory of money. Thus, in so far as Marshall developed the quantity theory of money, he contributed to the development of macroeconomics. In this, he was followed by his other Cambridge colleagues, namely Pigou and Robertson. Marshall however, failed to integrate the theory of money with the theory of income and output.

KEYNESIAN MACROECONOMICS

It was Keynes who successfully integrated the monetary theory with the theory of income, output and employment. Keynes's *General Theory*[4] (1936) is a very significant landmark in the development of macroeconomics and marks the beginning of modern macroeconomic analysis.[5]

The most distinguishing feature of Keynesian macroeconomics is its clear exposition of how an economy may be in equilibrium at less than full employment level. It meant an almost outright rejection of the classical economic theory which denied such a possibility.

This fundamental difference between the Keynesian and classical approaches is of vital importance from the point of view of economic policy. If the basic Keynesian argument, that, left to itself, the economy would not automatically attain full employment, is accepted, a positive role for the government, which Keynes envisages, also becomes acceptable. By giving a new direction to fiscal policy and by defending a massive public works programme by the government during depression, Keynesian economics has been responsible for the development of macroeconomic theory during the past five decades.

The most important contribution, however, of Keynes's *General Theory* to the development of macroeconomic theory is the clear and specific formulation of the consumption function. Other significant contributions of Keynes include the theory of the rate of interest indicating

4. The full title of the work is *General Theory of Employment Interest and Money* popularly known as *General Theory*.
5. Keynesian Economics is also called New Economics.

its great importance in the effective implementation of fiscal policy, the clear exposition of the concept of the marginal efficiency of capital and its vital relationship with business cycles, the multiplier analysis, the theory of money and prices and liquidity preference analysis.

POST-KEYNESIAN MACROECONOMICS

Keynes's thoughts on macroeconomic theory and analysis stimulated much of the later developments. Post-Keynesian developments in macroeconomics have been many and varied. Most of the developments have been in substance, either refinements or extensions or critique of basic Keynesian theories. Critical analysis or alternative theories have been prompted by limitations or insufficiency of Keynesian theories to explain source of the contemporary issues and developments.

Three main developments in post-Keynesian macroeconomics are:

(a) Monetarism
(b) Supply side economics
(c) Rational expectations theory

Monetarism

During 1970s, limitations of Keynesian theories were becoming apparent, or rather clear, to explain the problems of low growth, high unemployment and high rate of inflation in many developed countries. The failure of Keynesian fiscal theory or measures were becoming increasingly evident to solve these problems. This led to the growth of a new school of thought termed "monetarism". A group of economists called "monetarists" was led by Milton Friedman, a Nobel Laureate, who were the exponents or champions of monetarism.

The contention of monetarists is that role of money is key to stability of the economy, and, also economic growth (growth of national output or income) as against aggregate demand for real output as argued by the Keynesians. According to the monetarists, money supply is the prime determinant of output and employment, and, also the price level. This theory emphasised the role and need for better monetary management rather than demand management. This led to a long debate between the Keynesians and the monetarists. The debate continues.

Supply Side Economics

Stagflation[6] became characteristic of many economies during the '70s and early '80s. Keynesian economics could not explain stagflation in which both high unemployment and high rate of inflation coexisted. This led to the emergence of a new school of thought known as "supply side economics". Supply side economists, led by Arthur Laffer, focused on the role of supply side factors in the market to explain changes or fluctuations in output, employment and the price level.

Supply side economists argued that, given the aggregate demand curve, *supply shocks* in the form of either increase or decrease in supply, cause fluctuations in output, employment and the price level. This is explained through Laffer curve. According to the supply side economists, high rates of income tax work as disincentive to work more, save and invest. On the other hand, reduction is tax rates becomes an incentive to work more, save and invest. This leads to increase in output (aggregate supply), income and employment. This way, supply side economics can explain fluctuations in income and output, and, also work as anti-cyclical or stabilisation mechanism.

6. *Stagflation* characterises an economic situation in which stagnation in output and employment coexist with high rate of inflation.

Rational Expectations Theory

Rational expectations theory challenges the efficacy of conventional monetary and fiscal policies and instruments in producing economic stability. These policies and measures do not become effective because people—producers and consumers—anticipate such measures because of their *rational expectations* and regulate or adjust their behaviour accordingly. The rational expectations theory has been developed and popularised by Robert Lucas, a Nobel Laureate in economics.

The genesis of the rational expectations theory is as follows: producers, workers and consumers exhibit rational expectation and anticipation of government policies and actions. They have complete information about the prevailing economic situation of environment and the policies the government is likely to adopt and implement. Because of their rational expectations and anticipations, they take decisions in advance. Because of this, when the policies are actually implemented, they become largely ineffective. For example, if there is an inflationary situation in the economy, the government is likely to increase the rate of interest to discourage borrowing and spending. In anticipation, people—producers, workers and consumers—will borrow when the interest rate is still low so that when the interest rate is actually raised, it may not have the desired effect on borrowing and spending. This also implies inefficacy of the government's role in regulating the functioning of the economy.

Rational expectations theory is also known as new classical macroeconomics because the theory emphasises source of the theories or thoughts of classical economics like self-adjustment process of the economy and full employment.

Monetarism (modern monetarism), supply side economics and rational expectations theory will be analysed in detail in Chapter 25.

GROWING IMPORTANCE OF MACROECONOMICS

In the section on 'Why Macroeconomics?' discussed above, we had mentioned about the relevance and usefulness of the study of macroeconomics. In this section, we analyse the growing importance of macroeconomics in the current national and international perspective.

Interest in and importance of macroeconomics have increased significantly over the last few decades. Samuelson puts it like this: "no area of economics today is more vital.... than macroeconomics".[7]

Major factors which contribute to growing importance of macroeconomics are:

1. Increasing complexity of economic system(s)
2. Persistence of macroeconomic issues/problems
3. Frequency of economic fluctuations or business cycles
4. Growing need for government intervention in economic and market system
5. Formulation of government's economic policy
6. Growing of interface between macroeconomics and business decisions.

Increasing Complexity of Economic System(s)

Economic systems in different countries are becoming more complex. Various factors—both national and international—have contributed to this. Major contributory factors are:

7. P.A. Samuelson and W.D. Nordhaus, *Economics*, McGraw Hill Publishing Co., 1989, p. 76.

(a) Growing complexity of political and social systems;
(b) Increasing demand for sophisticated consumption goods or "conspicuous" consumption;
(c) Growing interdependence of economies—effect of globalisation;
(d) Increasing international transfer of capital, labour and technology;
(e) Growing pressure of international trade groups or regional formations.

These and such other factors and their repercussions on national economies call for high order of macroeconomic management both at national level and international level. This implies increasing demand for macroeconomic tools, techniques and policy instruments.

Persistence of Macroeconomic Issues/Problems

Increasing complexity of economic systems give rise to various macroeconomic issues or problems. There are also persistent or unsolved macroeconomic issues and problems in most of the countries. These relate to unemployment, income distribution or income inequality, inflation, recession, balance of payments, foreign exchange management, debt servicing, etc. These issues/problems exist in most of the developing countries, and, also some developed countries in different degrees or order.

These issues/problems are receiving increasing attention of international organisations like the IMF and the World Bank. International economists are seized with these. To resolve these issues/problems, macroeconomists and national governments have to play an increasingly important role. How well these are managed determine the political and economic success of a country.

Frequency of Economic Fluctuations or Business Cycles

Economic stability is key to economic success and growth. Frequent economic fluctuations disrupt stability. Economic or business fluctuations have become the biggest concern of modern market economies.

Different theories have been forwarded to explain the occurrence of business cycles. These will be discussed in Chapter 12. More theories or explanations may be forthcoming. But, none of these are able to adequately explain or forecast economic fluctuations. Such fluctuations disturb functioning of economic systems and planning of growth. The sub-prime crisis or global recession, 2008[8] had upset many economies.

To deal with unpredictable economic fluctuations, monetary and fiscal policies and instruments have been developed and are being applied. Some success has been achieved. But, much more requires to be done. Macroeconomics has to devise new methods and solutions.

Growing Need for Government Intervention in Economic and Market System

Failure of the market mechanism to effectively deal with economic fluctuations, inflation, recession, unemployment, etc. has necessitated government intervention in every country. Depending on the nature of economic systems, different national governments play different roles to manage the economies. Government intervention has delivered different results in different countries.

To be successful, government machinery or government system requires clear understanding of functioning of the economic system. The government also needs to adopt appropriate macroeconomic policies and instruments—whether monetary, fiscal or physical. This indicates an increasing role of macroeconomics to provide the right framework, perspective and direction.

8. Global Recession, 2008, will be discussed in Chapter 12 (Appendix).

Formulation of Government's Economic Policy

Government intervention and role imply, or, more appropriately, lead to formulation and implementation of government's economic policy. Formulation and implementation of government's economic policies emanate from macroeconomic base; or, we can even say that government's economic policies are essentially macroeconomic policies. This shows the significance of macroeconomics in government's policy formulation; and, this is increasing over the years.

Government's macroeconomic policies are expressed in the form of monetary policy, fiscal policy and, also, physical policy. These will be discussed in detail later (Chapters 19, 20 and 21). Government's formulation and implementation of economic policy depends heavily on these policies—whether to deal with recession, inflation or economic development. This is why the central bank of every country is staffed with high class macroeconomists.[9] Governments also have macroeconomists on their panels for policy and planning. The effectiveness or success of policy formulation and implementation depend, to a large extent, on how well they adopt or adapt inputs or lessons from macroeconomics. And, this is a continuous process.

Growing Interface between Macroeconomics and Business Decisions

In an earlier section, we had discussed the relationship between macroeconomics and business management. This is elaborated further here to highlight the close proximity or growing interface between macroeconomics and business decisions.

Like demography (subject of population studies), management is a hybrid or derived subject or discipline. Its origin depended on or borrowed heavily from economics, particularly macroeconomics. The relationship is becoming more intimate over time.

Business management or business decisions are largely guided or governed by business environment in the country which is primarily macroeconomic environment. This includes demand pattern or consumption levels, investment climate, inflationary or recessionary conditions, etc. Investment decisions are highly influenced by the prevailing rate of interest, rate of return and government's policy on new business ventures. Business diversification is also guided by such factors.

Business environment or macroeconomic environment keeps changing, and, with this, business conditions also change. For example, in India at present (2019), the business or macroeconomic environment is not very inviting or conducive, and, investment decisions are shy. This shows the growing interface or interaction between macroeconomics and business decisions.

Keeping the importance of this in view, a separate chapter (Chapter 22) on the subject has been included in this book.

LIMITATIONS OF MACROECONOMICS

The fact that importance of macroeconomics is growing does not mean that it has no limitations. Every subject or field of study has its own limitations. So has macroeconomics.

Major factors which are considered as limitations of macroeconomics are:

1. Macroeconomics/macroeconomic analysis depends on different assumptions;
2. Macroeconomic analysis or aggregates ignore or conceal micro-level variables or behaviours;
3. Macroeconomic analysis ignores structural factors or changes in the economy;

9. The central bank of a country is not a department of the government; it is an autonomous organisation. But, it is an integral part of government functioning.

4. Divergence between macroeconomic models and realities;
5. Macroeconomic analysis is more relevant for developed economies/countries than for developing economies/countries;
6. Estimation or measurement problem of macroeconomic variables or magnitudes.

These are explained or elaborated below.

Macroeconomics/Macroeconomic Analysis Depends on Different Assumptions: Macroeconomic analysis—in fact, all economic analysis including microeconomic analysis—is based on *ceteris paribus* assumption, i.e., other things being equal. Most often, pattern of movement of a particular macroeconomic variable, say, national income (GOP) is analysed assuming that many other variables or factors like economic environment remains unchanged. But, this is not generally true. Related macroeconomic variables and factors tend to vary simultaneously.

Macroeconomic Analysis or Aggregates Ignore or Conceal Micro-level Variables or Behaviours: Macroeconomic variables or magnitudes are aggregates and, these do not take into account micro-level factors or behaviours. Behaviours or propensities (of consumers, individuals) are micro-level factors and not macroeconomic phenomena. Let us take the case of consumption function. Aggregate consumption in a country is a macro variable. This does not reflect the differences in income levels, different tastes and preferences, castes, religious\affiliations of individual consumers which compose the aggregates. Let us take another example—of wages and employment. Macroeconomics considers the average wage level in the country. But, the average wage level is derived from wages of a heterogeneous cross-section of individuals in the country or society including managers or executives, office assistants, college and school teachers, nurses, etc. The average level does not properly or adequately reflect these individual variations or diversities. These tend to limit the value of macroeconomic or aggregative analysis.

Macroeconomic Analysis Ignores Structural Factors or Changes in the Economy: Let us explain this. Economic growth in a country may lead to the conclusion that the economy is performing well. But, high growth may be associated with structural change like high or excessive substitution of capital for labour resulting in displacement of labour or unemployment and/or transfer or redistribution of income from low-income to high-income segment of the population. Another example may be given. The general price level may be stable, but, there may be sectoral changes in the price structure; prices of agricultural goods may be decreasing, but, prices of industrial products may be increasing to balance the general price level. But, all these structural changes do not portray healthy economic and social trends.

Divergence between Macroeconomic Models and Realities: Macroeconomic models are mostly built in theoretical frameworks, and, these do not represent actual economic situations. Macroeconomic models, including forecasting models, are developed under controlled conditions or certain assumptions. Once the assumptions are relaxed or dropped, the models do not work. So, these become, at best, approximations to realities. This, in fact, is a general criticism against most of the models, whether macroeconomic or microeconomic. These create problems for policy makers.

Macroeconomic Analysis is more Relevant for Developed Economies/Countries than for Developing Economies/Countries: Macroeconomic theories, analyses and models have been developed mostly by economists in developed countries keeping the conditions in those countries in view. So, these are more suitable or appropriate for those countries than for developing countries or economies. Economic conditions in developing countries are significantly different from those in developed countries. Therefore, theories, analyses and models for these countries should be different from those for developed countries. Otherwise, the difference or gap between macroeconomic analysis and models and realities become more pronounced for these countries.

Estimation or Measurement Problem of Macroeconomic Variables or Magnitudes: It is generally recognised that major macroeconomic variables or magnitudes like national income (GDP), inflation, employment/unemployment are subject to estimation or measurement problem. J.R. Hicks puts it like this: "Most of the macro magnitudes which figure so largely in economic discussions (Gross National Product, Fixed Capital Investment, Balance of Payments, Employment—and so on) are subject to errors and (what is worse) to ambiguities."[10] In India, at present, questions are almost regularly being raised about authenticity or correctness of estimation or measurement of national income (GDP) and related aggregates by National Statistical Organisation (NSO).

We may summarise the limitations of macroeconomics in the words of Sir Eric Roll: "..... We may be in the danger of succumbing to 'macroeconomics' in economic policy: it is almost as if we had completed a cycle; and, having become used to the notion that government economic management had to rely on the economic analysis to which Keynes had introduced us, we began to realise its limitations and the need to add to it a more selective approach."[11]

Limitations of macroeconomics, however, do not minimise its importance in economic analysis of a country. It continues to play a vital role in economic management and growth and development of various countries—developed as well as developing.

B. BASIC MACROECONOMIC CONCEPTS

Any student of macroeconomics should acquaint himself or herself with some basic macroeconomic concepts which have direct relevance to, or bearing on, the study of macroeconomics. Twelve basic macroeconomic concepts are explained below.

OUTPUT AND INCOME

There is a general misconception or misunderstanding that 'output' is same as 'income'. This is not true.

"Income" is 'value added', 'output' is not. In fact, income is derived from output. This is the difference between the two. Let us explain this.

Output is produced by inputs—raw materials and intermediate products. Output is the final product. Output includes all raw materials and intermediate products. *Income or value added is equal to output minus all raw materials and intermediate products*. So, income eliminates the problem of double counting. Actually, income is the contribution of the four factors of production—land, labour capital and organisation or entrepreneurship.

This can be better explained with an example. Let us take the case of bread production. Bread is the output or final product. Basic raw material for this is wheat. Wheat is processed into flour; this an intermediate product. This is processed further to produce bread which is the final product. Income or value added from bread production is equal to

Income/value added = Bread *minus* flour *minus* wheat

---

10. *Capital and Growth*, Clarendon Press, 1965, p. 90.
11. R.G.D. Allen, *Macroeconomic Theory: A Mathematical Approach*, 1970, Preface, p. xii.

Let us explain this further with a numerical example. This is given in the table below:

Income/Value Added by Bread Production

Stage of Production	Value of Output	Cost/Value of Intermediate Products	Income/Value Added
Wheat	200	00	200
Flour	240	200	40
Bread	300	240	60
Total	740	440	300

As shown in the table, total value of output of bread is ₹ 740: wheat is ₹ 200, flour is ₹ 240, bread is ₹ 300.

Income or value added = ₹ 740–200–240 = ₹ 300

The difference between output and income or value added is more elaborately explained in Chapter 3.

VARIABLE AND PARAMETER

Dictionary of Economics and Business defines *variable* as "A term that can take different values".[12] A *parameter*, in contrast, does not take different values; it remains constant in an economic relationship or equation or analysis. For example, income, consumption, saving, investment are variables; parameters specify the relationship among these variables. In a consumption (C)-income (Y) relationship

$$C = a + b\,Y$$[13]

C and Y are variables and *a* and *b* are parameters.

In macroeconomic analysis, we study the behaviour or movements of variables like income, employment, price, consumption, savings, etc.

A variable can be a *dependent variable* or an *independent variable*. A variable is a *dependent variable* if its value depends on, or varies with, variation in the value of some other variable or variables. An *independent variable*, on the other hand, is one which determines the value of the dependent variable given certain values of the parameters. Variations in the independent variable(s) lead to changes or variations in the dependent variable. It should also be made clear that the dependent variable is always one, but, the independent variable can be single or multiple.

In the consumption-income relationship mentioned above, consumption (C) is the dependent variable and income (Y) is the independent variable.

EQUATION

An equation specifies the relationship between two or more variables—one dependent variable and the other (or others) independent variable or variables. The dependent variable is always on the left-hand side of the equation and the independent variable or variables are on the right-hand side. The relationship between consumption (C) and income (Y)

$$C = a + b\,Y$$

is an equation. C is the dependent variable, Y is the independent variable, and, they are linked through the parameters *a* and *b*.

12. S.E. Stiegeler (Ed.), *Dictionary of Economics and Business*, Gower Publishing Co., England, 1985, p. 448.
13. The consumption-income relationship or consumption function has been explained in Chapter 4.

An equation can also be called a functional relationship in which the dependent variable is a function of the independent variable. In the equation shown above, C is a function of Y.

An equation can be linear or non-linear. This is the form of the equation. A *linear equation* is of the form or shape of a straight line; a *non-linear equation* is of the form or shape of a curve. The equation $C = a + b\,Y$ is a linear equation.

Be it linear or non-linear, an equation can be written in a general functional form as, say

$$C = f(Y)$$

The specific form of the equation will determine the nature of the exact relationship.

AGGREGATION

Aggregation is basic to macroeconomics because macroeconomics is the study of aggregates. *Aggregation*, in simple terms, means 'summing up' or 'adding up'. This is more clearly explained here.

This can be done with the example of the household sector. Every household (micro level) in a country consumes goods and services of particular value during a particular period (month, quarter, half-year or year). If we add up the consumption of all the households (given the problems of aggregation or measurement), we get aggregate consumption, i.e., consumption at macro level. This is numerically shown in Table 1.1.

Table 1.1: Individual (Micro level) Consumption and Aggregate (Macro Level) Consumption of Households

Household	Consumption (₹)
Household 1	20,000
Household 2	40,000
Household 3	10,000
. . .	. . .
Household 10	30,000
Aggregate Consumption (Macro)	2,00,000

In reality, the number of households in a country are many more. Taking account of this, the relationship between consumption of individual households and aggregate consumption may be written in the form of a simple equation as

$$C = c_1 + c_2 + c_3 + \ldots + c_n$$

where C = Aggregate consumption

c_1 = consumption of household 1

c_2 = consumption of household 2

c_3 = consumption of household 3

and n is the number of households in the country. Using summation notation, this can be rewritten as

$$C = \sum_{i=1}^{n} c_i$$

The concept or principle of aggregation can also be explained through estimation of national income of a country. There are different approaches to estimation or determination of national income. We shall use the product approach. 'Product' here means 'value of final output' (this would be explained further in Chapter 3).

Every firm in the country produces some quantities of final output. If we multiply all these quantities by respective prices and add them up, we get national income. If we denote quantities of each of the goods and services produced in the country during a year as $Q_1, Q_2, Q_3 \ldots Q_n$ and their prices as $P_1, P_2, P_3 \ldots P_n$, then national income through aggregation is calculated as

National income (Y) = $P_1Q_1 + P_2Q_2 + P_3Q_3 + \ldots P_nQ_n$

where n stands for total number of final goods and services produced in the country.

By using summation notation, this may be rewritten as

$$C = \sum_{i=1}^{n} P_i Q_i$$

This is the principle or method of aggregation.

STOCK AND FLOW

The two most frequently used concepts, which are also of fundamental importance in economic analysis, are the concepts of 'stock' and 'flow'. The basic distinction between the two is that the stock variables are measured *at a given point of time,* while flow variables are measured *over a period of time.* The macro stock variables are total money supply, total bank deposits, wealth, debts, inventory, capital stocks, etc., while the flow variables include national income and output, consumption, investment, wages, profits, etc. Both stock and flow quantities are, however, generally expressed in money units. But, while stocks may be expressed as just 'rupees', the flows are expressed as 'rupees per month', 'rupees per year' or per some other time unit.

Between the two, flow variables are of greater significance and use in macroeconomic analysis. But, many times, it would be difficult, if not impossible, to define flows meaningfully or accurately without referring to stocks. In fact, in many cases, a net flow is measured as either the instantaneous rate of change of stock or as the change in stock occurring over a given period of time. For example, investment over any given time period is defined as the change in capital stock during the same period. Similarly, saving may be defined as an increase in net worth over a given period of time.

The distinction between stock and flow may be made more clear with some examples. Total deposit shown in a bank balance sheet, say on December 31, is a *stock* quantity. But, income of either a corporate body or a nation, either per month or per annum, is a *flow* concept. Total money supply is a stock quantity, but the change in money supply is a flow quantity.

This shows that there are certain macroeconomic variables which have both stock and flow magnitudes, e.g. money supply, while there are others which have only flow magnitudes, e.g. income, wages, dividends, etc.

CAPITAL AND INVESTMENT

Besides money supply, the other very important macroeconomic concept which has both stock and flow magnitudes is capital.

Capital, which is always measured at a point of time, is a stock concept while investment is the change in capital stock over a period of time. Let us make this point more clear.

Let us assume that K_t is total capital stock at any time point t and K_{t-1} was the capital stock at time t – 1. Investment (I_t) then, is defined as

$$I_t = K_t - K_{t-1}$$

It should also be stated to clear any doubts that 'investment' and 'capital formation' are synonymous words. Therefore, changes in capital stock may be designated as either investment or capital formation.

EX POST AND EX ANTE

These two terms are generally used in the context of savings and investment. *Ex ante* means 'planned' or 'desired'; *ex post* on the other hand, means 'actual' or 'realised'. Savings and investment are always equal *ex post,* although the two are not necessarily equal *ex ante. Ex post* saving can diverge from *ex ante* investment; likewise, *ex post* investment can be different from *ex ante* investment. But, in equilibrium (we will explain equilibrium) *ex post* savings and investment will be equal.

Ex ante and *ex post* magnitudes will be equal only when all the expectations or plans are realised.

EQUILIBRIUM

The concept of equilibrium, just referred to, is very fundamental to economics and economic analysis; and, therefore, an understanding of this concept is very necessary.

Equilibrium may be defined as 'a state of balance between two opposite forces', or a situation in which economic forces, as they exist at the time, have no tendency to change.

The concept is more extensively used in micro or managerial economics and the students of business management may get a clearer understanding of the concept through their study of managerial economics.

We will illustrate the concept here with the help of microeconomic demand and supply analysis. In a commodity market, a supply curve for the commodity shows the various quantities that would be supplied at various prices, and a demand curve,[14] shows the various quantities demanded at various prices. At the point of intersection of the two, the quantity demanded is equal to the quantity supplied and both the buyers and sellers are satisfied with the price. This is the equilibrium price, and, there will, generally, be no tendency for the price to change!

If there is a departure from the equilibrium situation caused by market forces and forces are so generated that equilibrium is not restored, then, equilibrium is said to be *unstable*. If, however, the market forces are such that, even if there is a departure from the equilibrium point, the original equilibrium will be restored through the interplay of demand and supply factors, then, equilibrium is said to be *stable*.

Equilibrium may also be general or partial. In *partial equilibrium* analysis, like the example given above, it is confined to a sector or market of the economy and everything else occurring in the economy outside the sector or market is assumed as constant. *General equilibrium* analysis,[15] on the other hand, assumes that everything depends on everything else. It emphasises the interdependence between different markets or sectors of the economy. General equilibrium indicates equilibrium in all the markets or sectors of the economy simultaneously.

MODEL

Economists, more often economic planners, make use of models to depict the functioning of a part or whole of the economic system. An understanding of the concept or meaning of a model

14. The supply curve is upward sloping and the demand curve is downward sloping, and therefore, there is a point of intersection.
15. The concept of general equilibrium analysis was pioneered by French engineering economist Leon Walras.

is, therefore, important. There have been various attempts to define a model by economists, econometricians and statisticians; but, there does not seem to be a single definition which has been accepted by all—not even all economists. We would, therefore, try to analytically describe a model or an economic model rather than exactly define it.

A *model*, or an economic model, generally means specification of the relationships or rather the interrelationships among the variables or events or phenomena under study; the specification should be explicit enough to enable us to study the behaviour of the variables or events under a variety of circumstances or assumptions and to draw conclusions or derive results which are economically meaningful.

In short, mostly, the economic models state assumptions, derive or specify relationships that inhere in the body of assumptions, and, derive conclusions from the relationships. Such definition or description of models include not only economic but also econometric models.

An economic model may be either a macroeconomic model attempting to depict the working of the economic system as a whole or a microeconomic model relating to a particular commodity, market or segment of the economy.

As an illustration of an economic model, we may state the simple equilibrium (micro) market model leading to the determination of market price. The conclusion that market price equates the supply and demand is the best known result of an equilibrium model. The model consists of a demand equation, a supply equation and a market clearing or equilibrium condition that the total quantity supplied eventually equals the total quantity demanded.[16]

All economic models are not equilibrium models. Many macroeconomic models are purely forecasting models where the concept or conditionality of equilibrium is not very pertinent or relevant.

STATICS AND DYNAMICS

Macroeconomic analysis or analysis of macroeconomic variables can be *static* or *dynamic*; the basic or fundamental difference between the two is time factor or change. *Static analysis* ignores the time factor or change, whereas *dynamic analysis* takes into account the time factor or change. This also means that static analysis takes place at a *point of time* and dynamic analysis takes place *over time*.

There are different definitions of economic dynamics, but, they all focus on the essential element of dynamic analysis, i.e., time. We mention here Baumol's definition: "Economic dynamics is the study of economic phenomena in relation to preceding and succeeding events".[17]

The definition shows that *dynamics* relates to the process of change. In contrast, *statics* pertains to stationary analysis.

---

16. A simple equilibrium micro market model may be expressed as

$Q_d = a - bP$ (Demand function)

$Q_s = c + dP$ (Supply function)

$Q_d = Q_s$ (Market clearing condition)

where Q_d, Q_s, and P stand for quantity demanded, quantity supplied and price, respectively. The relationships are assumed as linear (expressed as straight lines).

17. W.J. Baumol, *Economic Dynamics* (Third Edition), Macmillan, 1970, p. 4.

Between statics and dynamics, there is comparative statics. *Comparative statics* relates to analysis of economic variables or events at *two points of time*, say, the preceding year and the current year.[18] This makes possible some analysis of change.

Statics, comparative statics and dynamics can be applied to analysis of different macroeconomic variables like income, employment, price level. These can also be meaningfully applied to models and analysis of equilibrium positions.

TIME SERIES AND CROSS-SECTION

Time series and cross-section relate to data for economic or macroeconomic analysis.

A *time series*, as the name indicates, gives statistical information or data relating to movements of economic variables over time, say, months, quarters, years.[19] For example, we talk of or analyse movement of national income, employment, inflation, etc. over a period of time. Time series analysis helps to ascertain trends in the behaviour or movement of macroeconomic variables or events.

Cross-section analysis pertains to data relating to different or many members of the same population at a particular point or unit of time; for example, study of individuals, households, firms, industries, etc., during the same reference period.[20] In macroeconomics, cross-sectional studies may relate to income and revenue positions of different states, profit patterns in different industries, etc., in a country or inflation levels across countries during a particular year.

Sometimes, time series and cross-sectional data are combined for certain economic analysis. These are called "pooled" data. Often, pooled data provide a stronger base for economic or macroeconomic analysis.

CONTINUOUS AND PERIOD ANALYSIS

Analysis of macroeconomic variables can be continuous or period analysis. Both continuous analysis and period analysis are dynamic analyses. But, they differ in terms of use of the time factor. In *period analysis*, time is divided into successive discrete periods of equal intervals of units. In *continuous analysis*, time flows continuously: there is no legged relationship among the variables under consideration.

The differences between period analysis and continuous analysis can be better explained with an example. Let us take the case of investment multiplier. Investment multiplier has been discussed in Chapter 4.

In period analysis, the effect of a one-time increase in autonomous investment (i.e. investment not induced by income) on additional income generation is shown in Table 1.2.

Table 1.2: *Period Analysis:* Effect of One-time Increase in Investment on Additional Income Generation

Variable	Time Period						
	0	1	2	3	4	...... $t-1$	t
I	ΔI	$b\Delta I$	$b^2\Delta I$	$b^3\Delta I$	$b^4\Delta I$	... $b^{t-1}\Delta I$	$b^t\Delta I$
C	0	$b\Delta I$	$b^2\Delta I$	$b^3\Delta I$	$b^4\Delta I$	... $b^{t-1}\Delta I$	$b^t\Delta I$
Y	0	ΔI	$b\Delta I$	$b^2\Delta I$	$b^3\Delta I$	... $b^{t-2}\Delta I$	$b^{t-1}\Delta I$

18. See also Edward Shapiro, *Macroeconomic Analysis* (Fifth Edition), Galgotia Publications, New Delhi, 1984, pp. 61-62.
19. The famous Malthusian theory of population is based on decennial time series data of population and food supply.
20. Cross-sectional analysis is very common in consumer and household surveys.

I = Autonomous investment; C = consumption; Y = Income; b = Marginal propensity to consume; ΔI = Increase in autonomous investment. If we assume that ΔI = 100 and b = 0.8, additional income generation (ΔY) because of one-time increase in autonomous investment through period analysis is as below:

$\Delta Y = \Delta Y_1 + \Delta Y_2 + \Delta Y_3 + \ldots + \Delta Yt$

Or, $\Delta Y = \Delta I + b. \Delta I + b^2\Delta \ldots + b^{t-1} \Delta I$

$= 100 + 0.8 \times 100 \times 0.8^2 \times 100 + \ldots + 0.8^{t-1} \times 100$

= ₹ 500 crore

In continuous analysis, increase in autonomous investment is continuous over time and time (t) tends to ∝.

The effect of an increase in autonomous investment (ΔI) of ₹ 100 on additional income (ΔY) generation through continuous analysis (assuming b = 0.8) is shown in Table 1.3.

Table 1.3: *Continuous Analysis*: Effect of Increase in Investment on Additional Income Generation

1	100	0				100.0
2	100	80				180.0
3	100	80 + 64				244.0
4	100	80 + 64 + 51.2				295.2
5	100	80 + 64 + 51.2 + 41				336.2
6	100	80 + 64 + 51.2 + 41 + 32.8				369.0
7	100	80 + 64 + 51.2 + 41 + 32.8 + 26				395.0
8	100	80 + 64 + 51.2 + 41 + 32.8 + 26 + 20.8				415.8
...	...	...	...	...	...	...
...	...	...	...	...	...	...
...	...	...	...	...	...	...
t = ∝	100	80 + ...	...	...	... +0	500.0

Source: M.C Vaish, *Macroeconomic Analysis*, Allied Publishers, 1987, p. 220.

ACCOUNTING AND FUNCTIONAL RELATIONSHIP

In macroeconomics, the difference between accounting relationship and functional relationship is important.

An accounting relationship[21] is an identity. It is a relationship that is true by definition. Such a relationship is a *truism* or identity which holds in all cases by definition of the terms. For example, personal saving is equal to the difference between disposable personal income and personal expenditure. This is an accounting relationship which follows from the definition of saving and indicates nothing about the behaviour of savers. The statement that the total amount bought on a particular day is equal to the total amount sold on that day is also a mere identity. Similarly, the statement that the net production of an economy of final goods and services measured in money terms, or its net national product for any given period is identical with the total money expenditure incurred on those final goods and services expresses an accounting relationship.

21. This is also known as definitional relationship.

An accounting relationship is a tautology and may be expressed as:

Personal saving ≡ Disposable Personal Income – Personal Expenditure

It is to be noted that an accounting relationship is denoted by the equality sign (≡).

A functional relationship is different from an accounting relationship. Such a relationship is derived for economic explanation and analysis. Such a relationship may either be proved or disproved through empirical testing. For example, the familiar demand function is a *schedule* that relates the amount demanded to the price of a commodity. This demand schedule is a statement of the market behaviour of consumers or buyers and can be either verified or falsified by means of actual market observations. It is a verifiable or testable proposition. Similarly, the statement that aggregate consumption depends upon or is a function of aggregate income or national income is a testable relationship. This may be expressed in the form of the following equation:

$$C = a + bY$$

where C is aggregate consumption expenditure, a is a positive constant, Y is aggregate income and b is the constant proportion or ratio of income spent on consumption. The numerical value of b is positive, but less than one. For the linear consumption function, b is the familiar marginal propensity to consume. It should be noted that, in the equation, equality sign is expressed as '='.

Functional relationships which express certain empirical facts about individual or collective behaviour in the economic system are not necessarily true while the identity or accounting relationship must necessarily be so. Functional relationships derive their validity from the empirical observations that but this does not apply to accounting relationships.

TRANSACTION ANALYSIS[22]

In macroeconomics, we study transaction analysis to understand the pattern of transactions that take place between different sectors of the economy. Taking an economy with the household, business and government sectors, the transactions between these three classes of transactors may be summarised by means of the following transaction analysis matrix or flow-of-funds analysis (Table 1.4).

The transaction matrix or the flow-of-funds diagram shows the transactions which take place between three classes of transactors—households, business firms and government—in the economy. Moving across the row, we find the sales made by each transactor to the other transactors while a movement down the column shows the purchases made by each transactor from the other transactors. A cell-wise study of this matrix shows the following activities.

Cell 1 shows that the households sell their domestic labour services to other households. *Cell 2* shows that the households sell labour services to the business firms. They also sell to the firms old bonds (debentures) when the firms retire these bonds on maturity. *Cell 3* shows that the households sell labour services to the government. They also sell bonds to the government when the government retires these bonds on maturity. *Cell 4* (the sum of cells 1, 2 and 3) shows the total amount of money which flows into the household sector because of the sale of their labour services to themselves, to the firms and to the government and the sales of bonds to the business firms and the government.

22. This is mostly based on M.C. Vaish (1987), pp. 47-49.

Table 1.4: Transaction Matrix or Flow-of-Funds

	Sector	*Transactors Buy* Households	Firms	Government	*Funds Flow*
Transactors Sell	Households	1. Domestic labour services	2. Labour services, Retired bonds	3. Retired bonds Labour services	4. Total money inflow to households. Sum of 1, 2 and 3
	Firms	5. Consumer goods New bonds	6. Investment goods	7. Collective consumption and investment goods	8. Total money inflow to firms. Sum of 5, 6, and 7
	Government	9. New money, New bonds, Collective goods and services (for taxes)	10. New money	11. Nil	12. Total money inflow to government. Sum of 9 and 10
		13. Total money expenditure by households. Sum of 1, 5 and 9	14. Total money expenditure by firms. Sum of 2, 6 and 10	15. Total money expenditure by government. Sum of 3 and 7	16. Total money inflow and expenditure in the economy by the three sectors

Cell 5 shows that the firms sell consumption goods and services to the households and they also sell new bonds to the households. *Cell 6* shows that the firms sell investment or capital goods to the other firms in the economy. *Cell 7* shows that the firms also sell goods to government. These goods are either collectively consumed or are added to the community or public capital stock. This shows that in certain cases the free market mechanism fails as resource allocation device because some goods cannot be efficiently produced or consumed privately. Such goods are called the *collective* or *public goods* and can be charged for their costs only in the form of taxes if these are produced by the government. *Cell 8* shows that the total money inflow to the firms (business sector) is the sum of the total money expenditure of cells 5, 6 and 7—the total purchases made from the firms by the households, firms and government.

Cell 9 shows that the government makes available to the households the services of public goods/commodities discussed for cell 7. Although the government does not directly charge any price for these goods, it nevertheless, levies an indirect charge in the form of taxes which it collects from the users of public utility goods and services. *Cell 10* which shows only 'new money' reveals that the government may finance the purchase of goods and services by paying the firms with its new money issues. *Cell 11* is 'Nil' showing that the government does not transact with itself. *Cell 12* shows the total money inflow to the government and this amount is the composite of cells 9 and 10.

Cells 13, 14 and 15 are the sums of the respective columns above them. *Cell 16* is the sum of the cells in the last total column (i.e., cells 4, 8 and 12) as also the sum of the last total row (i.e., cells 13, 14 and 15).

REVIEW QUESTIONS

1. What is macroeconomics? Distinguish between macroeconomics and microeconomics.
2. Discuss the relevance of macroeconomics to business management or the relationship between the two.
3. What are the major stages in the development of macroeconomics? Name them.
4. Mention three main developments in post-Keynesian macroeconomics and briefly explain them.
5. Distinguish between the concepts 'stock' and 'flow'.
6. What is 'model'? Explain a simple equilibrium model.
7. Distinguish between statics, comparative statics and economic dynamics.
8. Explain time series and cross-sectional analysis. What is pooled data?

SUGGESTED READINGS

- F. Machlup, "Micro and Macroeconomics: Contested Boundaries and Claims of Superiority" in *Essays on Economic Dynamics*, K.K. Norton, New York, 1977.
- Gardner Ackley, *Macroeconomics: Theory and Policy*, 1978, Chapter 1.
- M.C. Vaish, *Macroeconomic Theory*, 1987, Chapters 1, 2, 3.
- M. Adhikary, *Economic Environment of Business* (Revised Edition), 1997, Chapter 1.
- S.E. Stiegeler, Dictionary of Economics and Business (Second Edition), Gower Publishing Co., England, 1985.
- W.J. Baumol, *Economic Dynamics*, Macmillan, New York, 1962, Chapter 1.

Chapter 2

Classical Theory and Keynesian Economics

In the previous chapter, while discussing the development of macroeconomics, we had mentioned about the key roles of classical economics and Keynesian economics in this process of development. In fact, most of the present macroeconomic analysis uses either classical or Keynesian theories as base. Most of the development is either extensions or modifications of either classical thoughts or Keynesian theories—more of Keynesian thoughts and theories. During the analysis of different subjects or topics of macroeconomics later in different chapters, we will be making references to both classical and Keynesian theories.

In this chapter, we start with the basic thought or theory of the classical school, namely the theory of output and employment. Later, we shall present a comparative analysis of classical economics and Keynesian economics.

A. CLASSICAL THEORY OF OUTPUT AND EMPLOYMENT

Classification or identification of the classical economists or the classical school has been a matter of some opinion in macroeconomics. We had mentioned in Chapter 1 that 'classical economics' does not refer to the economic thought of any particular individual or author, and; it has to be comprehended or distilled from the writings of a number of economists Karl Marx used the term to refer to the economists from Adam Smith to David Ricardo. Keynes, in *General Theory* used 'classical economists' to include almost all the pre-Great Depression economists like David Ricardo, J.S. Mill, Alfred Marshall, A.C. Pigou and others. There are, however, some common names in those groupings like Ricardo, J.B. Say and J.S. Mill which give a good or more clearer indication of the composition or leading members of the classical school.

Classical theory of output and employment marks the beginning of a theory of national income determination. The classical economists, however, did not develop a formal theory or model of income determination. A more well-known or modern theory of national income determination was laid down by Keynes in *General Theory*. But, the classical economists had given their own thoughts on how aggregate output is determined in an economy along with employment. This is known as the classical theory of output and employment. The analysis of this should logically start with Say's Law of markets.

SAY'S LAW OF MARKETS

The basic or fundamental proposition of Say's Law of markets is that "supply creates its own demand". This also implies that there is no general overproduction or underproduction in the economy. This is explained below.

Say's Law or the logic of supply creating its own demand can be explained both in terms of a barter economy and a money or monetised economy.

A barter economy is characterised by the absence of any medium of exchange like money. Goods are exchanged for goods. In such a system, people produce goods for their own consumption and also for exchange for other goods which they require for their living or consumption. As they exchange goods, they create both demand for and supply of goods. When they require goods from other producers or people, they create demand to them: when they meet the requirements of or deliver goods to others, they create supply of goods.

This can be explained with an example. A farmer may be producing rice. But, he may be producing more rice than his requirement or consumption, that is, there is surplus rice production. He exchanges the surplus rice to cloth from/with another producer who makes cloth. This happens because the producer of cloth also requires rice for his living or consumption. So, he creates demand for rice. This way, supply of rice creates demand for rice; the same applies to cloth. This can be generalised for all goods or commodities which are used for consumption.

In a monetised economy, Say's Law of markets operates through the market or the market mechanism. It works like this. Production or output of goods is sold in the market; this constitutes the supply side. But, production of goods involves employment of factors of production—land, labour, capital and organisation. Factors of production earn their incomes—wages (for labour), rent (for land), interest (for capital) and profit (for organisation). Income or money income is spent on goods by the factors of production or the owners of factors. So, they create demand. So, production of goods leads to income (of factors of production); income is spent on consumption of goods; consumption of goods means demand for goods. This is how supply creates its own demand.

This can be stated in a more logical or sequential manner or steps as follows:

Supply of goods = Total production (value)

↓

Employment of factors of production

↓

Factor incomes
(Wages, rent, interest, profit)

↓

Consumption of goods

↓

Demand for goods

∴ Supply = Demand

CLASSICAL REFORMULATION OF SAY'S LAW

A group of classical economists, led by Ricardo, made some finer modifications or conceptual change in the original version/formulation of Say's Law to make it more appealing or acceptable. This can be called classical reformulation of Say's Law. According to the reformulated law, in a capitalist or free market economy, total supply of goods equals total demand and, there cannot be either 'general overproduction' or 'general underproduction' in the economy.

The classical economists do not rule out transitory or temporary overproduction or underproduction of goods and services. According to them, this can happen and this is caused by external or foreign factors. This actually implies business cycles or fluctuations. But, this is implicit in the classical system; they did not make any explicit mention or reference about this.

The classical economists mentioned about the self-correcting mechanism to set right imbalances in the economy. There can be short-term imbalances between demand and supply of goods caused by exogenous factor or shocks. But, the imbalances are automatically corrected and equilibrium is restored between demand and supply through interplay of market forces. If there is temporary overproduction, i.e., excess supply, it has effect on price. Price tends to decline. Price decline works on both supply and demand; there is decrease in supply and increase in demand induced by the fall in price. Similarly, if there is underproduction, there is excess demand. Excess demand induce rise in price; this encourages or leads to increase in supply and, simultaneously, discourages or leads to reduction in demand. In either case, the demand supply adjustment process works through the market mechanism to restore the equilibrium position. Thus, according to Say's Law or classical economics, the market is always in equilibrium in the long-run.

'Supply creates its own demand' means, by implication, that aggregate supply (equal to output) is determined irrespective of the price level and aggregate demand. Aggregate demand affects or determines the price level. Samuelson and others make this clear in their statement of Say's Law and its graphical illustration.[1] This is presented in Fig. 2.1.

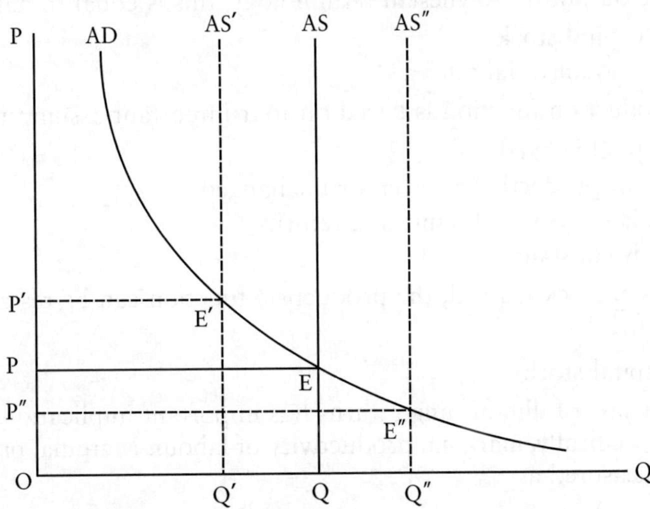

Fig. 2.1: Say's Law of Markets: Graphical Presentation

In Fig. 2.1, the aggregate supply curve (AS) is a vertical line indicating that aggregate supply is given or fixed, i.e., independent of aggregate demand and the price level. Given the aggregate demand curve (AD), equilibrium is reached at point E with equilibrium quantity OQ and price P. Short-term imbalances between demand and supply are shown by backward or forward shifts in the AS curve. If there is overproduction (QQ″), AS curve shifts to the right (AS″). Price falls to P″. Because of fall in price, demand increases, but supply is discouraged and supply decreases. Market interaction or the adjustment process between demand and supply (demand increases, supply decreases) continues. This pushes up the price till point E is reached at P. The opposite

1. P.A. Samuelson and W.D. Nordhaus, *Economics*, Indian Adaptation by S. Chaudhuri and A. Sen (9th Edition), Tata McGraw Hill, 2010, p. 831.

forces work when there is underproduction, and, the AS curve shifts temporarily backwards to AS′.

Say's Law, particularly in the reformulated form, is considered as the 'beginning of sound thinking in macroeconomics', and, also the core of classical macroeconomic thought.

THEORY OF OUTPUT AND EMPLOYMENT DETERMINATION

The classical theory of output and employment determination is derived from two separate, but, interrelated functions:

(a) The aggregate production function.
(b) The labour market: demand and supply functions.

These, along with simultaneous determination of equilibrium output and employment in the classical system, are explained below.

The Aggregate Production Function

In classical economics, aggregate production is expressed as a function of capital and labour. In terms of symbols, this can be expressed as

$$Y = f(K, L)$$

where Y = aggregate output (in Keynesian terminology, this is equal to national income)
K = capital stock
L = amount of labour

The classical production function is based on four important assumptions:

(a) Stock of capital is fixed
(b) Technology of production is given or unchanged
(c) Production is subject to diminishing returns
(d) Population is constant.

Because the capital stock is fixed, the production function can be restated as

$$Y = f(\bar{K}, L)$$

where $\bar{K}$ is fixed capital stock

Operation of the law of diminishing returns has important implication for production and productivity, more specifically, marginal productivity of labour. Marginal productivity of labour may be defined or measured as

$$MP_L = {}^{\Delta Y}/_{\Delta L}$$

where MP_L = marginal productivity of labour
ΔY = incremental output
ΔL = increases in the doses of labour

Operation of the law of diminishing returns means that marginal productivity of labour = MP_L, decreases as output increases and also with increase in doses of labour or employment. In diminishing returns, total production increases, but, at a decreasing rate. Productivity continues to increase till the point of MP_L= 0. After this point, total output starts declining. At this point, both output and employment reach the maximum levels. This is shown in Fig. 2.2.

In Fig. 2.2, at point M, MP_L = 0. Therefore, this is the point at which both output and employment are maximum. Total output = ML and total employment = OL. After point M, as shown by the slope of the aggregate production function, total output will start declining with employment of additional labour.

In the classical system, the assumption that capital stock is fixed, technology remains unchanged, and population is constant mean that the aggregate production function is essentially a short-run function. These factors do not remain unchanged or constant in the long-run.

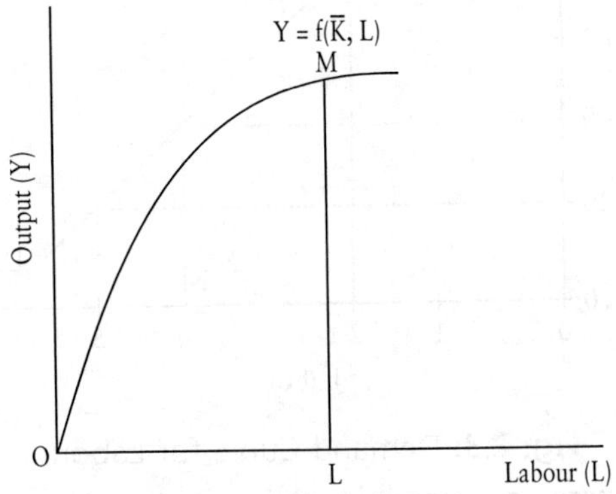

Fig. 2.2: The Classical Production Function

Labour Market: Demand and Supply Functions

In classical economics, labour market equilibrium determines full employment. Full employment is reached at the intersection of labour demand curve and labour supply curve. We shall first explain the demand curve for labour, and then discuss the supply curve for labour.

Labour Demand Function

Demand for labour depends on productivity of labour, or, more correctly, marginal productivity of labour. Marginal productivity of labour can mean either marginal physical productivity of labour, or, marginal revenue productivity of labour. Both, however, are closely interrelated and can be linked through price:

$$MRP_L{}^{2} = MPP_L{}^{2} \times P$$

where MRP_L = Marginal revenue productivity of labour

MPP_L = Marginal physical productivity of labour

P = Price

For derivation of labour demand curve, we need to introduce one more concept or variable, that is of marginal wage (MW). For hiring or engaging labour, produces or firms have to pay wages, which is the cost or price of labour. But wages paid by firms have to be related to productivity of labour, or, rather marginal productivity of labour. In fact, for the profit maximising of firm.

$$MRP_L = MW$$

Given this equation or condition, the demand curve for labour can be shown as below [Fig. 2.3].

2. Understanding of these concepts will be better if the student has read, or simultaneously read, Microeconomics or Managerial Economics where these concepts are more clearly explained.

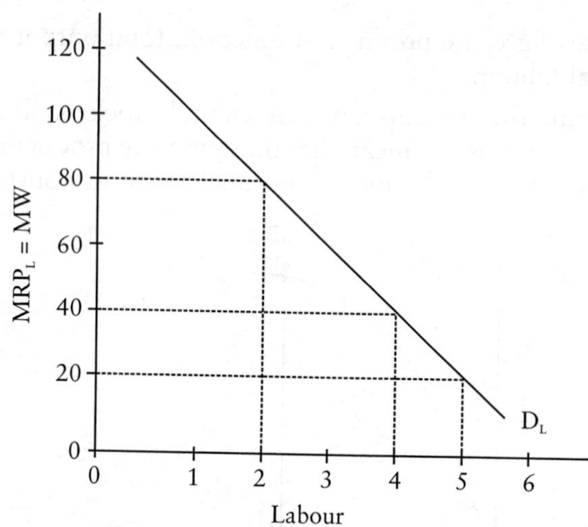

Fig. 2.3: Demand Curve for Labour

Figure 2.3 shows the inverse relationship between the wage rate and demand for labour. If the wage rate is ₹ 40, demand for labour is 4 units (workers). If the wage rate decreases to ₹ 20, demand for labour increases from 4 to 5 units (workers). But, if the wage rate increases from ₹ 40 to ₹ 80, i.e., becomes double, the demand for labour reduces to half, i.e., from 4 units to 2 units (workers).

Labour Supply Function

Supply of labour depends on the wage rate—the compensation or income for labour. Higher the wage rate, more is the supply of labour. This shows positive relationship between the wage rate and supply of labour.

The labour supply function can be stated as

$$S_L = f(W)$$

where S_L = Supply of labour
and W = Wage rate

The specific form of the function or the exact relationship between the wage rate and supply of labour would depend on the country concerned, the prevailing economic condition and the employment situation. For example, during recessionary condition with high unemployment, supply of labour would be more at a particular wage rate than during boom or prosperity.

The labour supply curve, as explained, is presented in Fig. 2.4.

In Fig. 2.4, the direct relationship between the wage rate and labour supply holds good up to a curtain point, i.e., up to a particular wage rate and the amount of labour supply. This is the point of labour-leisure substitution. This point is M. At this point, the wage rate is OW and labour supply is ON. At this point, the labour supply curve tends to become vertical; that is, any increase in the wage rate above this is not matched or responded by any further increase in labour supply (beyond ON) because the labour-leisure substitution. After achieving certain level of wage or income labourers substitute leisure for labour, because, at this level, most of their necessities or requirement of life have been fulfilled.

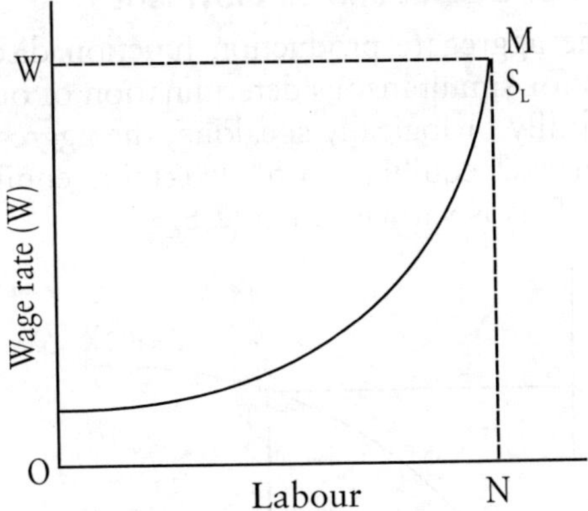

Fig. 2.4: Supply Curve for Labour

Equilibrium of Labour Market

We have explained the labour demand function; we have also just discussed the labour supply function or derivation of the labour supply curve. Given these two functions or curves, equilibrium of the labour market can be logically determined. This is presented in Fig. 2.5.

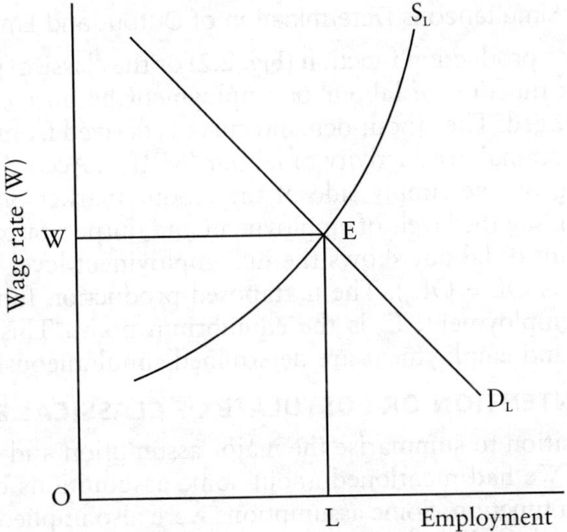

Fig. 2.5: Equilibrium in the Labour Market

As shown in Fig. 2.5, equilibrium in the labour market is the point of intersection of the labour demand curve (D_L) and labour supply curve (S_L). This is point E. At this point, the equilibrium wage rate is OW and OL is equilibrium amount of labour; this is the full employment level. Any disturbance or departure from the equilibrium point either because of excess supply or shortfall of demand, or, short supply or surplus demand is automatically correlated through interaction of market forces and equilibrium is restored. This means that equilibrium of the labour market is stable in classical economics.

Simultaneous Determination of Output and Employment

We can now combine the aggregate production function discussed earlier (Fig. 2.2) and the labour market conditions for simultaneous determination of output and employment in the classical system. More specifically or logically speaking, the aggregate production function can be juxtaposed with labour market equilibrium to determine equilibrium levels of output and employment in the economy. This is shown in Fig. 2.6.

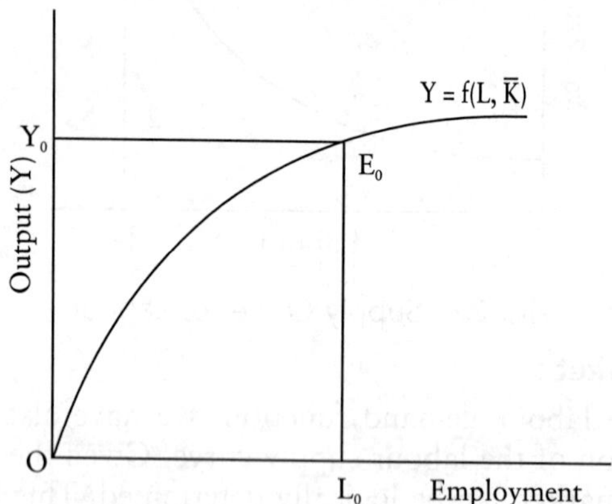

Fig. 2.6: Simultaneous Determination of Output and Employment

To recall the aggregate production function (Fig. 2.2) or the classical production theory output becomes almost a direct function of labour or employment because capital stock is fixed and technology is also unchanged. The labour demand curve is derived from the production function because it depends on marginal productivity of labour (MRP_L). According to classical economic theory, factors operating on the supply side of the labour market play a more important or dominant role in determining the levels of employment and output. Supply of labour depends on the wage rate. OL amount of labour shows the full employment level (Fig. 2.5). This is shown as OL_0 in Fig. 2.6 (that is $OL = OL_0$). The juxtaposed production function shows OY_0 as the output at this level of employment; E_0 is the equilibrium point. This is how, in the classical model, national output and employment are determined simultaneously.

MAJOR CONTENTION OR POSTULATE OF CLASSICAL ECONOMICS

We are now in a position to summarise the major assumption and contention or postulates of classical economics.[3] We had mentioned about some assumptions during our discussion of the aggregate production function. Some assumptions were also implied and certain conclusions reached during analysis of the labour market equilibrium and simultaneous determination of output and employment. It is time to put all these together or as assumptions and postulates of classical economic theory. These are important for better or clearer understanding of classical economics. We shall first mention the major assumptions and then the main contentions or postulates.

Major Assumptions of Classical Economics

Certain assumptions form the basis or foundation of the classical school. The Key assumption are:

(a) The economy functions on the principle of *laissez-faire* or free market mechanism;

3. It is actually Keynes who used the phrase "postulates of the classical economics" to describe the main contention or conclusion of classical economic theory.

(b) The principle of *laissez-faire* means that market forces take their own course depending on demand and supply conditions;
(c) Both consumers and producers have complete freedom in taking decisions on their purchases and production;
(d) No government control or regulation of operation of private enterprises; government control/regulation may however exist for ensuring free and fair competition;
(e) No monopolies or restrictive trade practices exist or are allowed to operate. These are prevented or eliminated by law.

Main Postulates of Classical Economics

Given the above assumptions, the main conclusions or postulates of classical economics follow almost deductively. There are

*1. Economy is always in a state of equilibrium;
*2. There is always full employment;
3. Optimal allocation of resources among all industries;
4. Actual output equals potential output in the economy;
*5. Real variables, and not money, matter.

*these are the more important postulates. These are briefly explained or elaborated below.

Economy is Always in a State of Equilibrium

This is one of the fundamental postulates of classical economics. The classical economists believed that an economy is always in a state of equilibrium. Disequilibrium, if any, is purely a temporary phenomenon.

As mentioned earlier, the classicists rule out any general overproduction or general underproduction of goods and services. This happens because aggregate demand is equal to aggregate supply—whatever is produced is consumed (may be with certain time lag). If there is any departure or deviation from the equilibrium situation or point, the "invisible hand"[4] comes into operation and restores equilibrium. This indicates and also ensures stability of equilibrium.

There is Always Full Employment

In the classical system, equilibrium of the economy also implies full employment of resources. Two employable resources are labour and capital. But, with capital stock as fixed, it is labour whose employment can vary. With equilibrium in the economy (equality of aggregate demand and aggregate supply) labour is also fully employed. In fact, as explained earlier, equilibrium in the commodity market and the labour market is determined simultaneously. However, in classical economic theory, full employment of labour does not exclude frictional unemployment and voluntary unemployment. In modern macroeconomic analysis also, definition of full employment in consistent with the existence of frictional unemployment and voluntary unemployment in the economy.

Optimal Allocation of Resources Among all Industries

This follows deductively from the *laissez-faire* principle or free market mechanism. Because of free market mechanism, there is free flow or movement of resources between different industries. This finally leads to optimal allocation of resources among all industries. This

4. The classicists used the phrase 'invisible hand' to denote automatic market mechanism or the demand-supply adjustment process.

has an important implication for or effect on productivity of factors of production. Optimal allocation of resources eventually means, or rather ensures that marginal productivity of factors in all industries becomes same. Till this happens, movement or transfer of resources from one industry to another will continue.

Actual Output Equals Potential Output in the Economy

Divergence between actual output and potential output in an economy occurs if there are market imperfection flow of resources is restricted, and, there are large productivity differentials among industries. These also imply that bottlenecks are mostly absent and potential output is always achieved. This means, in other words, that actual output is equal to potential output.

Real Variables, and not Money, Matter

This is a key postulate of classical economics. The classical economists strongly believed that real variables and factors play very significant or dominant roles in economy. Money plays only a passive or secondary role. Real output (and not nominal or money output), real resources (labour and capital), physical productivity of labour and real wages are the key determining factors of the course of an economy. Money is used only as a medium of exchange or a common denominator. It does not play any important role in determining the levels of output and employment. Therefore, the classical postulate: only *real variables* matter; money does not matter.

B. CLASSICAL ECONOMICS VERSUS KEYNESIAN ECONOMICS

In Chapter 1, we had mentioned that classical economics, neoclassical economics and Keynesian economics are three important phases in the evolution of economic thought. Classical economics and Keynesian economics are, however, two more distinctive stages in the development of macroeconomic theory and analysis. We had stated this in the beginning of the chapter. We had also mentioned that Keynes's contribution is considered to be more significant in influencing post-Keynesian or modern macroeconomics. We present here a comparative analysis of the main tenets of classical economics and Keynesian macroeconomics. This will bring out the contrasts or differences between the classical school and Keynes's thoughts or theories.

BACKGROUND TO KEYNESIAN ECONOMICS

Before we proceed with the comparative analysis, it may be in order, and, also informative or instructive, to give a brief introduction to the origin or background of formulation of Keynes's thoughts and theories on macroeconomics.

It may be said that Keynes was initially groomed or trained in the classical tradition.[5] But he broke away from classical thoughts. Keynes's break from the classical tradition was, however, not sudden or abrupt. It was gradual and spread over a period of more than a decade.

Before his well-known and more acclaimed *General Theory*, Keynes wrote *A Treatise on Money*—which was published in 1930. Keynes's thoughts on economics/macroeconomics started with the *Treatise*. In the *Treatise*, he was initially 'moving along the traditional line' of thinking—'money' as distinct or separate from the theory of demand and supply of goods and services (real output). But, in course of writing the *Treatise*, transition in his thoughts started taking place. This was apparent from his attempts to integrate monetary theory with the theory of

5. Keynes was one of the ardent students of Alfred Marshall. He had studied and also taught his students at Cambridge University for many years from Marshall's well-known book *Principles of Economics* which was first published in 1890.

real output. But he was not successful—he felt it was 'left incomplete'. His ideas were, however, changing. He wrote in the *Treatise*:

> This book has occupied use for several years...during which my ideas have been developing and changing.... The result is, I am afraid, that there is a good deal...which represents the process of getting rid of the ideas which I used to have.... I felt like someone who has been facing his way through a confused jungle. Now that I have emerged from it, I see that I might have taken a more direct route.
>
> —Preface, *A Treatise on Money*

The *Treatise* was published before the *Great Depression of the Thirties (1929-1935). The General Theory* was written during the Great Depression. This made a basic or fundamental change in Keynes's thoughts on demand, output, employment and money. The Great Depression was characterised by lack of demand, fall in output, widespread unemployment wage rigidity and lack of purchasing power. These environmental factors moulded Keynes's thoughts immensely. These also prompted his theories to depart from those of the classical school. His disposition towards classical economics changed almost drastically.

After the publication of *The General Theory*, a long controversy arose. It was not unexpected by Keynes. He wrote in *The General Theory* that he could not achieve his "object of persuading the economists to re-examine critically some of their basic assumptions except by a highly abstract argument, and, also by made controversy, although he wished that there was less of the latter."[6]

KEYNES AND THE CLASSICS: MAJOR CONTRASTS

Major contrasts or differences between the classical school and Keynes can be explained in terms of the following:

1. Real and monetary sectors of the economy,
2. Wage-price flexibility or rigidity,
3. Full employment or unemployment,
4. Market equilibrium or disequilibrium.

These are analysed below.

According to the classicists, the economy consists of two sets of market—the commodity market and the labour market. In the commodity market, the forces of demand and supply determine equilibrium levels of output and prices. An increase in the market price of any commodity over the equilibrium or market-clearing price will cause excess of supply over demand, and, vice versa if market price decreases. In the labour market, if the market wage rate becomes higher than the wage rate at which supply of labour equals demand, a situation of excess supply arises and unemployment sets in. The solution to the unemployment problem is a flexible wage-price system in which the labour market automatically moves towards full employment equilibrium.

If all the commodity markets and the labour market (rather the factor market) are simultaneously in equilibrium, there will be general equilibrium in the economy. This may easily happen because of flexible prices, i.e., each commodity price will increase or decrease to bring about equality of demand and supply. Because of complete wage-price flexibility, there will be a set of relative prices which will correspond to equilibrium in all the markets—both commodity markets and the labour market. Thus, according to classical economists, general equilibrium and full employment in the economy are almost automatic.

6. J.M. Keynes, *The General Theory of Employment, Interest and Money*, 1936, Preface.

In the classical system, relative prices[7] and, not money prices, are of real significance in an economy. Relative prices support or sustain the real sector of the economy. Relative price holds good at any level of absolute money prices. This can be explained with an example. In terms of relative prices or real exchange rates or ratios, a mango may be worth twice of an apple or two apples holds good whether money prices of mango and apple are ₹ 10 and ₹ 5 or ₹ 8 and ₹ 4 or ₹ 6 and ₹ 3 respectively. This shows the indeterminacy of money prices.

By implication, this means that money plays a nominal role in an economy—a role which is not related to the real sector of the economy. The role of money however is reflected in classicists' quantity theory of money. The quantity theory of money is expressed as MY = PT (Fishermen equation) or M = KYP or M = PY/V (The Cambridge equation). The quantity theory of money states that changes in money supply affect the absolute price level, and, not relative prices which are determined outside the monetary system in the commodity market. This shows that in the classical economic system. There is clear or complete dichotomy between the monetary and real sectors of the economy.

Keynes launched a direct, almost frontal, attack on all these classical propositions—automatic full employment, relative prices, dichotomy between the monetary and real sectors, etc.

As mentioned earlier, Keynes's thought and writing were greatly influenced by the prevailing economic environment in the United Kingdom and the *Great Depression of the Thirties* (*General Theory* was published in 1936). Keynes had witnessed massive unemployment in England and elsewhere during that time.

In this perspective, Keynes contended that full employment equilibrium was only one of the possible situations and, the classicists contention that the economy always tended to move towards full employment was fallacious or erroneous Keynes was of the strong view that competitive economy, governed by market forces, always tended to generate involuntary unemployment. This happened also because of wage rigidity, in contrast to wage flexibility which characterises most of the modern economies.

One of the greatest contributions of Keynes to economic theory and analysis is considered to be the consumption function. Alvin Hansen calls it the "heart of the Keynesian analysis". According to Hansen: "This is an epoch-making contribution to the tools of economic analysis, analogous to, but even more important than Marshall's discovery of the demand function. The consumption function is the most powerful instrument which has been added to the economist's kit of tools in our generation."[8] In Keynesian analysis, the level of aggregate output and income, saving and full employment or unemployment are all primarily determined by the nature and slope of the consumption function.

Keynes challenged the classical dichotomy between monetary and real sectors of the economy. He argued that the two sectors are not separate; they are rather interrelated or interdependent. According to him, interactivity between the two sectors works like this: Changes in money supply affect the rate of interest; the rate of interest affects aggregate investment; through this, money supply influences aggregate demand, output and employment. The magnitude of increase in aggregate income and output because of increase in money supply would depend on three factors:

7. Relative prices are exchange ratios between different goods and services. These equations are explained in Chapter 11.
8. A.H. Hansen, "The General Theory" in S.E. Harris (Ed.). *The New Economics*, 1947, p. 135.

(i) slope of the consumption function; (ii) interest elasticity of the investment demand schedule; and (iii) interest elasticity of the liquidity preference curve or the speculative demand for money.

In fact, inclusion of the speculative demand for money in the monetary system or transaction is another major contribution of Keynes. He added the speculative demand to the classical transactions demand for money. The speculative demand for money introduces interest as an additional explanatory variable in the demand for money, and, generally has inverse relationship with it. The speculative demand is inelastic at high rate of interest, becomes elastic as interest rate falls and becomes perfectly elastic at very low level of interest. The rate at which the speculative demand for money becomes perfectly elastic or infinite is the Keynesian "liquidity trap" (explained in Chapter 14).[9]

With the introduction of the speculative demand, total demand for money becomes a function of income and the rate of interest. This leads to a refutal of the quantity theory of money which postulates a relationship of proportionality between the general price level and total money supply. Once the rate of interest falls to the 'liquidity trap' level, there will be no increase in the general price level even if money supply increases because the entire increase in money supply will be absorbed by the speculative demand for cash balance. This results in a situation in which an unchanged or stable price level is consistent or can coexist with an increase in money supply—a conclusion which is in conflict with or contradicts the quantity theory of money. In the classical system, liquidity trap occurs at zero rate of interest. This assumes that there is no cost of holding money. This and the zero rate of interest are however hardly likely in reality.

Keynes also questioned the classicists' assumption of flexible wage which is/was the 'foundation of full employment equilibrium'. Keynes' argument is that money wages are rigid and not flexible particularly in the downward direction. Because of this, employment cannot be increased, let alone reaching full employment, through a general wage cut. In the Keynesian system, the feasibility of wage cut itself is questionable. According to Keynes, wages are fixed through collective bargaining and any move towards reduction of wages is subject to minimum wage legislations and would be resisted by the trade unions.

Keynesian position on output, employment, savings, investment and equilibrium may be briefly summarised as follows: money wages are inflexible downward below the minimum wage decided either by the government or fixed through collective bargaining; speculative demand for money is significant and highly interest-elastic (in the relevant zone); both savings and investment are interest-inelastic and the economy is imperfectly competitive. Given these conditions, Keynesian and not the classical-economic theory and analysis are required to ascertain the level of aggregate output and employment which can be achieved in the short-run. The Keynesian model, however, is considered static; it is concerned with only short-run equilibrium conditions. As Gardner Ackley puts it: "The Keynesian model is too static for the analysis either of the business cycle or of problems of growth".[10] The Keynesian model is also considered to be too aggregative.

CONCLUDING OBSERVATIONS

The contrasts and differences between the classicists and Keynes are based on the fundamentals of their economic thoughts, theories and principles. These were governed by the economic and social conditions or environment prevailing during those two periods. These render logic to the respective thoughts and theories.

9. The actual slope of the curve is rectangular hyperbola (Fig. 14.2).
10. Gardner Ackley, *Macroeconomic Theory*, 1961, p. 415.

But the perceptual differences remained. Given this perspective, we may conclude with Keynes's own observation on classicism and Keynesianism:

> ...If the classical theory is only applicable to the case of full employment, it is fallacious to apply it to the problems of involuntary unemployment—if there is such a thing (and who will deny it?). The classical theorists resemble Euclidean geometry in a non-Euclidean world, who, discovering that, in experience, straight lines apparently parallel often meet, rebuke the lines for not keeping straight.... Yet, in truth, there is no remedy except to throw over the axiom of parallels and to work out a non-Euclidean geometry. Something similar is required today in economics. We need to work out the behaviour of a system in which involuntary unemployment in the strict sense is possible.[11]

REVIEW QUESTIONS

1. "Classical Theory of output and employment marks the beginning of a theory of national income determination". Explain.
2. What is 'Say's Law of Markets'? Explain and also give a graphical presentation of Say's law.
3. Explain the classical production function clearly stating the assumptions involved. Also state the implications of the assumptions.
4. "In classical economics, labour market equilibrium determines full employment". Discuss this in terms of the demand curve for labour and supply curve of labour.
5. Classical postulates are based on certain important assumptions. Mention and analyse these assumptions.
6. What are the main postulates of classical economics? State and explain them, focus on the more important ones.
7. Discuss the background to Keynesian economics contained in *A Treatise on Money* and *The General Theory.*
8. What are the major contrasts or differences between Keynesian and the classical school? State and explain them.

SUGGESTED READINGS

- E.E. Hagen, "The Classical Theory of the Level of the Output and Employment" in M.G. Mueller (Ed.). *Readings in Macroeconomics*, 1969.
- H.G. Johnson, "The General Theory after Twenty-Five Years", *The American Economic Review*, May 1961.
- J.R. Hicks, "Mr. Keynes and the Classics: A Suggested Interpretation", M.G. Mueller (Ed.), *Readings in Macroeconomics*, 1966.
- M. Blaug, *Economic Theory in Retrospect* (3rd Edition), Vikas Publishing House, 1976.
- M.C. Vaish, *Macroeconomic Theory* (8th Edition), Allied Publishers, 1987, Chapter 30.

11. J.M. Keynes, *The General Theory*, 1936, pp. 16-17.

PART–II

NATIONAL INCOME AND RELATED AGGREGATES

In this part, we have discussed, in great details, concept and measurement of national income (Chapter 3). All the related aggregates—GDP, GNP, NDP and NNP—at both factor cost and market prices have been explained at length. Personal income and personal disposable income have also been analysed. The concept of value addition which is key to measurement of income has been clearly explained. Hypothetical examples of national income accounting have been given to help understanding of the concepts through applications. At the end of the chapter, national income estimation in India has been discussed.

Two most important components of national income are consumption and investment. Consumption and investment have been separately discussed in Chapters 4 and 5. Various theories of consumption-income relationship have been discussed. Concepts of APC, MPC, APS, MPS and the multiplier have been explained and illustrated with examples. Determination of the level of investment, roles of income and the rate of interest, marginal efficiency of capital and the acceleration principle have all been adequately explained and illustrated with examples and empirical investment functions.

Chapters 6, 7 and 8 are extensions of determination of national income. Chapter 6 presents the basic Keynesian model; in Chapter 7, national income determination with the government sector is discussed; Chapter 8 is devoted to determination of national income with the foreign sector (open economy model).

Chapter 3

Concept and Measurement of National Income

In Chapter 1, we had mentioned that national income is the 'most macro' of the macroeconomic concepts. It is also the most important of the macroeconomic concepts (because an understanding of this leads to an easier understanding of many other macroeconomic concepts) and the best indicator of the state of economy of a country. Therefore, an awareness and understanding of the concept and methods of measurement of national income is an essential prerequisite for learning and appreciating the many facets of macroeconomic analysis and also the economic environment of the country.

In Chapter 1, while discussing stock and flow concepts, we had mentioned that national income is a 'flow' concept. We make this the starting point of our discussion of the concept and measurement of national income.

To begin with, we may define national income as the total or aggregate value of the annual flow of final goods and services in the national economy. The concept of the 'final' is very important here, and, in fact, fundamental to the concept and measurement of national income. The important distinction here is between 'final' and 'intermediate' products. If this distinction is not made, the intermediate product will be counted twice, first as output of the firm or industry which produces this intermediate product and also in the final product of the firm or industry which uses this intermediate product, and, this will lead to duplication or double counting. We shall return to the problem of double counting later.

CIRCULAR FLOW OF GOODS AND INCOME

Let us consider a simple economy in which there are only two sectors—the business sector and the household sector. The business sector can also be called the producing sector and the household sector, the consuming sector. The business sector employs the factors of production (land, labour, capital and organisation) and produces the final output for sale, whereas the household sector supplies the factor services and consumes the output produced by the business sector.

These activities imply two sets of transactions between producers and consumers. For producers, these mean (i) purchase of services of factors of production from the household sector and (ii) sale of final output to the household sector. For the household sector, these transactions mean (i) sale of factor services to the business sector and (ii) purchase of goods and services from the business sector. These two-way transactions give rise to circular flow of goods and services in the economy. This can be clearly explained with the help of a flow chart (Flow Chart 3.1).[1]

The two sector flow chart can be extended to a three sector flow chart by introducing the government sector and to a four sector flow chart by incorporating the international sector, i.e. making the economy 'open'.

It can be seen in the chart that there are two kinds of flows; one is of *real* goods and services and, the other money flows of income and expenditure. *Real flows* are in the inner loop, and, the *money flows* in the outer loop. These two flows move in reverse direction and counterbalance each other.

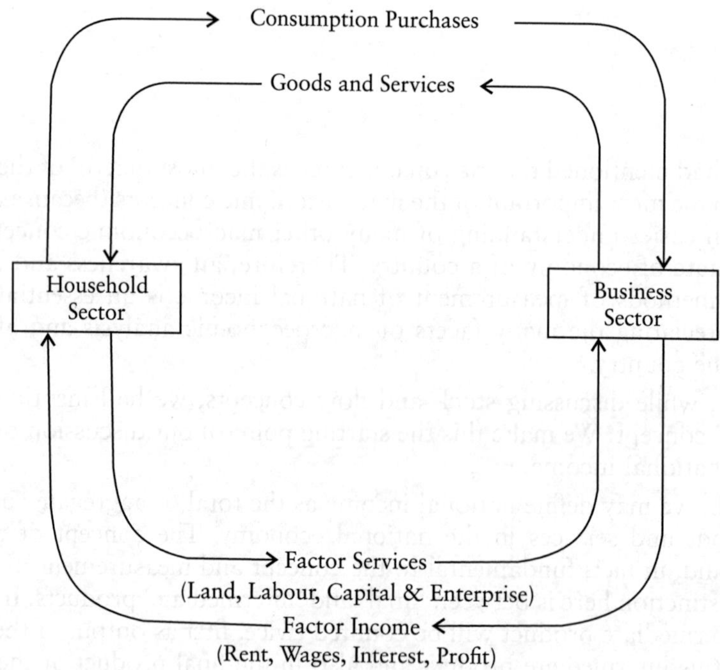

Flow Chart 3.1

DEFINITION AND MEASUREMENT OF NATIONAL INCOME

From the simplified model of the economy shown in the chart, it would be evident that definition and measurement of national income of a country essentially involves the measurement of the size of the circular flow.

The genesis of the circular flow is: production (in the business sector) creates income (for factors of production); income (of the household sector) leads to spending, and, spending generates

1. The flow chart is based on certain simplifying assumptions. These are:
   (i) The economy has no international sector, i.e. it is a 'closed' economy.
   (ii) Production takes place only in the business sector.
   (iii) Producers sell all that they produce, i.e. there is not stock build-up.
   (iv) Consumers spend their entire income on consumption expenditure, i.e. there is no saving.
   (v) There are no government operations (government expenditure, taxes, etc.), in the economy.

   If we drop some or all of these assumptions, the flow chart would not remain as simple as shown, but the basic mechanism of circular flow of goods and income would remain essentially the same.

demand which, in turn, induces production and the flow goes on. Correspondingly, there are three ways to measure the size of the circular flow and national income: product approach, income approach and expenditure approach.

PRODUCT APPROACH

According to this approach, we can estimate national income of a country by measuring the total value of final output. The final output in an economy consists of a large number of goods and services produced in the country. Let us denote the amounts of each of these goods and services produced in a given year as Q_1, Q_2, Q_3, ... Q_n, and their prices as P_1, P_2, P_3, ... P_n where n stands for the total number of final goods and services. Then, the size of national income (Y), according to product approach, would be:

$$P_1Q_1 + P_2Q_2 + P_3Q_3 + \ldots + P_nQ_n$$

or, using summing up notations, national income (Y) may be estimated as:

$$Y = \sum_{i=1}^{n} P_iQ_i$$

INCOME APPROACH

In the income approach, national income can be measured by annual flows of factor earnings (wages, rents, interest and profits which are the earnings of labour, land, capital and organisation, respectively) accruing during the process of production of final output. For a particular good, value of final output can also be expressed as total factor earnings from this output, that is, say for goods 1:

$$P_1Q_1 = W_1 + R_1 + I_1 + P_1$$

or, by generalising,

$$P_iQ_i = W_i + R_i + I_i + P_i$$

where W, R, I and P stand for wages, rent, interest and profits, respectively. Total income generated this way or national income estimated by using income approach may be expressed as:

$$Y = \sum_{i=1}^{n} (W_i + R_i + I_i + P_i)$$

EXPENDITURE APPROACH

In the expenditure approach, national income can be estimated by aggregating flows of expenditure on final goods and services. In the simplified model depicted in the chart, the only kind of expenditure shown is household consumption expenditure. But, in any economy, in terms of sectors, two other major categories of expenditure take place, viz. expenditures by the business sector and the government sector.

In national income accounting using expenditure approach, therefore, the flow of total expenditure should be measured by aggregating the flows of expenditure on final goods and services incurred by each of the three major sectors, viz. the household sector, the business sector and the government sector. Thus, using the expenditure approach, national income, Y, is estimated as

$$Y = E_h + E_b + E_g$$

where E_h, E_b and E_g denote the annual flows of expenditure by the household sector, the business sector and the government sector, respectively.

An alternative way to look at the expenditure approach is to consider the kinds or components of total expenditure. Expenditure incurred on final goods and services should be either consumption expenditure or investment expenditure so that national income, in expenditure form, may also be written as

$$Y = C + I$$

where C is expenditure on consumption goods and I expenditure on investment goods.

Y = C + I is the famous Keynesian income equation.

This income equation is for a closed economy, i.e. without foreign transactions as either exports or imports. If we consider the economy to be an open economy with exports and imports, then the income equation will change. This is a very realistic assumption because most of the economies today are open economies. If we also consider government expenditure as a separate component of aggregate expenditure, then national income by expenditure approach may be rewritten as

$$Y = C + I + G + X - M$$

where C is expenditure on private consumption, I is total investment expenditure—both public and private, G is government expenditure, X is expenditure of foreign countries on a country's exports and M is home country's expenditure on imports from abroad.

For logical reasons, the three approaches to the definition and measurement of national income discussed above give identical results. They provide three alternative methods of measuring essentially the same thing. If we follow the expenditure approach, we are trying to measure national income by the size of the income flow in the upper half of the loop. If we follow the income approach, we are trying to measure the flow in the lower half of the loop, the product approach sort of mediating between the two or balancing the two. This may be designated as the 'link flow', but essentially of the same order and magnitude as the other two flows.

NATIONAL INCOME AND RELATED CONCEPTS

If we obtain the aggregate flow using any of the above three approaches, what we should get (under normal assumptions) is Gross Domestic Product (GDP) at market prices. It is 'Gross' because, presumably we have not made allowance for depreciation of capital goods wherever relevant or applicable; a 'Domestic Product' because these represent the aggregate of flows within the country or domestic economy; and 'At Market Prices' because it is assumed that the final flows include all taxes including indirect taxes which are levied on products when those are marketed at certain prices. We shall now explain these concepts in greater details to provide a clear understanding of the concept and measurement of national income.

GROSS AND NET INCOME

Fixed capital used in any production process is subject to wear and tear over a period of time and generally has prescribed life. It is, therefore, necessary to make allowance for used-up capital every year. Such allowance referred to as depreciation, indicates the extent to which capital goods have been consumed in the process of production. The term 'Gross' is used to indicate that no allowance for capital depreciation has been made; 'Net' is used to mean that provision for capital depreciation has already been made.

Depending on the allowance for depreciation, we can make a distinction between gross and net income, i.e. between Gross Domestic Product (GDP) and Net Domestic Product (NDP). The relation between the two is:

Gross Domestic Product (GDP) *minus* Depreciation
= Net Domestic Product (NDP)

DOMESTIC AND NATIONAL INCOME

In the definition of gross domestic product, the term 'domestic product' denotes the value of total output or income originating within the specified geographical boundaries of a country or a nation. Therefore, the resulting measure is called a 'domestic' product. It includes all income generated through factor services within the physical limits of the domestic economy irrespective of whether these services have been provided by or supplied by normal residents of the country or others, i.e. non-nationals of the country. So, when national income of the country is estimated, adjustments have to be made for factor services rendered or income generated by the non-national factors of production. Actually, income generated by the non-nationals should be deducted from 'domestic product or income' to arrive at 'national income' of the country.

Similarly, national income of a country would include all income which accrues to the inhabitants or normal residents of the country due to their participation in production activities in the rest of the world. The term 'national' is used to indicate all factor incomes accruing to normal residents of the country irrespective of whether the factors of production supplied by them are located at home or abroad.

For measurement purposes, then, 'national' product differs from 'domestic' product by the amount of factor income received from abroad and factor income paid abroad or by net factor income abroad (total factor income received from abroad—total factor income paid abroad). We can now introduce the concept of Gross National Product (GNP) which is related to Gross Domestic Product (GDP) in the following way:

Gross Domestic Product (GDP)
plus Net Factor Income Abroad
= Gross National Product (GNP)

where Net Factor Income Abroad
= Factor Income Received from Abroad
minus Factor Income Paid Abroad

MARKET PRICES AND FACTOR COSTS

The market value of all final products will exceed total income accruing to the factors of production by an amount equal to indirect taxes levied on commodities less subsidies paid on commodities. National product at market prices indicates the total amount actually paid by the final consumers, whereas national income at factor cost measures the total amount earned by the factors of production for their contribution to the final output.

The relationship between the two may be shown as:

GDP or GNP at Market Prices
= GDP or GNP at Factor Cost
plus Indirect Taxes less Subsidies

GDP, GNP, NDP AND NNP

We are now in a position to define national income more exactly. We start with GDP and go down the steps till we arrive at what is defined or understood as national income. This can be done in two ways:

GDP *plus* Net Factor income abroad = GNP	GDP *minus* Depreciation = NDP
GNP *minus* Depreciation = *Net National Product (NNP) at Factor Cost*	NDP *plus* Net Factor Income abroad = *Net National Product (NNP) at Factor Cost*
or National Income at Factor Cost	*or National Income at Factor Cost*
NNP at Factor Cost *plus* Indirect Taxes less Subsidies = *NNP at Market Prices or National Income at Market Prices*	NNP at Factor Cost *plus* Indirect Taxes less Subsidies = *NNP at Market Prices or National Income at Market Prices*

(It is assumed above that GDP is also calculated at Factor Cost.)

Net National Product (NNP) of a country is its National Income, and NNP can be measured either at Factor Cost or at Market Prices. So, National Income can be defined and measured either at Factor Cost or at Market Prices, and we have seen the difference between the two.

NOMINAL INCOME AND REAL INCOME

It would be appropriate now to make a distinction between nominal income and real income with reference to the prices prevailing during different time periods that are used for estimation of national income. National income of a country can be estimated by using either current prices or constant prices. Current prices refer to those which prevail during the same reference period (usually a year) for which national income is estimated. Constant prices refer to prices prevailing during a particular base year and remain unchanged till the base year is changed. National income computed in terms of current prices is nominal income and income calculation based on constant prices is real income. In terms of symbols, by using the product approach, these can be presented as

$$\text{Nominal income} = \sum_{i=1}^{n} P_i^c Q_i^c$$

$$\text{Real income} = \sum_{i=1}^{n} P_i^b Q_i^c$$

where P_i^c = price of product i in the current year

P_i^b = price of product i in the base year

Q_i^c = output of product i in the current year

The distinction between nominal income and real income is made essentially to show or eliminate the effect of price change or inflation on growth of national income—whether GDP, GNP or NNP. If during two consecutive periods, national income in current prices of a country has doubled and prices have also doubled during the same period, output of goods and services would have actually remained unchanged (composition of the goods and services might have changed to some extent). In such a case, growth of national income would be only due to the price mechanism with no change in the output of goods and services. If income is measured at constant price, growth in national income in this case would be zero. This is the reason why, during any period of time, national income at current prices and constant prices shows big divergence in terms of numbers. For example, for India, GDP at current prices during 2001-02 was ₹ 20,94,013 crores; during the same year, GDP at 1993-94 prices was ₹ 12,65,429 crores. India's GDP, GNP and NNP at current prices and at constant prices during 2001-02 are shown in Table 3.3.

In calculation of national income at constant prices, i.e. real income, choice of the base year is very significant because this can lead to a difference in the growth rates. For example, if a negative growth year is chosen as a base year, future growth rates will always be shown higher than if a normal year or a positive growth year is taken as the base. In fact, this became a point of controversy in the mid-1980s in India. During this period, income calculations were made with 1979-80 as the base. Policy makers claimed higher growth rates, but, critics who included distinguished academicians, contended that 1979-80 was a negative growth year, and, therefore, higher growth rates based on that year were misleading or wrong. During this period, some economists also talked about 'Hindu Rate of Growth' explaining that the rate of growth was actually constant around 3.5-4.0 per cent during the period.

PURCHASING POWER PARITY (PPP) INCOME

The concept of purchasing power parity (PPP) was coined by Gustav Cassel in early 1920s. The concept is used to convert nominal income into income in terms of purchasing power of a country. Purchasing power parity (PPP) income of a country, many times, shows a sharp contrast to its nominal income. PPP of a country's currency is first determined in terms of US dollar, and, then PPP income is calculated. Purchasing power parity of Indian Rupee can be defined as

PPP of Rupee = No. of rupees required to purchase a representative basket of goods in India which one $ can buy in the US

Because US $ is taken as the benchmark, PPP of a country would generally depend on its currency's parity with $. The definition of PPP also implies that PPP of US $ is 1.

The concept of PPP can be used to convert nominal incomes of different countries into PPP incomes and make meaningful comparisons of inter-country income levels. Since price levels and purchasing power of local currency vary widely in different countries, comparisons of country-wise national income data may not lead to very useful conclusions. However, PPP income data make such comparison meaningful. That is the reason the World Bank has designed a scheme of converting nominal incomes of different countries into PPP incomes. Comparison of nominal income and PPP income of 15 selected countries is shown in Table 3.1.

Table 3.1: International Comparison of Nominal Income and PPP Income, 1998

Country	*GNP 1998 (Billion US $)*			
	Nominal		*PPP*	
	Income	*Rank*	*Income*	*Rank*
USA	7,903	1	7,903	1
India	427	6	2,018	4
UK	1,264	3	1,200	5
Canada	581	5	691	6
Malaysia	81	12	171	12

Country	*GNP 1998 (Billion US $)*			
	Nominal		*PPP*	
	Income	*Rank*	*Income*	*Rank*
China	924	4	3,779	2
Japan	4,089	2	2,982	3
Australia	387	8	409	9
Switzerland	284	9	191	11
Republic of Korea	399	7	616	7
Singapore	96	11	80	14
Nigeria	36	14	89	13
Pakistan	62	13	217	10
Sri Lanka	15	15	55	15
Indonesia	131	10	490	8

Source: World Development Report (World Bank), 1999-2000.

Nominal income and PPP income of different countries, shown in Table 3.1 depict some interesting data. The US has the highest nominal income and, also, by definition, the highest PPP income. Japan is second in terms of nominal income, but, third in PPP income. For China, it is almost the opposite; it is positioned fourth in nominal income and second in PPP income. India ranks sixth in nominal income, but, fourth in PPP income. For majority of countries, PPP income is higher than nominal income. The exceptions are UK, Japan, Australia and Singapore.

PERSONAL INCOME

We now introduce another concept related to National Income, i.e. Personal Income. National Income is the total income accruing to the factors of production. It does not straightaway represent the total income the individuals actually receive. The latter is referred to as Personal Income. It represents the flow of aggregate income to the household sector from other sectors.

Let us more clearly understand the difference between national income and personal income. First, the whole of income which accrues to the factors of production is not actually paid out to the individuals who own the factors of production. Part of this total income is deducted or retained. Two forms in which this income gets reduced are (a) corporate taxes, and, (b) the undistributed or retained profits. Both of these constitute a part of the factor income, but these are not received by the owners as their personal income.

Secondly, total income that individuals actually receive generally includes some amount which cannot be regarded as payment for the factor services rendered. Typical examples of this kind of payments received by individuals are gifts, pensions, relief payments and various welfare payments. Such payments are known as 'transfer payments' because these are merely transfers and do not represent payments made for any direct contribution made by the factors to the production process. So, transfer payments which do not constitute part of current production are excluded from national income.[2]

2. It may be mentioned here that besides gifts and all kinds of welfare payments transfer payments also include one special item, viz. interest on public debt. It has been a controversial issue as to whether this should be included in national income. But, it is a fairly universal custom now to treat interest on public debt as a transfer payment and, hence, not to include it in national income.

So, three factors which account for the difference between national income and personal income are corporate taxes, undistributed or retained profits and transfer payments, the first two being deducted from and the last one added to national income for computation of personal income. The relationship between the two, then, may be shown as:

Personal Income = NNP at Factor Cost
minus Undistributed Profits
minus Corporate Taxes
plus Transfer Payments

PERSONAL DISPOSABLE INCOME

Disposable income is income that is actually available with individuals to dispose of as they wish. It differs from personal income by the amount of direct taxes which may also be called personal taxes paid by individuals. The relationship between personal disposable income and personal income then, is:

Personal Disposable Income = Personal Income – Personal Taxes

FINAL ACCOUNTING OF NATIONAL INCOME AND RELATED AGGREGATES

We have developed all the concepts related to national income. We can now pull together all the components and present the final accounting of national income and related aggregate. As we did earlier, we start with GDP, again.

Gross Domestic Product (GDP)
plus Net Factor Income abroad
= Gross National Product (GNP)
minus Depreciation
= Net National Product (NNP) at Factor Cost or National Income at Factor Cost
minus Undistributed Profits
minus Corporate Taxes
plus Transfer Payments
= Personal Income
minus Personal Taxes
= Personal Disposable Income
Net National Product (NNP) at Factor Cost
plus Indirect Taxes less Subsidies
= Net National Product (NNP) at Market Prices or National Income at Market Prices

Alternatively, we may start with GDP and NDP and proceed further as we did earlier.

DISTINCTION BETWEEN FINAL AND INTERMEDIATE PRODUCTS: THE CONCEPT OF VALUE ADDED

The discussion on national income accounting and analysis would remain incomplete if we do not explain the concept of *value added* which plays a vital role in national income estimation. The concept of *value added* emanates from the distinction between final and intermediate products and is related to the problem of double counting.

Not all goods and services produced can be aggregated (in value terms) to derive estimate of national income; because, as mentioned in the beginning of the chapter, adding up the value of all that is produced irrespective of the product being 'final' will involve duplication and double counting. It is necessary to draw a clear distinction between the final products and 'intermediate' products for estimating national income.

A final product is defined as one produced and/or purchased, but not *resold* or *reused* during the current accounting period. Intermediate products, on the other hand, are defined as those produced and/or purchased and resold or reused with or without further processing during the same accounting period. *Intermediate products are used up in the process of production of the final products.*

In practice, however, it may be difficult, if not impossible, to classify goods produced in an economy into two mutually exclusive categories of final and intermediate products. Many times, output of a particular goods may be used partly for the production of other goods and, partly, for final use. For example, part of coal output or electricity is used by the steel producers as an intermediate input whereas part of it is purchased for/used in domestic consumption which is final use.

VALUE ADDED

If the difference between final product(s) and intermediate product(s) is clearly understood, the concept of *value added* is more easily defined and explained. *Value added* by a business firm (total or at any stage of production) can be defined as the difference between the value of output of the firm and the total expenditure incurred by it on materials and intermediate products purchased and used. Or, in other words, value added by a particular production process is obtained by deducting the value of material inputs or intermediate products from the corresponding value of total output. Thus,

(Gross) value added = (Gross) value of output
minus value of inputs or
intermediate products

In an extended or more elaborate definition, value added may be expressed as:

Value added = Total sales
plus closing stock of finished and semi-finished goods
minus total expenditure on raw materials and intermediate products
minus opening stock of finished and semi-finished goods

Total *value added* by a particular production process is obtained by aggregating value added at each stage of production. This is illustrated in Table 3.2.

Table 3.2: Value Added by Bread Production

(₹)

Stage of Production	*Value of Output*	*Cost/Value of Intermediate Products*	*Value Added*
Wheat	200	0	200
Flour	240	200	40
Bread	300	240	60
Total	740	440	300

Value added at a particular stage of production shows the contribution made by the factors of production at that stage to the value of final output. Therefore, it follows, that *value added* at a particular stage of production (or total value added) is exactly equal to the sum of wages, rent interest and profits earned by the factors of production at that stage of production (or all the stages of production put together).

HYPOTHETICAL INCOME ACCOUNTING

We have discussed above, in detail, the concept of National Income and the related aggregates, and each of the individual components which play a role in the measurement of these aggregates. To clarify the concepts and the methods of measurement further, some hypothetical income accounts are presented below. These would closely acquaint the students with national income derivation and estimation processes.

COUNTRY A

Total gross output of the country is valued at ₹ 1,000. Raw materials and inputs used amount to ₹ 600. Total wages paid is ₹ 100. Inflow of income from foreign countries is ₹ 50 (there is no income outflow). Depreciation of capital goods is estimated as ₹ 50. What is national income of the country?

Estimated National Income = ₹ 400.

COUNTRY B

Gross Domestic Product (GDP) at Factor Cost of the country is ₹ 2,000. Net income inflow from foreign countries is ₹ (–) 50 (number of countries including, India, have negative 'net factor in income abroad'). Indirect taxes levied in the country yield ₹ 150. Estimate the nearest approximate aggregate to national income.

In this case; we cannot estimate Net National Product (NNP) or National Income because no information on capital depreciation is given.

We can estimate Gross National Product (GNP) either at Factor Cost or at Market Prices.

GNP at Factor Cost = ₹ 1,950

GNP at Market Prices = ₹ 2,100

COUNTRY C

Total gross amount of wages, rent, interest and profit paid out to the factors of production amount to ₹ 3,000. Depreciation of capital goods is estimated as ₹ 200. Undistributed profits equal to ₹ 140 and corporate taxes yield to ₹ 60. Direct taxes on individuals yield a revenue of ₹ 50. Estimate National Income, Personal Income and Personal Disposable Income, and, also state the assumption necessary to derive these aggregates.

Because no information on factor income abroad is given, the first important assumption necessary to estimate national income aggregates is that the country has a closed economy. Given this assumption, we can estimate Net National Product (NNP) or National Income at Factor Cost. To estimate personal income we need to know the amounts of undistributed profits, corporate taxes and transfer payments. We know the first two, but we have no information on transfer payment. If we assume that there are no transfer payments in the economy, we can estimate personal income, and because, we know the amount of direct taxes on individuals or personal taxes we can also estimate Personal Disposable Income.

National Income at Factor Cost = ₹ 2,800
Personal Income = ₹ 2,600
Personal Disposable, Income = ₹ 2,550

NATIONAL INCOME ESTIMATION IN INDIA

From hypothetical accounting, we now move on to actual accounting of national income in India. In India, national income accounts are prepared by the Central Statistical Organisation (CSO), Department of Statistics, Ministry of Planning, Government of India. These accounts are contained in 'National Accounts Statistics', popularly known a the 'White Paper' published annually by CSO.

Any annual publication of 'National Accounts Statistics' gives a time series of national income and related aggregates for a period of generally fifteen years expressed in both current and constant prices. 'Current Prices' indicate the prices prevailing during the year for which the national income aggregates are estimated; these aggregates are also expressed in constant prices of a particular year by using appropriate price deflators.

National income and related aggregates as discussed above are presented in Part I of 'National Accounts Statistics'. There are five other parts of NAS which present various components and transactions related to national income aggregates. Contents of six parts of NAS are described here:

Part I : National Product
Part II : Factor Incomes
Part III : Consumption, Saving and Capital Formation
Part IV : Public Sector Transactions
Part V : Disaggregated Tables
Part VI : Consolidated Accounts of the Nation

We present national income and related aggregates of India for 2001-02 both at current and at constant prices in Table 3.3 (contained in Part I of NAS). These would give an exact idea of the size of India's national income, magnitudes of the related aggregates and the roles current and constant prices play in determining the size and variations in national income.

Table 3.3: National Income and Related Aggregate for India, 2001-02

(₹ *Crores*)

National Income Aggregate	*At Current Prices*	*At 1993-94 Prices*
Gross Domestic Product at Factor Cost	20,94,013	12,65,429
Gross National Product at Factor Cost	20,81,350	12,57,043
Net National Product at Factor Cost	18,64,292	11,15, 157
Net National Product at Market Price	20,43,264	12,24,442

The methodology for estimation of national income in India has gone through significant changes over time. A note on development of national income accounting in India is given in the Appendix.

REVIEW QUESTIONS

1. Explain the concept and three approaches to measurement of national income.
2. Distinguish between GDP, GNP, NDP and national income.
3. Analyse the difference between personal income and personal disposable income with reference to national income.
4. Explain the concept of 'value added' and illustrate with example.
5. Discuss the development of national income accounting in India.

SUGGESTED READINGS

- P.A. Samuelson and W.O. Nordhaus, *Economics* (Seventeenth Edition), Tata McGraw-Hill, 2003.
- Gardner Ackley, *Macroeconomics: Theory and Policy*, 1978, Chapter 2.
- C. Rangarajan and B.H. Dholakia, *Principles of Macroeconomics*, 1980.

APPENDIX

DEVELOPMENT OF NATIONAL INCOME ACCOUNTING IN INDIA

Publication of national income and related aggregates in 'National Accounts Statistics' (NAS) by CSO in their present form is a very recent phenomenon. This is the result of evolution of methodological issues and estimation procedures over a number of years.

In 1949, the Government of India appointed the National Income Committee (NIC) under the chairmanship of Professor P.C. Mahalanobis to make recommendations regarding the estimation of national income, improvement of the statistical data on which the estimates were to be based, and promotion of research in the field of national income. It submitted its final report in 1954 which contained a detailed account of limitations of the available data, gaps in the existing data base, and, an outline of suitable methods which can be used for estimating national income in India. Since then the Central Statistical Organisation (CSO) prepares and publishes, on a regular basis, the annual estimates of India's national income.

CSO also brought out a study report in 1961 titled "Proposals for a Revised Series of National Income Estimates for 1955-56 to 1959-60". It contained an analysis of the improvements considered necessary and possible and invited comments on the recommendations of the study. The discussion stimulated by this report resulted in another publication in 1967 entitled "Brochure on Revised Series of National Product for 1960-61 to 1964-65". This discussed the limitations of the estimates prepared before 1967, now known as the *conventional series* and outlined the revised methodology to be followed by CSO in constructing what is now known as the '*Revised Series*' of national income estimates in India. The revised methodology was developed in the light of the recent changes in the availability and quality of various statistical data relating to the Indian economy.

Chapter 4

Consumption Function Analysis

In the previous chapter, we had mentioned that one of the approaches to measurement of national income is the expenditure approach. We had stated that, using the expenditure approach, national income may be measured as

$$Y = E_h + E_b + E_g$$

where E_h, E_b and E_g denote expenditure on final goods and services by the household sector the business sector and the government sector respectively.

We had also mentioned that an alternative way to look at the expenditure approach is to consider the components of total expenditure. Expenditure incurred on final goods and services be either consumption expenditure (C) or investment expenditure (I) so that national income, in expenditure form, may also be written as

$$Y = C + I$$

In the present chapter, we shall discuss the relationship between consumption (C) and income (Y), the related propensities and the role consumption plays in the income determination process. In the next chapter, we shall discuss investment decisions.

CONSUMPTION FUNCTION HYPOTHESIS

The relationship between consumption and income is shown or hypothesised through the consumption function. The consumption function states consumption as a function of income, that is

$$C = f(Y)$$

where C is consumption and Y is income.

In its simplest form, consumption is expressed as a linear function of income (the consumption function is expressed as a straight line), that is

$$C = a + bY$$

where C is consumption, Y is income, b is the consumption-income ratio or the average propensity to consume and 'a' is the level of consumption which would exist even if income is nil or 0. The intercept 'a' indicates that when income is nil, consumption will be financed out of past savings, i.e. dissaving will take place. The level of consumption 'a' may also be described as autonomous consumption unrelated to income.

The linear consumption function, as described above, is shown in Fig. 4.1.

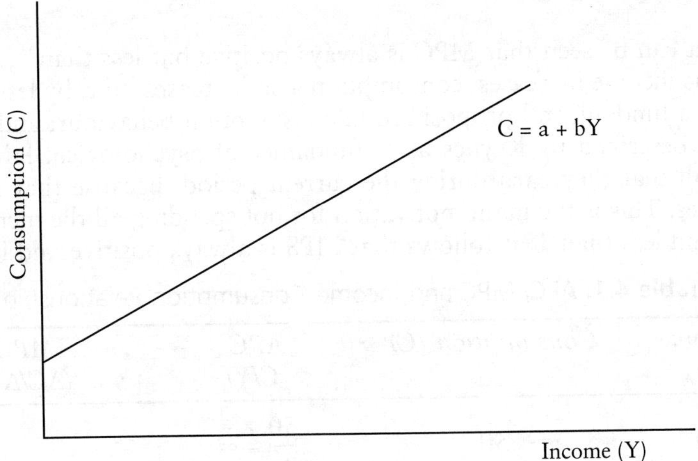

Fig. 4.1: Consumption Function

AVERAGE AND MARGINAL PROPENSITIES TO CONSUME (APC AND MPC)

The ratio of total consumption to total income (the parameter 'b' in the consumption function as described above) is the average propensity to consume (APC). APC may, therefore, be written as

$$APC = \frac{\text{Total consumption}}{\text{Total income}} = \frac{C}{Y}$$

$1 - \frac{C}{Y} = \frac{S}{Y}$ is the average propensity to save (APS). Since consumption plus savings equal income, APC + APS = 1 at all income levels.

Marginal propensity to consume (MPC), in contrast to average propensity to consume, is the ratio of *change* in total consumption to *change* in total income. MPC, may, therefore, be defined as

$$MPC = \frac{\text{Change in total consumption}}{\text{Change in total income}} = \frac{\Delta C}{\Delta Y}$$

MPC is the slope of the consumption function. For a linear consumption function like the one shown in Fig. 4.1 (C = a + bY), the slope is constant. Therefore, for a linear consumption function.

$$MPC = Slope^1 = \frac{\Delta C}{\Delta Y} = Constant$$

$1 - \frac{\Delta C}{\Delta Y} = \frac{\Delta S}{\Delta Y}$, i.e. marginal propensity to save. In the same way, as APC and APS add up to 1, MPC and MPS also add up to 1.

Table 4.1 illustrates the concepts of APC and MPC at different levels of income and their effects on consumption-income relationship. The illustration corresponds to the linear

1. In terms of differential calculus, the slope is written as dc/dy.

consumption function C = a + bY. The average propensity to consume varies at different levels of income. But, the marginal propensity to consume (i.e. slope of the consumption function) is constant.

In Table 4.1, it can be seen that MPC is always positive but less than 1, i.e. $0 < MPC < 1$. This means that, as income increases, consumption also increases, but, by less than the increase in income. This is a fundamental proposition in consumption behaviour; and, this behavioural characteristic was described by Keynes as 'a fundamental psychological law'. Human beings do not consume all that they earn during the current period, because they must save for the future contingencies. This is the main motivation for not spending all the increase in income. If MPC is positive and less than 1, it follows that MPS is always positive and is also less than 1.

Table 4.1: APC, MPC and Income-Consumption Relationship

Income (Y)	*Consumption (C)*	*APC (C/Y)*	*MPC (ΔC/ΔY)*
0	50	$\frac{50}{0} = \infty$	
100	125	$\frac{125}{100} = 1.25$	$\frac{75}{100} = 0.75$
200	200	$\frac{200}{200} = 1.00$	$\frac{75}{100} = 0.75$
300	275	$\frac{275}{300} = 0.92$	$\frac{75}{100} = 0.75$
400	350	$\frac{350}{400} = 0.88$	$\frac{75}{100} = 0.75$

In Table 4.1, we have shown that APC is falling. Depending on the nature of the linear consumption function. APC may be either falling, or remain constant, or may even be rising. Accordingly, the relationship between APC and MPC would also vary. Three possible forms of the linear consumption function are shown in Figs. 4.2, 4.3 and 4.4.

All the consumption functions we have shown so far are linear, that is, they depict consumption behaviour in which MPC is constant. Theoretically, it is possible that consumption behaviour is such that MPC is not constant, but falling (MPC cannot be rising). This means that out of an increase in income, not a constant proportion, but a *falling proportion*, is spent on consumption. In this case, the consumption function becomes non-linear (with changing slope). Such a consumption function is shown in Fig. 4.5.

Table 4.2 shows income, consumption and savings relationship (APC, MPC, APS and MPS) corresponding to the above consumption function.

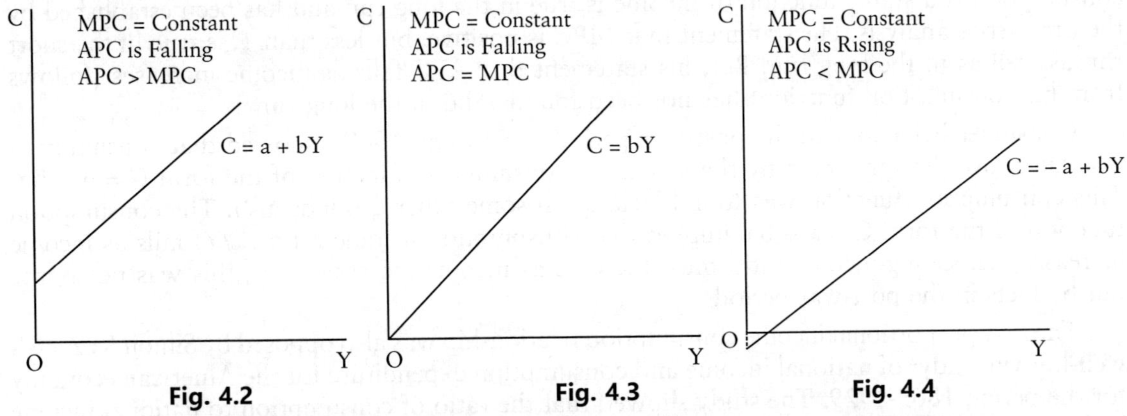

Fig. 4.2 **Fig. 4.3** **Fig. 4.4**

CONSUMPTION-INCOME RELATIONSHIP: SHORT RUN AND LONG RUN

The linear consumption function of the form C = a + bY described above is really the Keynesian form of the consumption function with the properties as discussed. Keynes indicated that this form of the consumption function is valid in the short run as well as in the long run. This implies that there is non-proportional relationship between consumption and income both in the short run and in the long run.

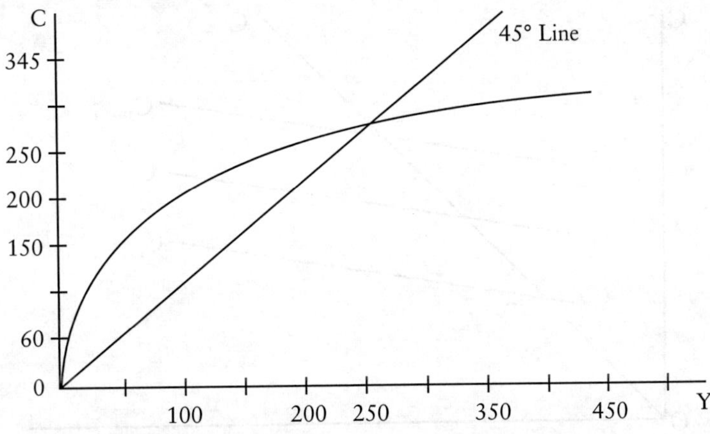

Fig. 4.5: Non-linear Consumption Function

Table 4.2: Income, Consumption and Savings Relationship in a Non-linear Consumption Function

Income (Y)	*Consumption* (C)	*Savings* (S)	*APC* (C/Y)	*APS* (S/Y)	*MPC* (ΔC/ΔY)	*MPS* (ΔS/ΔY)
0	60	– 60	–	–	–	–
100	150	– 50	1.50	– 0.50	0.90	0.10
200	220	– 20	1.10	– 0.10	0.70	0.30
250	250	0	1.00	0	0.60	0.40
350	300	50	0.89	0.11	0.50	0.50
450	345	105	0.77	0.23	0.45	0.55

Empirical findings have not verified all of Keynes's statements. Some of his argument hold in the short run but not in the long run and vice versa. For example, his statement that consumption is a stable function of income is true in the long run and has been established by the time series analysis. His statement that MPC is positive, but less than 1, is true in the short run as well as in the long run. But, his statement that APC falls as income increases (follows from his consumption function) has not been found valid in the long run.

Consumer behaviour in the post-war period—1946 and 1947—showed that consumption was far above that predicted by the simplified consumption function of the form C = a + bY. This consumption function was found lacking on some other grounds also. The consumption function of the form C = a + bY implies that consumption income ratio (C/Y) falls as income increases, i.e. saving-income ratio must increase as income increases. But, this was not borne out by facts in the post-war period.

The non-proportional income consumption relationship was also opposed by Simon Kuznets's well-known study[2] of national income and consumption expenditure for the American economy for the period 1869-1929. The study showed that the ratio of consumption to national income had remained constant while income bad increased four times. Kuznets's finding was supported by Goldsmith's study of income, consumption and savings in the United States.[3]

In short, the empirical findings confirm the Keynesian hypothesis of non-proportional relationship between consumption and income in the short run, but establish a proportional relationship between the two in the long run. Figure 4.6 illustrates the short-run and long-run linear consumption functions.

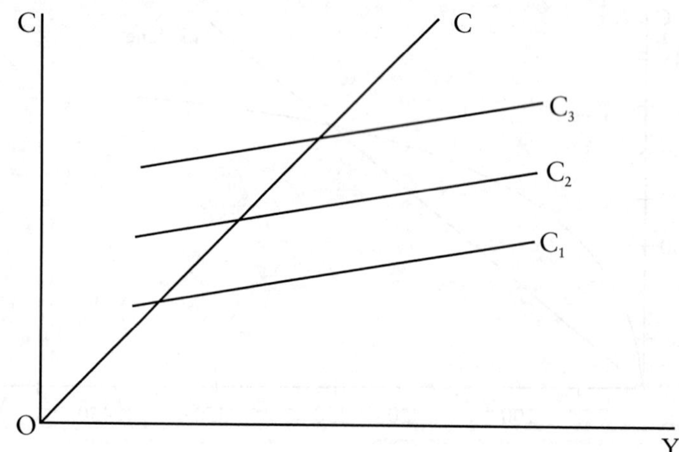

Fig. 4.6: Short run ($C_1 = a_1 + b_1V_1$, $C_2 = a_2 + b_2Y_2$ and $C_3 = a_3 + b_3Y_3$) and Long run (C = bY) Consumption Functions

Different hypotheses have been developed in the post-Keynesian era to explain the apparent contradiction between the short run non-proportional and long run proportional income-consumption relationship. Three well-known hypotheses are Absolute Income Hypothesis, Relative Income Hypothesis and Permanent Income Hypothesis, formulated and published in this order.

2. Simon Kuznets, *Uses of National Income in Peace and War*, NBER, 1942.
3. R. Goldsmith, *A Study of Saving in the United States*, 1955, Vol. 1.

ABSOLUTE INCOME HYPOTHESIS

According to Absolute Income Theory[4] (AIT), the level of consumption expenditure depends on the absolute level of income, with APC declining as the absolute level of income increases. Since the level of national income grows over time, the AIT concludes that APC should diminish continuously. Thus, the AIT argues that the consumption income relationship is non-proportional.

To rationalise the difference between theory and reality (observed proportional relationship), exponents of AIT argue that there are upward shifts in the consumption function—for example, the shift from C_1 to C_2 (and finally to the proportional path indicated by C_3) in Fig. 4.7—caused by factors other than income.

The upward shifts in the consumption function are explained to be the results of such factors such as: (i) consumer spending a larger proportion of any given level of income because of increased accumulation of wealth; (ii) individuals becoming less frugal, and pending a larger proportion of current income as they migrate from rural to urban areas (there is some statistical evidence suggesting that MPC of urban workers is higher than that of rural workers); and (iii) households spending more at every level of income in order to purchase newly introduced consumer goods which they regard as necessities.

The AIT explains that these factors cause the short run non-proportional consumption function to shift upward in such a manner that creates an illusion of proportionality, and thereby obscures or disturbs the basic non-proportional relationship. Thus, the AIT argues that it is the influence of these factors (other than income) which causes changes in consumption and income to appear proportional; but, if all other things were held constant, consumption and income would vary proportionally.

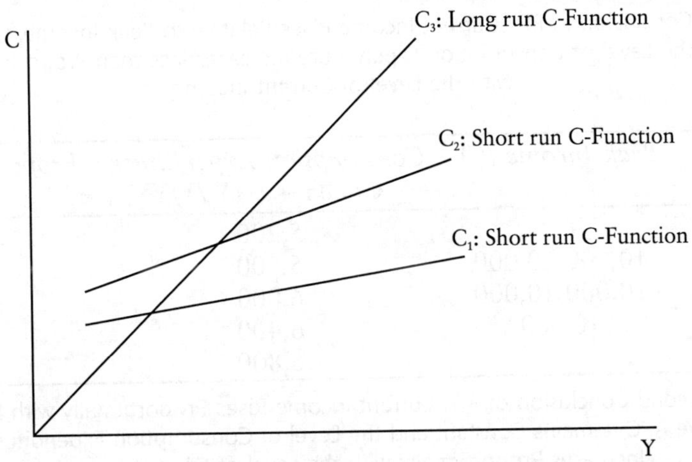

Fig. 4.7: Consumption Functions: Short run (C_1, C_2) and Long run (C_3)

RELATIVE INCOME HYPOTHESIS

Relative Income Theory (RIT)[5] states that the level of consumption expenditures is determined not by the absolute level of income but the *relative level* of income with the APC declining as

4. The development of the Absolute Income Theory is usually credited to A. Smithies, "Forecasting Post-War Demand", *Econometrica*, January 1945; and, also J. Tobin, "Relative Income, Absolute Income and Saving" in *Money, Trade and Economic Growth*, 1951.
5. The development of Relative Income Theory is credited to J.S. Duesenberry, *Income, Saving and the Theory of Consumer Behaviour*, 1949.

relative income increases, and remaining constant as absolute income increases. More specifically, RIT argues that the level of consumption spending is determined by the households' level of current income relative to the highest level of income previously achieved. The consumption function, according to RIT, may therefore, be shown as

$$C = Ay + b\left(\frac{Y_h}{Y}\right)Y$$

where C represents the current level of consumption expenditures, Y represents the current level of income, Y_h represents the highest level of income previously earned, and, 'a' and 'b' represent parameters which relate income to consumption.

From the above consumption function, we can establish two major conclusions of RIT. First, when a household (and all households in the aggregate) experiences a temporary, short run increase in current income above its previous peak level of income, it increases its consumption expenditure by an amount which is less than proportional to the increase in total income. Second, when a household (and all households in the aggregate) experiences current and peak income growing by the same percentage, it increases consumption expenditure by an amount which is proportional to the increase in current income. Consequently, the APC remains constant and the increase in total consumption expenditure is proportional to the increase in total income.

Both these conclusions can be derived mathematically from the RIT consumption function. These conclusions are illustrated below with numerical examples (Tables 4.3 and 4.4).

Thus, according to the exponents of RIT, it is continuous growth in current income and, thereby, growth in peak income by the same percentage which gives rise to the long run, proportional consumption function.

Table 4.3: First Conclusion of RIT: Current Income Rises Relative to Peak Income, the APC Declines, and the Level of Consumption Expenditure Increases less than Proportionally with the Level of Current Income

(₹ *Crores*)

Current Income (Y)	*Peak Income (C)*	*Consumption Expenditure* $C = aY + b\,(Y_h/Y)Y$	*Propensity to Consume (C/Y)*
6,000		5,200	0.866
8,000	10,000 10,000	5,600	0.700
10,000	10,000 10,000	6,000	0.500
12,000	10,000	6,400	0.633
14,000		6,800	0.485

Table 4.4: Second Conclusion of RIT: Current Income Rises Proportionally with Peak Income, the APC Remains Constant and the Level of Consumption Expenditure Increases Proportionally with the Level of Current Income

(₹ *Crores*)

Current Income (Y)	*Peak Income (C)*	*Consumption Expenditure* $C = aY + b\,(Y_h/Y)Y$	*Propensity to Consume (C/Y)*
10,000		6,000	0.600
11,000	9,090 10,000	6,200	0.563
12,100	11,000 12,100	6,820	0.563
13,310	13,310	7,502	0.563
14,641		8,252	0.563

There is a final point to note about the Relative Income Theory. It works for decreases as well as increases in the level of current income. According to RIT, as current income falls relative to peak income, each household (and all households in the aggregate), is forced to reduce its level of consumption. However, the reduction in consumption is less than the reduction in income. Consumers attempt to maintain as much of their previous level of consumption—or standard of living—as possible. They prevent consumption from declining too far by drawing down their past savings. In this way, the reluctance to reduce consumption spending in proportion to the loss in current income acts as a ratchet which prevents the economy from slipping backwards and losing all its previous gains in income and standard of living. This may be called the 'ratchet effect', and one can see it operate by working backward through Table 3.2. Evidence shows that consumers have followed a ratchet pattern in four post-World War II recessions.

Thus, the RIT concludes that it is the temporary deviations in current income from peak income which cause short run non-proportional variations in consumption and income and obscure the basic, long run relation between consumption and income.

This also show that there is a fundamental difference between RIT and AIT. RIT explains away the short run consumption function as a result of temporary deviations in current income, while the AIT explains away the long run consumption function as the result of factors other than income.

PERMANENT INCOME HYPOTHESIS

According to the Permanent Income Theory[6] (PIT), the level of consumption expenditures is not determined by absolute or relative levels of income, but by the level of permanent income, with the APC out of *permanent income* remaining constant as permanent income increases, and the APC out of current income declining as current income increases above permanent income in the short run.

Let us clearly understand the concept of permanent income. Most family budget studies indicate that one appropriate measure of income is the average of the amount received in the current year and the preceding year, or an average of the amounts received in the current and preceding years and the amount expected in future years. The measure of income determined as an average of current, past and future is called permanent income. But, what is the time horizon of permanent income, particularly with respect to future income? The time horizon in an individual case would depend on a large number of socio-economic factors such as health, education, job security, accumulated wealth and so on. For determining permanent income, the time horizon is usually taken as greater than one year, but less than the lifespan of the household (individual).

Since permanent income is defined as an average of current, past and future incomes, a household's level of current income may be larger or smaller than its permanent income. Current income, according to the PIT, is divided into two components; a permanent income component and a transitory income component, such that

$$Y = Y_p + Y_t$$

where Y is current income, Y_p is permanent income and Y_t is transitory income. Consequently, current income is greater or less than permanent income as transitory income is positive or negative.

6. The development of the Permanent Income Theory is credited to Milton Friedman, *A Theory of the Consumption Function*, 1957.

Similarly, PIT argues that current consumption is divided into two components: permanent consumption and transitory consumption such that

$$C = C_p + C_t$$

where C is current consumption, C_p is permanent consumption, and C_t is transitory consumption. Like income, current consumption is larger or smaller than permanent consumption depending on whether transitory consumption is positive or negative.

The PIT argues that permanent consumption is proportionate to permanent income—that the basic relationship is summarised by a proportional consumption function. In other words, the APC out of permanent income (i.e. the ratio C_p/Y_p) is constant. The PIT further states that the APC out of permanent income depends on the level of interest rates, the ratio of 'non-human' wealth to total wealth (i.e. non-human plus human wealth) and consumer tastes and preferences, and is independent of the level of income. Thus, the permanent consumption may be written as

$$C_p = b(i, w, \mu)\ Y_p$$

or

$$C_p/Y_p = b$$

where b represents the APC (and the MPC out of permanent income, and i is the interest rate, w is the ratio of non-human wealth to total wealth and μ the taste and preference factor.

The PIT also assumes that correlation between permanent and transitory components and also between the transitory components is zero. Thus,

$$\gamma(Y_p, Y_t) = 0$$

$$\gamma(C_p, C_t) = 0$$

$$\gamma(Y_t, C_t) = 0$$

The consumption function hypothesis of PIT leads to a startling conclusion. The PIT argues that the ratio C_p/Y_p is independent of Y_p itself—the APC out of permanent income does not change as Y_p changes. If all the households had the same tastes with the same interest rates and the same ratio of non-human to total wealth, each would spend exactly the same proportion of its permanent income on consumption regardless of its position on the income distribution scale. A 'rich' household is supposed to consume the same proportion of its permanent income as a 'poor' household.

Another controversial conclusion of the PIT is that transitory consumption is not related to transitory income. When a household experiences a transitory decline in income, its consumption expenditures do not decline. Likewise, when a household experiences a transitory increase in income, its consumption expenditures do not increase. According to PIT, unexpected changes in income do not produce changes in consumption; instead, they produce equivalent changes in savings. This means that the MPC out of transitory or 'windfall' income is zero, and the MPS out of transitory or 'windfall' income is unity.

According to PIT, if current consumption is uncorrelated to transitory income, the consumption-income relationship is non-proportional in the short run. For example, suppose that APC b in the permanent consumption function equals 0.90, the permanent income of a particular household is ₹ 1,000 and its level of permanent consumption is ₹ 900. Therefore, the APC declines (from 9/10 to 9/11) as income increases (from ₹ 1,000 to ₹ 1,100).

The PIT explains the existence of two consumption functions in a manner similar to the RIT. However, the two theories are not identical nor are they comparable. The RIT is based on a relationship between current consumption and current income; while the PIT is based on a relationship between permanent consumption and permanent income.

It may be noted here that the differences between the PIT and the RIT are still the source of considerable controversy among economic theorists.

EMPIRICAL CONSUMPTION FUNCTIONS

Given the various hypotheses regarding consumption-income relationship in the short run and in the long run, we are faced with the problem of choosing a proper form of the consumption function for empirical analysis. Should we employ a short run consumption function or a long run consumption function for such analysis? Since our objective is to analyse economic activity when income levels rise as well as fall, it may be more meaningful, and easier also, to use the form of a short run consumption function, i.e. a linear consumption function with average propensity to consume decreasing as income creases.

Table 4.5 gives estimates of MPC for various countries based on consumption functions fitted for these countries. In general, the MPC is high for low income countries. MPC for India is estimated as 0.80. Japan has the lowest MPC of 0.66.

Table 4.5: Estimated Marginal Propensity to Consume (MPC) for Selected Countries

Country	*MPC*	*Country*	*MPC*
Argentina	0.81	India	0.80
Australia	0.76	Iraq	0.75
Belgium	0.80	Israel	0.90
Brazil	0.83	Italy	0.78
Canada	0.77	Japan	0.66
Chile	0.89	Pakistan	0.89
Cyprus	0.86	South Korea	0.88
Ethiopia	0.90	Sri Lanka	0.87
France	0.76	Taiwan	0.83
Ghana	0.87	West Germany	0.72

In India, some studies have been conducted to estimate the empirical consumption functions, and through this, to more clearly specify the income-consumption relationship. All these studies are attempts to estimate the short run consumption function. Most of these studies do not confirm either the relative income model or the permanent income model for income-consumption relationship in India. Instead, the studies lend support to the Keynesian type of absolute income hypothesis.

CONSUMPTION AND INCOME DETERMINATION

The concept of the consumption function or consumption function analysis makes important contribution to the income determination process. Given the consumption function, and a level of investment, the appropriate or equilibrium level of income in the economy can be determined.

The equilibrium income may be defined as that income at which the total of consumption and investment expenditures will be equal to the aggregate output (income). If the total planned expenditure is either higher or lower than income, the level of income cannot be maintained. If the planned expenditures are higher than income, the latter will grow to make them equal. Similarly, if planned expenditures are less, income will fall to equal total expenditures at equilibrium level. This is shown diagrammatically in Fig. 4.8.

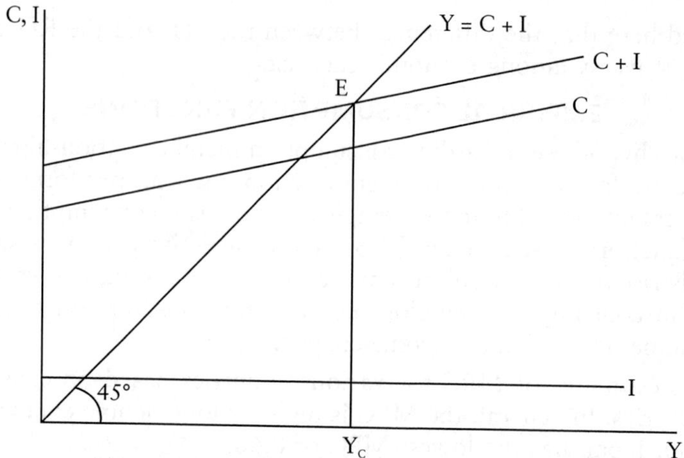

Fig. 4.8: Determination of Equilibrium Income

The equilibrium level of income is Y_0. Equilibrium is reached at E, where Y = C + I. The consumption function is linear and a fixed level fill vestment is assumed.

Let us explain the equilibrium income determination process mathematically. The linear income determination model may be written as

$$C = 30 + 0.8Y \quad \text{(i)}$$
$$I = 40 \quad \text{(ii)}$$
$$Y = C + I \quad \text{(iii)}$$

Equation (i) is the consumption function. Equation (ii) specifies the investment at all income levels. Equation (iii) is the equilibrium condition. By substituting equations (i) and (ii) in equation (iii), we get the solution the model as

$$Y = 30 + 0.8Y + 40; \text{ or } Y = 350$$

At an income of ₹ 350, consumption will be ₹ 310. The condition that planned expenditures will be equal to income will be satisfied by adding to it the investment of ₹ 40.

Table 4.6 more clearly shows equilibrium and non-equilibrium levels of income.

Only when income is ₹ 350, the condition that aggregate demand (expenditure) is equal to total income is satisfied. Therefore, in the table, only ₹ 350 is the equilibrium level of income.

Table 4.6: Aggregate Demand (Expenditure) and Equilibrium and Non-equilibrium Levels of Income

Income	*Consumption*	*Investment Demand*	*Aggregate Demand*	*Aggregate Demand-Income*
100	110	40	150	+50
200	190	40	230	+30
300	270	40	310	+10
350	310	40	350	0
400	350	40	390	–10

THE MULTIPLIER

The concept of the multiplier plays an important role in the income determination process. This determines how, or more specifically, by what amount income increases as the result of an increase in the level of investment. The multiplier, or the investment income multiplier as it is sometimes described, is in short, the ratio of Y to I. The ratio is always greater that I. Hence, the use of the expression *multiplier*. The multiplier shows the impact of an increase in investment on income through the savings function and, therefore, through the consumption function.

Let us explain the working of the multiplier. That is, we explain why or how an increase in investment leads to an increase in income that is a multiple of the increase in investment Since investment is part of income, an increase in investment will lead to an increase in income equal to it. But a rise in income following an increase in investment induces an increase in consumption spending also. Thus, the ultimate increase in income is composed of the original increase in investment and the induced increase in consumption brought about by it.

Let us assume that a firm enlarges its business by making an additional investment of ₹ 100 by buying a machine and installing it. This investment expenditure will become income for the machinery manufacturer and the workers employed to manufacture it. These income earners will spend this income on consumption expenditures. If the MPC is assumed to be 0.8, they will spend ₹ 80 on new consumption goods. The producers of these goods will have an additional income of ₹ 80 and they will, in turn, spend ₹ 64 (₹ 80 × 0.8) on additional goods, assuming that their MPC is also 0.8. Thus, there is a chain of income and consumption expenditure generated by an initial increase in investment. The total increase in income can be calculated as the sum of the increase in income at each stage. In the present example, it will be 100 + 100 × 0.8 + 100 × 0.8 × 0.8 + 1 × 0.8 × 0.8 × 0.8 and so on. Using the formula for geometric progression this will be equal to

$$\frac{100}{(1-0.8)} = 500, \text{ or } 500\,(\Delta Y) = \frac{1}{1-0.8}.100(\Delta I)$$

Therefore, $\frac{1}{1-0.8}$[7] is the multiplier and is equal to $\frac{1}{(1-MPC)}$ or $\frac{1}{MPS}$. It follows, then, that the larger the MPC, the higher is the MPS multiplier, because, the larger the MPC, the smaller is the MPS, and, therefore, the higher is the inverse of MPS. Analytically, larger MPC means that secondary expansion of income at each stage is higher.

The value of the multiplier can be directly derived from the income equation Y = C + I

$$Y = C + I$$

$$\therefore \quad \Delta Y = \Delta C + \Delta I$$

Dividing both sides by ΔY, we get

$$1 = \frac{\Delta C}{\Delta Y} + \frac{\Delta I}{\Delta Y}$$

7. This can be derived in terms of symbols as follows:

$$\Delta Y = \Delta Y_1 + \Delta Y_2 + \Delta Y_3 + \ldots + \Delta Y_t$$
$$= \Delta I + b\Delta I + b^2\Delta I + \ldots + b^{t+1}\,\Delta I \qquad (b = MPC)$$
$$= \Delta I\,(I + b + b^2 + \ldots + b^{t+1})$$

The sum in the bracket is a converging geometric series and is equal to $\frac{1}{1-b}$

$$\therefore \Delta Y = \frac{1}{1-b}.\,I \text{ or } \Delta Y/\Delta I = \frac{1}{(1-b)}$$

or $$\frac{\Delta I}{\Delta Y} = 1 - \frac{\Delta C}{\Delta Y}$$

or $$\frac{\Delta Y}{\Delta I} = \frac{1}{1 - \frac{\Delta C}{\Delta Y}}$$

REVIEW QUESTIONS

1. Explain the consumption function hypothesis.
2. What is APC and MPC? Explain these in terms of income, consumption and savings relationship.
3. Analyse consumption-income relationship in the short run and long run with diagrams.
4. Discuss and compare absolute income hypothesis, relative income hypothesis and permanent income hypothesis of consumption.
5. What is multiplier? Illustrate the role of the multiplier in the income determination process.

SUGGESTED READINGS

- R. Dornbusch and S. Fisher, *Macroeconomics*, International Edition, McGraw-Hill Inc., 1994.
- Gardner Ackley, *Macroeconomics: Theory and Policy*, 1978, Chapters 16 and 17.
- Edward Shapiro, *Macroeconomic Analysis*, Fifth Edition, 1997.

Chapter 5

Investment Decisions

In the preceding chapter, we assumed that the level of investment was autonomous, that is, independent of the level of income. In fact, we implicitly assumed that the level of investment was constant and as such, was independent of all variables. This is an oversimplification. The level of investment does fluctuate and there are many variables such as the interest rate, the level of income or output the wage rate the level of technology, and the corporate tax rate which influence the size and frequency of fluctuations. In this chapter, we shall discuss investment decisions and factors governing them.

INVESTMENT AND THE RATE OF INTEREST

The decision to invest depends upon whether or not the expected rate of return on investment is greater than the cost of borrowing the necessary funds; or if the finds are already available whether the expected returns are higher than interest earned by lending out the funds that is, the opportunity cost.

Let us restate the principle. The decision to invest in a machine (or any capital good or project) depends upon whether or not the investment is expected to yield more revenue over its lifetime than it costs to purchase and operate, i.e. whether it is expected to add to total profits. If the expected total revenue exceeds total cost the machine should be purchased. But, a machine or any capital good usually has a lifetime which extends over a number of years. Then how do we know what revenue will it earn in future years? What is the present value of all the future returns? Once we know these answers the machine should be purchased if the *present value* of the returns exceeds the cost.

For example, suppose that we expect (through market surveys and econometric forecasting) a particular machine to yield a return of ₹ R (say, ₹ 100) in each of the next n years. Therefore, we expect the total net returns from the machine over the next n years to be

$$R_1 + R_2 + R_3 + \dots + R_n + J$$

where J represents the scrap or salvage value of the machine after n years of use. Using this information, we can calculate the present value of the stream of returns[1] as,

1. We can demonstrate the method for calculating the present value of an asset. Suppose that the rate of interest is i and an individual lends out ₹ 100. After one year he will receive back ₹ 100 + ₹ 100i or ₹ 100 (1 + i). We may say, in general, that if the amount of money lent is P_0, the lender will receive at the end of one year

$$P_1 = P_0(1 + i)$$

$$V = \frac{R_1}{(1+i)} + \frac{R_2}{(1+i)^2} + \frac{R_3}{(1+i)^3} + \ldots + \frac{R_n}{(1+i)^n} + \frac{J}{(1+i)^n} \qquad \text{(i)}$$

where V represents the present value of the stream of returns and i is some appropriate interest rate. Further suppose that the machine initially 1,000; i is 0.05 and J equals 0. Then, we have

$$V = \frac{100}{(1.05)} + \frac{100}{(1.05)^2} + \ldots + \frac{100}{(1.05)^n}$$

or $$V = \frac{100}{0.05} \cong 2{,}000 \text{ as n gets very large}^2$$

Since V approaches ₹ 2,000 and C = ₹ 1,000, the decision to invest is a simple one. Since the present value of the expected stream of returns is greater than the cost of the machine, the entrepreneur should invest. So, with known life of a machine and the returns also known, V is easy to calculate, and hence, V can easily be compared to C.

RETURN ON INVESTMENT: MARGINAL EFFICIENCY OF CAPITAL

We have stated above that the rational entrepreneur will invest in a machine whenever the rate of return exceeds the cost of borrowing, or, in the absence of borrowing, the opportunity cost of the available funds. If the rate of return is r and, r is greater than i, then, the machine should be purchased even if it is necessary to borrow the funds.

But, how do we determine r? The expected rate of return r on any investment is simply the *discount rate which* exactly equates the value of all expected future earning to the cost of the machine. We say that

$$C = \frac{R_1}{(1+r)} + \frac{R_2}{(1+r)^2} + \frac{R_3}{(1+r)^3} + \ldots + \frac{R_n}{(1+r)^n} + \frac{J}{(1+r)^n} \qquad \text{(ii)}$$

where r is the expected rate of return on investment. It should be clear that r would be the discount factor in a present value problem; compare equation (ii) with equation (i). In economic jargon, r is called the marginal efficiency of capital (MEC), a concept introduced by Keynes.[3]

If the new sum is loaned out for another year, the amount received at the end of the second year is

$$P_2 = P_1(1 + i) = P_0(1 + i)(1 + i) = P_0(1 + i)^2$$

Following this procedure, a loan in n years would become

$$P_n = P_0(1 + i)^n$$

From this, it follows that $$P_n = \frac{P_n}{(1+i)^n}$$

P_0 is the present value of the claim, that is, value at maturity duly discounted by the rate of interest. But, an asset or a machine will yield a stream of returns over the years (same or different returns) and, the total present value of the returns will be equal to the sum of the expected returns in every year discounted by the rate of interest so that

$$V = \frac{R_1}{(1+i)} + \frac{R_2}{(1+i)^2} + \frac{R_3}{(1+i)^3} + \ldots + \frac{R_n}{(1+i)^n} + \frac{J}{(1+i)^n}$$

2. This involves summing of an infinite series using the formula $S = \frac{a}{(1-r)}$ where S is the sum of the series, a the first term in the series, and, r the ratio between terms.

3. J.M. Keynes, *The General Theory of Employment, Interest and Money*, 1936, p. 135.

It is the expected rate of return; it is also the discount rate which exactly equates the value of all expected returns to the initial cost of the investment.

Let us consider a simple example. Suppose that on an investment, the return is ₹ 100 per year and the initial cost of the machine is ₹ 1,000. Assuming that the machine has an infinite life, there is no salvage value to consider. Thus,

$$1000 = \frac{100}{1 + r} + \frac{100}{(1 + r)^2} + \ldots + \frac{100}{(1 + r)^n}$$

or, $$1000 = \frac{100}{r}$$

∴ $$r = 0.10$$

If i = 0.05 so that lending ₹ 1,000 yields ₹ 50 as return, it is wise to invest in the machine. The return from the machine or the MEC is twice as much as the interest payment, since r = 2i. It is generally quite difficult to calculate r particularly in cases in which returns differ from year to year and, when life expectancy of the machine is not infinite. But, whenever r is greater than i, V will exceed C. And, as long as the MEC (r) is greater than the rate of interest (i), or, as long as the present value of the stream of future returns (V) exceeds the cost (C), investment should take place.

Suppose that a business manager sees an array of potential investment projects available to his firm. Since each investment project is different, each has a different stream of returns, a different initial cost, a different present value, and a different rate of return (MEC). Suppose that the firm can borrow unlimited funds at a constant rate of interest. The business manager can array each investment project according to the amount by which r (MEC) exceeds i; after all, the higher the rate of return above the cost of borrowed funds, the more profitable is the investment. Such a situation is illustrated in Table 5.1.

The business manager should invest in Project 1 because it adds more to the firm's revenues than it does to costs, and, thereby, increases total profits of the firm. He should invest in Project 2 for the same reasons. He should be indifferent about Project 3 because it adds equally to revenue and cost, and, thereby leaves the total profits of the firm unchanged. He should not invest in Projects 4 and 5 because they add more to costs than to revenues, and, thereby decrease total profits of the firm. Therefore, investment should take place to the point where the marginal efficiency of capital (r) equals the cost of borrowing.

Table 5.1: Investment Criteria

Investment Project	*r*	*i*	*(r – i)*
1	0.10	0.05	0.05
2	0.08	0.05	0.03
3	0.05	0.05	0
4	0.04	0.05	– 0.01
5	0.03	0.05	– 0.02

CHANGES IN INTEREST RATE AND INVESTMENT

Let us now see what happens if the rate of interest falls. If the rate of interest falls from 5 to 3 per cent, investment opportunities with rates of return just over 3 per cent now become profitable. Under these circumstances, the businessman should increase his level of investment up to, but not beyond, Project 5.

Thus, we conclude that as the rate of interest falls, the level of investment increases, assuming that the MEC remains unchanged.

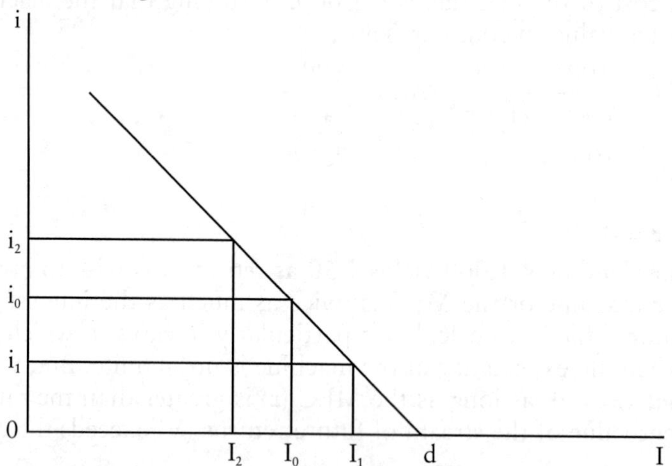

Fig. 5.1: Rate of Interest and Investment

Hence, we can graphically show an investment function relating the level of investment to the rate of interest (Fig. 5.1).

In Fig. 5.1, we have shown (for simplicity) a linear investment function. The equation of such an investment function is

$$I = d + ei$$

where d is positive and e is negative. The fact that e is negative indicates that the level of investment increases as the rate of interest falls (that is investment and interest rate are negatively correlated), and, the fact that d is positive shows that when the rate of interest falls to zero, the level of investment will reach some maximum level, d.

For a given level of interest i_0 the level of investment would be I_0. If the rate of interest increases to i_2 investment level will fall to I_2. If interest rate falls to i_1, investment will increase to I_1, and, eventually increase to d when $i = 0$.

INVESTMENT AND THE LEVEL OF NATIONAL INCOME

In addition to the rate of interest, the level of national income is also an important determinant of the level of investment. As the level of national income increases, investment opportunities become more plentiful, and, so the level of investment, for any given rate of interest, will increase. Thus, there would be an upward shift in the investment function shown in Fig. 5.1.

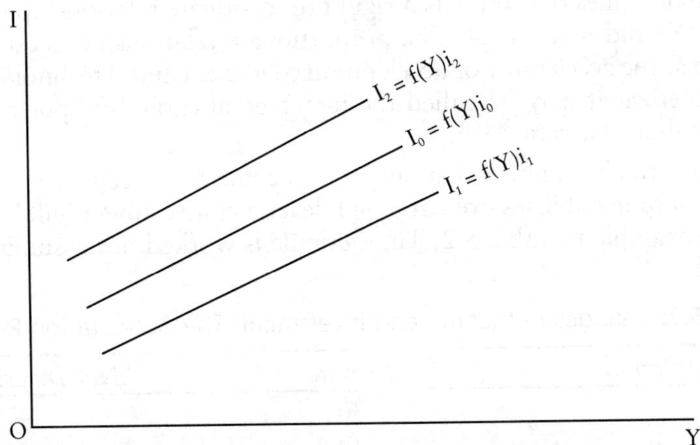

Fig. 5.2: Investment and the Level of National Income

Likewise if the level of national income falls, the investment function would shift to the left indicating that, at all levels of the interest rate, the level of investment will go down. This implies lack of investment opportunities. We can graphically show the relationship between the level of investment and the level of national income in Fig. 5.2.

In Fig. 5.2, it may be seen that for a given level of the rate of interest i_0, the investment function (relating investment to income, the two being positively correlated) is

$$I_0 = f(Y)i_0$$

If the interest rate increases to i_1, the investment function would shift downwards to I_1; and if the rate of interest decreases to i_2, the investment function would shift upwards to I_2.

CHANGES IN THE LEVEL OF INCOME AND INVESTMENT: THE ACCELERATION PRINCIPLE

We have explained above that national income is an important determinant of the level of investment. It may be more correct to say that *changes in the level of income* is a more direct determinant of the level of investment. This is stated by the Acceleration Principle. Let us explain the principle.

A firm decides to make an investment when it expects its sales to increase. Assuming the same inventory levels, sales can increase only when output increases. Thus, investment in any period by a firm may be taken as a function of the expected increase in output. If the expected increases can be treated as similar to the past changes, investment in any given period can be made a function of past changes in output. This is stated by the acceleration principle. Thus, according to the acceleration principle

$$I_t = f(O_t - O_{t-1})$$

where I stands for investment and O for output. This is a general functional form. A specific formulation of this functional form would be

$$I_t = v(O_t - O_{t-1})$$

For a national economy, the principle would be stated as

$$I_t = v(Y_t - Y_{t-1})$$

This formulation implies that there is a rigid proportionate relationship between changes in output or income (Y) and investment. The proportionate relationship is established through v which is referred to as the accelerator or acceleration coefficient and is technologically determined. The acceleration coefficient may be called the incremental capital-output ratio which is quite similar to the capital-output ratio.[4]

The acceleration principle implies that output or income must keep growing if net investment[5] is to be positive. If output stabilises even at a high level, net investment will become zero. This is illustrated with an example in Table 5.2. The example is worked out assuming the acceleration coefficient to be 2.

Table 5.2: Changes in Income and Investment: The Acceleration Principle

Time Period	*Income*	*Net Investment*
t	30	—
t + 1	40	20
t + 2	60	40
t + 3	70	20
t + 4	80	20
t + 5	95	30
t + 6	95	0
t + 7	90	–10

It would be seen in Table 5.2 when income stabilises at 95, net investment drops to 0. When income falls, net investment becomes negative, although output itself is at a high level. This example also indicates why induced investment (that is investment induced by increase in income) fluctuates, sometimes violently, as income fluctuates.

The rigid proportional relationship between investment and increase in income as stated by the acceleration principle may not always hold good. For example, if there is excess capacity in an industry, investment need not be made to keep pace with increase in output. The accelerator operates with greater force when all capacity has been used up, and, therefore, an increase in output will compel businessmen to invest.

The proportionate relationship between increase in output and investment may not also be maintained because of the lumpiness of capital. Because capital is not always divisible (plant and machinery are made with certain minimum capacity), not every increase in output can be matched by an appropriate level of investment. Sometimes, it pays to install a capacity larger than that required by the change in output and to let the increase in output catch up with capacity later.

INVESTMENT AND THE WAGE RATE

Does the wage rate influence the level of investment? It may not influence investment as directly as the rate of interest or the level of income, but, is likely to influence investment decisions by affecting the profitability of a particular investment project.

4. The capital-output ratio is given as K_t/Y_t where K is capital stock. Incremental capital-output ratio is estimated as $K_t - K_{t-1}/Y_t - Y_{t-1}$. The concept of capital-output ratio and its empirical use is discussed in Chapter 13.
5. The acceleration principle applies only to net investment. Replacement investment (that is, investment for replacement of machines which have become worn out) is not influenced by changes in income or output. Even if income remains at the same level, it will be necessary to replace worn out machines.

If we assume that the wage rate increases and the level of employment does not fall, then the wage bill must increase. For any particular producer, such a situation might make a particular investment less profitable than if the wage rate had not increased. This would also be true in the aggregate.

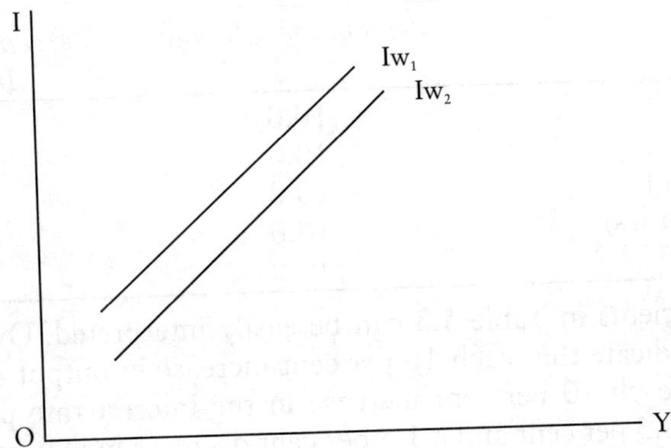

Fig. 5.3: Income, Investment and the Wage Rate

Under such situations, the inducement to invest at a particular level of income will be less; or, in other words, if the wage rate increases (from say w_1 or w_2) this would cause the investment function (relating investment to income) to shift downwards, i.e. for the same level of income, investment will be less, because the increase in the wage rate has made any investment now less profitable than before (Fig. 5.3).

TECHNOLOGY AND THE LEVEL OF INVESTMENT

In addition to the various factors mentioned above, the level of technology also plays a positive role in investment decisions. It may be difficult to establish a direct relationship between technological changes and the level of investment; the former generally influence investment decisions by causing a shift in the investment function. Inventions may make existing capital equipment obsolete. This will create need for new capital equipment which will generate demand for additional investible funds. In such a case, there will be an upward shift in the investment function, but it will be less pronounced. So, we can say that, in general, the effect of technological changes will be to cause an upward shift in the investment function.

EMPIRICAL INVESTMENT FUNCTIONS

Many empirical attempts have been made to estimate the relative statistical significance importance of the various factors which influence the level of investment or investment the ns. A complete discussion of the investment function requires that we analyse some of correlampts or results. More recent studies have attempted, through regression analysis, to the rates nges in investment with changes in such variables as output (acceleration principle), rate of price erest paid on debt (bonds) and equity (stocks), the corporate tax rate and the tion.

In order to as

of investment to ea in the relative roles of the variables, we examine the sensitivity or elasticity percentage change in in f the variables individually. The elasticity of investment measures the variables; for example, the ment induced by a given percentage change in one of the independent investment induced by every p sticity of investment to output measures the percentage change in percentage point increase in outpu entage change in output—if this elasticity equals 4, everyone vould produce a 4 percentage point increase in investment.

The elasticity coefficients derived from some regression analysis based on data for the period 1975 to 1990 for the US economy are summarised in Table 5.3.

Table 5.3: Determinants of Investment: Empirical Analysis

Change in Independent Variable		
Variable	*Percentage Change*	*Percentage Change in Investment*
Output	10.0	8.3
Corporate tax rate	10.0	– 4.0
Interest rate (bond)	10.0	– 3.5
Interest rate (equities)	10.0	– 1.5
Price inflation	10.0	1.6

The elasticity coefficients in Table 5.3 can be easily interpreted. Over the period, 1975 to 1996, the coefficients indicate that each 10 per cent increase in output results in a 8.3 per cent increase in investment; each 10 per cent increase in the interest rate paid to debt and equity instruments results in a 3.5 per cent and a 1.5 per cent decrease in investment respectively; every 10 per cent increase in the corporate tax rate results in a 4.0 per cent decrease in investment; and, every 10 per cent increase in the rate of price inflation results in a 1.6 per cent increase in investment.

Using these elasticity coefficients, we can draw a number of conclusions about the relative importance of each variable in determining the level of investment. Over the period 1953 to 1968, changes in the level of output was the most significant factor influencing investment decisions. The corporate tax rate was the second most significant variable followed closely by the interest rate paid on bonds. This was followed by the interest rate on equities and the rate of price inflation (these two factors being of equal significance).

The above empirical analysis, therefore, suggests that the accelerator principle dominates the investment demand function. It also suggests that a complete investment demand function must include the corporate tax rate as an important explanatory variable. The rate of price inflation, though not as important as the corporate tax rate, should also be included in empirical analysis of investment demand functions.

REVIEW QUESTIONS

1. Explain the relationship between investment and the rate of interest with reference to a capital project.
2. What is marginal efficiency of capital? Analyse marginal efficiency of capital in an investment project.
3. Define the acceleration principle. Explain its working with example.
4. Is there any relationship between technology and the level of investment? Comm
5. Discuss some empirical investment functions.

SUGGESTED READINGS

- R. Dornbusch and S. Fisher, *Macroeconomics*, International Edition, 1994.
- Edward Shapiro, *Macroeconomic Analysis*, Fifth Edition, 1997.
- N.F. Keiser, *Macroeconomics*, 1971, Chapters 9 and 11.

Chapter 6

Determination of National Income: Basic Keynesian Model

In Chapter 2, we had discussed the classical theory of output and employment. In this and the next chapter, we analyse the Keynesian theory of income determination which is the basis for most of modern macroeconomic analysis. Keynesian theory of income determination is an attempt to develop a new theory of income and employment in contrast to the classical theory. In the classical theory of output and employment, the emphasis was on the supply side ('supply creates its own demand'); in the Keynesian theory, the focus was on demand or aggregate demand in the income determination process. Aggregate demand consists of both consumption and investment. We shall see this more clearly as we proceed.

Keynesian theory of income determination is discussed in three forms or models: the two-sector model: the three-sector model and the four-sector model. The basic or simple Keynesian model consists of two sectors: firms and the households; in the three-sector model, the government sector is added to the two sectors; in the four-sector model, the foreign sector or foreign trade is included. The first and second models are *closed economy* models; the third model is *open economy* model.

The basic or simple Keynesian model of income determination is discussed in this chapter. The extended model including the government sector and the foreign sector is presented in the next two chapters.

IMPORTANT VARIABLES AND FUNCTIONS

To clearly understand the Keynesian model of income determination, it is necessary to know the important concepts or variables and functions used in the model. These variables and functions are:

1. Aggregate supply
2. Aggregate demand
3. Consumption
4. Savings
5. Investment (autonomous or constant)

Aggregate Supply (AS)

In the simple Keynesian model, the aggregate supply curve is assumed to be perfectly elastic till the full employment level of output or income is reached. Once the full employment level of output has been reached, the aggregate supply (AS) curve becomes perfectly inelastic or vertical. The AS curve is shown in Fig. 6.1.

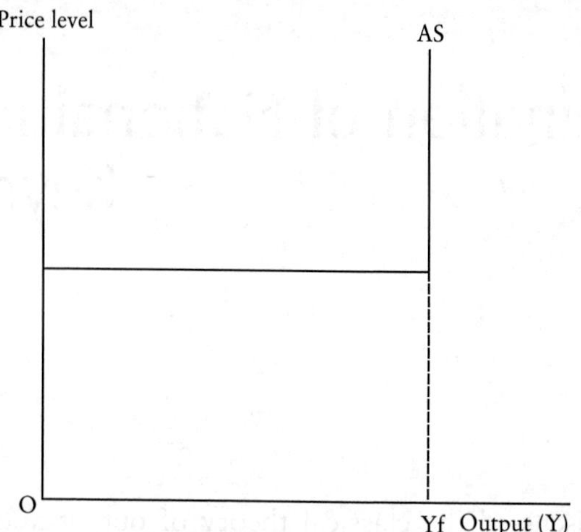

Fig. 6.1: The Aggregate Supply Curve in Keynesian Theory

The special shape of the aggregate supply curve (Fig. 6.1) means that the equilibrium level of output or income is determined entirely by aggregate demand, i.e., the point of intersection of the aggregate demand (AD) curve and aggregate supply (AS) curve. This shows the predominant role of aggregate demand or spending in the Keynesian system of income determination.

Aggregate supply, in the Keynesian theory, is aggregate output or Y. As an income concept, this closely approximates to personal disposable income.[1] As personal disposable income, two components of Y are consumption (C) and savings (S). In terms of an equation, this can be written as

$$Y = C + S$$

Some economists would like to call this an accounting identity. Then, this can be restated as an accounting identity as

$$Y \equiv C + S$$

Aggregate Demand (AD)

Aggregate demand (AD), in Keynesian theory, is same as aggregate expenditure. Aggregate expenditure consists of private final consumption (C), i.e., total consumption of the household sector and the business sector. Aggregate demand and aggregate expenditure (C + I) are accounting identities. In terms of equation or identity, this can be written as

$$AD \equiv C + I$$

We had mentioned in Chapter 3 that one approach to measurement of national income (Y) is the expenditure approach according to this Approach

$$Y = C + I$$

As mentioned in Chapter 3, this is the famous Keynesian income equation

In $AD \equiv C + I$ or $Y = C + I$

$$C = a + by$$

1. The concept of personal disposable income has been explained in Chapter 3.

This is the consumption function. This has been explained in Chapter 4; therefore, not explained here again.

In the simple Keynesian theory of income determination, investment is assumed as autonomous or given or constant. This can be written as

$$I = \overline{I}$$

With these conceptual clarifications of the variables constant involved, the aggregate demand is graphically shown in Fig. 6.2.

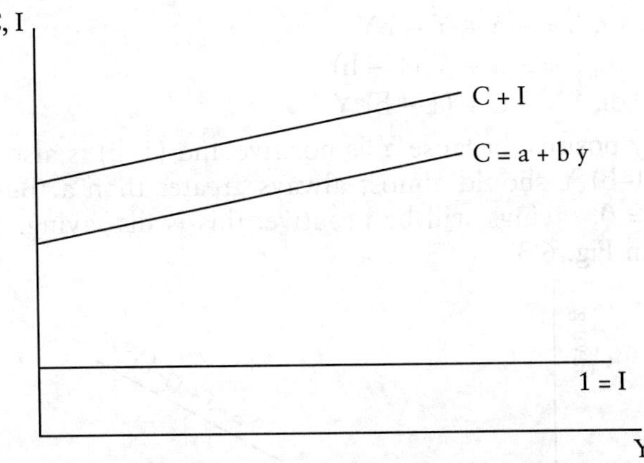

Fig. 6.2: The Aggregate Demand Curve

Consumption (C)

Consumption and the consumption function play a key role in the Keynesian theory of income determination. Because investment is assumed as constant, aggregate demand is mostly determined by consumption and fluctuations in aggregate demand depend on changes in consumption or the consumption function.

Consumption, consumption function (short run as well as long run) and related parameters had been elaborately discussed in Chapter 4. The consumption function used, as just mentioned, is linear of the form

$$C = a + bY^2$$

The consumption function has been graphically shown Fig. 6.2. In the equation, 'a' is autonomous consumption, that is consumption level even if income (Y) is zero; 'b' is marginal propensity to consume (MPC). MPC is expressed as $\Delta C/\Delta y$ and is always positive, i.e., $0<MPC<1$. The MPC plays an important role in the 'multiplier'. We will be discussing the use of multiplier in the income determination process in a later section. In addition to MPC, average propensity to consume (APC) is also an important concept and parameter in the consumption function. APC is expressed as C/Y.

Saving (S)

Saving, we all know, is the opposite or counterpart of consumption or spending. Like consumption, savings is also a function of income, or more correctly, disposable income and can be expressed as

2. The original Keynesian theory postulates a non-linear consumption function. The Keynesian economists, have, however, used a linear consumption function to reconstruct and present the Keynesian theory of income determination. They have also empirically estimated the consumption function which is linear in form.

$$S = f(Y)$$

The saving function can be derived from the consumption function. We start with the income equation or identity

$$Y = C + S$$

Substituting (a + bY) for C, we get

$$Y = a + bY + S$$

or, $S = Y - a - bY$
or, $S = -a + Y - bY$
or, $S = -a + Y(1 - b)$
or, $S = -a + (1 - b)Y$

Savings is normally positive because Y is positive and (1–b) is also positive, i.e., $0 < (1-b) < 1$ (b is MPC) and (1–b) Y should almost always greater than a. But, theoretically, if (1–b) Y is less than a or Y = 0, savings will be negative; this is dis-saving. The savings function is graphically presented in Fig. 6.3

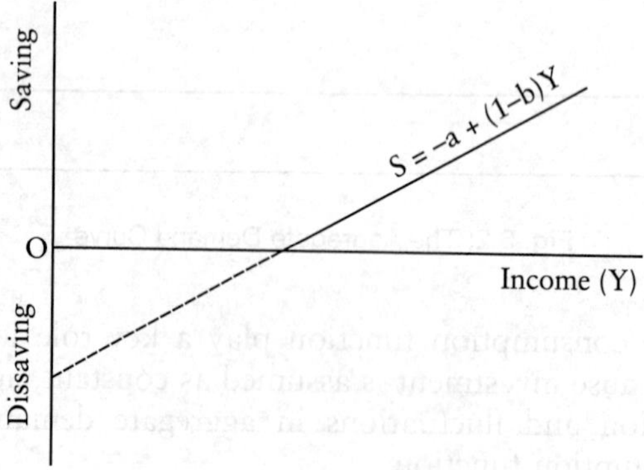

Fig. 6.3: The Savings Function or Curve

In the savings equation, (1–b) is the marginal propensity to save (MPS) which is expressed as $\Delta S/\Delta Y$. MPS plays a key role in working of the multiplier. The average propensity to save (APS) is written as S/Y. It should also be clear by now, as already mentioned in Chapter 4, that APC + APS = 1 and, also, MPC + MPS = 1.

Investment (I)

Investment and factors governing decision to invest were discussed in the previous chapter. The level of investment—and fluctuations in this—depends on many factors or variables like the interest rate, the level of output or income, the wage rate, technology level, etc. The nature of relationship—functional relationships—between investment and these variables was discussed in details in Chapter 5. The acceleration principle which specifies and measures the relationship between changes in income and the level of investment was also explained.

In the Keynesian theory of income determination, however, investment plays a limited role. This is because, in the income determination process, investment is assumed to be exogenously given or constant (I). It neither influences nor is influenced by other variables in the system. But, a change (increase) in the amount of autonomous investment has definite impact on the income generation or determination process. The impact is created through the multiplier. This is discussed later.

SIMPLE KEYNESIAN MODEL

We have defined/explained different variables and constants involved in the simple Keynesian income determination process. We can now present the model.

Assumptions of the Model

The model is based on certain inherent assumptions. Some of these assumptions are explicit, some are implied or implicit. We shall first mention these assumption and then present the model. Some of these assumptions have already been indicated or implied.

The important assumptions in the simple Keynesian theory of income determination are:

(a) In the simple economy, there are only two sectors: household and business; there is no government;
(b) Because there is no government, there are no government operations—no government expenditure or taxes;
(c) The business sector does not have retained earnings, i.e., there is no corporate savings; the entire profit is paid out as dividend;
(d) Supply of capital is fixed; this is implied in the constancy of investment;
(e) The level of technology is given, that is, there is no technological change;
(f) All prices (includes both commodity and factor prices) are constant, i.e., there is no price effect;
(g) The economy is closed economy; this means that there is no foreign trade and also no funds inflow from or outflow to foreign countries.

Equilibrium Income and Output: Two Approaches

In the Keynesian theory, equilibrium level of national income and output is determined at the point or level where aggregate demand (C + 1) becomes equal to aggregate supply of output (income) (C + S). So, equilibrium income is reached where

$$\text{Aggregate demand} = \text{Aggregate supply}$$
$$\text{or, } AD = AS$$
$$\text{or, } C + I = C + S$$

From this, it also follows that

S = I (because C is common to both sides).

So, it can be said that, in the Keynesian theory/system, there can be two approaches to determination of national income. The two approaches are:

1. Aggregate demand—Aggregate supply (AD-AS) approach
2. Saving-Investment (S-I) approach

We shall separately discuss the two approaches.

Aggregate Demand-Aggregate Supply (AD-AS) Approach

According to Keynesian theory, aggregate demand need not always or automatically be equal to aggregate supply. Aggregate demand depends on the plans of the household sector and business sector to consume, save and invest. Aggregate supply is determined by manufacturers' plans to produce. Aggregate demand will be equal to aggregate supply if and only when consumption and investment plans of the household sector and the business sector completely match or become identical with the manufacturers' plans to produce and supply. This will happen only at *one particular level* of output or income. This, according to Keynesian theory, is equilibrium income.

Let us see the determination of the equilibrium level of income in terms of equations. The equilibrium condition is

$$AD = AS$$
$$\text{or, } C + I = C + S$$

We also have (as stated earlier)

$$Y = C + I$$
$$C = a + bY$$
$$I = \bar{I}$$

With these equations, Y = C + I can be rewritten, with substitutions for C and I as

$$Y = a + bY + \bar{I}$$
$$\text{or, } Y - bY = a + \bar{I}$$
$$\text{or, } Y(1 - b) = a + \bar{I}$$
$$\text{or, } Y = a + \bar{I}/1 - b$$
$$\text{or, } Y = 1/(1 - b)\cdot(a + \bar{I}) \qquad (6.1)$$

Y is the equilibrium level of income. Value of Y can be estimated by putting appropriate values of a, b and $\bar{I}$. Once the value of Y is determined, the value of C also can be worked out. This can be done though algebraic analysis or numerical solution.[3]

Keynesian theory of income determination is conventionally explained through graphical presentation. The consumption function or curve, the investment function or curve, the aggregate demand curve, the AD-AS equality (45°) line are all presented in a single diagramme to show the equilibrium level of income in the Keynesian theory or model. This can be seen in Fig. 6.4.[4]

Equilibrium and Disequilibrium

It is seen in Fig. 6.4 that equilibrium level of income is reached at point E where the aggregate demand curve intersects with or cuts the 45° (AD = AS) line. Equilibrium level of income is Y_O. All other points in the diagramme other than E show disequilibrium levels of income, i.e., either AD > AS or AD < AS. At all points to the right of EY_O, AD < AS and at all points to the left of EY_O, AD > AS.

All points to the right of EY_O mean that the producers or the business sector has overproduced. If aggregate demand is less than total output or aggregate supply, excess production will add to inventories. If this happens period after period, the producer will be under pressure to liquidate inventories and cut-back production. With cut-back in production, output will fall and income also will fall. This process will continue till output and income fall to Y_O level and equilibrium is restored. Aggregate demand will become equal to aggregate supply or output. Opposite forces will work at all points to the left of EYO where aggregate demand is more than aggregate supply or output. This will induce producers to increase output to meet the unfulfilled demand. The process continues till output reaches Y_O level and equilibrium is restored.

3. Y and C are the only two unknowns in this equation system.
4. It is to be noted that the aggregate supply curve shown in Fig. 6.1 is not used for analysis of the equilibrium level of income.

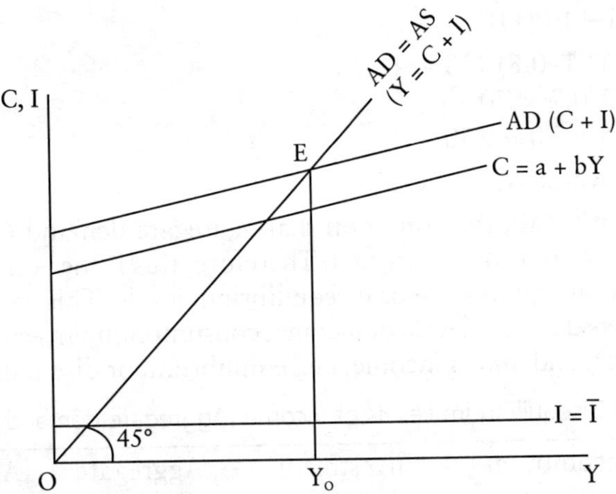

Fig. 6.4: Determination of Equilibrium Level of Income

Income Determination Model: Application Analysis

Equilibrium and disequilibrium situations will be more clear through application analysis of the Keynesian income determination model.

We state again the income determination model

$C = a + bY$	Consumption function	(6.2)
$I = \bar{I}$	Investment level (constant)	(6.3)
$Y = C + I$	Equilibrium condition	(6.4)

To find the equilibrium level of income, let us put the values (hypothetical) for the constants/parameters a, b and $\bar{I}$. Let a = 30, b = 0.8 and $\bar{I}$ = 40.

With these values of a, b and $\bar{I}$, Equation (6.2), Equation (6.3) and Equation (6.4) may be rewritten as

$$C = 30 + 0.8\,Y \quad (6.5)$$
$$\bar{I} = 40 \quad (6.6)$$
$$Y = C + I \quad (6.7)$$

By substituting Equation (6.5) and Equation (6.6) in Equation (6.7), we get

$$Y = 30 + 0.8\,Y + 40$$

or, $Y = 70 + 0.8Y$

or, $Y - 0.8\,Y = 70$

or, $Y(1 - 0.8) = 70$

or, $Y(0.2) = 70$

or, $1/5\,Y = 70$

or, $Y = 350$

∴ Equilibrium level of income is ₹ 350.[5] Consumption ₹ 310 derived from Equation (6.5)

Equilibrium level of income can also be directly estimated from the formula for Y or Equation (6.1) by putting the values of a, b and $\bar{I}$. This is worked out below:

5. For a real economy, the actual values of a, b and $\bar{I}$ will be taken from national income statistics. Correct estimation of national income in the simple Keynesian model will depend on availability of proper data base.

$$Y = 1/(1-b)\cdot(a+\bar{I})$$
$$\text{or, } Y = 1/(1-0.8)\ (30 + 40)$$
$$\text{or, } Y = 1/0.2 \times 70$$
$$\text{or, } Y = 5 \times 70 = 350$$

So, we get the same value of Y = ₹ 350.

Only when income is ₹ 350, the condition that aggregate demand (expenditure) is equal to aggregate supply (income or output) is satisfied. Therefore, this is the equilibrium level of income. All other incomes show non-equilibrium or disequilibrium levels. This can be more clearly seen in Table 6.1. The table shows different levels of income, consumption, investment demand, aggregate demand and aggregate demand *minus* income, i.e., equilibrium or disequilibrium levels of income.

Table 6.1: Equilibrium and Disequilibrium Levels of Income (Aggregate demand ***minus*** output or income)

Output/ Income	Consumption	Investment Demand	Aggregate Demand	Aggregate Demand – Income
100	110	40	150	+ 50
200	190	40	280	+ 80
300	270	40	310	+ 10
350	310	40	350	0
400	350	40	390	–10

Only at income level ₹ 350, aggregate demand *minus* income is equal to 0. Therefore, only ₹ 350 is the equilibrium level of income with particular values of a, b and $\bar{I}$ as mentioned.

Savings-Investment (S-I) Approach

As mentioned earlier, equilibrium level of income in the Keynesian theory can also be determined through the savings-investment approach. This is discussed below.

In this approach, we have to first state or derive the savings function. Like consumption, savings is also a function of income; in fact, as stated earlier, consumption and savings are counterparts of each other in disposable income. The savings function may be stated as

$$S = f(Y)$$

We have stated earlier that

$$Y = C + S$$

$$\text{or, } S = Y - C \qquad (6.8)$$

The consumption function is

$$C = a + b\,Y \qquad (6.9)$$

Substituting Equation (6.9) in Equation (6.8), we get

$$S = Y - C$$
$$\text{or, } S = Y - (a + bY)$$
$$\text{or, } S = Y - a - bY$$
$$\text{or, } S = -\,a + Y\,(1-b)$$
$$\text{or, } S = -\,a + (1-b)Y$$ [6]

Investment in the Keynesian theory is autonomous or constant ($\bar{I}$). Therefore, the equilibrium condition in the savings-investment approach may be stated as

$$S = \bar{I}$$

6. The savings function was derived earlier also.

or, $\bar{I} = -a + (1-b)Y$

or, $Y = 1/(1-b)\cdot(a + \bar{I})$ (6.10)

The equilibrium condition in Equation (6.10) can also be derived directly from the equilibrium condition in AD-AS approach. In this approach, as shown earlier, the equilibrium condition is

$$AD = AS$$

or, $C + I = C + S$

C is common to both sides, and, therefore, cancels out and the equilibrium condition can be written as

$$I = S$$

or, $\bar{I} = S$

The equilibrium condition using the savings-investment approach is graphically shown in Fig. 6.5.

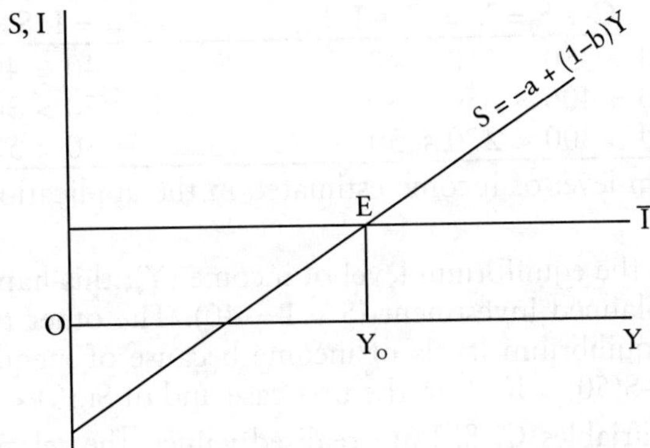

Fig. 6.5: Equilibrium Level of Income: Savings-Investment Approach

Equilibrium level of income Y_O shown in Fig. 6.5 is same as equilibrium level of income Y_O (in terms of value) as shown in Fig. 6.4 determined by the AD-AS approach. This will be clear when we do the application analysis of equilibrium income determination through savings-investment approach. Before that, clarification is required about the nature or meaning of savings and investment—in terms of planned and realised—used in this approach or the Keynesian model.

Savings and Investment: Planned and Realised

The distinction between *planned* and *realised* values or magnitudes—particularly for saving and investment should be clearly understood because this is linked to equilibrium and disequilibrium levels of income.

Conceptually, there can be planned consumption and actual or realised consumption; and, there can be difference between the two because consumption plans of the household and business sectors may not always materialise, i.e., realised consumption may be more or less than planned consumption. Because of the same reason, realised saving can be different than planned saving. However, in Keynesian theory, it is implicitly assumed that consumption plans are realised, and, therefore, savings plans are also realised at different levels of income during different periods.[7]

7. If this assumption is dropped, realised saving may be different (more or less) than planned savings and disequilibrium situations may arise.

But, this is not true of the relationship between planned saving and planned investment and also between planned investment and realised investment. Planned investment can be different than planned savings and realised investment can be different than planned investment. But, *realised savings is always equal to realised investment.* This is almost an identity. *Only at the equilibrium level of income, planned savings is equal to planned investment.* This can be clearly seen in numerical illustrations or examples of income, consumption planned savings, planned investment, realised savings and realised investment. This is shown in Table 6.2. The table presents planned supply (C + S), planned demand or expenditure (C + I), planned savings and planned investment (S = I or S ≠ I) and realised savings and realised investment (S ≡ I). The illustrations or examples have been given for three different time periods with equilibrium and disequilibrium levels of income with corresponding levels of consumption, savings and investment.

Table 6.2: Planned Income Levels (Y, C + S, C + I), Planned Savings and Investment (S = I or S ≠ I) and Realised Savings and Investment (S ≡ I)

Period	Planned C + S = Y = C + I	Planned S = I, S ≠ I	Realised S ≡ I
1.	310 + 40 = 350 = 310 + 40	40 = 40	40 = 40
2.	350 + 50 = 400 > 350 + 30	50 > 30	50 = 50
3.	270 + 30 = 300 < 270 + 50	30 < 50	30 = 30

This is the equilibrium level of income estimated in the application analysis and shown in Table 6.1.

In Table 6.2, ₹ 350 is the equilibrium level of income (Y); this happens because of equality of planned savings and planned investment (S = I = 40). The other two estimated incomes—₹ 400 and 300—are disequilibrium levels of income because of inequality of planned savings and planned investment—S(50) > I(30) in the first case and of S(30) < I(50) in the second case.

But, if all the three variables C, S, I are realised values, the relationships shown in Table 6.2 become identities rather than equations and all depict equilibrium situations. This is shown in Table 6.3.

Table 6.3: Realised Income Levels (Y, C + S, C + I) and Realised Savings and Investment (S ≡ I)

Period	Realised C + S ≡ Y ≡ C + I	Realised S ≡ I
1.	310 + 40 = 350 = 310 + 40	40 = 40
2.	350 + 50 = 400 = 350 + 50	50 = 50
3.	270 + 30 = 300 = 270 + 30	30 = 30

The difference between planned investment and realised investment (shown in Table 6.2) indicates that there is planned investment which may be positive or negative or even zero in special case. This also means that *realised investment is equal to planned investment plus unplanned investment.* This can be seen and derived from Table 6.2. Realised saving and realised investment, as already mentioned, are always equal. This can be clearly seen in Table 6.4.

Table 6.4: Planned Investment, Unplanned Investment, Realised Investment and Realised Saving

Period	Income	Planned Investment	+	Unplanned Investment	=	Realised Investment	=	Realised Saving
1.	350	40	+	0	=	40	=	40
2.	400	30	+	20	=	50	=	50
3.	300	50	–	20	=	30	=	30

The difference between realised investment and planned investment, i.e., unplanned investment, at each level of income is explained by changes in inventories. At income level of 400, unplanned investment is 20. This amounts to an increase in inventory which has not been planned, that is, some of the goods produced for sale could not be sold, and, therefore added to inventory of finished goods. The opposite happens at income level of 300. At this level of income, unplanned investment is (–) 20. This means that there is an unplanned decrease in inventories of 20, that is, goods not planned for sale have been sold. Both 400 and 300 are disequilibrium levels of income. This establishes that, if there is any unplanned investment, planned investment will not be equal to realised investment, the economy will be at disequilibrium levels of output or income. Only if unplanned investment is zero, the economy will be at equilibrium level of income. This happens at income level of 350.

Saving-Investment Approach: Application Analysis

For estimating the equilibrium level of income in saving-investment approach, we start the application analysis with the savings equation mentioned in Equation (6.8):

$$S = Y - C$$

We know that C = a + b Y (stated in Equation (6.9))

By substitution, we get

$$S = Y - (a + b\,Y) \tag{6.11}$$

We assume the same values of a and b as we did in the application analysis in the AD-AS approach, that is a = 30 and b = 0.8. Then equation (6.11) can be restated as

$$S = Y - (30 + 0.8\,Y)$$

or, $S = -\,30 + Y - 0.8\,Y$

or, $S = -\,30 + Y\,(1–0.8)$ (6.12)

The equilibrium condition in the saving-investment approach is

$$S = I = \bar{I}$$

We have assumed the value of $\bar{I}$ as 40 in Equation (6.6). Therefore, the equilibrium condition S = I can be restated in terms of numerical values as

$$-\,30 + Y\,(1–0.8) = 40$$

or, $Y\,(1–0.8) = 40 + 30$

or, $Y\,(0.2) = 70$

or, $1/5\,Y = 70$

or, $Y = 350$

∴ The equilibrium level of income is ₹ 350. This is the same value of income we had received in the application analysis in the aggregate demand-aggregate supply approach to income determination. This shows that both the AD-AS approach and the S-I approach give the same result or solution for equilibrium income.

THE MULTIPLIER AND INCOME DETERMINATION PROCESS

The concept and the mechanism of the multiplier plays an important role in the income determination process. The multiplier determines how, or more specifically *by what amount income increases as a result of an increase in the level of investment*. The multiplier, or the investment multiplier as it is often called, is the *ratio of change in income to change in investment*, or in short, ratio of ΔY to ΔI, i.e., ΔY/ΔI. The ratio is always greater than 1; hence, the name or expression *multiplier*. The multiplier shows the impact of a change in investment on income through the savings function, and, therefore, through the consumption function. It is actually the propensity to consume (MPC) and propensity to save (MPS) which are at work.

How the Multiplier Works

Let us explain how the multiplier or rather how the *mechanism* of multiplier works. That is, we explain why or how an increase in investment leads to an increase in income which is a multiple of the increase in investment. Since investment is part of income (Y = C + I), an increase in investment will initially lead to an increase in income equal to it. But, a rise in income following an increase in investment induces an increase in consumption spending also. Thus, the ultimate increase in income is composed of the initial increase in investment and induced increase in consumption brought about by this.

Let us explain this further. Let us assume that a firm expands it business by making an additional investment of ₹ 50 by buying a machine and installing it. This investment expenditure will become income of the machinery manufacturer and the workers employed to manufacture it. These income earners will spend a large part of this income on consumption expenditure. If the MPC is assumed to be 0.8, they will spend ₹ 40 on additional consumption of goods. The producers of these goods will receive an additional income of ₹ 40, and, they will, in turn, spend ₹ 32 (₹ 40 × 0.8) on additional consumption goods assuming the MPC of 0.8. This way, there is a sequence or chain of income and consumption expenditure generated by an initial increase in investment of ₹ 50. Because the MPC is 0.8, i.e., < 1, additional income generation during each successive stage goes on decreasing. The process of income generation continues, stage after stage, till additional income generation tends to or becomes zero. This is more clearly shown as a sequential process in Table 6.5.

Table 6.5: The Multiplier and the Income Generation Process

Stage of Income Generation	Consumption (₹)	Income Generation (₹)
Stage 1	–	50.00
Stage 2	40.00	40.00
Stage 3	32.00	32.00
Stage 4	25.60	25.60
Stage 5	20.48	20.40
Stage 6	16.38	16.38
. . .	. . .	. . .
. . .	. . .	. . .
. . .	. . .	. . .
Last Stage	0.00	0.00
Total Income		250.00

Total income of ₹ 250 shown in Table 6.5 needs to be explained. The total increase in income, i.e., 250 can be calculated as the sum of the increase in income at each stage. In the present example, if will be 50 + 50 × 0.8 + 50 × 0.8 × 0.8 + 50 × 0.8 × 0.8 × 0.8 and so on. This is actually giving a series is geometric progression. Using the formula for geometric progression, this will be equal to

$$50/(1-0.8) = 250$$

Therefore, 1/(1–0.8) or 5 is multiplier and is equal to 1/(1–MPC) or 1/MPS (MPS is the marginal propensity to save). It follows from this that higher the MPC, larger is the multiplier, because larger the MPC, smaller is the MPS, and, larger the inverse of MPS, i.e., the multiplier. Analytically, larger MPC means that secondary expansion of income at each stage is more.

The multiplier just worked out, i.e., (1/1–0.8) can be derived or expressed in terms of symbols or general formula as follows:

$$\Delta Y = \Delta Y_1 + \Delta Y_2 + \Delta Y_3 + ... + \Delta Y_t$$
$$= \Delta I + b\Delta I + b^2\Delta I + ... + b^{t-1}\Delta I \ (b = MPC)$$
$$= \Delta I + (1+b+b^2 + ... + b^{t-1})$$

The sum in the bracket is a converging geometric series and is equal to 1/1–b

$\therefore \Delta Y = 1/1\text{–}b.\ \Delta I$ or $\Delta Y/\Delta I = 1/(1\text{–}b)$ (1–b=MPS)

ΔY is total increase is income, ΔI is the increase in investment and 1/(1–b) (or, ΔY/ΔI) is the multiplier.

Therefore, *the multiplier is the inverse of the marginal propensity to save.*

Aggregate Demand and the Multiplier

To logically analyse the role and significance of the multiplier in the income determination process, one could start with aggregate demand or spending. More specifically speaking, it is the change in aggregate demand or spending which brings the multiplier into play. The theory of the multiplier answers two vital questions in macroeconomics:

(a) Is there any definite relationship between change in aggregate demand or spending and national income?

(b) If so, what is the magnitude of change in national income because of change in aggregate demand or spending?

According to the theory of the multiplier, the answer to the first question is *yes*, and, to the second, is *the exact measurement of the quantum of change.*

A change in aggregate demand or spending (C + I) can take place because of change in either consumption or investment or both. A change can mean either an increase or decrease in demand or spending. Let us take the case of an increase.[8] In a simple two-sector model, the increase is more likely in investment than in consumption.

Let us explain this. The consumption function is generally considered to be more stable than the investment function. Given the consumption function (C=a+bY) and the values of the parameters 'a' and 'b', at a particular level of income, consumption does not change or increase. If income changes or increases, consumption also changes or increases; but, income changes are not so frequent. Without change (increase) in income, consumption can, however, still change if either 'a' or 'b' or both change. For an increase in consumption, either 'a' or 'b' both have to increase. But, these parameters do not change in the short run. They change only in the long run. So, the consumption function and the consumption level are relatively stable. But, this is not true of investment. In the simple Keynesian theory of income determination, investment is autonomous and does not depend on income. Rather, it is the change or increase in the investment level which causes an increase in income. This happens through the mechanism or the instrument of the multiplier.

8. In case of a decrease in aggregate demand or spending, the logic of analysis will be same; only the movements of variables will be in opposite direction.

This means that the C curve does not shift in the short run nor does the S curve shift. But, the C+I curve may shift and this is caused by a quantum jump or shift in the I curve; and, this will have impact on the equilibrium level of income. Because of operation of the multiplier, total income will increase and a new equilibrium will be reached at the point of intersection of the new aggregate demand or spending curve and the aggregate supply (C+S) curve or the 45° equality line. This is shown in Fig. 6.6.

The graphical presentation in Fig. 6.6 may be compared with that in Fig. 6.4. Figure 6.4 shows the determination of the equilibrium level of income (Y_O) at the point of intersection (E) of the AD and AS curves. In comparison, Fig. 6.6 presents the effect of an increase in investment (ΔI) on the equilibrium level of income. Increase in investment may take place because of positive business or profit expectations. The increase in investment by ΔI causes a shift in the aggregate demand curve (C+I). Because of the shift, the aggregate demand curve now moves to ($C+I+\Delta I$). The additional investment ΔI sets in motion the multiplier. As a result of operation of the multiplier, additional income generation takes place. Total additional income generated is equal to $Y_O Y_1$, shown in Fig. 6.6. Because of an upward shift of the AD curve to ($C+I+\Delta I$) the new equilibrium point shifts to E_1 and Y_1 becomes the new equilibrium level of income.

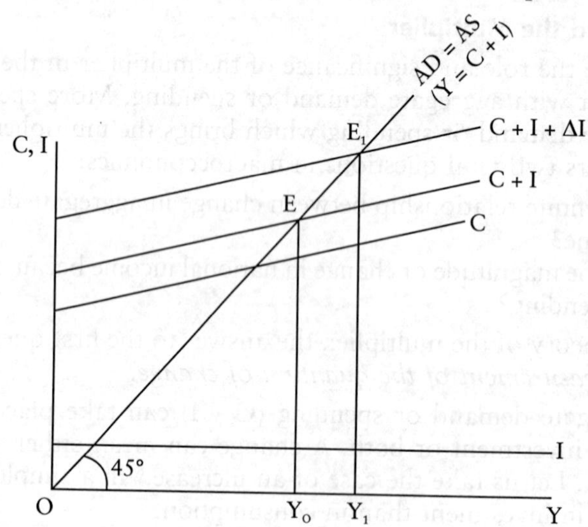

Fig. 6.6: Increase in Investment, the Multiplier and Equilibrium Income

Derivation of the Multiplier

We have just graphically illustrated (in Fig. 6.6) the effect of operation of the multiplier on equilibrium level of income, or, rather, the change in the equilibrium level of income. We now show the derivation of the multiplier from the equilibrium level of income. The equation for the equilibrium level of income is written as

$$Y = C + I \tag{6.13}$$

The equation for the new level of equilibrium income because of an upward shift in AD by ΔI may be written as

$$Y + \Delta Y = \Delta C + I + \Delta C + \Delta I \tag{6.14}$$

($Y + \Delta Y$) is new equilibrium income and $\Delta Y = \Delta C + \Delta I$

Subtracting equation (6.13) from Equation (6.14), we get

$$\Delta Y = \Delta C + \Delta I \quad (6.15)$$

The consumption function is $C = a + bY$

$$\therefore C + \Delta C = a + bY + b\Delta Y$$

or, $C + \Delta C = C + b\Delta Y$

or, $\Delta C = b\,\Delta Y \quad (6.16)$

By substituting $b\Delta Y$ for ΔC in Equation (6.15), we get

$$\Delta Y = b\Delta Y + \Delta I$$

or, $\Delta Y - b\Delta Y = \Delta I$

or, $\Delta Y\,(1-b) = \Delta I$

or, $\Delta Y = 1/1-b)\cdot\Delta I$

'b' is MPC and (1–b) is MPS. Therefore, the multiplier is the inverse of MPS.

Derivation of the Multiplier: Application

Application analysis, that is, numerical or algebraic derivation is done for better illustration or understanding of the concept or instrument of the multiplier.

For application analysis, we start with the incremental relationship between income, consumption and investment shown in Equation (6.15):

$$\Delta Y = \Delta C + \Delta I$$

Substituting $(b\Delta Y)$ for ΔC given in Equation (6.16), we get

$$\Delta Y = b\Delta Y = \Delta I \quad (6.17)$$

We assume $\Delta I = 30$. We take the value of b to be 0.8; it is the same value of b or MPC we had taken for application analysis of the AD-AS approach for determination of the equilibrium level of income and also shown in Equation (6.5). With these values of ΔI and b, Equation (6.17) may be rewritten as

$$\Delta Y = 0.8\,\Delta Y + 30$$

or, $\Delta Y - 0.8\,\Delta Y = 30$

or, $\Delta Y\,(1-0.8) = 30$

or, $\Delta Y = 1/(1-0.8)\cdot 30$

or, $\Delta Y = 1/1/5\cdot 30$

or, $\Delta Y = 150$

So, $\Delta I = 30$ and $\Delta Y = 150$

$\therefore$ the multiplier $= \Delta Y/\Delta I = 150/30 = 5$.

It is clear from here that the value or size of the multiplier depends on (1–b) or the MPS. Lower the MPS, larger is the multiplier. For example, if b or MPC is 0.9, MPS is 0.1 and the multiplier is 10. Given the value of the multiplier, the size or quantum of ΔI will determine total secondary income generation. In the present illustration, it is ₹ 150.

Theoretically, the value of the multiplier can vary between 1 and ∞ depending on the MPC or MPS. If MPC = 0, MPS = 1–0 = 1 and the multiplier is 1. If MPC = 1, MPS = 1–1 = 0 and the multiplier is ∞. Both these extreme values of MPC and MPS and the multiplier are unrealistic and, therefore, unlikely in practice. The most likely range of the multiplier is between 3 and 6.

Applicability of the Multiplier

We had mentioned earlier that the multiplier plays an important role in the income determination process. The most important role or use of the multiplier is in estimating or projecting future growth of national income and determining the investment requirement for this given the consumption level of the country. For multiplier analysis, the consumption level actually means or indicates the marginal propensity to consume (MPC).

Suppose a country has planned 5 per cent economic growth during next 10 years (approx). Economic growth is conventionally defined and measured in terms of growth of national income or GDP.[9] Economic growth of 5 per cent may mean an additional income generation of say, ₹ 1000 crores. If MPC = 0.8, additional investment requirement would be ₹ 200 crores. Let us put this in a tabular form:

Economic growth planned = 5.0 per cent
Additional planned income generation (ΔY) = ₹ 1000 crs
Multiplier (m) = 5
Additional investment requirement (ΔI) = ₹ 200

This also have important implication for, or affects, the fiscal policy of the government in terms of investment expenditure.

The role or use of the multiplier just explained is, however, more a theoretical presentation than a demonstration in practice. As happens with most theories, problems or issues arise during application in practice or implementation. These are the limitations of the multiplier.

Effective operation or working of the multiplier in practice is constrained or hindered by three major issues or factors:

1. Leakage from the income stream
2. Full employment situation
3. Availability of goods and services

The most important factor or issue relates to leakage from the income stream. In practice, in most of the economies, the proportion of additional income which should be spent on consumption expenditure is not actually done. This happens because people have non-consumption requirement or commitments to be met from additional income. They spend part of the additional income supposed to be spent on consumption as per MPC is used for or diverted to other essential requirements or spendings. These forms of spending constitute *leakages* from the income dream.

Such leakages can take place in different forms. Some of the common forms are repayment of past debts, acquisition of new assets or wealth and transfer payment to relatives or friends who may not spend the money on consumption goods. Repayment of part or outstanding debts is a common phenomenon among people. Most of the people usually have some loans or debts to repay, and, they use funds from additional income for such repayment. Acquiring new assets or wealth is also a common desire or tendency among people. New assets or wealth include property (land and building), shares, bonds, mutual funds, etc. The whole or part of additional income may be used to acquire such assets. All this income goes out of the consumption stream. Transfer payments to relatives or close friends either in the home country or abroad is third form of leakage of funds from the income stream.

9. Definition, measurement and issues of economic growth and planning are discussed in detail in Chapter 24.

These leakages reduce the value of the MPC and eventually of the multiplier. Therefore, additional income generation becomes less than planned. The leakages vary from country to country and depend on the non-consumption requirements or commitments of the population.

Full employment situation creates another problem for working of the multiplier. In the full employment situation, the multiplier process or system does not work. Full employment or near-full employment means that the productive resources in the economy (labour and capital) are almost fully employed and no further production may be possible, and, therefore, no additional output will be generated. Additional investment will generate new or additional demand, but with production or supply constraint, this is likely to lead to inflation.

Non-availability of the proper basket of consumption goods in time also acts as a constraint to effective working of the multiplier theory. Because of generation of additional income due to operation of the multiplier, demand for goods and services may be created immediately, but, production or supply of goods and services may not be able to respond so fast or instantly. There is usually a time lag between the two particularly if there are production problems or bottlenecks. This may lead to demand-pull inflation. If this happens, it reduces the value of consumption expenditure; this means reduction in the value of the real MPC, and, in turn, the effect of the multiplier.

We should also comment on the relative effectiveness of the three factors mentioned in curbing the intensity of the multiplier effect. In today's global economic environment, full employment is more a theoretical possibility than in existence in practice whether in developed economies or developing economies much less in the latter. Therefore, this may not be major constraint to operation of the multiplier principle. The time lag between creation of demand and production and supply of goods may be a possibility. But, it is also true that the full effects of a multiplier works itself out over a period of time as a series in geometric progression as explained earlier. The real constraint to effective operation of the multiplier may be the leakages from the income stream or consumption stream are quite common in various economies of the world. Such leakages can always reduce the effectiveness of the multiplier.

Because of various constraints, the multiplier is often found to have limited application. This can be illustrated with the example of the US. During the 1990s, the savings rate (APS or MPS) was estimated to be 20 per cent; if this is so, the multiplier should be about 5. But, it was actually found to be 1.4.[10] It has also been observed that the multiplier works differently during different phases of the business cycle. It is generally found to be more effective during early stages of recovery from recession than during boom or prosperity. This happens because there is usually excess capacity during recession and production responds fast to increase in demand resulting in consumption.

Multiplier and Developing Economies

If the multiplier has limited application in developed countries, it has more limited application in developing economies. In fact, in developing countries, the operation of the multiplier is faced with a paradoxical situation. This is explained below.

It is established economic fact that developing economies have a high propensity to consume (APC or MPC). This is because of low level of income or low per capita income in these countries. Because of low level of income a very large proportion of income is spent on consumption goods to cover or satisfy all consumption requirements. High propensity to consume means lower

10. E.C. Karl and C.F. Ray, *Principles of Economics* (6th edition). Pearson Education Asia, 2002, p, 450.

rate of savings (APS or MPS) in these countries. The World Bank's Development Reports also confirm this. The Development Reports state that less developed countries (LDCs) have lower per capita income and, because of this, lower rate of saving compared to developed countries.

This means that the multiplier should be higher in less developed countries. If the multiplier is higher, any additional investment should generate higher level of additional output and income, and, finally, higher rate of economic growth in these countries. But, this is not true. In LDCs or developing economies, both the multiplier and the rate of economic growth are lower than in developed economies. This is a paradoxical situation. This is often called "Keynes's MPC and the multiplier paradox".

Applicability of the Keynesian multiplier theory to the developing countries was examined by Rao with particular reference to India. Developing countries have same or similar characteristics; therefore, study results or findings for India should be generally applicable to other developing countries also. Less developed or developing countries possess characteristics most of which do not prevail in developed countries. Major typical characteristics of less developed or developing countries are:

(a) A large agricultural sector governed by monsoon and seasonality;
(b) Limited production capacity in the industrial or manufacturing sector;
(c) Lack of enough supply of inputs or resources;
(d) Low productivity level because of low level of technology;
(e) A vast sector producing goods for self-consumption;
(f) A very large non-monetised sector.

Because of these reasons or factors, considerable time lag exists between increase in demand and production or supply. "This tends to widen the difference between the multiplier linking up increments of money investment with increments of money income and that linking up increments of investment with increments of total output with the result that money incomes and prices rise much faster than real income and output."[11]

Rao concludes that "under these circumstances, the multiplier principle does not work in the simple fashion visualised by Keynes primarily for the industrialised economies". To illustrate or explain this further, we may mention the major assumptions behind the Keynesian theory of the multiplier. These key assumptions behind the Keynesian theory are:

(a) A high level of industrial and economic development;
(b) Existence of excess production capacity;
(c) Elastic aggregate supply curve till full employment output is reached.

These conditions hardly exist in developing economies.

REVIEW QUESTIONS

1. "Keynesian theory of income determination is an attempt to develop a new theory of income and employment in contrast to the classical theory". Explain.
2. Mention and explain the main assumptions in the Keynesian theory of income determination and their implications.
3. In the AD-AS approach to the income determination model, graphically explain the equilibrium and disequilibrium situations.

11. V.K.R.V. Rao, "Investment, Income and Multiplier in an Underdeveloped Economy", *Indian Economic Review*, Vol. 1, No. 1, 1952.

4. Do an application analysis (algebraic derivation) of the AD-AS approach to determination of the equilibrium level of income?
5. Explain the savings-investment approach to income determination. Does it give the same result as the AD-AS approach?
6. Clearly explain the differences between planned saving, realised saving planned investment and realised investment and their implications for determination of the equilibrium level of income.
7. Define the concept of the multiplier. Explain how it works in terms of a formula.
8. Discuss the applicability of the multiplier theory in practice and analyse the major constraints.
9. "If the multiplier has limited application in developed countries, it has more limited application in developing economies". Explain.

SUGGESTED READINGS

- E. Shapiro, *Macroeconomic Analysis* (Fifth Edition), Galgotia Publications, 1984, Chapters 4 and 5.
- P. Samuelson, "The Simple Mathematics of Income Determination" in *Income, Employment and Public Policy: Essays in Honour of Alvin Hansen*, W.W. Norton & Co. Inc., New York, 1948.
- V.K.R.V. Rao, "Investment, Income and Multiplier in an underdeveloped Economy," *Indian Economic Review*, Vol. 1, No. 1, 1952.

Chapter 7

Determination of National Income: Model with Government Sector

In the previous chapter, we had analysed the Keynesian theory of income determination including firms or the business sector and the household sector. This is the simple or basic Keynesian model. In this chapter, we extend the model by including the government sector. Income determination theory with the household sector, the business sector and the government sector is a closed economy model. The theory with the inclusion of the foreign sector becomes an open economy model. The open economy model of income determination will be discussed in the next chapter.

In any country, the government operates through the budget. Two main instruments of the budget are expenditure and tax. The government primarily uses these two instruments for macroeconomic management and growth.

In Chapter 3, while discussing different approaches to estimation of national income, we had mentioned about the government sector. In estimating national income by using the expenditure approach, inclusion of government expenditure as one of the components was mentioned. We shall analyse here the detailed implications of the role of the government sector in the income determination process.

GOVERNMENT EXPENDITURE AND NATIONAL INCOME

In Chapter 3 and also in Chapter 6, the income equation using the expenditure approach was written as

$$Y = C + I$$

where Y is national income, C is aggregate consumption and I is investment.

The consumption function is given as

$$C = a + bY$$

This was explained in Chapter 4.

If we add government expenditure to

$$Y = C + I$$

The income equation may be rewritten as

$$Y = C + I + G$$

where G is government expenditure.

Investment (I) is assumed to be autonomous. Government expenditure (G) is also assumed to be autonomous and constant.

We adopt the demand-supply approach,[1]

$$Y = C + I + G$$

represents aggregate demand including government expenditure.

Aggregate supply is given as

$$Y = C + S$$

where S is aggregate saving.

In equilibrium, aggregate demand is equal to aggregate supply, i.e.,

$$Y = C + I + G = C + S$$

This is graphically shown in Fig. 7.1.

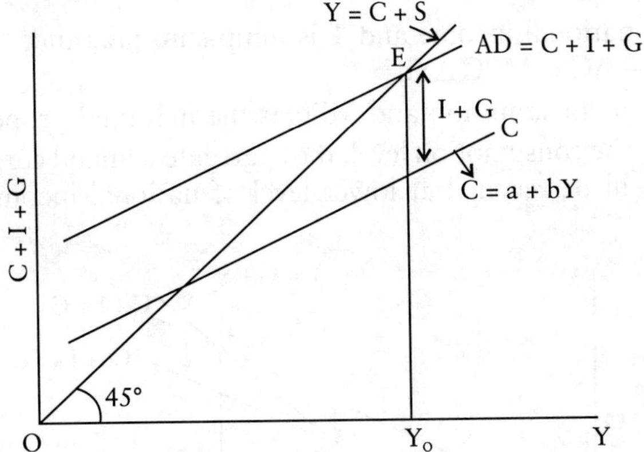

Fig. 7.1: Determination of National Income Including Government Expenditure (Three-sector Model)

It may be seen in Fig. 7.1 that the equilibrium level of national income is determined at point E—the point at which the aggregate expenditure curve (C+I+G) intersects the 45° line; that is, aggregate demand (C+I+G) is equal to aggregate supply (G+S). The equilibrium level of national income with government expenditure is OY_O. At levels of national income less than OY_O, aggregate expenditure is more than aggregate output or supply. These are situations of disequilibrium. In these situations, equilibrium is achieved or restored by increasing production or output. Similarly, at levels of national income more than OY_O, aggregate expenditure is less than aggregate output. These are also situations of disequilibrium. In these situations, equilibrium will be restored by curtailing production or output.

It should be mentioned that, because of government expenditure, national income is determined at the level at which saving is equal to investment plus government expenditure. This can be shown as below.

In equilibrium,

$$Y = C + I + G$$

or,

$$Y - C = I + G$$

because,

$$Y = C + S$$

1. Aggregate demand and aggregate supply were discussed in detail in Chapter 6.

$$Y - C = S$$

$\therefore$ in equilibrium,

$$S = I + G$$

GOVERNMENT EXPENDITURE, TAX AND NATIONAL INCOME

Given government expenditure, we shall now analyse the effect of imposition of tax on determination of national income. The tax is assumed to be only in the form of direct tax on individuals, i.e., income tax. The tax is also assumed to be one-time lump-sum tax. The direct or income tax affects the disposable income of individuals or households; and, this, in turn, affects the consumption level.

Because of imposition of the tax, disposable national income will be reduced by the amount of tax; and, given the marginal propensity to consume (MPC), aggregate consumption will decline proportionately.

$$\Delta Yd = T$$

where Yd is disposable national income and T is lump-sum tax, and,

$$-\Delta C = MPC \cdot \Delta Yd$$

where (–ΔC) in decline in consumption and MPC is the marginal propensity to consume.

Because of decline in the consumption level, the aggregate demand curve will shift downwards, and, new equilibrium will be reached at lower level of national income. This is illustrated in Fig. 7.2.

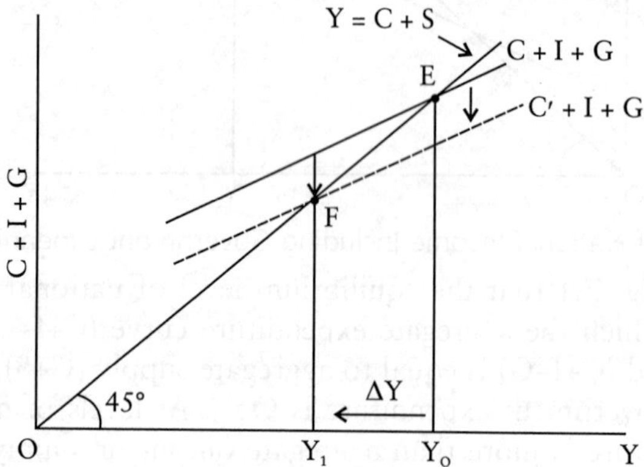

Fig. 7.2: Effect of Lump-sum Tax on Determination of National Income

In Fig. 7.2, the effect of lump-sum tax on equilibrium level of national income may be clearly seen. The downward shift in aggregate demand curve is shown by (C′+I+G). The aggregate supply curve remains the same. The new equilibrium is reached at point F—the point at which the new aggregate demand curve (C′+I+G) intersects the 45° line; that is, aggregate demand is equal to aggregate supply. The new equilibrium level of national income is OY_1.

It should be noted that OY_1 is less than OY_0 (seen in Fig. 7.1)—the equilibrium income before or without tax. So, we can say that *national income with government expenditure and lump-sum tax is less than national income with government expenditure but without tax*. This will be more clear with numerical examples given in the application of the three-sector model presented in the next section.

We have shown above (Fig. 7.2) the effect of imposition of lump-sum tax on determination of national income. If, however, instead of levy of new tax, existing amount of tax is reduced, the effect or situation will be different. If tax is reduced, disposable income will increase and given the MPC, consumption will also increase. This may be shown as

$$\Delta C = MPC \cdot \Delta Yd \ (\Delta Yd = (-T))$$

Because of increase in consumption, the aggregate demand curve will shift upwards (say, C″+I+G), new equilibrium national income will be determined at a level higher than OY_O.

A lump-sum tax is usually imposed to finance government expenditure. If government expenditure is equal to tax revenue, it is a balanced budget; if government expenditure is less than tax revenue, it is a surplus budget: and, if government expenditure is more than tax revenue, it is a deficit budget. In our analysis of the effect of government expenditure and taxation on national income, we have assumed a balanced budget, i.e., government expenditure is equal to tax revenue. It is also assumed that there is no transfer payments (pensions, subsidies, etc.) by the government.

APPLICATION OF THE THREE-SECTOR MODEL

We shall present the application of the three-sector model separately for government expenditure and determination of national income, and, government expenditure, lump-sum tax and national income.

Government Expenditure and Determination of National Income

We start with application of the basic Keynesian model given in Chapter 6.

The Keynesian income determination model is given as

$$C = a + bY$$
$$I = \bar{I}$$
$$Y = C + \bar{I} \text{ (Equilibrium condition)}$$

Let a = 30, b = 0.8 and $\bar{I}$ = 40

With these values, equilibrium income is given as

$$Y = C + I$$

or, $Y = 30 + 0.8\ Y + 40$

or, $Y = 70 + 0.8\ Y$

or, $Y\ (0.2) = 70$

or, $Y = 350$

If we add government expenditure to C + I, the aggregate demand becomes equal to

$$C + I + G$$

Government expenditure, G, is assumed equal to 50.

The new equilibrium condition is

$$Y = C + I + G$$

or, $Y = a + bY + I + G$

or, $Y = 30 + 0.8\ Y + 40 + 50$

a = 30, b = 0.8, I = 40; we have assumed the same values of the parameters/constants as in Chapter 6 for consistency and comparability.

Equilibrium level of income with government expenditure is

$$Y = 30 + 0.8\ Y + 40 + 50$$

or, $Y = 120 + 0.8\ Y$

or, $(Y - 0.8\,Y) = 120$
or, $Y\,(1 - 0.8) = 120$
or, $Y\,(0.2) = 120$
or, $1/5/Y = 120$
or, $Y = 600$

The equilibrium level of national income with government expenditure is 600 compared to 350 without this. So, *national income with government expenditure is higher than national income in the absence of government expenditure.* This shows the positive effect of government expenditure on the level of national income.

Government Expenditure, Lump-sum Tax and Determination of National Income

In our graphical presentation (Fig. 7.2), we have assumed a balanced budget, i.e., government expenditure is equal to tax revenue (G = T). We shall work out the application model in this basis.

We have assumed that G = 50

$$\therefore T = 50$$

Because of tax, we introduce disposable income Yd.

$$Yd = Y - T$$

We now rewrite the consumption function as

$$C = a + bYd$$

or, $C = a + b\,(Y - T)$

With revised consumption function, the new equilibrium level of income with government expenditure and lump-sum tax may be rewritten as

$$Y = 1 + b\,(Y–T) + I + G$$

or, $Y = 30 + 0.8\,(Y–50) + 40 + 50$
or, $Y = 30 + 0.8\,Y - 0.8 \times 50 + 40 + 50$
or, $Y = 30 + 0.8\,Y - 40 + 40 + 50$
or, $Y = 30 + 0.8\,Y + 50$
or, $Y = 80 + 0.8\,Y$
or, $Y - 0.8\,Y = 80$
or, $Y\,(1 - 0.8) = 80$
or, $Y\,(0.2) = 80$
or, $1/5/Y = 80$
or, $Y = 400$

Equilibrium level of national income with government expenditure and lump-sum tax is 400 compared to 600 with expenditure but without lump-sum tax. So, *national income with government expenditure and lump-sum tax is less than national income with government expenditure but without tax.* It is, however, is still higher than national income without government expenditure, i.e., 350.

DEFICIT BUDGET AND DETERMINATION OF NATIONAL INCOME

We now move away from balanced budget to deficit budget which is a more common phenomenon. This means that government expenditure is more than tax revenue (G > T). Let us see the impact of deficit budget on determination of national income.

Let us assume that T = 35

The consumption function will now be modified as

$$C = a + bYd$$

or, $C = a + b\ (Y–T)$

or, $C = 30 + 0.8\ (Y–35)$

The new equilibrium level of national income with budget deficit may be given as

$$Y = a + b\ Yd + I + G$$

or, $Y = a + b\ (Y–T) + I + G$

or, $Y = 30 + 0.8\ (Y - 35) + 40 + 50$

or, $Y = 30 + 0.8\ Y - 0.8 \times 35 + 40 + 50$

or, $Y = 30 + 0.8\ Y - 28 + 40 + 50$

or, $Y = 30 - 28 + 40 + 50 + 0.8\ Y$

or, $Y = 92 + 0.8\ Y$

or, $(Y - 0.8Y) = 92$

or, $Y\ (1 - 0.8) = 92$

or, $Y\ (0.2) = 92$

or, $1/5/Y = 92$

or, $Y = 460$

Because of lower tax (35 instead of 50), disposable income is higher, and, because of this, consumption level is also higher. This increases aggregate demand, and, consequently, equilibrium national income—460 compared to 400.

So, to conclude, equilibrium national income without government expenditure is the lowest (350); equilibrium income with government expenditure is the highest (600); this is followed by national income with government expenditure and budget deficit (460); and, this is followed by national income with government expenditure and balanced budget (400). These, along with consumption levels and investment, are presented in Table 7.1.

Table 7.1: Consumption, Investment, Government Expenditure, Lump-sum Tax and Equilibrium National Income

Consumption (C)	Investment (I)	Government Expenditure (G)	Lump-sum Tax (T)	Equilibrium National Income (Y)
310	40	0	0	350*
410	40	50	0	600
310	40	50	50	400
370	40	50	35	460

Parameters/Constants : a = 30; b = 0.8

* Worked out in Chapter 6.

FISCAL MULTIPLIERS

Government's fiscal operations have certain multiplier effects—be it government expenditure or taxation. The multiplier effects of the fiscal operations have impact on the level of national income. The actual effects of the multipliers depend on the magnitudes of fiscal operations. To ascertain these effects, we consider three forms or types of multipliers:

1. Expenditure multiplier
2. Tax multiplier
3. Balanced budget multiplier.

Expenditure Multiplier

To derive the expenditure multiplier, and, work out its effect on national income, we start with the income equation, with government expenditure, presented above:

$$Y = C + I + G$$

or, $$Y = a + bY + I + G \quad \text{(i)}$$

We have shown above that effect of government expenditure is to increase national income. If government expenditure, G, increases by ΔG, and, increase in income is ΔY, the income Equation (i) may be rewritten as

$$Y + \Delta Y = a + bY + b\,\Delta Y + I + G + \Delta G \quad \text{(ii)}$$

Subtracting Equation (i) from Equation (ii), we get

$$\Delta Y = b{\cdot}Y + \Delta G$$

or, $$\Delta Y - b{\cdot}\Delta Y = \Delta G$$

or, $$\Delta Y(1-b) = \Delta G$$

or, $$\Delta Y = \Delta G{\cdot}1/1-b$$

or, $$\Delta Y/\Delta G = 1/1-b$$

So, the expenditure multiplier Gm is given as

$$Gm = 1/1-b$$

where b is the marginal propensity to consume (MPC).

Illustration Example: Let us now see the impact of the expenditure multiplier on increase in income through a numerical example.

Let us assume that ΔG = 20 and b = 0.8.

Then the increase in income ΔY is given as

$$\Delta Y = 1/1-b{\cdot}\ \Delta G$$

or, $$\Delta Y = 1/1-0.8{\cdot}20$$

or, $$\Delta Y = 5 \times 20$$

or, $$\Delta Y = 100$$

where the expenditure multiplier is 5.

So, *given the marginal propensity to consume as 0.8 and increase in government expenditure of 20, the multiplier effect of this is to increase national income by 100.*

Tax Multiplier

We have seen above that the effect of a lump-sum tax is to reduce income. So, the multiplier effect of an increase in tax on national income will be negative.

To derive the tax multiplier and work out its effect on national income, we start with the income equation with government expenditure and lump-sum tax

$$Y = a + b\,(Y-T) + I + G \qquad (Y-T = Yd) \quad \text{(iii)}$$

If lump-sum tax increases by ΔT and change in national income is ΔY, income Equation (iii) may be revised as

$$Y + \Delta Y = a + b\,(Y-T) + b\,(\Delta Y - \Delta T) + I + G \quad \text{(iv)}$$

Subtracting Equation (iii) from Equation (iv), we get

$$\Delta Y = b\,(\Delta Y - \Delta T)$$

or, $\Delta Y = b\,\Delta Y - b\,\Delta T$

or, $\Delta Y - b\,\Delta Y = -\,b\,\Delta T$

or, $\Delta Y\,(1-b) = -\,b\,\Delta T$

or, $\Delta Y/\Delta T = -b/1-b$

So, the tax multiplier Tm is expressed as

$$Tm = -\,b/1-b$$

It is to be noted that the tax multiplier is negative.

Illustration Example: Let us see the effect of the tax multiplier on change in income through a numerical example.

Let us assume that $\Delta Y = 25$ and $b = 0.8$.

Then the change in ΔY is given as

$$\Delta Y/\Delta T = b/1-b$$

or, $\Delta Y = b/1-b \cdot \Delta T$

or, $\Delta Y = 0.8/1-0.8 \times 25$

or, $\Delta Y = -0.8/1-0.8 \times 25$

or, $\Delta Y = -\,4 \times 25$

or, $\Delta Y = -100$

where the tax multiplier, Tm, is (–4).

So, *given the marginal propensity to consume as 0.8 and increase in lump-sum tax of 25, the multiplier effect of this is to reduce national income by 100.*

Balanced Budget Multiplier

We have seen above the effect of expenditure multiplier, i.e., the effect of an increase in government expenditure, without changing tax, on increase in national income. We have also seen the effect of the tax multiplier, i.e., the effect of an increase in lump-sum tax, without changing government expenditure, on reduction of national income. We now see the multiplier effect of simultaneous increase in government expenditure and tax.

Balanced budget means that government expenditure is equal to tax revenue (G = T), and, also, by implication, that increase in government expenditure is equal to increase in tax revenue, i.e., $\Delta G = \Delta T$. We shall see the effect of this through the balanced budget multiplier.

We start with the income equation with government expenditure and lump-sum tax.

$$Y = a+b\,(Y-T) + I + G \tag{v}$$

If government expenditure increases by ΔG, lump-sum tax increases by ΔT, and, change in national income is ΔY, income Equation (v) may be rewritten as

$$Y + \Delta Y = a+b\,(Y-T) + b(\Delta Y - \Delta T) + I + G + \Delta G \tag{vi}$$

Subtracting equation (v) from Equation (vi), we get

$$\Delta Y = b\,(\Delta Y - \Delta T)\,\Delta G \tag{vii}$$

In a balanced budget, $\Delta G = \Delta T$ in Equation (vii), we get

$$\Delta Y = b\,(\Delta Y - \Delta T) + \Delta G$$

or, $\Delta Y = b\,(\Delta Y - \Delta G) + \Delta G$

or, $\Delta Y = b\cdot\Delta Y - b\cdot\Delta G + \Delta G$

or, $\Delta Y - b\,\Delta Y = \Delta G - b\cdot\Delta G$

or, $\Delta Y = \Delta G$

or, $\Delta Y/\Delta G = 1$

So, the balanced budget multiplier BBm is given as

$$BBm = 1$$

∴ the balanced budget multiplier is always equal to unity.

Illustration Example: Let us assume that $\Delta G = \Delta T = 20$

Then, $\Delta Y/\Delta G = 1$

or, $\Delta Y = \Delta G$

or, $\Delta Y = 20$

So, *the balanced budget multiplier shows that, if increase in government expenditure is equal to increase in tax, national income increases exactly by the amount of increase in government expenditure.* Larger the increase in government expenditure, higher will be the increase in national income; vice versa, smaller the increase in government expenditure, lower will be the increase in national income.

REVIEW QUESTIONS

1. What is the three-sector model of income determination? Mention the additional variables in the three-sector model
2. Explain, graphically, determination of national income with government expenditure.
3. If tax is added to government expenditure, how will it affect equilibrium national income?
4. Work out the application (algebraic solution) of the three-sector model with only government expenditure.
5. Work out the application (numerical solution) of the three-sector model with government expenditure and tax. Compare the results with that of the three-sector model with only government expenditure and comment.
6. What is balanced budget multiplier? How does its effect on national income differ from that of the expenditure multiplier and tax multiplier? Explain.

SUGGESTED READINGS

- E. Shapiro, *Macroeconomic Analysis* (Fourth Edition), Harcourt Brace Jovanovich, 1994, Chapter 7.
- Gardner Ackley, *Macroeconomics: Theory and Policy*, 1978, Chapter 3.
- P. Samuelson, "The Simple Mathematics of Income Determination" in *Income, Employment and Public Policy: Essays in Honour of Alvin Hansen*, W.W. Norton & Co., New York, 1948.
- P. Samuelson and W.D. Nordhaus, *Economics* (Seventh Edition), Tata-McGraw Hill, 2003.
- T.F. Richard, *Macroeconomics: Theories and Policies*, Macmillan, New York (Third Edition), 1990, Chapter 5.

Chapter 8

Determination of National Income: Open Economy Model

In the last chapter, we had mentioned about the open economy model and the foreign sector. In this chapter, we discuss the open economy model of income determination including the foreign sector. This makes it a model of four sectors—the household sector, the business sector, the government sector and the foreign sector. This makes the income determination process complete and more realistic.

Addition of the foreign sector opens up the economy. This essentially means inclusion of export and import in the income determination process. With the foreign sector, the three-sector (household, business and government) *closed economy* model becomes a four-sector *open economy* model.

In Chapter 3, while discussing determination of national income by expenditure approach, we had mentioned about export and import national income, by expenditure approach, for an open economy was written as

$$Y = C + I + G + X - M$$

where X is export and M is import. It is assumed that export is more than import, i.e., (X – M) is positive. In reality, however, in many countries including India, imports are more than exports, i.e., (X–M) is negative.[1]

To complete the role of the government in the four-sector model, we introduce tax in the system. If we include tax in the system, the consumption function

$$C = a + bY$$

will be modified as

$$C = a + b\ Yd$$

or, $$C = a + b\ (Y-T)$$

With the modified consumption function, national income by expenditure approach or aggregate demand will be written as

$$Y = a + b\ (Y-T) + I + G + X - M$$

1. This is called negative balance of trade. This is discussed later in Chapter 23.

EQUILIBRIUM WITH THE FOREIGN SECTOR

Equilibrium national income with the foreign sector will be reached at the point at which the aggregate demand curve intersects the aggregate supply curve. This is graphically shown in Fig. 8.1.

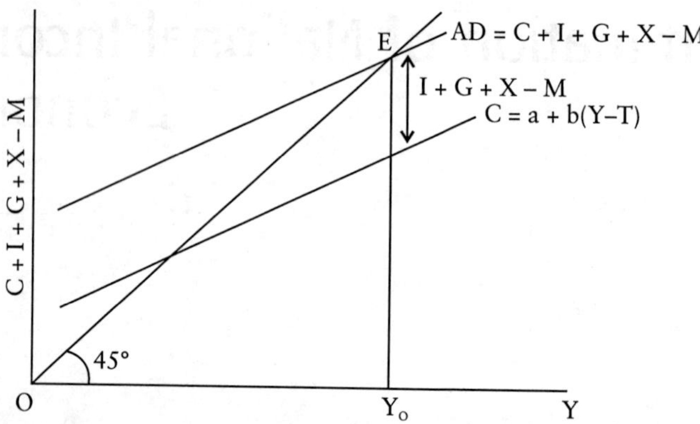

Fig. 8.1: Determination of National Income with Foreign Sector

In Fig. 8.1, it may be seen that equilibrium is reached at point E—the point at which the aggregate demand curve (C+I+G+X–M) intersects the 45° line—the line of equality of aggregate supply and aggregate demand. The equilibrium level of national income is OY_O.

In Fig. 8.1, we have assumed that (X–M) is positive. So, (C+I+G+X–M) is higher than C+I+G. But, if imports are more than exports (X–M) is negative. In that case, aggregate demand will be lower than C + I + G and the aggregate demand curve would shift downwards, and equilibrium will be reached at a level of national income less than OY_O. The exact downward shift of the aggregate demand curve, and, the new equilibrium would depend on the values of X and M.

APPLICATION OF THE FOUR-SECTOR MODEL

We shall consider application of the four-sector model as an extension of the three-sector model with inclusion of foreign trade, i.e., export and import. We shall present the application of the four-sector model under two situations:

Situation 1. Export is more than import (X > M)

Situation 2. Export is less than import (X < M)

Application of the Four-Sector Model: X > M

We start with the equilibrium income equation in the four-sector model

$$Y = a + b\,(Y–T) + I + G + X – M$$

We assume the same values of the parameters/constants as in the three-sector model. So, a = 30; b = 0.8; I = 40; G = 50 and T = 50

Then, the equilibrium income equation may be written as

$$Y = 30 + 0.8\,(Y–50) + 40 + 50 + X – M$$

or, $$Y = 30 + 0.8\,Y – 0.8 \times 50 + 40 + 50 + X – M$$

or, $$Y = 30 + 0.8\,Y – 40 + 40 + 50 + X – M$$

or, $$Y = 30 + 0.8\,Y + 50 + X – M$$

or, $$Y – 0.8\,Y = 30 + 50 + X – M$$

or, $Y (1–0.8) = 80 + X – M$

Let us assume that X = 20 and M = 10.

Then the income equation is finally written as

$$Y (1–0.8) = 80 + 20 – 10$$

or, $0.2 Y = 90$

or, $1/5 Y = 90$

or, $Y = 450$

So, *equilibrium national income for an open economy with export more than import (that is, positive balance of trade) is higher than equilibrium income for a closed economy, other things remaining the same (assuming a balanced budget)*. The application model also shows that, higher the positive balance of trade (X > M), more will be the increase in income. For example, in the present case, the balance of trade is 10; if the balance of trade is 20, equilibrium national income will be 500 and so on.

Application of the Four-Sector Model: X < M

We start with the equilibrium income equation in the four-sector model

$$Y = 1 + b (Y–T) + I + G + X – M$$

We assume the same values of the parameters/constants as in situation 1, that is,

a = 30; b = 0.8; I = 40; G = 50 and T = 50.

Then, the equilibrium income may be written as

$$Y = 30 + 0.8 (Y – 50) + 40 + 50 + X – M$$

or, $Y = 30 + 0.8 Y – 0.8 \times 50 + 40 + 50 + X – M$

or, $Y = 30 + 0.8 Y – 40 + 40 + 550 + X – M$

or, $Y = 30 + 0.8 Y + 50 + X – M$

or, $Y – 0.8) = 30 + 50 + X – M$

or, $Y (1– 0.8) = 80 + X – M$

Let us assume that X = 10 and M = 20.

Then, the income equation may be finally written as

$$Y (1–0.8) = 80 + 10 – 20$$

or, $0.2 Y = 70$

or, $1/5/Y = 70$

or, $Y = 350$

So, *equilibrium national income for an open economy, with export less than import (that is, negative balance of trade), is lower than equilibrium income for a closed economy, other things remaining the same.*[2] The application model also shows that, more the negative balance of trade (X < M), larger will be the decline in income. For example, in the present numerical illustration, the balance of trade is (–10); if the balance of trade is (–20), equilibrium national income will be 300.

Incidentally, it should be noted that equilibrium income in the four-sector model with negative balance of trade (X–M= –10) is the same as in the basic Keynesian model (see Table 7.1). Both

2. National income in a closed economy with balanced budget and deficit budget are 400 and 460 respectively (Table 7.1).

are 350. This means that, for particular values of investment (I), government expenditure (G), tax (T), export (X) and import (M), equilibrium income in the basic Keynesian model (two-sector) is equal to equilibrium income in the open economy (four-sector) with negative balance of trade. This, however, should not be taken as a basis for a general conclusion or generalisation.

The application results of the two-sector, three-sector and for sector models make interesting comparisons of equilibrium levels of income because of different determining or explanatory variables. The results are summarised in Table 8.1.

Table 8.1: Equilibrium Levels of Income in Two-Sector, Three-Sector and Four-Sector Models: Application Results

Sector	C	I	G	T	X	M	Y
Two-Sector	310	40	0	0	0	0	350
Three-Sector	410	40	50	0	0	0	600
	310	40	50	50	0	0	400
	370	40	50	35	0	0	460
Four-Sector	300	40	50	50	20	10	450
	220	40	50	50	10	20	350

Parameters/Constants: a = 30; b = 0.8.

FOREIGN TRADE MULTIPLIER

The foreign trade multiplier essentially shows the effect of an increase in export on increase in national income given certain level of import. So, the foreign trade multiplier can also be called the export multiplier.

A distinction can be, and, is often, made between the foreign trade multiplier and the export multiplier. The export multiplier is defined as one which shows the effect of an increase in export on income with autonomous import, i.e., import independent of income. The foreign trade multiplier is one which works out the effect of an increase in export on income with an import function, i.e., import as a function of income. This, in other words, means working out the export multiplier under two situations or assumptions—autonomous import and import as a function of income.

We shall derive the export multiplier, and, work out its effect on income under two situations or assumptions:

Situation/Assumption 1. Export multiplier with autonomous import.

Situation/Assumption 2. Export multiplier with import function.

Export Multiplier with Autonomous Import

To derive the export multiplier, we start with the equilibrium income equation

$$Y = a + b\,(Y-T) + I + G + X - M$$

or, $$Y = a + bY - bT + I + G + X - M \qquad \text{(vii)}$$

Let us assume that export increases by ΔX, and, the resultant increase in income is ΔY. Then, Equation (vii) may be rewritten as

$$Y+\Delta Y = a+b\,(Y+\Delta Y-T)+I+G+X+\Delta X-M$$

or, $$Y+\Delta Y = a+bY+b\cdot\Delta Y-bT+I+G+X+\Delta X-M \qquad \text{(viii)}$$

Subtracting Equation (vii) from Equation (viii), we get

$$\Delta Y = b\,\Delta Y + \Delta X$$

or, $\Delta Y\,(1-b) = \Delta X$

Dividing both sides by (1–b), we get

$$\Delta Y = \Delta X/1-b$$

or, $\Delta Y = 1/1-b\cdot\Delta X$

So, the export multiplier (Xm) is

$$Xm = 1/1-b$$

where b is the marginal propensity to consume.

It is to be noted that the export multiplier is the same as the expenditure multiplier (Gm) explained in the three-sector model in Chapter 7. The export multiplier is also same as the investment multiplier discussed in Chapter 4.

Illustration Example: We shall see the effect of the export multiplier on increase in income through a numerical example.

Let us assume that $\Delta X = 10$ and $b = 0.8$.

Then the increase in income ΔY is given as

$$\Delta Y = 1/1-b\cdot\Delta X$$

or, $\Delta Y = 1/1-0.8 \times 10$

or, $\Delta Y = 1/1-0.2 \times 10$

or, $\Delta Y = 1/1/5 \times 10$

or, $\Delta Y = 5 \times 10$

or, $\Delta Y = 50$

Where the export multiplier (Xm) is 5.

So, *with the increase in export of 10 and given the marginal propensity to consume as 0.8, the multiplier effect of this is to increase national income by 50.*

Export Multiplier with Import Function[3]

To derive the export multiplier with an import function, we need to first introduce the import function in the income determination process. The import function may be written as

$$M = \overline{M} + m\cdot Y$$

where $\overline{M}$ is autonomous import independent of income and m is the marginal propensity to import.

With the import function, the income Equation (vii) may be rewritten as

$$Y = a + bY - bT + I + G + X - (\overline{M} + m\cdot Y)$$

or, $Y = a + bY - bT + I + G + X - \overline{M} - mY$ (ix)

Let us assume that export increases by ΔX, and, increase in income is ΔY. Then, Equation (ix) may be rewritten as

$$Y + \Delta Y = a + b\,(Y+\Delta Y) - bT + I + G + X + \Delta X - \overline{M} - m(Y+\Delta Y)$$

or, $Y + \Delta Y = a + bY + b\Delta Y - bT + I + G + X + \Delta X - \overline{M} - mY - m\cdot\Delta Y$ (x)

3. This is alternatively called the *Foreign Trade Multiplier* (Fm).

Subtracting Equation (ix) from Equation (x), we get

$$\Delta Y = b\cdot\Delta Y + \Delta X - m\cdot\Delta Y$$

or, $\Delta Y - b\Delta Y + m\cdot\Delta Y = \Delta X$

or, $\Delta Y\ (1-b+m) = \Delta X$

or, $\Delta Y = 1/1-b+m)\cdot\Delta X$

So, the export multiplier (Xm) with an import function is

$$Xm = 1/1-b+m$$

where b is the marginal propensity to consume and m is the marginal propensity to import.

If m = b, the export multiplier becomes equal to unity. This, however, is a purely theoretical possibility because the marginal propensity to import is hardly ever likely to be equal to the marginal propensity to consume. In all real macroeconomic situations, the marginal propensity to import should be always less than the marginal propensity to consume.

Illustration Example: Let us see the effect of the export multiplier, with an import function, on increase in national income with a numerical example.

Let us assume that $\Delta X = 10$, $b = 0.8$ and $m = 0.05$.

Then the increase in income ΔY is given as

$$\Delta Y = 1/1-b+m\cdot\Delta X$$

or, $\Delta Y = 1/1-0.8+0.05\cdot\Delta X$

or, $\Delta Y = 1/0.2+0.05\cdot\Delta X$

or, $\Delta Y = 1/0.25\cdot\Delta X$

or, $\Delta Y = 1/0.25 \times 10$

or, $\Delta Y = 1/25/100 \times 10$

or, $\Delta Y = 1/1/4\cdot 10$

or, $\Delta Y = 4 \times 10$

or, $\Delta Y = 40$

where the export multiplier is 4.

So, the increase in national income with the same increase in export is less (40 compared to 50) with an import function than without it. This shows that the marginal propensity to import has a dampening effect on increase in national income. Higher the propensity to import more will be the dampening effect on national income.

REVIEW QUESTIONS

1. Explain, graphically, determination of equilibrium national income with the foreign sector.
2. Work out the application (numerical solution) of the four-sector model with the assumption X>M. Compare the result with that of the three-sector model.
3. Work out the application (numerical solution) of the four-sector model with the assumption X<M. Compare the results with that of the three-sector model.
4. Derive equilibrium levels of income in two-sector, three-sector and four-sector models. Work this out as application results. Make necessary assumptions.
5. Derive the export multiplier with autonomous import. Does the export multiplier increase national income? Show the numerical illustration.
6. Work out the export multiplier with an import function. What is the effect it has on national income? Compare the effect with that of the export multiplier with autonomous import.

SUGGESTED READINGS

- E. Shapiro, *Macroeconomic Analysis* (Fourth Edition), Harcourt Brace Jovanovich, 1994, Chapter 7.
- Gardner Ackley, *Macroeconomics: Theory and Policy*, 1978, Chapter 3.
- P. Samuelson, "The Simple Mathematics of Income Determination" in *Income, Employment and Public Policy: Essays in Honour of Alvin Hansen*, W.W. Norton & Co., New York, 1948.
- P. Samuelson and W.D. Nordhaus, *Economics* (Seventh Edition), Tata-McGraw Hill, 2003.
- T.F. Richard, *Macroeconomics: Theories and Policies*, Macmillan, New York (Third Edition), 1990, Chapter 5.

PART–III

PRODUCTION, POVERTY AND UNEMPLOYMENT

This part deals with aggregate production, income distribution, poverty and unemployment. Production depends on the factors of production. Therefore, factor conditions, demand for and supply of factors of production and factor market equilibrium have all been discussed. All this is done in Chapter 9. Chapter 10 deals with income distribution, inequality and poverty. Production or increase in production or income does not indicate anything about equality or inequality of income of the people. This is ascertained through distribution of national income among various sections of the society. Measurements of inequality of income will be covered in the chapter. Poverty is related to income inequality. Definition of poverty will be given in an international perspective. Also, analysis of poverty in India, which involves some debate or controversy, will be elaborately covered. Chapter 11 deals with unemployment which is closely related to poverty. Definition of unemployment has been given. In fact, unemployment or employment has been defined and analysed in a broader perspective; full employment, voluntary unemployment, involuntary unemployment, frictional unemployment, seasonal unemployment have all been covered.

Chapter 9

Production Function and Aggregate Supply and Market Equilibrium

We had discussed aggregate demand (expenditure), the major components of aggregate demand and their determinants in Chapters 3, 4 and 5. We shall discuss here aggregate supply and its determinants. We shall discuss the aggregate supply curve in the short run and long run under different wage-price conditions. Like the supply curve of an individual firm (dealt with in microeconomics), the aggregate supply curve is derived from the production function. As we talk of production or the production function, we shall also discuss demand for and supply of factors of production, because, given the technology level, the factors of production determine the production function or production relationships.

It is necessary to distinguish between the industry supply curve and the aggregate supply curve. The industry supply curve is derived from the supply curves of individual firms through an aggregation process. The industry supply curve shows the quantity of output a particular industry is willing to supply at different prices of the product. The aggregate supply curve depicts the quantity of all goods and services which all industries in the economy together, that is, at an aggregate level, are willing to supply at different general price levels. So, the industry and aggregate supply curves are similar in definitions (except the levels of aggregation), and, both the curves are upward sloping under all normal circumstances. But their slopes would generally differ because of different factors or influences which govern them or determine their slopes.

PRODUCTION FUNCTION

A production function specifies the relationship between inputs and outputs whether at micro level or macro or aggregate level. But the inputs are not raw material inputs which are consumed in the production process, but factor inputs which contribute to productivity and value addition. So, a production function specifies the relationship between factor inputs or factors of production, and, output, given certain technology level.

In macroeconomic analysis, output is represented by income (Y). The factors of production are land, labour, capital and organisation or enterprise or entrepreneurship. Because land, which is a natural resource, is mostly fixed, it is not generally considered as a factor for explaining changes in output or production. Also, for simplicity, organisation or entrepreneurship is often combined with labour input (although income of organisation or entrepreneurship is profit and not wages). Then the production function of an economy, for a given technology level, can be stated as

$$Y = f(L, K)$$

where Y is output, L is labour input and K capital input.

If we consider technology also as not fixed, but variable which would be more realistic in many production processes, then the production function would be

$$Y = f(L, K, T)$$

where T is technology.

As in microeconomics (that is, production function for individual firms), the law of diminishing returns applies to the aggregate production function also. This means that marginal physical product (MPP) of each factor of production decreases as more and more of that factor is used, other factors remaining constant. Given this fundamental characteristic, the aggregate production function can be graphically presented as in Fig. 9.1.

In Fig. 9.1, the production function has been presented by assuming capital and technology as fixed or constant ($\overline{K}$ and $\overline{T}$), that is making the production function a direct relationship between labour and output. The production curve is first convex (up to point A) and, then, concave to the x-axis, later reaches the peak or saturation point at B, and, finally slopes downwards. This particular shape of the production curve is due to operation of the law of diminishing returns. Because of the law of diminishing returns, MPP of the variable input labour first increases, then decreases, falls to zero, and eventually becomes negative.

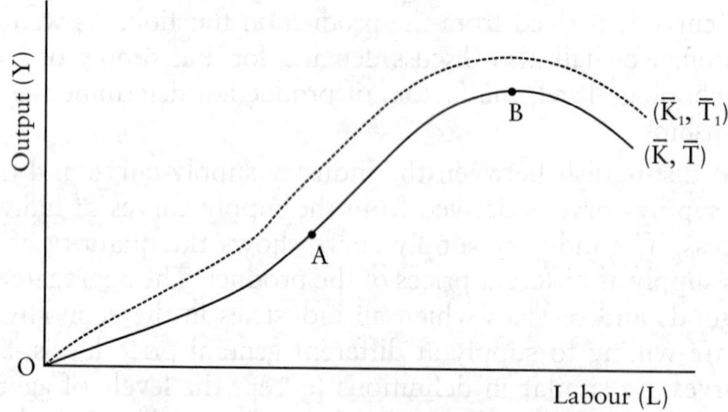

Fig. 9.1: Aggregate Production Function

The production function would shift upward if either capital increases or technology level improves or there is increase/improvement in both. Similarly, the production function would shift downwards if either capital decreases or technology level falls or both are reduced. For example, if capital increases to K_1 and technology level improves to T_1 the production function would shift upwards as shown by the curve corresponding to ($\overline{K}_1$ and $\overline{T}_1$).

DEMAND FOR AND SUPPLY OF FACTORS OF PRODUCTION

Because the production function is directly governed by the factors of production, particularly labour, it is necessary to understand the actor market in terms of demand for and supply of factors of production. Demand for labour would depend on the level of output or production and the productivity (MPP) of labour. Supply of labour would generally depend on the wage rate—money or nominal wage rate or the real wage rate.[1]

1. Demand for labour also depends, to some extent, on the wage rate because the wage rate is the cost of labour—demand for labour varying inversely with the wage rate.

Because demand for labour is based on MPP of labour, we can say that the factor demand function follows from the production function. Any change in the production function would cause a corresponding change in the factor demand function. For example, if the technology level improves or there is increase in land or natural resources, the production function would shift upwards, and because of this, the factor demand curve (labour or capital) would also shift upwards. This implies that what holds good for an individual firm also holds good for the economy as a whole. The only difference would be in terms of the actual configurations of MPP, prices and wages. For an individual firm mpp, p and w relate to its marginal physical product, price of its product and the wage (rate) it pays to its workers. For the economy as a whole, P = general price level, W = nominal/money wage rate in the economy, and MPP is derived from the aggregate production function.

The demand curve for labour is actually the MPP curve for labour, because, given the wage rate, different points on the MPP curve will show demand for labour at those levels of MPP. We know from microeconomics that a profit-maximising firm would employ a factor up to the point where marginal revenue productivity (MRP) of the factor equals its marginal cost. This means that, for labour

MRPL = W (W is money wage rate)

or $MPP_L = W/P$ (P is product price)

We can call this the demand for labour equation.[2] The slope of the curve will be governed by the law of diminishing returns. The demand curve for labour is shown in Fig. 9.2.

If there is free play of market forces, that is, if there is wage-price flexibility, supply of labour would vary directly with the real wage rate. This means that the supply curve for labour will slope upwards because more and more labour would be supplied as the wage rate increases. This is the view of the classical economists.

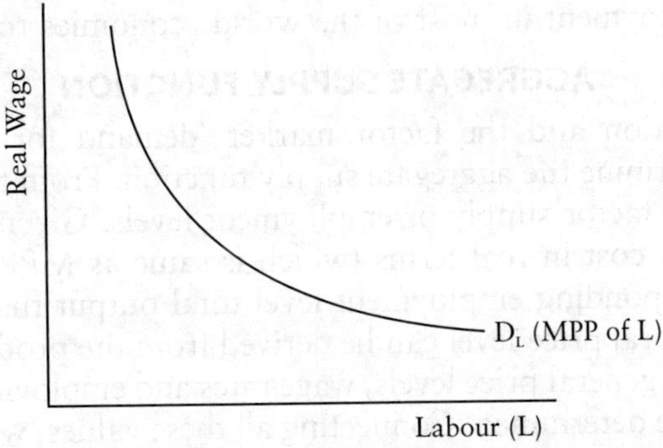

Fig. 9.2: Demand for Labour

Given the demand curve for labour and the supply curve for labour as defined above, labour market equilibrium under wage-price flexibility is shown in Fig. 9.3.

---

2. Similarly demand for capital can be expressed by the equation $MPP_K = R/P$ (R is nominal capital rental) and the demand curve for capital can be drawn accordingly.

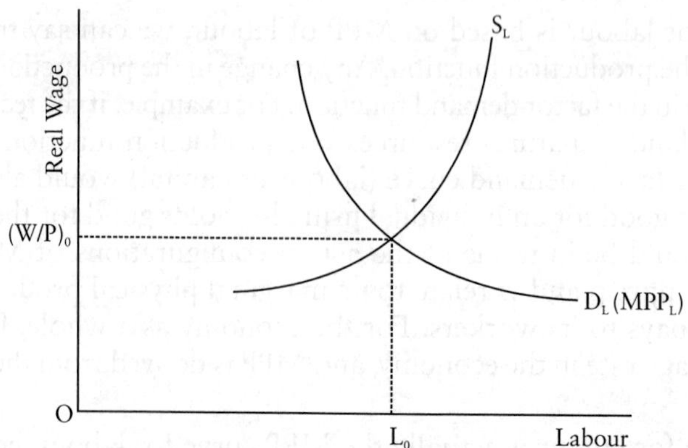

Fig. 9.3: Labour Market Equilibrium

As shown in Fig. 9.3, because of free play of market forces, equilibrium will be reached at L_0 (L_0 is equal to full employment level L_f) and the real wage rate $(W/P)_0$. This equilibrium situation assumes perfect competition in the labour market. The assumption is that all labour units are homogeneous, inter-occupational and spatial mobility of labour within the economy are perfect and other conditions of perfect competition prevail in the labour market.[3]

If there is wage price rigidity, the situation would be different with possibilities of unemployment and market disequilibrium. If there is wage rigidity that is, fixed money wage rate (W_0), then the real wage rate and employment will vary according to the general price level (P). If for example the price level increases to P_1 from P_0, then, given the fixed money wage rate W_0, real wage rate will decrease to W_0/P_1 and, employment will increase to say L_1 from L_0 (L_0 # L_f). So, higher the price level lower would be the real wage rate and higher will be the level of employment and vice versa. This is the thought of the Keynesian economists. We also find wage rigidity and unemployment in most of the world economies today.

AGGREGATE SUPPLY FUNCTION

The production function and the factor market (demand for and supply of factors of production) together determine the aggregate supply function. From the factor market we know factor prices or costs and factor supply or employment levels. Given a particular general price level, real wage or labour cost in real terms (which is same as MPP) can be known. For each real wage rate and corresponding employment level total output that would be produced and supplied at particular general price level can be derived from the production function. Similarly, corresponding to different general price levels, wage rates and employment levels, different values of aggregate output can be determined. Connecting all these values, we will obtain the aggregate supply (AS) curve, because these values actually represent different points on the AS curve.

The aggregate supply function is obtained on the assumption that labour is the only factor of production as we have assumed for the production function. But as we know, in reality, capital, raw materials, electricity or energy are all essential for producing output. This implies that when we say that the wage rate is flexible or rigid, we also assume that prices or costs of all other inputs are also flexible or rigid. This is done for the sake of simplicity. We can formulate

3. This means that a single firm or employer entering the labour market as a buyer, and, a single worker entering as a seller has no influence on the wage rate which is determined by total demand for and total supply of labour in the economy.

a sophisticated production function by making some of these inputs and their prices or costs variable because these prices or costs need not move parallel to labour costs. Such production function can be worked out through an appropriate mathematical function or model.

Depending on the state of wage-price flexibility or rigidity, three different forms of supply curve can be obtained. These are:

1. AS curve under wage (nominal wage) rigidity,
2. AS curve under price rigidity,
3. AS curve under wage-price flexibility.

The above three situations indicate three different forms or structures of the product and labour markets. Situation 1 signifies perfect competition in the product market and imperfect competition in the labour market. Situation 2 reflects imperfect competition in the product market and perfect competition in the labour market. Situation 3 holds when there is perfect competition in both product and labour markets.

AGGREGATE SUPPLY CURVE: SHORT RUN AND LONG RUN

The wage rate and the price level are generally fixed in the short run but flexible in the long run. Therefore, the AS curves in situations 1 and 2 depict two different forms of the short-run supply curve. The AS curve in situation 3 shows the long-run supply curve. We shall discuss these three forms of the aggregate supply curve below.

AS CURVE UNDER NOMINAL WAGE RIGIDITY: SHORT RUN

This situation typically reflects wage settlement or wage agreement—pattern in most of the companies today. In most companies, wage settlements or agreements between the management and the labour unions are generally made for a period of five years (three years in some cases) and the nominal wage rate remains fixed[4] during the period of the agreement. Under such circumstances, the labour market becomes subject to wage rigidity. The product market, however, remains fully competitive with flexible prices. The AS curve under such situation is shown in Fig. 9.4.

As shown in Fig. 9.4, the AS curve is upward sloping till the point J which corresponds to the full employment level of output (Y_f) and is vertical or perfectly inelastic after that. Let us explain this. Let us assume that the nominal wage rate is fixed at W_0 and P_0 is the price level at full employment (L_f) and corresponding output level Y_f. If $P = P_0$, the real wage rate is W_0/P_0. At this real wage rate, demand for labour is L_f which corresponds to output Y_f. Now, let us assume that the price level increases to P_1 ($P_1 > P_0$) because of increase in aggregate demand. Because $P = P_1$, the real wage rate decreases to W_0/P_1. At this lower wage rate, demand for labour increases to, say, L_2($L_2 > L_f$). But, because, full employment level has already been reached, there is no supply of labour beyond L_f. Therefore, although the real wage rate is lower, supply of labour still remains restricted to L_f because no excess labour is available for employment and output remains constant at Y_f level. This is shown by point K. It is, therefore, evident that for any $P > P_0$, the AS curve will be vertical or perfectly inelastic at Y_f level.

4. In most of the agreements, however a provision is made for increase in dearness allowance (called variable dearness allowance) linked to the cost of living index or the price index. But this constitutes a very small proportion of total monthly or annual wages/salaries.

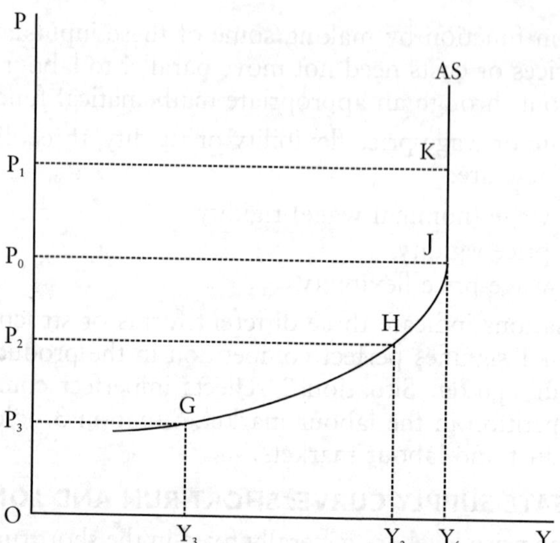

Fig. 9.4: Short Run AS Curve under Nominal Wage Rigidity

Let us now assume that the price level falls to P_2 ($P_2 < P_0$). This can happen if aggregate demand falls. If price falls from P_0 to P_2, the real wage rate increases to W_0/P_2. At this real wage rate, demand for labour decreases to, say, ($L_2 < L_f$). Corresponding to labour employment of L_2 output would fall to Y_2 (known from the production function). This is shown by point H on the AS curve. Similarly, if the price level falls further to P_3, the real wage rate will increase further to W_0/P_3 demand for labour will fall further and output will fall to Y_3. This is shown by point G on the AS curve. In other words, output levels Y_3 and Y_2 show that the AS curve is upward sloping till the full employment level of output is reached.

AS CURVE UNDER PRICE RIGIDITY: SHORT RUN

If there is imperfect competition in the product market, prices will not move freely. In fact, the price level may remain rigid during a particular period (short run). This will happen particularly if there is dominance of monopoly firms. The labour market, however, still remains perfectly competitive with flexible wages. The AS curve representing such situation is shown in Fig. 9.5.

Because of price rigidity, but flexible wage rate, the AS curve is horizontal or perfectly elastic up to a point, and after that becomes vertical or perfectly inelastic. In Fig. 9.5, the AS curve is perfectly elastic up to point J, and perfectly inelastic after that with corresponding price, wage, employment and output levels.

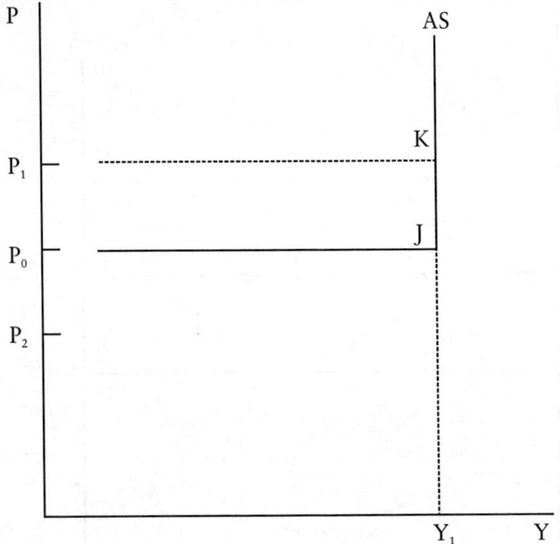

Fig. 9.5: Short Run AS Curve under Price Rigidity

Let us explain this. Let P_0 be the fixed price level. If aggregate demand increases (from the existing level); firms can increase output to meet the additional demand. They can do this by employing more labour by paying higher nominal, and also real, wage till the full employment level (L_f) is reached. Firms can pay higher nominal wage because the wage rate is flexible and, also higher real wage rate because price is fixed and, therefore, higher nominal wage would also mean higher real wage. So, at fixed price level P_0, output will increase till the full employment level of output Y_f is reached. This is shown by the perfectly elastic part (P_0J) of the AS curve. After the full employment level of output is reached, there will be no further increase in production and supply even if aggregate demand increases, because no more labour is available for employment. This is shown by the perfectly inelastic part (JK) of the AS curve.

AS CURVE UNDER WAGE-PRICE FLEXIBILITY: LONG RUN

In the long run, neither the price level is fixed nor the wage rate is rigid; both are flexible and move according to market conditions. With no imperfections in the labour market, the money wage rate would be flexible downwards. This means that, at any time, if supply of labour exceeds demand for labour, competition for jobs among workers would result in a fall in the money wage rate and vice versa. With the price level also flexible, the AS curve in the long run would be perfectly inelastic. This is shown in Fig. 9.6.

As shown in Fig. 9.6, the most important feature of the AS curve in the long run is that aggregate supply or output is independent of the price level. Supply remains constant at full employment output Y_f. Because of flexibility in the labour market, full employment (L_f) will be always ensured through adjustment in the nominal wage rate. This is the classical theory of full employment equilibrium.

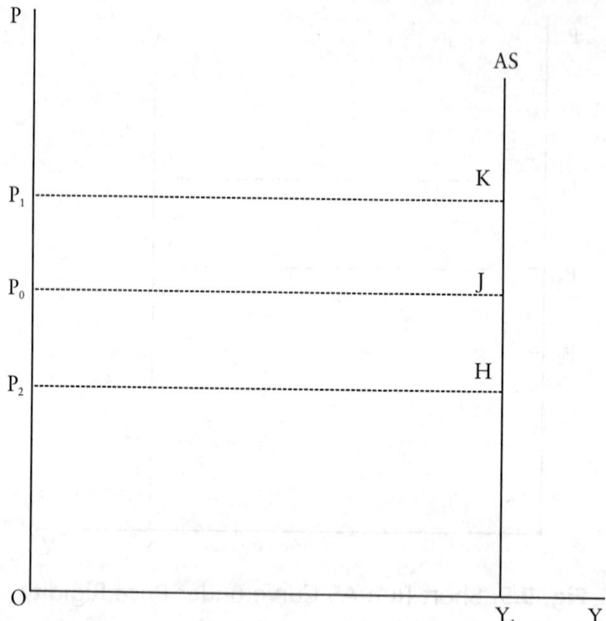

Fig. 9.6: Long Run AS Curve with Wage-Price Flexibility

Let us explain this. If the price level is P_0 and the corresponding money wage rate is W_0, full employment real wage rate is $(W/P)_0 = (W/P)_f$. This is shown by point J. If the price level increases to P_1, because of increase in aggregate demand, output should increase to meet the additional demand, and, demand for labour should increase. But, because output is constant at Y_f level, excess demand for labour would lead to an increase in the nominal wage rate to W_1 which is proportional to P_1 so that real wage rate is maintained at the full employment level $(W/P)_1 = (W/P)_f$. Similarly, if price falls to P_2, excess supply of labour will push down the nominal wage rate to W_2 so that $(W/P)_2 = (W/P)_f$ and full employment is maintained.

This shows that equilibrium in the labour market is consistent with different price levels, but only one level of output, that is, Y_f. Any change in the price and, in aggregate demand would cause a proportional or equal change in the money wage rate so that constancy of the real wage rate and full employment level is maintained.

Figures 9.4, 9.5 and 9.6 show that differences in the shapes of AS curve under nominal wage rigidity (short run), price rigidity (short run) and, wage-price flexibility (long run) exist till full employment output is reached.[5] At the full employment output level, all the three AS curves are perfectly inelastic. Because of wage and price rigidity in the short run, full employment equilibrium may not be reached, and, output may remain below the full employment level. Once the full employment level of output (Y_f) is reached, there will be no further increase in output because of diminishing marginal productivity of labour. Output will not increase further even if there is constant marginal productivity of labour. With full employment labour supply, output can increase beyond Y_f only if there is increase in labour productivity, that is, if there is increasing marginal productivity of labour, but, this is very unlikely.

5. Because of wage-price flexibility, the long-run AS curve is always perfectly inelastic because full employment is always maintained and, therefore, we do not see any shape or form of the AS curve below the full employment level.

Aggregate supply or output can increase if there is a rightward shift in the AS curve. This can happen because of change in a number of factors which have so far been assumed to remain constant. Three major factors which can cause a rightward shift in the AS curve are increase in the labour force, increase of capital and improvement in the level of technology. All these changes are likely to take place in the long run and not in the short run.

The assumption of wage rigidity in the short run may appear quite reasonable as explained earlier. Wage/salary contracts are very common in most of the business organisations and wages/salaries change only once in two or three years. But the assumption of price rigidity or fixed price seems to be unreasonable even in the short run. If there is an increase in the costs of variable inputs like raw materials, intermediates, fuel or electricity, firms may be under compulsions to increase prices of their products; otherwise, their margins may be reduced or eroded. Also, inflation (cost push or demand pull) is a common characteristic of most of the economies today.

AGGREGATE DEMAND AND AGGREGATE SUPPLY

We had mentioned about aggregate demand during our analysis of aggregate supply above. We had also talked about aggregate demand (expenditure) in Chapter 3. We shall now discuss aggregate demand and aggregate supply together in some details, and, see their interaction or intersection for determination of equilibrium levels of price and output.

We start with aggregate demand. During our analysis of aggregate supply and AS curve, we had mentioned about decrease or increase in aggregate demand because of rise or fall in the general price level. Let us see how this actually happens, that is, how the process of change in demand for real output (at constant prices) takes place.

The process works through the monetary system, or, more precisely, through demand for and supply of money—real money or real cash balances—and, the interest rate.[6] Real money supply is defined as money supply (M3) divided by the price level (P). Let us assume that the price level falls. Given a particular level of money supply, if price falls real money or real cash balances increase. This means that the public is now holding larger real money balances than it wishes to hold. The excess real money balances will be used/diverted to purchase of bonds by the people. This will push up the bond prices and lower the interest rate. As the interest rate falls; investment increases.[7] This means that, other things being equal, total amount of goods demanded (to meet the new investment demand), i.e., aggregate demand increases. Similarly, the opposite happens when the price level increases. Because of the inverse relationship between the price level and aggregate demand, the AD curve will be downward sloping. (Note that the general shape of the AD curve is same as that of the demand curve facing an individual firm.)

Once the AD curve has been derived, its intersection with the AS curve will determine equilibrium price and output. But the AS curve may have more than one form and shape as we have seen above depending on whether we make the Keynesian assumption of wage/price rigidity or the classicists assumption of wage-price flexibility. We shall show equilibrium levels of price and output corresponding to two different forms of the AS curve—one with wage rigidity (and flexible prices) and the other with wage-price flexibility.

6. We have also discussed this in Chapter 16 (IS and LM curves and integration of monetary and real sectors).
7. We had discussed the inverse relationship between investment and the rate of interest in Chapter 5.

Equilibrium levels of price and output with wage rigidity is shown in Fig. 9.7.

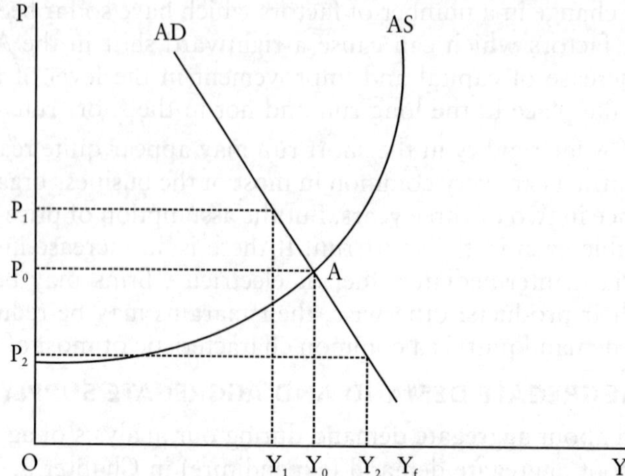

Fig. 9.7: Equilibrium Price and Output: Keynesian Model

As shown in Fig. 9.7, equilibrium is at point A and equilibrium levels of price and output are P_0 and Y_0. It is to be noted that equilibrium output Y_0 is less than the full equilibrium level Y_f. The shape of the AS curve, however, shows that, if there is a significant rightward shift in the AD curve, both price and output will increase, and, there is possibility of full employment equilibrium. In fact, although the Keynesian approach stipulates that equilibrium below full employment is a realistic possibility, it does not completely rule out full employment equilibrium.

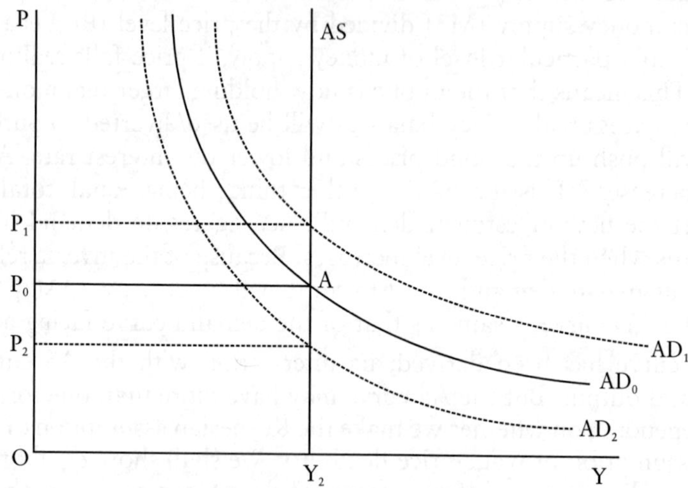

Fig. 9.8: Equilibrium Price and Output: Classical Model

The classical approach, on the other hand, states that full employment equilibrium is the only possibility. This is shown in Fig. 9.8.

In the classical model, the AD curve is a rectangular hyperbola as shown in the figure. The AS curve, as explained earlier, is vertical or perfectly inelastic at full employment level of output (Y_f). AD intersects AS at point A which gives the equilibrium price as P_0.

The relevance of the classical model of almost automatic full employment equilibrium is being questioned today. With high rates of unemployment in countries like India and many other countries, less than full employment equilibrium output, wage/price rigidity and market imperfections seem to more realistically characterise most of the modern economic systems.

REVIEW QUESTIONS

1. Define and analyse production function. Make a graphical presentation.
2. What determines demand for and supply of factors of production? Discuss the equilibrium situation.
3. State the aggregate supply function. Discuss the AS curve under three wage-price conditions.
4. Analyse the Keynesian model of equilibrium of aggregate demand and aggregate supply.

SUGGESTED READINGS

- Edward Shapiro, *Macroeconomic Analysis*, Fifth Edition, 1997, Chapters 8 and 13.
- R. Dornbusch and S. Fisher, *Macroeconomics* (International Edition), 1994.
- N.G. Mankiw, *Principles of Economics*, 2001.

Chapter 10

Income Distribution, Inequality and Poverty

A country's GDP or GNP or national income (NNP) may increase; its per capita income may also increase. But this does not ensure equality of income or well-being of all the people in the country or society; it depends on the nature or pattern of income distribution among different levels or strata of society. Only income distribution tells about equality or inequality of income of people and poverty. A related issue is unemployment. This will be discussed in the next chapter.

INCOME DISTRIBUTION AND INEQUALITY

Income equality or inequality is defined and measured in terms of percentile distribution of national income among different income groups (poor, middle class, rich, etc.) of population of a country. The concept or meaning of income distribution and inequality can be more clearly understood through graphical presentation. This is shown in Fig. 10.1.

In Fig. 10.1, the 45° line (OB) is the income equality line. Every point on this line shows equal distribution of income, i.e., 20% of population receives 20% of income, 40% of population gets 40% of income, 60% of population receive 60% of income, etc. The curve OCB shows inequality of income distribution—The first 20% of population receives less than 20% of income first 40% of population gets less than 40% of income, 60% of population receives less than 60% of income. But last 20% of population receives more than 20% of income. Steeper the OCB curve, more unequal is income distribution of a country.

To know the degree of inequality, one should be able to measure the pattern of income distribution among the population. How do we measure income inequality? The best known and very widely used method for this is the Lorenz Curve. The Lorenz Curve is presented in Fig. 10.2. The Lorenz Curve is similar to that shown in Fig. 10.1, but this is the standardised form.

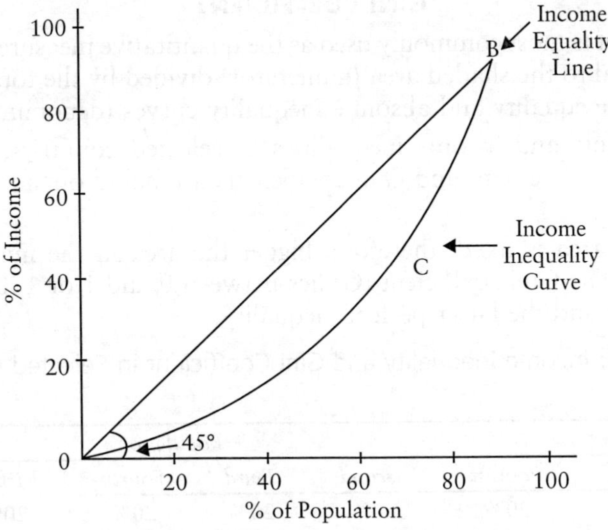

Fig. 10.1: Income Distribution: Income Equality and Income Inequality

MEASUREMENT OF INCOME INEQUALITY

Two extremes shown in the Lorenz Curve are the curves of absolute equality and absolute inequality. Actual income distribution of any country lies between these two extremes. The shaded area in the curve (Fig. 10.2) shows the deviation from absolute equality; this gives the nature and extent or degree of inequality of income distribution. This varies from country to country.

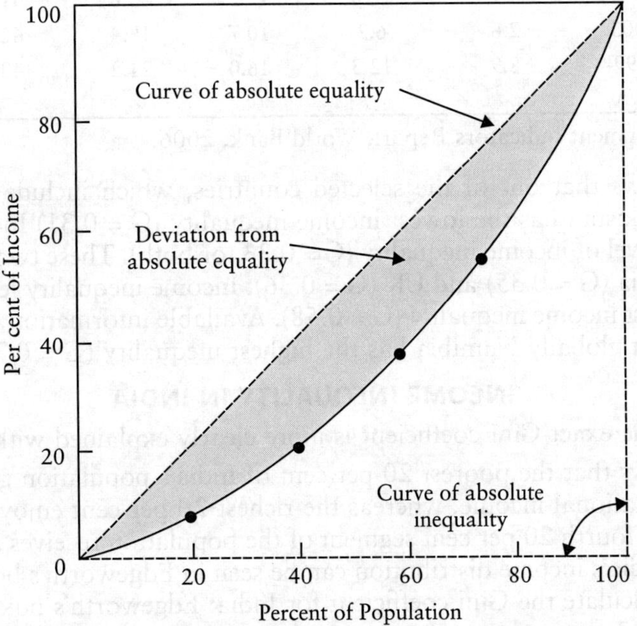

Fig. 10.2: Lorenz Curve for Income Distribution

GINI COEFFICIENT

The Gini coefficient is most commonly used as the quantitative measure of income inequality. Gini coefficient is equal to the shaded area (numerator) divided by the total area of the triangle formed by the absolute equality and absolute inequality curves (denominator) in Fig. 10.2.

The Gini coefficients and income inequalities of selected countries, including India, are presented in Table 10.1. The data and Gini coefficients are based on surveys and estimates by the World Bank.

The denominator area is fixed; therefore, bigger the area in the numerator, larger is the inequality of income. The Gini coefficient (G) lies between 0 and 1 or 100 per cent; the former means perfect equality and the latter perfect inequality.

Table 10.1: Income Inequality and Gini Coefficient in Selected Countries

(% Share in Income)

Country	*Population*						
	Year	*Poorest* 20%	*Second* 20%	*Third* 20%	*Fourth* 20%	*Richest* 20%	*Coefficient* (G)
USA	2000	5.4	10.7	15.7	22.4	45.8	0.411
UK	1999	6.1	11.4	16.0	22.5	44.0	0.361
Canada	2000	7.2	12.7	17.2	23.0	39.9	0.313
Russian Fed	2002	6.1	10.5	14.9	21.8	46.6	0.340
China	2001	4.7	9.0	14.2	22.1	50.0	0.415
Pakistan	2002	9.3	13.0	16.3	21.1	40.3	0.311
Nigeria	2003	5.0	9.6	14.5	21.7	49.2	0.414
Australia	1994	5.9	12.0	17.2	23.6	41.3	0.351
Brazil	2003	2.6	6.2	10.7	18.4	62.1	0.580
India	1999-2000	8.9	12.3	16.0	21.2	43.3	0.30

Source: World Development Indicators Report, World Bank, 2006.

Table 10.1 shows that out of the selected countries, which include both developed and developing ones, Pakistan has the lowest income inequality (G = 0.31) India and Canada have the second lowest level of income inequality (G = 0.33 for both). These two countries are closely followed by Australia (G = 0.35) and UK (G = 0.36). Income inequality level of the US is 0.41. Brazil has the highest income inequality (G = 0.58). Available information for various countries, however, shows that globally Namibia has the highest inequality (G = 0.74).

INCOME INEQUALITY IN INDIA

Estimation of the exact Gini coefficient is more clearly explained with reference to India.

Table 10.1 shows that the poorest 20 per cent of India's population gets a very low of 8.9 per cent of India's national income, whereas the richest 20 per cent enjoys as high as 43.3 per cent of income. The fourth 20 per cent segment of the population receives almost proportionate income (21.2%). India's income distribution can be seen in Edgeworth's box diagram. This will also enable us to calculate the Gini coefficient for India. Edgeworth's box diagram for India is presented in Fig. 10.3.

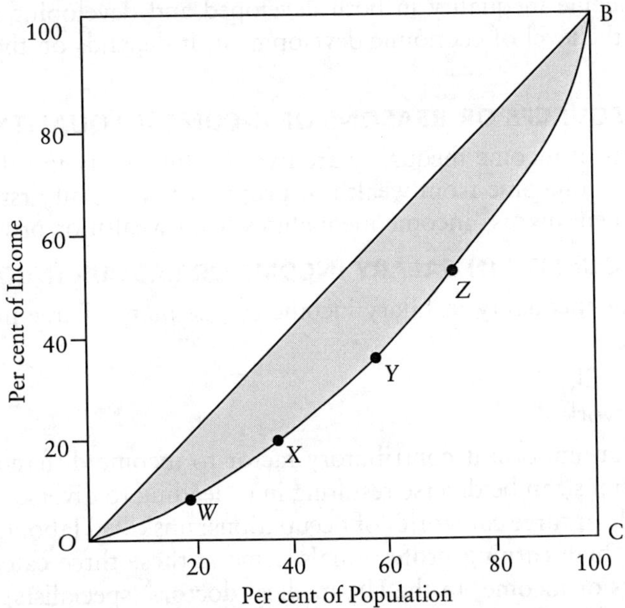

Fig. 10.3: Edgeworth's Box Diagram for India

Notes: '% of income' means '% of national income'; '% of population' means '% of total population'.

Points W, X, Y, Z show different percentages of national income held by different percentages of population; in other words, these represent the nature of income inequality in India.

Point W shows that 20 per cent of the population (poorest) holds about 9.0 per cent of national income; point X shows that 40 per cent of the population (poor) holds about 20 per cent of national income; point Y shows that 60 per cent of the population (poor) holds about 37 per cent of total income; point Z shows that 80 per cent of the population holds about 58 per cent of total income; this means, in other words, that balance 20 per cent of the population holds about 42 per cent of national income.

Income inequality is conventionally measured with the help of the Gini coefficient (G). The Gini coefficient is calculated from Edgeworth Box diagram as

$$\text{Gini Coefficient (G)} = \frac{\text{Area OWXYZB (shaded)}}{\text{Area } \Delta\text{OCB}}$$

$$= 0.325 \text{ or } 32.5\%$$

So, 32.5 per cent is the Gini coefficient for India. Similarly, Gini coefficient can be calculated for different countries for comparison. This is shown in Table 10.1.[1]

The Gini coefficient for India during 2010-11 was 36.8 per cent. In terms of Gini coefficient, income inequality in India is lower than developed countries like the US and many developing countries. Compared to 36.8 per cent of India, Gini coefficient for the US was 40.8 per cent. The Gini coefficient for selected developing countries are: Brazil (53.9%), South Africa (57.8%), Thailand (53.6%), China (41.4%), Malaysia (46.2%), Turkey (40.8%), Sri Lanka (40.3%) and

1. For details of calculation of the Gini coefficient, refer G.S. Gupta and R.D. Singh, "Income Inequality Across Nations Over Time: How Much and Why", *Southern Economic Journal*, July 1984, pp. 250-57.

Vietnam (37.6%). Income inequality in both developed and developing countries proves that this is not related to the level of economic development. It depends on the nature or pattern of income distribution.

SOURCES OR REASONS OF INCOME INEQUALITY

Sources or reasons of income inequality are two: (a) Inequality in salary income or labour income; (b) inequality in income from wealth or properties. We shall first analyse inequality in salary income, and, then, discuss income inequalities from wealth or properties.

INEQUALITY IN SALARY INCOME OR LABOUR INCOME

Reasons of income inequality in salary income can be many. Three major factors are:

1. Occupations,
2. Ability and skill,
3. Intensity of work.

Occupations are an important contributory factor to income differentials or inequality in any country. Occupations can be diverse resulting in or leading to diverse differences in income. Let us take an example of three categories of occupations: unskilled labour, average professional and highly trained or high-earning professionals. Among these three categories, there are vast differences in earnings or income. In the US, medical doctors (specialists) have average annual income of more than $2,00,000; an average unskilled American worker may not earn more than $20,000 (annual). In India also, the difference between the two classes/categories may be as much. In India, however, the doctors are not very highly paid. Different reasons explain vast differences in income among people with different occupations. The most important is education or specialised education and training; another important reason is financial condition or support of parents or families; other reasons include availability of facilities or opportunities, etc.

Ability and skill are personal traits or qualities. These differ enormously among people. Given certain level of education or training, ability and skill can make major differences in income. Abilities have different dimensions or forms—physical, mental, intellectual, temperamental, etc. Skill is inherent or acquired (through training) capability of individuals to do their jobs or perform their duties. Skills can be many and varied. Both abilities and skills contribute to income differential—potential as well as actual.

> "Skills valued in the marketplace are varied and often difficult to measure. Markets tend to reward willingness to take risks, ambition, luck, strokes of engineering genius, good judgement and hard work—none of which is equality measured in standardised tests."—Paul A. Samuelson

Intensity of work is another contributory factor to earning or incomes. Intensity of work also includes application to job or the task. Some may work just enough to earn a livelihood or necessities of life or some minimum comfort. Some others may work 60 hours a week or through the weekends to earn large sums of money. Work effort or intensity is guided by different objectives or motives for earning money by different people.

Other factors relate to miscellaneous reasons for inequality of personal income. These include exclusion to women from certain occupations or jobs like medical surgery, flying aircraft, driving heavy vehicles, etc., workplace discrimination and social or family origin—differences between individuals from poor families and the affluent society. Social origin is a very significant factor.

Some economists feel that technology also can be an important factor. Fast changing technology makes differences in individual performances, and, also incomes, particularly in industries/sectors like IT, ITES, software, BPO and also KPO. Immigration is also considered by some as a reason for personal income inequality—differences in earnings of local workers and immigrant workers.

INEQUALITIES IN WEALTH OR INCOME FROM ASSETS/PROPERTIES

Major factors which cause inequalities in wealth or income from assets or properties are:

1. Entrepreneurship (for profit)
2. Inheritance of wealth/assets
3. Savings (through thrift)

Entrepreneurship or lack of it makes all the difference in creation and accumulation of wealth or assets. History of various countries, including both developed and developing ones, is evidence to rise of entrepreneurship and its association with or contribution to building of wealth including rags to riches stories. Entrepreneurs take risks and create profitable new businesses in different products or industries. Henry Ford (Ford Motor Co.) Bill Gates (Microsoft), Sam Walton (Walmart), Warren Buffett (Investment Guru), Dhirubhai Ambani (Reliance Industries), Ratan Tata (Tata Group), Aditya Birla (AV Birla Group) are some of the dominant examples of entrepreneurial leadership and wealth and asset building.

Inheritance of wealth or assets or property is a major source of income inequality. Descendents of royal families invariably inherit wealth or properties. Members of rich families inherit assets or properties from parents or predecessors. According to available estimates, two-thirds of top one per cent wealth-holders in the US received a significant proportion of their wealth through inheritance. This is true of many other countries including India. This partly explains concentration of wealth in the hands of small number of people. This usually does not depend on growth or level of development of a country.

Savings, differently by different individuals, also accounts for certain account/degree of income inequality. Savings are made out of personal income, but once made, contribute to assets or properties. Savings is definitely not as important a factor as either entrepreneurship or inheritance; but, savings through thrift or by thrifty individuals can ultimately make a difference in assets or properties compared to those who hardly save. It is the degree of thriftiness or level of savings which matters.

POVERTY: NATURE AND INCIDENCE

Poverty is almost a natural concomitant of economic growth. It is difficult to say whether it is a necessary evil or unnecessary evil. There is a clear trade-off. Arthur Okun has observed: "The conflict between equality and efficiency (is) our biggest socio-economic trade-off, and, it plagues us in dozens of dimensions of social policy. We can't have our cake of market efficiency and share it equally."[2] Policy makers dilemma is: efficiency or equality or poverty?

POVERTY: MEANING AND MEASUREMENT

The concept of 'poverty' seems simple but in reality, poverty means different things to different people and countries. This also means that there is no single or unique definition of poverty. Individuals, countries and source international organisation have given their own definitions and measurements of poverty, and accordingly, estimates of proportions of people below the poverty line or above the poverty line.

2. A. Okun, *Equality and Efficiency: The Big Trade-off*, Brooking Institution. Washington D.C., 1975.

In simple or common sense terms, poverty indicates a financial condition or situation of inadequate income of people for living. But what is inadequate or adequate income? Differences or disagreements hover around this.

The US had defined poverty[3] as income insufficient for food, clothing, shelter and other necessities of life.[4] But, which are basic necessities? These would be definable and measurable in quantitative terms to render some precision or exactness to the definition, and, also for comparison between different periods and among countries. Quantification had been done in the US definition of the poverty line. The US had defined poverty line as $1/day/person. This definition or measurement is based on family budget data. From time to time, the family budget and the poverty line have been revised and updated by the government based on changes in the consumer price index which reflects or represents cost of living.

The common international poverty line had in the past been approximately $1 per person per day. It is estimated that about one-fifth (1.3 billion) of world population survives on $1 per day. In 2008, The World Bank gave a revised estimate of the poverty line at $1.25 at 2005 purchasing power parity (PPP).[5] The poverty line in the developed countries, as expected, is significantly higher than in the developing countries.

The definition and measurement of poverty line mentioned above are in absolute terms (head count) and not in relative terms. Many economic experts feel that poverty should be defined and measured in relative terms. In 1995, the National Academy of Science in the US suggested that poverty should reflect relative income position. The Academy recommended that a family should be considered poor if its consumption is less than 50 per cent of the median family's consumption of food, clothing and housing.[6] Poverty, measured this way, would decline when inequality of income distribution would decrease.

An extension of measurement of poverty in relative terms is the poverty gap. The *poverty gap* is the mean shortfall from the poverty line usually expressed as a percentage of the poverty line. In this definition or measurement, the non-poor will have zero shortfall from the poverty line. The poverty gap shows both the incidence and depth of poverty. A related measure is the Sen index which indicates income inequality among the poor population. The Sen index uses the Gini coefficient for measuring income inequality of poor people.[7]

ANTI-POVERTY POLICIES AND INCOME REDISTRIBUTION

Early classical economists held the view that distribution of income, once taken place, was not alterable. Many contended that government intervention in economic activities for reduction of poverty were "foolish endeavors that would simply end up reducing total national income". This view was, however, challenged by J.S. Mill, also among the classical economists. Mill generally agreed with non-interference by the government with the free market mechanism. But he strongly felt and argued that government policies and actions could reduce poverty.

The end of the nineteenth century witnessed almost a historic turning point in the role of the government in dealing with poverty. Political leaders in Europe—Gladstone and Disraeli in Britain, Bismarck in Germany—and, also Franklin Roosevelt in the US introduced a new

3. Poverty was first officially defined in the US in 1960's.
4. P.A. Samulson and W.D. Nordhaus (2002), p. 392.
5. Wikipedia.org/Wiki/Poverty-Threshold
6. P.A. Samuelson and W.D. Nordhaus (2002), p. 382.
7. For details on the Sen index, refer A.K. Sen, "Poverty: An Ordinary Approach to Measurement", *Econometrica*, 44, No. 2, 1976.

concept of the role of the government for welfare of the people of their countries. In their role and responsibility, the government overstepped market forces to guarantee a minimum standard of living or a "safety net" for the people. This, in fact, marked the beginning of the concept of the welfare state.

During this era, many policies were introduced by different governments. More important of these policies and measures include food and housing programme family allowance, health insurance, unemployment insurance and public pension. These and similar policies and programmes were implemented in different countries in phrases since 1880. Today also, many of these policies and programmes are being introduced/implemented by different countries with some changes or modifications.

The US is one of the leading countries in introducing implementing anti-poverty policies and programmes. One of the major anti-poverty programmes implemented by the US is income-security programme. But, most of the income-security programmes are designed or meant for the old people and not the poor. Two major income-security programmes are for social security and medical care. The social security measure is a contributory retirement programme, and, the medical care scheme designated Medicare, is a subsidised health programme for people over 65 years of age. These two are the biggest programmes introduced in the US and most other developed or high-income countries.

Programmes specifically designed or meant for the poor included cash assistance, food subsidy and some in kind. Food subsidization was done in the form of coupons given to poor families which allow them to buy food at a small percentage of the market price. Assistance "in kind" included schemes like medicine through which poor families received free health care or medicine. But, many of the programmes for poor families have either been withdrawn or discontinued during the last two decades.

All anti-poverty programmes have cost. We can say that this is the cost of income redistribution. This has also raised some questions and controversies.

In most of the countries, a large proportion of the national budget is channelled to anti-poverty or income support programmes. Taxes have been used as a major instrument of income redistribution; and, taxes have increased steadily over the years. This incidence of tax is invariably on the rich Many economists contend that policies to redistribute income from the rich to the poor through measures like taxation may affect economic efficiency and may even lead to reduction of national income.

Arthur Okun is one of the most vocal of the exponents of this view. Okun expressed his argument through the "leaky Bucket" phenomenon. His argument or logic is: we may tax a dollar from the very rich and put it in a bucket for giving to the very poor. But, the bucket of re-distribution has a leakage; only a fraction—may be half—of every dollar paid by the rich may actually reach the poor. If this is so, redistribution of income for the sake of equality is taking place at the expense of economic efficiency. According to Okun, redistribution measure like progressive income tax may reduce incentives to work and save, and, may eventually, lead to reduction of real output or income.[8]

POVERTY IN INDIA

The issue of poverty and definition of poverty or poverty line were first officially deliberated upon in India in the Indian Labour Conference in 1957. Since then, the Planning Commission has been regularly addressing this matter.

8. A.M. Okun, *Equality and Efficiency: The Big Tradeoff*, Brookings Institution, Washington D.C., 1975.

The Planning Commission (Working Group) estimates poverty and poverty line every five years using data on household consumer expenditure based on sample surveys conducted by the National Sample Survey Office (NSSO). The poverty line is defined/estimated on the basis of monthly per capita consumption expenditure (MPCE). The methodology followed by the Planning Commission for estimation of poverty or; poverty line has been based on recommendation made by experts from time to time.

The Expert Group on poverty, also known as the Tendulkar Committee, estimated all India poverty lines and MPCE of ₹ 447 for rural areas and ₹ 579 for urban areas based on sample survey data for 2004-05. The Expert Group or the Committee also submitted a detailed report on poverty in India and related issues. Based on the recommendation of the Tendulkar Committee, the Planning Commission revised the estimates of the poverty lines (rural and urban) during 2009-10. The revisions were based on 66 the round (2009-10) of household Consumer Expenditure survey of the NSS. The revised estimates of poverty lines for 2009-10 were MPCE of ₹ 673 for rural areas and ₹ 860 for urban areas.

The poverty line has progressively improved in India during the last four decades, particularly during the last decade. The poverty lines (at current prices)—rural and urban—for the period 1972-74 to 2009-10 are presented in Table 10.2.

Table 10.2: Poverty Lines in India (at Current Prices), 1973-74 to 2009-10

(₹/month/Person)

Year	*Poverty Line (at Current Prices)*	
	Urban	*Rural*
1973-74	57	49
1977-78	75	65
1987-88	152	132
1993-94	264	229
1999-2000	454	327
2004-05	579	447
2009-10	960	673

Source: Government of India, *Economic Survey, 2012-13.*

Along with the poverty line, the Planning Commission has also estimated the poverty ratio, i.e., the ratio between the poor people or people below the poverty line and total population. The estimates show that the percentage of people below the poverty line in India has declined from 37.2 per cent in 2004-05 to 29.8 per cent during 2009-10. On an average, poverty had fallen annually by 1.5 percentage point between 2004-05 and 2009-10. The annual average rate of decline during 2004-05 to 2009-10 is twice the rate of decline during the period 1993-94 to 2004-05. In absolute terms also, the number of people below the poverty line had declined by 52.4 million—48.1 million in rural areas and 4.2 million in urban areas—during 2004-05 and 2009-10.

Number of poor people—total, rural and urban—and poverty ratio—also total, rural and urban—for the years 1993-94, 2004-05 and 2009-10 are shown in Table 10.3. The table also shows the average annual decline (in per cent) in the poverty ratio during 1993-94 and 2004-05 and between 2004-05 and 2009-10.

Table 10.3: Number of Poor People and Poverty Ratio during 1993-94, 2004-05 and 2009-10 and Decline in Poverty Ratios

Year	*Number of Poor (million)*			*Poverty Ratio (%)**		
	Rural	*Urban*	*Total*	*Rural*	*Urban*	*Total*
1993-94	328.6	74.5	403.7	50.1	31.8	45.3
2004-05	326.3	80.8	407.1	41.8	25.7	37.2
2009-10	278.2	76.5	354.7	33.8	20.9	29.8
Annual Average Decline: 1993-94 to 2004-05 (percentage points per annum)				0.75	0.55	0.74
Annual Average Decline: 2004-05 to 2009-10 (percentage points per annum)				1.60	0.96	1.48

* Estimated by Tendulkar Committee Method.

Source: Government of India, *Economic Survey, 2012-13.*

The above analysis shows that there has been almost radical improvement in the poverty line and significant decline in the poverty ratio or percentage of people below the poverty line particularly after the economic reforms of the 1990s. There is, however, disagreement, debate and controversy among economists, politicians and social activists regarding the estimates and statistics of poverty and poverty line in India.

REVIEW QUESTIONS

1. Define income inequality. Explain the Lorenz curve for income distribution.
2. Explain Edgworth's box diagram for India for measurement of income inequality.
3. What is Gini coefficient? How do you measure it? Measure the Gini coefficient for India.
4. What are the sources or reasons for income inequality? Analyse in details.
5. How do you define 'Poverty'? Discuss different definitions and measures of poverty and poverty line.

SUGGESTED READINGS

- A.K. Sen, "Poverty: An Ordinary Approach to Measurement," *Econometrica*, 44, No. 2, 1996.
- A.M. Okun, *Equality and Efficiency: The Big Tradeoff*, Brookings Institution, Washington D.C., 1975.
- B. Bluestone and B. Harrison, *The Industrialisation of America*, Basic Books, New York, 1982, Chapter 3.
- B.S. Gupta and R.D. Singh, "Income Inequality Across Nations and Over Time: How Much and Why", *Southern Economic Journal*, July 1984.

Chapter 11

Unemployment: Meaning, Measurement, Impact

> Unemployment is an unnecessary evil; it should be removed at all cost...
> Full employment is like a mirage-more an illusion....

Unemployment exists in every country today, with differences of magnitudes. This exists more in developing countries. Of the various problems facing a country or society, unemployment may be the most significant, or, may be just next to poverty. This is one of the most concerning macroeconomic issues for the policy makers and the government. It is, therefore, important to understand unemployment in the right perspective—its meaning, measurement types, impact and implications. All these are discussed here.

MEANING OR DEFINITION OF UNEMPLOYMENT

In general terms, unemployment means absence or lack of jobs for all those who are able and willing to work. In terms of symbols, unemployment (U) may be defined as

$$U = W_f - E_p$$

and where W_f = workforce, E_p = employed people.

Workforce = population – people not in workforce

"People not in workforce" needs proper classification or definition. Certain categories of people, both men and women, are not included in the workforce. These are people of certain age groups—both on the lower side and the upper side. According to ILO, those belonging to the age group of 15 to 65 year should be included in workforce or labour force of a country. People below the age of 15 are children and students and those above 65 are superannuated or retired people. The eligible age group varies, to some extent, from country to country. In India, the eligible age group is 15 to 60 year. In the US, the minimum age limit is 16 years.

UNEMPLOYMENT RATE

Two concepts related to unemployment are the work participation rate and the unemployment rate. The *work participation rate* is defined as

$$w_p = \frac{W_f}{\text{Population}}$$

where w_p is the work participation rate and W_f is the workforce. The work participation rate is alternatively, and more appropriately defined as workforce as a proportion of adult population (15-65 year as per ILO).

The unemployment rate is a vital concept because this is what the countries and the governments are most concerned with. The *unemployment rate* is defined and measured as

$$u = \frac{U}{W_f}$$

When u is the unemployment rate, U is total unemployment and W_f the workforce.

So, the unemployment rate is measured as the proportion or percentage of the unemployed in the total workforce. This is the most commonly understood used definition and measurement of the unemployment rate.

There is another definition of the unemployment rate given by Milton Friedman. He calls it the natural rate of unemployment. This is linked to inflation. The *natural rate of unemployment*, according to Friedman, is the rate of unemployment which is consistent with the non-accelerating rate of inflation. This is why, this is also known as the non-accelerating inflation rate of unemployment (NAIRU). NAIRU is the rate of unemployment which alone is consistent with stable or constant, i.e., non-accelerating rate of inflation. This is also called the lowest sustainable unemployment rate (LSUR).

TYPES OF UNEMPLOYMENT

Unemployment can be classified or distinguished at two ways or bases—voluntary and involuntary, and, open and hidden. Both classifications and distinctions are important. We shall first analyse voluntary unemployment and involuntary unemployment, and, then discuss different forms of open and hidden unemployment.

VOLUNTARY UNEMPLOYMENT AND INVOLUNTARY UNEMPLOYMENT

The distinction between voluntary unemployment and involuntary unemployment owes it to Keynes. Since Keynes first mentioned the distinction, it has occupied economists and policy makers in their analysis of unemployment. The distinction, however, is not easy. *Voluntary unemployment*, as the term indicates, is willful unemployment or unemployment by choice or desire. A person may not get a job of his/her choice or liking, either in terms of financial compensation or job specification or job location, and, therefore, he/she may like to remain unemployed for some time. This is voluntary unemployment. *Involuntary unemployment*, on the other hand, is forced unemployment. A person needs a job, or, may be desperately seeking a job, and, he/she is willing to work at prevailing wages/salaries, but, he/she is not getting a job. This is involuntary unemployment.

So, the distinction between voluntary unemployment and involuntary unemployment is apparently quite clear. But, it may not be as clear as it appears. This can be explained with an example. An engineer, also an MBA, is looking for a placement. He has an offer for ₹ 10,000 per month in a metropolitan city. He does not accept the offer. Is he voluntarily unemployed or involuntarily unemployed? He may be said to be voluntarily unemployed because he has not accepted the job offered to him. But, he may also be logically involuntarily unemployed because the market rate for a person with such qualification/degree is not less than ₹ 20,000. So, accepting a job for just ₹ 10,000 may be highly embarrassing, and humiliating for him.

But, in spite of conceptual ambiguity and some marginal cases, the distinction between voluntary unemployment and involuntary unemployment is important and should exist voluntary unemployment does not pose any macroeconomic problem. But, involuntary unemployment creates serious economic and social problems. It has, therefore, important implications for the policy makers and the government.

OPEN UNEMPLOYMENT AND HIDDEN UNEMPLOYMENT

Open unemployment is explicit or visible; hidden unemployment exists, but, is not easily or clearly visible. Open unemployment is of three types; hidden unemployment also is of three kinds. These are

Open unemployment

1. Structural unemployment
2. Cyclical unemployment
3. Frictional unemployment

Hidden unemployment

1. Underemployment
2. Disguised unemployment
3. Seasonal unemployment

Each of these type or form of unemployment is explained below. Along with these, we shall also discuss 'full employment' which requires some definitional or conceptual clarify.

Structural Unemployment

This means unemployment caused by structural changes in an economy. Structural changes can take place in a number of ways. With economic growth, changes occur in the sectoral composition of industries—shift from primary industries to secondary industries, and, with more growth, progressive shift from secondary to tertiary industries. Structural change takes place also because of technological growth and innovation. Fast development of information technology has also contributed to this process.

Because of structural changes nature of job or job specifications and skill requirements change, and, as a consequence of this, mismatch develops between new capability requirements, and, old skills and training. Because of this, and, also depending on the pace or speed of structural change, some or many people get unemployed, and remain so for, sometime till they acquire new skills and capabilities. This may be considered as a cost of economic growth.

Cyclical Unemployment

Business cycles cause unemployment, this is called cyclical unemployment.

We would analyse business cycles in Chapter 12. We would explain that, during downturn or recession, economic and business activities slow down; production declines; there is fall in output or income, and, because of this, unemployment occurs or increases. The opposite happens during upswing and boom.

We are, however, concerned here with the impact of recession on unemployment. A direct consequence of recession is an increase in the unemployment rate. As production declines, there is lesser demand for labour: firms do not hire new labour, and, some present workers may be laid off. This increases the unemployment rate. At the end of the recession of 1981-82, about one of every 10 American workers was unemployed. During the recession in Europe in the mid-1990s, unemployment level was more than 10 per cent of the workforce. The unemployment situation in the US after the onset of recessionary conditions during 2008 has been quite bad. The Indian Economy is also currently experiencing this.

The inverse relationship between output and unemployment was first clearly identified by Arthur Okun, and studied in quantitative terms. His study result, based on output and employment data of 1950s and early 1960s, established that, for every 2 per cent fall in real GDP relative to potential GDP, the unemployment rate increases by about 1 per cent point. This is known as Okun's Law. This means that if real GDP falls to 98 per cent of potential GDP (100 per cent), the unemployment rate increases by 1 percentage point, say from 7 to 8 per cent.

Frictional Unemployment

This means unemployment which occurs between the period of change of jobs by people. Many people leave a job and decide to take a break, i.e., remain unemployed, before joining the second job. Such unemployment is quite common in developed countries because, in these countries, jobs are usually very demanding (requiring break) and new jobs are more easily available. So, frictional unemployment is purely a temporary phase. Because of its nature, frictional unemployment can also be considered as voluntary unemployment.

Both classical economists and neoclassical economists had their own views or notions of frictional unemployment. We shall discuss there both the notions or thoughts.

According to the classical economists, there is always full employment in an economy. If any unemployment occurs, it is purely temporary. This can happen because in a free economy, the labour market is "always in a state of flux". New firms create fresh demand for labour; some old/existing firms close down resulting in reduction in demand for labour. Because of these reasons, mismatch develops between demand and supply in the labour market leading to excess supply for a short or transitional period. This temporary excess supply is frictional unemployment. But, this is quickly wiped out through an automatic market adjustment process and restoration of full employment equilibrium.

The neoclassical economists emphasised imperfections in the market mechanism (both commodity and labour markets), and because of this, emergence and existence of frictional unemployment. The imperfection in the labour market is caused by many reasons or factors. These include insufficient and imperfect market information, cost of information, slow occupational mobility, cost of transportation and spatial movement of labour, cost of training, labour unions and collective bargaining, etc. In an imperfect market, there is upward flexibility in wages, and, therefore, adjustment in wages in response to rise in prices is fast; but, there is downward inflexibility in wages and, because of this, downward adjustment in wages in response to fall in prices is slow and rigid particularly because of resistance by the unions. The firms may not be willing to hire labour at the old or higher wages. This leads to frictional unemployment. According to neoclassical economists, under imperfect market conditions, frictional unemployment is almost a regular feature in an economy.

The neoclassical school, however, contends that, even with the existence of frictional unemployment, the economy is "deem to be in the state of full employment". This is explained with reference to the US economy. Many economists think that frictional unemployment in the US economy is about 4 per cent and full employment occurs at the employment level of about 96 per cent. With 4 per cent frictional unemployment and 96 per cent regular employment in the 1970s, the US economy was considered to be in full employment.[1]

1. F.R. Glahe, *Macroeconomics: Theory and Policy*, Harcourt Brace Jovanovich, 1973, p. 231.

Underemployment

This is a situation or a state of employment in which people are not fully employed. This means that work done is for lesser than full employment hours or for periods lesser than full working days. Most of the full-time labourers in agriculture and part-time workers in the secondary sector and services typically constitute the 'underemployed' category. Underemployment is very common in developing countries; and, this is most common in the agricultural sector. In many agricultural farms, the entire family, of say 5, may be working in the field, but, work involved may be for three persons on full time basis. Because five people are working, none of them is fully employed, i.e., they are underemployed.

Disguised Unemployment

This is similar to underemployment. Some people are visibly or apparently employed, but, the work can be completed or the same output can be produced without them. These people are 'disguisedly unemployed' like underemployment. This also happens typically in the agricultural sector. We can take the above example of an agricultural family of five persons. Three members of the family may be able to complete the farming job. This means that, if two people are withdrawn from the field, production or output will remain the same, that is, the marginal product of these two people are zero. These two people are a typical case of disguised unemployment.

Disguised unemployment also exists in the public sector and the government in mixed and socialist economies. A country like India, with a very large public sector—both central and state undertakings—is a good example. It is commonly agreed that there is over employment in the public sector industries companies in India. Over employment means underemployment for all or disguised unemployment for certain percentage of the employed people. This also exists is the government sector.

Seasonal Unemployment

This refers to unemployment during off-seasons (particular months or periods of the year) and employment during seasons. Some economic activities or industries or occupations are seasonal in nature. The best example is agricultural employment. In agricultural farming in a country like India there are two main seasons—Kharif (June-October) and Rabi (December-March). Farmers or agricultural labourers remain employed during these months, but become mostly unemployed for the rest of the months or periods during the year. This is seasonal unemployment. Next to agriculture, seasonal unemployment exists in industries like food processing, sugar, textiles, tea, etc. which use inputs from the agricultural sector. Seasonal unemployment also exists, to some extent, in some consumer durable industries which have seasonal demand and peak production operations take place during particular months or periods of the year. Examples are fans, coolers and air conditions for the summer season and heaters or air blowers, and geysers for the winter season.

Full Employment

In simple terms, or apparently, full employment means that nobody is unemployed in the economy or country, i.e., there is zero unemployment. But, it is not so in reality. In the real world, full employment is presumed to exist with certain level of unemployment of different forms. Economists differ on what should be the proper or realistic level of unemployment. Because of such differences of views, there is no single or unique definition of unemployment.

In macroeconomic theory, full employment is reached when demand for labour is equal to supply of labour, and the labour market is in equilibrium at a particular wage rate. But, most often, this does not happen in reality because of market imperfections and bottlenecks. Equality of demand and supply at the aggregate level ignores inequality of demand and supply at disaggregated or sectoral levels. For example, there may be excess demand for labour in one industry or occupation, and, excess supply in another industry or occupation. These two 'excesses' may be equal in terms of pure numbers, but, these two are not matchable, i.e., not adjustable against each other. Again, there may be excess demand of labour in one market (geographical region) and excess supply of equal number in another market, but, there may be lack of mobility of labour because of various reasons or problems including bottlenecks in movement. Also, wage rates may not be uniform—those are usually not—across occupations and markets (places) because of occupational and spatial (regional a local) factors. Because of many such factors or reasons, full employment is said to exist along with some unemployment.

Such unemployment should be mostly frictional, and, to some extent, structural, and, generally voluntary. There may be a very small percentage of involuntary unemployment. For the US economy, as mentioned above, the acceptable unemployment is about 4 per cent which is consistent with the full employment level. For other developed countries. This is estimated to be 3-4 per cent.

MEASUREMENT OF UNEMPLOYMENT

Because of different kinds of unemployment, some being hidden, measurement of unemployment always becomes a difficult task. For such reason, unemployment data in different countries and also over time are not easily comparable.

Certain bases or criteria have been suggested for measurement of unemployment. Four major ones are:

1. Income or earning
2. Time spent on (or hours of) work
3. Willingness to work
4. Productivity or output

The income criterion requires that a worker should earn a minimum income during a defined period, and if the prescribed income level cannot be achieved, the worker is at least partly unemployed. As per the productivity standard, a worker should achieve a minimum productivity level, i.e., output per unit period; if he (she) cannot achieve the minimum level, he (she) is unemployed. 'Time' criterion states that a person has to work for certain number of hours per day/week as required by law of the country to be fully employed; if he (she) works for less number of hours, he (she) is partially unemployed. "Willingness" means that only those who are willing to work are to be considered for measurement of employment and unemployment. Voluntarily unemployed people are not willing to work, and, therefore, they are not counted as unemployed.

Productivity is very difficult to measure for every individual worker who is not fully employed in various industries or occupations. This is more difficult in services and high technology production processes. Income is also difficult to measure for the self-employed for classification of these into fully employed or partially employed. For other occupations also there may bias and possibilities of understatements and over statements. Because of these reasons, methodology for measurement of unemployment does not usually take these two factors into account, and, mostly use 'willingness' and time criteria. Measurement method or criteria are, however, not uniform in all countries.

The methodology used in India for measurement of unemployment is briefly discussed here. In India, collection, analysis and publication of data on workforce, employment and unemployment are done by NSSO. The first survey on employment and unemployment was carried out by NSSO in the 27th round (1972-73), and, the second survey was conducted in the 32nd round (1977-78). Since then, more surveys have been carried out by NSSO. During these surveys, people (respondents) are asked about their employment unemployment status.

There are four possible categories: willingness to work or availability for job, actively looking for a job, employed or unemployed. The first two categories of people constitute the workforce. Based on the nature of responses, estimates of the employed and unemployed are made. Some people may simultaneously belong to three categories, viz., unemployed, actively to searching a job and willingness to work. Compilation and analysis of response data have to be carefully done to avoid double counting or duplication of numbers. Many other countries use same or similar methods for measurement of employment or unemployment.

IMPACT OF UNEMPLOYMENT

Full employment or employment has positive or good impact on the economy and society. Conversely, unemployment has negative or bad or ill effect on the economy as well as the society. High unemployment has serious economic and social implications. Most direct or immediate economic impact is the loss or waste of valuable human resource. There are other significant economic impacts. The social affect is clearly reflected in human suffering because of lack of job and substandard living. Economic and social impacts are often interactive. The combined effect of these two produces the socio-economic impact. This is also shown in Fig. 11.1.

The biggest economic impact of unemployment is loss of output or income, and the resultant consequences or effects on other economic variables or factors. We have mentioned above Okun's Law. This can be restated as follows: for every increase in the unemployment rate by one percentage point, the fall in GDP or GNP is 2 per cent below the potential level. The unemployment rate always increases during recession; loss of output is, therefore more during recession, and this affects almost all industries including housing, consumer durables, food, clothing, etc.

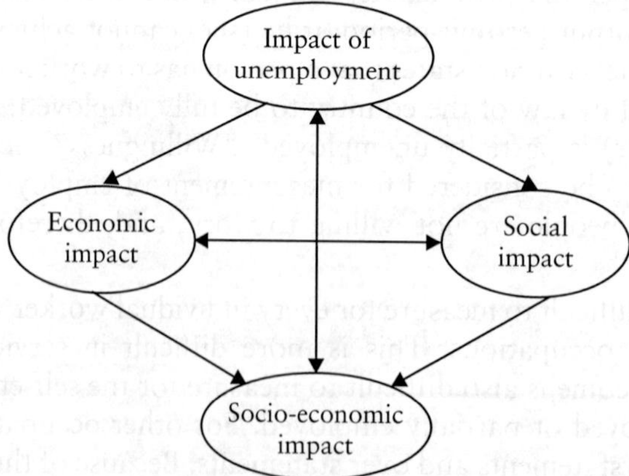

Fig. 11.1: Economic, Social and Socio-economic Impact of Unemployment

ECONOMIC IMPACT

Some estimates of high rates of unemployment and loss of output or income (GDP) during last half century are available. These are shown in Table 11.1. The table shows average unemployment rates, loss of GDP, and GDP loss as percentage of GDP during the selected periods.

Table 11.1: Average Unemployment Rate, GDP Loss and GDP Loss as per cent of GDP during 1930-39, 1975-84, and 1985-99

Period	*Average Unemployment Rate (%)*	*Loss of Output*	
		GDP loss ($ Billion, 1999 Prices)	*% of GDP of the Period*
Great Depression (1930-39)	18.2	2420	27.6
Oil and inflation crises (1975-84)	7.7	1480	9.0
New Economy Period (1985-99)	5.7	240	0.3

Source: P.A. Samuelson and W.D. Nordhaus (2002), p. 668.

As shown in Table 11.1, and, as is universally known, the biggest output (GDP), loss happened during the Great Depression (close to $2.5 trillion). During the oil and inflation crises of 1970s and 1980s, GDP loss was about 1.5 trillion. Even during comparatively good times (1985-99), loss of output was $240 billion. Average unemployment rate during the Great Depression was undoubtedly the highest (18.2 per cent), and, output loss as per cent of GDP was a staggering 27.6 per cent economic history tells us that many industries closed down during this period.

Social Impact

The economic (output) loss of unemployment may be measurable (even if not perfectly), but, the social impact in terms of "human and psychological toll of long periods of involuntary unemployment" is not easily measurable. People live sub-human lives. And, worse, there are losses of human lives.

Some economists have made attempts to estimate human sufferings and deaths during periods of high rates of unemployment. Bluestone and Harrison have estimated different forms of human suffering and death in the US during 1981-82 recession. The estimates of human sufferings and deaths for every 1 per cent increase in the unemployment rate are as follows: 4,000 people were admitted to mental hospitals: 3800 people were sent to prisons; 650 committed homicide; 920 committed suicide; and, 500 people died of heart attack and liver cirrhosis. In all, for every 1 per cent increase in the unemployment rate, 37,000 more deaths occurred.[2] These are the human costs of unemployment.

Human misery and sufferings are more common in developing countries because of higher rates of unemployment. It is estimated that one-quarter to one-third of the population in these countries live with prolonged joblessness or unemployment. In countries like India with a large agricultural sector, underemployment and disguised unemployment are quite common in addition to the official estimates of unemployment. Certain number of farmers (sometimes along with their family members) commit suicide every year—Thousands of farmers would have done so

2. B. Bluestone and B. Harrison, *The Deindustrialization of America*. Basic Books, New York, 1982, Chapter 3.

during last few years. A large proportion of the population, particularly in rural areas, have got used, or, rather forced to live in poverty, malnutrition and starvation.

Socio-Economic Impact

The economy cannot be isolated from the society. In repercussions of serious national problems like unemployment, economic and social effects interact with each other, and, this ultimately results in the socio-economic impact.

The socio-economic impact of unemployment can be seen in the 'vicious circle of unemployment' similar to the 'vicious circle of poverty' in the theory of economic underdevelopment. In terms of the elements or components/constituent, the vicious circle of unemployment can be stated as: unemployment, loss of output, loss of job, poverty and starvation (Fig. 11.2).

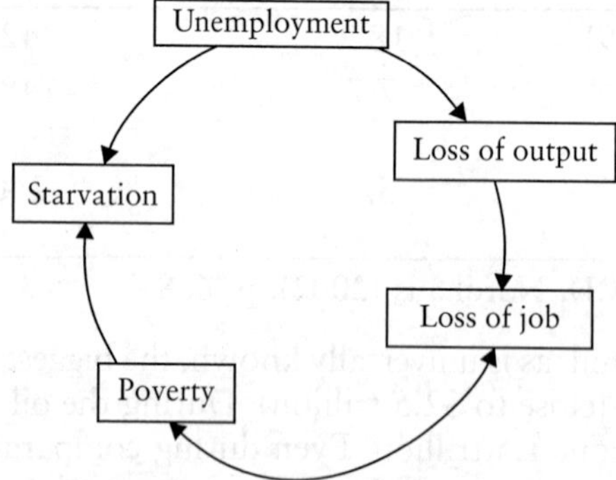

Fig. 11.2: The Vicious Circle of Unemployment

The vicious circle starts with the economic impact of unemployment: first is loss of output; loss of output leads to loss of job: loss of job creates poverty; loss of job and poverty are both economic and social problems; loss of job and poverty ultimately cause starvation (also death) which is a serious social problem. This way, the vicious circle of unemployment perpetuate itself with profound socio-economic impact.

INFLATION AND UNEMPLOYMENT

A relationship exists between inflation and unemployment—a relationship of trade-off. According to some economists, the relationship may be a matter of contention and debate. According to some others, "the foremost macroeconomic concern of the past decade or more—is the relationship between the inflation rate and the unemployment rate."[3] The simple (inverse) relationship between inflation and unemployment in terms of the Phillips curve will be mentioned in Chapter 13. In this section, the relationship is analysed in more detailed perspective including extension of the original Phillips model or curve into a definite relationship (short run as well as long run) between inflation and unemployment and closely related issues.

Analysis of the relationship between inflation and unemployment begins with explanation of the relationship between the wage rate and the price level. If an increase in the wage rate is not matched or neutralised by an equal increase in labour productivity. This results in an increase of the inflation rate. This can be explained with a numerical example. If money wage rate is increasing by 8 per cent annually and labour productivity is increasing by 4 per cent, the result will be 4 per cent rate of inflation (wage-push). If the money wage rate increases

3. E. Shapiro, *Macroeconomic Analysis* (Fifth Edition), Galgotia Publications, 1984, p. 514.

from a rate of 8 per cent to 10 per cent, but the rate of increase of labour productivity remains unchanged at 4 per cent, the resultant increase in the rate of inflation will be 6 per cent (10 per cent *minus* 4 per cent).

From the relationship between the rate of increase of the wage rate and the rate of inflation, we move to another relationship. This is between the rate of increase of the wage rate and the unemployment rate. There is inverse relationship between these two, i.e., if the wage rate increases, the unemployment rate decreases. Because there is direct relationship between movements in the wage rate and the inflation rate, it follows that there is inverse relationship between movements in the inflation rate and the unemployment rate. Inflation and unemployment data of different countries and time periods also corroborate this inverse relationship.

Investigation and analysis of the relationship between the wage rate and the unemployment rate was pioneered by the British economist A.W. Phillips as early as middle of the last century. His study was based on data of the United Kingdom.[4] Ever since, this is known as the Phillips curve. Samuelson and Solow, among others, popularised the Phillips curve and extended it to a relationship between the inflation rate and the unemployment rate. The inverse relationship clearly establishes the trade-off between the two.

Short-Run Relationship

The Phillips curve, along with extension to or incorporation of the inflation rate, is graphically shown in Fig. 11.3. Inflation ($^{\Delta P}/_{P}$) and increase in the wage rate ($\Delta W/W$) are both shown in the vertical (Y) axis, and, the unemployment rate in the horizontal (x) axis. The trade-off between the rate of inflation and the unemployment rate can be more clearly seen in this.

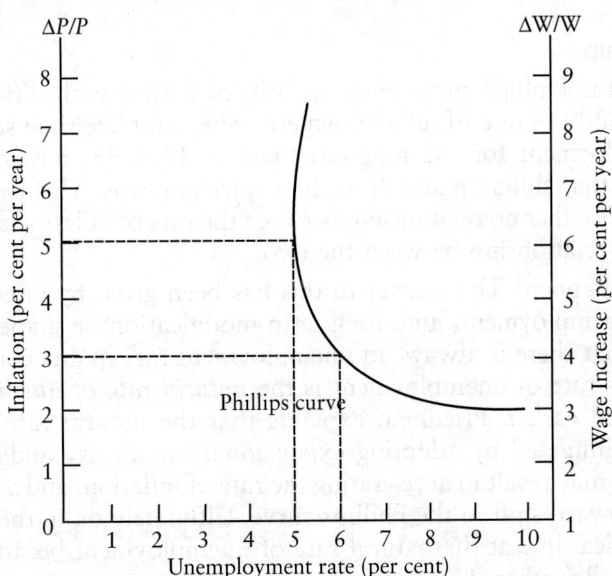

Fig. 11.3: Extended Phillips Curve: Inflation Rate, Wage-Rate and the Unemployment Rate

As shown in Fig. 11.3, the trade-off between the inflation rate and the unemployment rate works like this: a 2 per cent (5 per cent – 3 per cent) increase inflation can be traded for

4. A.W. Phillips, "The Relation between unemployment and the Rate of change of Money Wage Rates in the United Kingdom 1862-1957", *Economica*, November 1958.

1 per cent (6 per cent – 5 per cent) decrease in unemployment. This has an implication for policy or the policy makers. If unemployment is to be reduced from 6 per cent to 5 per cent, an increase in the inflation rate from 3 per cent to 5 per cent has to be accepted. A target for either inflation rate or the unemployment rate has to be decided by the policy makers; the other will automatically follow as a trade-off (Phillips curve).

This means, in other words, that inflation and unemployment cannot be controlled simultaneously. If inflation is controlled, it may result in a higher rate of unemployment; conversely if unemployment is controlled, it may lead to a higher rate of inflation. The policy makers may have to choose between the two or seek a proper balance between the rate of inflation and the unemployment. This is a macroeconomic challenge. Economists like Samuelson have put it like this: "The search for a way to resolve the cruel dilemma of needing high unemployment to contain inflation continues to be one of the most pressing concerns of modern macroeconomics."[5]

The trade-off between inflation and unemployment shown by the Phillips curve (Fig. 11.3) is, however, considered to be a short-run relationship. More recent studies tend to corroborate this. Different studies showed that the Phillips curve (trade-off relationship) held good only for short periods like 1961-69, 1970s and late 1980s at different rates of inflation and unemployment. A number of economists used the US data to establish the short-run relationship between inflation and employment (unemployment. Dennburg used the data for 1951-61 Ackley for (1955-69) Dornbusch and Fisher for 1961-69, and Glahe for 1961-70.[6] These studies found a positive relationship between the rate of inflation and the rate of employment; this, in other words, means the inverse relationship between the inflation rate and the unemployment rate during these periods.

Long-Run Relationship

In the long-run, the Phillips curve tends to shift over time with different combinations of the rate of inflation and the rate of unemployment. The complete time series of the wage rate, inflation and unemployment for the long-term period 1961-93, put together and analysed, gives a Phillips curve that shifts up and down in a spiralling way. This leads to the inference or conclusion that there is either no relationship between the rate of inflation and the unemployment rate or there is weak relationship between the two.

But, why does it happen? The answer to this has been given by Friedman in his theory of the natural rate of unemployment, and, long-term modification or shape of the Phillips curve. Friedman contends that there is always an unemployment rate in an economy whatever be the rate of inflation. This rate of unemployment is the *natural rate of unemployment* (also called NAIRU) as mentioned earlier. Friedman explains that the natural rate of unemployment or NAIRU cannot be eliminated by adopting expansionary monetary and/or fiscal policies. The expansionary policies may result in accelerating the rate of inflation, and a higher unemployment rate by causing an upward shift in the Phillips curve. Ultimately or, in the long run, the Phillips curve becomes a vertical line at the natural rate of unemployment because the unemployment level or rate cannot fall further. This is shown in Fig. 11.4.

5. P.A. Samuelson and W.D. Nordhaus (2002), p. 597.
6. D.N. Dwivedi, *Macroeconomics* (3rd Edition), McGraw Hill India, 2010, p. 499.

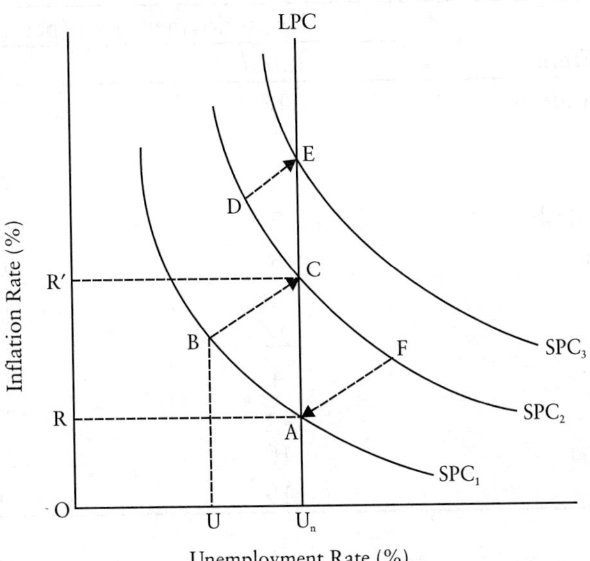

Fig. 11.4: Long-Run Phillips Curve

Note: SPC_1, SPC_2 and SPC_3 are the short-run Phillips curves corresponding to certain levels of inflation and unemployment LPC is the long-run Phillips curve.

UNEMPLOYMENT IN INDIA

Like poverty, unemployment is a serious problem in India as in many other countries. As mentioned earlier estimates of unemployment in India are made by NSSO during its different surveys or rounds. Because of definitional and methodological issues involved, it is generally felt that there may be bias in the official estimates—bias in the form of under reporting or underestimation. In spite of this, the unemployment rate in India is quite high. During 2009-10, for which the last official estimate is available, the unemployment rate was 6.6 per cent. This marked a decline over 2004-05 during which the unemployment rate was 8.2 per cent.

For 2009-10, unemployment rates (per 1000) are separately available for rural and urban areas. For the year all India unemployment rate was 16 (per 1000) in rural areas and much higher 34 (per 1000) in urban areas. Unemployment rate, all India and by major states, during 2009-10 for rural and urban areas is shown in Table 11.2.

Table 11.2: Unemployment Rate (Per 1000), All India and Major States, for Rural and Urban Areas, 2009-10

State	Unemployment rate (per 1000)*	
	Rural	*Urban*
All India	16	34
Andhra Pradesh	12	31
Assam	39	52
Bihar	20	73
Gujarat	8	18
Haryana	18	25

State	Unemployment rate (per 1000)*	
	Rural	Urban
Himachal Pradesh	16	49
Karnataka	5	27
Kerala	75	73
Madhya Pradesh	7	29
Maharashtra	6	32
Odisha	30	42
Punjab	26	48
Rajasthan	4	22
Tamil Nadu	15	32
Uttar Pradesh	10	29
West Bengal	19	40

* NSS (66th Round)

Source: *Economic Survey*, 2012-13, Government of India.

REVIEW QUESTIONS

1. Define the work participation rate and the unemployment rate. Also explain Friedman's natural rate of unemployment.
2. What are the different kinds of unemployment? Mention the basis and different classifications.
3. What is full employment? Mention the definition in macroeconomic theory, and, also market imperfections and bottlenecks which dilute such definition.
4. What are the bases or criteria for measurement of unemployment? Comment on the applicability of such criteria.
5. Analyse the impact of unemployment on the economy, the society and the socio-economic impact.
6. What is the relationship between inflation and unemployment? Discuss both the short-run and long-run relationship.
7. Discuss the methodology for estimation of unemployment in India. Also comment on the unemployment rate.

SUGGESTED READINGS

- A.M. Okun, *Equality and Efficiency: The Big Trade-off*, Brookings Institution, Washington D.C., 1975.
- A.W. Phillips, "The Relation between Unemployment and the Rate of Change of Money Wage Rates in the United Kingdom, 1862-1957", *Economica*, November 1958.
- B. Bluestone and B. Harrison, *The Industrialisation of America*, Basic Books, New York, 1982, Chapter 3.
- M. Friedman, "Nobel Lecture: Inflation and Unemployment", *Journal of Political Economy*, 85, June 1977.

PART–IV

BUSINESS CYCLES AND INFLATION

In this part, two closely related topics have been discussed, viz., business cycles and inflation. Chapter 12 deals with fluctuations in output or income and the price level, i.e., business cycles. Nature of business cycles, phases of business cycles, various theories of business cycles including the multiplier-acceleration model have been discussed; finally, synthesis of various business cycle theories has been covered in the chapter. Different anti-cyclical or stabilisation measures have been discussed at length. Chapter 13 is devoted to a detailed analysis of inflation—its nature, causes, effects and control of inflation through various anti-inflationary measures. Inflationary gap has been defined and explained. Special focus has been given on the nature and measurement of inflation in India in terms of different price indices. Inflationary trend in India, as a time series, has also been covered.

Chapter 12

Business Cycles and Stabilisation Policies

INTRODUCTION

Economic or business activity implies fluctuations in such activity. In business, there is good time—high turnover, good profit and growth; there is also bad time—slack demand, low sales, less or no profit and growth gives way to decline or downswing. This is at micro-level, i.e., for individual business or organisation. Business fluctuations of individual firms or enterprises cumulate at macro-level, i.e., for the economy or country as a whole. Periods of high investment, income and economic growth alternate with periods or phases of downturn-low demand, low or no new investment, less income and deceleration of economic activity. This keeps happening with certain frequencies or periodicities.

If fluctuation in economic or business activity occurs, its nature and causes need to be understood. Also to cut the intensity of fluctuations and their adverse effects on functioning of the economic system, appropriate anti-cyclical or stabilisation policies and measures are required to be applied. In all these, the government of the countries concerned has a very important role to play in terms of timely intervention and action. But, sometimes, such timely actions are not forthcoming earlier because of inability or complacency of the government to effectively deal with such situations. Let us look at the following observation:

> ...men who wish to serve democracy faithfully must recognise that the roots of business cycles go deep in our economic organisation, that the ability of government to control depressions adequately is not yet assured, that our power of forecasting is limited and, that true foresight requires policies for coping with numerous contingencies.[1]

The global recession of 2008 is a good example. Neither the onslaught of the recession could be predicated or signalled through any forecasting mechanism or system nor the corrective actions or measures have been very effective or successful. The recession has been a major setback for global economic management. We will be talking more about the recession of 2008 later.

All these very clearly emphasise the significance of business cycles as disturbing economic phenomena, and, the necessity for appropriate anti-cyclical or stabilisation policies and measures. We shall discuss the subject in the present chapter in two parts:

A. Business Cycles: Meaning, phases, theories

B. Anti-cyclical or stabilisation policies

1. R.A. Gordon, *Business Fluctuations*, Harper and Brothers, New York, 1952, p. 4.

A. BUSINESS CYCLES: MEANING, PHASES, THEORIES

MEANING OF BUSINESS CYCLES

As explained, business conditions hardly remain steady. There are periods of flourishing activity leading to prosperity and growth. There are also periods of recession which lead to decline in output and employment. Usually, periods of prosperity and recession alternate in some cyclical pattern. Prosperity or boom is generally followed by downswing and recession which are, in turn, followed by recovery leading to a new boom. Such fluctuations in national income, employment, investment and related macroeconomic aggregates are called business cycles.[2]

Different economists have given different definitions or descriptions of the concept and nature of business cycles. These definitions show the various ways we can look at the phenomenon of the business cycle. We reproduce below two such definitions, including one given by Keynes, which are quite illustrative.

"A (business) cycle consists of expansions occurring at about the same time in many economic activities followed by similarly general recessions, contractions and revivals which merge with the expansion phase of the next cycle; this sequence of change is recurring but not periodic."

"By a cyclical movement, we mean that as the system progresses in, e.g. the upward direction, the forces propelling it upward first gather force and have a cumulative effect on one another, but gradually lose their strength until at a certain point, they tend to be replaced by forces operating in the opposite direction, which, in turn, gather forces and accentuate one another until they too, having reached their maximum development, wane and give place to their opposite. We do not, however, merely mean by a cyclical movement that upward and downward tendencies, once started, do not persist for ever in the same direction, but are ultimately reversed; we also mean that there is some recognisable degree of regularity in the time sequence and duration of the upward and downward movements."[3]

The available time series of important economic aggregates such as national income, employment, investment and prices of various countries generally show a systematic pattern of cyclical fluctuations. To identify and measure the business cycle, it is necessary to remove certain factors from the reported economic time series such as seasonal patterns and long-term trends, if any. First, the time series are adjusted for seasonal variations by smoothening the series. Then, the underlying trend is established. If the time series reveals a significant long-term trend, the deviations of the reported or actual observations from the estimated trend line are measured and plotted separately to ascertain the existence and extent of cyclical fluctuations. If, however, no long-term trend exists, the business cycles and their amplitude are measured with respect to the line of steady growth (a horizontal line indicating a given, steady level of economic activity).

PHASES OF THE BUSINESS CYCLE

All business cycles generally have some common characteristics in terms of phases of the cycle.[4] Normally, there are four phases of a typical business cycle. These phases are: expansion,

2. It is difficult to precisely say when systematic study of business fluctuations or fluctuations in aggregate economic activity started. According to Schumpeter, C. Juglar (1860) was the first to begin a systematic analysis of business cycles in terms of three phases of prosperity, crisis and liquidation spread over an average period of 9-10 years. Refer J.A. Schumpeter, *History of Economic Analysis*, Oxford University Press, 1954, pp. 1123-24.
3. J.M. Keynes, *The General Theory of Employment, Interest and Money*, 1936, pp. 313-14.
4. No two business cycles are, however, likely to be exactly identical, because, factors or economic circumstances governing one cycle may not exactly be the same as those governing another cycle.

peak, recession and trough. *Expansion and recession* are really the two important phases; *peak* and *trough* are the turning points.

Expansion is characterised by a high level of economic activity and is also referred to as the period of prosperity or boom. The expansion phase implies a continuous upward movement. This comes to an end and passes into the recession phase at the upper turning point or peak. During recession, production, employment, investment, prices, profit, etc., show a continuous downward movement till the recession phase gives way to the expansion phase at the lower turning point or trough. Thus, four phases of the cycle keep alternating themselves as shown in Fig. 12.1.

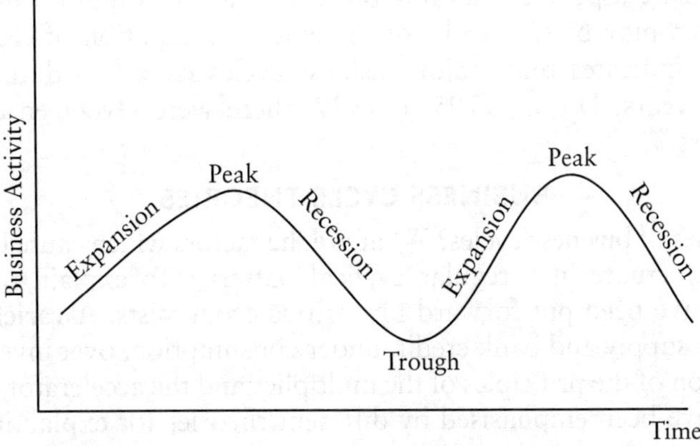

Fig. 12.1: Phases of the Trade Cycle

Schumpeter, the well-known economist, has given a slightly different description of the phases of the business cycle.[5] He has defined various phases of the cycle in terms of fluctuations in business activity reflected in fluctuations in national income around an equilibrium or trend level. Four phases of the cycle defined by Schumpeter are: prosperity, recession, depression and recovery. The business cycle, according to Schumpeter, is divided into two parts—the upper half and the lower half. The upper half of the cycle above the equilibrium or trend line is divided into two phases, namely prosperity and recession. The lower half of the cycle below the trend line is also divided into two phases—depression and recovery. Figure 12.2 illustrates the four-phase Schumpeterian trade cycle.

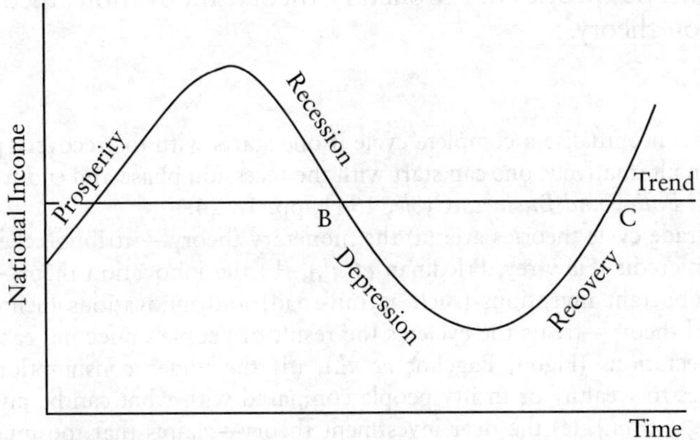

Fig. 12.2: Four Phases of the Schumpeterian Cycle

5. J.A. Schumpeter, *Business Cycles*, 1939, Vol. 1, pp. 207-09.

In Fig. 12.2, prosperity and recession phases indicate that the level of aggregate economic activity is above the trend level while depression and recovery phases imply that the economy is operating below the trend level. In the prosperity phase, employment continues to increase, but, at a diminishing rate till the cycle peak is reached. In the recession phase, employment decreases at an accelerating rate till point B is reached. After this, the cycle moves into the lower half. In the depression phase, employment continues to fall, but the rate of fall gradually decreases till the cycle trough is reached. In the recovery phase, employment continues to increase at an increasing rate till point C is reached. This is how a cycle completes itself.[6]

It is difficult to make a generalisation about the length or duration of a business cycle. A normal cycle, however, may be said to be of the length or duration of eight to ten years. The American experience indicates that major business cycles have had durations on an average of a little over eight years. During 1795 to 1937, there were seventeen cycles of an average duration of 8.35 years.[7]

BUSINESS CYCLE THEORIES

What are the causes of business cycles? What are the factors which cause income, employment, investment, etc., to fluctuate in a regular cyclical pattern? To explain these factors, a large number of theories have been put forward by various economists. A variety of factors such as fluctuations in money supply and bank credit, under consumption, over investment, clustering of innovations, interaction of the principles of the multiplier and the accelerator, people's expectation about future, etc., have been emphasised by different theories for explaining business cycles.[8]

Various theories of business cycles may be broadly classified into two categories, *external* theories and *internal* theories. In external theories, the basic cause of business cycles is found in events or factors outside the economic system like wars, revolutions, political events, growth and fluctuations in population, discoveries of new lands and resources, and finally, scientific and technological innovations. The internal theories emphasise mechanisms or factors within the economic system (like money supply, over investment, under-consumption; changes in consumption propensities and inducement to invest, etc.), which produce self-generating cycles so that every expansion breeds recessions, and, recession or contraction breeds revival and expansion, and so on.

We shall discuss here three important business cycle theories which include both external and internal theories. The theories are Monetary theory, Innovations theory, and, Multiplier—accelerator Interaction theory.

---

6. It would be easy to conceptualise a complete cycle if one starts with the recovery phase and ends with the depression phase, or, alternatively, one can start with the recession phase and end with the prosperity phase.
7. A.H. Hansen, *Fiscal Policy and Business Cycle*, 1941, pp. 18-24.
8. The better known trade cycle theories are: (a) the monetary theory—attributes the cycle to expansion and contraction of bank credit (Hawtrey, Friedman *et al.*), (b) the innovation theory—attributes the cycle to the clustering of important inventions (such as rail-road) and innovations (Schumpeter, Hansen *et al.*), (c) the psychological theory—treats the cycle as the result of people's infecting each other with pessimistic and optimistic expectations (Pigou, Bagehot *et al.*), (d) the under consumption theory—assumes that much of income goes to wealthy or thrifty people compared with what can be invested (Hobson, Sweezy, Foster and Catchings, *et al.*), (e) the over investment theory—claims that too much rather than too little investment causes recessions (Hayek, Mises, *et al.*), (f) the multiplier-accelerator interaction theory—states that interaction of the principles of the multiplier and the accelerator causes cycles (Samuelson, Hicks).

MONETARY THEORY[9]

According to this theory, expansion and contraction of bank credit are the central causes of business cycles, and bank credit affects business operations through the rate of interest. The business sector which is dominant in monetarist explanation is that of merchants, particularly wholesalers. A rise in the rate of interest charged by the banks on their loans to merchants raises the cost of holding inventories. This leads to a reduction in the desired ratio of stocks to sales. The opposite happens when the interest rate falls. Fluctuations in the desired ratio of stocks to sales finally leads to fluctuations in business activity.

When banks possess excess cash reserves and are anxious to utilise these reserves, they reduce the rate of interest to induce entrepreneurs to borrow funds to increase their inventory. When merchants decide to increase their desired ratio of stocks to sales because of a fall in the rate of interest, they book fresh orders with the manufacturers who, in turn, increase their scale of operations and production levels. This creates additional demand for factors of production resulting in the increase in incomes of factory owners who, in turn, spend a part of their additional income for purchase of consumer goods. This results in fast depletion of merchants' inventories inducing them to place further orders with the manufacturers. The cumulative expansion, or boom, continues as long as banks continue to extend liberal credit facilities at low rates of interest to the merchants.

In the process of credit creation, however, the limit as reached, eventually, when the banks can lend no more; in fact, they begin to recall their old loans and raise the rate of interest. This is enough to create panic and merchants start reducing their inventory levels and cancel the unexecuted orders pending with the manufacturers who, in turn, take no time in curtailing their scale of operations throwing workers out of employment. Faced with unemployment, labourers and other factory owners curtail their spending, reducing aggregate effective demand in the process. Soon the markets for consumer goods present a deserted look with many merchants sitting idle. The recession grips fast the economy.

In the process of cumulative contraction, bank loans are paid back which gradually leads to excess reserves and banks once again lower the rate of interest. At this point, the process of revival, and subsequently expansion, begins.

The monetary theory rightly emphasises the credit creation capacity (also credit contraction capacity) of the banking system and changes in interest rates as important factors causing business fluctuations.

But, the monetary theory, by its very definition, does not emphasise the roles of any of the non-monetary factors (which are also important) and, therefore, does not offer a complete explanation of the phenomenon of business cycles.

INNOVATIONS THEORY[10]

This theory makes innovations the central cause of occurrence of business cycles in modern industrial economies. An innovation is different from an invention. An invention is the discovery or development of a new process, product or service by scientists or engineers; and an innovation is the initial application of an invention to commercial production. Despite the fact that inventions might appear continuously through time, innovations—initial commercial

9. We present here Hawtrey's version of the monetary theory. Refer R.G. Hawtrey, *Good and Bad Trade*, 1913.
10. This theory is due to Schumpeter. Refer J.A. Schumpeter, *Business Cycles*, 1939.

application of inventions—show marked discontinuities. This happens because the majority of businessmen are reluctant to innovate because of the risks involved.

An innovator is one who is the first to go for commercial exploitation and consequently bears the risks involved in introducing a new good or service or process in the market. The innovators are formally designated as entrepreneurs and play the leading role in the entire process of modern industrial growth. They consist of a small group of enterprising and pioneering individuals in the business community who are constantly on the lookout for something new and different. They translate inventions into innovations by using their business acumen. When the innovation proves successful, extraordinary profits accrue to the innovator. But very soon the innovation is imitated by others who adopt similar processes of production, and produce and market goods and services similar to those produced and marketed by innovators. The imitators imitate the innovator because they cannot allow themselves to lag behind for too long. As more firms imitate, the pressure on those not imitating increases. Bright profit opportunities stimulate investment, and a surge of investment activity seizes the economy. Moreover, the innovation, especially if it comes at a time when the economy is operating at or near full employment level, causes a rise in prices because entrepreneurs compete for the available supply of resources. For some time, business activity continues to expand as the innovators, and the imitators, reap large profits.

The expansion process comes to an end as the course of introducing innovations in the economy also comes to an end for the time being. Every innovation takes some time to work itself out in the form of construction of new factories, installation of new plant and equipment, etc. When this has happened, the advantage of the innovation disappears. That is, all the investment, whether to produce new goods or services, reduce costs, open new markets or develop new sources of supply, eventually would have been made. The boom comes to an end because investment outlays generated by the innovations slow down and ultimately get exhausted. The upswing turns into a downswing as the maladjustments which were built into the system during the process of innovational activity begin to manifest themselves. This happens because innovational activity is 'lopsided, discontinuous, disharmonious by nature.'[11] The prosperity being imbalanced cannot be sustained and 'depression is nothing more than the economic system's reactions to the boom or adaptation to the situation into which the boom brings the system.'[12]

The lower turning point of the cycle, i.e., recovery, occurs when the period of readjustment to the changed economic circumstance begins. Prices would have fallen to a point where the pioneering businessmen hope that any further fall is unlikely, and once again, start innovating. The introduction of innovation marks the beginning of recovery which soon leads to the expansionary phase.

It is true that innovations lead to spurt in business activity, and as the effect of the innovations die out, recessionary trends may set in. But, the nature and intensity of changes in business activity would depend on the force of the innovation, that is, the extent to which the innovation can cause imbalance in the economic system; or, in other words, the extent to which it can cause shifts from the equilibrium level. In addition, effectiveness of an innovation depends on the existence or operation of a number of other factors or conditions which govern the economic system at a particular point of time. For example, when the economy is operating at or near full employment the innovation theory may be effective. During such times, the nature of the expansion process emphasised by the theory may actually take place. But, in an economy with

11. J.A. Schumpeter, *Business Cycles*, 1939, Vol. 1, p. 102.
12. J.A. Schumpeter, *The Theory of Economic Development*, 1934, p. 224.

vast unemployed resources, the introduction of an innovation may not lead to any competition for available resources (because resources are freely available), and therefore, prices may not rise, and there may not be any inflationary boom. Similarly, when innovations are financed through real savings, and not by bank credit (as assumed by the theory), there is unlikely to be any inflationary price increase.

MULTIPLIER-ACCELERATOR INTERACTION MODEL[13]

An interesting explanation for the occurrence of business cycles has been given by Samuelson. The explanation is based on interaction of the multiplier and the accelerator.

The acceleration principle explains that net investment I_t during any given time period t depends upon the value of accelerator v and the change in income during time period t and t – 1, i.e.

$$I_t = v(Y_t - Y_{t-1})$$

Assuming a change in income Y, net investment I_t in any time period t will differ from net investment I_{t-1} of the preceding time period t – 1 as stated by the acceleration principle. But an increase or decrease in investment will affect income during subsequent time periods as stated by the multiplier principle. The change in income will, in turn, affect net investment because of the operation of the accelerator which, in turn, will affect income because of the operation of the multiplier and so on. The process may continue (sometimes endlessly) because of interaction of the multiplier and the accelerator. Samuelson's model may be presented as

$$Y_t = G_t + C_t + I_t$$
$$C_t = bY_{t-1}$$
$$I_t = v(C_t - C_{t-1})$$

where Y is income, C is consumption, I is induced investment and G is government expenditure autonomously determined. Substituting for C_t and I_t, equilibrium income Y_t can be rewritten as

$$Y_t = G_t + bY_{t-1} + v(C_t - C_{t-1})$$
$$= G_t + bY_{t-1} + bv(Y_{t-1} - Y_{t-2})$$

This equation states that income Y(t) in time t is the sum of autonomous government expenditure G_t, consumption expenditure C_t which depends upon the marginal propensity to consume b and income of the preceding period Y_{t-1}, and, investment expenditure I_t, which depends on the capital output ratio or the accelerator v and change in consumption during t and t – 1, i.e. $C_t - C_{t-1}$, which can, in turn, be expressed in terms of Y_{t-1} and Y_{t-1}. In other words, given the values of b and v, and C_t and C_{t-1} or Y_{t-1} and Y_{t-2} we can determine the level of Y_t.

Although in the original multiplier accelerator model developed by Samuelson, investment was related to change in consumption (*as shown above*), Hicks' version of the model in which investment is related to change in income has become more common.[14] We shall discuss here Hicks' version of the multiplier-accelerator model which may be presented as

13. P.A. Samuelson, "Interaction between Multiplier Analysis and the Principle of Acceleration", *The Review of Economics and Statistics*, Vol. XXI, May 1939, reprinted in M.G. Muller (Ed.) *Readings in Macroeconomics*, 1966.
14. It can be easily shown that there is no fundamental difference between Samuelson's and Hicks' versions of the multiplier-accelerator model. It can be seen that if we convert Hicks' version of the model into Samuelson's version, the value of the accelerator v according to Hicks will be lower than the value of the accelerator in Samuelson's version since b < 1. It will be evident from the following two equations:

$$Y_t = G_t + bY_{t-1} + bv(Y_{t-1} - Y_{t-2}) \quad \text{(According to Samuelson)}$$

$$C_t = bY_{t-1}$$
$$I_t = v(Y_{t-1} - Y_{t-2})$$
$$Y_t = C_t + I_t + G_t$$

Fluctuations in Y around its equilibrium value may be initiated by an exogenous shock (say, an increase in government expenditure). The shape of the time path of Y will depend upon the values of b and v. In general, higher the value of v, greater is the possibility of an explosive time path of Y; higher the value of b, smaller the possibility that oscillations will occur. Such analysis is based on the assumption that

$$0 < b < 1 \text{ and } v > 0$$

In this model, no trade cycle can be generated without an accelerator relationship and a second order lag (first order lag cannot produce a cycle). The multiplier itself will not cause a cycle. In fact, as the value of b increases, the possibility of generation of the cycle is diminished. The model

$$I_t = v(Y_{t-1} - Y_{t-2})$$
$$Y_t = C_t + I_t + G_t$$

will generate cycles for any value of v ranging between 0 and 4. But, with the inclusion of the multiplier, this simple model becomes more realistic and causes cycles which are more similar to those which actually occur in an economy.

With or without a consumption function, two time periods after an initial increase in the exogenous variable—an increase in autonomous government expenditure—has raised the level of income Y, the negative term $v(Y_{t-2})$ will exert a negative effect on investment. Unless the accelerator is very strong or the marginal propensity to consume is very close to 1, this will result in a slight decrease in investment and slackening of the rate of increase in income. This will generally be sufficient to cause a fall in investment (I) and, in the rate of increase in income (ΔY).

Soon ΔY becomes negative and a turning point is reached. When this happens, the forces of reversal begin to operate. The low values of Y tend to reduce the negative effect of the term ($- vY_{t-2}$) on investment with the result that investment ceases to fall rapidly. As this happens, ΔY increases and with it I also increases. Consequently, the economy begins to move upward. This process will be repeated until the economy either reaches a new equilibrium or continues to fluctuate so widely that negative values of Y are reached. Such explosive cycles are, however, not actually to occur.

Table 12.1: Interaction of the Multiplier and the Accelerator

Time Period	*Damped, b = 0.5*	*No Oscillations v = 0.05*			*Damped, b = 0.5*		*No Oscillations v = 0.8*	
	C +	I +	G =	Y	C +	I +	G =	Y
t − 2	50	0	50	100	50	0	50	100
t − 1	50	0	50	100	50	0	50	100
t	50	0	60	110	50	0	60	110
t + 1	55	0.5	60	115.5	55	8.0	60	123
t + 2	57.7	0.3	60	118.0	63	12.8	60	135.8

$$Y_t = G_t + bY_{t-1} + v(Y_{t-1} - Y_{t-2}) \quad \text{(According to Hicks)}$$

Both these equations are identical except the presence of b (in bv in the first equation); since b is less than 1, the value of bv will be less than the value of v.

Time Period	Damped, b = 0.5		No Oscillations v = 0.05		Damped, b = 0.5		No Oscillations v = 0.8	
t + 3	59.0	0.1	60	119.1	67.9	7.8	60	135.7
t + 4	59.5	0.1	60	119.6	67.9	0.0	60	127.9
t + 5	59.8	0	60	119.8	63.9	– 6.2	60	117.7
t + 6	59.9	0	60	119.9	58.9	– 8.2	60	110.7
t + 7	60.0	0	60	120.0	55.3	– 5.6	60	109.7
t + 8	–			–	54.8	– 0.8	60	114.0
t + 9	–	–	–	–	57.0	– 3.4	60	120.4
t + 10	–	–	–	–	60.2	5.1	60	125.3
t + 11					62.7	3.9	60	126.6
t + 12					63.3	1.0	60	124.3
t + 13					62.2	– 1.8	60	120.4
Y_{eq}	60	0	60	120	60	0	60	120
Time Period	**Explosive, b = 0.5**		**No Oscillations v = 1.5**		**Explosive, b = 0.5**		**No Oscillations v = 3.0**	
	C +	I +	G =	Y	C +	I +	G =	Y
t – 1	50	0	50	100	50	0	50	100
t	50	0	60	110	50	0	60	110
t + 1	55	15	60	130	55	30	60	145
t + 2	65	30	60	155	72.5	90	60	222.5
t + 3	77.5	37.5	60	175	111.2	232.5	60	403.7
t + 4	87.5	30	60	177.5	171.9	363.6	60	595.5
t + 5	88.8	3.7	60	152.5	297.8	775.4	60	1,133.2
t + 6	76.2	–37.5	60	98.7				
t + 7	49.4	–80.7	60	28.7				
t + 8	14.4	–105.0	60	–30.6				
t + 9	15.3	–89.0	60	–44.3				
t + 10	22.2	–20.6	60	17.2				
t +11	8.9	40.7	60	91.8				
t + 12	45.9	163.5	60	269.4				
t + 13	134.7	266.4	60	461.1				
Y_{eq}	–	–						

Y_{eq} = Equilibrium income = Y_0.

Note: The table has been reproduced from Michael K. Evans, *Macroeconomic Activity*, 1969, p. 365.

Table 12.1 shows how, with different combinations of the values of b and v, interaction of the multiplier and the accelerator generates different patterns of income oscillations or movements.

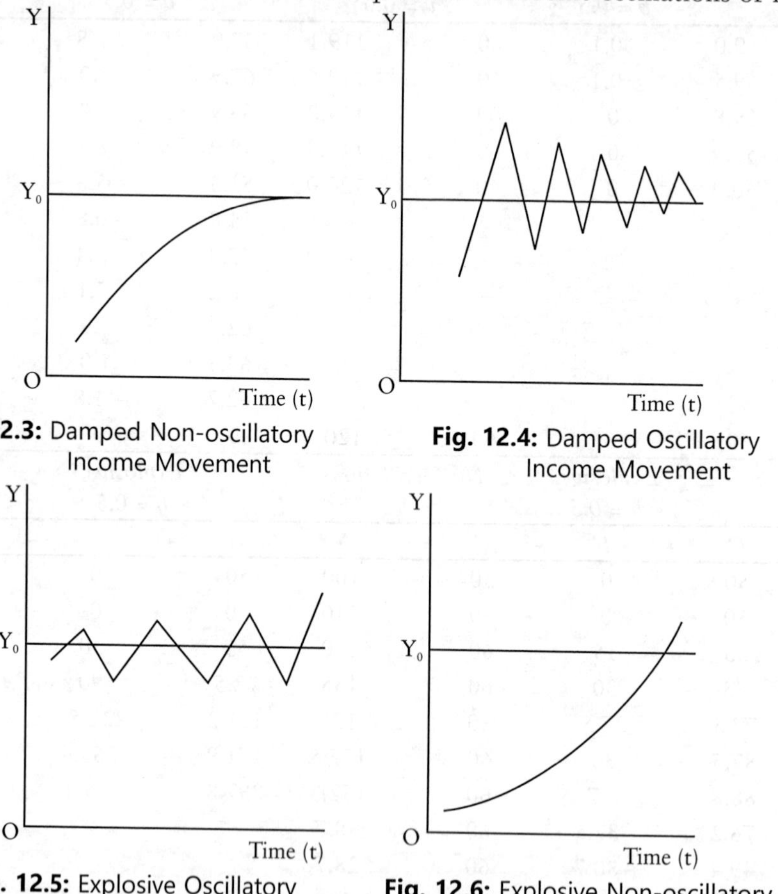

Fig. 12.3: Damped Non-oscillatory Income Movement

Fig. 12.4: Damped Oscillatory Income Movement

Fig. 12.5: Explosive Oscillatory Income Movement

Fig. 12.6: Explosive Non-oscillatory Income Movement

Four types of income movements are shown: damped non-oscillatory, damped oscillatory, explosive oscillatory and explosive non-oscillatory. These four types of income movements are graphically shown in Figs. 12.3, 12.4, 12.5 and 12.6 respectively.

The basic criticism of the multiplier-accelerator model is in terms of the rigid acceleration principle which does not always hold good in practice. A critic has rightly stated that although the basic concept of multiplier-accelerator interaction is an important one, we cannot really explain observed cycles by a mechanical application of the concept.[15]

SYNTHESIS OF BUSINESS CYCLE THEORIES

We have discussed above the major business cycle theories—monetary theory, innovation theory, multiplier accelerator theory—and their limitations or shortcomings—theoretical and also empirical. Each theory is important in its own way because it gives a particular perspective and focus on business cycles or economic fluctuations. But, none of these theories, by itself, is able to completely explain the occurrence and, also recurrence, of business cycles. The existence

15. J.S. Duesenberry, "Hicks on the Trade Cycle", *The Quarterly Journal of Economics*, August 1950, pp. 464-76.

of multiple theories also indicate, in a way, the incompleteness or insufficiency of individual theories to correctly explain the forces or factors or crises of business cycles or fluctuations.

In fact, most economists today agree that occurrence of business cycles is ideally explained, not by a single theory, but by a combination of theories, or more appropriately, by a combination of external and internal theories. In explaining all major business cycles, primary emphasis is put on fluctuations in investment which eventually lead to income movements. Initial causes of investment fluctuations are many times found in external factors like technological innovation, population growth, territorial growth, etc. With these external factors, one must combine the internal factors which cause any initial change in investment to be amplified into a cumulative process—factors such as propensities to consume, inducement to invest, availability of bank credit, etc.

It is also true that the general economic situation arising out of changes or fluctuations in investment levels, in turn, reacts on investment. If high consumption levels make businessmen optimistic, they are more likely to embark upon new investment programmes. Inventions or scientific discoveries may take place independently of the business cycle, but, their economic exploitation will certainly depend on business conditions. When national income moves to or is at a high level, it is reasonable to expect that a considerable amount of capital formation (new machines, added inventories, construction) would be induced. Therefore, especially in the short run (when business cycles occur), investment is in part an effect as well as a cause of income movements.

B. ANTI-CYCLICAL OR STABILISATION POLICIES

Different theories or models, discussed above, try to explain the reasons for occurrence of business cycles or economic fluctuations in various countries. We may always try to analyse the factors which cause business cycles, but, the fact is that such cycles do occur and are continuing to occur. The global recession of 2008 is one of the latest examples. If business cycles or economic fluctuations occur, those have to be controlled for stabilising the economy and steady growth.

According to classical economic thought, the fluctuations in the economy should be left to themselves or the market forces. Any imbalance arising in the working of the economic system would be set right by the 'invisible hand' (i.e., market forces themselves) and economic balance would be restored. But, the Great Depression of the thirties (1929-33) revealed/proved the inadequacy of the classical thought and the 'invisible hand' mechanism.

Keynes pointed out the insufficiency of classical thought and inability of the invisible hand to control economic fluctuations. He emphasised the significance of business cycles, and the need for anti-cyclical or stabilisation policies and measures for economic stability and growth. In fact, in *General Theory*,[16] Keynes dealt with the concept, characteristics and the necessity for controlling and regulating the economy for preventing the occurrence of business cycles.

After the Second World War, the subject received more attention of the economists. There was greater concern by both economists and national government for policies for controlling economic fluctuations. Lee's observation is very relevant here:

> ...by an evolutionary process, economic thought has progressed from a strong conviction that the economy should be left to run its own course to a general and non-partisan acceptance of the need for a stabilising policy which would prevent excessive fluctuations in the private economy.[17]

16. J.M. Keynes, "Notes on the Trade Cycle". *General Theory*, 1986, Chapter 22.
17. M.W. Lee, *Economic Fluctuations*, Richard D. Irwin, 1955, p. 422.

BUSINESS CYCLES AND STABILISATION PERSPECTIVE

We can explain business cycles in terms of fluctuations in investment as mentioned above. We can also look at business cycles in a different way, that is, in terms of demand shocks and supply shocks. Economists generally agree that business cycles are caused by both demand shocks and supply shocks. But, economists differ with regard to the relative roles of these two types of shocks. The classical economists emphasise more on the role of supply shocks; the Keynesian economists stress more on the demand shocks.

Demand shocks can emanate from the private sector as well as the government. Fluctuations in private sector consumption and investment can generate instability and demand shocks.[18] Demand shocks can also be caused by government actions—government expenditure, taxation and money supply. Supply shocks can, however, be generated both by the private sector and the government sector. In the private sector, cartel formations or monopolies, technological progress and trade unions are important factors; wage-price rigidity is considered by many as a very important causative factor for business cycles. The government can cause supply instability or shocks through credit policy, physical controls and regulations and proclamation of emergencies or wars.

Demand shocks and supply shocks bring in the roles of stabilisation policies for moderating business cycles or reducing the intensities of fluctuations in income, investment and consumption spending. Stabilisation policies, conventionally, take the form of fiscal and monetary policies.[19] But there are differences of opinion among economists about the role and effectiveness of stabilisation policies in moderating business cycles.

There are two schools of thought on this: the Keynesian school and the monetarist school. The Keynesians believe that a private enterprise economy needs to be stabilised, can be stabilised, and therefore, should be stabilised by appropriate monetary and fiscal policies. Monetarists take the contrasting view that there is no serious need to stabilise the economy, and even if there were a need, it should not be done because stabilisation policies would be more likely to increase rather than decrease instability.

The monetarists' contention that the economy is inherently stable does not mean that the economy is not subject to fluctuations. But they attribute such fluctuations primarily to destabilising variations in money supply caused by monetary authorities. According to Friedman and other monetarists, much of the instability actually experienced by world economies since World War II has been the result of active fiscal and monetary intervention by the respective governments. The Keynesians argue that the economy need not be always unstable, but it is subject to frequent, and sometimes erratic, shocks primarily due to variations in investment spending; and these shocks are sufficiently strong to produce business cycles or destabilisations.

To correct or reduce such destabilisations, appropriate corrective measures in terms of monetary and fiscal policies are required.

Both schools of thought agree or admit that counter-cyclical monetary and fiscal policies affect output, employment, and prices. But, what should be the appropriate form, content and intensity of such policies to be really effective as counter-cyclical or stabilisation measures may be the real issue for discussion or debate between the two schools. In fact, this is a more general issue which macroeconomists and policy makers are facing today.

18. Keynesian economists particularly emphasise the role of private investment expenditure.
19. We will be discussing fiscal and monetary policies in detail in Chapters 19 and 20. Here, the roles of these two policies are discussed only as anti-cyclical policies.

We will be discussing below the roles—effectiveness and limitations—of fiscal and monetary policies in detail. We shall then mention the less known or minor anti-cyclical or stabilisation measures. At the end, we will analyse the global recession of 2008 and stabilisation policies and measures adopted for dealing with this.

ROLE OF FISCAL POLICY

Fiscal and monetary policies are the two most important and commonly used anti-cyclical policies.[20] We shall first discuss the role of fiscal policy and instruments, and then monetary policy and instruments.

Fiscal policy and measures of the government operate through instruments of fiscal policy. Four tools or instruments of fiscal policy are:

1. Government expenditure
2. Government taxation
3. Subsidies by the government
4. Transfer payments by the government

Government expenditure and taxation are the two main instruments of fiscal policy, and these two operate through the government budget.

In contra-cyclical fiscal policy, two major approaches are adopted: liberal or expansionary policy means increase in government expenditure, reduction in taxation, and also increase in subsidies and increase in transfer payments. This has implication in terms of its impact on the government budget. An increase in government expenditure without simultaneous increase in taxation (and other sources of revenue or income) results in an increase in budget deficit. There are three ways to finance budget deficit; these are internal public borrowing, external borrowing (foreign exchange and exchange rate problems are involved) and deficit financing. *Deficit financing*[21] means or involves issue of new currency or money. All the three ways or forms of financing budget deficit add to public debt.

Dear or contractionary fiscal policy is opposite of liberal or expansionary policy. This indicates reduction in government expenditure, increase in taxation, withdrawal of subsidies and decrease in transfer payments. This essentially means reducing purchasing power in the economy. This has positive impact on the government budget. A reduction in government expenditure without simultaneous reduction in taxation leads to budget surplus or reduction of budget deficit. If there is budget surplus, the government does not require borrowing; if can, in fact, resort to lending or repayment of loans. This, in turn, leads to reduction in public debt.

As anti-cyclical fiscal policy, liberal or expansionary policy is followed during downswing or recession, and tight or contractionary policy is pursued during upswing or booms. During recessions demand becomes slack and unemployment increases. This requires boosting of industrial and economic activities. This is done through two major expansionary fiscal instruments: increase in government expenditures and reduction in taxation. During economic expansion or boom, there is usually excess demand in relation to supply or production capacity, and there is threat of inflationary conditions. To curb or discourage excess demand and tame inflationary situation, two major contractionary fiscal instruments—cut in government expenditure and increase in taxation—are adopted.

20. Fiscal and monetary policies are also sometimes known as demand management policies because they operate primarily through their influence on aggregate demand.
21. Deficit financing is also known as *monetisation*.

Both the fiscal instruments—public expenditure and taxation—have final impact on aggregate output or national income or GDP. An increase in government expenditure increases GDP. The amount of increase in GDP because of increase in government expenditure would depend on the size or value of the expenditures multiplier. Similarly, as a contractionary fiscal instrument, a decrease in public expenditure will have negative impact on GDP. The extent of reduction in GDP would be determined by the size or value of the negative expenditure multiplier.

Taxation always has a deflationary or negative effect on the economy. Increase in taxation reduces disposable income. Given the MPC, this reduces household spending or consumption, and finally the GDP. This becomes contractionary fiscal policy. The actual reduction in GDP would depend on the value or size of the tax multiplier. Used as an expansionary fiscal instrument, a reduction in tax will have positive effect on GDP. The actual increase in GDP would be determined by the size of the tax multiplier. Because the expenditure multiplier and the tax multiplier work in opposite direction, both increase in government expenditure and reduction in tax (expansionary policy) will have positive multiplier effect on GDP. Similarly, both reduction in public expenditure and increase in taxation (contractionary policy) will have negative multiplier effect on GDP.

CONSTRAINTS OF FISCAL POLICY

Formulation and implementation of fiscal policy suffer from certain constraints. These reduce the effectiveness of fiscal instruments as anti-cyclical measures. Three major constraints are:

(a) Differential multiplier effect
(b) Time lag factor
(c) Asymmetry in implementation

Multiplier effects of government expenditure and taxation are not uniform. Government expenditure in the form of investment in production, projects and construction activities generate direct demand for goods and services for consumption and create multiplier effects. But, subsidies and transfer payments do not produce the same effect. Also, sometimes, public expenditure may only be a replacement of private expenditure (in sectors like healthcare, education, rural development), and therefore, no multiplier effect. Taxation can also have differential multiplier effect. Taxes paid by lower income groups have higher multiplier effect than those paid by the higher income groups because of differences in the MPCs of the two income groups—the lower income groups always have higher MPC compared to that of higher income groups. Multiplier effects of indirect taxes are not clearly known or measurable.

Time lag between formulation of a fiscal policy and its implementation also acts as a constraint to its effectiveness. There are two types of lag: first, between formulation of policy or policy change and its implementation, and second, between implementation of a particular policy and, the time by which the policy has impact on the economy in terms of the desired change. Government departments and machinery are involved in formulation and implementation of fiscal policy. This generally causes delay. Experience of many countries show that six months or more may elapse between conception and formulation of policy and actual result in terms of required change or effect. In the meantime, economic conditions may change at last to some extent. This reduces the effectiveness of the policy instrument. More details on the lag factor are given in Chapter 17.

Asymmetry in policy implementation is another factor. For effectiveness, it should be possible to implement fiscal policies with equal speed and force during both unpowing and downswing or expansion and recession. But, in reality, this does not always happen. Experience of fiscal administration of different countries shows that expansionary policies are welcome and easy to implement, but, restrictive or contractionary policies are not so easy to implement. Employees welcome increase in salaries and compensations, firms are happy with new subsidies, individuals like more transfer payments, but reduction in financial benefits, withdrawal of subsidies and cut in transfer payments (retirement benefits, etc.) usually face resistance. This gives rise to asymmetry in fiscal policy implementation.

ROLE OF MONETARY POLICY

Formulation and implementation of monetary policies are undertaken, monitored and controlled by the central bank of the country (RBI in case of India). Major instruments of anti-cyclical monetary policy are:

1. Bank rate (or Repo rate)
2. Open market operations
3. Cash reserve ratio (CRR)
4. Statutory liquidity ratio (SLR)
5. Selective credit control[22]

As anti-cyclical measures, more important of these instruments are open market operations and the bank rate (or the repo rate). Both open market operations and the bank rate are used to regulate money supply which, in turn, is intended to control spending or purchasing power in the economy. Some economists feel that money supply itself is the only or the most important monetary policy instrument. In any case, money supply is the most critical factor or weapon in/for monetary management of an economy both as an expansionary instrument and as a contractionary instrument.

Open market operations, i.e., purchase and sale of securities in the open market can directly control money supply. Purchase of securities increases total availability of money and credit by putting more money in the market or in circulation. Conversely, sale of securities leads to withdrawal of money from the market; this means contraction of money supply. Therefore, through open market operations, the central bank can effectively control the expansion or contraction of money and credit.

The bank rate operates primarily through its effect on cost of credit. Through the bank rate, the central bank tries to control the interest rate structure in the country, i.e., interest rates at which commercial banks lend funds or extend credit to firms or industries and the public. During economic expansion or boom threatening inflation, the central bank increases the bank rate. The commercial banks respond by raising their interest rates increasing the cost of funds or credit. This discourages borrowing by firms and the public, and in effect, reduces money supply with its impact on purchasing power, spending or consumption. During recession, the opposite forces work. It starts with reduction in the bank rate to encourage and facilitate borrowing of funds, and stimulate demand for goods and services by increasing the purchasing power. Federal Reserve Bank in the US and Reserve Bank of India (RBI), along with some other central banks, have been effectively using the bank rate to regulate money supply in the economy.

---

22. Detailed analysis of instruments of monetary policy—effectiveness and limitations—are presented in Chapter 19.

CONSTRAINTS OF MONETARY POLICY

Like fiscal policy, formulation and implementation of monetary policy also are subject to certain constraints. According to some economists, monetary policy has lesser constraints than fiscal policy. Three major constraints of monetary policy as anti-cyclical measure, are:

(a) Time lag factor
(b) Growth of financial intermediaries
(c) Structure of money and capital markets

Time lag involved in formulation, implementation and result of monetary policy is a major constraining factor. Three types of time lag are involved: first, recognition lag; second, action lag; and third, effect lag. As a problem or imbalance in the economy arises either because of cyclical boom or recession, some time may elapse before the central bank feels or recognises the need for an appropriate monetary policy or action. Sometime will inevitably be lost before the course of action (general or selective and the degree or dose) is decided and actual action taken. Finally, there is always a time, and sometimes it can be considerable, between the action taken and the result or impact is seen. The compounding effect of these three types of time lag can often be quite significant.

Growth of non-banking financial intermediaries is quite common in various economies and this dilutes the functioning or operation of commercial banks. This, in turn, affects the policy measures of the central bank which are mostly implemented through the banking system. *Financial intermediaries* are non-banking financial institutions like industrial development banks, industrial finance corporations, insurance companies, mutual find companies, etc. These financial institutions do not have credit creation capacity or power like commercial banks, but, they hold and manage a significant proportion of total credit in an economy. Because such credit or funds are not within the preview of the central bank's control system, this reduces the effectiveness of monetary policy and instruments. Financial intermediaries are more developed and operational in developed economies than in developing economies where money and financial markets are not so organised. Because of this, credit or cash flow leakages through the financial intermediaries create a bigger problem in developed economics than in developing economies for monetary management of the central bank.

As just mentioned, money and capital or financial markets are comparatively less organised in developing economies than those in developed economies. One important implication of this is relative insensitiveness of these markets to policy change and implementations of the central bank. For effectiveness or success of monetary policy and instruments, it is essential that money and capital or financial markets are well developed and responsive and interactive. Otherwise, monetary policy implementations can only be partially successful.

FISCAL POLICY VIS-À-VIS MONETARY POLICY

A comparison of effectiveness and constraints of fiscal and monetary policies as anti-cyclical measures may make their relative roles more clear.

There "Fiscalists" contend that fiscal policy is more effective than monetary policy as a counter-cyclical measure. There is enough logic in such contention. Fiscal policy or instrument works directly on investment and purchasing power, but, monetary policy acts only indirectly by controlling money supply and the interest rate. An increase in public expenditure (except transfer payments) will have multiplier effect on output or income through consumption or MPC during a recessionary phase. Similarly, a reduction in public expenditure will have the opposite effect during an expansionary phase. Also, the countering expansionary or boom conditions, contractionary fiscal policy is generally more effective and sustainable. Contractionary fiscal policy reduces budget deficit or leads to budget surplus which reduces public debt, and therefore, more sustainable from the budgetary point of view.

Advocates of monetary policy contend that formulation and implementation of monetary policy are easier because they do not suffer from the same constraints as fiscal policies do. Fiscal policy is formulated and implemented by the government or government departments. There is always an issue of interdepartmental coordination—sometimes even conflict—about priorities, timing and modalities of implementation. In case of monetary policy, only the central bank of the country is involved. The Governor of the central bank is appointed by the government, but, he and his team enjoy a large degree of autonomy in policy making and implementation. This is true in most countries including the European common currency area. The central bank (RBI in India) as an institution, is a fairly straight forward official machinery. Also, monetary policy has more symmetry in implementation compared to fiscal policy. We had earlier mentioned about asymmetry in implementation of fiscal policy. This hardly exists in case of monetary policy. The central bank can frame and implement, almost with equal ease and speed, both an easy or liberal money policy (increase in money supply or decrease in the interest rate) and a tight money policy (decrease in money supply or increase in the interest rate).

So far, we have discussed *pure fiscal policy* and *pure monetary policy*, i.e., each policy in isolation or alone as anti-cyclical measure, and not as a mix or combination of the two policies. Many policy economists have suggested the use of these two policies as complementary measures rather than as competitive or conflicting instruments. Senior government officials in policy making for controlling business cycles in different countries have also realised this.

The two sets of policies can be applied alternatively or simultaneously depending on the situation, i.e., intensity of the cycle (boom or recession). Both policies have their strengths and weaknesses. A proper mix of the two policies is likely to enable the policy makers to overcome the limitations or constraints of one policy with the other. For example, an expansionary fiscal policy often leads to an increase in the interest rate because of increase in budget deficit and public debt and debt servicing; therefore, this can be simultaneously combined with expansionary monetary policy which causes the interest rate to fall. Also, complementary or combined use of the two policies in the same direction make them a more potent anti-cyclical force. For example, combination of increase in public expenditure and increase in money supply gives a big boost to liquidity and purchasing power in the economy, and this can be highly effective or successful in countering recession. A combination of the opposite policies (reduction in government expenditure and contraction of money supply) can be effectively used to fight a runaway expansion or inflation.

But, this requires, rather presupposes, close coordination between departments in the government, particularly the Finance Ministry, and the central bank. Policy making and decision in the government are sometimes influenced by political considerations or balancing factors. If this happens, certain objectivities or priorities may be sacrificed or lost. Also, thinking of the Finance Ministry and the central bank may be on similar same lines, but, policy announcement and action may have to be initiated by the central bank, and the bank may not consider the timing most appropriate. This can often happen if it comes to interest rate cut. This needs to be sorted out, and an agreement or consensus should be reached in time. If this happens, and there is desired understanding and cohesiveness between the government and the central bank a judicious mix of fiscal and monetary policies can be a powerful weapon for dealing with business cycles or fluctuations and ensuring economic stability.

OTHER ANTI-CYCLICAL OR STABILISATION MEASURES

We have so far analysed the two most important and commonly used anti-cyclical measures, that is, fiscal and monetary policies—their applications, constraints and complementarity for more effectiveness or success. There are few other anti-cyclical measures, which can also be used, and in fact sometimes used.

Three such measures should be considered:

1. Built-in or automatic stabilisers,
2. Incomes policy,
3. Physical policy.

BUILT-IN OR AUTOMATIC STABILISERS

Automatic stabilisers are built in the functioning of the economic system, and work as a spontaneous or self-generating mechanism during both recessionary and expansionary phases.

Built-in or automatic stabilisers work like this. During recession, employment falls, income falls, and, therefore, tax revenue falls and transfer payments (unemployment compensation, social security payments, etc.), increase. As a result of this, disposable income (including receipts from transfer payments) increases, and given the MPC, aggregate demand and consumption increase. This helps to arrest the downswing. According to many economists, MPC increases during recession because savings (or MPS) falls. This has double effect on boosting demand and consumption. When the economy is moving high on the upswing, the opposite forces work. Employment increases, income level increases, tax revenue increases and disposal income and, also transfer payments decrease. Also, the MPC may decrease. The combined effect of all these is to set the deceleration process through fall in aggregate demand and consumption.

If all these happen the way we have described, built-in stabilisers can be a potent anti-cyclical force. But, history of business cycles and stabilisation measures show that this is not really true. Built-in stabilisers can, at best, work well for controlling very short-term fluctuations in the economy and, also fluctuations of smaller magnitude. For controlling longer cycles or fluctuations of larger magnitude, built-in stabilisers may prove inadequate. The policy makers may have to look for stronger measures like the fiscal policy or the monetary policy or a combination of the two.

INCOMES POLICY

Incomes policy is one of the lesser known anti-cyclical policies, but, this is well known in the US governmental system.

Incomes policy is not construed to be an alternative either to fiscal policy or monetary policy. The exponents of incomes policy do not doubt or question the important roles played by fiscal and monetary policies. They argue that these policies are necessary, but, not sufficient as anti-cyclical measures. These need to be supplemented by incomes policy which goes "right down to the microeconomics of what determines the prices of goods." Determination of prices leads to costs (because of close relationship between the two), and through costs, incomes policy, seek to regulate wages or incomes. Prices and wages (i.e., incomes) are sought to be regulated by laying down price and wage standards. By controlling prices and wages (incomes), incomes policy can be both anti-inflationary and anti-deflationary depending on the prevailing economic situation.

For number of years, incomes policy has been pursued in conventional form, i.e., in terms of laying down price and wage standards or guidelines. In the 1970s, a number of tax-based incomes policies (TIPs) were developed which received enough attention of economists and policy makers as anti-cyclical measures. Foremost among these were the Wallich-Weintraub (W.W.) plan and the Okun plan. Both the approaches propose taxes instead of conventional measures for controlling wage increases. But, the two approaches or methods have suggested two contrasting bases or control instruments—one uses 'carrot', and the other 'stick'. The W-W approach recommends a 'stick' or penalty; this is to be implemented in the form of imposition of a tax (a tax increase) for failure to comply with prescribed standards or guidelines. The Okun plan suggests the opposites—a "carrot" or reward or incentive in the form of a tax credit for complying with the prescribed norms or standard.

Incomes policy has not become a regular or common macroeconomic policy like fiscal policy and monetary policy. But, incomes policy appears to be a more direct instrument for controlling inflation compared to fiscal and monetary policies. The US has, over a long period, made serious attempts to implement incomes policy with different degrees of success.

The US experience shows the usefulness, and, during certain periods, effectiveness of incomes policy as an anti-cyclical or anti-inflationary measure. Both President Nixon and President Carter found incomes policy-wage and price standards—both useful and effective. Nixon's mandatory standards programme was relatively more effective. The point is not whether incomes policy is useful. Hardly anybody doubts or questions its relevance or usefulness. The main insure is: what should be the nature and exact form or content of incomes policy to be effective. This is what the US experience has shown. There can be discussion or deliberations on this.

The exponents of income policy—rather tax-based incomes policy (TIP)—are correct in their contention that economic administrators and countries have often to look beyond monetary and fiscal policies for controlling inflation. In this context, the benefits of incomes policy cannot be overlooked. And, in incomes policy, the tax-based variant should be more seriously considered. Also, in tax-based incomes policy (TIP), the choice should be more for Okun's plan than for Wallich-Weintraub plan. A 'carrot' or reward or incentive is always a more progressive policy instrument than a surcharge or penalty or 'stick'.

PHYSICAL POLICY

Physical policy indicates methods of direct control—price control, production control, trade control, etc.—through regulatory measures. Physical policy has been analysed in detail in Chapter 21.

Unlike fiscal and monetary policies which has impact on the entire economy, physical policies are meant to affect only strategic points of the economy; they are specifically designed for particular sectors or business or economic activities. They are formulated and executed to overcome specific problems with regard to say, pricing of particular commodities, shortages or surpluses developing in the economy through over-production or under-production, distribution, etc. Such controls or regulatory measures exist in almost all countries—developed as well as developing. Different countries adopt different types of control depending on their political, social and economic system.

Major areas where physical policies are more commonly applied are investment (includes capital issues), production and distribution, wages, prices, foreign trade and foreign exchange control. Some or all of these regulatory controls can be usefully deployed as anti-cyclical measures during expansionary and recessionary phases. For example, zero investment including IPOs (*Initial Public Offers* of shares by companies) can be encouraged or discouraged depending on the economic situation, production can be accordingly regulated, upward or downward movement of wages and prices may be allowed or stimulated as anti-inflationary or anti-deflationary measures to stabilise or revive the economy.

GLOBAL RECESSION, 2008 AND STABILISATION MEASURES

The global recession of 2008 posed big challenges to economic administrators and policy makers in both developed and developing countries, and, a vital test for stabilisation measures. Different countries responded by formulating and economic administrators and policy makers in both developed and developing countries, and, a vital test for stabilisation measures. Different countries responded by formulating and implementing their own stabilisation measures or stimulus packages for economic revival. Most of these revival packages are a mix of fiscal and monetary instruments with differences in relative emphasis in different countries. According to some of the most recent reports and opinion surveys, global economic recovery is still sub-trend; this means that it is growing slower than it grew before the recession (sub-prime crisis). The Eurozone is of major concern. Also see Appendix below.

APPENDIX

GLOBAL RECESSION, 2008

> The global economy may be slipping into a Great Depression; Governor, RBI
> —*Times of India*, June 27, 2015

In this note, we analyse the origin of the global economic recession, 2008 (some call it 2008-09), its impact on economies of different countries, the revival process and some of the most recent reports and surveys on the state of recovery.

Origin of the Recession

The global recession, 2008 originated in the US in the later half of 2008. The recession was caused by a financial crisis. The cause of the financial crisis was burst of the housing boom in the US. This is widely known as the *sub-prime crisis*.

The Sub-prime Crisis

The sub-prime crisis owes its name to sub-prime borrowers of housing loans which ultimately caused the burst of the housing boom. The sub-prime borrowers are the poor or economically weaker segments of the American society who have low creditworthiness and track records of defaults in repayment of loans. The housing boom was the result of excessive, one can even say indiscriminate, housing loans given to sub-prime borrowers by banks (including their subsidiaries) and non-banking financial institutions who were also extending housing finance or loans. The collapse of the housing boom was triggered by excess supply of houses which were far more in number compared to demand. Following the laws of demand and supply, excess supply of houses caused sharp decline in housing prices. Housing prices had fallen by over 50 per cent during 2008 from their peak level in 2006.

The deterioration in financial and economic conditions in the US was compounded by large scale defaults by sub-prime borrowers in repayment of their housing loans. Banks and other financial institutions were unable to recover their loans from collaterals by sub-prime borrowers or mortgages which were sometimes 'junk houses.' Failure of banks, and, non-banking lending institutions to recover their loans resulted in massive financial losses to them. Repercussion of this was drastic. Many banks, including leading banks of the US, started closing down. Lehman Brothers declared bankruptcy in September 2008, and, this made the financial condition in the US worse.

The financial crisis marked the beginning of the downturn of the US economy. Availability of finance or credit to industry (manufacturing and trading firms) became scarce. Consequently, production suffered and industrial output declined sharply. This had very adverse effect on the economy. There was a sharp fall in GDP. According to US Commerce Department, GDP decline was estimated at 6.3 per cent in the fourth quarter of 2008 compared to the corresponding period of 2007. This was one of the severest downswings in the US economy.

Sharp fall in GDP meant declining production, output, income and demand. Continuous decline in production resulted in large-scale unemployment. All the symptoms or consequences of a recession were clear. The downswing continued during 2009.

Global Impact of the US Recession

The recession in the US had far reaching effect on the global economy because of strong economic linkages of the US with the rest of the world, particularly the European Union or the Eurozone. The US recession spread to the global economy because of two major causative factors: first, decline in international flows of goods and services, i.e., world trade, and, second, decline in international capital flows. World trade was estimated to decline by over 2 per cent. This led to decline in global output and growth rate of the world economy. This meant the onset of global recession.

International organisations have made their own assessments and estimates of decline in global economic growth and, increase in unemployment. The World Bank has projected the decline in world GDP growth rate to be 0.9 per cent in contrast to growth rate of 2.5 per cent during 2008. According to the UN Department of Economic and Social Affairs, the negative growth rate of the world economy is estimated to be 2.6 per cent during 2009 (the earlier estimate was only (–)0.5 per cent). The IMF had also forecast that global growth rate could be negative for the first time in 2009—"the worst performance in our lifetime." The global recession has been attributed to two major factors: global financial crisis and recession in many developed economies.

The International Labour Organisation (ILO) has made detailed analysis of the effect of the global recession on global employment, or rather, global unemployment. ILO has estimated that global unemployment may be over 6.0 per cent during 2009. Global loss of jobs is estimated to be about 30 million. The loss of jobs is spread across different economic and geographical regions including both developed and developing countries. The highest unemployment rate—estimated as 10.3 per cent—would be in North America. In terms of loss of jobs (numbers), bigger losers are developing countries including Latin America, sub-Saharan Africa and South Asia.

According to the Global Wage Report (2008/09) of ILO: "For the World's 1.5 billion wage earners, difficult times lie ahead...wages growth has lagged behind overall economic growth during upswing and slowed down more rapidly during economic downswing. ...if this pattern were to be in rapidly spread global downturn, it will deepen the recession and delay the recovery."

Different countries have been affected differently by the global recession in terms of decline in output or GDP and the growth rate. The Japanese economy has been the worst affected by the global recession (outside the US). For the first time since 2001, the Japanese economy was in recession. GDP declined by more than 15 per cent during January-March 2009—the highest fall since 1955. Consequent to sharp fall in GDP, investment in industrial production—particularly in automobiles and consumer electronics—declined considerably. The most important reason for the Japanese recession, according to official sources—is drastic fall in global demand for Japanese goods (automobiles and consumer electronics). In addition to Japan, all other developed economies suffered including the Eurozone.

Among the developing economies, India and China have been comparatively less affected by the global recession. This, however, is only a matter of degree or intensity. Between the two countries, China has been affected more because its GDP or economy is more dependent on export than that of India. India's problems were more in its financial markets. A study by Subbarao reveals that India's money markets, credit markets, forex markets and equity markets—all were under pressure because of global liquidity squeeze and reversal of capital flows.[23] RBI projected that economic slowdown in India may continue till 2010 primarily because of decline in consumer demand, increase in unemployment and low business confidence. In China, according to official estimates, because of drastic decline in export, more than 2450 manufacturing units in Guangdong—"the heart of China's economic miracle"—closed down. As a consequence, China's export suffered a drastic decline of more than 27 per cent. This had its inevitable impact on employment, industrial production and GDP.

The Revival Process

The global recession of 2008 posed big challenges to economic administrators and policy makers in both developed and developing countries, and, a vital test for rehabilitation or stabilisation measures. Different countries responded by formulating and implementing their own stabilisation measures or stimulus packages for economic revival. Most of these revival packages are a mix of fiscal and monetary instruments with differences in relative emphasis in different countries.

Japan, the worst hit economy (outside the US) depended primarily on fiscal instruments for countering the recession. It announced a public expenditure of about $ 120 billion in 2009 to be channelled to different sectors or activities for economic revival. The objectives of the large public expenditure were two-fold: first, to prevent further economic slowdown or downturn, and, second, to promote investment, encourage and increase production, create new employment opportunities and boost demand.

The US announced a bigger and more comprehensive revival package—$ 1.8 trillion. The revival package included both fiscal and monetary measures. The basic objective of the package was to bail out or revive banks and financial institutions badly affected by the crisis. The government also extended relief to corporates by buying shares of ailing companies.[24] The most important monetary policy implemented was reduction of key interest rate (federal reserve rate) to close to zero to stimulate investment, industrial activities and production and demand.

Developing countries like India and China were comparatively less affected by the crisis; India was lesser affected than China because it was more insulated against the world economy.

India adopted its own revival package; the package included both fiscal and monetary policies. Two major fiscal policies were increase in public expenditure (included allocation of funds for infrastructure development) and reduction in indirect taxation—total fiscal package

23. D. Subbarao, "Impact of the Global Financial Crisis on India: Collateral Damage and Response", *RBI Bulletin*, March 2009.
24. The government bought 70% shares of General Motors (GM).

was of the value of 3 per cent of GDP. The most important monetary policy instrument was significant reduction in the interest rate. This was combined with liberalised financing of export and ₹-$ swap facility to banks. The combination of fiscal and monetary measures produced quick results. The core sector industries—electricity, coal, cement and fuel oil—were on the path to recovery. Other important sectors gradually followed the course.

China's revival package was also a mix of monetary and fiscal measures. The most significant monetary measure was a reduction of the bank rate by more than 1 per cent—the highest reduction since the Asian financial crisis of 1999. The reserve rate was also reduced. The objective of interest rate cut was to ensure "...ample liquidity in the banking system and promoting stable credit growth to make the monetary policy play an active role in supporting economic growth". China's fiscal policy for economic revival was equally strong. This included government expenditure of $ 587 billion for labour intensive infrastructure projects. This was combined with schemes for creating new jobs in housing construction (for 12 million families) and health care services.

Revival schemes or stimulus packages announced and implemented by Japan, US, India, China and other countries created both the base and pace for revival of the world economy. To supplement the revival packages of individual countries, the World Bank announced a $ 50 billion trade liquidity fund in 2009. In an opinion survey conducted by the National Association of Business Economists in the US, 90 per cent of the participating economists predicted that the recession would come to an end by 2009, although there may be some oscillations in the revival path. The two key international institutions—the World Bank and IMF—and, number of economic research organisations in different countries also pitched for revival of the world economy during 2009-10. The global GDP growth during 2010 was projected at 3 per cent.

Latest Developments, Reports, Surveys

Since 2010, a number of international organisations have undertaken analysis, review and assessment of the lingering global recession and the state of recovery. The general conclusion emerging from these analyses and review is that the recovery process has been lopsided. Lopsidedness in recovery has been observed both in developed countries or regions and developing countries or regions. This has happened primarily because of the economic structure—demand pattern, GDP movements and employment or unemployment situation—of different regions/countries and the revival or stimulus packages adopted by the governments of the respective regions/countries.

One of the most recent reviews has been made through Bloomberg Global Poll of International Investors.[25] The review (November 2014) points to the lopsidedness of the recovery process and generally projects a global environment of economic pessimism.

The US economy is improving and the US market is again becoming attractive for business. According to the US Labour Department, unemployment in the US dropped (in October 2014) to the lowest level in six years, and, 200,000 new jobs have been created. The US, however, is still not considered immune to "growing nervousness among investors" about slow increase in consumer prices. Disinflation or deflation is a bigger risk for the US than inflation during next one year or so.

25. The Bloomberg Global Poll was conducted by Selzer & Co., of US. It has a margin of error of plus minus 4.3 percentage points. Refer R. Miller, *The Economic Times* (World View), New Delhi, November 17, 2014.

Japan's revival process has also been generally satisfactory. The Japanese economy is seen to be mostly stable in terms of important parameters or indicators. But, like the US, Japan is also anticipated to face the problem of a depressed price level. The danger of disinflation or deflation is likely to pose a bigger threat than inflation during the next year or more.

But, in terms of economic rehabilitation or revival, the Eurozone is a matter of real concern. The study observes that the Eurozone economy has deteriorated, and, may get worse if there are no proper fiscal policy actions from core European countries particularly Germany. The present fiscal policies of the region are considered too tight. The European Central Bank's (ECB) monetary policies are also considered to be too restrictive. It is also felt that "the ECB measures are coming up too little and too late". The Governor of Bank of England observes that the specter of economic stagnation is haunting Europe.

The Bloomberg Global Poll concludes that the world economy is in its "worst shape" in two years with the euro area and emerging markets deteriorating and the danger of deflation increasing.[26]

Another opinion survey[27] observes that the global economy is still sub-trend; this means that it is growing slower than it grew during pre-Lehman (sub-prime crisis) period. The survey further observes that there was very sharp downward trend during 2009, a sharp V-shape recovery during 2010, and, then steady recovery during 2011-14. But, this is tricky recovery; it is essentially slower growth. The faster growth markets are growing slower than they used to but, faster than the slower growth markets.

The survey concludes that the US and UK are recovering, but, Germany, France, Italy and Spain still have enough issues and people are worried about the Erozone. So, we have Eurozone, and, then Middle East, problems in BRIC (Brazil, Russia, India, China) economies and the US debt.[28] All these pose enough problems for balanced global economic recovery.

REVIEW QUESTIONS

1. What is business cycle? Explain graphically, the four phases of a typical business cycle.
2. Distinguish between external and internal theories of business cycle. Explain the innovations theory of business cycle. Is it an external theory or an internal theory or a combination of both?
3. "Occurrence of business cycles is ideally explained, not by a single theory, but, by a combination of theories." Elucidate.
4. What are the major anti-cyclical fiscal policies? Analyse their effectiveness and limitations.
5. Mention the major instruments of anti-cyclical monetary policy, focusing on the more important ones, and, their effectiveness and constraints.
6. "Constraints of pure fiscal policy and pure monetary policy suggest consideration of a mix or combination of the two." Explain in a perspective of comparison or complementarity.
7. Explain anti-cyclical or stabilisation measures other than monetary and fiscal policies. Comment on their applications.

26. R. Miller, *The Economic Times*, New Delhi, November 17, 2014.
27. V. Mahanta, "Good Luck Growth", *The Economic Times* (Corporate Dossier), November 7-13, 2014.
28. *Ibid*.

8. Explain the stabilisation measures or revival packages adopted by different countries for dealing with the global recession of 2008 with your comments on their effectiveness or success.

SUGGESTED READINGS

- C. Rangarajan and D.K. Srivastava, "Dynamics of Debt-Accumulation in India: Impact of Primary Deficit, Growth and Interest Rate", *Economic and Political Weekly*, November 15, 2003.
- D. Hamberg, *Business Cycles*, Macmillan Company, New York, 1951.
- G.S. Gupta, "Economic Fluctuations and Stabilisation Policies," *Vikalpa*, January-March 2003, pp. 1-10.
- T.J. Clark and M. Cohan, *Business Fluctuations, Growth and Economic Stabilisation*, Random House, 1968.
- M.W. Lee, *Economic Fluctuations*, Richard D. Irwin, Inc., Minois, 1955.
- P.A. Samuelson, "Interaction Between the Multiplier, and, the Principle of Acceleration," *Review of Economic Studies*, May 1939.
- R.A. Gordon, *Business Fluctuations*, Harper and Brothers Publishers, New York, 1952.
- R. Miller, *The Economic Times* (World View), November 17, 2014, p. 15.

Chapter 13

Inflation: Meaning, Causes and Control

In one of the important textbooks on macroeconomics, the author felt in 1961 that "it may well be argued that inflation is currently, has been for a decade or more, and threatens to be in future, one of the most crucial macroeconomic problems for most countries of the world."[1] If the observation was valid in 1961, it is much more so today. Both developed and developing countries are equally concerned with the phenomenon of inflation. This is regarded as one of the major economic problems of the day.

Therefore, an investigation into the nature, causes, effects and control of inflation, including the inflationary situation in India, is important for an understanding of the major macroeconomic issues.

WHAT IS INFLATION?

In the layman's understanding, inflation signifies a situation which is characterised by a rising trend in the general level of prices. The complete meaning of inflation may not be clear from this simplistic definition or understanding because, inflation can be looked at from a number of angles, and depending on how one looks at it, a definition may be attempted accordingly.

Some possible definitions are stated here. According to one definition, inflation exists 'when money income is expanding relatively to the output of work done by the productive agents for which it is the payment", leading to a rise in the price of goods. According to a second definition, inflation is characterised by an "undue increase in quantity of money in proportion to buying power", resulting in the rise of prices. A third definition states that "inflation is a state in which the value of money is falling, i.e. prices are rising". A fourth definition sees inflation "as a persistent and appreciable rise in the general level or average of prices". This definition further elaborates: "We define inflation as *rising* prices, and, not as *high* prices. In some sense, then, inflation is a disequilibrium state; it must be analysed dynamically rather than with the tools of statics."[2]

All the above definitions have one point in common; that is, of identifying inflation with rising prices whatever be the other factors associated with it (the role of the factors associated with inflation would be more clear when we discuss the causes of or factors leading to inflation). It should be made clear that inflation is *not just high prices, it is rising prices*; that is, inflation *is a process and not a state* of prices. It is conventional to measure price increase or inflation per year, but it may be measured per month also. It generally depends on the rate of inflation.

1. Gardner Ackley, *Macroeconomic Theory*, 1961, Chapter 16.
2. Gardner Ackley, *Macroeconomic Theory*, 1961, Chapter 16. Also Gardner Ackley, *Macroeconomic Theory and Policy*, 1978, Chapter 13.

When the rate of inflation is high (the increase in prices between two months is significant), monthly measure of the rate of inflation becomes important. Otherwise, when the increases are small, it may be more meaningful to talk of the annual rate of inflation.

CREEPING AND GALLOPING INFLATION

Depending on the intensity of price increase or the rate of inflation, inflation may be classified as 'creeping' or 'galloping'. A sustained price rise of, say, 2 per cent per year may be described as creeping inflation to distinguish it from the other extreme of galloping inflation (more commonly known as hyperinflation) which occurs when the annual price increase is of the order of 600 or 700 per cent or more or the monthly increase (which may be more relevant here) is of the order of 50 to 60 per cent or more.[3]

The basic characteristic of creeping inflation is that the annual price rise is almost imperceptible, likely to be overlooked by many observers. But creeping inflation, if not controlled in time, may eventually accelerate and develop into galloping or hyperinflation. Hyper inflation which is characterised by almost astronomical rise in prices makes complete nonsense of the monetary and economic system of the country and leads to almost chaotic conditions. Such inflation occurred in Germany in 1923, in Hungary in 1947 and in China in 1949. During hyperinflation, all motives for holding money disappear, and there are frantic efforts for procuring and holding goods and real assets.[4]

OPEN AND SUPPRESSED INFLATION

Sometimes inflation, i.e. price rise, may be suppressed through government's control on prices and distribution of commodities. The symptoms of inflation like shortages (demand outstripping supply) would exist, but because of administered prices, inflation would not be visible. The phenomenon of price increase would be replaced by long queues of waiting buyers at government-controlled distribution centres. If only, and as soon as, restriction on prices and rationing of supplies are removed, inflationary situations would develop. Suppressed inflation really implies postponement of present demand to the future, and diversion of demand from one good to another (to the extent commodity substitution is possible) from those goods whose prices are controlled, and supply is rationed to those whose prices and supply are not administered. Against suppressed inflation, open inflation signifies a process in which prices are permitted to rise commensurate with market forces.

The post-war inflation in many countries and hyper-inflations of the 'Twenties' in Germany, Austria and Russia and of the 'Forties' in China are examples of open inflation. This is the type of inflation that we normally observe. A good illustration of suppressed inflation may be given by the post-Second World War situation in Germany. In the post-war period in Germany, prices were not allowed to increase, although by usual standards, there existed significant inflationary potential. If prices were allowed to rise freely, the price level might have shot up sufficiently (some say, it might have quadrupled), and there could be an inflationary spiral. Suppression of price or inflation through controls really means weakening or suspension of the market economy and this may disrupt the normal functioning of the economic system.

---

3. When the price rise occurs at intermediate rates between creeping and galloping inflation, the situation is sometimes designated as 'trotting' inflation.
4. It is said that during hyperinflation in Germany in 1923, money had lost so much value that if two cartloads, one of coins (money) and the other of bread, were in the street, people would run after the cart of bread rather than that of coins.

DISINFLATION AND DEFLATION

Disinflation and deflation are two stages or phases in the decline or fall of the inflation rate. Inflation, as explained above, is a steady increase in the price level. *Disinflation* means a reversal of the price increase, i.e., a fall in the rate of inflation. *Deflation* means a further fall—actually fall in the price level below the base level. Suppose, the inflation rate in a particular year is 5% (base=100). If the rate of inflation falls to 4% or 3%, there is disinflation. If the price level (index) falls below 100, i.e., (–2%) or (–3%), there is deflation. Therefore, deflation means that the price level goes down below the base year level.

This can be more clearly explained with the help of an hypothetical example. This is presented in Table 13.1.

Table 13.1: Inflation, Disinflation and Deflation

(base year = 2005-06)

Year	Price Index	% change in price (index) (Annual)	Inflation/disinflation/ deflation
2005-06	100	–	–
2006-07	106	6.0	Inflation (6%)
2007-08	104	(–) 2.0	Disinflation (2%)
2008-09	100	(–) 4.0	Disinflation (4%)
2009-10	100	0.0	Zero rate of inflation
2010-11	98	(–) 2.0	Deflation (2%)

The decline of the price level from inflation to disinflation is a gradual process. It may not take long for inflation to change to disinflation, but, deflation is not very common or usual. This can happen occasionally during periods of recession. This happens more in the weekly or monthly movement of the price level than in the annual movements.

In India, this was visible during second week of September 2008 and first week of June, 2009. In the second week of September 2008, the inflation rate was about 12.0%. Since then, the price level had been falling fast (weekly basis). The inflation rate declined to about 6.6% in the second week of December 2008. This was disinflation. The price level fell further and declined to (–) 1.6% in the first week of June 2009. This was deflation.

CAUSES OF INFLATION

Having discussed the meaning of inflation, that is, its nature and the various forms in which it may occur, the next question one may like to ask naturally is 'why does inflation occur?' or 'What are the causes of inflation?' The answer to this question leads to the identification of the basic sources of inflationary pressures. This is important because once causes or sources of inflation are known, the government or the authorities concerned may be in a position to formulate appropriate policies for the control of inflation.

Depending on the causes or the source of inflationary pressures, we may distinguish between three types of inflation, viz., demand pull, cost push and structural.

DEMAND PULL OR EXCESS DEMAND INFLATION

An increase in the price level (i.e. inflation) may be caused by excessive demand far outstripping supply of goods or commodities. Generation of additional or excess demand would raise the level of aggregate demand and would cause the aggregate demand function curve to shift upward. Supply may respond to this through additional production till full employment is reached. As soon as full-employment is reached, aggregate supply tends to become inelastic and the price level increases. This is the Keynesian analysis of excess demand inflation.

Let us explain this with the help of a diagram (Fig. 13.1). In Fig. 13.1, the horizontal axis (x-axis), represents real national income, Y (i.e. national income in terms of physical goods and services) and the vertical axis (y-axis) shows the general price level (P). The aggregate supply curve, S, is horizontal or perfectly elastic initially, then slopes upwards and finally becomes completely inelastic at income Y_0 corresponding to full employment level. The aggregate demand curve, D, slopes downwards (shown as linear or a straight line for convenience of presentation). When the aggregate demand curve shifts from D_0 to D_1 the price level rises from P_0 to P_1. If demand increases further, the demand curve will shift upward again, say, to D_2, causing the price level to rise further. Thus, continuous shift in the aggregate demand curve results in a price spiral.

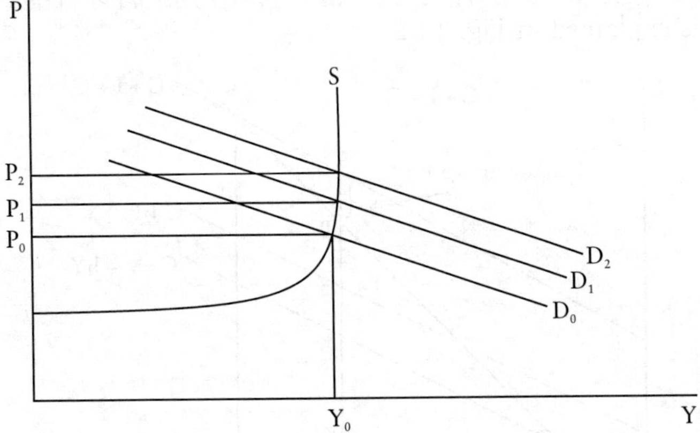

Fig. 13.1: Demand Pull Inflation

Increase in demand or expenditures and the resulting shifts in the aggregate demand curve is generally closely linked to money supply. A shift in the aggregate demand curve can take place because of an increase in either private or government expenditures leading to an increase in total expenditures. In either case, increased expenditures are facilitated or financed by increase in money supply. When the government, for various reasons, attempts to maintain aggregate demand (expenditure) at a high level or wants to increase it, and these expenditures cannot be financed by taxation or borrowing from the public, and resorts to borrowing from the central bank, new additional purchasing power is created, and this pushes up prices. Similarly, there may be increase in, demand (expenditures) of the private sector financed by additional credit from the commercial banking system and, if the credit creation by the commercial banks is supported by the central bank, there is increase in money supply, purchasing power, and prices rise.

We have mentioned above (and shown in the diagram) that inflation occurs after the full employment income level has been reached. But the experience of recent years shows that it is not essential, and may not be necessary, that the economy should be operating at full employment level for the inflationary situations to develop. Most of the economies in the world today are operating at less than full employment level and many of them, including India, are experiencing inflation. So long as the aggregate supply curve is sloping upwards, an increase in demand and shift in the demand curve will lead to inflationary situations. The genesis of an inflationary situation is: 'too much money chasing too few goods'.

INFLATIONARY GAP

Excess demand inflation can also be explained in terms of the inflationary gap. Inflationary gap is measured as the excess of aggregate demand C + I + G (C = consumption, I = investment and G = government expenditure) over full employment aggregate output or supply Y_0. In other words, the situation $(C + I + G) > Y_0$ indicates presence of an inflationary gap. Correspondingly, if $(C + I + G) < Y_0$, there exists a deflationary gap in the economy.

The concept of inflationary gap may be defined as the excess of the actual level of aggregate demand that exists in the economy at full employment level of income and the amount of aggregate demand that is required to attain full employment. Since the amount of aggregate demand required to attain full employment should be equal to aggregate supply at full employment, we may also say that the *inflationary gap is the excess of the actual aggregate effective demand in the economy over the aggregate supply at the full employment level.* The concept and measure of inflationary gap is explained in Fig. 13.2.

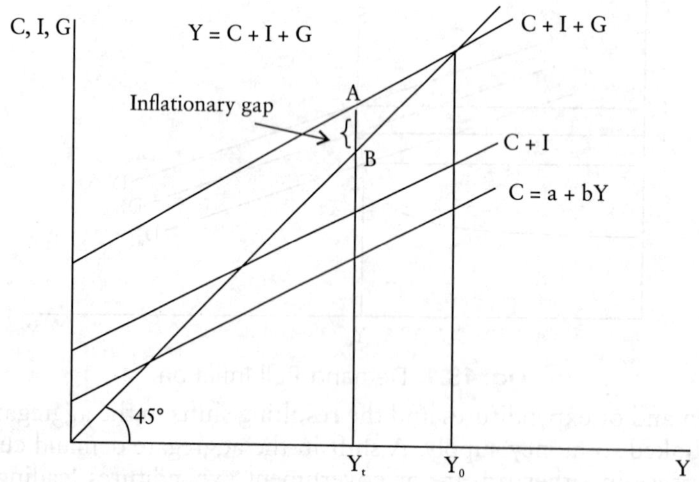

Fig. 13.2: Inflationary Gap

In Fig. 13.2, the consumption function is of the form C = a + bY. Aggregate investment I and government spending G are autonomously determined so that the aggregate demand function C + I + G is shown parallel to the consumption function, the distance between the two being I + G. The line C + I + G represents aggregate demand or spending corresponding to different levels of income. If aggregate real output could increase without limit, aggregate real income would then increase to Y_0, i.e. the equilibrium level. But aggregate real output or supply cannot increase beyond Y_1, the full employment limit. At Y_1 aggregate demand (C + I + G) exceed aggregate supply by AB, i.e. $(C + I + G) - Y_1 = AB$. Thus, AB is the inflationary gap which raises the price level.

COST-PUSH INFLATION

The cause of inflation many times may not be excess demand, but increase in the cost of production or supply. Increase in cost would push the price level up through an upward shift in the aggregate supply curve. So, while in excess demand or demand-pull inflation, increase in the price level is caused by an upward shift in the aggregate demand curve, cost-push inflation occurs because of an upward shift in the aggregate supply function. Cost-push inflation is illustrated in Fig. 13.3.

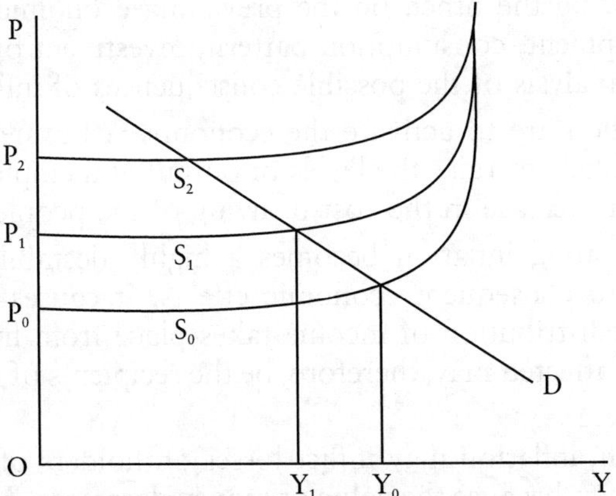

Fig. 13.3: Cost-push Inflation

Because of increase in costs, either raw material cost or wage cost, if the aggregate supply curve shifts from S_0 to S_1, price rises from P_0 to P_1. If costs increase further, there will be further upward shift in the supply function, say to S_2, and the price level will escalate to P_2.

The shift in the aggregate supply curve can occur as a result of increase in any one of the major cost elements, but cost-push inflation is generally ascribed to increase in wage costs. Cost-push inflation, therefore, often becomes a case of wage-push inflation. Trade unions may be able to achieve higher money wages through collective bargaining without corresponding increases in productivity causing an upward shift in the aggregate supply curve through increase in total costs.

Sometimes monopolistic and oligopolistic producers may increase prices to increase profitability or total profits. This may be designated as profit-push inflation against cost-push inflation as described above. Many times, cost-push inflation occurs as a result of the combination of wage-push and profit-push inflation. This happens particularly when entrepreneurs try to maintain the same margin of profit when there are cost escalations. Certain constant margin or mark-up is added to computed costs to yield a given target rate of return on the invested capital. This kind of inflation is sometimes described as 'mark-up inflation'.

STRUCTURAL INFLATION

Structural inflation may develop when there are structural imbalances in the various sectors of the economy. There is a possibility that, although there is no excess aggregate demand, the price level may rise because of excess demand in certain specific sectors of the economy. Initially, prices will rise in those sectors where there is excess demand. This may lead to wage increases in the same sectors. The rise in wages in these sectors may then spread to sectors where there is no excess demand for labour. Also, the output of the industries with rising prices may enter as rising cost (of inputs) into the cost structure of industries with deficient demand. This will tend to shift the supply curve of these industries. Thus, finally, a general shift in the aggregate supply curve can take place because of structural imbalances in the economy, and the inflation thus occurring is, therefore, described as structural inflation.

EFFECTS OF INFLATION

It is difficult to exactly enumerate the effects of inflation on the economy or economic life of a community or country. Such effects would depend, on the one hand, on the nature and intensity of inflation, and, on the other, on the prevailing economic situation reflected in the levels of industrial development, consumption pattern, investment opportunities, etc. One can only make some general analysis of the possible consequences of inflation.

Initial effects of inflation are to activate the economy. A business boom, which generally accompanies inflation, is likely to raise the levels of output and employment. And this may not cause more than a modest increase in the cost of living of the people.

Continuous or accelerating inflation becomes a highly destabilising force. Starting with price instability, it leads to consequent economic effects. It causes inequitable redistribution of income and wealth. Redistribution of income takes place from fixed income groups to the business sector. The worst affected may, therefore, be the recipients of fixed incomes like salaries, pensions and annuities.

With respect to wealth, inflation may inflict losses on holders of government bonds, fixed deposits in banks and money, because the value of money decreases: A continuous and spiralling inflation may reduce the value of money to almost nothing in the extreme case.

Inflation reduces savings substantially, if not wipe out completely. During periods of inflation, debtors may liquidate their past debts by offering currency, which is fast losing its value, to their creditors. The value of accumulated cash savings also decreases fast, and, in the process of liquidating savings, the velocity of circulation of money increases. The velocity of circulation reaches its climax during hyperinflation when the flight from money is such that the velocity approaches infinity. In Germany, during the hyperinflation in the 1920s, there were cases where life's entire savings could not buy a cup of coffee. Such periods are also characterised by very low public morale.

Inflation may also cause misallocation and waste of a country's resources. During the German hyperinflation, much of the industrial plant and equipment set up in desperation during the inflation was found subsequently to be technically inefficient. These are clear examples of misallocation of resources (no allocation of resources should really have been made to such projects or sectors). Such misallocation leads to waste of resources also. Depending on the intensity and duration of inflation, the magnitudes of misallocation and wastes would vary.

CONTROL OF INFLATION

Mild or moderate inflation (say, about 2%) may be good for an economy and economic growth. But continuous and accelerating inflation has adverse effects on an economy. We have just mentioned above the ill-effects of inflation. Possible serious consequences of inflation call for effective measures to control or curb it. Inflation should be controlled before it assumes serious proportions and becomes a highly destabilising force. In fact, control of inflation through appropriate anti-inflationary measures is a major concern of economists and governments in almost all countries all over the world. Presently, in India, control of inflation is a very major issue; in fact, both the Ministry of Finance and RBI are almost grappling with it.

There may also be a paradoxical situation. Some studies have shown that a fall in the rate of inflation may increase the rate of unemployment. This becomes the policy-makers' dilemma. Along with anti-inflationary measures, we will also be discussing this issue in this section.

Various anti-inflationary measures or policy instruments are generally classified under three heads:

1. Monetary policy or measures
2. Fiscal policy or measures
3. Incomes policy or wage and price control

Monetary and fiscal policies or instruments are the conventional and most common measures adopted by policy-makers or governments for controlling inflation. Monetarists content that monetary policy or instruments play a more important role in controlling inflation. Fiscalists, also known as Keynesians, on the other hand, argue that fiscal policy or instruments are more effective as anti-inflationary measure. We shall comment on the relative roles or effectiveness of these two policies as we proceed.

MONETARY POLICY OR INSTRUMENTS

Three major instruments of monetary policy most commonly used as anti-inflationary measures are:

(a) The bank rate
(b) Open market operations
(c) Cash reserve ratio (CRR)

The roles and effectiveness of these three policy instruments in controlling inflation are discussed below.

The *bank rate* is actually the 'rediscount rate' of the central bank of a country; RBI uses the term 'Repo rate' (Repurchase operation rate) for the bank rate. The central bank rediscounts bills of exchange and other approved securities for lending money to commercial banks. The central bank plays this important role in its capacity as the 'lender of the last resort'. The bank rate or the *repo rate* provides the base or the basis for lending rates of commercial banks. To control inflation, the central bank increases the bank rate to control money supply (by increasing the cost of borrowing, because, according to the monetarists, the key to controlling inflation is to control money supply). Increase in the bank rate by the central bank, in turn, leads to increase in the lending rate of commercial banks. This is commonly known as 'dear money policy'.[5] In a developed or integrated money market, increase in the bank rate sets the trend for the general market rate of interest.

The bank rate essentially controls or regulates the credit creation process or lending by commercial banks to control money supply. Therefore, the effectiveness of this instrument depends on the extent to which it succeeds in achieving this objective. The bank rate is generally not effective, or it can succeed to a very limited extent, under the following situations:

(a) Banks may maintain their lending rates because they are not under any compulsion or obligation to increase their lending rates even if the central bank increases the bank rate;
(b) Banks may have excess liquidity so that they are not constrained to extend credit or lend funds;
(c) Demand by firms or the industry for commercial credit may be low.

Open market operations is a more direct instrument for control of money supply compared to the bank rate and also the cash reserve ratio. The central bank undertakes open market operations as banker of the government. For controlling inflation through open market operations, the central bank sells government securities to the public through authorised commercial banks and other financial institutions. Through this operation, money flows from the public to the central bank, and, this leads to contraction of money supply in the market. Contraction of money supply or money in circulation, in turn, reduces purchasing power of people; this results in reduction of effective demand which becomes anti-inflationary.

5. If the bank rate is reduced, it is called 'cheap money policy'.

An advantage of open market operations is that it is flexible unlike the bank rate which cannot be changed frequently (to avoid destabilisation of the financial and capital markets). Open market operations can be undertaken almost any time, or intermittently, i.e. in doses, in appropriate amount, and can also be reversed without causing much problem in the market. Open market operations are generally considered an efficient instrument and more effective than other instruments of monetary control. The effectiveness or success of open market operations, however, assumes a well-organised and developed money and financial market. This is the reason why open market operations is more effective or successful in development economies like the US, UK and some other European countries than in developing countries like India.

Cash reserve ratio (CRR), also known as variable reserve ratio, is similar to the bank rate, but, is little more direct in effect because it has direct impact on the liquidity position of commercial banks. The central bank determines and regulates the CRR. For controlling inflation, CRR is raised so that commercial banks have less funds at their disposal for lending to the public and firms or industry. This reduces money in circulation in the economy, and, therefore, purchasing power of people and demand for goods and services; less or fall in demand prevents prices from rising. This is how CRR can become anti-inflationary.

But, CRR has more or less the same limitations as the bank rate. For example, if commercial banks have excess liquidity, they are not constrained by increase in CRR. Their lending operations may still continue as prior to increase in CRR. Only if the increase in CRR is very significant or high, the liquidity and lending operations of banks may be affected. But large or disproportionate increase in CRR is not very common because this may have destabilising effect on the monetary and financial system and the economy.

FISCAL POLICY OR INSTRUMENTS[6]

As mentioned above, according to the fiscalists, inflation is caused by fiscal factors or reasons. Therefore, inflation should also be controlled with the help of fiscal instruments or measures. Two major instruments of fiscal policy are:

(a) Government expenditure
(b) Taxation

Both these instruments operate through the government budget and are regulated by the Ministry of Finance of the country.

Government expenditure is generally considered to be a more direct instrument of fiscal policy compared to taxation. Fiscalists contend that inflation is caused by excess of aggregate demand over aggregate supply (i.e. demand-pull inflation). Excess demand results from increase in or excessive expenditure by the government sector or the business sector or the household sector, or, often, by two or all the three sectors. Inflation caused by excess demand can be controlled through reduction in expenditure or increase in taxation. If excess demand is the result of increase in government expenditure, the direct anti-inflationary measure is proportionate cut in public expenditure. The amount or magnitude of cut would depend on the extent of excess demand or the intensity of rate of inflation.

The reduction in government expenditure not only reduces government demand for goods and services, but also has impact on private consumption expenditure. The effect on reducing private consumption or demand comes through working of the expenditure multiplier; correctly

6. Fiscal policy—its meaning, scope, role, limitations, etc. in a broader macroeconomic framework will be discussed in Chapter 20.

speaking, it is the *negative or reverse multiplier* which gets into operation when there is a cut in government expenditure. Therefore, a reduction in government expenditure reduces total expenditure or demand not only by the amount of government expenditure, but by a larger amount because of the (negative) multiplier effect.

If excess demand is the result of increase in private final consumption or expenditure, i.e. expenditure by the business sector and the household sector, the appropriate or more direct fiscal instrument is increase in taxation. This is intended to have direct effect on controlling inflation. Taxation (direct tax) reduces disposable income, and, this, in turn, reduces purchasing power and, hence, demand or consumption expenditure of the household sector and the business sector. This means reduction in aggregate demand, and, this has anti-inflationary effect. The reduction in consumption expenditure, however, would depend on the MPC.

There are generally two arguments against increase in taxation and reduction in consumption expenditure. The first is an economic one. Reduction in consumption expenditure may affect growth process of an economy. Even with additional investment desired increase in output or income may not take place because of fall in the consumption level. The second argument is related to a social factor or reason. Any increase in taxation, particularly direct taxes, faces social resistance. It may also have political implications, and, may reflect on the government.

INCOMES POLICY

Income policy is also known as wage-price control policy because its objective is to have direct impact on wages and the price level. One important variant of incomes policy is tax-based incomes policy (TIP); tax-based incomes policy is also known as 'carrot' and 'stick' policy. Incomes policy is intended to play more a supplemental role in controlling inflation, but a more direct one.

Income policy works through government intervention in wage and price movement process. Depending on the level or rate of inflation, the government intervenes with appropriate guidelines or control measures. Incomes policy takes one of the three forms:

(a) Wage-price guidelines or "guideposts";
(b) Mandatory wage-price controls;
(c) Tax-based incomes policies (TIPs).

Wage-price guidelines mean that appropriate guidelines or standards are laid down by the government for wages and prices so that inflation can be removed or mitigated. This includes different kinds of measures. For example, firms with excess capacities may be asked or persuaded to increase production so that supply can be increased to meet demand to avert price rise. Also, firms making profits may be required to absorb increase in cost in profit, and, not to increase prices of their products. This helps to control cost-push inflation.

Mandatory wage-price controls are issued when the government wants to implement stronger measures to control inflation. In fact, the government passes resolutions or legislations to control price rise. This may include different types of steps or measures. Prices or costs of public utilities and services—electricity, water, post and telegraph, railways, etc.—which are mostly fixed or regulated by the government may be reduced. All forms of wage-price increase may be stopped or suspended for a particular period except in very special cases. Commercial banks may be instructed to adopt a liberal credit expansion policy or measure to stimulate investment and boost production. There can be some other similar measures.

Tax-based incomes policy (TIP) uses tax as an instrument as a 'carrot' (reward or incentive) or 'stick' (penalty or punishment) for controlling wage-price increase. In 'carrot'—or reward or incentive plan (Okun plan), firms which adhere to prescribed government guidelines and do not increase wages are rewarded with rebates in corporate tax. Similarly, workers (or workers' unions) who agree to work at the existing or original wage rate, and, do not press for an increase may be rewarded with personal income tax rebates or tax credit. In the 'stick' or penalty plan (Wallich-Weintraub plan), a penalty is imposed in the form of an additional tax or tax increase for non-compliance with prescribed standards or guidelines. This applies to both firms and individual workers (or worker groups).

The US was the first country to experiment with, or, rather make serious attempts to implement, incomes policy. The US experience—during Presidents Nixon, Carter, Kennedy—shows the usefulness of incomes policy as an anti-inflationary measure. Both President Nixon and President Carter found incomes policy—wage and price standards—both useful and effective. Nixon's mandatory standards programme was relatively more effective.

In addition to the US, many other countries have used incomes policy in different forms to control inflation. Malaysia is one such country which should be mentioned. In Malaysia, firms were instructed to absorb cost increases in profits and not to increase their selling prices. As additional control measures, allowances of government employees were reduced, increase in salaries of staff in corporatised universities, and some other organisations was postponed for some time and import of goods and services was closely monitored and controlled. In India, administered prices including those of public utilities and in public distribution systems[7] are forms or extensions of incomes policy.

Today, the issue about incomes policy is not whether it is useful; hardly anybody doubts its relevance or usefulness. The main issue is: what should be the nature or exact form or content of incomes policy to be more effective. This is what the US experience has shown. There can be debate or discussion on this.

COMPLEMENTARITY OR MIX OF MONETARY POLICY, FISCAL POLICY AND INCOMES POLICY

The type of anti-inflationary measures to be adopted should generally depend on the type of inflation to be controlled, i.e. whether it is demand-pull or cost-push. If the primary cause of inflation is demand-pull or a shift in the aggregate demand curve, monetary authorities may attempt to curb both private and government expenditures through the use of the monetary instruments of the bank rate, cash reserve ratio, open market operations, etc. The monetary controls may be supplemented by appropriate fiscal or tax policy by the government.

If the major cause of inflation is a cost-push factor and results in a shift in the aggregate supply function, the application of normal monetary and fiscal policies may not be adequate. In fact, it is being increasingly realised in recent years, particularly because of the complexities of the nature of inflation that occurs, that present-day governments should look for more effective methods of control than rely-entirely on traditional instruments of policy. To curb or contain cost-push inflation, resulting from wage increases, monetary and fiscal policies may have to be supplemented by appropriate incomes policy to directly control prices, wages and income.

7. Strictly speaking, administered prices in public distribution systems are more of "fair prices" for the common people than for controlling inflation.

As indicated above, incomes policies, including wage-price freezes, have been implemented on several occasions in a number of countries including Canada and the US.

There is, however, one danger with wage-price freezes. Such strong controls or freezes may sometimes only suppress inflation temporarily rather than contain or control it. For example, the US anti-inflation programme adopted in the latter half of 1971 partly suspended the market system and succeeded in suppressing inflation rather than controlling it. Nevertheless, all situations or intensities of inflation have to be controlled. Such situations do require a pragmatic mix of policies—a set of policy measures which should include a restrictive or contractionary monetary and fiscal policies, an appropriate wages or incomes policy, and, some degree of direct control on prices. This also requires close coordination among various government machineries—different departments of the government and the central bank—who are responsible for formulation and implementation of anti-inflationary policies or measures.

POLICY-MAKERS' DILEMMA: PHILLIPS' CURVE

In pursuing anti-inflationary policies leading to wage and price controls, the policy-makers face a dilemma. The dilemma is that such an anti-inflationary policy may result in fall of output and employment. A study conducted by the British economist, A.W. Phillips, on the relation between unemployment and rate of change in money wage rates in the United Kingdom (based on actual changes in wages and unemployment rates during 1862-1957) revealed an inverse relationship between the two. This is shown in the 'Phillips' Curve'. The modified Phillips' curve establishes relationship between percentage rise in prices and the unemployment rate. The modified Phillips' curve is shown in Fig. 13.4.

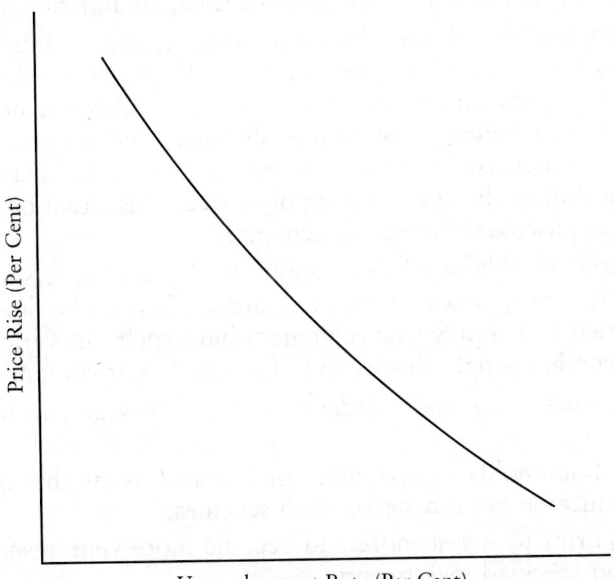

Fig. 13.4: Modified Phillips' Curve

The curve shows that as the rate of increase in the price level increases, the unemployment rate falls; or, conversely, as the price level decreases (in per cent), the rate of unemployment increases. The curve clearly reflects the dilemma of the policy-makers. The dilemma is: how to choose the best combination of unemployment rate and wage-push inflation? It is quite likely that the extent of unemployment which may be necessary to avoid wage-push inflation may be higher than what may be considered socially or economically acceptable. For example, if a sustained high percentage of unemployment is necessary to achieve price stability or avoid inflation, it might appear to society that the lesser of the two evils is to accept mild inflation with a low unemployment rate of 2 to 3 per cent rather than a high unemployment rate with no inflation in the economy.

SUPPLY SIDE ECONOMICS AND INFLATION

We had seen earlier that inflation can be caused by demand factors (demand pull) or supply factors (cost-push or profit-push). Supply factors can sometimes take the form of supply shocks. We shall discuss here the role of supply side economics in dealing with supply shocks and inflation.

A supply shock is a sudden change in input costs or productivity which affects supply sharply and causes shift in the aggregate supply curve. Supply shocks can be of two types, favourable and unfavourable, with two different effects on the price level (upward or downward movement). A favourable supply shock would increase the supply of goods and services, caused by increase in factor supplies and, also, factor productivities brought about by improvement in technology. This would lead to fall in factor prices and cost saving (or cost reduction) in raw material input and energy. Increase in the supply of goods and services or the favourable supply shock would shift the aggregate supply curve downward. This would mean a decrease in the price level. An unfavourable or adverse supply shock would produce the opposite effect caused by decrease in factor supplies and productivities and increase in input costs or prices. This would result in decrease in supply of goods and services resulting in an upward shift in the aggregate supply curve. This would mean increase in the general price level, i.e. inflation and fall in real income.

Let us give an example of an unfavourable supply shock leading to inflation. The Organisation of Petroleum Exporting Countries (OPEC) had increased the price of crude oil significantly during 1973-74—oil price went up by almost 80 per cent. Because oil is a major fuel or energy input (directly or indirectly) for production of almost all goods and services, its price hike caused a sudden and significant increase in the cost of production. This unfavourable supply shock resulted in an upward shift in the aggregate supply curve. This situation is more appropriately described as stagflation (discussed later in the chapter).

Remedy for an unfavourable or adverse supply shock lies in reversing or neutralising it by instituting a favourable supply shock of the same order. This can be done through supply side economics. The exponents of supply side economics have spelt out various components of the supply side policy to combat supply shocks and inflation. Major components of this policy are:

1. Encouraging workers to work harder and longer through cuts in personal income tax rates;
2. Encouraging households to save more in financial assets through savings promotion schemes like income tax rebates on such schemes;
3. Encouraging firms to invest more and become more venturesome through corporate tax rebates on specified investments.

Policy measure 1 would increase effective supply of labour and, also, productivity. This would, therefore, lead to increase in output and cause the aggregate supply curve to shift downwards. If policy measure 2 is implemented, savings would increase thus leading to increase in the available funds for investment. This, along with policy 3, would ensure increase in investment and output and, cause a downward shift in the aggregate supply curve. If the policy measures

1, 2 and 3 are effectively used, this may cause downward shift in the aggregate supply which is strong or sufficient to ensure that the post-supply shock supply curve (S_1) would shift back to pre-supply shock position (S_0). This would mean that supply side policies would restore the original equilibrium and cure inflation and unemployment simultaneously.

It is the effectiveness of supply side economics that made it very popular during the 1970s and later to control stagflation and general inflationary situations. President Reagan had implemented these policies in the US during 1981-89. Margaret Thatcher had employed these policies in the UK during her Prime Ministership in the 1980s. In India also, these policies were put into practice during 1984-89. Many other governments have employed supply side economics/policies to combat inflation or stagflation.

INFLATION IN INDIA AND ITS MEASUREMENT

Conventional measures of inflation are given by indices of wholesale prices. The same is true in India also. In addition to the wholesale price index, however, there are three other measures of inflation in India.[8] These are: consumer price index for industrial workers, consumer price index for urban non-manual employees and consumer price index for agricultural labourers. These four indices are explained below.

WHOLESALE PRICE INDEX (WPI)

Wholesale price index is the index of the weighted average price of all goods produced and/or transacted in the economy at the *wholesale* level. This includes the prices of intermediate or semi-finished goods, and, also raw materials which are transacted at the wholesale level. The WPI, however, excludes prices of services such as education: health, financial (banking, etc.), transport and communication.

For calculation of WPI, weights are assigned to all prices included in the index on the basis of relative values of wholesale transactions of various goods. The weighted arithmetic mean is used for computation of the index, WPI is computed at all-India level only. The index, however, is available for major groups, sub-groups and individual commodities/products. The WPI is presently available with 1981-82 (= 100) and 1993-94 (= 100) as bases—till 1993-94 with 1981-82 as base and since 1993-94 with 1993-94 as base.

CONSUMER PRICE INDEX FOR INDUSTRIAL WORKERS (CPI-IW)

CPI-IW is the index of average retail price of goods and services which comprise the consumption basket of industrial workers. Because the consumption basket consists of only consumer goods and services used by industrial workers, the index excludes the prices of capital goods and all intermediate products. The consumption basket is determined based on the consumption pattern, nature of work/profession, level of income of industrial workers, etc. The CPI-IW series is available with 1982 (= 100) as base.

CONSUMER PRICE INDEX FOR URBAN NON-MANUAL EMPLOYEES (CPI-UNME)

CPI-UNME is based on the consumption pattern of the middle-class families. The consumption basket consists of 180 items sold in open market through cooperative stores and fair price shops. The consumption basket is reviewed from time to time and, necessary changes made in

8. Some economists mention 'GDP Deflator' as also a measure of inflation. GDP deflator is the index of the average price of all final goods and services, and, excludes intermediate goods and raw materials.

the composition of the basket to make it as representative as possible. CPI-UNME is published with 1984-85 (= 100) as base.

CONSUMER PRICE INDEX FOR AGRICULTURAL LABOURERS (CPI-AL)

Because of the special role of agriculture and agricultural labourers in the Indian economy, a separate index is prepared to show inflation affecting this sector. Number of items in the consumption basket for agricultural labourers varies between 27 and 38 from state to state. CPI-AL is first prepared at state level, and, then aggregated at national level. CPI-AL is presently published with base 1986-87 (= 100).

The three consumer index members—CPI-IW, CPI-UNME and CPI-AL represent the levels of inflation facing these different consumer groups. In other words, three CPs indicate the cost of living indices of the respective consumer groups.

As has been mentioned above, the wholesale price index is the most conventional, and, also the most common measure of inflation or movement in the general price level. Therefore, the measure of inflation in India has been given by WPI. The nature of inflation in India by WPI, along with food inflation and non-food manufacturing inflation, during April, 2010 and December, 2012 is shown in Fig. 13.5.

If one analyses the developments in the economic scene in India during last ten or fifteen years, one is led to the conclusion that inflation in India during recent years has been primarily demand-pull inflation.

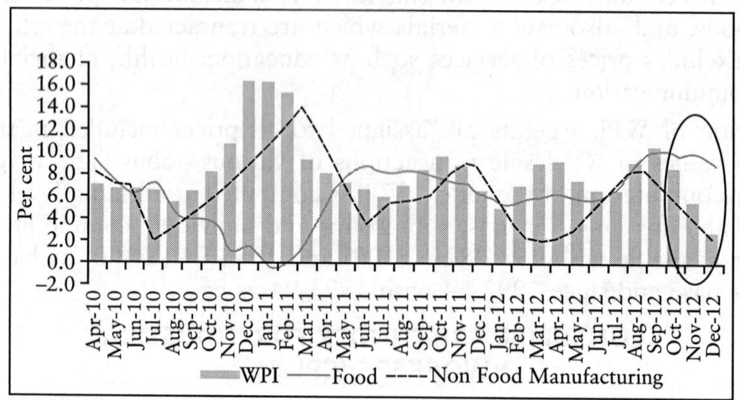

Fig. 13.5: Inflation in India, April 2010–December 2012
Source: Economic Survey, Government of India, 2012-13

Increase in neither agricultural production nor industrial production kept pace with increase in demand, particularly monetary demand, and this led to development of an inflationary situation in the country. There was significant increase in the money supply during the period and with money supply increasing, aggregate monetary demand increased considerably during the period. Demand pressures have been sustained because in addition to private demand, the government has been maintaining its expenditure at a high level even through deficit financing, whenever necessary.

ANTI-INFLATIONARY POLICIES IN INDIA

In the early phases of inflation, attempts were made to control the rise in prices through policy measures, mostly monetary policies, aimed at discouraging demand. The Reserve Bank of India brought into use a large variety of general instruments of credit control. The bank rate was raised many times. The cash reserve ratio to be maintained by banks was increased several times. Limits were also set on the total volume of credit expansion during the busy season. It was also felt that an attempt should be made to restrain demand through measures aimed at restricting incomes. Several actions were taken to impound some part of wage income as well as dividend income. But these had only temporary or short-term effects.

Actually, the pursuit of a restrictive monetary policy highlights the dilemma faced by the monetary authorities. In spite of the Reserve Bank of India bringing into operation a large variety of instruments of credit control, money supply tended to rise at a fairly fast rate. The explanation for this is like this. During a period of rising prices, business units may legitimately demand a larger amount of credit from the banking system because of the increase in the cost of raw materials and inventories. If the central bank allows the business units to obtain more credit from the banking system, what it achieves, in effect, is credit expansion required to compensate the increase in prices rather than support or finance any expansion in real output. Thus, a cycle of rise in price and rise in credit is set in motion and the monetary authority loses all effective control over the prices. And the vicious cycle continues. Inflation in India was often caught in vicious cycles like these.

Since 1991-92, however, with the initiation of economic reforms, inflation has been brought under control. The economic reforms have laid greater emphasis on the supply side encouraging production and investment including foreign investment. Some of the specific measures undertaken are: substantial reduction in excise duties on a number of items expected to accelerate the pace of industrial growth; strengthening of public distribution system; and, supplementing supplies under liberal import policy for essential commodities like sugar, edible oil and pulses.

Because of various economic reforms and steps taken to augment supply, the rate of inflation fell from double digit (13.7 per cent) in 1991-92 to single digit (8.7 per cent) in 1993-94. The rate of inflation came down further to 5.5 per cent during 1996-97. The rate of inflation was 7.2 per cent during 2000-01.

It was 5.5 per cent during 2003-04, 5.4 per cent during 2006-07, but, increased to 8.4 per cent during 2008-09. The inflation rate remained above 7.0 per cent since 2009. Very recently (2014) inflation had come down to below 5.0 per cent. This is WPI inflation. But, CPI inflation continues to remain high.

Therefore, inflation continues to be a major cause of concern both for the government and the RBI. Both the government and the RBI have implemented a number of measures to curb or control inflation. More important of these measures are: containing demand by restricting money supply and keeping interest rates high, increasing supply with incentives to producers, protecting vulnerable section of consumers with subsidies for below-poverty-line families or households, protecting almost all consumers against price rise with subsidy on diesel, etc.

Inflation, however, continues to persist. Because inflation has been almost persistent, this indicates a significant mismatch between demand and supply. The government is fully aware of this. Therefore, the government plans to curb demand through fiscal consolidation, and, the RBI likes to do so through high interest rate and 'dear money policy'. In the short-run, curbing demand to a reasonable extent may enable supply to catch up; this can be an appropriate step. But, in the long-run, measures for increasing supply may be the only way for non-inflationary growth. Anti-inflationary policies or measures have to be compatible with the government's commitment for steady growth. These are what the government is planning and implementing at present.

STAGFLATION

Inflation characterises an economic situation in which the price increases, and induced by this, there is increase in output and employment till the full employment level is reached (in most of the economies today, full employment is hardly reached, because some degree of unemployment always exists). So, inflation is generally associated with a boom in economic activity. But the experience of many countries during recent years has shown a rather unusual combination of increase in prices and stagnation or decline in output and employment. To describe this rather paradoxical situation of the co-existence of 'inflation' (sustained price increases) and economic 'stagnation' the economists have coined the phrase 'stagflation'.

During the early 1970s, governments in many countries were under political pressure to undertake expansionary economic programmes to reduce unemployment; and one of the major objectives of economic policies, and, particularly those relating to foreign trade, were to achieve a higher rate of growth in output associated with a higher rate of price increase than before 1971. But the large and erratic changes which followed acted as a check on increase in real output by increasing uncertainty, and finally contributed to the unexpectedly severe downturn in economic activity in 1975. Restrictive policies, both fiscal and monetary, adopted to curb the high rates of inflation experienced during 1973 and early 1974 had little or no effect on wages and prices, but there were unusually severe declines in output and employment. In short, substantial declines in output co-existed with price and wage inflation in most economies, particularly in the industrially advanced countries of the West. Such economic conditions are being designated as stagflationary situations.

In India, a similar situation arose in recent years when on the one hand prices rose while on the other, there was stagnation or curtailment of output in a large number of industries leading to unemployment of labour. Between 1990-91 and 1991-92, for example, the price level increased by about 4 per cent, but real net national product declined by 1 per cent. Manufacturing activities as a whole registered negative growth. There were a number of industries like textile, leather and rubber products and engineering industries like electrical machinery, non-electrical machinery and transport equipment where output declined—the decline ranging between 2 to 12 per cent.

REVIEW QUESTIONS

1. Define inflation. Can any increase in price be called inflation? Distinguish between creeping and galloping or hyperinflation.
2. Explain the difference between inflation, disinflation and deflation. Give some numerical examples of the difference.
3. What are the causes of inflation? Clearly distinguish between demand-pull inflation and cost-push inflation.
4. What is inflationary gap? Explain with the help of a diagram.
5. Analyse the effects of inflation. Are there also some good effects of inflation? Mention them, and, discuss the detailed effects or consequences of inflation.
6. Explain supply side economics and supply shocks in relation to inflation. Do supply shocks have favourable or unfavourable effects on inflation?
7. Analyse major anti-inflationary policies or measures, and, mention the relative effectiveness and limitations of these policies or measures.

8. "The type of anti-inflationary measures to be adopted would generally depend on the type of inflation to be controlled." Elaborate this in terms of complementarity or mix of major policies or measures.
9. What are the different measures of inflation. Comment on the suitability or appropriateness of these measurements in correctly reflecting the state of inflation. Do this with reference to India.
10. What is 'stagflation'? Do we observe stagflation in both developed and developing countries?

SUGGESTED READINGS

- EPW Research Foundation, "Wholesale and Consumer Prices", *Economic and Political Weekly*. September 18, 1999.
- G. Ackley, *Macroeconomics: Theory and Policy*, Macmillan New York, 1978, Chapter 15.
- N. Mankiw, *Macroeconomics*, Worth Publishers, New York, 2004, Chapter 4.
- Reserve Bank of India, "New Series of Consumer Price Index Numbers for Industrial Workers (Base: 1982 = 100)", *RBI Bulletin*, May 1989.
- W.E. Diewert, "Index Number Issues in Consumer Price Index," *Journal of Economic Perspectives*, Winter, 1998.
- W.J. Baumol and A.S. Blinder, *Economics: Principles and Policy* (4th Edition), Harcourt Brace Jovanovich Publishers, New York, 1988, Chapter 6.

PART–V

MONETARY SYSTEM AND REAL SECTOR

The monetary system—functions of money, demand and supply of money, velocity of circulation of money, central and commercial banks—plays an important role in any economy. The entire monetary system is discussed in Chapters 14 and 15. Chapter 14 analyses the monetary system excluding the banking sector (covered in Chapter 15). Chapter 15 discusses, in details, functions of the central bank, the commercial banks and different monetary instruments of credit control. Roles of the central bank in developing economies like India has also been highlighted. Chapters 16 and 17 deal with integration of the monetary and real sector (income, consumption savings, investment) which is a very important aspect of macroeconomic analysis. Integration of monetary and real sectors shows simultaneous determination of income and the rate of interest through IS-LM analysis.

Chapter 14

Money: Definition, Demand, Supply

Almost all of us make use of money in our daily lives. We know that money consists of coins and currency notes. But economic interpretation of money is something more than this. We apparently know why we want money. But we should clearly know the economic motives for demanding or holding money. We should also know what constitutes money supply and what is the relationship between the supply of money and the price level. We shall discuss here these and related matters.

DEFINITION OF MONEY

In the economic sense, money means more than the coins and currencies people hold. Coins are issued by the government. Currency notes are issued by the central bank (Reserve Bank of India in case of India) of the country. Both coins and currencies, as we all know, are of different denominations.

In addition to coins and currency notes, money, in the economic sense, also includes demand deposits in commercial banks. Demand deposits in banks are also considered as money, because, whenever we issue a cheque on demand deposits (current accounts and savings accounts), the cheque is payable immediately on demand. Demand deposits are, therefore, considered almost as good as cash. Money consisting of currency with the public (coins and currency notes) and demand deposits in banks is generally expressed in symbols as M_1.

But M_1 is considered to be money narrowly defined. Money, broadly defined, should also include time deposits in banks. Time deposits are deposits kept for a fixed period in banks. Such deposits include fixed deposits, special term deposits, etc. One cannot draw cheques on these deposits. But these can be converted into cash at short notice, sometimes at very short notice. It is, therefore, felt that such deposits should also be considered money. Money, broadly defined, which includes time deposits also is symbolised as M_2 and including other deposits is denoted as M_3.[1]

FUNCTIONS OF MONEY

Money performs four important functions. First, and the most important, is its function as a medium of exchange. In earlier times, there was barter system. In the barter system, commodities

1. Some economists feel that, in addition to M_2 money should also include all interest-bearing assets which can be ultimately converted into cash. M_2 plus all interest-bearing assets together constitute total monetary resources of a country and may be designated as M_3.

used to be exchanged for commodities. But various problems of working with the barter system gave rise to the need for a common medium of exchange, and this led to the introduction of money. In the present monetary system which has been adopted by all countries of the world, money is the common medium of exchange. All goods and services can be exchanged for money and vice versa.

The fact that money acts as a medium of exchange also implies that it is a measure of value of goods and services. This is the second important function of money. All goods and services are expressed in terms of money and their value is measured in monetary units. As soon as a monetary unit (such as a rupee, a dollar or a pound) is adopted by the country, the value of each commodity and service is expressed as a *price* which indicates the number of money units for which, it will exchange or sell.

But, in order to measure something, there must be a unit of account in terms of which the value may be expressed; and, this brings us to the third important function of money, that is, its role as a standard of measure or unit of account. The rupee in our system is the common unit of account—the numeraire. When we say a book is worth ₹ 10, we have a measure of value in terms of the basic unit of account which is the rupee.

It would be clear, then, that the three functions of money, viz., to act as a medium of exchange, a measure of value, and, a unit of account, are closely interrelated.

The fourth important function of money is its role as a store of value. Because of its general acceptability as a medium of exchange, one can preserve his wealth or savings in the form of money; and, the same can be utilised at a future date either to buy goods or services or to acquire assets.

Money, however, is not the only form in which wealth may be preserved. Wealth or savings may be preserved in the form of various assets (government bonds, shares, debentures, etc.) also. And some of these assets are close substitutes for money as a form of store of value. Consequently, money has to compete with many of these assets and the proportion in which money is held in relation to the assets depends on the relative advantages and disadvantages in terms of returns, risks, etc.

DEMAND FOR MONEY[2]

There are three kinds of demand for money or motives for holding money, namely the transactions demand, the precautionary demand, and, the speculative demand.

The transactions demand for money arises from the function of money as a medium of exchange. Because money is used as a medium of exchange or method of payment people require to hold money for the purchase of goods and services. *Holding* of money is necessary because purchase of goods do not synchronise with receipt of income. Income may be received in the beginning of the month, but purchases may be made throughout the month and, in future also out of the same income. Holding of some money balances is, therefore, necessary, and this is the transactions demand for money.

The transactions demand for money is closely related to the level of income. This can be illustrated by an example. A family with an income of ₹ 5,000 per month can and is likely to make more transactions (purchases) involving larger amounts of money than a family with an income of ₹ 3,000 per month; accordingly, its demand for transaction balances will be higher. The household which keeps transactions money balances of

2. Demand for money implies holding of money in M_1 sense, i.e. cash and demand deposits.

₹ 1,000 when its monthly income is ₹ 5,000 may hold transaction balances of ₹ 1,200 if its monthly income increases to ₹ 6,000. The relationship between transactions demand for money and income may be algebraically shown as

$$L_T = kY^{*,**}$$

where L_T represents transactions demand, k the proportion of income which is kept as transaction balances, and, Y the income. The equation is illustrated graphically in Fig. 14.1.

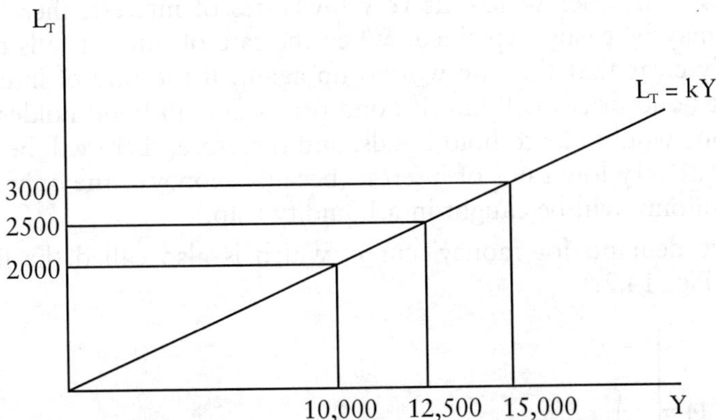

Fig. 14.1: Transactions Demand for Money

A second reason for holding money is to guard against contingencies. There is always the possibility that an unexpected need to incur expenditures may arise and, since, expected future income can never be known with certainty, or will occur with some time lag, there is a precautionary motive for holding money. As with the transactions demand, the demand for precautionary balances will depend on the level of income and will be generally interest-inelastic. At very high rates of interest, however, the demand for precautionary cash balances may fall as individuals and business firms may be tempted by high returns on investment in assets. The precautionary demand for money, therefore, is nothing more than a variant of the transactions demand for money, and the total of transactions-precautionary demand for money may be represented by the same equation as for transactions demand for money ($L_T = kY$) and, by the same Fig. 14.1, except that the value of k in transactions-precautionary demand will be higher than in the case of transactions demand alone.

Transactions-precautionary demand does not explain the existence of all money balances in the economy. Individuals and business firms do hold money in excess of transactions-precautionary requirements. The demand for money in excess of transactions-precautionary needs is called the speculative demand for money.[3]

The essence of the speculative demand for money is that the investor's expectations of future changes in the rate of interest create expectations about future capital gains and losses and give rise to changes in the demand for money. A current fall in the rate of interest creates expectations of a future increase while a current increase in the rate of interest creates expectations of a future fall. If the interest rate rises, investors switch over from money to bonds because they expect a future decline in the interest rate and a possible capital gain. Conversely, if the interest rate falls, investors switch over from bonds to money because they expect a future rise in the interest

3. The speculative demand for money is a Keynesian concept and signifies the difference between the classical theory and the Keynesian theory of demand for money.

rate and a possible capital loss. This shows that the speculative demand for money increases as the rate of interest falls and vice versa. The relationship between the speculative demand for money and the rate of interest may be shown as

$$L_s = L_s(i)$$

where L_s is speculative demand for money and i is the rate of interest.

It is often argued that speculative demand for money becomes perfectly elastic at very low rates of interest.[4] In other words, at very low rates of interest, there is a *liquidity trap.* The liquidity trap may be easily explained. When the rate of interest falls to a very low level, it becomes perfectly clear that the rate will go up again. If the rate of interest is sure to rise, then it follows that bond prices will fall. If bond prices fall, all bond holders will incur capital losses. Hence, no one would like to hold bonds, and therefore, there will be an infinitely elastic demand for money at very low rates of interest (because money is the only close substitute for bonds) and, the economy will be caught in a liquidity trap.[5]

The 'speculative demand for money' curve, which is also called the liquidity preference curve, is shown in Fig. 14.2.[6]

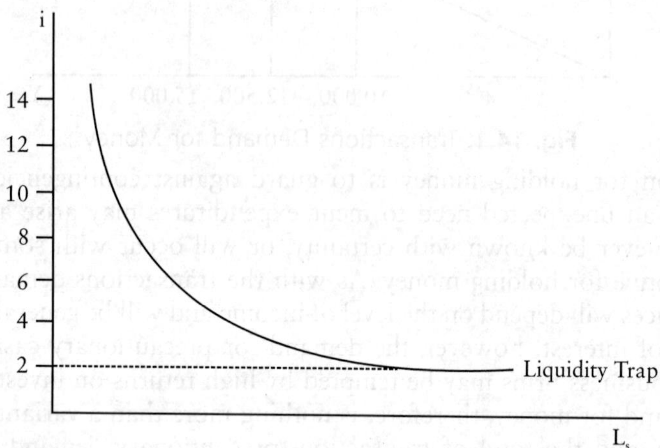

Fig. 14.2: Speculative Demand for Money or the Liquidity Preference Curve

We can put together the transactions-precautionary demand for money and speculative demand for money to determine the total demand for money. Total demand for money may be written as

$$L = L_T + L_s$$
$$L = L_T(Y) + L_s(i)$$
$$L = L\ (Y, i)$$

where L represents total demand for money. The relationship between total demand for money, income and the rate of interest is illustrated graphically in Fig. 14.3.

4. For perfect elasticity, the percentage change in the dependent variable divided by percentage change in the independent variable becomes infinite.
5. This is the reason why the curve representing speculative demand for money is also called the liquidity preference curve.
6. In Fig. 14.2, at 2 per cent rate of interest there is liquidity trap.

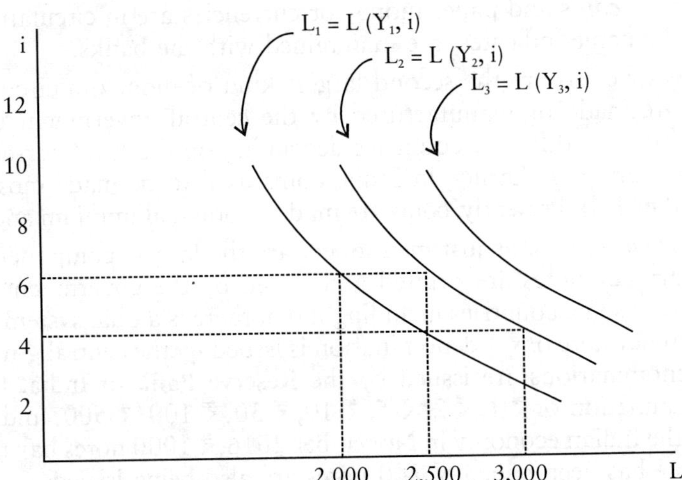

Fig. 14.3: Total Demand for Money

In Fig. 14.3, curve L_1 represents a hypothetical total demand for money where income (Y_1) = ₹ 10,000. It shows that at ₹ 10,000, level of national income, demand for money would be ₹ 2,500 at 4 per cent rate of interest; but the demand would be ₹ 2,000 at 6 per cent rate of interest. If the level of income, increases to Y_2 (= ₹ 12,500), at 4 per cent rate, demand for money would be ₹ 3,000, and, at 6 per cent rate, demand for money would be ₹ 2,500 (shown by curve L_2); both demand levels are substantially higher than for comparable interest rates at the lower income level. This reflects the fact that the transactions-precautionary component of total demand for money increases with income. Curve L_3 represents demand for money when the income level is Y_3 = ₹ 20,000. It should be noted that the three curves tend to converge and flatten out at the extreme right. This is the Keynesian liquidity trap area.

Some empirical demand functions for money are discussed in the Appendix.

SUPPLY OF MONEY

Before we discuss the details of supply of money, we should introduce or understand the concept of money supply.

Concept of Money Supply

In simple terms, money supply in any country/economy refers to *total stock of money held by the public at any point of time.*

This simple definition requires some clarification or explanation. First, money supply indicates total sum of money at a *particular point of time*, that is, on a date. This means that money supply is a *stock* concept in contrast to output or national income which is a *flow* concept and measured per unit of time (normally yearly, half-yearly or quarterly). Second, money supply means stock of money *held by the public*. 'Public' stands for or includes individuals, families/ households, firms, and organisations other than banks and the government. Third, stock of money includes different kinds or types of money.

Total stock of money at any point of time primarily consists of three types:

1. Metallic money or coins
2. Paper money or currency
3. Bank deposits

Metallic money or coins and paper money or currencies are in circulation in the economy. Bank deposits, as the name indicates, are maintained with the banks.

Metallic money or coins are the second largest kind of money in circulation next only to currencies. Coins are made or manufactured by the central government units. Coins are of different denominations in different countries depending on the local currency. In India, coins are of ₹ 10, ₹ 5, ₹ 2 and ₹ 1. Earlier, in India, coins used to be made mostly of cupro-nickel (alloy of copper and nickel). Presently, coins are made of brass, aluminium and stainless steel (ss).

Paper money or currencies, as just mentioned, are the largest component of money supply in any country. Currency notes are printed and issued by the government and/or the central bank of the country. In some countries including India, there is a dual system of issuing currency notes. In India, currency note of ₹ 1 denomination is issued by the central government. Currency notes of higher denominations are issued by the Reserve Bank of India. Currency notes are commonly of denomination of ₹ 1, ₹ 2, ₹ 5, ₹ 10, ₹ 50, ₹ 100, ₹ 500, and ₹ 1000. But, after demonetisation of the Indian economy in November 2016, ₹ 1000 notes have been discontinued. Instead, ₹ 2000 note has been issued. ₹ 200 notes are also being issued.

Bank deposits, as the name indicates, are not in circulation. Those are kept with the banks. Bank deposits can be of three types: savings account deposits, current account deposits and time deposits. Time deposits can again be of two types: term deposit or fixed deposit and recurring deposit. Recurving deposits are not very common. Savings account deposits and current account deposits are almost as liquid as cash because these can be withdrawn instantly and cheques can also be issued for payment against these deposits. That is why these deposits are also known as *demand deposits*.

Measurement of Money Supply

The concept of money supply leads us to measurement of money supply. Also, in the definition of money given in the beginning of the chapter, we had mentioned about M_1, M_2 and M_3. These indicate that different measures of money supply are conceivable or possible. Different measures of money supply are also relevant or necessary because of different functions of money.

Four measures of money supply can be distinguished:

1. Money supply M_1
2. Money supply M_2
3. Money supply M_3
4. Money supply M_4

Money Supply M_1: This is also called *narrow money*. This consists of money with the public or in circulation, i.e., coins and currency notes, and, demand deposits with banks, i.e., current account deposits and savings account deposits. M_1 also includes other deposits by the public with the central bank. So,

M_1 = Money with the public (coins and currency notes) + demand deposits with banks + other deposits with the central bank

Money Supply M_2: This consists of three components of money supply mentioned above and savings accounts with post offices. So,

$M_2 = M_1$ + savings deposits with post offices

Money Supply M_3: This is also known as *broad money*. This consists of three components of money supply mentioned under M_1 and time deposits with banks. So,

$M_3 = M_1$ + time deposits with banks

Money Supply M_4: This is an extended concept and measure of money supply. This consists of all components of money supply under M_3 and total deposits with post office savings organisation. This includes time deposits in post offices like the Senior Citizen Savings Scheme, 2004 in India. So,

$M_4 = M_3$ + total deposits with the post office savings organisation

The four measures of money supply are prevalent in some countries including few developed countries. The Reserve Bank of India adopted these four measures since April 1977. M_1 and M_3 measures of money supply are, however, predominant and quantitatively more significant.

Different measures of money supply have some important economic or financial implications. For example, if M_1 is increasing, it means that people are spending more money for transactions or consumption. How much more people are spending will depend on the rate at which M_1 is increasing. But, in any case, this will have some effect on the propensity to consume. If, on the other hand, time deposits in M_3 are increasing, this indicates that people are tending to save more and consume less, and, this is likely to have impact on the propensity to save. This shows that changes in money supply or stock of M_1 and stock of M_3 are likely to affect or alter the consumption-savings balance in the economy. These have implications for the policy makers. So, different measures of money supply have significance for monetary policy formulation by the central bank and the government for macroeconomic management of the country.

Supply of money at any point of time, or changes in money supply are generally determined by the monetary authorities—commonly the central bank of the country. The size of the currency component is not directly under the control of the monetary authorities and is largely determined by the choice the public makes between bank deposits and cash balances. However, the relationship between deposits and cash generally remains constant so that any action by the monetary authorities to regulate bank deposits usually has a corresponding effect on the currency component. But, balance cannot be, or is not, always maintained. That is where the role of policy makers come in.

MONEY MULTIPLIER

Money multiplier is an important concept and tool in analysis of money supply. Let us understand the meaning, estimation and effect of this on money supply.

Money multiplier is defined and estimated as the rate at which high-power money gets multiplied to determine total money supply.

Let us explain 'high-power' money and clarify total money supply M. Let us first define M. *M approximates M_1*. More precisely, M is equal to currency (notes and coins) with the public plus demand deposits with the banks, that is,

$$M = C + D$$

where C is currency with the public and D is demand deposits with the banks.

High-power money (H) is defined and estimated as

$$H = C + R$$

where C is currency with the public and R is cash or currency reserves maintained by banks as certain ratio to their deposits

The money multiplier is conventionally denoted by m. Let us work out the money multiplier. By definition of money multiplier

$$M = m\,H$$

or, $m = M/H$

We know that $M = C + D$ and $H = C + R$

$$\therefore M/H = C{+}D/C{+}R$$

Dividing both the numerator and denominator by D, we get

$$\frac{M/D}{H/D} = \frac{C+D/D}{C+R/D}$$

or, $M/H = C/D{+}1/C/D{+}R/D$

C/D is currency-deposit ratio and R/D is reserve-deposit ratio. We can denote C/D by c and R/D by r. Then the money multiplier m is written as

$$m = M/H = 1{+}c/c{+}r$$

or, $m = 1{+}c/c{+}r$

So, *the two determinants of money multiplier are currency deposit ratio and reserve-deposit ratio. The value or size of the money multiplier depends on these two factors.*

The money multiplier (m), currency-deposit ratio (c) and reserve-deposit ratio (r) are all positive; m is > 1 and c and r are each < 1. If c = 1 and r = 1, m = 1. This, however, is a purely theoretical possibility.

Let us illustrate the money multiplier with a numerical example. If we assume that, in a country, c = 0.3 and, r = 0.05, then the money multiplier m is equal to

$$m = 1{+}c/c{+}r$$

or, $m = 1{+}0.3/0.3{+}0.05$

or, $m = 1.3/0.35$

or, $m = 3.7$ (approx)

So, in a country, given the amount of high-power money, and, currency-deposit ratio of 0.3 and reserve-deposit ratio of 0.05, total money supply (M) will be 3.7 times of high-power money (H). In India, the money multiplier varies approximately between 4 and 4.5.

Determinants of Money Supply

Analysis of money multiplier shows that determinants of money supply are three:

(a) High-power money
(b) Currency-deposit ratio
(c) Reserve-deposit ratio

Money supply varies directly with high-power money and inversely with currency-deposit ratio and reserve-deposit ratio. Lower the currency-deposit ratio or reserve-deposit ratio, and, given certain value of high-power money, more will be the money supply. Similarly, given the currency-deposit ratio and the reserve-deposit ratio, more the high-power money, more will be the money supply. If the currency-deposit ratio and/or the reserve-deposit ratio decrease and high-power money increases simultaneously, higher will be the money supply.

VELOCITY OF CIRCULATION OF MONEY

A concept closely related to money supply is the velocity of circulation of money. In understanding the functioning of the monetary system, it is important to understand this concept or element. Let us explain this concept with an example. If a person purchases a book and pays ₹ 100 in exchange, the hundred rupee note passes from the hands of the buyer to the bookseller. If the bookseller uses that currency note for buying groceries worth ₹ 100, it passes from the bookseller to the grocer. The total value of transactions completed with the aid of the currency note is ₹ 200. Thus, the currency note of ₹ 100 by passing hands twice has been able to fulfil transactions worth ₹ 200. This means that the velocity of circulation of money in this case is 2. The velocity of circulation of money may, therefore, be defined as the *number of times money changes hands*. The supply of money *over a period of time* is equal to the amount of (stock) of money multiplied by its velocity of circulation.

Money is used not only for buying and selling of goods and services, but also for borrowing and lending. To calculate the velocity of circulation of money, we should know the total value of all these transactions. But this is difficult to obtain. Therefore, for practical purposes, we divide national income by total money supply to obtain what is known as income velocity of circulation of money. In India, income velocity of circulation of money is currently estimated to be about 5.0.

QUANTITY THEORY OF MONEY

During any period of time, total value of transactions must be equal to the total value of money exchanged. Total value of all transactions will be equal to the total value of goods and services traded (T) multiplied by their average price (P). Total value of all monetary payments during any period will be equal to the amount of money (M) multiplied by its velocity of circulation (V). Thus, by equating what is paid with what is received, we get $MV = PT$. This is known as the equation of exchange. The equation of exchange is a truism, that is, it holds good under all circumstances.

The quantity theory of money is derived from the equation of exchange with the help of certain assumptions. The quantity theory assumes that in the equation of exchange V and T remain constant. Then, it follows as the quantity theory argues, that a change in M will lead to a proportionate change in P. This is the cash transactions approach to the quantity theory of money.[7]

A second approach to the quantity theory is the cash balance approach.[8] The cash balance approach rests on the assumption that people desire to hold a fixed proportion of their income in the form of money. The cash balance equation may be written as

$$K = M/YP$$

where M is the stock of money, Y is real national income, P the price level, and, K the proportion of income to be held as money assumed to be constant. If, in addition, Y is also assumed to remain constant, it follows from the equation that a change in M must lead to a proportionate change in P.

It can be shown, with some manipulation, that the cash balance approach to quantity theory is not different from the cash transactions approach. The cash balance approach can be written as

$$M = K \times Y \times P$$

7. The cash-transactions approach to the quantity theory of money, which is also sometimes known as Fisher's Equation, is associated with the name of Irving Fisher and others. Refer Irving Fisher, *The Purchasing Power of Money*, 1926.
8. The cash balance approach to the quantity theory, also known as the Cambridge Approach, is associated with the names of the Cambridge economists Alfred Marshall, A.C. Pigou, D.H. Robertson and J.M. Keynes.

The transactions approach also may be rewritten as

$$M = PY/V$$

By comparing the two equations, we find that K = 1/V. This should be so because when people desire to hold a larger proportion of income in the form of money, the velocity of circulation decreases. So, the cash balance approach to the quantity theory of money does not differ in substance from the transactions approach.

Uses of the Quantity Theory

To analyse the usefulness of the quantity theory of money, we shall consider the cash transactions approach of the quantity theory which is also known as the classical quantity theory of money. The quantity theory has important implications for macroeconomic theory. Specifically speaking, the quantity theory implies or contributes to two important macroeconomic theories:

(a) Theory of price level

(b) Theory of demand for money

Theory of Price Level: The quantity theory mentioned above is of the form

$$MV = PT$$

where M is the quantity of money in circulation

If we include bank deposits, i.e. demand deposits (which can be withdrawn or transferred by cheque) in money supply, the quantity theory may be modified or expanded as

$$MV + M'V' = PT \tag{14.1}$$

where M' is bank deposits (demand deposits) and V' is the velocity of their circulation

Equation (14.1) may be rewritten as

$$\frac{MV + M'V'}{T} = P$$

or, $$P = \frac{MV + M'V'}{T} \tag{14.2}$$

Equation (14.2) shows that, if V, V' and T are constants (assumed in the quantity theory), P varies directly or proportionately with M and M', i.e., changes in supply of money. In other words, the quantity theory establishes that *the quantity of money determines, ceteris paribus, the general price level*. To put it in the words of Fisher. "The mechanism makes clear the fact that the average price increases with the increases of money or bank deposits and with the increase in the volume of trade."[9]

Theory of Demand for Money: The theory of demand for money is not explicitly stated in the classical quantity theory of money. But, this is implicit and can be derived from the quantity theory. It can be derived or established that demand for money, in equilibrium, is equal to supply of money. As Laidler has stated: "The demand for money depends on the value of transactions to be undertaken in the economy and is equal to a constant fraction of those transactions," and, "in equilibrium, the demand for money must be equal to its supply."[10]

9. Irving Fisher, *The Purchasing Power of Money*, 1926, p. 9.
10. D.E.W. Laidler, *The Demand for Money: Theories and Evidence*, Monetary Economics Series, Allied Publishers, 1972, p. 45.

To show this, let us start with the basic quantity theory of money

$$MV = PT$$

or, we can write

$$M\overline{V} = P\overline{T} \quad (14.3)$$

where $\overline{V}$ and $\overline{T}$ are constants.

We can call Equation (14.3) an equilibrium equation

From Equation (14.3), we get

$$M = \frac{1}{\overline{V}} . P\overline{T} \quad (14.4)$$

We know that in equilibrium, demand for money (*Md*) is equal to supply of money (*Ms*). In Equation (14.4), *M* can be taken as *Ms* and $\left(\frac{1}{\overline{V}} PT\right)$ as *Md*.

If follows from Equation (14.4) that, in equilibrium, demand for money is a fraction $(1/\overline{V})$ of the total value of transactions, i.e., $P\overline{T}$. It should be noted that $(1/\overline{V})$ is the inverse of the velocity of circulation of money. This means that, at any point of time, *the amount of money demanded is determined by the inverse of the velocity of circulation of money* given P and $\overline{T}$.

If we denote $(1/\overline{V})$ by K, the demand for money derived from the quantity theory can be expressed, in a more simplified form, as

$$Md = K.P\overline{T}$$

where Md = demand for cash balance.

Criticism of the Quantity Theory

The quantity theory of money has been subject to criticism on both theoretical and empirical grounds. The assumption that velocity (or the inverse of velocity) is constant has been disputed. Historically, in the developed countries, velocity has shown a tendency to decline. It has also been varying according to the phase of the business cycle. During periods of hyper-inflation, people lose so much faith in money that they do not like to hold it at all. This results in a sharp increase in the velocity of circulation.

The assumption that output (T or Y) remains constant is also subject to criticism. An increase in money supply is likely to lead to an increase in demand for goods and services through an increase in purchasing power of the people; this, in turn, is likely to lead to an increase in output. It is, therefore, not correct to assume that output will not change.

Analytically, the chief weakness of the quantity theory of money is that it does not explain how an increase in the quantity of money leads to an increase in the price level. The explanation implicit in the quantity theory seems to be that an increase in M leads to an increase in aggregate monetary demand. With output remaining constant, this should result in an increase in the price level.

Since its formulation, there have been many modifications of the quantity theory of money. Most of the economists today do not adhere to the rigid statement of a proportionate increase in the price level corresponding to an increase in money supply. But, if the assumption of constancy of V is abandoned, then, a new exposition is required to explain the behaviour of velocity. Many such attempts have been made recently.

REVIEW QUESTIONS

1. Define money in terms of different components.
2. Explain demand for money—transactions demand, precautionary demand and speculative demand using equations.
3. Explain the concept of money supply.
4. Which are the different measurements of money supply? Comment on them.
5. What is 'Money Multiplier'? Explain and illustrate.
6. What is the quantity theory of money? Explain the cash balance approach.

SUGGESTED READINGS

- P.A. Samuelson and W.D. Nordhaus, *Economics*, Seventeenth Edition, Tata McGraw-Hill, 2003.
- R.A.M. Bilas and F.J. Alessio, *Essentials of Macroeconomic Analysis*, 1995, Chapter 8.
- S.B. Gupta, *Monetary Economics*, S. Chand & Company, 1995.

APPENDIX

SOME EMPIRICAL DEMAND FUNCTIONS FOR MONEY

Theoretical discussion of the demand for money in the text raises a number of empirical questions like: how sensitive is the demand for money to changes in the level of national income? How sensitive is demand for money to changes in the rate of interest? Is there a liquidity trap in the real world?

There are several statistical studies of the demand for money in economic literature. Most of these studies have tried to determine how strongly demand for money is correlated to changes in interest rates and national income, and, have used the regression analysis to do so.

One such study used time series data for the period 1900 to 1958 to estimate the regression equation

$$\ln Md = a - 0.95 \ln i + 1.11 \ln Y$$

$$R = 0.99$$

where ln Md represents the log—to the natural base e—of the demand for money, ln i stands for the log—to the national base e—of national income and R is the coefficient of correlation.

The above equation suggests that every 10 per cent change in the interest rate (for example, a change from 5 to 5.5 per cent) produced a 9.5 per cent change in the demand for money over the period 1900-58. (A rise in the interest rate by 10 per cent led to a fall in the demand for money by 9.5 per cent.) The equation also suggests that each 10 per cent change in the level of national income produces an 11 per cent change in the demand for money over the same period. (An increase in national income by 10 per cent led to an increase in the demand for money by 11 per cent.) Finally, the equation implies—through the correlation coefficient—that 97 per cent of the variation in the total demand for money over the period 1900-58 was due to variations in the level of interest rates and national income.

It follows, then, that the demand for money function developed in the text appears to have enough statistical validity: the demand for money is primarily determined by the rate of interest and national income with the demand for money falling as the interest rate rises and rising as national income increases.

Another study—using interest rate as the only independent variable in the demand for money function—was conducted for the period 1909-58, and, established the regression equation

$$Md/Y = a + 0.08(1/i)$$

$$R = 0.91$$

where Md/Y represents the proportion of national income held as idle cash balances, i stands for the rate of interest, add R, the coefficient of correlation.

The equation indicates that the interest elasticity of demand for money function is higher at low interest rates, and lower, at high interest rates, but never perfectly elastic. In other words, it means that the curve representing the total demand for money function becomes flatter as the rate of interest declines.

We may, therefore, conclude that the theoretical demand functions developed by us during our discussion of demand for money in the text appear to be generally valid except that the liquidity trap has not been empirically established.

Chapter 15

Monetary and Credit System: Commercial and Central Banking

In understanding the functioning of the monetary system, it is necessary to understand not only the nature and functions of money, but also the role credit plays in the economic system. And, related to the role of credit are various credit institutions of which commercial banks are the foremost, next, however, to the central bank which is the apex monetary institution in any country. We shall discuss here the concept of credit, the role of commercial banks with particular reference to credit creation and expansion, and the functions of the central bank including its role in formulating and implementing various monetary controls.

MONEY AND CREDIT

Money and credit are related concepts. Credit means borrowing and lending of money. Every credit involves a commitment to pay money, and, therefore, creates a claim. Thus, the instrument of credit has given rise to various money lending or credit institutions. There are various kinds of institutions which specialise in borrowing and lending. Credit institutions differ according to the type of credit being made available by them. There are institutions which lend exclusively to agriculture. There are others which provide credit to industry alone. Credit institutions may also be differentiated according to whether they provide short-term or long-term credit.

The commercial banking system is the most important segment of the entire credit system of a country. Commercial banks are similar to other credit or financial institutions so far as borrowing and lending operations are concerned. But there is a very important difference between commercial banks and other credit institutions which are generally called financial intermediaries.[1] The difference is that while commercial banks can create credit (we shall soon see how they do this), other financial institutions cannot do it.

COMMERCIAL BANKS

The primary function of commercial banks, like all financial intermediaries, is to mobilise surplus funds in the country and lend the same to various kinds of borrowers.

In this process, banks earn their income. Banks earn some income by providing services—remittance facilities, encashment of cheques, safe deposit lockers, etc., to their customers. But the bulk—over 75 per cent—of income of commercial banks is earned from interest on loans

1. Various credit institutions are called financial intermediaries because they act as an intermediary between the savers and the investors. They borrow surplus funds of the public, private and governmental bodies and transfer or lend the same to the prospective investors without being able to create or generate credit.

and advances. The commercial banks are able to use depositors' money in this productive or profitable manner because, on any normal working day, the difference between total deposits and withdrawals is likely to be either very close to zero or the deposits may marginally exceed the withdrawals.

In order to meet those rare days when withdrawals exceed deposits, the banks keep cash reserves equal to a certain fraction or percentage of their total deposit liabilities. This fraction is called the Cash Reserve Ratio (CRR) or the Reserve Ratio. It is essential for a bank to maintain the ratio or otherwise, it may not be able to meet the withdrawal demand of all its depositors, and, failure to do so may eventually result in failure of the bank. The cash reserve ratio in India generally varies between 10 and 11 per cent.

Besides the cash reserve ratio, the commercial banks are also required to maintain a certain Net Liquidity Ratio (NLR) which is determined by the central bank. NLR is defined as the ratio of a bank's net liquid assets comprising cash in hand, balances with the central bank of the country, balances in current account with other banks, and, all investments in government and other approved securities minus a bank's total borrowings from the central bank and other sources[2] to its total deposit liabilities. The net liquidity ratio in India fluctuates around 30 per cent.

MULTIPLE EXPANSION OF DEPOSITS

One of the most distinguishing functions of the commercial banks is creation of credit which finally leads to multiple credit expansion. We shall discuss this phenomenon now.

Let us suppose that an individual, X, who is a government employee, receives a pay cheque of ₹ 3,000. The cheques issued by the government are drawn on the Reserve Bank of India. We assume that X deposits this cheque in his account in Bank A. The bank then presents the cheque to the Reserve Bank of India and collects cash. As a result of this transaction, the deposits of Bank A will go up by ₹ 3,000 and its cash will also increase by ₹ 3,000. The balance sheet of Bank A will now appear as shown below.

Balance Sheet of Bank A

Liabilities		*Assets*	
Deposit (of X)	+3,000	Cash	+3,000
	+3,000		+3,000

Let us assume that Bank A has found by experience that only 10 per cent of this deposit will be demanded by X in the form of cash. This means that Bank A can lend ₹ 2,700 out of this deposit of ₹ 3,000. The bank can lend in two ways. It can either allow the borrower, if he has an account with the bank already, to overdraw on his account or open an account in the name of the borrower to the extent of the loan taken if he is a new customer. Hence, the maxim *every loan creates a deposit*. We assume that Bank A grants a loan of ₹ 900 to Y and thereby opens an account in his favour. Then, the balance sheet of Bank A will appear as follows.

Balance Sheet of Bank A

Liabilities		*Assets*	
Deposit (of X)	+ 3,000	Cash	+ 3,000
Deposit (of Y)	+2,700	Loan	+2,700
	+5,700		+5,700

2. Other sources in India are State Bank of India and Industrial Development Bank of India (IDBI).

This can only be a temporary situation because no one borrows from a bank just to maintain an account. He borrows to utilise the money. Let Y who has taken the loan from Bank A issue a cheque to Z from whom he has bought goods. Let Z deposit this cheque in his account in Bank B. At this point, the balance sheets of Banks A and B will appear as shown below:

Balance Sheet of Bank A

Liabilities		*Assets*	
		Cash	+ 300
Deposit (of X)	+3,000	Loan	+2,700
	+3,000		+3,000

Balance Sheet of Bank B

Liabilities		*Assets*	
Deposit	+2,700	Cash	+2,700
	+5,700		+5,700

The cash of Bank B goes up because it has collected the cash from Bank A. Thus, we see that deposits in the banking system now become (+) ₹ 5,700.

Bank B which has a deposit of ₹ 2,700 and cash of ₹ 2,700 may react to the situation in the same way as was done by Bank A. If Bank B also finds by experience that only 10 per cent of the deposits needs to be kept in the form of cash, it can grant a loan of ₹ 2,430. If the borrower of Bank B draws a cheque of ₹ 2,430 and this cheque is deposited with Bank C, cash of Bank B will go down by ₹ 2,430, and that of Bank C will go up by ₹ 2,430. Bank deposits have now increased by another ₹ 2,430.

Bank C, if it needs to keep only 10 per cent of the deposit in the form of cash, will be in a position to lend ₹ 2,187 which will become the deposit in the next bank. Thus, at each successive stage, every bank which receives deposits from the previous bank, will be able to lend 90 per cent of the deposits. In this way, total increase in deposits will be

$$3{,}000 + 2{,}700 + 2{,}430 + 2{,}187 + \ldots$$

The sum of this series will be equal to[3]

$$3{,}000/0.10 = 30{,}000$$

Thus, with an initial increase of deposits of ₹ 3,000, the banking system has been in a position to create a total deposit of ₹ 30,000 which is 10 times the initial increase in deposits, even though each bank lends only 90 per cent of the deposits it receives.[4,5] There are three limits to the banks' capacity to create deposits. First, is the amount of cash the banks have to maintain against the deposits—the larger the proportion of deposits to be kept in the form of cash (the cash reserve ratio), the smaller is the secondary expansion.

3. This is an infinite geometric series and the sum, S, of an infinite geometric series is expressed as $S = a/1 - r$ where a is the first term and r the common ratio.
4. This is based on the assumption that the cash reserve ratio is 10 per cent; if the reserve ratio is lower, total credit creation will be higher, and if the reserve ratio is higher, total credit creation will be smaller.
5. The above account of multiple expansion of deposits shows that bank deposits are created in two ways. First, deposits are created through customers depositing money. Second, deposits are created through the process of lending. Deposits created through deposit of money by customers are called 'passively created deposits' and deposits created through the process of lending are called 'actively created deposits'; these are also referred to as 'primary deposits' and 'secondary deposits' respectively.

The second limit on deposit expansion is set by the cash drain or cash leakage. In describing the process of multiple expansion of deposits, we had assumed that neither the borrower from a bank nor the person to whom the borrower pays requires any cash. The entire amount of loan is assumed to be re-deposited in another bank. This is not a realistic assumption. Borrowers may like to take out a percentage of the loan in the form of cash or the person(s) to whom the borrower pays may like to do so. The desire of the depositors at each stage to withdraw cash is referred to as cash drain or cash leakage.

The larger the cash leakage, the smaller will be the secondary expansion of credit.[6]

The third limit to multiple credit expansion may be imposed by lack of enough borrowers. In the examples given above, it has been assumed that banks can lend to the full extent of the excess reserves. There may be occasions when banks may not find enough borrowers. This may be a rather unusual situation. Nevertheless, the possibility exists, and, therefore, the opportunity for lending may also set a limit to the banks' ability to expand deposits.

FUNCTIONS OF CENTRAL BANK

The most important function of the central bank is to regulate money supply and credit in the country. But, besides credit control, the central bank performs four other important functions. These are: (i) issue of currency notes, (ii) banker to the government, (iii) bankers' bank, and (iv) lender of last resort. We shall discuss these four functions first, and then, discuss at length, the various instruments of credit control.

In today's monetary system, the central bank has the monopoly power to issue currency notes.[7] This has been found necessary, both to prevent malpractices and to regulate the total volume of money supply. In most countries, the power to issue notes is subject to certain statutory regulations.

One of the systems of note issue is known as the proportional reserve system. Under this system, the central bank of a country is required to maintain a certain percentage of the notes issued in the form of gold and foreign exchange securities. The rest of the note issue could be backed by domestic securities. In India, the proportional reserve system was in operation for some years and, the Reserve Bank of India was required to keep 40 per cent of the notes issued in the form of gold and foreign exchange securities. Since 1956, this system has been abolished.

The Reserve Bank of India is now required to maintain only a minimum value of gold and foreign exchange securities. Experience has shown that it is better to leave the amount of notes to be issued to the discretion of the central bank than to regulate it through such statutory restrictions.

The central bank usually acts as a banker to the government. Besides maintaining the deposit accounts of the government, the central bank also helps the government in floating public loans and advises the government on when the latter should enter the market for floating the loan. The central bank also manages public debt by taking the responsibility of redeeming the securities at the time of maturity or converting one security into another.

6. The extent of cash drain or cash leakage depends very much upon the popularity of the cheque system. The more widespread the use of cheques in a society, the less the amount of cash that will be withdrawn. Cash leakage in a country like India is much higher than in a country like the United States. This is reflected in the ratio of currency to demand deposits. This ratio for India is 1 : 1 as compared to 1 : 3 in the United States.
7. In India, except for the issue of one rupee notes, the Reserve Bank of India has the monopoly power to issue notes.

The central bank of a country also performs the function of being a bank to the bankers. All the commercial banks maintain accounts with the central bank. This facilitates settlement of claims among banks.

The central bank of the country usually plays the role of a clearing house. At the clearing house, the claims of banks are settled among themselves. The settlement can be done easily when the banks maintain accounts with the central bank. In this sense, the central bank plays the same role in relation to the commercial banks as the latter plays in relation to the general public. Another important service provided by a central bank in acting as a bankers' bank is remittance facilities at cheap rates.

It was mentioned earlier that the commercial banks operate on the fractional reserve system. Even the most well-managed bank can run into difficulties if there is a sudden rush of demand for funds. Therefore, the central bank of a country should be always willing to come to the assistance or rescue of commercial banks whenever they are in dire need of funds. In this case, the central bank plays the role of the lender of last resort. It is understood in such cases, that the central bank is convinced that these difficulties were not due to any fault of the banks, and that the banks' bad explored all other avenues of obtaining funds before approaching the central bank. One way to ensure this is to make the rate at which the central bank provides funds a penal rate. This, however, is not the universal practice. There are many countries, including India, where the bank rate (the rate at which the central bank provides finance to commercial banks) is not the highest rate prevailing in the market.

INSTRUMENTS OF CREDIT CONTROL

We have already mentioned that the most important function of the central bank is to control money supply and credit in the country. To control or regulate total volume of credit, the central bank uses a number of methods or instruments. These are called the instruments of credit control. The instruments of credit control can be broadly divided into two categories—general and selective. The general instruments are intended to regulate the total volume of credit. The selective instruments are used to regulate credit in a particular area or sector of the economy. The general instruments are also called *quantitative methods* and selective instruments *qualitative methods*. We shall first discuss the general instruments of credit control which are: (a) the bank rate, (b) open market operations, and (c) legal reserve ratio, and then, discuss the methods of selective credit control.

BANK RATE

Bank rate is the rate at which the central bank of a country provides finance to the commercial banks. This is also known as the discount rate, because, in the earlier days, the central banks used to provide financial assistance to commercial banks by rediscounting bills of exchange.

We shall explain how the bank rate operates as an instrument of credit control. When the bank rate is raised, the cost of borrowing by the commercial banks from the central bank goes up. This, in turn, leads to an increase in the lending rates of commercial banks. Increase in the lending rate may compel the borrowers of commercial banks to borrow less. The bank rate is usually raised when there is an inflationary situation in the country. Although the immediate effect of a rise in the bank rate is on the borrowings by the banks' customers, the final effect is expected to be on the price level through a decline in aggregate monetary expenditures. A fall in the bank rate similarly leads to a lowering of the lending rates of commercial banks which, in turn, leads to an expansion of bank credit. This expansion in bank credit may have the effect of raising income and output.

Changes in the bank rate may have some external effects also. Such effects, may, however, be relevant only to countries which allow free flow of funds into and out of the country. A rise in the bank rate has the general effect of raising all the rates in the market. A rise in deposit rate may attract funds from outside, and, also prevent outflow of funds. If this happens, it is likely to have a favourable effect on the balance of payments of the country.

The bank rate can be effective as an instrument of credit control only if certain conditions are fulfilled. First, for the bank rate to influence all other rates prevailing in the market, there should be a well-organised money market. Only in a well-organised (well-linked) money market, a change in one rate will produce similar changes in other rates in the market. Secondly, the working of the bank rate depends on the reaction of the borrowers to changes in the lending rates. Some empirical studies have shown that changes in interest rates do not always have strong influence on investment decisions. Unless interest rates are increased very sharply, they may not significantly affect the willingness to borrow. A rise or fall in the bank rate may not, then, produce the desired effects on output, expenditures and prices. Thirdly, the bank rate can become an effective instrument of credit control only if the commercial banks are in the habit of borrowing from the central bank. Only then can a rise or a fall in the bank rate affect the lending operations of the commercial banks. Finally, the bank rate may not be very effective as an instrument of credit control if availability of credit rather than cost of credit becomes the important factor in the credit market. The bank rate as an instrument of credit control operates by altering the cost of credit. Recent studies on the working of the bank rate have revealed that availability of credit itself is an important factor apart from cost of credit. If the central bank restricts the funds made available to commercial banks, it may be able to produce necessary effects on commercial bank credit. In such cases, cost of credit or bank rate does not become very important.

OPEN MARKET OPERATIONS

Open market operations involve purchase and sale of securities by the central bank. When the central bank buys securities, it pays the seller with a cheque drawn upon itself. When this cheque is deposited with a commercial bank, its reserves increase. Thus, purchase of securities by the central bank leads to an increase in bank reserves. An increase in bank reserves provides a basis for multiple expansion of bank credit. Similarly, sale of securities by the central bank has the effect of reducing bank reserves, and consequently leading to multiple contraction of credit.

Open market operations are considered a primary instrument of credit control in developed countries, but not so in developing economies. Open market operations do not play the role of an instrument of credit control in India. This is primarily because the government securities market in India is very narrow. The commercial banks, the Life Insurance Corporation, the General Insurance Corporation and the Provident Funds hold about 85 per cent of government securities. Also, the rate of interest offered on government securities is not very competitive. In such situations, any attempt to sell government securities is likely to have the effect of lowering the value of government securities which may not be desirable from many other points of view. Thus, sale of securities is almost ruled out because of a likely fall in prices. Open market operations have been employed by the Reserve Bank of India primarily to assist the government in the borrowing operations, and to maintain orderly conditions in the government securities market.

LEGAL RESERVE RATIO

Commercial banks are required to maintain a percentage of their deposits in the form of balances with the central bank. This is known as the legal reserve ratio. The central bank has the power to vary this ratio and thereby use it as an instrument of credit control. An increase in the legal reserve ratio will reduce the excess reserves available to a bank for lending. This will, therefore, have the effect of contracting credit. On the other hand, a lowering of the reserve ratio will enable banks to expand credit because the excess reserves will increase.

The variable reserve ratio may appear to be the easiest way to control credit, but it has its practical limitations. In many cases, the legal reserve ratio cannot be altered except by law. Besides, there is no reason why the member banks should always be strongly influenced by such a ratio. For example, if their cash reserves position is very good, they may not care so much for increase in the legal reserve ratio unless the increase is very high. The banks might also conduct their operations with a lower cash reserve ratio (cash to deposit ratio) if they are optimistic about the future. Likewise, a mere decrease in the legal reserve ratio during depression may not be enough inducement for banks to lend.

Besides these considerations, a counteracting force to effective operation of the legal reserves ratio may arise from a change in banking practices. It can be particularly true in countries like the United States where the percentages of legal reserves required to be kept differ for different kinds of deposits held by the banks. Thus, with a reserve ratio of 10 per cent required against demand deposits and 3 per cent required against time deposits, a shift of funds from the former to the latter would enable the member banks to expand credit and consequently disregard the policy of the central bank.

SELECTIVE CREDIT CONTROLS

Selective credit controls are used to regulate flow of credit to specific sectors or activities. Theoretically, they can be both positive and negative. The central bank can encourage the flow of credit to a particular sector or sectors by charging a rate of interest lower than the bank rate on the borrowings of commercial banks and other financial institutions meant for refinancing such operations. Selective credit controls are, however, primarily negative in character. They are generally intended to discourage activities which are regarded as inessential or undesirable.

Selective credit controls originated in the United States to regulate stock market credit. They have also been used during war time to restrict the flow of credit for buying durable consumption goods. In India, these controls have been used primarily to prevent speculative hoarding of commodities like food grains and other essential raw materials.

Selective credit controls, in general, are more effective when they are accompanied by general credit controls. Also, the ultimate effect of selective credit controls on prices is very difficult to measure. While total bank credit given against a commodity may be reduced as a result of imposition of selective credit controls, it does not follow that the holder of these commodities can obtain credit by offering other securities. This implies that the entire credit market has to be monitored properly if selective credit controls are to be effective.

ROLE OF CENTRAL BANK IN DEVELOPING ECONOMIES

In developing economies, commercial banking practices are not generally as developed as in developed economies. Money and capital markets also are not so organised and the bill market is almost non-existent. Therefore, in developing countries, the central bank has to play a more positive role in the development of a sound commercial banking system and money and capital markets than it is expected to play in developed countries. In developing countries where the commercial banking system is not developed, the central bank is required to provide ordinary banking facilities to the country. And, in countries in which the commercial banking system is inadequately developed, there is need for the central bank to supplement ordinary commercial banking facilities in addition to performing its accepted central banking functions.

Besides performing the traditional functions and some supporting functions as described above, the central bank in a developing country has to perform many developmental functions in order to initiate and accelerate the economic development of the country.

The central bank must promote term lending institutions to make available adequate investible funds for development of agricultural, industrial and export sectors of the economy. The central bank must also create agencies to develop money and capital markets because it is through these markets that the community's surplus funds are mobilised and made available to productive sectors of the economy. This is how the central bank can encourage mobilisation of savings and help the process of capital formation in the developing countries.

Since most of the developing countries have a large rural sector where agriculture is the mainstay of the population, modernisation of this sector is essential for development of these countries. This cannot be done in the absence of provision of adequate credit facilities at low cost for the agriculturists. The central bank should provide credit facilities in the form of medium- and long-term loans to the agricultural sector of the economy. Adequate supply of credit at low interest rates and repayable in easy instalments requires the promotion of agricultural credit institutions like the land development banks and agricultural refinance and development corporations. The central bank should subscribe to the share capital of agricultural credit institutions, and, may also provide support for the debenture floatation programmes undertaken by these institutions.

In the developing countries, the modern industrial sector is either absent or in its infancy. The central bank can and should assist development of this sector by promoting specialised industrial finance institutions like the Industrial Development Bank of India (IDBI), Industrial Finance Corporation and State Finance Corporations. The function of these financial institutions is to provide financial assistance in the form of loans, subscription to equity capital and purchase of debentures of the industrial units in the country. Judged from these angles, the Reserve Bank of India has been playing the role of a dynamic central bank in the developing economy of India.

REVIEW QUESTIONS

1. Explain, with examples, multiple expansion of deposits by commercial banks.
2. Enumerate the major functions of central bank of a country with special reference to the Reserve Bank of India.
3. What are the major instruments of credit control? Distinguish between the general and selective instruments of control.
4. Analyse the role of the central bank in developing economies with special reference to RBI.

SUGGESTED READINGS

- P.A. Samuelson and W.D. Nordhaus, *Economics* (Seventeenth Edition), Tata McGraw-Hill, 2003.
- S.B. Gupta, *Monetary Economics*, 1995.
- C. Rangarajan and B.H. Dholakia, *Principles of Macroeconomics*, 1980, Chapters 6 and 7.

Chapter 16

Integration of Monetary and Real Sector: IS-LM Analysis

In Chapter 14, we had analysed the monetary system in terms of demand for and supply of money, velocity of circulation of money, the quantity theory and the cash balance approach. In Chapter 15, we had discussed the monetary and credit system in terms of commercial and central banking, functions of commercial banks and role of the central bank particularly in formulating and implementing monetary policies. It is now time to talk about the real sector, and, make a distinction between the monetary and real sectors, and, finally, about synthesis or integration of the two sectors.

In every economy, there is monetary sector and the real sector. We have just mentioned about the monetary variables or factors. Demand for and supply of money determine the rate of interest. Therefore, the rate of interest also is a monetary factor. The real sector consists of real output or income, consumption, savings and investment. Consumption (includes government expenditure) and investment constitute aggregate demand. According to Keynes, the whole of macroeconomic analysis is done in real terms. Real consumption depends on real income, and similarly every economic variable is measured in real terms, i.e., in constant prices or wage units.

Let us now put the relationships in the monetary and real sectors together. Consumption is a function of income. Investment is a function of the rate of interest. Investment determines the level of income through the multiplier which depends on consumption (MPC). The interest rate is determined by the money market. Supply of money is fixed or controlled by the monetary authorities, but, demand for money depends on income and the rate of interest. This shows interdependence of monetary and real factors or variables, and, implies the need for simultaneous determination of major monetary and real sector variables. This commonly done through the IS-LM analysis.

The IS-LM analysis can be done as a simple two-sector (business and consumer) model or a more detailed multi-sector model including the government sector, and, also, the foreign sector.

In this chapter, the IS-LM analysis is done as a two-sector model. The more detailed multi-sector model including the government sector and the foreign sector will be undertaken in the next chapter.

IS-LM ANALYSIS: A TWO-SECTOR MODEL

Hicks and Hansen have explained (and also analysed) the integration of the real and monetary sectors of an economy with the IS-LM analysis or model. In IS-LM analysis, IS stands for the real or product sector equality or equilibrium condition I=S (I is investment and S is savings) and LM denotes the money market equilibrium condition L=M (L represents liquidity preference or demand for money and M stands for money supply). The two sectors, as just mentioned, are the business (or firm) sector and the consumer or household sector.

The interconnection or interdependence between the product market (real sector) and the money market (monetary sector) is a logical phenomenon in any economy. The interconnection or interdependence takes place through two important variables: one is *investment*—a product market or real sector variable, and, the other is *interest*—a money market variable. The interdependence of the two sectors will be more clear through the IS and LM curves and IS-LM analysis for simultaneous determination of income and the rate of interest.

IS AND LM CURVES

The first step in IS-LM analysis is derivation of IS and LM curves. We shall first explain the derivation of IS curve, and, then discuss derivation of the LM curve, and, finally, analyse the intersection of the IS and LM curves for determination of the equilibrium situation.

Derivation of IS Curve

The IS curve shows the relationship between income and the rate of interest with equality or equilibrium levels of savings and investment (I=S). Let us see the derivation of the IS curve.

The IS curve can be derived deductively from the product market equilibrium.

Let us recall (Chapter 3) the Keynesian income equation

Y = C + I (C is consumption, I is investment)

Also, as shown in Chapter 4.,

$$Y = C + S \text{ (S is savings)}$$

$$\therefore \quad Y = C + I = C + S$$

$$\text{or,} \quad I = S \text{ (in equilibrium)}$$

Investment (I) depends on the rate of interest. There is inverse relationship between investment and the rate of interest (i)—lower the rate of interest, more is investment. Savings (S) depends on income (Y)—given the average propensity to save (APS) or the marginal propensity to save (MPS), higher is income (Y), more is savings (S). These two relationships—between investment and the rate of interest and savings and income—are graphically presented in Figs. 16.1 and 16.2 respectively. Figure 16.3 shows the equality or equilibrium condition I=S. From these three relationships or equations or curves, IS curve will follow or can be derived.

In Fig. 16.1, the investment function (I = I(i) shows the downward sloping curve or inverse relationship between investment and the rate of interest, in Fig. 16.2; the savings function (S=s(Y)) shows the upward sloping curve or positive relationship between savings and income; in Fig. 16.3, the equality (45°) line or equilibrium condition of I = S is shown.

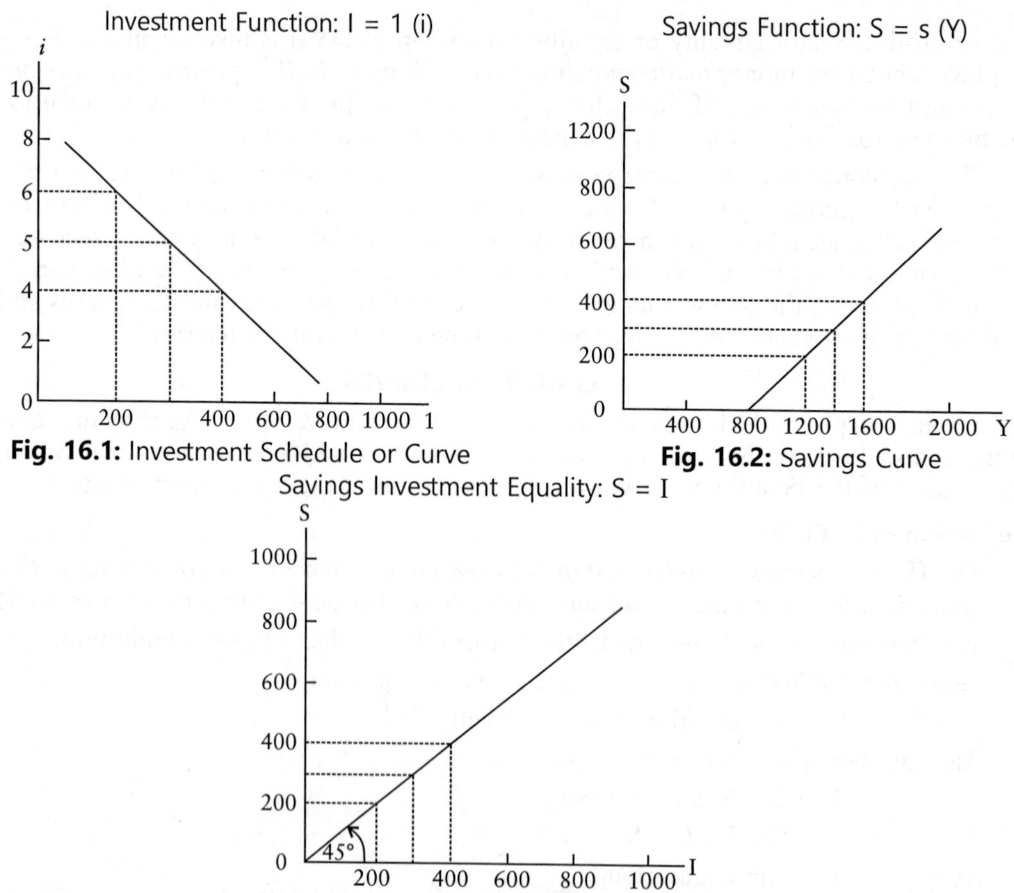

Fig. 16.1: Investment Schedule or Curve

Fig. 16.2: Savings Curve

Fig. 16.3: Savings Investment Equality Curve

Let us now see how the IS curve is derived from these three functions or curves. This is shown in Fig. 16.4. Let us assume that the interest rate is 6 per cent meaning that investment is ₹ 200 (Fig. 16.1). Savings will be ₹ 200 if income is ₹ 1200 (Fig. 16.2); the figure also shows that below a certain level of income (₹ 800), there is no savings. Equality of savings and investment at ₹ 200 is shown is Fig. 16.3. By putting together these numbers, we get one combination of income (Y) and the rate of interest (i)—income of ₹ 1200 and interest rate of 6 per cent at which 1 = S (Fig. 16.4). Similarly, if the rate of interest is 5 per cent, following the same chain of logic as just explained, we get another combination of income and the rate of interest—income ₹ 1400, interest rate 5 per cent and 1 = S = ₹ 300. If the rate of interest is 4 per cent, the combination will be Y = 1600, i = 4 per cent and 1 = 5 = 400. If the rate of interest is more than 6 per cent (say 7 or 8 per cent), the combinations of Y and 1 = S will change accordingly. This can be clearly seen in Fig. 16.4.

Product Market Equilibrium: I(i) = S(Y)

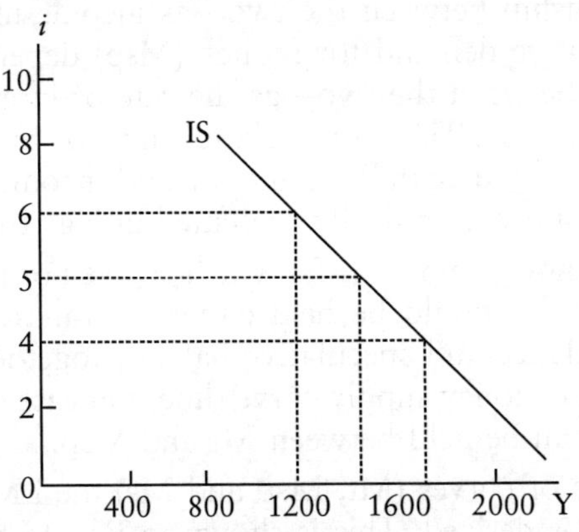

Fig. 16.4: The IS Curve

Figure 16.4 shows the shape of the IS curve. This is downward sloping depicting the particular relationship between income and the rate of interest. The relationship is inverse. This can be explained. A high interest rate indicates low investment; low investment, through the multiplier, leads to low income. Similarly, a low rate of interest means high investment; high investment, through the multiplier effect, means high income. The relationship between income and the rate of interest can also be explained in another way. We start with income. High income means high savings. Because of the equality or equilibrium condition 1 = S, high savings means high investment. High investment is the result or effect of low interest rate. So, high income indicates low rate of interest.

Derivation of LM Curve

The LM curve shows the relationship between income and the rate of interest with equality or equilibrium levels of demand for money and supply of money (Md = Ms). Let us see the derivation of the LM curve.[1]

The LM curve can be derived deductively from the equilibrium of the money market.

Let us recall our discussion of demand for money and supply of money in Chapter 14.

Let us start with demand for money. Demand for money can be written as

$$Md = Mt + Msp$$

(Md is total demand for money, Mt is transaction demand for money and Msp is speculative demand for money)

$$Mt = k(Y) \qquad \text{(Y is income)}$$
$$Msp = l(i) \qquad \text{(i is interest rate)}$$

Money supply is determined or fixed by monetary authorities.

$$Ms = \overline{M}s \text{ (Ms is money supply)}$$

In equilibrium,

$$Md = Ms$$

i.e.,
$$Ms = Mt + Msp$$

or
$$Ms = k(Y) + l(i)$$

1. In Chapter 14, total demand for money was represented by L, Mt was written as Lt and Msp was written as Ls.

Transaction demand for money (Mt) (includes precautionary demand) depends on income (Y); there is positive relationship between the two—as income increases, transaction demand for money increases. Speculative demand for money (Msp) depends on the rate of interest(i); there is inverse relationship between the two—as the rate of interest falls speculative demand for money increases and vice versa. These two relationships or functions—between transaction demand (including precautionary demand) for money and income and speculative demand for money and the rate of interest are graphically presented in Fig. 16.5 and Fig. 16.6 respectively.

Figure 16.7 shows total money supply (Ms) which is given or fixed, i.e., determined outside the system; total money supply should be held either as transactions balance or speculative balance, i.e., transactions balance and speculative balance together should be equal to money supply. Different points on the money supply curve (line) indicate different ways or proportions in which the money supply can be held between Mt and Msp.

From the three equations or curves (Mt, Msp and Ms) the LM curve will follow or can be derived. Let us see how this is derived. This is shown in Fig. 16.8. It can be seen in Fig. 16.5 that at an income level of ₹ 1200, transaction demand for money is ₹ 600. It follows then that speculative demand for money is ₹ 400. It has to be so because total demand for money is ₹ 1000 which is equal to total supply of money, i.e., Md = Ms = ₹ 1000. This is shown in Fig. 16.7.

Transaction Demand for Money: Mt = k(Y)

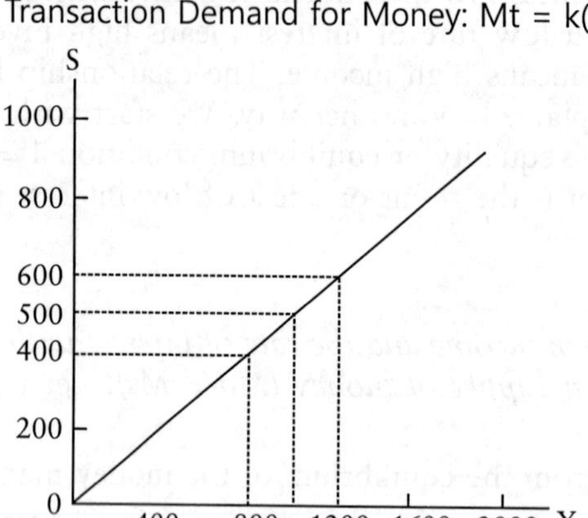

Fig. 16.5: Transaction Demand for Money

Speculative Demand for Money: Msp = l(i)

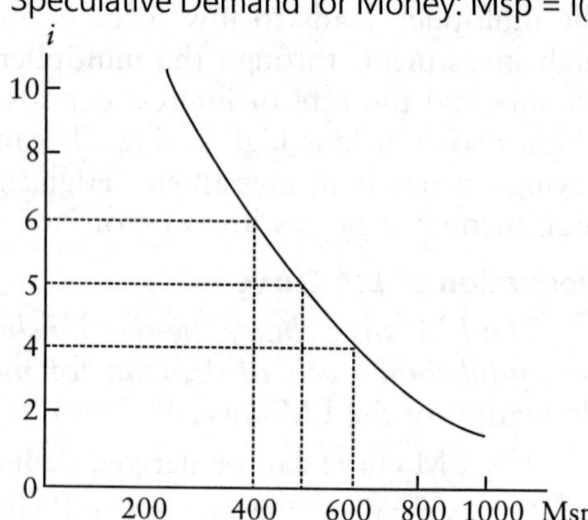

Fig. 16.6: Speculative Demand for Money

Money Supply: Ms = Mt + Msp

Fig. 16.7: Supply of Money

In Fig. 16.6, we see that speculative demand for money of ₹ 400 is made at the interest rate of 6 per cent. Putting together Fig. 16.5, Fig. 16.6 and Fig. 16.7, we get one combination of income and the rate of interest—₹ 1200 and 6 per cent—at which the money market is in equilibrium (Md = Ms = ₹ 1000). This is shown in Fig. 16.8. At an income level of ₹ 1000, transaction demand to money is ₹ 500 (Fig. 16.5). Therefore, speculative demand for money is also ₹ 500 because total demand for money is ₹ 1000 (Fig. 16.7). From Fig. 16.6, we see that speculative demand of ₹ 500 is made at an interest rate of 5 per cent. Putting these information together, we get another combination of income and the rate of interest—₹ 1000 and 5 per cent—at which the money market is in equilibrium. Similarly, a third combination of income and the rate of interest will be ₹ 800 and 4 per cent respectively. Accordingly, if income level is ₹ 1600, the rate of interest will be 8 per cent (transaction demand for money is ₹ 800 and speculative demand is ₹ 200).

Money Market Equilibrium: Md = Ms

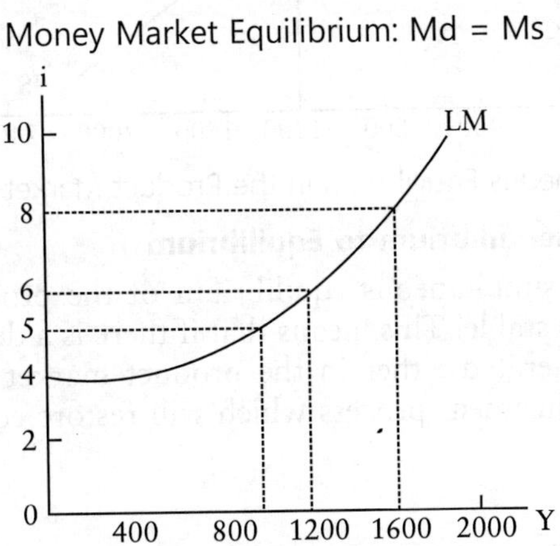

Fig. 16.8: The LM Curve

The shape and logic of the LM curve can be explained. The LM curve is upward sloping to the right. With given money supply (here ₹ 1000), money market equilibrium is reached at different combinations of high income and high interest rate or low income and low interest rate. This is depicted in Fig. 16.8. To see this, we can either start with income or the interest rate. Let us start with income. High level of income indicates high transaction balances given the transaction demand for money. With fixed money supply, high transaction balances mean low speculative balances which imply high interest rate, or, in other words, high transaction balances can be drawn from the stock of speculative balances which will push up the interest rate. So, the combination of high income and high interest rate follows. We can see this by starting with the interest rate also. High interest rate means low speculative balances; low speculative balances indicate high cash balances which will be held at high level of income.

IS-LM MODEL: SIMULTANEOUS EQUILIBRIUM IN THE PRODUCT MARKET AND MONEY MARKET

The IS curve shows equilibrium in the product market with different combinations of income (Y) and the rate of interest (i). The LM curve shows equilibrium in the money market with different possible combinations of Y and i. But, there is only one combination of income and the rate of interest at which both the product market and the money market are simultaneously in equilibrium. We can call this *general equilibrium*. Simultaneous equilibrium in the product market and the money market is reached at the point of intersection of the IS and LM curves. This is shown by point E in Fig. 16.9. The equilibrium level of income is ₹ 1200 and the rate of interest is 6 per cent.

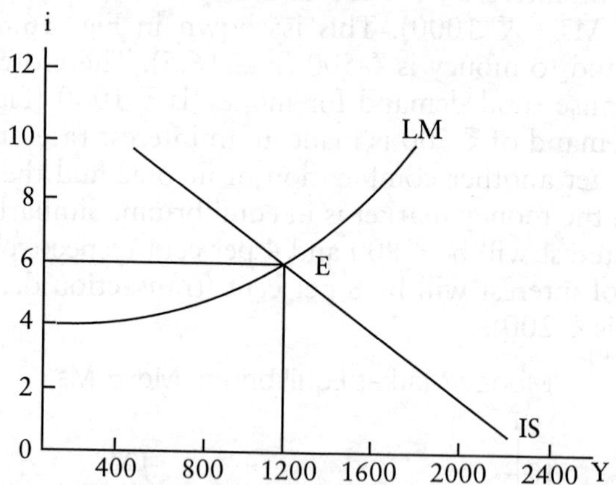

Fig. 16.9: Simultaneous Equilibrium in the Product Market and Money Market

Stability of Equilibrium: Disequilibrium to Equilibrium

General equilibrium or simultaneous equilibrium of the product market and the money market shown in Fig. 16.9 is stable. This means that if there is a deviation from the equilibrium situation, forces will be generated either in the product market or in the money market or both to set in motion an adjustment process which will restore equilibrium at point E. This is illustrated in Fig. 16.10.

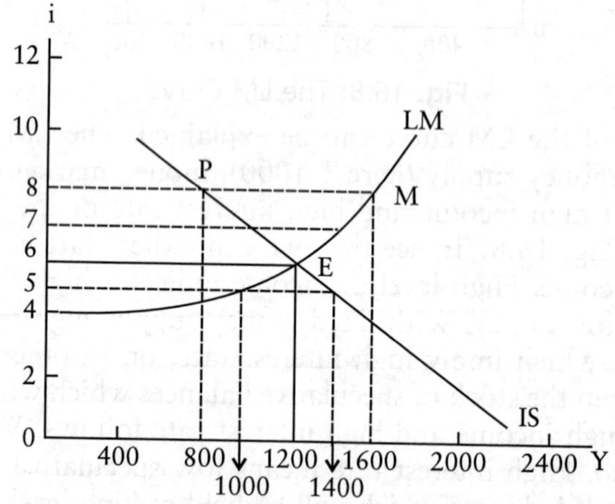

Fig. 16.10: IS-LM Model: Equilibrium and Disequilibrium

All combinations of Y and i in Fig. 16.9 other than the one of intersection of the IS and LM curves (i.e., point E) are the situations of disequilibrium either in the product market or in the money market or in both. This is explained in Fig. 16.10. Let us consider an interest rate of 8 per cent. With 8 per cent rate of interest, the product market is in equilibrium at an income level of ₹ 800. This follows from the IS curve. But, at 8 per cent rate of interest, the money market is in equilibrium at an income level of ₹ 1600. This can be seen from the LM curve. This means that 8 per cent rate of interest is not consistent with simultaneous equilibrium in the product market and the money market. The same result with follow if we start with income. Let us consider an income level of ₹ 1400. At this income level the product market is in equilibrium at an interest rate of 5 per cent (see IS curve). But, at ₹ 1400 level of income the money market is in equilibrium at the interest rate of 7 per cent (see LM curve). This shows that ₹ 1400 level of income is not compatible with simultaneous equilibrium in the product market as well as the money. Let us consider an interest rate below 6 per cent, say 5 per cent. At this interest rate, the product market is in equilibrium at the income level of ₹ 1400. But, at the same rate of interest, the money market is in equilibrium at an income level of ₹ 1000. This shows the incompatibility or inconsistency of 5 per cent rate of interest with simultaneous equilibrium in the product market and the money market. These are situations of general disequilibrium.

Let us more clearly understand the deviations from the equilibrium point and their implications; this will help understanding the process of adjustment and restoration of equilibrium at point E.

Any point away from the LM curve means a situation of disequilibrium since Md ≠ MS. At all points which lie to the right and below the LM curve, Md > Ms. Similarly, at all points which lie to the left and above the LM curve. Ms > Md. As in the money market, so also is in the product market. Any point away from the IS curve indicates situation of disequilibrium because I ≠ S. At all points lying to the left and below the IS curve 1 > S. Similarly, at all points lying to the right and above the IS curve, S > I.

To understand the market adjustment process, let us start with a situation or point at which Ms > Md, i.e., there is excess supply of money. P in Fig. 16.10 is one such point. At P, the interest rate is 8 per cent. The excess supply of money (not demanded either for transaction or speculative purposes) will flow to the bond market. This will push up bond prices. This will push-down the interest rate because bond prices and the interest rate are inversely correlated. The reduction in the interest rate will have effect both on the product market and the money market. We shall first see the implication of the impact of reduction in the interest rate on the product market, and, then see the implications for the money market.

In the product market, a decline in the interest rate will lead to increase in investment because investment and interest rate are inversely correlated (Fig. 16.1). Increase in investment will lead to increase in income. Because of these three effects—decline in i, increase in I and increase in Y—the product market equilibrium point will shift downwards along the IS curve. Both increase in income and decrease in interest rate will have effect on the money market. The effect will be on demand for money. Total demand for money will increase because of increase in both transaction demand and speculative demand; transaction demand will increase because of increase in income (positive correlation) and speculative demand will increase because of fall in the interest rate (negative or inverse correlation). The effect of all these will be on money market equilibrium M which will also shift downwards along the LM curve. The processes of adjustment in the product market and money market will continue till the general equilibrium point E is reached.

We can also start with a situation where there is Md > Ms, i.e., there is excess demand for money and the rate of interest is below 6 per cent, say 5 per cent or 4 per cent. In such a situation, opposite forces will work in both the product market and money market—opposite for what we have mentioned above is terms of bond prices, interest rate, investment, etc.—for restoration of equilibrium at point E.

Shift in IS and LM Curves

The general equilibrium position, however, will shift if there is a shift in either the IS curve or the LM curve or both. The IS and LM curves may shift upwards or downwards. The direction of shift will depend on the nature of movements of the determining variables. These variables are savings and investment for IS curve and demand for and supply of money for the LM curve. Because of shifts in IS and LM curves (either one of them or both), there will be changes in the point of general equilibrium. There will be three situations: new equilibrium because of shift in the IS curve, new equilibrium because of shift in the LM curve and new equilibrium because of shifts in both the IS curve and the LM curve. These are analysed in this section.

Shift in IS Curve and New Equilibrium

We consider here a shift in the general equilibrium position because of a shift in the IS curve with no change in the LM curve. A shift in the IS curve can take place because of either an increase or decrease in investment.[2] Let us consider the case of an increase in investment. The increase should be in the form of autonomous investment (that is, not related to or induced by income). Autonomous investment may be made because of introduction of new or improved technology and likely increase in productivity or possibility of market or business expansion or in the form of foreign investment (assuming an open economy).

Because of increase in investment, savings also will increase because of equality of savings and investment in equilibrium (I = S). Increase in savings will also lead to an increase in the equilibrium level of income. This completes the shift in the IS curve. The shift will be upwards or to the right. The new IS curve will be parallel to the existing IS curve, i.e., the shift will take place at all levels of interest. This is shown by IS, in Fig. 16.11. The new equilibrium point is Et. The new equilibrium levels of income and the rate of interest are ₹ 1400 and 7 per cent respectively. This means that the result of an upward shift in the IS curve is simultaneous increase in income and the rate of interest.

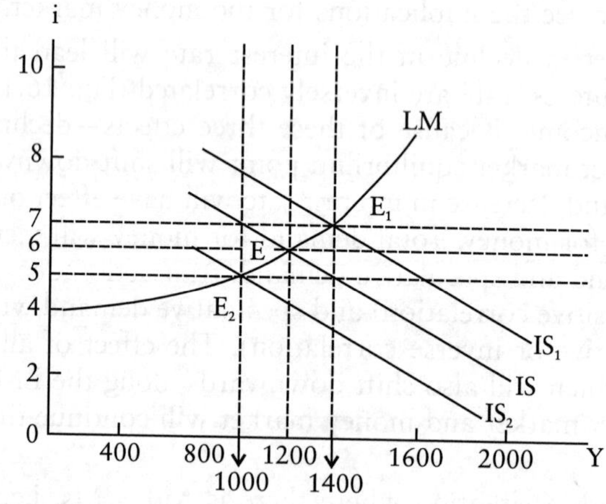

Fig. 16.11: Shift in IS curve and New Equilibrium

Instead of increase in investment, there can be decrease, i.e., withdrawal of investment or funds because of reasons opposite to those mentioned above—outdated technology and likely fall in productivity, business recession or withdrawal of foreign investment. If there is decrease

2. There are also other factors which may cause a shift in the IS curve. But, a change in investment is one of the most important factors or causes.

in investment, the opposite forces or the process of market adjustment will be at work. Because of decrease in investment, income will fall. Fall in income will have effect on both the product market and the money market. In the product market, fall in income will cause savings to fall; equilibrium level of savings also has to fall to maintain equality with investment. In the money market, fall in income will reduce transaction demand for money. The excess cash or liquidity (with given supply of money) will flow into the bonds market. This will push up bond prices and, as a result, the interest rate will fall. This will complete the downward shift of the IS curve. The new IS curve is IS_2. The new equilibrium point is E_2 and the equilibrium levels of income and the rate of interest are ₹ 1000 and 5 per cent respectively.

Shift in LM Curve and New Equilibrium

A shift (either to the right or to the left) in the LM curve occurs because of developments or changes in the money market. More specifically, the LM curve can shift for three reasons: first, change (either increase or decrease) in transactions demand for money; second, change (either increase or decrease) in speculative demand for money; and, third, change (either increase or decrease) in money supply. Of these three reasons or factors, money supply is generally considered to be the most important one. We shall, therefore, consider here a shift in the equilibrium position due to shift in the LM curve because of change in money supply, given the IS curve.

Let us start with an increase in money supply. Money supply may increase because of a decision by the government or the monetary authority, i.e., the central bank (RBI in case of India). Increase in money supply indicates an equal increase in the demand for money (Md) to satisfy the equilibrium condition Md = Ms. If there is no change in the interest rate (and, therefore, also, no change in the speculative demand for money), the entire increase in the demand for money has to be in the form of transaction balances. Given the value of k, this will mean proportionate increase in income Y. Because of increase in income, there will be rightward shift in the LM curve at all levels of interest rate. This is shown by LM_1 in Fig. 16.12. But, no new equilibrium can be reached at the existing equilibrium rate of interest of 6 per cent. This can be seen in Fig. 16.12.

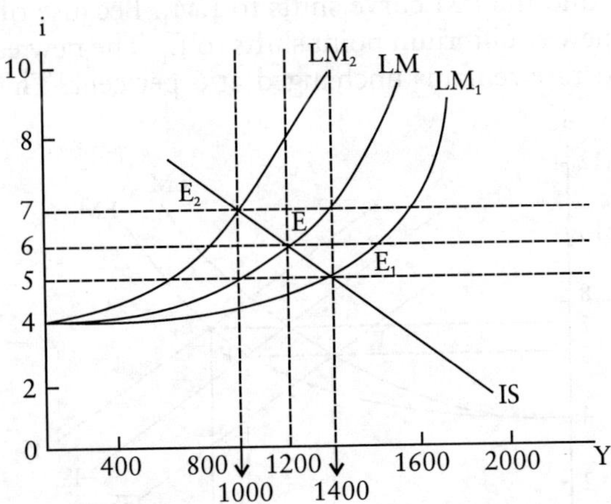

Fig. 16.12: Shift in LM Curve and New Equilibrium

This happens because there is no change in the position of the IS curve. For the present equilibrium point E to shift to a new position or point, the interest rate has to fall. A fall in the interest rate will increase the speculative demand or balances (this will actually complete the increase in total demand for money). Fall in the interest rate will also increase investment, and, through the multiplier increase in investment will lead to increase in income. The increase in income now explains the required increase in transaction balances. The result of all these is increase in Y, decrease in *i* and a rightward shift of the LM curve to a new equilibrium position. This is shown by point E_1 in Fig. 16.12. The new equilibrium levels of income and the rate of interest are ₹ 1400 and 5 per cent respectively.

If, instead of increase, there is a decrease in money supply, the opposite forces will work. A decrease in money supply will mean an equal decrease in demand for money because of the equilibrium condition Md = Ms. As explained above (for increase in demand for money), the decrease in total demand for money will be accounted for by decrease in both transaction demand for money and speculative demand for money. This will happen because of increase in the interest rate, fall in investment, and, consequently, fall in income. Given the IS curve, all these will cause a leftward shift in the LM curve and a new general equilibrium will be reached. The new LM curve will be LM_2 and the new equilibrium point will be E_2. The new equilibrium level of income will be ₹ 1000 and the new interest rate will be 7 per cent. All these can be seen in Fig. 16.12.

Shifts in both IS Curve and LM Curve and New Equilibrium

We have discussed above different factors or variables which cause a shift in the IS curve, and, the resultant new equilibrium, given the LM curve. We have also just discussed factors which lead to a shift in the LM curve and, the resultant new equilibrium, given the IS curve. We now drop the assumptions of 'unchanged IS curve' and 'unchanged LM curve' and allow both the curves to shift simultaneously, and, see the resultant new equilibrium.

A shift in the IS curve can be either upwards or downwards depending on whether there is an increase or decrease in investment. Similarly, a shift in the LM curve can be either rightwards or leftwards depending on whether there is an increase or decrease in money supply. We consider here the case of increase in investment and increase in money and shifts in both IS and LM curves in the same direction, i.e., an upward shift in the IS curve and rightward shift in the LM curve. The IS curve shifts to IS_1, and the LM curve shifts to LM_1. Because of these simultaneous shifts in IS and LM curves, the new equilibrium point shifts to E_1. The new equilibrium level of income is ₹ 1600, but the interest rate remains unchanged at 6 per cent. This is shown in Fig. 16.13.

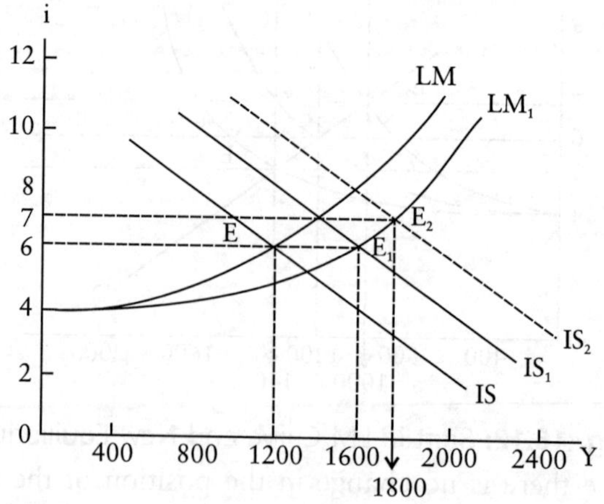

Fig. 16.13: Simultaneous Shifts in IS and LM Curves and New Equilibrium

The new equilibrium at E_1 (Fig. 16.13) because of simultaneous shifts in IS and LM curves is explained as follows. An increase in investment will lead to an increase in income and also the rate of interest because of a shift in the IS curve (see Fig. 16.11) if there is no increase in money supply and no shift in the LM curve. But, because of increase in money supply and simultaneous shift in the LM curve, the increase in interest rate will be prevented so that the new equilibrium at E_1 will be reached at the old interest rate of 6 per cent.

The unchanged rate of interest (6 per cent) needs to be explained further. The interest rate remains unchanged because the magnitudes of shift in both IS and LM curves are same. The equal shift is indicated by the horizonal distance between E and E_1. The shift or distance between the IS and LM curves need not, however, be always be equal. The shifts in IS and LM curves may be in the same direction, but, of different magnitudes. If this happens, the rate of interest will change. Let us assume that, in Fig. 16.13, the LM curve shifts to LM_1, but the IS curve shifts to IS_2. In this case, the new equilibrium shifts to E_2 with new equilibrium income ₹ 1800 and the rate of interest 7 per cent. This happens because the increase in investment, and, the consequent increase in the rate of interest are more pronounced or stronger than can be fully offset by increase in money supply and fall in the interest rate.

If the IS and LM curves shift in opposite directions, the changes in income and the rate of interest will depend on both the direction and magnitude of shifts. A new equilibrium will be reached depending on the changes in investment and money supply and the related variables or factors like savings and demand for money (both transaction and speculative), and, finally, new equilibrium levels of income and the rate of interest will be determined.

APPLICATION OF THE IS-LM MODEL: ALGEBRAIC PRESENTATION

The IS-LM model is not only a theoretical formulation. It has very important empirical significance. Variables involved in the IS-LM model are key factors or indicators in an economy; levels of income, investment, interest rate, etc.—and changes in them—cause market movements, and, determine the course of an economy—its development and fluctuations. It is, therefore, important to understand the application of the IS-LM model in terms of real numbers. This is done here in terms of an algebraic or numerical presentation of the model.

Application of the IS-LM model is discussed here in terms of hypothetical values or numbers of income, consumption, savings, investment, demand for money, supply of money and the rate of interest. The algebraic formulation or presentation will show the nature of inter-relationships among the variables, the magnitude of their interactions and impacts on the product market, the money market and finally on the equilibrium situation. For a real economy, the hypothetical numbers can be substituted by actual values of different variables during a particular period for analysing the process of integration of the product market and money market and determination of general equilibrium.[3]

IS and LM Functions

We shall proceed the same way as we did for development of the theoretical model above, i.e., first derive or discuss the IS and LM functions, and, then state the general equilibrium situation or condition and determination of the equilibrium values of income (Y) and the rate of interest (i).

3. This will, however, be subject to availability of data, timeliness of data, correctness or accuracy of data and issues or problems of measurement.

IS Function

Let us start with the Keynesian income equation Y = C + I

In functional form, consumption (C) is written as

$$C = a + b\,Y^{4} \quad (16.1)$$

Assigning values to 'a' and 'b' equation (16.1) may be rewritten as

$$C = 520 + 0.5\,Y \quad (16.2)$$

We also know that

$$Y = C + S$$

or, $$Y = 520 + 0.5\,Y + S$$

∴ $$S = Y - 520 - 0.5\,Y \quad (16.3)$$

Equation (16.3) is the savings function

Let us now turn to the investment function. The investment function may be written as

$$I = d + ei^{5} \quad (16.4)$$

Where *d* is positive and *e* is negative meaning that investment varies inversely with interest rate i

Assigning values to 'd' and 'e', equation (16.4) may be rewritten as

$$I = 200 - 2000\,i \quad (16.5)$$

The product market equilibrium condition is I = S.

This can be written in terms of equation (16.3) and equation (16.5) as

$$200 - 2000\,i = Y - 520 - 0.5Y$$

or, $$Y = 200 - 2000\,i + 520 + 0.5Y$$

or, $$Y - 0.5Y = 520 + 200 - 2000\,i$$

or, $$Y/2 = 520 + 200 - 2000\,i$$

or, $$Y = 2\,(520 + 200 - 2000\,i)$$

$$= 2\,(720 - 2000\,i)$$

$$= 1440 - 4000\,i$$

∴ IS function is $Y = 1440 - 4000\,i$

LM Function

To derive the LM function, we have to consider demand for money including its two components, transaction demand for money and speculative demand for money—and supply of money.

Let us start with demand for money. Demand for money equation is written as

$$Md = Mt + Msp \quad (16.6)$$

where Md is total demand for money, Mt is transaction demand and Msp is speculative demand

Transaction demand for money Mt is written as

$$Mt = kY\ (k > 0) = 0.5Y \quad (16.7)$$

Speculative demand for money Msp can be written as

---

4. Refer Chapter 4.
5. Refer Chapter 5 for brief explanation of this function or equation. The equation is assumed as linear.

$$Msp = L - li^{6} \qquad (16.8)$$

Assigning values for 'L' and '*l*', equation (16.8) may be rewritten as

$$Msp = 1500 - 10000\ i \qquad (16.9)$$

By combining equation (16.7) and equation (16.9) a we get

$$Md = 0.5\ Y + 1500 - 10000\ i \qquad (16.10)$$

The money market equilibrium condition is Md = Ms

$$\text{Let } Ms = 1500 \qquad (16.11)$$

The money market equilibrium can be stated in terms of equation (16.10) and equation (16.11) as

$$0.5Y \times 1500 - 10000\ i = 1500$$

or, $0.5Y = 1500 - 1500 + 10000\ i$

or, $Y/2 = 1500 - 1500 + 10{,}000\ i$

or, $Y = 2(1500 - 1500 + 10000\ i)$

$= 2\ (10000\ i) = 20{,}0000\ i$

∴ LM function is $Y = 20{,}000\ i^{7}$

Simultaneous Equilibrium of the Product Market and the Money Market or General Equilibrium

We have derived the IS function. We have also derived the LM function. We can now combine these two function or equations to determine the conditions (that is, values of Y and i) for simultaneous equilibrium in the product market and the money market or general equilibrium.

The condition for general equilibrium is IS = LM

$$\text{IS function is } Y = 1440 - 4000\ i \qquad (16.12)$$

$$\text{LM function is } Y = 20000\ i \qquad (16.13)$$

These are two linear equations with two-unknowns Y and i. Therefore, determinate solution is possible.

Subtracting equation (16.13) from equation (16.12), we get

$$0 = 1440 - 4000\ i - 20000\ i$$

or, $1440 - 4000\ i - 20{,}000\ i = 0$

or, $1440 = 24{,}000\ i$

or $i = 0.06$ or 6 per cent

Substituting the value of i (i.e., 0.06) in equation 16.13, we get

$$Y = 20{,}000\ i$$

$$= 20{,}000 \times 0.06$$

$$= 1200$$

So, the general equilibrium solution for the IS-LM model is

Y = ₹ 1200 and i = 6 per cent

This is the same solution or equilibrium values of Y and i we obtained in Fig. 16.10. This shows the compatibility of graphical analysis and algebraic solution.

---

6. The speculative demand for money function is non-linear or, rather curvilinear as shown in Fig. 16.6. For simplicity, equations (16.8) and (16.9) are written as linear.
7. For simplicity, the LM function is assumed as linear. In reality, this is usually non-linear. In Fig. 16.8 and Fig. 16.9, the LM function or curve is shown as non-linear.

REVIEW QUESTIONS

1. Mention the monetary and real sectors in an economy in terms of different variables and also explain the relationship or interdependence between the two sectors. What is IS-LM analysis?
2. What is the IS curve? Explain, in stages or steps, derivation of the IS curve.
3. What is the LM curve? Explain, in stages or steps, derivation of the LM curve.
4. Develop the Hicks-Hansen two-sector IS-LM model. Explain the equilibrium situation.
5. Analyse the results of a shift in the IS curve, a shift in the LM curve, and, also shifts in both the IS and LM curves in terms of equilibrium values of income and the rate of interest.
6. Discuss application of the two-sector IS-LM model using hypothetical values of different variables, propensities and constants, and, final equilibrium solution in terms of income and the rate of interest.

SUGGESTED READINGS

- E. Shapiro, *Macroeconomic Analysis* (Fifth Edition), Galgotia Publications, 1984, Chapter 14.
- G. Acklay, *Macroeconomics: Theory and Policy*, Macmillan, 1978, Chapter 11.
- J.R. Hicks, "Mr. Keynes and the Classics: A Suggested Interpretation" in M.G. Mueller (Ed.) *Readings in Macroeconomics*, 1966.
- M. Friedman and W. Heller, *Monetary vs. Fiscal Policy*, New York University Press, 1969.
- T.F. Dernberg, *Macroeconomics: Concepts, Theories and Policies*, McGraw Hill, 1985, Chapter 9.

Chapter 17

IS-LM Analysis: Model with Government Sector and Foreign Sector

In the previous chapter, we had analysed the IS-LM model with two sectors—the household sector and the business sector. In this chapter, we extend the model to two more sectors—the government sector and the foreign sector. Because of inclusion of these two sectors, we see the new equilibrium situations, and, resulting changes in determination of the levels of income and the rate of interest. This makes the analysis more comprehensive.

The IS-LM analysis with the government sector and the foreign sector will be conducted in two parts:

A. IS-LM model with government Sector
B. IS-LM model with foreign Sector

A. IS-LM MODEL WITH GOVERNMENT SECTOR

In this part, we introduce the government sector in the IS-LM model and discuss appropriate changes or modification in the model because of incorporation of this sector. Introduction of the government sector makes the model more broad based and realistic because markets and economies do not function without a government.

Introduction of the government sector implies incorporation of the variables related to operation of the government. Two sets of variables are implied or included. These are:

(a) **Fiscal variables:** Includes government expenditure and taxes or taxation;
(b) **Monetary variables:** Includes money supply and demand for money and related factors or variables like the rate of interest and other monetary instruments or measures like the bank rate, CRR, SLR, etc.

The fiscal variables or operations primarily affect the product market, and, therefore, the IS function or curve; the monetary variables and measures essentially influence the money market, and, therefore, the LM function or curve.

IS AND LM CURVES

As in the case of the two-sector model, we start will derivation of IS and LM curves. We shall first explain derivation of the modified IS curve (because of introduction of the government sector). Two forms of the LM curve will be considered—one without any change in money supply, and, the other a shift in the LM curve because of increase in money supply. Corresponding to these two LM curves, two equilibrium situations will be discussed: first, with modified IS curve and unchanged LM curve; second, equilibrium situation taking into account fiscal and monetary changes and, their effects on both the IS and LM curves and the resultant general equilibrium situation.

Derivation of IS Curve

Let us start with the Keynesian income equation

$$Y = C + I$$

Because of introduction of government expenditure, this will be modified as

$$Y = C + I + G$$

where G is government expenditure.

Also because of introduction of government taxation the equation

$$Y = C + S$$

will be modified as

$$Y = C + S + T$$

where T is taxes.

Because of these changes, the equilibrium condition for the product market for a three sector (government, business, consumer) economy will be modified as

$$S + T = I + G$$

Because of government expenditure, the investment function or curve shown in Fig. 16.1 will shift to the right (and upwards) by the amount of government expenditure G. Because G is independent of the rate of interest, the I-curve, i.e. (I+G) curve will shift to the right at all interest rates. This means that I + G curve will shift parallel to the original I curve (Fig. 16.1). This is shown in Fig. 17.1.

Let us now explain the savings function. The savings function or curve will be modified because of introduction of taxes (T). The immediate impact of taxation (assuming direct taxes) is reduction in personal disposable income. Reduction in disposable income has effect on both consumption and savings. Given certain propensity to consume (APC or MPC) and the propensity to save (APS or MPS), there will be fall in both consumption and savings. This means a rightward (or downward) shift in the savings curve indicating less savings at a given level of income. This is shown by shift of the savings curve from S to S_1 in Fig. 17.2. Savings has another meaning; it is like a 'leakage' from income, that is the amount not available for spending or consumption. Taxes are also like leakages—not available for consumption spending. If T is added to S_1, the resultant curve (S_1 + T) shifts leftwards or upwards to complete the equation Y = C + S + T. The S_1 + T curve is shown in Fig. 17.2.

The modified savings investment equality curve is shown in Fig. 17.3. The two axes are S+T and I+G.

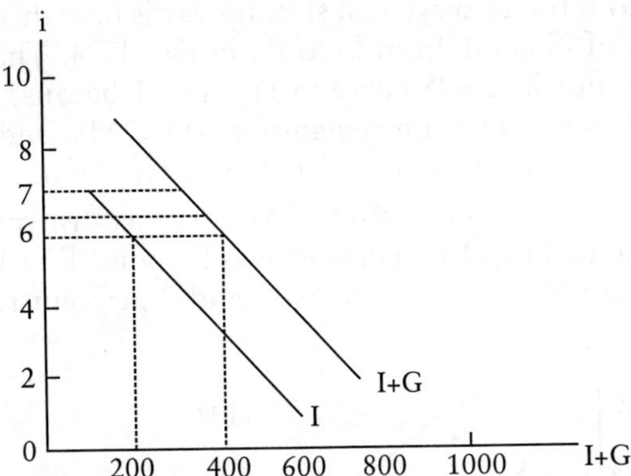

Fig. 17.1: The Modified Investment (I+G) Curve in Three-sector Model

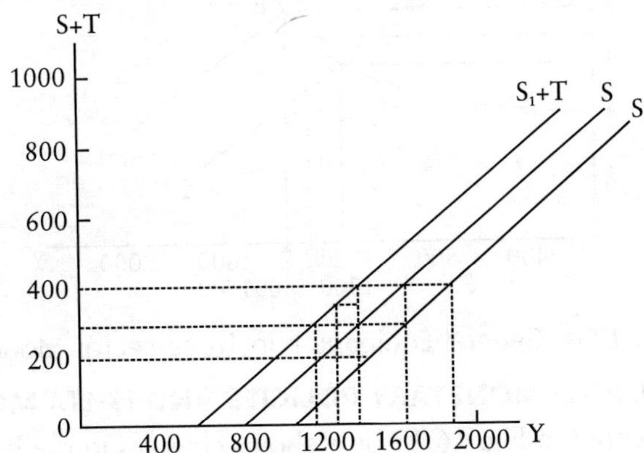

Fig. 17.2: The Modified Savings (S+T) Curve in Three-sector Model

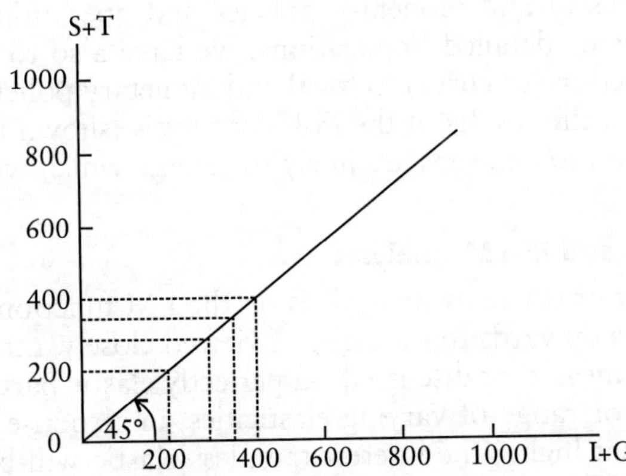

Fig. 17.3: Savings (S+T) Investment (I+G) Equality Curve in Three-sector Model

General Equilibrium in the Three-sector Model with Given Ms

We can now restate the new general equilibrium condition in the IS-LM model because of these changes. Because of changes in the investment function or curve and the savings function or curve, the IS curve will be modified. We may call the modified IS curve as IG-ST curve. However, for simplicity and continuity of terminology, we may continue to call it the IS curve.

Because of addition of G to I, the IS curve will shift upwards or rightwards by the amount of G. This is shown by the shift of IS curve from IS to IS_1 in Fig. 17.4. The shift is to be interpreted/understood to be same as shift in the IS curve in Fig. 16.11 because of increase in investment. The money market equilibrium condition remains as Md = Ms, and, therefore, the LM curve or function is retained as same as derived and shown in Fig. 16.8.

With the new IS (IG-ST) curve IS_1 and the LM curve as just mentioned, the new general equilibrium in the three-sector IS-LM model is shown by point E in Fig. 17.4. The equilibrium levels of income and the rate of interest are ₹ 1400 and 7 per cent respectively.

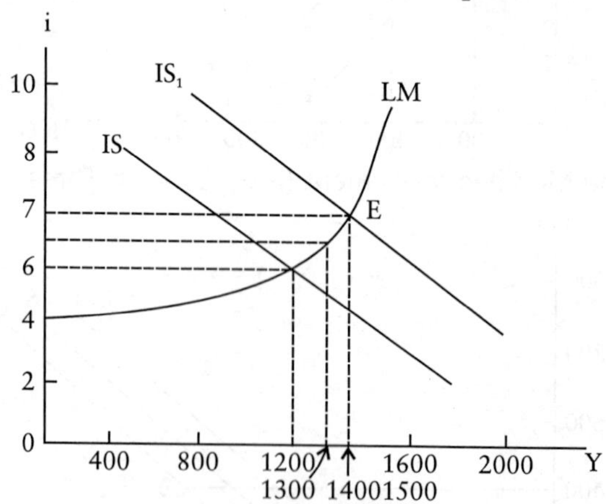

Fig. 17.4: General Equilibrium in Three-sector Model

FISCAL AND MONETARY POLICIES AND IS-LM MODEL

The equilibrium presented in Fig. 16.17 only shows changes in the IS function (LM function unchanged) because of introduction of government expenditure and taxes; but, it does not reflect the full effects of fiscal and monetary policies and operations on IS-LM analysis. To understand the full effects or detailed implications, we have also to consider the elasticity or responsiveness of LM function (or curve) to fiscal and monetary policies and change in them. If we consider the elasticities, the results of the IS-LM analysis (shown in Fig. 17.4) will undergo change because new situations/solutions are likely to emerge which would require modification of the existing results.

Elasticity of LM Function and IS-LM Analysis

The immediate impact of elasticity analysis is on the LM function or curve. The LM curve shown in Fig. 16.17 slopes upwards to the right. If viewed closely, three parts of the curve may be apparent or may be delineated or discussed—a perfectly elastic part, a perfectly inelastic part and an intermediate part or range of varying elasticities, in response to the interest rate. This means, in other words, that higher the interest rate, less elastic will be the corresponding part or point on the LM curve eventually becoming perfectly inelastic at very high rates of interest. The three parts of the LM curve are appropriately called the "Keynesian range" (the perfectly elastic part), the "classical range" (the perfectly inelastic part) and "intermediate range" (part or range of varying elasticities). These are depicted in Fig. 17.5.

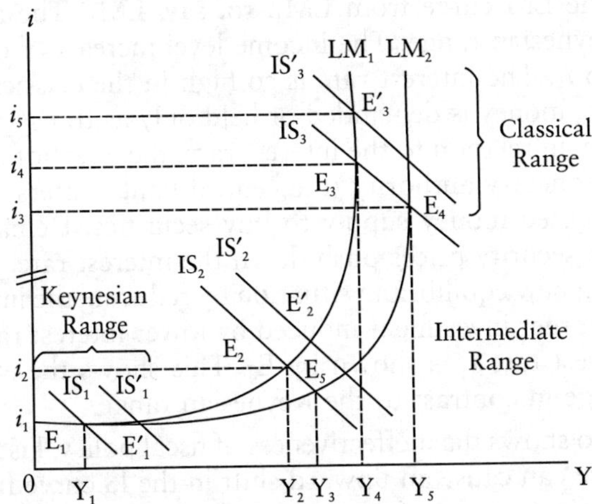

Fig. 17.5: Elasticities, Fiscal and Monetary Policies and IS-LM Analysis

The "Keynesian range", the "classical range" and the "intermediate range" of the LM function and their implications for IS-LM analysis should be clearly explained.

The Keynesian Range

Let us first analyse the *Keynesian range*. Let us consider equilibrium point E_1 with equilibrium level of income Y_1 and interest rate i_1. An increase in money supply causes a shift in the LM curve from LM_1 to, say, LM_2. This should mean that for each level of income, the interest rate should fall for new equilibrium as shown in Fig. 16.12. But, this cannot happen in the Keynesian range because of "liquidity trap" (explained in Chapter 14). The interest rate is already at the minimum or bottom level and the demand for money is perfectly elastic at this rate. An increase in money supply can shift the LM curve to the right, but, the lower end of the curve, i.e., the relevant Keynesian range, would still remain under the liquidity trap. This shows the ineffectiveness of monetary policy to reduce the interest rate and a movement downwards along the IS (here IS_1) curve to a higher level of equilibrium income.

According to Keynes, here comes the role of fiscal policy or instruments.[1] If monetary policy cannot succeed in increasing the level of income, fiscal policy can do it. Fiscal measures like increase in government expenditure or reduction in taxes can shift the IS curve along the perfectly elastic LM curve (liquidity trap range) from IS_1 to, say, IS'_1. This makes possible a new equilibrium (at E'_1) at a higher income level. Liquidity trap, the foundation of the Keynesian range, is, however, not a common phenomenon. It may happen only very occasionally during depression. The liquidity trap does not occur in progressive or prosperous economy. This is why some economists are prompted to call Keynesian economics the economics of depression.[2]

The Classical Range

Let us now turn to the *classical range*. The classical range is a contrast to the Keynesian range. Let us start with the equilibrium point E_3 and equilibrium levels of income and the interest rate of Y_4 and i_4 respectively. Let us now see the effect of increase in money supply. An increase

1. Keynes's emphasis on or prescription of fiscal policy was induced or prompted by his belief or thought that the economy (in Europe and the US) was in the liquidity trap during the early thirties or the Great Depression of the Thirties.
2. J.R. Hicks, "Mr Keynes and the classics: A suggested Interpretation" reproduced in W. Fellner and B.F. Haley (Ed.), *Reading in the Theory of Income Distribution*, Irwin, 1946, p. 472.

in money supply shifts the LM curve from LM_1, to, say, LM_2. The result of this produces a contrast to that in the Keynesian range. The income level increases from Y_4 to Y_5 and the rate of interest falls from i_4 to i_3. The interest rate is so high in the classical range that speculative demand for money is zero; money is demanded or held only as transaction balances. Given this demand pattern for money in relation to the interest rate, the effect of increase in money supply will be as follows. The monetary authority (the central bank) enters the security market with additional money or increased money supply to buy securities. Demand for securities pushes up security prices. Higher security prices push down the interest rate. This way, an increase in money supply will lead to a new equilibrium situation by reducing the interest rate and increasing the income level through larger investment induced by lower interest rate. The new equilibrium with income Y_5 and interest rate i_3 is shown by E_4. This shows the effectiveness of monetary policy in the classical range in contrast to the Keynesian range.

The classical range also shows the ineffectiveness of fiscal policy. Fiscal measures like increase in government expenditure can cause an upward shift in the IS curve from IS_3 to, say, IS'_3. But, this can only increase the interest rate from i_4 to i_5, but, the income level remains unchanged at Y_4 because of the perfectly inelastic LM curve. This proves that, in the classical range, only monetary policy, and not fiscal policy or methods, can become a powerful instrument for controlling the income level.

The Intermediate Range

Let us finally consider the *intermediate range*. This range combines some of the features or characteristics of both the Keynesian range and the classical range.

Let us start with equilibrium at E_2 with equilibrium income Y_2 and interest rate i_2. Let us now see the effect of a shift in the LM curve from LM_1 to LM_2 because of an increase in money supply. The increased money supply is partly absorbed in transaction balances and partly absorbed in speculative balances. The income level increases, but, not as much as in the classical range. The interest rate falls, but, again, not as much as in the classical range. This is shown by the equilibrium point E_5. This means that monetary policy is partially, and, not fully, effective in the intermediate range.

Fiscal policy is also partially effective in the intermediate range causing changes in both the level of income and the rate of interest. An upward shift in the IS curve because of fiscal measures from IS_2 to IS'_2 increases both the income level and the rate of interest to a new equilibrium situation shown by E'_2. The fiscal policy is effective throughout the intermediate range in varying degrees depending largely on the elasticity of the IS function.

To conclude, it can be said that monetary policy is more effective closer the equilibrium point to the classical range; and, monetary policy is less effective closer the equilibrium point to the Keynesian range. Conversely, fiscal policy is more effective closer the equilibrium to the Keynesian range, and, fiscal policy is less effective closer the equilibrium to the classical range. This means that both monetary and fiscal policies are effective (in different degrees) in the intermediate range in contrast to the Keynesian range and classical range where either the monetary policy is effective or the fiscal policy is effective but not both.

APPLICATION OF THE THREE-SECTOR MODEL: ALGEBRAIC PRESENTATION

During our analysis of application of the two-sector model, we mentioned that the IS-LM model is not only a theoretical formulation, it has great practical or empirical significance. This is more true of the three-sector model because introduction of the government sector makes it more realistic. Application of the three-sector model is discussed here in terms of hypothetical values or numbers of different constants, propensities and variables—income, consumption, savings, investment, government expenditure, taxes, demand for money, supply of money and the rate of interest. For a real economy, the hypothetical numbers have to be substituted by actual values of different variables during a particular period to analyse the process of integration of the product market and the money market and determination of general equilibrium.[3]

In the theoretical or graphical analysis above, some function or curve like the LM function is non-linear (because of varying elasticities). But, for simplicity and easier understanding, all equations, including the LM function, are assumed as linear.

We first derive the IS and LM functions or equations, and, then, proceed to the equilibrium situation.

IS Function or Equation

We start with the Keynesian income equation in a three-sector economy with government expenditure (G):

$$Y = C + I + G$$

Also, in a three-sector model with taxes (T):

$$Y = C + S + T$$

We use the consumption function developed in Equation (16.2)

$$C = 520 + 0.5\ Y$$

or, $$Y = 520 + 0.5\ Y + S$$

or, $$S = Y - 520 - 0.5\ Y$$

or, $$S + T = Y - 520 - 0.5\ Y + T \qquad (17.1)$$

Assigning value of 40 to T

Equation (17.1) can be rewritten as

$$S + T = Y - 520 - 0.5\ Y + 40 \qquad (17.2)$$

We now turn to the investment function. We use the investment function developed in Equation (16.5).

$$I = 200 - 2000\ i$$

or, $$I + G = 200 - 2000\ i + G \qquad (17.3)$$

Assigning value of 160 to G, Equation (17.3) can be rewritten as

$$I + G = 200 - 2000\ i + 160 \qquad (17.4)$$

The product market equilibrium condition in a three-sector model is I+G = S+T. This can be written in terms of equation (17.2) and equation (17.3) as

$$200 - 2000\ i + 160 = Y - 520 - 0.5\ Y + 40$$

or, $$Y = 200 - 2000\ i + 160 + 520 + 0.5\ Y - 40$$

or, $$Y - 0.5\ Y = 200 - 2000\ i + 160 + 520 + 0.5Y - 40$$

or, $$Y/2 = 200 - 2000\ i + 640$$

or, $$Y = 2(200 + 640 - 2000\ i)$$

$$= 2(840 - 2000\ i)$$

$$= (1680 - 4000\ i)$$

∴ IS function is $Y = 1680 - 4000\ i$

3. This, however, is subject to availability of proper data base.

LM Function or Equation

We start with demand for money: Md = Mt + Msp

We use the transaction demand for money (Mt) function and speculative demand for money (Msp) function developed in equation (16.7) and equation (16.9)

$$Mt = kY \ (k > 0) = 0.5\ Y \tag{17.5}$$

$$Msp = 1500 - 1000\ i \tag{17.6}$$

By combining equation (17.5) and equation (17.6), we get

$$Md = 0.5\ Y + 1500 - 1000\ i \tag{17.7}$$

The money market equilibrium condition is Md = Ms

$$\text{Let} \quad Ms = 1500 \tag{17.8}$$

The money market equilibrium can be stated in terms of equation (16.20) and equation (17.8) as

$$0.5\ Y + 1500 - 10000\ i = 1500$$

or, $0.5\ Y + 1500 - 1500 + 10000\ i$

or, $Y/2 = 1500 - 1500 + 10000\ i$

or, $Y = 2(1500 - 1500 + 10000i)$

$= 2(10{,}000\ i)$

$= 20000\ i$

$\therefore$ LM function is Y = 20000 i

Simultaneous Equilibrium of the Product Market and the Money Market

We have derived the IS function or equation. We have also derived the LM function or equation. We can now combine these two functions or equations to determine the conditions, that is values of Y and *i*, for simultaneous equilibrium in the product market and the money market.

The condition for simultaneous equilibrium in the product market and the money market is IS = LM

$$\text{IS function is } Y = 1680 - 4000\ i \tag{17.9}$$

$$\text{LM function is } Y = 20000i \tag{17.10}$$

These are two linear equations with two unknowns Y and *i*. Therefore, determinate solution is possible.

Subtracting equation (17.10) from equation (17.9), we get

$$1680 - 4000\ i - 20000\ i = 0$$

or, $1680 = 4000\ i + 20000\ i$

or, $1680 = 24{,}000\ i$

or, $i = 0.07$ or 7 per cent

Substituting the value of i (i.e., 0.07) in equation (17.10) we get

$$Y = 20{,}000\ i$$

$= 20{,}000 \times 0.07$

$= 1400$

So, the general equilibrium solution for the three-sector IS-LM model is

Y = ₹ 1400 and i = 7 per cent

This is the same solution or the equilibrium values of Y and *i* we obtained in Fig. 17.4. This shows the compatibility of graphical analysis and mathematical solution.

B. IS-LM MODEL WITH FOREIGN SECTOR

So far, we have discussed the IS-LM model for a closed economy (i.e., no foreign sector). In part A, we have introduced the government sector and discussed the impacts or the implications of government expenditure, taxes, fiscal policies and monetary policies for IS-LM analysis. Accordingly, the three-sector model has been developed with necessary changes or modifications required in the two-sector model. In this part, we introduce the foreign sector, and, discuss the model for an open economy with four sectors—business, consumer, government and the foreign sector.

IS AND LM CURVES

As in the case of two-sector model and three-sector model, we start with derivation of IS and LM curves and then proceed with the equilibrium analysis. We shall first explain derivation of the modified IS curve because of introduction of the foreign sector.

Derivation of IS Curve

Introduction of the foreign sector essentially means inclusion of export and import activities in the economy and consequent changes in the IS curve and, finally, in the IS-LM analysis. *Export* means outflow of goods and services from the country/economy and *inflow of revenue and income. Import* means inflow of goods and services and *outflow of income.* Export, import and balance of trade (export-import) have been discussed in detail in Chapter 23.

Export and import affect the IS curve through impacts on the investment function or curve and the savings function or curve. Let us see how this works out.

Let us start with the investment function or curve. To derive this, we restate the Keynesian income equation for a three-sector economy

$$Y = C + I + G$$

Because of introduction of the foreign sector, this gets modified as $Y = C + I + G + X$ where X is export

Therefore, the modified investment function or curve for a four-sector IS-LM model is

$$I + G + X$$

Export (X) is determined outside the product market and, also, by factors outside the domestic economy, i.e., foreign market demand, international business environment, etc., and, therefore, is assumed to be exogenously given.[4] Export is independent of the rate of interest because the general rate of interest in the domestic economy does not have any effect on export (only the special interest rate on export credit may have some effect). Therefore, the I+G+X curve runs parallel to the I+G curve at different rates of interest. The I+G curve in the three-sector economy actually shifts rightward or upward by the amount of given X to become the I+G+X curve. This is shown in Fig. 17.6.

We now turn to the savings function, or, more correctly, the modified savings function or curve because of introduction of imports.

4. In a multivariate analysis of an open economy involving many sectors and variables, export may be related to some of the sectors and variables. But, such analysis is outside the scope of the present IS-LM model.

Imports of a country depend on many factors the most important being the need for a country's requirement of either finished goods or industrial inputs or raw materials. Therefore, imports can be partly autonomous[5] (that is, not related to income) and other imports which depend on or a function of income. So, the import function or equation can be written as

$$M = Ma + mY$$

where M is total import, Ma is autonomous import and m is the average propensity or marginal propensity to import out of national income (Y).

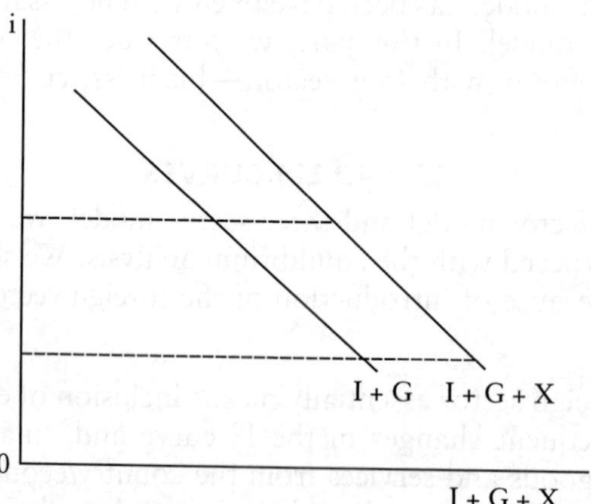

Fig. 17.6: Modified Investment (I+G+X) Curve in a Four-sector Model

To introduce import in IS-LM analysis, M is added to S+T of three-sector model. For a four-sector model, this is modified as S+T+M. The three-sector S+T curve shifts leftwards to become the four-sector S+T+M curve. This means that, for each level of income, (Y), S+T+M is more or higher than S+T by the amount of M (M as defined). This is shown in Fig. 17.7.

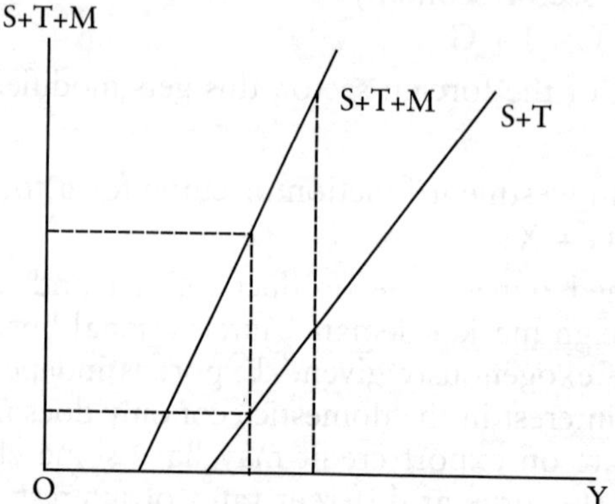

Fig. 17.7: Modified Savings (S+T+M) Curve in Four-sector Model

In Fig. 17.7, the widening gap between S+T and S+T+M needs to be explained. The gap between the two widens as Y increases. This happen because of M, or more specifically, because of the mY component in the import function. It is clear that the gap between S+T and S+T+M arises because of M. M has an autonomous or fixed component Ma and a variable component

5. For example, a large proportion of India's crude oil import is autonomous; this is essential to meet the petrol and diesel requirements of the country.

mY which is positive and increases as income (Y) increases. This is why the gap between S+T and S+T+M widens as income increases.

With changes in the investment function and the savings function because of introduction of export and import, the product market equilibrium condition also changes. The modified product market equilibrium condition for the four-sector model now becomes

$$S + T + M = I + G + X$$

This is shown by the 45° line in Fig. 17.8.

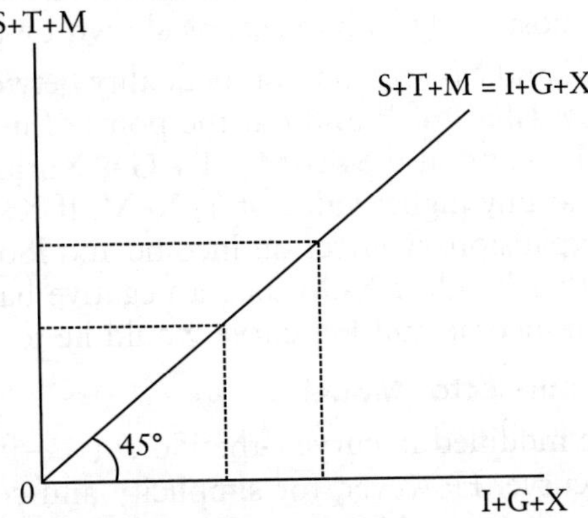

Fig. 17.8: Savings (S+T+M)—Investment (I+G+X) Equality Curve in the Four-sector Model

We have derived the investment (I+G+X) curve. We have also derived the savings (S+T+M) curve. We can now derive the modified IS curve for the four-sector model. The IS curve for the open economy (four-sector) is denoted as ISo to distinguish it from and compare it with the IS curve for a closed economy (three-sector) which is marked as ISc.

Both ISo curve and ISc curve slope downwards to the right, but, the slopes of the two curves are different. The slope of the ISo curve is more (i.e. the ISo curve is steeper) than that of the ISc curve. This is explained as follows. A fall in the interest rate increases investment. An increase in investment leads to increase in income. But, increase in income required to make I+G+X = S+T+M is less compared to that in the three-sector model. This is because import is added to savings. The autonomous import (Ma) will have strong effect. To this will be added import resulting from increase in income. This is shown in the ISo curve and the ISc curve (and their slopes) in Fig. 17.9.

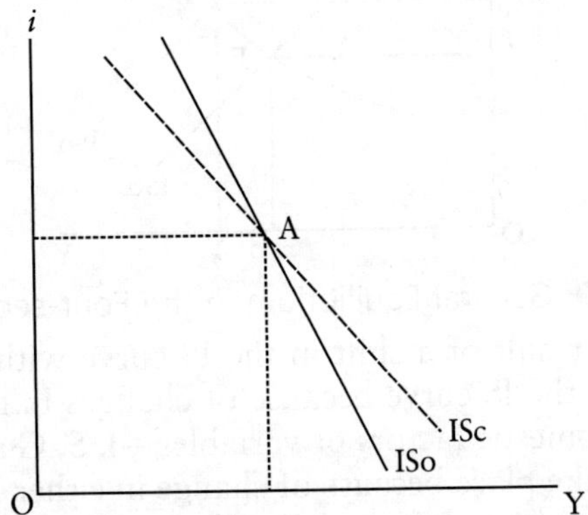

Fig. 17.9: The IS Curve (ISo) for the Four-sector Model vis-a-vis the IS Curve (ISc) for the Three-sector Model

The relationship between the curves ISo and ISc should be explained. It is seen in Fig. 17.9 that there is a point of intersection (A) between the two. Whether the two curves would intersect or one would lie to the right or left of the other would depend on the modified investment curve (I+G+X) shown in Fig. 17.6 and the modified savings curve (S+T+M) shown in Fig. 17.7. If the gap between the I+G and the I+G+X curves in Fig. 17.6 is more than that between the S+T and S+T+M curves in Fig. 17.7, the ISo curve will always lie to the right of the ISc curve. If, on the other hand, the gap between the I+G and I+G+X curves is less than that between the S+T and S+T+M curves, the ISo curve will lie to the left of the ISc curve. But, there is a range of income in which the two curves are most likely to intersect as shown by point A.

It actually boils down to X and M—equality or inequality between the two or which is larger or smaller than the other. The values of Y and *i* at the point of intersection are a combination (of Y and *i*) at which S+T = I+G and also S+T+M = I + G + X; this means that X = M. At any lower value of Y, X>M, and, at any higher value of Y, X<M. If X>M, i.e., a positive balance of trade, foreign trade has an expansionary effect on income and ISo curve would lie to the right of the ISc curve; if, on the other hand, if X<M, i.e., a negative balance of trade, foreign trade has a contractionary effect on income and ISo curve would lie to the left of ISc curve.

General Equilibrium in the Four-sector Model

We have now derived the modified IS curve—the ISo curve—for the four-sector model. We may call this the IGX-STM curve. However, for simplicity and continuity of terminology, we may continue to call it the IS curve as in the case of the three-sector model. The money market equilibrium condition remains as Md = Ms (because this is not affected by foreign trade or the foreign sector), and, therefore, the LM function or curve is retained as same as derived and shown in Fig. 16.8.

With the new IS (ISo) curve as derived and the LM curve as just mentioned, the new general equilibrium in the four-sector IS-LM model is shown by point E in Fig. 17.10. The equilibrium levels of income and the rate of interest are Yo and *i*o. The equilibrium is stable. There would, however, be a change in the equilibrium situation or point if there is a shift in the IS curve or the LM curve. We will discuss this later.

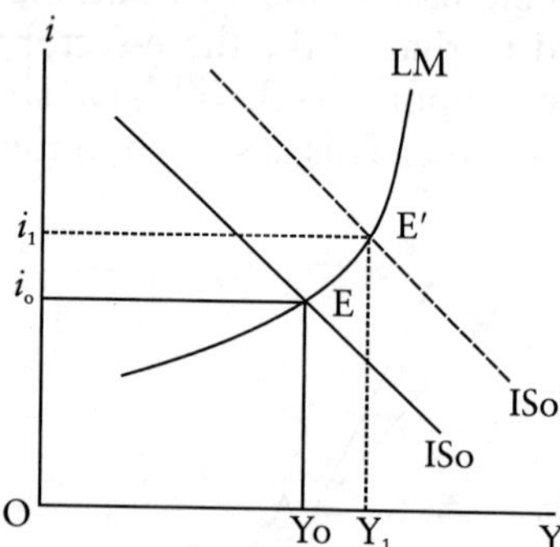

Fig. 17.10: General Equilibrium in the Four-sector Model

Let us now examine the result of a shift in the IS curve with no change in the LM curve. We are considering a shift in the IS curve because of changes in the foreign sector variables or factors X and M assuming domestic factors or variables—I, S, G and T—to remain unchanged. A shift in the ISo curve can take place because of change in either X or M or both. The shift can be either rightwards (or upwards) or leftwards (or downwards). If X increases or M decreases, the ISo curve shifts rightwards or upwards. If X and M both change simultaneously, ISo curve will still shift rightwards or upwards if increase in X is more than the increase in M, i.e., $\Delta X > \Delta M$. This is shown by ISo′ curve in Fig. 17.10 and the new equilibrium point is E′. So, because of rightward (or upward) shift in the ISo curve, equilibrium levels of both income and the rate of interest increase. The new equilibrium levels of income and interest are Y_1 and i_1.

Under the opposite circumstances, that is, if X decreases or M increases the ISo curve will shift leftwards (or downwards). The ISo curve will also shift leftwards (or downwards if both X and M decrease but decrease in X is more than the decrease in M, i.e., $\Delta X < \Delta M$. In this situation, the new equilibrium point will also shift downwards. The new equilibrium levels of income and the rate of interest will be lower than the original equilibrium levels of income and the rate of interest shown by point E.

APPLICATION OF THE FOUR-SECTOR MODEL: ALGEBRAIC PRESENTATION

Application of the four-sector IS-LM model is discussed here on lines similar to those for the two-sector model and, the three-sector model with required changes or modifications because of introduction of the foreign sector (export and import). Application of the four-sector model is analysed here in terms of hypothetical values or numbers of different constants, propensities and variables—income consumption, savings, investment, government expenditure, taxes, export, import, demand for money, supply of money and the rate of interest. For a real economy, the hypothetical numbers have to be substituted by actual values of different constants/variables during a particular period. Based on these values/data, the process of integration of the product market and the money market can be analysed and general equilibrium determined. This, however, is subject to availability of proper data base.

We shall first derive the modified IS function or equation for the four-sector model and then proceed with the equilibrium analysis or solution.

IS Function or Equation

We start with the savings function for the three-sector model and then modify it for four sectors. The savings function/equation for the three-sector model was derived in equation (17.2) as

$$S+T = Y-520-0.5\ Y + 40 \qquad (17.11)$$

We now introduce the import function or equation (mentioned in the text above)

$$M = Ma + mY$$

Assigning value of 50 to autonomous import (Ma) and 0.1 to average or marginal propensity to import (m), we get

$$M = 50 + 0.1\ Y \qquad (17.12)$$

Combining equation (17.11) and equation (17.12), we get

$$S+T+M = Y - 520 - 0.5\ Y + 40 + 50 + 0.1\ Y \qquad (17.13)$$

We now bring the investment function for the three-sector model from equation (17.4):

$$I+G = 200 - 2000\ i + 160$$

Export (X) is now added to this. Assigning value of 50 to X, the modified investment equation for the four-sector model becomes

$$I+G+X = 200 - 2000\ i + 160 + 50 \qquad (17.14)$$

The product market equilibrium condition for the four-sector model is I+G+X = S+T+M. This can be written in terms of equation (17.13) and equation (17.14) as

$$200–2000i+160+50 = Y–520–0.5Y+40+50+0.1Y$$

or, $Y = 200–2000i+160+50+520+0.5Y–40–50–0.1Y$

or, $Y–0.5Y+0.1Y = 200+2000i+160+50+520+0.5Y–40–50$

or, $Y–Y(0.5–0.1) = 200–2000i + 640$

or, $Y–0.4Y = 840–2000i$

or, $Y(1.0–0.4) = 840–2000i$

or, $0.6Y = 840–2000i$

or, $3/5Y = 840–2000i$

or, $3Y = 4200–10000i$

or, $Y = 1400–3333i$ (approx.)

∴ *IS function for the four-sector model is* $Y = 1400 – 3333i$.

LM Function or Equation

We had mentioned in the text that there is no change in the LM function, that is, in the demand for money and supply of money. Therefore, the LM function remains same as in the three-sector model. The money market equilibrium condition is Md=Ms. This can be written in terms of equation (17.7) and equation (17.8) as

$$0.5Y + 1500 – 10000\ i = 1500$$

or, $0.5Y = 1500 – 1500 + 10{,}000i$

or, $Y/2 = 1500 – 1500 = 10{,}000i$

or, $Y = 2000i$

∴ *LM function for the four-sector model is* $Y = 20{,}000i$

Simultaneous Equilibrium of the Product Market and the Money Market

The condition for simultaneous equilibrium of the product market and the money market is IS = LM

IS function is $Y = 1400 – 3333i$ (17.15)

LM function is $Y = 20{,}000i$ (17.16)

These are two linear equations with two unknowns Y and *i*. Therefore, determinate solution is possible.

Subtracting equation (17.16) from equation (17.15), we get

$$1400 – 3333i – 20{,}000i = 0$$

or, $1400 = 3333i + 20{,}000i$

or, $1400 = 23{,}333i$

or, $i = 0.06$ or 6 per cent

Substituting the value of i (0.06) in equation (17.16) we get

$$Y = 20{,}000i$$
$$= 20{,}000 \times 0.06$$
$$= 1200$$

So, the general equilibrium solution for the four-sector IS-LM model is

Y = ₹ 1200 and i = 6 per cent

Equilibrium values of Y and i in the four-sector model are different than those (Y = ₹ 1400 and i = 7 per cent) in the three-sector model. This is explained by the foreign sector factors or variables, that is, values of X and M. If we assume values of X, Ma and m different than those used in the present solution, equilibrium values of Y and *i* would also be different. In the real world, the solution or equilibrium values for every economy would be different.

REVIEW QUESTIONS

1. Develop the three-sector IS-LM model taking into account government expenditure and taxes. Also take into account fiscal and monetary changes and their effects on the equilibrium situation.
2. Consider elasticity of the LM function or curve and its impact on IS-LM analysis. Analyse the impact in terms of the "classical range", the "Keynesian range" and the "intermediate range".
3. Work out the application of the three-sector model in terms of hypothetical values of different variables, propensities and constants and compare the solution (in terms of value of Y and *i*) with that of the two-sector model.
4. Explain modifications in the IS-LM model because of introduction of the foreign sector. Also mention the effect of a shift in the IS curve.
5. Discuss the application of the four-sector IS-LM model in terms of hypothetical values. Compare the solution with that of the three-sector model and mention the reason for difference in results.
6. Do you think the IS-LM model (two-sector, three-sector or four-sector) is only a theoretical formulation or it has enough practical significance? Comment in terms of application of the model.

SUGGESTED READINGS

- E. Shapiro, *Macroeconomic Analysis* (Fifth Edition), Galgotia Publications, 1984, Chapter 14.
- G. Ackley, *Macroeconomics: Theory and Policy*, Macmillan, 1978, Chapter 11.
- J.R. Hicks, "Mr. Keynes and the Classics: A Suggested Interpretation" in M.G. Mueller (Ed.) *Readings in Macroeconomics*, 1966.
- M. Friedman, and W. Heller, *Monetary vs. Fiscal Policy*, New York University Press, 1969.
- T.F. Dernburg, *Macroeconomics: Concepts, Theories and Policies*, McGraw Hill, 1985, Chapter 9.

PART–VI

MACROECONOMIC RATIOS AND POLICIES

Macroeconomic ratios and policies are of special relevance to business and management. Various macroeconomic ratios—capital-output ratio, output-labour ratio, input-output ratio, cash reserve ratio and such others—determine the operational level and efficiency of business units. Twelve such ratios have been discussed in Chapter 18. These ratios also include those on income distribution.

Chapters 19, 20, and 21 are devoted to different macroeconomic policies—monetary policy, fiscal policy, and physical policy. Various instruments of monetary policy, roles of monetary policy in controlling inflation and recession/depression and, in economic growth and development, have been discussed in details in Chapter 19. Chapter 20 is devoted to fiscal policy—instruments of fiscal policy, roles of fiscal policy, roles of fiscal policy during inflation and recession/depression, built-in fiscal stabilisers, etc. Chapter 21 deals with physical policy which has a very direct bearing on business and management of enterprises. Major physical policies or controls like MRTP Act, Capital Issues Control Act, and FERA have been discussed and their implications given.

Chapter 18

Macroeconomic Ratios

In this chapter, we shall discuss some ratios which play vital roles in macroeconomic and business analysis. These are ratios spread over a wide range and relate to consumption patterns, production structure of the industry or of the entire economy, income distribution, etc. Some of these ratios like the capital-output ratio or the incremental capital-output ratio is often talked about, but not always clearly understood; or, the ratios may be known conceptually, but the empirical forms may not be known. A discussion of these ratios would also help in the better understanding of growth economics or growth models which make extensive use of many of these ratios. We state below twelve major macroeconomic ratios.

TWELVE MACROECONOMIC RATIOS

1. Consumption-income ratio
2. Savings-income ratio
3. Capital-output ratio
4. Capital-labour ratio
5. Output-labour ratio
6. Value added-output ratio
7. Input-output ratio
8. Cash reserve ratio
9. Cash-income ratio
10. Labour's share of income
11. Capital's share of income
12. Land's share of income

The above twelve ratios may be classified into four groups or categories based on the meaning and structure of these ratios. The ratios, in classified form, are shown below.[1]

Propensities or Behavioural Ratios

Consumption-income ratio (propensity to consume)
Savings-income ratio (propensity to save)

Production Structure Ratios

Capital-output ratio (acceleration principle)
Capital-labour ratio (factor proportion)

1. The description in brackets indicates the meaning and implication of a particular ratio.

Output-labour ratio (productivity)
Value added-output ratio (value added coefficient)
Input-output ratio (technical coefficient of production)

Cash or Credit Ratios

Cash-income ratio (reciprocal of the velocity of circulation)
Cash reserve ratio (credit creation capacity of commercial banks)

Factor Income Ratios or Distributive Shares[2]

Labour's share of income (income distribution)
Capital's share of income (income distribution)
Land's share of income (income distribution)

Some of the above ratios have already been discussed earlier. Propensities or behavioural ratios were discussed in detail in Chapter 4. The monetary (cash or credit) ratios were also explained in Chapters 14 and 15. We shall not deal with these ratios here. We shall discuss here the production structure ratios and factor income ratios or distributive shares which have not been dealt with so far. The concept of the capital-output ratio was mentioned during our discussion of the acceleration principle in Chapter 5, but not elaborated upon. We shall discuss this ratio in some details here because this is of great significance in macroeconomic analysis.

We shall briefly discuss the capital-labour ratio, output-labour ratio and value added-output ratio and then deal with capital-output ratio and input-output ratio.

CAPITAL-LABOUR RATIO

The capital-labour ratio is defined as

$$K/L$$

where K is capital stock expressed in value terms and L is labour or employment expressed in number so that the ratio gives the value of capital employed per unit of labour, that is, per person employed.

Capital-labour ratio, as already mentioned, indicates factor proportion or combination, i.e. the proportion in which capital and labour are combined in the production process. This ratio measures the relative capital and labour intensities of the process of production. If between two production processes, the capital-labour ratio is higher in the first compared to the second, we may say that the first process is more capital intensive than the second process; or alternatively, we may say that the second process is more labour intensive than the first process.

For example, capital-labour ratio in chemical industries which is highly capital intensive is always higher than that in the textile industry which is labour intensive rather than capital intensive.

If the capital-output ratio increases between two periods, which happens during the initial years of industrialisation, we can say that the capital intensity of the productive process has, in general, increased.

OUTPUT-LABOUR RATIO

Output-labour ratio may be written as

$$Y/L$$

2. One can also include in this category the 'organisation's' share of income because the 'organisation' is the fourth factor of production.

where Y is net national product (or national income) and L is employment so that the ratio, in effect, gives value added-labour ratio as a measure of labour productivity.

If a production process is highly capital intensive, labour productivity also would be high. In general, higher the capital intensity, the higher is the productivity of labour. For example, in manufacturing of petroleum products which is highly capital intensive, labour productivity is many times more than in textiles or printing and publishing which are generally labour intensive.

VALUE ADDED-OUTPUT RATIO

Value added-output ratio or the value-added coefficient may be put as

$$Y/O$$

where Y is net national product or total value added (net) and O is gross value of output which includes intermediate products.

The value added-output ratio shows the extent of value added in the productive process; or, in other words, the ratio shows raw material (including intermediate products) intensity of a particular process of production. If the value-added coefficient is very low, it indicates that the industry is highly raw material intensive. For example, in food products manufacturing which is highly raw material intensive, value added-labour ratio is very low (say, about 0.10), whereas in high technology sectors like generation of electrical power, the value-added coefficient is very high (sometimes as high as 0.40).

CAPITAL-OUTPUT RATIO

The capital-output ratio is defined as

$$K/Y$$

where K is the capital stock (expressed in values) and Y is net national product (also expressed in values).

A parallel concept of the capital-output ratio is the incremental capital-output ratio (ICOR). This ratio, at any time t, is defined as

$$\frac{K_t - K_{t-1}}{Y_t - Y_{t-1}} = \frac{I_t}{Y_t - Y_{t-1}}$$

where I_t is investment[3] or incremental capital and $(Y_t - Y_{t-1})$ is the increment in output.

Like the capital-labour ratio, the capital-output ratio or the incremental capital-output ratio indicates the capital intensity of the productive process.[4] High capital-output ratio indicates a capital-intensive method of production. Sectors with high capital-output ratios are chemical products, petroleum products, generation of electrical power, etc. These are highly capital-intensive industries. Sectors with low capital-output ratios are textiles, rubber products, printing and publishing, etc. These are industries with low capital intensities.

Empirical studies have shown a certain cyclical variability in the capital-output ratio. The capital-output ratio generally rises during recessions because output falls during such periods, but the stock of capital remains nearly stable. It can, at most, fall no faster than depreciation. Similarly, it takes time to increase capital during an upswing, but output may be growing rapidly; hence, the ratio falls during this phase of the cycle.

3. We had explained the conceptual difference between capital and investment in Chapter 1. Capital is actually measured as the cumulation, from a fixed starting value of annual net investment.
4. Net capital-labour ratio is a more direct measure of the capital and labour intensities of a particular process of production.

Some empirical studies have tried to establish the secular or long-run constancy of the capital-output ratio which is consistent with its cyclical variability. Constancy of this ratio would mean that all investments are 'induced' investments, that is, induced by expansion of output. This assumes the operation of the acceleration principle. It is true that in the long run, additional net investments do create additional capacity to produce, and this capacity, must be utilised fully for steady growth; hence, capital and output both would increase. But the question remains whether they increase in the same proportion resulting in constant capital-output ratio (as some studies have tried to establish) or in different proportions resulting in increasing or decreasing capital-output ratio. On this point, there is no clear agreement among economists.

We shall now discuss some capital-output ratios for India. But, before we do so, we shall distinguish between fixed capital and working capital. At any point of time, total capital stock is made up of two components, fixed capital and working capital or circulating capital. *Fixed capital* comprises fixed assets like land,[5] buildings, machinery, etc., while *working or circulating capital* comprises inventories. Capital-output ratios can be estimated for these two components of capital stock separately. Capital-output ratio for fixed capital will always be higher than that for inventories. The capital-output ratios can also be estimated for major sectors like agriculture, manufacturing and tertiary services (and also for subsectors within these major sectors). These are called sectoral capital-output ratios.

The capital-output ratio for India is approximately 3 : 1[6] (K/Y, i.e. K : Y). This may also be written as only 3 because the capital-output ratio is always expressed as capital units per unit of output. The incremental capital-output ratio (ICOR) for India is about 1.70. Corresponding to the ICOR of 1.70, incremental fixed capital-output ratio is 1.40 and incremental inventories-output ratio is 0.30.[7]

Among all the sectors, the capital-output ratio is most important for the manufacturing sector; because, it is in this sector that the concept is most relevant and is most extensively used and has important implications in terms of technology level, labour productivity, etc. The capital-output ratio in the Indian manufacturing sector is about 3.5, fixed capital-output ratio is 2.7 and inventories-output ratio is 0.8.

INPUT-OUTPUT ANALYSIS

Input-output ratio may be written as

$$X_i/X$$

where X_i is any input (expressed in value) and X is the value of output in which the input is used. It should be made clear here that X_i *is not a factor input, but raw material input*. This distinction is important.

An input-output ratio may also be called a coefficient. We may write

$$X_i/X = a_i$$

where a_i is called the technical coefficient of production because this is largely determined by technological factors.[8]

5. Views differ as to whether land should be considered as a capital asset or not.
6. Net capital stock to output ratio.
7. ICOR is defined as Net Domestic Capital Formation (NDCF) to output ratio.
8. The amount of a particular input or input mix used in producing a particular output is determined by the kind or the level of technology used.

The input-output ratio or the technical coefficient of production is the starting point of a wider framework of input-output analysis which has been widely accepted as an important analytical tool in economics in general and quantitative economics in particular. We shall briefly discuss here the origin, complete meaning and applications of input-output analysis, and also, of developments in input-output analysis in India.

Input-output analysis originated from the famous American economist, W.W. Leontief.[9] The concept is based on the fundamental fact of interdependence of industries or economic activities in a country or a nation. The interdependence is expressed through the fact that almost every industry uses, in its production process, some inputs which are the outputs of some other industries like many engineering industries using iron and steel or iron and steel using coal.

The input-output relationships may be more clearly illustrated with an example. Let us assume that there are only two industries or sectors in an economy, namely agriculture and manufacturing. Then, the input and output flows may be shown as below (Table 18.1).

Table 18.1: Input-Output Flows (Numbers)

Industry	*Inputs to Agriculture*	*Inputs to Manufacturing*	*Final Demand*	*Total Output*
Agriculture	25	175	50	250
Manufacturing	40	20	60	120

Final demand would consist of final consumption (private plus government), investment and exports.

If we use symbols and designate agriculture as industry (sector) 1 and manufacturing as industry (sector) 2, the input-output flow process may be shown as in Table 18.2.

If instead of actual flows, we use input coefficients, the numerical example shown in Table 18.2 may be rewritten as in Table 18.3.

In, terms of symbols, the input coefficients may be written in more general form in Table 18.4.

Table 18.2: Input-Output Flows (Symbols)

Industry	*Inputs to Industry 1*	*Inputs to Industry 2*	*Final Demand*	*Total Output*
Industry 1	X_{11}	X_{12}	C_1	X_1
Industry 2	X_{21}	X_{22}	C_2	X_2

Note: In the input flow symbol, the first subscript indicates the sector in which the input originates and the second subscript stands for the sector to which the input flows.

Table 18.3: Input Coefficients (Numbers)

Industry	*Inputs to Industry 1*	*Inputs to Industry 2*	*Final Demand*	*Total Output*
Industry 1	0.10	1.46	50	250
Industry 2	0.16	0.17	60	120

9. Leontief's original concepts are contained in *The Structure of American Economy*, 1919-39 published in 1951. Further elaboration and extensions of Leontief's basic ideas are to be found in *Studies in the Structure of the American Economy* by Leontief and others published in 1953. There have been many extensions later.

Table 18.4: Input Coefficients (Symbol)

Industry	*Inputs to Industry 1*	*Inputs to Industry 2*	*Final Demand*	*Total Output*
Industry 1	a_{11}	a_{12}	C_1	X_1
Industry 2	a_{21}	a_{22}	C_2	X_2

where $a_{11} = x_{11}/X_1$, $a_{12} = x_{12}/X_2$, $a_{22} = x_{22}/X_2$, etc., or, in more general notations

$$a_{ij} = x_{ij}/X_i$$

Table 18.4 shows the basic input-output framework in which the elements a_{11}, a_{12}, etc. (or a_{ij}) are the fixed input coefficients or the technical coefficients of production.

In Table 18.5,[10] we present an actual input-output flow table for the United Kingdom for three sectors, namely agriculture, industry and services.

It would be noticed in Table 18.5 that the total value of each of the sectors, i.e. the row total (50,430) is equal to the total value of inputs, i.e. the column total (50,430). This is a consistency criterion in input-output analysis.

Table 18.5: An Input-Output Flow Table for the United Kingdom

(Unit: Million $)

Input/Output	*Agriculture*	*Industry*	*Services*	*Final Demand*	*Total Output*
Agriculture	277	444	14	1,209	1,944
Industry	587	11,148	1,844	16,605	30,224
Services	236	2,915	1,572	13,539	18,262
Total input	1,100	14,507	3,470	31,353	50,430

Note: This table is abstracted from R. O'Connor and E.W. Henry, *Input-output Analysis and its Applications*, 1975, p. 23, Table 2.3.

INPUT-OUTPUT MODEL

The input-output model, as it is sometimes called, may be written (in terms of two-industry case) as

$$X_1 = X_{11} + X_{12} + C_1$$
$$X_2 = X_{21} + X_{22} + C_2$$

or, more correctly as

$$X_1 = a_{11}x_1 + a_{12}x_2 + C_1$$
$$X_2 = a_{21}x_1 + a_{22}x_2 + C_2$$

where a_{11}, a_{12}, etc., represent fixed input and technology levels. This is one of the assumptions of the original input-output model.[11]

These are two equations in two unknowns X_1 and X_2 (a_{ij}s are given and C_1 and C_2 also are given or exogenous), and, therefore, a solution exists for the model.

10. This is an input-output table in highly aggregated form, that is, for only three sectors. Some of the actual input-output tables now constructed in various countries pertain to more than two hundred sectors.
11. Later, attempts have been made to forecast changes in input coefficients, that is, to allow variability in input coefficients or technology levels.

The two-industry model discussed above can easily be generalised to n number (i.e. any number) of industries.

APPLICATIONS OF INPUT-OUTPUT TECHNIQUE

Input-output (I-O) analysis, through various developments, has evolved into a useful technique for many applications. Major applications of input-output analysis are mentioned below.

(a) Input-output analysis is found most useful in understanding the complexities of interdependence or interactions in any economic system.
(b) It helps the national income analyst because it provides a detailed breakdown of the macroeconomic aggregates and money flows.
(c) An important application of I-O technique consists of providing a framework for inter-sectoral money flow or cash flow analysis. Instead of commodity flows, the technique is many times used in analysing or explaining cash flow patterns in modern business processes.
(d) The technique has found useful applications in regional economic analysis. It has been successfully used by many in analysing interregional inter-sectoral flows of commodities and money and their effects on regional income determination.
(e) Input-output can also be, and is sometimes used as, a projection technique. Given the final demand estimates for any period, I-O model can forecast future production levels of various industries.
(f) Finally, the input-output approach can be used in optimisation analysis. The theory of input-output can be regarded as a simple form of linear programming. In the simplest Leontief system, in which no substitution of inputs are possible, the optimising solution is the one and only efficient solution possible.

INPUT-OUTPUT ANALYSIS IN INDIA

In India, input-output analysis has been generally confined to construction of I-O tables at national and regional (State) levels either for understanding the nature of sectoral interdependence or estimation of the input coefficients themselves or for developing I-O model for projection purposes.

Three organisations which have prepared I-O tables for India are the Indian Statistical Institute (ISI) Calcutta, the Gokhale Institute of Politics and Economics, Pune and the Planning Commission, Government of India.

The Indian Statistical Institute (ISI) started construction of I-O table for India in 1954. The first table prepared by ISI was for 36 × 36 sectors for 1951-52. The Institute subsequently prepared a table for 1953-54.

The Gokhale Institute had constructed a 238 × 238 table for 1963, and also an aggregated 84 × 84 table for the same year. Later (1979 and after) the Gokhale institute has also prepared some regional (State level) input-output tables.

The Planning Commission had prepared an I-O table (66 × 66 sectors) for 1965-66 (at 1970-71 prices) during the Fifth Plan period which was used for future projections. I-O tables have been prepared during subsequent plans also.

One common limitation of input-output tables prepared in India is that in these tables, there is excessive emphasis on the manufacturing sector (which contributes only about 25 per cent of India's GNP) compared to the agricultural sector (which contributes about 35 per cent of GNP) and the tertiary sectors—trade, transport and communications and services (which contribute about 40 per cent of GNP). This phenomenon is generally explained by non-availability of a proper database for agriculture and various tertiary activities.

INCOME DISTRIBUTION

In Chapter 3, we had shown that value added by a manufacturing process, and also in the aggregate, consists of wages, rent, interest, and profits, that is, incomes of the four factors of production. In other words, income generated in a country is distributed among the four factors of production in certain proportions which determine their income shares.

Among the four factor incomes, measurement of labour's share has been the primary concern of the economists in empirical analysis. Labour's share of income may be written as

$$W/Y \text{ or } wN/Y$$

where W[12] is wages (w is the wage rate and N employment) and Y is income. Among the four factors, labour's share in national income is always the highest. For India, this share is generally around 60 per cent.

A number of empirical studies have been conducted to determine the long-term trends in labour's share. Some have tried to establish long-term stability of the share (which may be consistent with short-run or cyclical variability) while others have shown a secular increase in the share. One of the comprehensive studies covering a period of about three decades has shown that the share of wages and salaries and investment income[13] increases, while that of unincorporated income decreases over time.[14]

In India also, some studies have been conducted on the long-term trend of distributive shares. We refer to the results of one of the studies which is quite comprehensive. This study demonstrates stability of labour's share (a small net increase between the initial year and the terminal year), increase in capital's share, and decrease in land's share in national income during a twenty-year period.[15] No recent studies are available.

REVIEW QUESTIONS

1. Enumerate twelve macroeconomic ratios. Give full descriptions.
2. Distinguish between capital output ratio and incremental capital-output ratio with reference to investment and income.
3. Give an introduction to input-output analysis and show its relevance to macroeconomics.

SUGGESTED READINGS

- W.J. Baumol, *Economic Theory and Operations Analysis*, Prentice Hall of India Pvt. Ltd., Fourth Edition, 1996.
- R. O'Connor and E.W. Henry, *Input-Output Analysis and its Applications*, 1975, Chapters 1, 2 and 4.
- Alpha C. Chiang, *Fundamental Methods of Mathematical Economics*, McGraw-Hill, International Editions (Economics Series), 1984.

---

12. There are some definitional problems associated with the determination of W or w. This has been discussed by some economists.
13. Investment income includes corporation profits and should also include income from investment in land resources.
14. The study considers various definitions of income and concludes that said movements in income shares would be valid only if income is defined as net national product. If, however, income is defined as gross domestic income, the trends in investment income may be different. Refer S.A. Goldberg, "Long-run Changes in the Distribution of Income by Factor Shares in Canada" published in *The Behaviour of Income Shares: Studies in Income and Wealth*, Vol. 27, National Bureau of Economic Research, Princeton, 1964.
15. Refer Bakul H. Dholakia, *The Sources of Economic Growth in India*, 1974, Chapter 11.

Chapter 19

Macroeconomic Policy: Monetary Policy

WHAT IS MONETARY POLICY?

Monetary Policy is one of those macroeconomic concepts which is more easily and frequently talked about but not so precisely defined.

To start with, it may be said that monetary *policy* stands somewhere mid-way between monetary *theory* and monetary *practice*. Monetary theory lays down principles which are concerned with the influence of the quantity or supply of money in the economy while monetary practice is concerned with actual monetary measures, generally based on monetary theories, which translate monetary policy decisions into action.

In most general terms, monetary policy may be defined as a "policy employing the central bank's control of the supply of money as an instrument for achieving the objectives of general economic policy."[1] This definition means that monetary policy is one which employs the central bank's control over the supply of money as an instrument for achieving certain given objectives of economic policy. Since the common objectives of economic policy are attainment of full employment, price stability, balance of payments equilibrium and rapid economic growth, monetary policy would be concerned with these objectives with certain given priorities fixed by the monetary authorities and the government of the country and, the effectiveness of monetary policy would depend on the degree to which it succeeds in achieving these objectives. According to a more comprehensive definition, monetary policy includes "all monetary decisions and measures irrespective of whether their aims are monetary or non-monetary, and all non-monetary decisions and measures that aim at affecting the monetary system."[2] This definition would include, within the scope of monetary policy, not only measures of every kind which are taken for the purpose of influencing the value, volume, etc., of money, but also monetary measures which pursue non-monetary economic, social, or political aim. Likewise, non-monetary measures such as incomes policy, control of prices or wages, physical controls, budgetary measures, etc., would be included within the scope of monetary policy in so far as their primary aim is to influence the monetary situation.[3]

OBJECTIVES OF MONETARY POLICY

This brings us to the objectives of monetary policy. Once we discuss the objectives, the meaning and scope of monetary policy may be more clearly understood.

---

1. H.G. Johnson, "Monetary Theory and Policy", *American Economic Review*, June 1962.
2. Paul Einzig, *Monetary Policy: Ends and Means*, 1964, p. 50.
3. This definition seems to be too comprehensive, and sometimes rather vague to be acceptable to many. This may, however, be understood to set an outer limit to the scope of monetary policy.

There is no fixed or single objective of monetary policy which has been held constant over the years. This is because monetary policy, like any other policy of a government or a country, at any point of time, is closely linked to the national and international economic situation prevailing during the period. The objectives of monetary policy, therefore, have been changing over the years, with the changing nature of economic development and economic problems of various countries.

During the period when the international gold standard system operated—a system under which a currency was convertible into gold according to a pre-determined rate, the primary concern of monetary authorities was to maintain the external value of the currency. The actions of monetary authorities in those days were guided by the objective of expanding credit when inflow of gold took place and contracting credit when there was gold outflow.

Gradually, there was a shift in the policy of monetary authorities from maintaining a stable external value of the currency to ensuring its stable internal value. (This incidentally was partially responsible for the collapse of the gold standard system.) There was abandonment of the principle of expanding credit and contracting credit according to gold flows. The new objective emerging out of this was to ensure a stable price level irrespective of the impact it might have on the external value of the currency. In the pre-Keynesian days, i.e. before 1930s, price stability was the single-established objective of monetary policy and monetary policy was the only instrument of macroeconomic policy.

Two events in the 1930s drastically changed the role of this policy. Firstly, the Great Depression which produced mass unemployment caused a major shift in the objective of national economic policies in favour of full employment. Secondly the Keynesian revolution following the publication of Keynes's *General Theory* in 1936 (also influenced by the economic situation during the Depression) brought to us the same economic policy objective, namely the maintenance of full employment, now more commonly known as economic stability.

Since the middle of 1950s, rapid economic growth has been added to the objectives of monetary policy. Rapid post-war recovery in Europe, Russia, and Japan led to high rates of economic growth in these countries surpassing even the growth rate of the American economy. But such high rates of growth also gave rise to balance of payments problems in many countries. Therefore, in the late 1950s and early 1960s, the balance of payments equilibrium has been added to the list of monetary objectives in a large number of affected countries.

In addition to the above objectives which have evolved over a period of time, in developing economies, monetary policy is expected to achieve some further objectives mostly necessitated by the structure of economies and the state of economic development in these countries.

The more important of these objectives are:

(i) to maintain continuously low rates of interest;

(ii) to force the community to save a larger fraction of its income;

(iii) to create a continuous market for government securities;

(iv) to help in the establishment and development of term financing institutions; and

(v) to provide credit at differential interest rates to weaker sections and other preferred borrowers of the community.

The above shows that in modern economies, monetary policy has before it a multiplicity of objectives. And multiplicity of objectives raises the problem of conflicting objectives, and therefore, of conflicting choice, because the pursuit of some objectives can be done only at the expense of some other objectives. The real dilemma of the monetary policy maker—the central bank—is not whether to direct its efforts towards the achievement of one rather than the other of these objectives, but rather, how much to sacrifice of one objective for a gain in the other in the event of conflict.

The best example of this conflict and trade-off may be seen in developing economies. In developing countries, economic growth is the overriding objective, but the monetary authorities cannot completely ignore the objective of price stability. However, the trade-off in a developing economy between these two objectives will be different from that of a developed country. A developing economy may be willing to accept a larger degree of inflation for a given rate of economic growth. The exact trade-off in a particular country, however, would depend on the choice between stability and growth, or rather, on a particular combination of the two.

INSTRUMENTS OF MONETARY POLICY

The central bank of a country (the Reserve Bank of India in India) is responsible for formulating and implementing the monetary policies of the country. The traditional instruments through which the central bank implements or enforces the monetary policies are the bank rate, open market operations, and variable reserve ratio. These are called the general or quantitative instruments of control. We have discussed the meaning and nature of each of these in Chapter 15. Besides these general instruments, there are also selective or qualitative instruments, which, as the name suggests, are used only selectively, that is, for selective sectors or purposes.

The three traditional instruments generally operate by influencing the credit creating capacity of the commercial banks directly or indirectly, and, thereby affecting total money supply.

Perhaps the most useful policy tool is open market operations, i.e. purchase and sale of securities in the open market. The central bank's purchase of securities in the open market increases total availability of money and credit, while a sale leads to contraction of money supply. Through open market operations, the central bank can effectively control the expansion or contraction of credit. It is also a very flexible tool, and therefore, favoured by many monetary economists and policy makers.

Another way to influence the creation of money in an economy is to control the level of required reserves the commercial banks must keep against their deposits. If the central bank adopts an expansionary policy, it will decide to reduce reserve requirements of the commercial banks. As a result of this, a part of the existing required reserves is reclassified as excess reserves and, consequently, becomes available for credit creation by the banks. The opposite happens when the central bank decides to increase reserve requirements, and the commercial banks may have to call in some of their loans and/or sell some of their securities to build up reserves. Although fixing reserves is a powerful tool, it may cause considerable dislocations in the economy; and therefore, as a policy tool, it is used much less frequently than open market operations and even the bank rate.

The bank rate, as an instrument of credit control, operates by controlling, or rather altering, the *cost of credit*, and is likely to affect the *level or availability of credit* only indirectly (unless cost and availability of credit are perfectly correlated). As a policy instrument, it is considered generally less efficient than either open market operations or variable reserve ratio.

Besides the three general instruments discussed above, there are selective or qualitative instruments of credit control employed by the central bank from time to time. Unlike the general instruments which affect the total volume of credit directly, the selective instruments of monetary policy affect particular types of credit extended by the banks.

The immediate object of imposing selective credit controls is to regulate both the amount and the terms on which credit is extended by the banks for selected purposes—say, for financing the speculative purchase of sugar or paddy which may be in short supply and stock-building by the speculators is likely to lead to price spurt—without at the same time curbing credit expansion in general. This is a case of selective credit contraction. The opposite would happen in case of selective credit expansion, that is, say, for financing procurement of certain essential commodities.

Selective credit controls—either credit expansion or contraction—may sometimes be contrary to the general policy of credit control. For, example, the central bank may be following a policy of general credit squeeze; but at the same time, may be enforcing selective credit liberalisation, say, for food procurement and distribution.

This way, elective credit controls, in certain situations, might prove more effective in meeting the goals of monetary policy where the general instruments of credit control may either fail or appear discriminatory.

MONETARY POLICY AND INFLATION

The above instruments of credit control (general or selective), in addition to being used as measures of general economic regulation are particularly employed in situation of economic imbalances arising out of either inflation or depression. Although there may be several objectives of monetary policy as outlined above, price stability, and resulting from it, economic stability, still remains one of the foremost objectives of monetary policy.

Let us first examine the effectiveness of monetary policy in controlling inflation. Inflation may be either demand-pull or cost-push and effectiveness of monetary policy, or for that matter, of any policy, would be different in controlling the two situations. It is generally known that monetary policy is more effective in controlling demand-pull inflation than cost-push inflation. Let us see the relative effectiveness.

In demand-pull inflation, prices rise because of rapid expansion of aggregate demand and the issue is: can the central bank control the increase in aggregate demand or purchasing power by controlling the supply and cost of money? Or, more fundamentally, can the central bank effectively control the money supply or credit availability? The answer to this may be obtained by analysing the effectiveness and limitations of a restrictive monetary policy.

The first limitation of a restrictive monetary policy is related to velocity of circulation of money. Given the volume or level of money supply (M), its velocity of circulation (V) mostly depends on public transactions. So, even if the central bank is able to keep the money supply constant or actually decrease it, the inflationary expansion of aggregate demand might still continue because the public might succeed in increasing the effective money supply (MV) by increasing the velocity of whatever quantity of money is available to them.

Besides this possibility, there are enough doubts about the effectiveness of a restrictionist monetary policy in controlling the composition or availability of credit which have important implications during inflationary situations.

Firstly, during periods of inflation, the commercial banks may be able to finance expanding business activity through portfolio adjustment (it does not increase the total amount of credit but changes its composition or structure) by selling government securities and lending the proceeds to the borrowers. If the banks expect that the rates of interest will rise (or continue to rise) in future (during inflation, interest rates will be generally high), they will clearly gain by shifting out of government securities into loans. And, when demand for bank loans begins to subside, the banks can again switch back into government securities. The changing composition of banks' asset portfolios over time reveals that banks do behave in this manner—shifting out of government securities into loans in times of restrictive monetary policy and moving into government securities in times of easy money policy pursued by the central bank.

Secondly, in recent times, the fast growth of non-bank financial intermediaries has considerably weakened the traditional monetary controls enforced by the central bank. The financial intermediaries are life and general insurance companies, various financial institutions, deposit and loan associations, etc. These intermediaries receive savings from the public and invest the same in securities and loans in much the same way as do the commercial banks. But the essential difference between the banks and the financial intermediaries is that, unlike banks, they do not, rather cannot, create credit. These are called 'intermediaries' because they merely channel savings into the hands of spenders. It is argued that the lending operations of the financial intermediaries can considerably weaken the effectiveness of monetary policy during inflation because these can offset, to a large extent, the credit squeeze imposed by the monetary authorities. This is generally done through portfolio adjustment in much the same way as done by the commercial banks.

Thirdly, large business corporations, both in the private corporate sector and public sector can reduce the effectiveness of restrictive monetary policy by directly mobilising public savings. In recent years, in India and many other countries, large business organisations, both in the public and private sector, have successfully mobilised large saving from the public. Funds are invited and accepted in the form of term deposits at rates of interest higher, very often much higher than those offered on such deposits by the commercial banks. High rates of interest make such deposits sufficiently attractive to the public. For the borrowing companies also, this is not a bad proposition because the high rates of interest paid to the public do not necessarily mean high 'effective borrowing rates' because the lending rates of the banks, whom the companies may have to approach otherwise, are at any rate substantially higher than their borrowing rates.

We have discussed above the limitations of monetary policy in controlling demand-pull inflation. In case of cost-push inflation, its effectiveness is even more limited. This is because the source of demand-pull inflation is increase in purchasing power which can be curbed, to some extent, by controlling the cash-flow or money supply; but, in the case of cost-push inflation, the source of price rise is a cost-push factor which is more difficult to control by restricting the money supply. In such situations, restrictive monetary policy is used or should be used in conjunction with fiscal policy and suitable wages and incomes policy, and also, if necessary, some direct controls.

MONETARY POLICY IN DEPRESSION

During the Great Depression of the 1930s, and for some time following that, economists felt that monetary policy was too weak to stimulate recovery from a depression. However, since the 1950s, the view has been slowly changing with changes in the effectiveness of monetary policy in fighting depression. And it is now generally recognised that monetary policy is more effective against depression than against inflation.

During business recessions, what is badly required by the business community is a stimulus; and monetary policy and monetary authorities can provide the necessary stimulus at such times. If credit is freely available during recessions at attractive terms, it is very likely to have a stimulating effect and in case of a mild recession or depression, it might prove sufficient to initiate recovery and, consequently, bring a certain amount of stabilisation in the economy. Recent experiences of employing monetary tools in moderate business cycles have given rise to enough confidence in the efficacy of monetary expansion in fighting a recession or a depression.

The effectiveness of monetary policy depends very much on the intensity of a recession and its effectiveness in a severe depression may still be very limited. During a severe contraction of business activities, the central bank may pump more and more money into the banking system and to almost all classes of borrowers through open market operations. But mere availability of credit at attractive terms may not be enough to induce borrowers—entrepreneurs and consumers—to borrow and spend if other conditions affecting spending decisions are so adverse as to more than offset the inducement of easy credit. When prospects of profit and good returns on investment are bleak and highly uncertain, businessmen may not like to borrow on short-term to build up inventories. In fact, they would like to reduce inventories. Nor would they like to borrow on long-term to finance plant and equipment when a large part of the existing plant and equipment is already idle or unutilised. At such times, the consumers too, faced with unemployment and fall in incomes, may be reluctant to increase their spending by borrowing from banks and other sources.

To say all this, however, is not to dismiss altogether the use of monetary policy during a severe depression; or, to say that, pursuit of monetary policy will not have any beneficial influence in the economy. If nothing else, it can certainly prevent a bad situation from becoming worse. In dealing with a crisis, it may be necessary to use monetary instruments in combination with other instruments and controls. This may bring out the best of monetary policy.

CONTRA CYCLICAL MONETARY POLICY AND THE LAG FACTOR

A general limitation of monetary policy, as either an anti-inflationary or anti-depression measure, lies in the lag factor. Success of any policy, monetary or otherwise, depends on the timing of the policy or the speed with which it is implemented. A lagged response is likely to reduce its effectiveness. Monetary policy suffers from this problem.

The lag problem in monetary policy may be explained as follows. Some imbalance may arise in the economy which may call for action or intervention by the monetary authorities. First, some time may lapse between *need for recognition* of the problem and *recognition* of it. This generally happens because the disturbance or the imbalance may not show up immediately but may be evident only after some time. This time lag may be called the 'recognition lag'. Secondly, even after the need for action has been recognised, sometime lapses before corrective action is actually taken. This time lag is almost inevitable because before taking any action, monetary authorities may take some time to decide about the course of action (general or selective), the intensity of the measures to be implemented, etc. This is the 'action lag'. Thirdly and finally, the effects of any action may take some time to work themselves out because monetary measures are not direct, but indirect controls, and, therefore, would not become effective instantaneously. This lag may be called the 'effect lag'.

Milton Friedman, who is a strong critic of flexibility in monetary policy, feels "that monetary policy may often move in the right direction, but such policies are applied too late and also in too much quantity". Talking about the monetary policy of the Federal Reserve System of the United States, he states that 'too late' and 'too much' have been the general practice. For example, in early 1966, it was the right policy for the Federal Reserve to move in a less expansionary direction—though it should have done so at least a year earlier. But, when it moved, it went too far, producing the sharpest change in the rate of monetary growth of the post-war era. Again, having gone too far, it was the right policy for the Fed to reverse course at the end of 1966. But, again, it went too far, not only restoring, but exceeding the earlier excessive rate of monetary growth. And the episode is no exception. Time and again, this has been the course followed—as in 1919 and 1920, in 1937 and 1938, in 1953 and 1954, in 1959 and 1960.[4]

The above not only emphasises the lag factor in monetary policy, but also the problem of intensities of monetary measures.

MONETARY POLICY AND ECONOMIC GROWTH

The fact that monetary policy has a certain role to play in controlling either inflation or depression implies that it has also relevance to problems of economic growth because business cycles and economic growth are not independent but related phenomena. In fact, we have already mentioned that one of the major objectives of monetary policy is to promote economic growth particularly in developing economies.

The classical economists regarded money as a veil which did not affect real output. A change in money supply had effect only on the price level. According to these economists, therefore, money plays a 'passive' role in the economy. The second view, which is a more recent development, on the relationship between money and economic growth is that money plays a 'permissive' role in the economy. As output, and resulting from it, income increases, a larger amount of money supply is needed in order to facilitate the larger volume of transactions, and therefore, money supply must keep pace with increase in real output. A third view on money and growth is that money plays an 'active' role in the economy and that by increasing money supply real output can be increased. We shall analyse the role of monetary policy in the context of the latter two views which are now more widely accepted.

In general, two conditions are essential for sustained economic growth. First, the economy's production capacity should increase. Secondly, demand for goods and services, particularly for those whose supply has increased, should correspondingly increase. This implies that proper balance should be maintained between the economy's total production capacity and aggregate demand. In other words, aggregate demand should be geared to the increase in total output which itself results from growth.

Monetary policy can promote economic growth mainly in two ways. Firstly, the monetary authority can try to maintain equilibrium between total money demand and total production or supply. This calls for a monetary policy which can restrict bank credit when total money demand threatens to raise prices because of the absence of corresponding increase in output and can enforce expansion of credit when lack of demand causes decline in prices, production, and employment in the economy. This implies measures geared to price stability.

Secondly, monetary policy can promote economic growth by creating a favourable environment for savings and investment. This can be done partly by ensuring price stability and partly by undertaking measures which induce savings directly and lead to mobilisation of the same. History tells us that rising prices discourage savings; and price stability encourages saving. By ensuring price stability, therefore, monetary policy can encourage savings. Also, it can induce savings directly through changes in the bank rate (and consequently interest rates which attract savings) and open market operations.

4. Milton Friedman, "The Role of Monetary Policy", *The American Economic Review*, March 1966.

To summarise, monetary policy can help in achieving economic growth by (a) minimising fluctuations in prices and business activity and (b) providing an economic environment conducive to high levels of savings and investment.

MONETARY POLICY IN INDIA

The Reserve Bank of India (RBI) is the central bank and the apex monetary and financial institution in the country. The Reserve Bank is responsible for efficient working of the monetary and banking system of the country.

The Banking Regulation Act, 1949, is an important landmark in the history of central banking in India. Before the passing of this Act, the Reserve Bank of India possessed mainly two instruments to control the operations of the money market in the country, namely to lend to the banks at the bank rate or discount bills of exchange and to engage in open market operations, that is, to buy and sell approved securities in the market.

The Banking Regulations Act, 1949, armed the Reserve Bank of India with extensive powers to control the activities of the commercial banks in the country. The RBI now possesses powers to determine the lending policy of the banks, to decide the ceiling and floor rates of interest they should charge on loans and advances; the rates of interest they have to pay on different kinds of deposits, the liquidity ratio the banks must maintain in order to be eligible to borrow from the Reserve Bank, etc. The RBI has also powers to prevent the banks generally or any particular bank from making certain types of investments.

We give below a brief account of the monetary policy of the Reserve Bank of India in terms of application of the bank rate. The bank rate had remained pegged to 3 per cent ever since 1935 before it was raised to 3.5 per cent in 1951. But, since 1951, the bank rate was continuously raised five times till it reached 6 per cent in 1965. The bank rate was lowered for the first time from 6 to 5 per cent in 1968. This was the final outcome of the policy of selective liberalisation followed by the Reserve Bank of India since the 1966-67 busy season. The bank rate was, however, raised from 5 to 6 per cent in 1971. In 1973, it was raised to 7 per cent. Now the bank rate is about 5.5 per cent.

Since 1951, the bank rate was raised from a mere 3.5 per cent gradually to the present level of about 5.5 per cent mostly to contain inflationary pressures which were developing in the economy (except 1968); and to curb inflationary pressures, the bank rate was many times used in conjunction with other general instruments of control. For example, in 1965, simultaneously with raising of the bank rate from 5 to 6 per cent, the net liquidity ratio for the scheduled banks was also increased from 28 to 30 per cent. Again in 1973, as the inflationary situation continued to cause concern, the Reserve Bank of India, along with increasing the bank rate (from 6 to 7 per cent) also raised the cash reserve ratio of the commercial banks from 3 to 5 per cent and the net liquidity ratio from 37 to 39 per cent. There are many other examples during recent years also when the general instruments of credit control were used simultaneously by the Reserve Bank of India.

Also, the general instruments, whether used singly or in combination, were throughout strongly supplemented by selective credit controls or liberalisations. In fact, in almost every year, the selective controls dominated over the general instruments.

Regarding the effectiveness of monetary policy in India, one can say that the policy pursued by the Reserve Bank of India reveals the dynamic role played by the Bank in the process of planned growth of the economy. The monetary policy of the Bank has been marked by flexibility to suit the changing conditions of the economy. The RBI has employed the instruments of both general and selective credit controls to contain inflationary pressures which have haunted the economy almost right through the planning era. The policy of selective credit controls which generally dominated the scene was not, however, very rigidly applied. In fact, within a restrictionist monetary policy, the Bank introduced pockets or segments of effective credit liberalisations whenever such liberalisations became necessary. The financing of the priority sectors on a large scale would never have been possible without the liberal financing facilities provided by the Bank.

In evaluating the overall success or failure of the Reserve Bank's monetary policy, we should keep in view the constraints imposed on it by other factors, governmental or non-governmental. It should be borne in mind that the Reserve Bank can control only those factors or forces which are associated with money supply. The Bank has nothing within its powers to control directly the non-monetary factors. The Bank's policies may be effective only when the fiscal operations of the government do not run counter to the goals of monetary policy. Therefore, in spite of the pursuance of general and selective credit controls by the Reserve Bank, if inflationary pressures continue in the economy, it may not be a sufficient ground to infer or conclude that the monetary policy of the Reserve Bank of India has failed to contain inflation in the economy.

REVIEW QUESTIONS

1. What are the major objectives of monetary policy? Explain the more important ones.
2. Mention the major instruments of monetary policy. Comment on their relative effectiveness.
3. Explain the role of monetary policy in controlling inflation and recession.
4. Explain the 'lag factor' in monetary policy. How much is it a limitation of the policy?
5. Discuss the evolution of monetary policy in India with the role of the Reserve Bank of India.

SUGGESTED READINGS

- Edward Shapiro, *Macroeconomic Analysis*, Fifth Edition, 1997.
- M.G. Vaish, *Macroeconomic Theory*. Tenth Revised Edition, 1995.
- S.B. Gupta, *Monetary Economics*, S. Chand & Company, 1995.

Chapter 20

Macroeconomic Policy: Fiscal Policy

In comparison to monetary policy, fiscal policy is a recent development in the context of economic regulation and management. Fiscal policy had its birth almost with the publication of Keynes's *General Theory* (its use was not very clear before that) and was prompted by ineffectiveness of monetary policy in the Great Depression of the 1930s. And, from its modest beginning in the 1940s, fiscal policy has today become a major instrument employed by governments to achieve price stability, generate employment opportunities and promote economic growth.

In this chapter, fiscal policy, its instruments and uses are discussed in two parts:

A. Meaning, objectives and instruments of fiscal policy,
B. Use or application of fiscal policy.

A. FISCAL POLICY: MEANING, OBJECTIVES, INSTRUMENTS

MEANING OF FISCAL POLICY

Generally, fiscal policy means a policy which affects aggregate output, employment, savings, investment, etc., through budgetary manipulations. We quote below three definitions which explain the nature of fiscal policy more clearly. According to one definition, fiscal policy refers to "a policy under which government uses its expenditure and revenue programmes to produce desirable effects and avoid undesirable effects on the national income, production and employment."[1] The other definition states that "by fiscal policy it meant the use of public finance expenditure, taxes, borrowing and financial administration to further our national economic objectives."[2] The definition given by Samuelson and Nordhaus focuses on more aspects or roles of fiscal policy. According to them, fiscal policy means "the process of shaping taxation and public expenditure to help dampen the swings of the business cycle and contribute to the maintenance of a growing, high employment economy, free from high or volatile inflation."[3]

We can suitably combine these definitions and give a more complete or comprehensive definition of fiscal policy:

Fiscal policy is the policy of the government using budgetary instruments or measures of public expenditure, taxation and borrowing to achieve economic objectives of controlling

1. Arthur Smithies, "Federal Budgeting and Fiscal Policy" in *A Survey of Contemporary Economics*, Vol. I, The Blakiston Co., Philadelphia, 1949, p. 174.
2. A.G. Buehler, "Government Finance in Stable Economy", *Annals*, 1947, p. 32.
3. P.A. Samuelson and W.D. Nordhaus, *Economics* (Fifteenth Edition), 1995, p. 626.

recession and inflation and business cycle, stabilising the economy, creating employment and, also contributing to the process of economic growth.

OBJECTIVES OF FISCAL POLICY

The objectives of fiscal policy are not very different from those of monetary policy as they are understood today. But, unlike objectives of monetary policy which have undergone periods of shifting emphasis, objectives of fiscal policy have been more or less uniform throughout.

The most important objective of both monetary and fiscal policy is maintenance of economic stability which implies two things; first, price stability and second, achievement of full employment. But experience of modern economies shows that it may be difficult to achieve both these goals simultaneously. In fact, full employment and rigid price stability may sometimes be even mutually inconsistent. (This has been demonstrated, among others, by the Phillips curve discussed earlier in Chapter 13.) Therefore, price stability and reduction of unemployment or generation of employment opportunities have become more acceptable objectives of both monetary and fiscal policies.

In addition, in developing countries, fiscal policy, like monetary policy, is also intended to contribute to the objective of economic growth through revenue or savings mobilisation and creation of investment potential.

INSTRUMENTS OF FISCAL POLICY

We have mentioned about instruments of fiscal policy in our definition. In fact, fiscal policy is implemented and operates through the instruments of fiscal policy. The government of a country, both at the centre and in the states, is directly responsible for formulating and implementing fiscal policy through different instruments or measures.

Four major instruments of fiscal policy are:

1. Budget mechanism (surplus/deficit budgeting)
2. Public expenditure
3. Taxation (direct and indirect)
4. Public borrowing

Budgetary Mechanism

Two major instruments of fiscal policy—public expenditure and taxation—operate through the government budget. But the budget itself can be, and, is quite often used, as an instrument of fiscal policy. There can be three kinds of budget: balanced budget, surplus budget and deficit budget. If total expenditure of the government is equal to its total receipts or revenue, it is a balanced budget; if total expenditure is less than total receipts or revenue, it is a surplus budget; if total expenditure is more than total receipts or revenue, it is a deficit budget. Deficit budget is more common among world economies. India also has a deficit budget.

Receipts and expenditure are the two constituents of a budget. An understanding of these two constituents or components and their sub-components helps to analyse the role of budget as a fiscal instrument. A hypothetical budget with details of receipts and expenditure for three years (with a gap of five years)—2005-06, 2010-11 and 2015-16—is shown in Table 20.1. Budget of India, with different components, during the period 2008-09 and 2012-13 is given in Table 20.2.

As shown in Table 20.1, expenditure in a budget is classified into two categories:

- Revenue and capital expenditure
- Plan and non-plan expenditure

Details of public expenditure are analysed in the next section.

Government receipts are also divided into two categories: revenue receipts and capital receipts. Revenue receipts are further classified into tax and non-tax (interest, profits of public sector enterprises, etc.) revenue. Capital receipts are divided into debt receipts (public borrowing and other liabilities) and non-debt receipts (recovery of loans, public disinvestments, etc.).

Differences between different kinds of receipts and expenditures are defined as various types of deficit/surplus. There are four important concepts:

- Fiscal deficit
- Revenue deficit
- Primary deficit
- Budget deficit

Fiscal deficit is defined as the difference between the government's total expenditure and total non-debt receipts. *Revenue deficit* is the difference between revenue expenditure and revenue receipts. *Primary deficit* is calculated by subtracting interest payments (a component of non-plan revenue expenditure) from fiscal deficit. This means that primary deficit is the deficit of the current year. *Budget deficit* is the fiscal deficit minus government borrowings and other liabilities (debt receipts). Calculations of all the four types can be seen in Table 20.1 also.

Table 20.1: Budget and its Components: 2005-06, 2010-11 and 2015-16 (Hypothetical)

(₹ billions)

Item	*2005-06*	*2010-11*	*2015-16*
1. Total Expenditure	1,067	1,783	3,752
1.1 Revenue expenditure	750	1,399	3,106
1.1.1 Plan	140	290	602
1.1.2 Non-plan	609	1,108	–
1.1.2.1 of which interest payment	219	500	1,123
1.2 Capital expenditure	318	384	647
1.2.1 Plan	159	174	349
1.2.2 Non-plan	158	211	248
2. Total receipts	959	1,685	3,752
2.1 Revenue receipt	574	1,101	2,317
2.1.1 Tax (net to centre)	443	819	1,630
2.1.2 Non-tax	131	282	687
2.2 Capital receipts	386	583	1,435
2.2.1 Loans recovery	60	65	152
2.2.2 Other receipts of which PSU disinvestment	–	14	120
2.2.3 Borrowing and other liabilities	326	504	1163
3. Deficit			
3.1 Fiscal (1 – 2.1 – 2.2.1 – 2.2.2)	453	602	1163
	(8.3)	(5.4)	(4.7)

Item	2005-06	2010-11	2015-16
3.2 Revenue (1.1 – 2.1)	176 (3.5)	297 (2.7)	788 (3.2)
3.3 Budget (3.1 – 2.2.3)	127 (2.1)	98 (0.9)	–
3.4 Primary (3.1 – 1.1.2.1)	234 (4.3)	102 (0.9)	40 (0.2)

* Numbers in parentheses are percentages of GOP.

Table 20.2: Budget (Receipts and Expenditure) of India, 2008-09 to 2012-13

Item	2008-09	2009-10	2010-11	2011-12 (P)	2012-13 (BE)
	(As per cent of GDP)				
1. Revenue receipts (a+b)	9.6	8.8	10.1	8.4	9.3
(a) Tax revenue (net of states' share)	7.9	7.0	7.3	7.0	7.7
(b) Non-tax revenue	1.7	1.8	2.8	1.4	1.6
2. Revenue expenditure	14.1	14.1	13.4	12.7	12.8
of which:					
(a) Interest payments	3.4	3.3	3.0	3.0	3.2
(b) Major subsidies	2.2	2.1	2.1	1.6	1.8
(c) Defence expenditure	1.3	1.4	1.2	1.1	1.1
3. Revenue deficit (2–1)	4.5	5.2	3.2	4.3	3.5
4. Capital receipts	6.1	7.0	5.2	6.0	5.5
of which:					
(a) Recovery of loans	0.1	0.1	0.2	0.2	0.1
(b) Other receipts (mainly CPSEs disinvestment)	0.0	0.4	0.3	0.2	0.3
(c) Borrowings and other liabilities $	6.0	6.5	4.8	5.7	5.1
5. Capital expenditure	1.6	1.7	2.0	1.8	2.0
6. Non-debt receipts	9.7	9.4	10.6	8.8	9.7
7. Total expenditure [2+5=7(a)+7(b)]	15.7	15.8	15.4	14.5	14.9
of which:					
(a) Plan expenditure	4.9	4.7	4.9	4.6	5.2
(a) Non-plan expenditure	10.8	11.1	10.5	9.9	9.7
8. Fiscal deficit (7-6)	6.0	6.5	4.8	5.7	5.1
9. Primary deficit [8-2(a)]	2.6	3.2	1.8	2.6	1.9

Sources: Union Budget documents and Controller General of Accounts.

CPSEs Central Public Sector Enterprises.

P. Preliminary, BE. Budget estimate

\# Based on provisional actuals for 2010-11.

$ Does not include receipts in respect of the Market Stabilization Scheme, which will remain in the cash balance of the central government and will not be used for expenditure.

Notes: 1. The ratios to GDP at current market prices are based on the CSO's National Accounts 2004-05 series.

2. The figures may not add up to the total due to rounding/approximations.

We shall discuss below the implications of the use of various budgetary instruments.

Government expenditure incurred on wages and salaries of its employees (including pension payments), interest paid on government debts, social security, etc., tend to increase the personal disposable income of people as a result of which aggregate demand for consumer goods increases. Thus, an increase in total government expenditure tends to expand aggregate economic activity in the economy. On the other hand, taxes levied on people to finance government expenditure tend to reduce disposable personal and corporate incomes which could have been spent either on consumption or channelled to capital formation through savings. Thus, taxes have the effect of reducing aggregate income and demand in the economy. These effects of government budget are valid for the central, state, and local government budgets, although the budget of the central government, particularly because of its size, is much more powerful in influencing the level of economic activity of the country than the combined budget of all the states and local bodies.

Government expenditure and revenue can be combined in various ways in order to stimulate or depress aggregate demand and economic activity in the country. A surplus in the budget will exert a deflationary effect on national income because aggregate government expenditure will be less than total tax collections. Conversely, a deficit in the budget will tend to become inflationary because total receipts through taxes will be less than aggregate government expenditure. It follows, therefore, that during a slump, when there is need for stimulating or expanding aggregate demand, a deficit budget will be effective; while during inflation, when the problem is of restricting aggregate demand and expenditure, a surplus budget will be the appropriate fiscal measure.

This generalisation regarding the roles of a surplus budget and a deficit budget also brings us to the question of a balanced budget and its role as a fiscal instrument. We should not be led to the conclusion that a balanced budget (which shows neither a surplus nor a deficit) is neutral in its effects on the level of national income and economic activity. A balanced budget may be no less important than an unbalanced—deficit or surplus—budget. This is so because, apart from the *magnitude* of government expenditure and revenue, their *composition* or *structure* is equally important in influencing the level or direction of economic activity.

A given amount of revenue can be raised by the government in several ways—by levying taxes, by increasing profits from departmental enterprises or undertakings and by borrowing from the public, and each of these methods will affect the economy differently. And, even in the case of taxes, the effect will be different for different tax levies, say, for income tax and excise duty. Similarly, the government can incur a given expenditure in various ways. It might, for example, spend on building a hospital or on slum clearance or on construction of a factory or on unemployment doles. The effect on the level of aggregate economic activity will be different, even though the total expenditure may be the same in each case. Expenditures incurred on constructing a new national highway or slum clearance is not likely to affect investment activity in the private sector materially; if anything, it will affect private investment by causing an increase in the demand for materials and equipment required for road construction or house building for slum dwellers. But if the same amount is spent for constructing a factory, it might cause an offsetting fall in aggregate private investment. Consequently, the beneficial effects of public expenditure on the level of aggregate economic activity will be partially lost.

Thus, a balanced budget is not neutral in its effects on national income and economic activity unless it is assumed that composition of income and expenditure remains unchanged from year to year.

Public Expenditure

As mentioned in the previous section, public expenditure can be classified into different categories: revenue and capital expenditure, plan and non-plan expenditure, developmental and non-development expenditure, and, expenditure on transfer payment and non-transfer payment.

Revenue expenditure is current expenditure incurred on civil administration (law and order/police), defence services, salaries of government staff, public health, education, etc. Revenue expenditure is recurring expenditure, i.e., incurred with regular periodicity-monthly, quarterly, yearly. *Capital expenditure* is expenditure incurred on developing durable or long-term assets like steel plants, roads and highways, river projects, capital equipment or machinery, etc. Capital expenditure, unlike revenue expenditure, is one-time or non-recurring in nature.

Plan expenditures are incurred on government's new programmes which have been planned.[4] *Non-plan expenditures* are incurred on past commitments, maintenance/recurring expenses.

Development expenditure is expenditure incurred on national development and economic growth. Such expenditure includes those on infrastructural facilities including transport and communications, investment in agricultural, industrial and services sectors, irrigation projects, etc. *Non-development expenditures* are those incurred on civil administration, defence, public health services, education, etc. It should be mentioned that development expenditure is almost same as plan expenditure and non-development expenditure is same as non-plan expenditure, although some may like to make a finer distinction between the two.[5] Another point is about classification of health services and education as non-development expenditures. Earlier, expenditure on public health and education were classified as non-development expenditure. But, more recently, if is increasingly being realised that educational and public health services are developmental activities which help to promote growth of human capital which, in turn, contribute to the process of economic growth.

Another classification of public expenditure is into transfer payment. *Transfer payments* are those against which the government does not receive any return or goods or services. These are merely transfer of cash or funds from the government to the recipients (of payment). A common form of transfer payment is old age or post-retirement pension. Other forms of transfer payment are social security payment, unemployment allowance, subsidies on goods or commodities, etc. Non-transfer payment includes call other forms of payment or expenditure by the government. For clarity, it should be mentioned that expenditure on defence, health and educational services are non-transfer payment because the government receives services of army, teachers and physicians surgeons. All forms of investment or expenditure on capital goods are non-transfer payments.

Growth of Public Expenditure

The importance of public expenditure as an instrument of fiscal policy has increased over time because of rising trend in public expenditure in various economies of the world. Two theories or hypotheses try to explain the reasons for significant growth of public expenditure: one is Wagner's Theory and the other is Wiseman-Peacock hypothesis.

Wagner's theory is about increasing activity of the state over time. Wagner, a German economist, contends that as an economy develops, activities or functions of the government expand. New functions or programmes are initiated and performed by the government which are

4. Expenditure made under five year plans in India are all plan or planned expenditure.
5. Classical economists had distinguished between productive and unproductive public or government expenditure. Development expenditure and non-development expenditure are new or modern names for productive and unproductive expenditures—developmental for productive and non-developmental for unproductive.

related to economic and social development of the state. This leads to increase in government expenditure. Wagner's theory or study is based on time series of government expenditure and economic development of Germany; but, the logic or argument applies equally to many other countries including India.

Wiseman-Peacock hypothesis emphasises a different reason for growth in public expenditure. This hypothesis is based on a study of the nature and growth of public expenditure in the UK economy. The authors contend that public expenditure does not increase at a steady and continuous pace or rate as indicated in Wagner's study, but, discontinuously in lumps over time. Such lumpy and discontinuous increase in public expenditure takes place during situations like depression (which requires large doses of public expenditure to stimulate economic activity for revival) and wars.

Given these two theories or arguments, a number of factors can be identified which explain most of the growth of public expenditure in recent times. Ten such factors are mentioned below:

1. Population growth
2. Urbanisation
3. Anti-cyclical measures
4. Economic development
5. Anti-poverty activities
6. Welfare measures
7. Subsidies
8. Debt servicing
9. Infrastructural facilities
10. Defence services

These factors generally play their roles in both developed and developing economies. But, many of these factors like urbanisation, economic growth and development, anti-poverty measures play a more important role in developing economies than in developed economies. Also, relative roles of these factors vary from economy to economy depending on the economic system, i.e., free enterprise, socialistic or mixed economic system. In the same economy or economic system also, the relative roles of these factors change over time with economic and social development and changes in government priorities for national development.

Taxation

A *tax* is a compulsory payment by the people to the government against which there is no direct return to them, i.e., taxpayers. A tax can be direct or indirect; this classification covers all taxes. A *direct tax* is one in which the incidence of the tax falls directly on the taxpayer, i.e., the taxpayer pays the tax directly to the government. Most common form of direct tax is personal income tax. Corporate income tax is another important form of direct tax. Other direct taxes are wealth tax and property tax. An *indirect tax* is one in which the incidence of the tax does not directly fall on the taxpayer, i.e., the taxpayer does not directly pay the tax to the government. The most common forms of indirect tax are sales tax, excise duty/value-added tax (VAT), customs duty and goods and services tax (GST).

Classification of Tax

Direct tax and indirect tax are only two classifications of tax, although the most important one. There are also other classifications of tax. These are different forms or variants of direct tax and indirect tax. Various classification of tax, including direct tax and indirect tax, are mentioned below:

1. Direct tax and indirect tax
2. Progressive tax, proportional tax and regressive tax
3. Specific tax and ad-valorem tax
4. Central tax, state tax and local tax

The concepts of direct tax and indirect tax, and, the differentiation between the two have already been explained.

Progressive tax, proportional tax and regressive tax primarily relate to personal income tax, and also to wealth tax.

A *progressive* (*income*) *tax* is one in which the rate of tax increases as the tax slab (in value) increases. For example, if the income tax slab is, say, ₹ 10,000-₹ 20,000, the tax rate is 10 per cent; but, if the tax slab increases beyond ₹ 20,000, say, ₹ 21,000-₹ 30,000, the tax rate increases to 15 per cent or 20 per cent, and, so on; however, beyond a certain level of income, there may not be any further increase in the tax rate. This means that, in a progressive tax system, higher income groups pay a higher rate of tax, and, lower income groups pay a lower rate of tax; in other words, the incidence or burden of tax is higher on richer sections of the population and, lesser on the middle income and lower income people. India has a progressive income tax system.

A *proportional tax* is one in which the same rate of tax is applied irrespective of the slab or level of income. For example, the rate of tax may be 20 per cent. If the income slab is ₹ 10,000-20,000, applicable tax is 20 per cent; if the income slab is ₹ 21,000-30,000 the same rate of 20 per cent will apply. So, the richer segment of the population and middle/lower income groups will pay the same rate of tax; but, the rich people will pay more tax in absolute terms because of higher income levels. A *regressive tax* is one in which the rate of tax decreases as income increases. This also means that, in a regressive tax system, the burden of tax is more on the middle and lower income groups than on the higher income groups. The regressive tax system is hardly used by any country or government.

Specific and ad-valorem taxes relate to indirect taxes like sales tax, excise duty and customs duty levied on commodities or manufactured products. A *specific tax* is one which is levied per unit of the commodity/product irrespective of price or value, i.e., ₹ per kg/tonne. *Ad-valorem tax*, in contrast, is one which is levied on the price or value of a commodity/product. Sales tax is an *ad-valorem tax* because it is levied on the price or value of a commodity/product. Excise duty and customs duty can be either specific or ad-valorem. For some commodities/products, the tax may be charged per unit of the commodity/product; for some others, it may be levied on the price or value of the product. For high-priced base metals like copper, nickel, tin, the customs duty is often specific because the price (invoice price) can be manipulated mutually by the buyer (importer) and the seller (exporter) to evade some tax. In such cases, in some countries including India, the customs authorities may levy ad-valorem tax, but, they decide the price (based on international price information) for assessment of import duty.

Classification of taxes into central tax, state tax and local tax is based on the authority which levies the tax. For example, income tax, corporate tax, wealth tax and customs duty are all charged by the central government; therefore, these are central taxes. Sales tax is generally a state tax collected in the state where the sales take place by the state government. But, there is also central sales tax (CST) on some commodities/products. Local taxes are levied by local authorities like municipal corporations. The most important local tax is house tax. Another local tax is octroi.

Characteristics of a Good Tax System

Classification of taxes as direct and indirect, progressive, proportional and regressive, specific and ad-valorem affect different businesses and sections of the population differently. This raises a question: what should be a good or equitable tax system? The primary objective of taxation is collection of revenue by the government. The modern governments also have the objectives—one can also say responsibilities—of maintaining economic stability, generating or increasing employment and promoting economic growth. Taxation can be used in different ways to achieve these objectives. On the other hand, businesses, industries and people should not feel too much of burden of taxation. This raises the question or issue of a balanced or equitable tax system.

This implies that a good tax system should follow certain principles. Adam Smith, in *The Wealth of Nations*, mentioned four principles of a good tax system; he called them 'canons' of taxation. The four Smithian principles or canons of a good tax system are: equality, certainty, convenience and economy.

The principle of *equality* means that every individual should pay tax proportional to his (her) income; in other words, all persons will pay the same rate or percentage of their incomes as tax. According to Adam Smith, the principle of equality also means the principle of 'ability to pay' because the tax payable is in proportion to income received. In essence, the principle of equality means the proportional tax system.

The principle or canon of *certainty* indicates that there should be no ambiguity or arbitrariness about the tax people have to pay. To put it in Adam Smith's own words: "The tax which each individual is bound to pay ought to be certain, and, not arbitrary. The time of payment, the manner of payment, the quantity to be paid ought all to be clear and plain to the contributor and to every other person".[6] The governmental system in a country has the responsibility to make all this very clear to businesses, industries and individuals who are taxpayers.

The principle or canon of *convenience* indicates ease of payment. This essentially relates to procedural or implemental system. The procedure for payment of tax should not be complicated or inconvenient to the taxpayer. In modern times, there are reports about problems faced by taxpayers in submitting income tax returns. This shows the relevance of Adam Smith's principle of convenience even today. However, in many countries including India, the procedure for submission of income tax returns has been sufficiently simplified with the introduction of e-filing of returns.

The principle of *economy* relates to cost of collection of tax, or, rather, cost-benefits of tax collection. In any country, the government has to incur expenditure for collection of tax. The cost depends on how elaborate or complicated the tax collection machinery is. If the tax is simple, and, is easy to calculate, collection is easy and the cost is also less. The norm or guiding principle for cost should be: the cost of collection of a particular tax should not be more than the revenue earned from it. Otherwise, a tax is not justified from the 'economy' perspective or principle.

The four canons or principles of a good tax system enunciated by Adam Smith have significance and applicability even in modern economies, although there may be disagreement with his principle of equality which essentially means a proportional tax system. Also, since

6. Adam Smith, *The Wealth of Nations*, Vol. II, p. 327.

the publication of *The Wealth of Nations*, there has been significant evolution in economic theory and policy, and, many developments have taken place in the objectives, approaches and activities or functions of governments. Because of these evolutionary changes or developments, some of the Smithian principles may be modified and new principles or requirements may be added which may characterise a good tax system in modern economies. Seven characteristics of a good tax system, covering both direct and indirect taxes, are mentioned below:

1. Taxes should be progressive, rather than proportional and, surely not regressive.
2. The tax system should improve income distribution.
3. Procedure for payment of tax should be simple and convenient to taxpayers.
4. Cost-benefit of collection of a tax should justify the tax.
5. The tax system should be elastic.
6. The tax structure should have diversity.
7. Taxation should help mobilisation of economic surplus.

Some explanations may make the seven characteristics more clear. Characteristic 2 follows from characteristic 1. Only progressive taxes (income tax, wealth tax, capital gains tax) can help redistribution of income from richer section of the society to lower income people to reduce income inequality. Characteristic 3 has been explained above in connection with Adam Smith's principle of convenience. The procedures have been largely simplified in many countries with the facility of e-filing. Characteristic 4 has also been explained above. If the cost of collection of a tax is more than or almost same as revenue generation from it, this means that the tax is too cumbersome or revenue earning is too small to justify the tax. Elasticity of a tax system (characteristic 5) means its responsiveness to increase in national income. In every country, tax revenue constitutes a certain proportion of national income. As national income increases over time with economic growth, the tax system should respond by increasing tax revenue to maintain its ratio with national income. This is particularly important in developing economies where the ratio of tax revenue to national income is lower than that in developed economies. Diversity of the tax system (characteristic 6) means that the government should adopt a multiple tax system and not try to generate all the revenue through a single or few taxes. Collection of the entire revenue through only few taxes is characteristic of a regressive tax system; it imposes high burden on selected businesses, industries or individuals. Instead, the tax base should be broad enough to cover all those who can and should pay taxes. A diversified or multiple tax system may include both direct and indirect taxes. One of the major objectives of a tax system should be mobilisation of economic surplus[7] for financing capital formation and economic growth (characteristic 7). Through an appropriate tax system, the government should discourage or control non-essential consumption and generate and mobilise economic surplus. This leads to increase in savings, and, may also be, the savings rate which, in turn, facilitates investment and economic growth.

The seven characteristics mentioned above may be necessary, but, not sufficient conditions for a good tax system. It is difficult, may be also not possible, to generalise the characteristics of a good tax system. It depends on many factors: level of development of a country or economy; the nature of economic system—free enterprise, mixed economy, socialistic system; government prioritisation of different development programmes; relative priorities between economic and social objectives, etc. Because of all these factors, it may be appropriate to say that the characteristics mentioned above may be taken as basic or necessary guidelines for developing a

7. *Economic surplus* is defined and measured as the surplus of national income over essential consumption.

good tax system. The appropriate or ideal characteristics of a good system should be different for different countries or economies.

Public Borrowing

Public borrowing is the fourth major instrument of fiscal policy next to budgetary mechanism, public expenditure and taxation. Public borrowing is usually resorted to if the first three instruments do not produce adequate results or fail to achieve all the fiscal objectives of the government.

Public borrowing can be of two kinds: internal borrowing and external borrowing. *Internal borrowing* means borrowing within the country or national territory. *External borrowing* means borrowing from sources outside the country, i.e., international sources.

Internal borrowing can be of two types:

(a) Borrowing from the public

(b) Borrowing from the central bank of the country

Borrowing from the public is done through sale of government bonds. The bonds are sold through the banking system and non-banking financial institutions. The issue or sale of bonds is primarily resorted to for financing budget deficit. Borrowing from the central bank, in effect, means issue of new currency; this is more commonly known as deficit financing.[8] Deficit financing usually has expansionary effect on the economy because it means increase in money supply.

External borrowing can be of three kinds:

(a) Borrowing from international financial organisations like World Bank and IMF,

(b) Borrowing from foreign governments,

(c) Borrowing from international financial or foreign currency market.

External borrowing is resorted to for financing budget deficit and also for development programmes. Borrowing from World Bank and IMF is particularly utilised for financing different economic and social development projects. Long-term borrowing from foreign governments on capital account is used, in addition to achieving some fiscal objectives, for settling balance of payments problems.

Of the two fiscal instruments for raising funds from the public or the market, i.e., taxation and borrowing, the latter is much faster in terms of execution and result than the former. Bonds can be issued or sold by the government almost any time during the year; banks, non-banking financial institutions, mutual funds and insurance companies may buy or invest in them. Assessment and collection of tax take more time.

There are, however, some major issues or problems associated with government borrowing. First, government borrowing results in increase in public debt; with increase in borrowing, public debt also increases. Accumulation of public debt can cause large revenue deficit in the budget. Second, following from the first, is interest payment on public debt. If public debt accumulates, interest payment increases. If this keeps recurring new borrowing may be required every year for payment of interest on accumulated debt, if not for any other purposes. This may eventually lead to a vicious cycle of high public debt, large interest payment and more borrowing. Third, borrowing by the government from the market, particularly large borrowing, leads to increase in demand for loanable funds, and, this may, in turn, lead to an increase in the interest rate. If the

8. *Deficit financing* means issue of new currency by the central bank of the country (RBI in India) for financing budget deficit.

interest rate increases, private investment is discouraged and may decline. So, large government borrowing tends to reduce private investment because of increase in the interest rate. This is known as the crowding-out effect of government borrowing—government borrowing *crowds out* private investment. If, however, the commercial banks have enough availability of loanable funds for lending to the corporate sector, the intensity of the crowding out effect will be less.

Crowding-out versus Crowding-in Argument

We have just mentioned about the crowding-out effect of public borrowing. We may mean the same thing by saying crowding-out effect of public debt (which arises from public borrowing), or, more specifically, debt-financed public spending or deficit spending. In economic literature, *crowding-out means negative effect of deficit spending by the government on private investment.* It works like this: High deficit spending by the government means that it is spending more than its tax revenue. Then the government needs to borrow funds from the public or the market to finance the deficit spending. Borrowing by the government leads to increase in demand for loanable funds, and, because of this, the rate of interest increases. This discourages private investment which may actually fall. This is the crowding-out effect.

Another group of economists or school of thought argues that deficit spending by the government has the oppositive, i.e., 'crowding-in' or positive effect on private investment. So, *crowding-in means an increase in private investment because of deficit spending by the government.* It happens like this. Deficit spending may lead to an increase in the interest rate, and, this may discourage private investment. But, deficit spending leads to an increase in aggregate demand. The additional demand is met by increasing output with unutilised production capacity and existing capital stock. Increase in output and income puts the acceleration principle into operation. Working of the acceleration principle means that additional income induces new investment, the amount of new investment depending on the acceleration coefficient. This way, deficit spending stimulates new investment. This is the crowding-in effect.

There is some empirical evidence of crowding-out effect and crowding-in effect of deficit spending. Empirical evidence relates to the US economy, and, also the Indian economy. In the US economy, there are examples of both crowding-out effect and crowding-in effect. During 1960s, deficit spending had crowding-in effect on private investment. The crowding-in effect was seen during 1974-75 also. The congressional budget office observed that deficit spending during the depression of mid-70s had crowding-in effect during 1974-75. But, deficit spending had crowding-out effect during 1980s. Business leaders and, also politicians, opined that "When the government spend people's money on entitlement programmes, these funds simply crowd-out private investment."[9] In India, deficit spending had crowding-in effect on private investment almost throughout the early periods of economic growth. Deficit spending led to increase in the price level, but, also created additional demand. This stimulated private investment. As a result, capital formation in the private sector increased very significantly during 1955-56 and 1970-71.[10] So, no clear conclusion can be reached about the occurrence or appropriateness of either crowding-out effect or crowding-in effect of deficit spending on private investment. Available empirical evidence is not enough for this.

9. P.A. Samuelson and W.D. Nordhaus, *Economics* (Seventeenth Edition), Tata McGraw Hill, 2009, p. 735.
10. D.N. Dwivedi, *Macroeconomics: Theory and Policy* (Third Edition) McGraw Hill (India), 2010, p. 618.

FISCAL MULTIPLIERS

Two of the fiscal instruments—government expenditure and taxation—have multiplier effects on output or national income. Expenditure has positive effect on income and taxation has positive or negative effect depending on whether it is tax reduction or tax increase. The expenditure multiplier and tax multiplier were explained in detail in Chapter 7. Those may be referred.

The multiplier effects of the two instruments of fiscal policy have important policy, as well as operational, implications for the economy. This should be kept in view while analysing the use or application of these instruments.

Policy Implications of Fiscal Multipliers

The size or magnitude of fiscal multipliers has important implication for formulation and implementation of macroeconomic policy. The important decision factor is to determine the precise or appropriate quantum of government expenditure and taxation keeping their multiplier effects in mind. As Samuelson has put it: "Just as a physician prescribing a painkiller must know the effect of different dosages, so an economist must know the quantitative magnitude of expenditure and tax multipliers. When the economy is growing too rapidly and a dose of fiscal austerity is prescribed, the economic doctor needs to know the actual size of multipliers before deciding how large a dose of tax increases or expenditure reductions to order."[11]

Economic and econometric models have been constructed to work out more precise impacts of fiscal multipliers, i.e., to ascertain the more exact responses of output or income to changes in government expenditure and taxation. Such analyses or models can provide a good basis for policy formulations and recommendations. Some of these models are more comprehensive in terms of formulation (multivariate analysis) and cover factors like movement of wages and prices, monetary variables and more realistic treatment of expenditure and taxes. The inclusion of such factors as additional explanatory variables tend to modify or reduce the size or intensity of fiscal multipliers in practice.[12]

Comparatively speaking, of the two fiscal multipliers, namely the expenditure multiplier and the tax multiplier, the former has a stronger effect on the economy in terms of output or income and related aggregates compared to the latter. This has been explained above. For either an increase or decrease in GDP, the tax multiplier effect is smaller in magnitude compared to the expenditure multiplier. This should be always kept in mind while either increasing (for stimulating the economy) or decreasing (for controlling inflation) public expenditure or increasing tax dose (for disinflationary effect) or reducing taxes for stimulating consumption and economic revival. This is how the full impacts of the two multipliers can be worked out properly or more correctly.

The related vital question is: in a given macroeconomic situation, whether public expenditure should be used as a fiscal instrument (with its multiplier effect) or the tax instrument should be adopted (with its own multiplier effect), or, a combination of the two should be used, and, if so, what should be the relative doses? These are for the government or the policy makers to decide.

B. USE OR APPLICATION OF FISCAL POLICY

The uses or applications of fiscal policy can be varied. The fiscal instruments can be used to achieve a number of macroeconomic objectives or goals. We start with the Keynesian thought on the application of fiscal policy.

11. P.A. Samuelson and W.D. Nordhaus, *Economics* (2003), p. 506.
12. For more elaborate analysis of implications of fiscal multipliers, refer Samuelson and Nordhaus, *Economics* (2003), pp. 506-08, and, also, Samuelson and Nordhaus, *Economics* (Indian adaptation) (Nineteenth Edition), 2010, pp. 574-75.

Keynes and Fiscal Policy

The emphasis or focus on systematic use or application of fiscal policy started with Keynes's *General Theory*. Three developments during 1930s led to the emergence of fiscal policy as an effective instrument of macroeconomic policy. First, failure of monetary policy and measures to deal with the severe unemployment problem of 1930s caused by the Great Depression; second, increasing role or use of public expenditure and taxation in government's macroeconomic planning and management, and, third, may be the most important, Keynes's *General Theory* or his "new economics" with its clear emphasis on aggregate demand for stimulating the economy, and, solving the unemployment problem.

With these developments, fiscal policy started making a beginning as an important instrument of public policy. Keynesian economics began moulding thoughts of governments and policy makers. In fact, the impact of Keynes's new economic theory was so strong that during next two decades (1940 to 1960), economists and public planners were almost convinced that aggregate demand (and related aggregates) could be increased or decreased through judicious use of public expenditure and taxation. Even today, Keynesian thoughts have significant influence on the application of fiscal policies and instruments for achievement of different macroeconomic objectives or goals.

Different Applications of Fiscal Policy

Two major applications of fiscal policy are for achieving economic stabilisation, i.e., dealing with recession and inflation, and, economic growth. But, fiscal policy instruments can also be used for employment generation and achievement of economic or income equality. So, fiscal policy can serve five important macroeconomic goals:

(a) Controlling inflation
(b) Dealing with recession
(c) Employment opportunities
(d) Economic equality
(e) Economic growth

Each of these application areas, and, relative effectiveness of fiscal policy in achieving these objectives or goals are analysed below. The analysis is done generally in the Keynesian framework. In formulation and implementation of fiscal policy in these areas, there is a lag factor. The lags in fiscal policy will also be discussed here.

Fiscal Policy and Inflation

We have mentioned above that for an economy plagued with inflation, the appropriate fiscal remedy is to create a budget surplus in order to reduce aggregate spending. If total tax collections exceed total government expenditure, the reduction in private spending caused by taxation is not fully offset by government expenditures. Consequently, total spending will be less than what it would have been had the budget been balanced. This policy will directly attack the cause of inflation, i.e. the rate of increase in aggregate spending exceeding the rate of increase in the supply of goods and services in the economy.

A budget surplus will have the biggest impact on total spending, and, therefore, on inflation, if the surplus is impounded by the government. Firstly, the surplus reduces total spending. Secondly, if the surplus is impounded, the quantity of money in circulation will fall causing aggregate spending to be reduced still further. Assuming that the taxes are paid in cheques drawn by the public on commercial banks, the net effect is to reduce the demand deposits in banks by the amount of budget surplus. Further, as the cheques are deposited by the government in its account with the central bank, commercial banks' deposits at the central bank are transferred from commercial banks to the government account. This reduces commercial banks' reserves, and to the extent these are reduced below the required or desired level, the commercial banks are forced to contract their loans and advances. All this will hold only if the surplus is impounded by the government.

It is also possible that the government may not impound the surplus, but uses this to pay off its debt, i.e. to purchase and retire outstanding government bonds. In this case, the effect of the surplus on total spending would vary depending on who owns the bonds that are retired. There are three possibilities. The bonds may be held by (a) the central bank, or (b) commercial banks, or (c) non-bank public.

If a budget surplus is used to retire outstanding government bonds which are held by individuals and business organisations (non-bank public), there can be two types of effects depending on how the money received for bonds is held or utilised. If the money is held as idle cash balances, the reduction in aggregate spending caused by the budget surplus would be the same as it would have been had the entire surplus been impounded by the government. The total stock of money in the economy will not change because of debt retirement, but the velocity of money would decrease. This would reduce aggregate spending. If, however, the money received by the public (individuals and business units) is not held as idle balances but is spent out, aggregate spending will not be reduced and budgetary surplus will be generally ineffective as an anti-inflationary measure.

If the government uses the budget surplus for retiring government bonds held by the commercial banks, as a result of this operation, cash reserves of commercial banks will increase. This would enable them to expand credit. Since commercial banks' cash reserves would increase by the full amount of the budget surplus, their reserves would also be raised to the same level at which they stood before the budget surplus had accrued. As a result, banks will be able to expand their loans and demand deposits to the same old level at which these stood before the budget surplus had occurred. The primary reduction in aggregate spending caused by the surplus is still effective; but, since there is no net fall in money supply, the secondary reductions would be eliminated.

Finally, if the budget surplus is used to retire outstanding government securities held by the central bank, the effect is precisely the same as when the government impounds the surplus.

Fiscal Policy in Recession

During recession, the economy suffers from rising unemployment, falling income and contracting economic activity. The aggregate demand for current output falls low, sometimes very low depending on the severity of the recession/depression. During depression, the objective of fiscal policy is to stimulate demand and promote spending.

This can be done in a number of ways. First, aggregate private spending can be increased by reducing taxes. Personal income tax and corporate taxes may be reduced to encourage spending by individuals and business firms. Tax-cuts would increase the disposable income of individuals and corporate bodies, and given the propensities to consume or spend, should increase private spending. Excise duties on consumer goods may be reduced. This would bring down the prices and induce buying. Price reduction can also be achieved by reducing or abolishing sales taxes. Secondly, government spending can be directly increased through budget deficit or deficit financing. One of the good ways of government spending is to undertake public works programmes. The great merit of public works programmes is that they not only raise personal income and consumption, but also generate additional employment, and income and consumption increase via the multiplier (rather by the size of the multiplier) without dampening investment activity in the private sector.

If the depression is severe, it may not be enough to increase aggregate consumption; aggregate investment also may have to be simultaneously raised. Fiscal policy can induce changes in aggregate investment by making appropriate changes in the tax structure. Since the objective is to raise the marginal efficiency of private investment (new investment can be attracted during recession/depression only if the marginal efficiency of capital is raised), business and corporate taxes may be reduced to achieve this. As a matter of policy, firms engaged in capital formation during depression may be allowed tax concessions.

Fiscal Policy and Employment

Keynesian theory of employment states that fiscal policies which contribute to economic growth also help in creation of employment opportunities, and, finally, for achieving full employment. This, however, may happen only under certain assumptions or conditions, and, may not hold good under all circumstances. For example, it labor-saving or capital-intensive technology is generally used[13] in production during the process of economic growth, this may not lead to creation of employment opportunities. This may be desirable from the growth point of view, but, this may not serve the employment objective. This is where the government may have to intervene with appropriate fiscal policy or measures. In this situation, the applicable tax policy may be taxation.

The objective of taxation in such situation would be to discourage capital-intensive processes of production or projects, and, encourage labor-intensive methods or technologies. This may be achieved by increasing excise duty or imposing new excise duty on production of capital goods,[14] and/or, extending duty concessions or exemptions to production of labour-intensive goods. Similarly, import of capital-intensive goods or technology can be discouraged by imposing or increasing customs duty and giving duty concessions to import of raw materials or inputs for production of labour-intensive goods. But, such policy may be in conflict with the objective of economic development or growth. Many engineering and capital goods industries are *basic industries*[15] with high industrial linkages which support or promote the growth of many other industries. So, growth of such industries may be required—may be essential—for sustained or faster growth of the economy. And, economic growth may have a higher priority than growth of employment for a country particularly in free enterprise economies.

However, employment generation can always take place through different 'linkage industries' of basic or capital goods industries. This may be a more positive or logical way for creation and promotion of employment than a negative policy of discouraging certain key industries. Tax concession or 'tax holiday' can be granted to basic or capital goods industries, particularly in

13. The focus is on engineering industries or capital-intensive projects with high capital-output ratio. Capital-output ratio and incremental capital-output ratio (ICOR) have been explained discussed in Chapter 9 and also Chapter 18.
14. In addition to discouraging production, consumption of capital goods can also be discouraged by imposing additional sales tax.
15. Basic industries are base or infrastructure industries like steel and power which support/promote the development of many other industries.

backward regions; such industries in these regions are most likely to have a direct employment generation effect in the neighbourhood areas. An ideal progressive tax policy may be to simultaneously offer concessions to both capital-intensive and, labour-intensive industries to create and increase employment both ways. In practice, a suitable package of tax (including excise and customs duties) concessions can be worked out keeping the budget position in the perspective.

A more direct method for creation of employment opportunities may be through the expenditure policy. The policy here should be to incur expenditure on public works programmes including construction of roads, bridges, canals, dams, and, also hospitals, schools and colleges. Such activities are naturally labour-intensive, and, almost automatically create employment. Several countries undertake such programmes to generate employment. In addition, the government may also undertake employment-specific programmes or projects. In 2006, the Government of India launched a comprehensive employment creation scheme—National Rural Employment Guarantee Scheme (NREGS). During the Tenth Five-Year Plan, the government had also implemented *Jawahar Rozgar Yojna* (work and earn). Many developing countries, including India, have taken recourse to external aids and/or borrowing from international sources like the World Bank for financing public works programmes for generating employment.

Fiscal Policy for Economic Equality

Economic equality means income equality. Income equality is the ultimate social goal. A more practical objective is to reduce income inequality or disparity. This can be achieved through redistribution of income from the richer sections of the society to lower income groups. Fiscal policy can be used as a powerful instrument for reducing inequality of income and wealth. Fiscal instruments of both taxation and public expenditure can be utilised for this. Economic or income equality is, to some extent, related to creation of employment because unemployed people get employed and receive income. This helps to reduce income inequality. We will be doing this linking in our present analysis. Linking of employment with income equality, however, is done though the expenditure policy.

We shall start with the taxation instrument. Between taxation and government expenditure, the former is a more direct instrument for reducing income inequality or for achieving income equality. The government may take the following steps in using the tax instrument:

(a) Taxation of personal income using progressive rates, appropriate income slabs and tax rates to be decided for more effective results;
(b) Personal income tax exemption limit to be revised upwards to exempt lower income people from the tax net;
(c) Taxation of corporate income at progressive rates; appropriate tax slabs and rates to be decided. In most countries, corporate tax is levied at a flat rate, but, slab system can be introduced with differential tax rates to make the system more progressive.
(d) Discriminatory taxation (i.e., at higher rate) of luxury goods to discourage consumption of non-essential goods and "conspicuous consumption".[16]
(e) Imposition or increase of wealth tax to prevent or discourage accumulation of wealth.
(f) Imposition or increase of tax on property above a minimum value to exempt low income/poor people from payment of house tax.

16. *Conspicuous consumption* is a kind of abnormal behavior by some consumers to make their purchase or consumption of some goods visible or conspicuous to a others; these are high value products or brands, bought to demonstrate to others that the buyers are rich people who may not care for the price.

Depending on the state of the economy or the stage of development, some or all the above steps may be implemented simultaneously as complementary measures. Exact details will vary from economy to economy, or, from government to government.

Expenditure policy, as indicated above, is a more indirect method for achieving income equality compared to tax policy. The expenditure policy works partly through allocation and spending of funds on projects and people and, partly through the employment route. For example, the government can allocate and spend funds on projects which help to increase earnings of people in real terms like free education and healthcare facilities; the government can make special plans or schemes, and, allocate funds for development of rural industries (village and cottage industries) for generation of income and employment; related to this, the government can offer financial assistance for self-employment of the unemployed people through micro-financing using the nationalised banks and related institutions; the government can formulate specially designed schemes for creation of employment opportunities for the unemployed; in India, schemes like NREGS are one of the best examples, and, the government can make financial allocations for special schemes like unemployment allowance or unemployment insurance.

Different instruments or schemes under expenditure policy can be implemented concurrently with those under the tax policy. Both sets of instruments or policies can be used as complementary measures because there is no conflict between the two sets of measures. The ultimate objective should be to uplift as many people as possible above the poverty line.[17] That is the best way to reduce income inequality or achieve economic or income equality.

Countries and governments may try to reduce income inequality through various fiscal instruments or measures. But, a note of caution should be sounded here. Too strong dose or excessive use of fiscal measures may sometimes turn out to be failure or even counter productive. There is a good example from India. During 1973-74, the Government of India had increased the personal income tax rate (including surcharge) to about 98 per cent for taxable income above ₹ 10 lakhs (per annum). The main objective was to reduce income inequality. But, it turned out to be counterproductive. There was large scale tax evasion, and, corruption in the tax collection system (to help tax avoidance); ultimately, this led to the emergence of parallel economy. It also seems that disparity of income between the rich and the poor had actually increased instead of getting reduced.[18] This suggests that fiscal instruments, particularly taxation, should be used with prudence and caution. The fiscal policy and measures should be compatible with the prevailing economic and social system in a country, and, ability or tolerance level of the system to absorb strong policy doses or shocks.

Fiscal Policy and Economic Growth

Fiscal policy has a definite role to play in controlling either inflation or depression; and this implies that it has also relevance to problems of economic growth, because business cycles and economic growth are not independent but related phenomena. In fact, one of the major objectives of fiscal policy today, like monetary policy, is to promote economic growth particularly in developing countries.

Fiscal policy can promote economic growth through the instruments of both taxation and government expenditure. Taxation policy can be used to create a favourable climate for savings and investment. This can be done partly by ensuring price stability (rising prices generally discourage savings while price stability encourages savings) and partly, by inducing savings

---

17. *Poverty line* has been defined and explained in Chapter 10.
18. D.N. Dwivedi, *Macroeconomics: Theory and Policy* (Third Edition), McGraw Hill (India), 2010, p. 614.

directly through suitable changes in the tax rates. Personal and corporate tax structures can be rationalised to encourage savings and investment. Besides this, firms engaged in capital formation may be given tax concessions. This will also encourage investment.

In addition to encouraging voluntary savings and investment, the government can also undertake programmes to enforce compulsory savings. The Compulsory Deposit (Income Tax Payers) Scheme, 1974, introduced in India to impound part of the income of higher income groups is an example of this. But such schemes should be resorted to only when sufficient mobilisation of savings is not taking place through voluntary methods.

Besides the taxation policy, government's expenditure policy can also contribute to the cause of economic growth. The expenditure pattern in the budget can be so designed as to give more emphasis to capital disbursements or development expenditure than to revenue expenditures. Expansionary effect of revenue or consumption expenditure tends to crowd out private investment (through increase in the interest rate). A fall in investment decelerates economic growth (assuming that fall in private investment is not more than compensated by public investment). Therefore, the right policy should be to concentrate on development expenditure. A proportionately larger allocation may be made in the budget for capital projects. This would generally mean generation of additional output, income and employment, i.e., economic growth.

In addition to taxation and expenditure, public borrowing can, and, in practice, often used by countries for promoting/financing economic growth. Public borrowing essentially means resource mobilisation for financing growth. Borrowing is usually resorted to if resource mobilisation through taxation is inadequate. Borrowing can be both internal and external. Internal borrowing can be from the public/market, and, through deficit financing. Deficit financing almost always tend to be inflationary. This should be treated as a constraint of deficit financing. External borrowing is normally done from three sources: first, international development institutions like the World Bank, IMF, second, international foreign currency market, and, third, foreign governments. External borrowing can lead to balance of payments problem which is very typical in developing economies.

Besides taxation, development expenditure and public borrowing, there can also be some other sources for financing economic development.[19] Bagchi has mentioned surpluses of public enterprises, and, other sources for financing India's economic development during the five year plans. Bagchi has mentioned six sources while analysing financing of India's economic development. The six sources are:

1. Balance from current revenue of government
2. Deficit financing
3. Borrowing
4. Surpluses of public enterprises
5. Additional resource mobilisation
6. External assistance[20]

'Additional resource mobilisation' needs clarification. 'Additional resource mobilisation' relates to resources which the central government, the state governments and public enterprises run

19. The terms 'economic growth' and 'economic development' are often used synonymously. But, there is a finer, but, important, distinction between the two. This is explained later in Chapter 24.
20. For Bagchi's complete study refer A. Bagchi, "Fiscal Policy for Financing Development: The Indian Experience" in U. Kapila (Ed.) *Indian Economy Since Independence* (seventh Edition), Academic Foundation, 1996.

by them can raise/mobilise through additional efforts like increasing the tax rates or intensifying the tax collection process/mechanism and/or reducing non-plan expenditures.

Lags in Fiscal Policy

Like monetary policy, formulation and implementation of fiscal policy also is subject to time lags. The time pattern involved in making changes in fiscal or monetary policy may be broken into two timing lags: the *inside lag* and the *outside lag*. The inside lag refers to the time between a change in economic conditions and the actual implementation of a new policy designed to offset the change. The outside lag, on the other hand, relates to the time between the policy change and the point at which the new policy has an impact on the economy.

The inside lag may be thought of as two separate lags. On the one hand, there is the 'recognition lag', while, on the other hand, there is the 'action lag'. It generally happens that when a situation is disturbed, it takes some time to recognise that this has actually happened (recognition lag). It may take upto three months or more to recognise the need for action. Even after the need for action is recognised, policy makers may not make a change till such time as they are convinced of the need for action (action lag). Thus, it is possible that before any action is taken, six months or more may elapse. This lag may, however, sometimes appear to be overestimated since there are leading economic indicators which predict or anticipate changes in economic events. Nevertheless, it must be recognised that there is always a lag of some indeterminate length from the time a need for action arises and the time when action is actually taken.

The action lag differs for monetary policy compared to fiscal policy. The Board of Governors or Directors of the central bank has full authority to change the discount rate, the reserve requirements and take decisions regarding buying and selling of securities. The exact delegation of authority, however, depends on the operational system of a particular central bank. In any case, because only one agency, namely the central bank, is concerned, the action or implementation process is likely to be faster than in case of fiscal policy. In case of fiscal policy, both the administrative and legislative branches of the government must first coordinate their views. The need for legislative action may come at a time when the legislature is not in session. The time when the need for action arises may be the time of an election. All kinds of possibilities exist which tend to make the action lag in fiscal policy quite long.

While the inside lag in monetary policy may be quite short, just the opposite seems to be true with regard to the outside lag (the 'effect lag'). A simple lowering of the discount rate may take a good amount of time to be effective. A lower rate of interest will tend to increase the level of investment but, new investment projects will have a minimum gestation period before becoming productive. The lag problem is generally true of other two instruments of monetary policy, namely reserve ratio and open market operations. The essential fact about these measures is that they are not direct, but indirect controls, and therefore, do not become effective immediately. Fiscal measures like tax increase or government expenditure are, in comparison, more direct, and therefore, take less time to work themselves out. This makes the outside lag in fiscal policy shorter than that of monetary policy. But the shorter outside lag in fiscal policy need not necessarily make up for its longer inside lag.

FLEXIBILITY IN FISCAL POLICY

To be effective or successful, any strategy or policy should have some flexibility or manoeuvrability, and, should not be too rigid in terms of formulation and implementation.

Flexibility is required to make the strategy or policy suitable for application in a particular situation. It is notable that fiscal policy and its application process has certain flexibilities. We shall explain here the nature and degree of flexibility in formulation and application of fiscal policy and instruments.

The flexibility aspect of fiscal policy can be analysed in three ways—we can also say three facts of flexibility:

1. Built-in flexibility/stabilisers
2. Discretionary flexibility
3. Formula or indicator flexibility

Built-in Fiscal Stabilisers

Our discussion of the role of fiscal policy during inflation and recession shows that the government can manipulate the budget (through the two instruments of taxation and expenditure) to generate contra-cyclical (anti-recession or anti-depression) behaviour. In fact, the concept of contra-cyclical behaviour is built into the fiscal mechanism. The built-in fiscal stabiliser is generally the instrument of taxation. Given the tax rates, any increase in national income means that a certain proportion of increased income will be taken away by taxes so that the inflationary effects of rising income and expenditure are curbed to some extent. The opposite mechanism works during periods of falling income.

The effectiveness of built-in stabilisers would partially depend on the taxation system. If it is a proportional tax system, i.e. if the tax rate is the same at all levels of income, the impact is the same both during inflationary phases or periods of rising income and during recession or periods of falling income. This, as a general rule, will be less effective than if the tax system is progressive. In a progressive tax system, during an economic boom with incomes at high levels, a larger proportion of income would be taxed away which may be necessary for reversing the inflationary trend. Correspondingly during recession/depression, with incomes at low levels, a smaller proportion of income is taxed so that the income level does not depress as much as it would normally do in a proportional tax system.

As an extension of the built-in mechanism some have suggested that tax rates should be so fixed as to normally balance the budget but provide for a surplus for debt retirement at certain defined high level of employment and national income. So, with a fall in national income during recession/depression government revenue will fall relative to outlays leading to budget deficit. This implies that, as a built-in stabiliser, fiscal policy cushions fluctuations by withdrawing more purchasing power from the economy than it puts into it during a boom and vice versa.

Having known about the built-in fiscal stabilisers and their possible impacts, we should also be clear about their limitations as a stabilisation factor. Built-in stabilisers can only be a first line of defence, and not sufficient in themselves to maintain complete stability.

Let us explain this point. When national income increases, the automatic tendency of taxes to take away a fraction of incremental income will mean that the size of the multiplier will be cut down via automatic effect on consumption or propensity to consume. This means that the destabilising effects of an increase in income and aggregate demand during periods of inflation (or fall in income and demand during recession) are only reduced by the built-in stabilisers, and not wiped out completely. A built-in stabiliser, therefore, acts to reduce part of any fluctuation in the economy, but cannot wipe out the whole (or most) of the disturbance. It is left to discretionary fiscal (and monetary) policy or action to eliminate the rest of the fluctuation or disturbance.

Discretionary Flexibility

As just indicated, discretionary flexibility or discretionary fiscal policy begins where built-in flexibility ends or fails to deliver the result. The distinction between the two should also be understood. As explained above, built-in stabilisers are self-correcting mechanisms during inflation and recession/depression through almost automatic effects of primarily taxation (and, also of expenditure), and, no government intervention is required. In contrast, in discretionary flexibility, government intervention is needed to correct imbalances in the economy (primarily cyclical) through use of discretionary fiscal policy. This is explained further below.

During a period of economic boom, as national income increases, the built-in fiscal mechanism ensures that a certain proportion of additional income would be automatically taken away by taxes. Personal disposable income would be reduced to that extent, and, so also aggregate consumption, given the MPC. But, if an inflationary trend has already set in, the built-in mechanisms may not be sufficient to curb inflation. The government may have to intervene with fiscal measures like increasing the personal income tax, corporate tax, and, also mopping up funds/liquidity from the market by selling bonds to reduce purchasing power of the people. These are discretionary policies or actions deliberately initiated/taken by the government to contain or curb inflation. The opposite forces and policies/actions will follow during periods of recession or depression.

However, how flexible the discretionary fiscal policy can be, i.e., how quickly or smoothly the government can implement discretionary policies or measures under the existing governmental or economic and social system in a country may be a matter of opinion or discussion. The US experience can be a good example of this. It has been observed that "although discretionary action is taken from time to time by Congress, such action has typically not been sufficiently flexible to be useful against short-run fluctuations in economic activity."[21] The 1964 tax cut is quoted as a "classic" example of delayed discretionary fiscal action. The proposed tax reduction was desired by President Kennedy during 1962 to increase the growth rate of the US economy. But, it was not implemented till 1964. Another example relates to a later period. This time, reverse policy or action was required to counter the inflationary threat arising because of large increase in military expenditure for Vietnam. This time also, it was almost two years before the fiscal measures could actually be implemented.[22]

The difference between automatic flexibility and discretionary flexibility may sometimes boil down to the frequency or speed with which fiscal policies or measures, i.e., changes in taxation and public expenditure are implemented. In automatic flexibility, changes and effects are instant or immediate because those are built into the system. But, the impact may not be as much as desired. In case of discretionary fiscal policy, changes and effects take time to work themselves out, but, the impact may be as desired or strong. But, because of the lag factor involved, by the time effects or results are visible, those may not be as relevant or appropriate as expected because economic factors or variables might have changed in the meantime. If implementation and results are fast or quick, distinction between automatic flexibility and discretionary flexibility may be just a matter of degree.

This is why some economists have commented on the line of distinction between the two. Peston has observed: "The literature on economic policy makes a great deal of fuss about

21. E. Shapiro, *Macroeconomic Analysis* (Fifth Edition), Galgotia Publications, 1984, p. 580.
22. *Ibid.*

discretionary versus automatic policy making"[23] It is not sure whether this issue of distinction can be called a matter of "fuss", but, this can always be a point of discussion or debate. There can be differences of opinion on this. We can also say that these are different approaches to macroeconomic policy analysis.

Formula or Indicator Flexibility

Formula or indicator flexibility relates to changes in fiscal policy in response to changes in selected economic indices or indicators like GDP, price increase or rate of inflation, unemployment rate, etc. Changes in such indices/indicators or signals trigger necessary or appropriate fiscal action. For example, if the unemployment rate increases—say, beyond 5 per cent in developed economies or more than 10 per cent in developing economies—this may require tax concession for setting up new firms/industries particularly in the labour-intensive category, government expenditure on new (labour-intensive) projects, and/or, transfer payment in the form of unemployment allowance; similar action, and, also a reduction in personal income rates may be required to increase purchasing power/consumption if GDP falls below a certain level during a period of recession. An increase in the price index (WPI or consumer price index) may trigger the opposite course of action. The exact fiscal policies or measures to be adopted would depend on the magnitude of the change in index and the prevailing economic, social and political situation in the country.

Some economists contend that built-in flexibility and formula flexibility are very similar to each other, because, in both, action takes place almost automatically. But, this may not be really true in reality. In built-inflexibility, action is really automatic, as we all know. But, in formula flexibility, action has to be planned and executed may be with urgency or high speed. There is another distinction between the two. In *automatic flexibility*, action takes place within the *existing fiscal structure*, i.e., tax system, revenue or development expenditure and transfer payments; but, in *formula flexibility*, *structure* itself *may be changed*. For example, tax slabs may be changed or new tax may be introduced or a tax may be abolished. Similar structural changes may take place in expenditure (including transfer payments) also.

In formula flexibility, the necessity of an action, or even the nature and course of an action, may be clear based on the formula or indices. But, there are two problems or issues associated with formulation and implementation of a particular fiscal policy. First, is the lag factor. This may be less pronounced than in discretionary fiscal policy, but, the lag still exists. Second, the cause of the formula may be a purely short-term signal, and, may die out or may not exist by the time the full fiscal action under formula flexibility has worked itself out. For example, there may be stoppage of production in the sort-run and consequent unemployment because of inventory liquidation programme by firms/industries. By the time, the unemployment (or increase in the unemployment rate) problem is tackled, the inventory liquidation phase may be over and the need for the formula flexibility action might have become redundant. This suggests that the formula or index should be more closely studied and understood based on pragmatic forecast of events in the firms, industries and the economy. Action based on formula flexibility should then follow.

Some economists have commented that formula flexibility is often supported or justified more on political grounds than for economic reasons. Such observation or comment may apply, with difference of degree, to discretionary fiscal policy also.

In conclusion of our analysis of flexibility in fiscal policy, it may be said that there are linkages between three forms of flexibility, viz., built-in flexibility, discretionary flexibility and

23. M.H. Peston, *Theory of Macroeconomic Policy*, Philip Alan, Oxford, 1974, p. 6.

formula flexibility. The starting point may often be formula flexibility, because the need for any government action including fiscal action begins with certain signals or indices relating to GDP, price level or employment. The first set of measures would be automatic because those are internally generated within the system. Action under discretionary flexibility and formula flexibility may follow with differences in approaches, speed and thrust. Action under discretionary flexibility may be generally a little slower than under formula flexibility.

The linkages among three forms of flexibilities may be diagrammatically shown as below (Fig. 20.1).

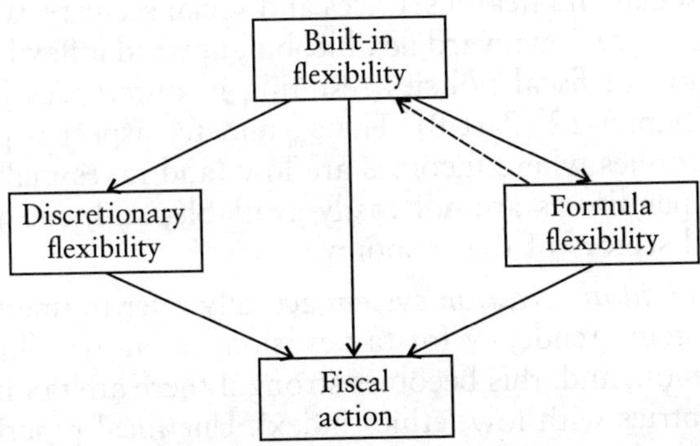

Fig. 20.1: Built-in Flexibility, Discretionary Flexibility, Formula Flexibility and Fiscal Action: Linkages

GENERAL CONSTRAINTS OF FISCAL POLICY

Flexibility in fiscal policy may make it more acceptable or amenable to policy makers and governments. But, fiscal policy is subject to certain constraints or limitations. During application or implementation, a particular fiscal policy or measure may face some specific problems. But, general constraints or limitations apply to all fiscal policies and their implementations with differences of degrees. It is useful to understand these constraints to appreciate the role of fiscal policy in an economy. Six such constraints or limitations are mentioned below:

(a) Data base and forecasting problem
(b) Fiscal multipliers do not always work
(c) Lags in policy formulation and implementation
(d) Asymmetry in implementation
(e) Leakages in fiscal administration system
(f) Problems in low income/developing economies

These are briefly explained/analysed below:

(a) All actions by the government, including fiscal action, is based on certain *data base and forecasting* of future events and behaviour or movements of macroeconomic variables like GDP, aggregate demand, consumption, investment and the price level. If the data base is inadequate and forecasting of economic variables is not correctly done, the fiscal actions taken on the basis of such data base or forecasting may not deliver the desired results. This, however, is a general limitation of macroeconomic data base and forecasting.

(b) *Fiscal multiplier* works out the total effect of a particular fiscal action whether it is increase/ decrease in taxation or expenditure. But, partly, because of data base or forecasting problem of propensities (like MPC), the full effects of fiscal multiplier may not be clearly known, and, therefore, the complete effect of a fiscal action may not also be known.

(c) *Lags in policy formulation and implementation* have been analysed in a previous section. 'Recognition lag', 'action lag' and 'effect lag' all reduce the effectiveness of a particular fiscal policy or instrument.

(d) *Asymmetry in implementation* refers to one-way flexibility in implementation of fiscal policies. In terms of implementation, reducing taxes is easy and welcome because there are no social repercussions; but, attempts to increase taxation face resistance from affected economic and social groups. Similarly, any increase in development expenditure is always welcome by the people; but, reduction in expenditure, particularly in sectors like education, social and health services and social security, will face strong resistance. So, generally, taxes are downward flexible, but, upward inflexible. This is the asymmetry in implementation of fiscal policies resulting in differences in effects. This was also mentioned in Chapter 12 (Part B). The asymmetry aspect is particularly important in developing economies where incomes are low (and taxes make them even lower) and development expenditures are not easily available, and, cut in expenditure may even affect some vital sectors of the economy.

(e) *Leakages in fiscal administration system* actually refer to unethical practices in the tax management system. Tendency for tax evasion, often in collusion with tax collection officials, is common, and, this becomes strong if there are tax increases. This is a major problem in countries with low 'ethics index'. Unethical practices and tax evasion are commonly observed in personal income tax and excise and customs duties. In customs duties, corrupt customs officials may even help tax evasion (or payment of lower customs duty) by manipulating definition/specification of imported products. If there are leakages in the tax administration system, particularly financial leakages or evasions, the purpose of increasing the tax rate or imposing a new tax (including import duty) is defeated to a large extent.

(f) *Problems in low income/developing economies* refer to structural issues affecting fiscal policy and its implementation in these countries. Fiscal policy is generally found to be more effective in developed or mature economies than in low income and developing economies because of structural differences. In low income/developing economies, proper working of fiscal policy and measures is constrained by four special factors compared to developed economies: (i) a large unorganised[24] and non-monetised sector; (ii) small proportion of population in the taxable income segment; (iii) low per capita income; and, (iv) skewed income distribution. Existence of these factors makes the operation of fiscal instruments, particularly taxation, in these countries, to a large extent, ineffective.

Such constraints have prompted economists to make observations on application of fiscal policy and instruments for achieving macroeconomic goals or objectives. One such observation is mentioned below:

> Achieving macroeconomic goals with fiscal policy is like "shooting through dense fog at an erratically moving target with an inaccurate gun."
> —W.J. Baumol and A.S. Blinder, *Economics: Principles and Policy*, Harcourt Brace, London, 1988, p. 123.

---

24. For example, almost 98 per cent of the retailing industry in countries like India is in the unorganised sector. This is insignificant compared to the level and scale of organised retailing in Japan. This makes large differences in policy implications.

COMPLEMENTARITY OF MONETARY POLICY AND FISCAL POLICY

Because of the limitations of fiscal policy, it is worthwhile to consider the possibility of using fiscal policy in conjunction with monetary policy, i.e., use both the policies as complementary to each other. Neither classical economists nor the Keynesians had considered such possibility. According to the classicists, fiscal policy has no effect on output/income, the price level and employment, it is the monetary policy which plays an important role in explaining and regulating the movements of these variables. In contrast, the Keynesians, as mentioned earlier, felt that fiscal policy plays an effective role in controlling economic aggregates; monetary policy plays only a passive role. Many of the post-Keynesian economists attempted to focus on the roles of both; they contended that both monetary and fiscal policies can together play effective role in regulating the behaviour/movements of macroeconomic variables. Experiences of many countries have also provided empirical evidence to this.

So, as instruments of regulatory economic policy, monetary and fiscal policies can be complementary to each other. Monetary policy influence the level of aggregate income and spending in the economy by regulating the level of money supply and the cost of borrowing. Fiscal policy affects income and spending through its effects on the size, composition and timing of government revenue and spending. These two policies can work together to produce a more effective contra-cyclical force than each can produce alone.

During inflation, economic stability can be achieved more successfully by combining the policy of surplus budgeting with dear money policy. Conversely, in a slump, recovery can be started faster by reinforcing the policy of deficit budgeting with cheap money policy. Thus, for achieving economic stability more effectively, it may be necessary to combine both monetary and fiscal policy instruments.

The two policies can also play complementary roles for promotion of economic growth. The two instruments, by working in the same direction, can lead to better economic stability which is conducive to savings. In promoting economic growth directly also, the two policies can work as complementary to each other. A rational or liberal tax policy may generate more investible surplus, and, simultaneously, lower rate of interest may stimulate investment, and eventually lead to the growth of the economy. This has been tried in India during some periods of planned development.

A note on the development and role of fiscal policy in India is given in the Appendix.

REVIEW QUESTIONS

1. Define fiscal policy. Try a complete definition taking into account different aspects of fiscal policy.
2. What are the major objectives of fiscal policy? Are they different from those of monetary policy?
3. Mention the instruments of fiscal policy. Which, among these, according to you, are more important from the point of view of fiscal management of a country?
4. Define 'balanced budget', 'surplus budget' and 'deficit budget'. Also, define and explain 'fiscal deficit', 'revenue deficit,' 'primary deficit' and 'budget deficit'.
5. What are the characteristics of a good tax system? Analyse including Adam Smith's views.
6. Distinguish between 'crowding-out' effect and 'crowding-in' effect of deficit spending. Comment on the applicability of these two effects in reality.
7. Define fiscal multipliers. The tax multiplier (M_T) is written as

$M_T = b.M_G$ (b = MPC; M_G = expenditure multiplier)
Explain this. Also explain why the tax multiplier is always negative.

8. Mention the major applications of fiscal policy. Analyse them with comments on their effectiveness.
9. Explain different lags in formulation and implementation of fiscal policy. Is there any connectivity among these lags? Comment.
10. Explain built-in flexibility, discretionary flexibility and formula or indicator flexibility in fiscal policy. "There are linkages among these three forms of flexibility." Comment.
11. What are the general constraints or limitations of fiscal policy? Which are the special constraints of fiscal policy in low-income/developing economies?
12. Do you think monetary policy and fiscal policy can play complementary roles in controlling inflation, recession and, also for achieving economic growth? Explain by mentioning classical and Keynesian views on this.

SUGGESTED READINGS

- A. Bagchi, "Fiscal Policy for Financing Development: The Indian Experience" in U. Kapila (Ed.), *Indian Economy Since Independence* (Seventh Edition), Academic Foundation, 1996.
- A.M. Okun, "Rules and Roles for Fiscal and Monetary Policy" in G.K. Shaw, *Fiscal Policy*, Macmillan, 1972.
- A.S. Blinder, *Fiscal Policy in Theory and Practice*, General Learning Press, New Jersey, 1973.
- A.S. Blinder and R.M. Solow, "Analytical Foundations of Fiscal Policy" in A.S. Blinder et.al. (Ed.), *The Economics of Public Finance*, The Brookings Institution, 1974.
- E. Shapiro, *Macroeconomic Analysis* (Fifth Edition), Galgotia Publications, 1984, Chapter 25.
- M. Feldstein, "Budget Deficits and National Debt" in *Monthly Bulletins*, Reserve Bank of India, February 2004.
- M.H. Peston, *Theory of Macroeconomic Policy*, Philip Alan, Oxford, 1974.
- P.A. Samuelson and W.D. Nordhaus et.al., *Economics* (Indian adaptation) (Nineteenth Edition), McGraw Hill Education (India), Pvt. Ltd., 2010, Chapter 22.
- R.A. Musgrave, *The Theory of Public Finance*, McGraw Hill, 1959, Chapters 2-4.
- W.J. Banmol and A.S. Blinder, *Economics: Principles and Policy*, Harcourt Brace, London, 1988.

APPENDIX
FISCAL POLICY IN INDIA

Development and role of fiscal policy in the Indian economy can be discussed during two periods or phases:

A. Fiscal Policy before economic liberalisation in 1991
B. Fiscal policy since economic liberalisation

Evolution, growth, role and effectiveness/success of fiscal policy in India during these two periods or phases are discussed in this note.

A. FISCAL POLICY IN INDIA BEFORE 1991

First fiscal policy of India was formulated by the government of independent India during 1950-51. The most basic problem facing the Indian economy during that period was very low level of growth, high poverty and unemployment. During that time, India had almost lowest per capita income and consumption in the world. During five decades, 1900-50, growth of the Indian economy was almost = zero. Therefore, the government's highest priority was economic development of the country. For this, the government had decided to launch five year plans.[25]

It is in this background that the new government had to formulate its first fiscal policy. The government's biggest problem was mobilisation of resources for financing the five year plans for growth. The fiscal policy had to address itself to this task. This was also the most difficult job. To fulfill this task, the government decided to use two primary instruments of fiscal policy, i.e., taxation and expenditure. The government's policy was twofold: to mobilise maximum revenue or resources through taxation—both direct and indirect; and, second, to allocate expenditure in a planned manner to create employment opportunities and promote economic growth. This has been the policy and strategy of the government during successive five year plans starting with the First Plan during the period 1951-56.

Plan outlays and additional resource mobilisation during First Plan (1951-56) to Sixth Plan (1980-85) are shown in Table 20.3.

Table 20.3: Public Sector Plan Outlay and Additional Resource Mobilisation during First to Sixth Five Year Plans (1951-56 to 1980-85)

(₹ crores)

Five Year Plan	Public Sector Plan outlay		Additional Resource Mobilisation	
	Original estimates (at pre-plan year prices)	Actuals (at constant prices)	Original estimates (at pre-plan year prices)	Actuals at constant prices
1	2	3	4	5
First Five Year Plan (1951-56)	2069	1840 (88.9)	–	239
Second Five Year Plan (1956-61)	4800	4011 (83.5)	850	903 (106.2)
Third Five Year Plan (1961-66)	7500	7429 (9.0)	1710	2505 (146.4)
Fourth Five Year Plan (1969-74)	15902	125727 (78.7)	3198	3318 (103.7)
Fifth Five Year Plan (1874-79)	39303	29797 (75.8)	14693	7539 (51.3)
Sixth Five Year Plan (1980-85)	97500	76000 (77.9)	21300	21800 (102.3)

Notes: 1. Figures within brackets indicate actuals as percentages of original estimates.
2. 'Additional resource mobilisation' has been explained in the text (section on 'Fiscal Policy and Economic Growth')
Source: ESCAP, The integration of Tax Planning into Development Planning in the ESCAP Region, reproduced in A. Bagchi, "Fiscal Policy for Financing Development: The Indian Experience" in U. Kapila (Ed.) *Indian Economy Since Independence* (1996), p. 126.

25. The five year plans of the Government of India are discussed in the Appendix to Chapter 24.

It is interesting to see the proportion of expenditure financed by taxes, i.e., the gap between tax revenue and expenditure by the government. This is shown in Table 20.4.

Table 20.4: Proportion of Expenditure Financed by Taxation during 1950-51 to 1980-85

(Per cent)

Centre/State	1950-51	1960-61	9170-71	1980-81	1980-85*
Centre	70.0	42.2	51.9	29.8	42.6
	(30.0)	(57.8)	(48.1)	(60.2)	(57.4)
Centre plus states	68.5	52.2	58.9	56.1	53.6
	(31.5)	(47.8)	(41.1)	(43.9)	(46.4)

* Revised Estimate

Note: Numbers or proportions in brackets show the gaps between tax revenue and expenditure during the respective periods

Source: Compiled/Adapted from *Indian Economic Statistics* (*Public Finance*), Government of India.

Another important aspect of the budget and fiscal management of the country during this period was the tax-GDP ratio. The ratio had increased significantly during this period—from 6.5 per cent during 1950-51 to 16.9 per cent during 1984-85. The increase took place primarily because of indirect taxes. Ratios of all the three major component of indirect tax, namely excise duties, sales tax and customs duty increased considerably—ratio of excise duty to GDP increased from 0.7 per cent during 1950-51 to 5.2 per cent during 1984-85; during the same period, ratio of sales tax to GDP increased from 0.6 per cent to 3.5 per cent and that of customs duty increased from 1.6 per cent to 3.3 per cent. This showed the government's increasing reliance on revenue collection from indirect taxes.

During the same period, the ratio of direct taxes to GDP increased only insignificantly—from 2.4 per cent during 1950-51 to 2.6 per cent during 1984-85. The ratios of personal income tax and corporate tax, in fact, declined during this period—the ratio of personal income tax to GDP declined from 1.2 per cent in 1970-71 to 0.8 per cent during 1984-85 and that of corporate tax to GDP declined from 1.8 per cent during 1950-51 to 1.3 per cent in 1984-85. Because of low income levels and high unemployment the government was not increasing direct taxes.

Tax-GDP ratios, for both direct and indirect taxes, for the Indian economy during 1950-51, 1970-71, 1980-81 and 1984-85 are given in Table 20.5.

Table 20.5: Tax-GDP Ratio for the Indian Economy during 1950-51, 1970-71, 1980-81 and 1984-85

(Per cent)

Direct/Indirect Tax	1950-51	1970-71	1980-81	1984-85
1. Direct taxes				
Personal income tax	NA	1.2	1.2	0.8
Corporate tax	1.8	0.9	1.0	1.3
Land revenue	0.5	0.3	0.1	0.2
Total: direct taxes	**2.4**	**2.5**	**2.6**	**2.6**
2. Indirect taxes				
Sales tax	0.6	2.0	3.2	3.5
Excise duty	0.7	4.4	5.1	5.2
Customs duty	1.6	1.3	2.7	3.3
Total: indirect taxes	**4.1**	**9.3**	**13.0**	**14.3**
3. Total: all taxes	**6.5**	**11.8**	**15.6**	**16.9**

Source: Government Budget Sources (Compiled).

Table 20.4 shows the shortfalls of tax revenue to finance development expenditure. Because of such shortfalls, the government had to resort to borrowing and other sources for resource mobilisation. This meant that the government followed a policy of deficit budgeting. Large borrowing took place from RBI, among other sources. This led to *deficit financing*. Deficit financing is generally inflationary. In fact, deficit financing and inflationary trend have been the characteristics of the Indian economy for many decades now.

B. FISCAL POLICY IN INDIA AFTER 1991

In view of the inflationary trend and deficit financing, significant changes were made by the government in the fiscal policy and fiscal management of the country during 1991. Fiscal reform was one of the major objectives of economic liberalisation policies announced during 1990-91. For stabilising the economy or to restore macroeconomic balance, it was necessary to reverse the expansionary fiscal process.

Accordingly, the government decided to reduce the fiscal deficit and deficit financing. Because of rigorous budgetary planning, fiscal deficit, expressed as a ratio of GDP, declined since 1990-91 till 2007-08 (with the exception of 1993-94). But, since 2007-08, the ratio started increasing again. This had been a matter of concern for the government and, also an indication of the inadequacy of fiscal management.

The nature of movements/fluctuations in the ratio of fiscal deficit to GDP since 1980-81 till 2012-13 is shown in Table 20.6.

Table 20.6: Fluctuations in Fiscal deficit-GDP Ratio during 1980-81 to 2012-13

Year	Fiscal deficit-GDP ratio (%)	Year	Fiscal deficit-GDP ratio (%)
1980-81	5.7	1996-97	4.1
1981-82	5.4	1997-98	4.8
1982-83	6.0	1998-99	5.1
1983-84	6.3	1999-00	5.4
1984-85	7.5	2000-01	5.7
1985-86	7.9	2001-02	6.2
1986-87	8.5	2002-03	5.9
1987-88	7.6	2003-04	4.5
1988-89	7.3	2004-05	4.0
1989-90	7.3	2005-06	4.1
1990-91	6.6	2006-07	3.4
1991-92	4.7	2007-08	2.5
1992-93	4.8	2008-09	6.0
1993-94	6.4	2009-10	6.5
1994-95	4.7	2010-11	4.8
1995-96	4.2	2011-12 (P)	5.7
		2012-13 (BE)	5.1

P: Provisional BE: Budget estimate

Source: *Economic Survey*, Government of India, 2012-13.

For proper fiscal management of the country, Fiscal Responsibility and Budget Management (FRBM) Act was passed by the Parliament in 2003. The FRBM Act laid down 3.0 per cent as the fiscal deficit-GDP ratio. This was to be achieved within five years, i.e., 2008-09 (the ratio during 2003-04 was 4.5 per cent). The target ratio was achieved during 2007-08 itself—the ratio was 2.5 per cent. But, the ratio shot up to 6.0 per cent next year (2008-09). The ratio had declined during subsequent years, but, it did not fall below 5.0 percent (Table 20.6). Management of fiscal deficit has remained a major challenge to the government.

During the presentation of the Budget for 2012-13 in the Parliament, amendments were introduced to the FRBM Act. The amendments related to two important aspects of revenue and expenditure reforms. The first is the concept of 'effective revenue deficit'; this is defined as conventional revenue deficit minus transfers for creation of capital assets. Because of this amendment, the objective of the government would be to eliminate or reduce effective revenue deficit. But, understating capital expenditure (because of transfer) may lead to a divergence between national accounts data on capital formation on government accounts and conventional public finance data compiled from budget.[26]

The second amendment in the FRBM Act relates to introduction of a new provision for 'Medium Term Expenditure Framework Statement' in the Act. This framework introduces rolling targets for expenditure and facilitates prioritisation of expenditure.

The government has also proposed measures to increase the share of taxes in total revenue envisaging bigger role for taxation as a source of revenue. The share of taxes in total revenue has been increasing over time. The tax-GDP ratio, however, has been fluctuating. As shown in Table 20.4, from a low of 6.5 per cent during 1950-51, tax-GDP ratio increased steadily to 16.9 per cent during 1984-85. But, after that, there was steady decline and recovery and the ratio reached 11.5 per cent during 2006-07. Since then, the ratio has been fluctuating around 10.0 per cent. Tax-GDP ratios for both direct and indirect taxes—during the period 2007-08 and 2012-13 are presented in Table 20.7.

Table 20.7: Tax-GDP Ratio (both Direct and Indirect Taxes), 2007-08 to 2012-13

Tax-GDP Ratio (%)

Tax	2007-08	2008-09	2009-10	2010-11	2011-12 (P)	2012-13 (BE)
Direct taxes	5.9	5.7	5.7	5.6	5.5	5.6
Indirect taxes	5.6	4.8	3.8	4.4	4.4	5.0
All taxes+	11.9	10.8	9.6	10.2	9.9	10.7

P: Provisional BE: Budget estimate
+ includes taxes of Union Territories
Source: *Economic Survey*, Government of India, 2012-13

The government has plans to increase the tax-GDP ratio. This and expenditure reforms, mentioned above, are together likely to lead to better fiscal marksmanship, and, thereby reduce key fiscal risks,[27] and, improve fiscal management of the country.

26. *Economic Survey*, Government of India, 2012-13, p. 57
27. *Ibid.*

Chapter 21

Macroeconomic Policy: Physical Policy

NATURE OF PHYSICAL POLICY

Fiscal and monetary policies constitute indirect or general controls; they affect aggregate demand or supply or operation of the economic system only indirectly. In contrast, there may be direct or physical controls; they affect particular sectors of consumers and producers. Such controls are imposed in the form of licencing, price controls, rationing, quality control, monopoly control, regulation of trade practices, anti-hoarding and anti-smuggling schemes, export incentives, import duties, import-export and exchange regulations, etc.

It is this complex and varied set of direct controls which is often referred as physical policy. Unlike fiscal and monetary policies which affect the entire economy, physical policies are meant to affect only strategic points of the economy; they are specifically oriented and discriminatory in nature. They are designed and executed to overcome specific problems with regard to, say, pricing of particular commodities, shortages or surpluses developing in the economy, export promotion, import substitution and the like. The enclosed chart would make more clear distinction between monetary policy, fiscal policy, and physical policy.

Areas in which physical policies are more commonly applied are investment and production, price and distribution, foreign trade and foreign exchange control.

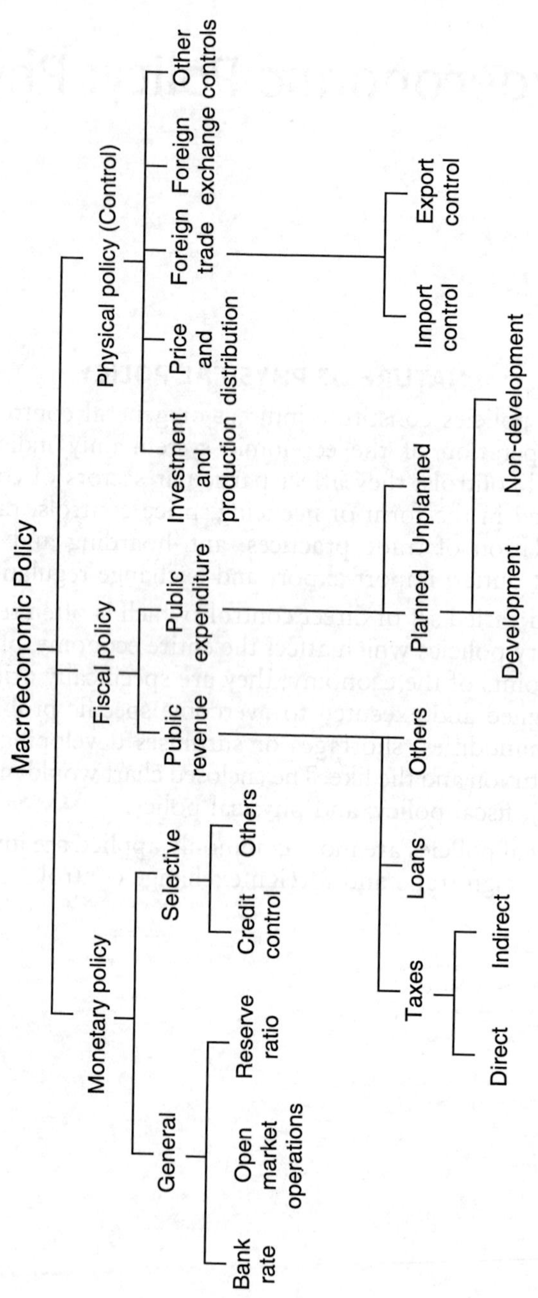
Macroeconomic Policy
Monetary policy
Fiscal policy
Physical policy (Control)
General
Selective
Bank rate
Open market operations
Reserve ratio
Credit control
Others
Public revenue
Public expenditure
Taxes
Loans
Others
Direct
Indirect
Planned
Unplanned
Development
Non-development
Investment and production
Price and distribution
Foreign trade
Foreign exchange
Other controls
Import control
Export control

For allocation and utilisation of scarce resources, control over investment and production becomes necessary. The usual methods of control here are issue of licences, demarcation of areas of different sectors like public, private, joint and cooperative sectors and, large, medium and small scale sectors; fixation of priorities, guidelines for foreign investment, etc. Such controls are usually exercised through industrial policy statements, industrial development and regulation acts, control of capital issues, etc.

Such controls are particularly relevant and necessary in developing economies with inflationary potential; in such economies, production of essential mass consumption goods, basic raw materials and capital goods must be controlled so that shortages and bottlenecks may not develop.

Price and distribution controls are exercised to regulate consumption and also to ensure supplies during periods of scarcities. Supplies are controlled or ensured through rationing. Price controls are sometimes less drastic and more comprehensive than rationing, and therefore, more useful as methods of distributing the goods equitably. Of course, a system of price controls and rationing should generally go together. Prices of essential goods are usually fixed at low levels. At such low levels of controlled prices, there always exists excess demand, and unless there is rationing, price controls may lead to queues, profiteering, hoarding, adulteration, black marketing and other unethical business practices. Thus, unless there is an efficient public distribution system, the purpose of price controls may get defeated. This implies the significant roles of fair price shops, super bazars, consumer cooperatives, state emporia, etc.

Price controls may operate at different levels and in different degrees. Sometimes, controls may be imposed statutorily on ex-factory prices of product. At the same time, consumer prices of the same product may be uniformly regulated. Sometimes the government introduces the system of dual pricing; one set of prices for producer goods (like steel) which are industrial inputs and a separate set of prices for consumer goods particularly for food articles (like rice or wheat) which directly influence the cost of living.

Price controls may be administered not only in the commodity market but also in the factor market. Profit or dividend control, interest control, rent control and wage control are all examples of factor price controls. Commodity prices and factor prices are interrelated: cost-push inflation (or a wage-price spiral) is a glaring example. Therefore, commodity price controls should be, and, are many times, combined with factor price controls.

The difference between domestic production and consumption accounts for either import or export. If there is a deficit, imports become necessary; if there is an exportable surplus, exports may be made. These are the two constituents of foreign trade. Foreign trade controls may, therefore, be of two types: import controls and export controls.

Import controls are imposed to keep a balance between indigenous availability and import requirements. Such controls may take the form of ban on import of certain non-essential items (or items which are indigenously produced) and liberalisation of import of certain essential raw materials and goods. Normally, import controls are executed through a system of quotas and licences.

The principal objectives of export control are (a) earning of foreign exchange and (b) fulfilling export commitments in accordance with trade agreements on the one hand, and conserving basic resources and raw materials of the country on the other. For purposes of export controls (export promotion rather) there are various measures like export incentive schemes, duty drawbacks, etc. Reduction, rationalisation or abolition of export duties are made from time to time in view of developments in national and international market conditions.

Foreign exchange control attempts to regulate the country's balance of payments directly. Most of the developing countries suffer from balance of payment difficulties because of low exports and large import requirements. Exchange controls are designed to attain the twin objectives of export promotion and import restriction.

Exchange controls are also designed to promote optimum utilisation of foreign exchange. Controls aim at rationing of a scarce currency and liberalisation of a currency which is in reserves in plenty; this way exchange controls may discriminate against imports from certain countries.

Another form of exchange control is the system of multiple exchange rates. Normal exchange rate may be used for essential imports and penalty exchange rate may be applied to non-essential imports.

GOVERNMENT CONTROLS IN VARIOUS COUNTRIES

Government regulation and control of private industrial development is a common phenomenon in almost all countries of the world, developing as well as developed. Different countries have adopted different types of control depending upon their political, social, and economic systems. A number of such types may be identified.

Japan and some other south-east Asian countries, e.g. South Korea, follow a system of controls which is as complete and pervasive as anything one can think of; but a form of control which is administered not through any discriminatory case by case scrutiny, but through a system of administrative guidance and supervision. The Japanese Government feels that private business is incapable of taking the best decisions by itself, and therefore, it is essential for the government to provide guidelines on virtually every aspect of operations.

Based on discussions between the government and the private enterprises, mutually determined national targets are worked out. A private enterprise pledges to carry these out. The government, on its part, promises special measures of favours such as rationalisation of taxation and grant of subsidies. Mutual consent and bilateral methods obviate the need for legal compulsion. The result is the emergence of a 'concerted economy' or 'consent economy'.

South Korea which has made remarkable industrial progress in recent years also provides an illustration of the same type of centrally controlled economy through administrative guidance.

Secondly, one can take the case of France where also there is very close government control over private industry exercised through the method of 'indicative planning'. The French approach to planning has aimed, from the beginning, at finding a new path between centralised control and individual market decisions. It is based on group consultation and persuasion. Unlike the coercive and highly directive planning of socialist countries, French planning operates by stimulating different segments of the economy towards accepted short-range sectoral goals. Thus, it is commonly called indicative, i.e. it *spells out goals* and provides help in achieving them as opposed to those forms of planning which *prescribe action* in certain direction.

A third type of close government control over industry is provided by countries like Singapore, Malaysia, Mexico, Brazil and a host of American countries. The countries seek to regulate private industry through a system of incentives and active promotional measures.

Among these countries, Singapore seems to have been the most successful. Malaysia and Indonesia also seem to have streamlined their administrative systems considerably and created specific agencies for stimulating and coordinating private industrial investment through incentives and promotional measures, e.g. Federal Industrial Development Authority (FIDA) in Malaysia, Foreign Investment Board in Indonesia.

Also significant are the 'investment codes' adopted by a number of African countries indicating the fiscal and promotional benefits and preferential treatment to be offered to eligible foreign and domestic companies which invest in specified categories of industries.

REGULATORY CONTROLS IN INDIA

India, in contrast, provides the model of a system of direct and discretionary control. Such control or regulation requires that applications be submitted in respect of a very large proportion of major business activities and approvals obtained for each before corporate management can actually undertake them.

The government is involved with business in India in many ways. First, it intervenes wherever business is likely to harm the interest of employees, customers, and shareholders. Secondly, it functions as a protector of the weaker sections of business, and takes measures to curb the excessive power of big business houses. Thirdly, government itself is the owner of many industries. Finally, the government has the overall responsibility in the management of the nation's resources, and has, therefore, to be concerned with their proper utilisation.

The degree to which business in the private sector is controlled by the government depends directly on the scope or freedom the business sector enjoys in functioning against the interest of society. The policies for intervention are formulated within the framework of the Constitution of India, the Five-Year Plans and the Industrial Policy Resolutions of 1948 and 1956. There is hardly any area of business activity affecting social interest which is not regulated by the government, and it is well-nigh impossible for an executive to take any decision in such areas without being familiar with the types of controls and their implications.

Government regulation of private industrial development in India has been in vogue for more than three decades now. While there are almost innumerable administrative controls over the working of private business emanating from various legislations and policies, we may broadly identify the following major areas:

1. Industrial licensing[1]
2. Control over concentration of economic power
3. Control over restrictive trade practices
4. Various controls under the company law
5. Commodity control (control over price and distribution)
6. Capital issues control
7. Import control
8. Export control
9. Foreign exchange control
10. Regulation of foreign investment and foreign collaboration agreements

We shall not enumerate each of the legislations or acts pertaining to each of the above areas of control, but discuss the legislations or acts relating to four major areas mentioned above, namely control of monopolies and restrictive trade practices, capital issues control, company law and regulations and foreign exchange regulation. The Acts relating to these areas give good illustrations of the nature of regulatory controls which are in force in India today.

1. In the economic liberalisation measures announced in 1991, many industries have been delicensed, and licensing procedures have been simplified to a great extent.

MONOPOLIES AND RESTRICTIVE TRADE PRACTICES (MRTP) ACT

The MRTP Act, enacted in December 1969 and brought into force with effect from June 1970 has three objectives:

(i) to control and regulate the concentration of economic power in a few business and industrial units;

(ii) to control monopolies and monopolistic trade practices;

(iii) to prohibit or curb restrictive trade practices unless any one of those can be justified in public interest.

The MRTP Act is a comparatively recent legislation in India, but similar legislations existed long before in developed countries like the United Kingdom, the United States and Canada. The Indian MRTP Act is patterned on the British model.

CONCENTRATION OF ECONOMIC POWER

The Monopoly Enquiry Commission (1965) had concluded that concentration of economic power is the central problem of the Indian economy and the monopolistic and restrictive trade practices are mere functions of such concentration. The Commission considered both 'productwise' or 'industrywise' concentration and 'countrywise' concentration, and it was felt socially desirable to control such concentration.

For purposes of such control, the MRTP Act identifies four types of undertakings:

(i) An undertaking which has gross assets of ₹ 20 crore and more;

(ii) Interconnected undertakings which together have assets of ₹ 20 crore or more;

(iii) A dominant undertaking—one which produces, supplies or controls one-third of any goods in the country; in the MRTP (Amendment) Bill, 1982, the criterion of dominance has been reduced from one-third to one-fourth of total capacity or production—which has assets of ₹ 1 crore and more; and

(iv) Interconnected undertakings constituting a dominant undertaking and having aggregate assets of ₹ 1 crore and more.

The Act makes it obligatory for all undertakings covered above to have the central government's prior approval for (a) merger and amalgamation and (b) for takeover of an undertaking by another through inter-corporate investment or purchase. No such approval is, however, necessary for a merger when the concerned undertakings are either already interconnected or produce the same goods or are not dominant undertakings.

MONOPOLISTIC AND RESTRICTIVE TRADE PRACTICES

Monopolistic practices are defined as practices adopted by, or are prevalent in any individual firm or a group of firms by virtue of its dominant market share. Monopolistic practices have been more specifically defined in terms of their effects on production, prices, competition, technical development or capital investment.

Circumstances have also been identified under which monopolistic trade practices are considered harmful or prejudicial to public interest.

These circumstances are:

(i) an unreasonable increase in the prices of goods sold;

(ii) unreasonable profits derived from the production, supply or distribution of goods and services;

(iii) undue reduction in competition in the market;
(iv) deterioration in the quality of goods and services; and
(v) unreasonable limitation on supply of goods and services to the consumers.

For the control of monopolistic trade practice (i.e. dominant firm's behaviour) the MRTP Commission has powers of investigation which it can undertake either on its own initiative or by a reference made by the government. But recommendations to control or curb monopolistic practices are not binding nor is the Commission empowered to enforce any regulatory measures or take any action leading or relating to such enforcement. The power to take action on its findings or recommendations lies with the government. In other words, the role of the MRTP Commission is advisory or recommendatory with no authority of decision-making.

The role of the Commission is similar with respect to restrictive trade practices also. Restrictive trade practices, in contrast to monopolistic practices, are those which result in preventing, distorting, or restricting competition in any manner and which, in particular, tend to obstruct the smooth flow of capital or resources into the production process or manipulate prices or conditions of delivery.

Restrictive trade practices, as defined above, are to be considered generally prejudicial to public interest unless undertaken under any one of the following circumstances:

(i) the character of the goods justifies restriction and the possibility of public interest being affected if it is withdrawn;
(ii) substantial benefits or advantages are likely to accrue to the consumers because of the existence of the restriction;
(iii) the need for contracting measures (imposed or enforced as restriction) to prevent or distort competition;
(iv) enabling two or more parties to negotiate fair terms for supply of goods;
(v) possible adverse effects of the withdrawal of the restriction on the general level of employment;
(vi) possible reduction in the volume or value of earnings from particular export business (balance of payments considerations);
(vii) the necessity of the restriction for enforcing or maintaining another restriction required in the public interest; and
(viii) relative insignificance of the relevant restriction for purposes of restricting or discouraging competition.

The government has been constantly aware of the need for removing all unnecessary and irksome procedural impediments to industrial growth. With this in view, important amendments have been made in the MRTP Act, first by an ordinance, and, subsequently, by law in 1991-92. The Act has been restructured to broaden its base and make it more progressive, without, at the same time, sacrificing its basic objectives.

CAPITAL ISSUES CONTROL ACT

This is an instrument of control to regulate the working of the capital market. In 1956, along with the Companies Act, two more enactments took place which were concerned with control of capital issues: the Capital Issues Control Act and the Securities Contracts Regulation Act. Both of these Acts recognise and pronounce the twin roles of the state as promoter of the capital market and protector of the shareholders.

The Capital Issues Control Act makes it obligatory for corporate units to obtain the central government's consent or approval for the issue of capital within the country in respect of:

(i) issue of capital in excess of ₹ 25 lakh during a period of twelve months;
(ii) issue of bonus shares of any amount by public or private limited companies;
(iii) a public offer of securities for sale at premium or discount;
(iv) renewal or postponement of the date of maturity or repayment of any security maturing for payment; and
(v) issue of debentures carrying conversion rights other than those privately placed with financial institutions.

Certain types of securities are exempt from the provisions spelt out in (iii), (iv), and (v) above; six such types of issues have been distinctly classified which are exempt from the capital issues control. The details of these exemptions are specified in the Capital Issues (Exemption) Order, 1969.

In addition to the general provisions listed above governing capital issues, the Capital Issues Control Act is specifically concerned with four important types of issues, viz.,

1. *Fresh issue of capital by new companies*. In this context, the Controller of Capital Issues, who is the competent authority to investigate into and sanction such issue, normally examines the viability of the venture in terms of total capital cost and scheme of finance, debt-equity ratio, equity-preference ratio, etc.

2. *Issue of right shares by the existing companies*. When an existing company likes to issue additional shares in order to finance any expansion or diversification programme, and limits the offer to its existing shareholders, such issue of capital is known as rights issue. Whether rights issue is to be allowed at par or at a premium is decided by the Controller of Capital Issues after examination of several factors like net value of assets, the market value, past dividends paid, etc.

3. *Issue of bonus shares by capitalisation of free reserves*. Companies are allowed to declare bonus only out of free reserves built either from past profits or share premiums collected in cash. The total amount to be capitalised from free reserves at any time should not exceed the amount of paid-up equity capital of the company. This is the well-known 1 : 1 formula. No declaration of bonus shares are allowed in lieu of dividends. And not more than two issues of bonus shares are permitted in a period of five years.

4. *Issue of debentures*. Cases for issue of debentures by companies are examined with reference to purpose of the issue, debt-equity ratio, adequacy of security, and, whether the company would be able to service the debentures without difficulty.

We have mentioned above that the Capital Issues Control Act has been designed to exercise control over the functioning of the capital market. But it should not give the impression that the Act is restrictive or prohibitive; in fact, it is intended to promote a healthy structure of the capital market in consistency with the objective of balanced industrial development of the country, and therefore, it has a positive role to play in national industrial and economic growth.

It should, however, be mentioned here that capital issues control is one of the many mechanisms which affect the capital market. Some of the important mechanisms of control are industrial policy statements, monetary and fiscal policies, lending policy of financial institutions, etc. The cumulative effect of all these control mechanisms or factors on the capital market and corporate capital growth is quite significant, and sometimes makes the role of the capital issues control rather secondary.

COMPANY LAW AND REGULATIONS

In the present economic and business environment in India, the Company Law is the principal law affecting the organisation, management and control of corporate business. Originally, the Law used to be concerned with joint stock companies only; but, overtime, its scope has been enlarged, and, it now covers different types of companies, their incorporation, constitution, management and also the manner of dissolution. Company Law today is represented/implemented through the Companies Act, 1956 and its amendment in 1960, 1963, 1969 and 1970.

The word 'Company' in the Companies Act refers to a business organisation with features of corporate personality, limited liability and transferability of shares. The Act defines and distinguishes three types of companies: (i) companies limited by share, commonly known as 'limited companies', (ii) companies limited by guarantee, known as 'guarantee companies' and, (iii) companies with unlimited liability (this is more in theory than in practice). Each of these three types of companies can again be classified or formed as either a public company or a private company.

Given the definitions of various types of companies, the Companies Act provides for certain degree of ultimate control by the shareholders, democratisation of company management, and, also, prevention of some known malpractices in corporate management. For example, the Act contains provisions for government's control over the appointment and remuneration of managing directors and whole-time directors of companies. In addition, the Act puts some restrictions on loans made or guarantees given by one company to another (interlocking of funds). The Act also contains provisions for maintenance of proper books of accounts, inspection and auditing of accounts.

Liberal but regulatory company enactments are in line with the emerging trends in India's economic and business environment. Growth of big businesses at national and multinational level has to be encouraged, but also properly regulated and directed. Secondly, growth of corporate giants such as SAIL, BHEL, ONGC, IOC, and MMTC has created a challenging public sector with its own objectives and priorities. Thirdly, social responsibility of the business sector is increasing, and, includes protection of interest of all shareholders, consumers, managers, workers, community and the government, that is, various stakeholders of companies. The Company Law—its enactments and amendments—is to be viewed in this perspective.

SEBI REGULATIONS ON CORPORATE RESTRUCTURING

In a competitive and free economy, takeovers, amalgamations, mergers, restructuring and also winding up are normal business phenomena. Amalgamations, mergers, reconstructions, winding up or dissolution take place under due process of law as per provisions of the Company Act and these (except voluntary winding up) require sanction of the court. Takeover or acquisition can, however, take place without sanction of any court or Company Law Board. But many of these are controlled through SEBI (Substantial Acquisition of Shares and Takeovers) Regulation, 1994.

Takeover can be of different kinds. Four major takeover types may be distinguished:

(a) *Friendly Takeover*: Takeover takes place with the approval and in agreement with the existing management. Shares and control are acquired through negotiations.

(b) *Hostile Takeover*: A person or a group of persons or a corporate body may acquire shares from the open market or by negotiations with or without knowledge of the existing management to obtain management control of the company.

(c) *Bailout Takeover*: In case of a potential sick company in which large amount of institutional funds are blocked and public interest is involved, takeover and change in management take place to help revival of the unit.

(d) *Substantial Acquisition of Shares without Change in Management*: This may happen under different circumstances. This may include a situation in which an Indian promoter may buy out shares of a foreign collaborator who may like to disinvest for a variety of reasons.

A distinction should be made between a takeover and a merger. In a takeover, direct or indirect control over the assets of the acquired company passes to the acquirer. In a merger, shareholding in the combined enterprise would be divided/spread between shareholders of the two companies. SEBI regulations, 1994 prescribes a takeover code and provides a framework for more open and orderly conduct of takeovers and mergers. The prescribed code is in the nature of business standards appropriate to Indian market conditions. In August, 1996, new guidelines for takeover have been suggested by a Special Committee of the government. These are more detailed and comprehensive.

FOREIGN EXCHANGE REGULATION ACT (FERA)

In today's economic and business environment in India, the FERA has emerged as a very important legislation which imposes control over (a) the activities of multinational business; (b) the flow of foreign capital, technology and management or entrepreneurial skill; and (c) foreign collaboration and joint ventures. In short, the FERA regulates the flow of foreign investment and foreign participation in business in India.

Foreign exchange control in India was introduced for the first time in the Defence of India Rules, 1939. Replacing that, the Foreign Exchange Regulation Act was introduced in 1947 as the basic law of exchange control and as the main legal instrument regulating the operation of foreign-owned or foreign-controlled companies in India. This Act was amended in 1957 and 1965; and major changes were effected in the provisions of the Act through the introduction of the Foreign Exchange Regulation (Amendment) Act of 1973. The guidelines laid down in the amendment of 1973 were further revised in 1975 to incorporate a major role for the Reserve Bank of India in administering foreign exchange regulations in the country. Six main features of the revised FERA guidelines, 1976 are:

(i) If the activities of a company together with activities requiring sophisticated technology and exports, account for not less than 75 per cent of its total annual turnover, such a company will be allowed to continue its activities subject to the condition that it will increase Indian participation within a specified period to not less than 26 per cent of the equity capital of the company.

(ii) If instead of 75, the percentage is 60, such a company also will be allowed to continue provided it increases, within a specified period, Indian participation to not less than 49 per cent of the equity of the company. The company should also undertake to export a minimum of 13 per cent of its total annual turnover within a period of two years commencing from the date of approval by the Reserve Bank of India.

(iii) If the exports of a company account for more than 40 per cent of the total annual turnover, such a company would be allowed to continue provided it increases, within a specified period, Indian participation to not less than 49 per cent of the equity of the company.

(iv) Cases of companies coming with proposals for substantial exports would be considered for higher level of equity participation provided such participation is in the overall interest of the economy of the country.

(v) A limit of ₹ 5 crore is fixed for permissible trading activity by multi-activity companies.

(vi) The ceiling of 25 per cent of the ex-factory value of annual production for permissible trading activity by multi-activity companies will be raised to 40 per cent and 60 per cent respectively in types of cases mentioned in (ii) and (iii) above.

Foreign investments in Indian enterprises which are branches or subsidiaries of foreign companies as well as joint ventures involving foreign collaboration (financial, technical or managerial) are subject to all the laws governing Indian enterprises—the MRTP Act, the Companies Act, Income Tax Act, the Industries (Regulation and Development) Act, etc., as well as the FERA.

The objective behind formulating and enforcing foreign exchange regulations is to encourage Indianisation of corporate ventures wherever feasible and attract foreign capital, technology and entrepreneurship wherever desirable. It is realised that foreign investment does play an important role in promoting industrialisation and generating income and employment in developing countries like India; foreign collaboration also helps transfer of technology and managerial skill. But while recognising all this, the Government of India likes to make sure that flow of foreign capital and technology does not stand in the way of indigenous growth of industries and self-sustained economic growth in the country, and therefore, its basic policy towards foreign investment and technical collaboration has been one of selectivity. It is in this perspective that one has to understand the implications of FERA guidelines.

The government has recently made far-reaching changes in FERA through a Presidential Ordinance (FERA Amendment Ordinance, 1993) to remove many restrictions on FERA companies in keeping with the liberalised regime. Reviewing recent experiences of FERA implementation, the government has felt the need for replacing FERA by FEMA (Foreign Exchange Management Act)—a change from 'regulation' to 'management'. The objective is to combine simultaneous loose-tight properties in the Act that is, generally managing the flow of foreign exchange and imposing controls and restrictions only in individual cases where violations of norms or guidelines are involved. This is the policy of liberalism with caution.

REVIEW QUESTIONS

1. What is physical policy? Explain with reference to its constituents.
2. What is the MRTP Act? Analyse, in detail, its operation with special reference to the MRTP Commission.
3. Explain FERA/FEMA. Comment on its effectiveness in regulating foreign exchange.

SUGGESTED READINGS

- M. Adhikary, *Economic Environment of Business* (Eighth Edition), S. Chand & Sons, 2000.
- A. Dasgupta and N. Sengupta, *Government and Business in India*, 1981, Chapters 4 and 19.
- N. Sengupta, *Government and Business* (Fourth Revised Edition), Vikas Publishing House, 1996.

PART–VII

MACRO-ENVIRONMENT, FOREIGN SECTOR, ECONOMIC GROWTH AND PLANNING

Macroeconomic environment which governs business decisions is analysed in Chapter 22. The nature of interaction between macroeconomic environment and business decisions (at micro level) has been explained through some interaction matrices.

Study of macroeconomics goes beyond national boundaries because most of the modern economies are open economies. A discussion on international economics and foreign trade is, therefore, necessary and has been presented in Chapter 23. Balance of trade, balance of payments, terms of trade, foreign exchange, exchange rate fluctuations have all been analysed.

The last chapter (Chapter 24) in this part deals with economic growth and planning. The discussion covers stages of economic growth, balanced and unbalanced growth, growth models, and economic planning. This is done in two parts (A and B). The chapter ends with analysis of the planning process in India in terms of the various five year plans—beginning with the First Five Year Plan and concluding with the Tenth Five Year Plan.

Chapter 22

Macroeconomic Environment and Business Decisions

In the preceding chapters, we have discussed different areas of macroeconomics. Some are indicators of the economic system like GDP, rate of savings, rate of inflation, etc., some are policy measures like various monetary and fiscal policies; some are regulatory measures or controls mostly the physical controls. All these indicators, measures, and controls affect management of business and business decision. Although precise quantification of their effects on the management process may be difficult, it is certain that they have clear impacts on management decisions: or, to put it in another way, there are interrelations or interactions between the two.

THREE BASIC PROPOSITIONS

We start our discussion of the interaction between macroeconomic environment and business decisions by stating three basic propositions.

These are:

1. Business is an economic activity.
2. A business firm is an economic unit.
3. Business decision-making is an economic process.

An *economic activity* is the task of adjusting the means (resources) to ends (targets) or the ends to means. Economic activities may assume different forms such as consumption, production, distribution and exchange. The nature of business differs depending upon the form of economic activity which is being undertaken and organised. For example, manufacturing business is primarily concerned with production. Stock exchange business is mainly concerned with buying and selling of shares and debentures. Wholesale or retail trading is the business of buying and selling goods. Banking business is to facilitate transactions in short-term and long-term funds. Many more such examples can be given. The essential point to note is that each business has a target to achieve; and for that each business has some resources at its disposal. Sometimes the level of targets has to be matched to given resources; sometimes, the use of resource has to be matched to given targets. Either way, the task of business is to optimise the outcome of economic activities.

A business firm is essentially a conversion or transformation unit. It converts or transforms a set of inputs into a flow of output either of goods or services. The nature of input requirements and the type of output flows are determined by the size, structure, location and efficiency of the particular business firm concerned. The business may be of different sizes and forms. They may undertake different types of activities such as mining, manufacturing, trading, transporting, banking, etc. The objective behind these activities is the same, viz. profit maximisation in the short-run as well as in the long-run.[1] The firm can grow further if the profit or surplus is productively invested. The firm, therefore, plans carefully and critically the optimum allocation of resources (inputs of men, money, materials, time, energy, etc.), and the optimum production mix (output combination). The entire process of creation, mobilisation and utilisation of surplus constitutes the economic activity of the business firm.

Making any decision involves undertaking a choice among a set of alternative courses of action. Choice is the essence of all economic decisions. The question of choice and valuation arises because of relative scarcity of resources. The business firm thinks of optimum allocation of resources because resources are limited in supply and same resource has alternative uses. The firm, therefore, intends to get the best out of given resources or to minimise the use of resources for attaining a given goal. In other words, when 'input' is the constraining factor, the firm's decision variable is 'output'. And when 'output' is the constraining factor, the firm's decision variable is 'input'. Whatever may be the decision variable, procurement or production, distribution or sale, input or output, the decision-making itself is the process of selecting the best available alternative. That is what makes it an economic pursuit.

BUSINESS ENVIRONMENT

Business environment or environment for business broadly implies the set of factors or forces which influence or affect the operations of an individual business firm or unit. Environment would imply both internal environment and external environment. Internal environment is made up of factors internal to the firm, like market standing, financial health, systems and procedures, work culture, etc., which have a direct bearing on the business unit's performance. External environment is constituted of the vast multitude of factors or forces—national as well as international—over which the firm has no control[2] and which are taken as 'given' by the management for taking business decisions as against internal environment which can be controlled to a large extent by the management. Therefore, when we talk of business environment, we generally mean external environment which determine the business climate at any particular moment of time.

Business environment may be classified on different criteria, such as time, space, forces and factors. Based on 'time', we may talk of past, present and future environment of business. Based on 'space', we may think of local, regional, national and international environment of business. Based on 'forces' of market such as demand, supply, price, etc., or non-market institution like government, we may distinguish between market and non-market environment of business. Finally, based on the relevance of economic or non-economic 'factors', we may specify economic and non-economic environment of business.

Such classification of environmental factors is mainly for reasons of analytical convenience to understand their pull and/or push. In real world situation, the environmental factors interact

1. The profit maximisation hypothesis has been empirically challenged. Alternative hypotheses have been put forward, i.e. sales maximisation, utility maximisation, welfare maximisation, etc. Such hypotheses do explain the short-run economic behaviour of the firm. But in the long-run, most of the firms aim at stable and secure profit. See M. Adhikary, *Managerial Economics*.
   This is true of the private sector. In the public sector, profit maximisation may not be the objective even in the long-run.
2. Although the firm individually does not have much control or influence on the external environment, collective behaviour/decisions of the firms may affect the environment.

with each other.[3] Because of the involved nature of these interactions, the environment often appears very complex, dynamic and sometimes beyond theoretical comprehension. But for efficient operation of the firm, there is no alternative to identification, description and explanation of its business environment, immediate and remote.

For business decisions, economic environment has the most immediate impact. But, as just mentioned, because of the close interaction between the economic and non-economic environment, the non-economic factors or environment also becomes important.[4] Before we discuss the economic environment in detail, let us have a look at the non-economic environment. Major non-economic factors of environment are physical, historical, political, sociological, legal, educational and cultural, the political factors being by far the most important.

We may all generally agree that economic stability, growth or fluctuations depend, to a large extent, on the prevailing political situation in a country—stability or instability; the nature of political ideology, foreign policy, etc. In fact, it may not be an exaggeration to say that the political climate or ideology contained in the policy prescriptions or announcements of the ruling government sets the tone of the economic and business environment. For example, various liberalisation measures of the present government—industrial, investment and trade policies—provide the ideal environment for growth of business. On the other hand, the disintegration of the former Soviet Union may pose the opposite problem in the immediate future, although, in the long run, transformation from 'command' economy to 'market' economies is likely to promote industry and trade. But, that is, only after the new states have sorted out the problems of regeneration and attained political stability.

Next in importance may be the sociological factors which give form and content to the system of values and culture. Sociological factors which essentially reflect customs, traditions, and conventions, would include matters such as social attitudes towards business and managers, ethics in business and management, attitude towards wealth including concentration, and income, view towards authority and responsibility, resistance or otherwise to change, occupational and labour mobility, inter-organisational or individual cooperation or conflict, etc. All these have important bearing on business environment and decisions.

Educational and cultural factors reinforce the social values because they are very closely interrelated. Legal environment or factors mainly pertain to labour laws, minimum wage legislations, etc. Physical and geographical environment is important because of ecological factors in general and conservation of forest resources, pollution problems and such others in particular. Finally, the historical factors provide the historical perspective or setting for economy and business. For example, the business environment in a number of newly independent nation/states has been largely determined by the colonial status which those countries enjoyed earlier. The French Revolution had much to do with the emergence of capitalist spirit of business and investment. The Soviet Revolution provided a perspective for setting up of a state-owned or state-controlled business system.

Because of the existence of a large number of environmental factors which impart enough complexity to business environment, environmental scanning becomes an important step towards corporate planning and business policy decisions. *Scanning of environment* essentially involves

3. Some authors have illustrated the interaction process through interaction matrics. See, for example, M. Adhikary, *Economic Environment of Business*, 1990, Chapter 1.
4. That is why we sometimes talk of politico-economic environment or socio-economic environment rather than just economic environment.

analysis of the strengths and weaknesses of an organisation vis-à-vis the environment. Scanning or analysis is done for both internal and external environment. Such analysis is done to ascertain the strengths (S), weaknesses (W), opportunities (O) and threats (T) or what is more popularly known as SWOT.[5] Strengths and weaknesses are analysed or assessed in terms of internal environment whereas opportunities and threats are provided by the external environment. SWOT analysis should generally precede the formulation of business or corporate plan and strategies.

ECONOMIC ENVIRONMENT

Economic environment is an amalgam; it comprises all sectors or areas of economic activity—the government sector, the household sector, the business sector[6] (including manufacturing and services), capital or financial sector, the foreign sector, etc. All these sectors together influence the structure and trends of the economy and determine the economic environment.

The government sector may be the most important because all the major policy decisions which determine the course of the economy, and, all regulations, controls in the form of government intervention emanate from this sector. Planning itself is a form of government intervention. The basic objectives of the economic policies of any government generally are: growth, efficiency, and equity. Specific policies of a particular government would determine the relative priorities between growth and equity and the pace or rate of growth itself. For example, the new economic and industrial policies of the present government are clear indicators of liberalised and fast growth of the economy, industry and trade.

The rate of growth of the economy (GDP or GNP) itself is an important determinant of the economic environment. The overall economic growth would also include or reflect the pattern of growth in individual sectors, namely the agricultural sector, the industrial sector, and the services sector—the three major constituents of economic growth. Related to the growth of these sectors are the respective policies, namely the agricultural policy, industrial policy, trade policy, fiscal policy, etc.

The pricing mechanism or system is also an important economic factor. In most of the economies, both free market mechanism and centralised planning exist in different degrees. By 'free market mechanism' or 'price mechanism', we mean the free play of the forces of demand and supply; market mechanism determines commodity prices, factor prices and income distribution. In the present-day world, planning is combined with free market pricing in arriving at many macroeconomic decisions. Thus, the economy in which a business operates is not exclusively a free enterprise economy using prices and markets, but to some extent, directed by a system of planning, control, regulation and coordination.

The financial sector is at the centre of economic activity. The financial sector represents the capital market on the one hand, and banks and financial institutions on the other as also the various financial instruments used by the government mostly through the central bank of the country. The financial policy of the government, including the monetary policy, would determine the investment climate, flow of funds for investment, etc., which would ultimately determine the pace of industrial and economic growth.

Because most of the modern economies are 'open' and not 'closed', international trade, international competition, tariff structure, etc., also significantly affect growth of business and industry essentially through export and import trade. Connected with this are international

5. Instead of SWOT, some would like to call it SCOT, substituting constraint (C) for weakness (W).
6. We are presently discussing interaction of the business sector (at micro level) with other sectors which really constitute the environment for the purpose of the present analysis.

trade and tariff organisations like the United Nations Conference on Trade and Development (UNCTAD), the General Agreement on Tariffs and Trade (GATT) (include the Uruguay Round Negotiations), the roles of non-resident Indians (NRIs), multinational corporations, direct foreign investment, transfer of technology, etc.

ECONOMIC ENVIRONMENT AND BUSINESS DECISIONS

As we have seen above, when we talk of economic environment, the immediate reference is to the macro-context within which the individual enterprise or the micro level unit operates. So whenever we talk of economic environment for business decisions, we essentially talk of macro-micro interaction.

Economic or macroeconomic environment implies certain 'givens' either as indicators, or policies, or controls—factors which are exogenous to the business firm. The major elements or constituents of this environment may be broadly classified as: (i) macroeconomic indicators; (ii) policy measures; (iii) regulatory or physical controls. Macroeconomic indicators are the macro-variables like national income (the net national product or NNP) or the related aggregates of NDP, GDP or GNP. Other important macroeconomic indicators are the general price level, the rate or process of investment or capital formation, indices of agricultural output or industrial production.

Let us start with the 'most macro' of the macroeconomic indicators, namely gross domestic product (GDP) or gross national product (GNP). GDP is the most commonly used (and also the most pervasive) index of economic growth of a country or nation and incorporates the effects of all the productive sectors, or rather, summarises the results of operation of the entire economic system. An increase or decrease in GDP or GNP of a country is also used as a synonym for growth or decline in industrial or business activity with its repercussions on individual business units.

Let us illustrate this point. The year 1988-89 was a year of economic boom in India caused primarily by the tremendous success of the agricultural sector. There was an all-time increase in GDP—a growth of 10.5 per cent. Industrial production also increased significantly. Because of the existence of input-output relationships or linkages, production of most of the industries also increased with direct effects on the demand for industrial inputs or raw materials. This can, however, happen many times with some lag due to production lag and also, because, many consuming industries may be carrying past inventories so that demand for inputs may pick up only after some time.

This has no immediate implication for business decisions for corporate units. Import planning should be closely linked with fluctuations in demand in the domestic market during periods of prosperity or recession as indicated by macroeconomic indicators like GDP or GNP. Careless planning may lead to unwarranted build of inventories or out-of-stock situation.

The GDP or GNP is a quantitative indicator. The overall economic environment would also be governed by macroeconomic policy parameters like monetary and fiscal policies, export and import policies. At any point of time, the corporate tax structure, the monetary controls like the bank rate, various lending rates of banks and financial institutions offer certain economic or business climate which influences or regulates investment decisions at corporate levels.

The policy parameters have wider ramifications and would also include wages, incomes and prices policy. The objectives of a policy on wages, incomes and prices is to supplement rather than substitute fiscal and monetary policies. The scope of such policy is obviously very wide. It encompasses direct controls over product prices, property incomes, dividends, wages and salaries.

When other policies fail to maintain certain balance in the economy, direct controls on wages, incomes or prices may become necessary. Many manufacturing enterprises and purely trading organisations have been subject to price controls in recent times. An extension of the regulatory controls is to be found in economic or business legislations, the best example of which is the MRTP Act (Monopolies and Restrictive Trade Practices Act).

Given these controls, the corporate management has to match these through appropriate strategies for cost control or effectiveness, inventory planning, marketing efficiency, etc. In doing so, the management of the corporate units has to look beyond the national frontiers; and, in some cases, international economic environment may become as much, or even more important than national economic environment.

We have made certain general observations above on the characterisation of economic environment and the possible impacts major economic parameters may have on the functioning of the corporate units. These generalisations should now be qualified because the three major elements or parameters of the environment will have impacts of different nature and intensities. Also, the impacts or interactions will not be uniform for all kinds of industries. For example, a very short-term increase or decline in the index of industrial production may not have the same kind of impact on basic industries or capital goods industries as on intermediate products.

The intensity of impacts of many policy measures, including regulatory controls would be more immediate on many consumer goods industries or finished products than on either capital goods, basic industries or intermediate products.

THE INTERACTION MATRICES

The closeness or precise nature of interaction between the various elements of environment and industries may be best approximated through an interaction matrix. A possible conceptual interaction matrix[7] is shown as follows:

Interaction Matrix 1: Elements of Macroeconomic Environment

	Indicators	*Policy Measures*	*Regulatory Controls*
Basic goods	1	2	2
Intermediate products	2	2	2
Capital goods	2	2	2
Consumer goods	3	2	1

Note: The elements in the matrix signify the closeness or intensity of interaction. '1' indicates the closest or most immediate interaction, '2' next immediate and '3' less immediate and so on.

A different kind of impact the elements of environment will have on corporate units would depend on the nature of business decisions involved. Certain decisions, which are predetermined pertaining to day-to-day business operations (sort of 'programmed decisions'), may be more immediately affected by the elements of environment, but there are non-programmed decisions relating to longer term changes in production targets, capacity utilisation rates, diversification programmes, changes in marketing strategies or networks which may be planned subject to the

7. The interaction matrix is more suggestive than exhaustive. Strictly speaking, the elements indicate certain *orders* rather than *magnitudes*.

'givens' of the environment and are likely to be less disrupted when the implementations take place. The interaction matrix, in this case, may be as below (Matrix 2):[8]

Interaction Matrix 2: Elements of Macroeconomic Environment

	Indicators	*Policy Measures*	*Regulatory Controls*
Programmed	2/3	2	1
Non-programmed	ND	ND	ND

'*ND*': Interaction is positive but cannot be defined.

A third kind of interaction will have space connotations. Certain policy measures or regulatory controls may be purely local or regional, others may be national while there may be still others which may be international in character.

Interaction matrices for indicators or policies or controls which may be either local/regional, national or international are formulated below (Matrix 3).[9]

Interaction Matrix 3: Elements of Macroeconomic Environment

Local/Regional[10]

	Indicators	*Policy Measures*	*Regulatory Controls*
Local/Regional	1	1	1
National	2	2	2
International	3	3	3

National

	Indicators	*Policy Measures*	*Regulatory Controls*
Local/Regional	3	2	1/2
National	2	1/2	1
International	2/3	2	2

International

	Indicators	*Policy Measures*	*Regulatory Controls*
Local/Regional	0	0	0/ND
National	2/3	2/3	2
International	1/2	1/2	1

'0' indicates 'no interaction'.

But, what is the process of interaction? Is the change in corporate behaviour instantaneous to changes in the elements of environment? Is there a critical path? What is the critical path? What are the critical activities?

8. Like Interaction Matrix I, this matrix is also only indicative. See Footnote 7.
9. *Ibid.*
10. Classification of industries as local/regional, national or international is generally made on the basis of their market spread, 'Local/regional' industries cater purely to local/regional market like some of the textiles and food products industries do. 'National industries', although those may be geographically located in a region, cater to a national market like most of the basic industries. 'International industries' are the ones which, in addition to domestic sales, also have an export market or are exclusively export-oriented, including those in export processing or free trade zones.

As a general rule, it may be said that regulatory controls, including ordinance and promulgations, will provoke more instant reactions or changes in corporate decisions in marketing and production controls. A change in the policy measure may induce a lagged response, the corporate units having to adjust to the policy changes during a certain time period. The indicators, obviously, provide the remote controls with certain signals about the state of things to come which the corporate units may like to take note of in immediate or short-term future planning of business activities. Given the general rule, specific repercussions will depend on particular industries.

The recent steel decontrol order and abolition of administered prices for steel would have immediate impacts on production planning and marketing of indigenous steel manufacturers, both in the public and private sector. But the impact may not be as immediate as in the case of finished products or consumer goods. Therefore, the interaction element has been shown as '2' in Matrix 1 (interaction between basic goods or industries and regulatory controls; if it was a directly marketable product or consumer goods the interaction element would have been '1').

Talking of policy measures, a series of liberalisation measures were announced by the government in July 1991 in the New Industrial Policy. In one of the measures, areas reserved for the public sector have been narrowed down from 17 to 8 (these eight areas are still reserved for strategic and security reasons) to encourage greater participation by the private sector in core and basic industries. This policy announcement will, no doubt, prompt the private sector to enter at least some of the areas now permitted, but, this may happen with certain lag because of planning, resource generation and project implementations involved.

We finally turn to economic indicators. Stagflationary situation has been in existence in the Indian economy for more than a year now. This is sort of negation of the interaction matrix (Interaction Matrix 1) because with sustained increase in the price level as an economic indicator, there should be concomitant (may be lagged) increases in aggregate output and employment which generally characterise an economic boom. But, what we have experienced during the year is some kind of economic recession (the industrial recession has been more pronounced). This only shows that there are exceptions to the general interaction process.

We have so far attempted to analyse the various facets of organisation—environment interaction focussing mostly on the way the 'macro' environment influences 'micro' decisions. But there is other side of the interaction process, that is, the micro level decisions affecting the macro particularly, the indicators, like GDP or GNP, which may, in tum, affect the policy measures and controls, because in final analysis, the 'macro' is built on the 'micros'.

Because of management by certain objectives by some corporate units or corporate priorities of some other units or even management by exceptions, individual firms or industries may undertake production activities or diversification programmes which may even be apparently contrary to prevailing economic environment. Such production decisions or diversification programmes may also be engineered by conscious decisions by some multinationals who may be more guided by international economic environment and the objective of generating 'net factor income abroad'.

And, depending on the progress of the economy (indicated by GDP or some related aggregates) which is the result of the state of corporate activities, the governmental authorities might like to review, relax or tighten certain policies or controls which are the elements of the environment.

The cycle is continuous (reaction time lags being allowed) in the sense that one may start either at micro level ('corporate decision' or corporate performance') or macro level ('state of the economy' or 'macro-environment') and complete the interaction process. This is to say that the cycle operates both ways.

During recessions, this becomes the vicious cycle of stagnation and deceleration; and, during upswings, this becomes the cycle of prosperity and economic growth.

REVIEW QUESTIONS

1. State and explain three basic propositions of business and economics.
2. Discuss the major elements of economic environment and their implications.
3. Explain the nature and process of interaction between economic environment and business decisions.
4. What is an interaction matrix? Illustrate with reference to Interaction Matrix 1 mentioned in the text.

SUGGESTED READINGS

- M. Adhikary, *Economic Environment of Business* (Eighth Edition) 2000, Chapter 1.
- A. Dasgupta and N. Sengupta, *Government and Business in India*, 1981.
- A. Nag, 'Factors Governing Business', *Financial Express*, January 4, 1983.

Chapter 23

International Economics, Trade and Balance of Payments

INTERNATIONAL TRADE

Trade means exchange of goods and services and *international trade* means exchange of goods and services among nations. When trade takes place among nations, a number of issues or problems crop up which do not exist when trading goes on within the nation. These issues or problems relate to balance of trade, balance of payments, terms of trade, foreign exchange, exchange control, etc. *International economics* is a study of all the issues which crop up when trade takes place between two or more countries. We shall discuss here some of the important issues or factors in international economics.

BALANCE OF TRADE

Balance of trade of a country shows its export and import of goods or commodities. The balance of trade may be defined as

Export – Import = Balance of Trade

'Balance of trade' may be either positive or negative (or nil which is normally not likely), that is, there can be either a surplus or a deficit in the balance of trade. If a country exports more goods or commodities than it imports, it is said to have a surplus in its balance of trade. If the country imports more goods than its exports, it has a deficit balance of trade.

Balance of trade may be understood either in the aggregate sense, i.e. as balance of total exports and total imports of a country, or with reference to only a particular country. For example, we can talk of the balance (surplus or deficit) of India's total trade with various countries, or her balance of trade with a particular country, say, Nepal.

BALANCE OF PAYMENTS

Balance of payments is a very important concept in international economics; because, unlike balance of trade which represents only the current trade account, the balance of payments summarises the results of all the transactions of a country with other countries. It includes all current transactions as well as long-term transactions. The balance of payments is like a balance sheet because for every transaction, whether current or long-term, there is a credit entry and a debit entry. That is why it is said that 'the balance of payments always balances'. We shall now explain this statement in terms of the various constituent of balance of payments.

The first constituent is balance of trade which we have just discussed. In addition to exchange of physical goods, a country can exchange (export or import) services with various countries.

Most important of these services is usually shipping services. Other services are professional and technical services, banking and insurance services, tourist services, etc. Receipts or payments of interest and dividends on investment (in shares, bonds, etc.), in foreign countries are also included in these services. Besides exchange of goods and services which always involves payments, there can be 'transfers' between two countries which are received free (the country receiving does not have to make any payment for it either at present or in the future). Transfers include gifts, assistance, indemnities, etc. Services and transfers are often classified as 'invisibles' against physical goods which are 'visibles'.

Balance of trade, balance of services and balance of transfers together constitute the 'balance of current account' because all these forms of transactions or transfers take place during a reference period of, say, one year which is considered the current period.

In contrast to the current account, there also exists a capital account between two countries. The capital account shows capital transactions or movements either in the short-term or in the long-term. Capital movement includes borrowing or lending, repayment of loan, etc.

'Balance of current account' and 'balance of capital account' together constitute the balance of payments of a country. To understand the concept of balance of payments more clearly, let us consider a hypothetical account of a country's balance of payments.

Account of a Country's Balance of Payments

Credit		*Debit*	
1. Export of goods	550	5. Import of goods	800
2. Export of services	150	6. Import of services	50
3. Transfer receipts	100	7. Transfer payments	80
4. Capital receipts	200	8. Capital payments	70
Total receipts	1,000	*Total payments*	1,000

In terms of various balances, the above account may be rewritten as below:

Balance	*Credit*	*Debit*	*Net Credit* (+) *Debit* (–)
1. Balance of trade	(+) 550	(–) 800 =	(–) 250
2. Balance of services	(+)150	(–) 50 =	(+) 100
3. Balance of transfers	(+) 100	(–) 80 =	(+) 20
4. Balance of current account (1 + 2 + 3)	(+) 800	(–) 930 =	(–) 130
5. Balance of capital account	(+) 200	(–) 70 =	(+) 130
6. Balance of payments (4 + 5)	(+) 1,000	(–) 1,000 =	0

The left or credit side shows all the ways in which a country can acquire foreign currency, that is, the ways in which it can acquire purchasing power which can be used in foreign markets. The right or debit side shows how foreign currency is spent and how the purchasing power over foreign goods is used.

It is possible that the sum of exports of goods, services and gifts (total credits in current account) need not be equal to the sum of imports of goods, services, indemnities, etc. (total debits in current account) and therefore, there is no reason why the balance of current account should be completely in balance or in equilibrium. The normal thing to assume is that it is not balanced, and in our example, we see that the country in question has a deficit of 130.

This deficit must be settled because if a country has a deficit on the balance of current account, the country has spent more abroad during the period than it has earned. A way to settle this is by a transaction on the capital account. The country can adjust its capital stocks by an amount equal to the deficit in the balance of current account. This can be done either by borrowing abroad or by depleting its reserves of foreign currency.

In our example, capital exports of the country in question are 70 and total capital imports are 200. The net inflow of capital is 130; this is exactly equal to the deficit in the balance of current account and required to equalise the two sides in the balance of payments. This way, either a surplus or a deficit in the balance of current account is matched or offset by a corresponding movement in the capital account so that, in a book-keeping sense, the balance of payments always balances or is always in equilibrium.

But if we deviate from the purely book-keeping sense, and think in the wider economic sense, we see that it may be appropriate to talk of either a 'surplus' or 'deficit' in the balance of payments, or an 'equilibrium' or 'disequilibrium' in the balance of payments. This would depend on the *nature* of capital movements.

Two types of capital movements may be distinguished, viz. accommodating and autonomous. *Accommodating capital flows* are those which take place specifically to equalise the balance of payments in the book-keeping sense and would not have otherwise taken place. *Autonomous capital flows*, in contrast, are those which take place regardless of balance of payments considerations. These transactions have an effect on the country's balance of payments but are no way induced, like accommodating flows, by balance of payments considerations.

We can now define equilibrium and disequilibrium in a country's balance of payments. If a country's autonomous receipts (these would include receipts in the current account also which are always autonomous) are either more or less than its autonomous payments, it will have a disequilibrium in the balance of payments (a surplus or a deficit, favourable or unfavourable, depending on whether the difference between autonomous receipts and payments is positive or negative). The difference will then be settled by an accommodating capital outflow/inflow equal to the surplus/deficit, thereby bringing the balance of payments into equilibrium in a book-keeping sense.

TERMS OF TRADE

The rate at which the goods of a country are exchanged against those of another is referred to as the 'terms of trade'. The terms of trade depend on the prices of goods entering into foreign trade. Thus, terms of trade generally explain the relation between import prices and export prices. When the prices of a country's exports are high relatively to the prices of its imports, the terms of trade are said to be favourable. On the other hand, when the prices of a country's imports are high relatively to the prices of its exports, the terms of trade are deemed to be unfavourable to that country. In other words, terms of trade indicate or measure gains from trade.

There are a number of measures of terms of trade. Measurement in terms of export and import price, as mentioned above, is only one of the methods, although most commonly referred to or used.

Different terms of trade concepts or measures developed so far, may be divided into three distinct categories: (i) those that relate to the ratio of exchange between commodities—the net barter, the gross barter and income terms of trade; (ii) those that relate to the interchange between productive resources—the single-factoral and double-factoral terms of trade; and, (iii) those that measure the gains from trade in terms of utility analysis—the real cost and utility terms of trade.

Of the various measures, we shall discuss here three methods which are more commonly used and more easily understandable. These are net barter terms of trade, income terms of trade and single-factoral terms of trade. The other methods are given in the Appendix.

Net barter terms of trade: The net barter or commodity terms of trade refer to the ratio of price index numbers of exports and imports, respectively. If P is price, x is exports, m is imports, o is initial period and t is any given period, the net barter terms of trade, N, may be written as

$$N = \frac{Pxt}{Pmt} : \frac{Pxo}{Pmo} = \frac{Pxt}{Pmo} : \frac{Pmt}{Pmo} = \frac{Px}{Pm}$$

where Px (Pxt/Pxo) and Pm (Pmt/Pmo) are price index numbers of exports and imports, respectively. A rise in N means that a larger volume of imports can be obtained, on the basis of price relations only, in exchange for a given volume of exports. A rise in N, therefore, indicates a favourable trend (gains) in international trade and vice versa. This, as mentioned above, is the most commonly used terms of trade concept or measure.

Net barter terms of trade or commodity terms of trade may be more clearly understood with numerical examples. Commodity terms of trade of a hypothetical country A is shown below (Table 23.1).

Table 23.1: Commodity Terms of Trade of Country A (2012 = 100)

Year	*Index of Import Prices*	*Index of Export Prices*	*Terms of Trade**
2012	102	100	97
2013	100	100	100
2014	99	101	102
2015	103	104	101
2016	107	106	99
2017	107	108	102
2018	109	112	103
2019	109	114	105

*Export price index as per cent of import price index.

Income terms of trade: One major shortcoming of net barter terms of trade or commodity terms of trade is that those may be misleading if the volume of exports has changed significantly. For this reason, the net barter terms of trade are modified by multiplying them with the quantity of exports. The terms of trade, thus expressed, are called income terms of trade. In symbols,

$$I = N \times Qx = Px/Pm \times Qx$$

where Qx is the export volume index. An increase in I means that the country can obtain larger volume of imports from the sale of its exports. The net barter terms of trade may rise thereby showing an improvement; but the rise in export prices may cause a large decline in exports so that the country becomes worse off, rather than better off, in its command over foreign goods. This means that I and N may move in opposite directions, depending on the direction and magnitude of changes in Px and Qx. Let us assume, for example, that import prices Pm remain unchanged, while export prices Px falls, but export quantities Qx increases by a greater percentage than the decrease in Px. This means that while commodity terms of trade, N, have deteriorated, the income terms of trade I have improved.

The income terms of trade are also referred to as a country's capacity to import; for (Px × Qx/Pm) determines Qm. A country can make more imports, if there is (a) a rise in the price of exports, or (b) a fall in the price of imports, or (c) a rise in the volume of exports, other things remaining constant.

Factoral terms of trade: The commodity terms of trade or income terms of trade fail to take account of changes in productivity in export goods sector. Some have, therefore, devised the concept of factoral terms of trade which represent the ratio of the export price index and the import price index adjusted for changes in the productivity of a country's factors of production in the export goods sector. That is, if the commodity terms of trade index is multiplied by the reciprocal of the export commodity technical coefficient index, the resultant index will provide a better guide to the trend of gain from trade than the commodity terms of trade index by itself. In symbols,

$$S = \frac{Pxt/Pxo}{Pmt/Pmo} \times \frac{Fxo}{Fxt} = N \times Zx$$

where Zx (= Fxo/Fxt) which represents reciprocal of the index of cost or technical coefficient of production in the export sector), is the export productivity index. A rise in S indicates a favourable movement in the sense that a greater quantity of imports can be obtained per unit of factor input used in the production of export goods. Under conditions of changing productivity—conditions generally encountered in a developing economy—the commodity terms of trade are an inadequate measure of gains from trade. If export prices fall relative to import prices, but productive efficiency increases, a country will definitely be better off in real terms despite a deterioration in the commodity terms of trade.

We have discussed above some of the major concepts or measures of terms of trade and their specific limitations and advantages. We should also be aware of some of their general limitations as indices or measures of gains from trade. One limitation is that terms of trade measures reflect almost exclusively trade in commodities. Unilateral transactions and invisibles are taken care of only by gross barter terms of trade (discussed in the Appendix) and income terms of trade, and even in these cases, only imperfectly. Another general limitation is that changes in quality of exports and imports are ignored by all measurements of terms of trade.

Further, Px is usually measured at f.o.b. prices (excluding international transport costs) and Pm at c.i.f. prices (including international transport costs). As a result, all measures of imports and exports are subject to an asymmetry with respect to transport costs; and, therefore, terms of trade may reflect, many times, changes in international transport costs rather than real changes in the prices received for exports or paid for imports.

FOREIGN EXCHANGE

Every country has its own currency which is legal tender within its boundaries only. If an Indian wants to buy foreign goods from England, he will have to pay in pounds sterling because Englishmen will not like to be paid in any other currency except in their own. Hence, it is essential for the Indian importer first to buy pounds, and then use pounds for buying his requirements from England. The rupee, therefore, can buy goods in a foreign country not directly, but indirectly, through the help of foreign currency. Foreign currency is called foreign exchange (because the currency has to be obtained in exchange for domestic currency), and the rate at which one currency buys or exchanges for another currency is known as the rate of exchange.

FIXED AND FLEXIBLE EXCHANGE RATES

How is exchange rate determined? One way of determination of the exchange rate is to look upon it as a commodity, and then, equilibrium exchange rate, like equilibrium price, will be determined by supply and demand conditions.

Determination of the equilibrium exchange rate through demand and supply is shown in Fig. 23.1.

Demand curve DD shows how many pounds India demands depending on the exchange rate, and supply curve SS shows how many pounds Britain is willing to supply as the exchange rate varies. The supply and demand curves cut each other at point P. The equilibrium exchange rate is r_1 and at this rate, oq_1 of foreign exchange is demanded and supplied.

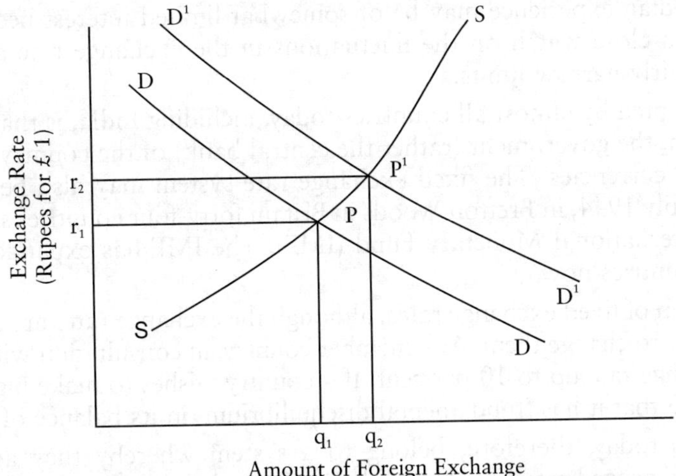

Fig. 23.1: Determination of Equilibrium Rate of Exchange

Let us assume that a shift occurs in the Indian demand curve for foreign exchange from DD to D^1D^1. There may be many reasons for this shift. One could be a change in taste, causing Indian consumers to demand, at any given exchange rate, more imported goods than before. Another reason could be an increase in national income of India, giving rise to an increase in imports. Whatever be the reason for the shift, the result is the establishment of a new equilibrium at P^1 with a new exchange rate r_2 and a new amount of foreign exchange supplied and demanded. This shows that the exchange rate is flexible and varies with varying supply and demand conditions; and it is always possible to find an equilibrium exchange rate which clears the foreign exchange market and creates external equilibrium.

If there is a shift in the demand curve from DD to D^1D^1 as illustrated in Fig. 23.1, this will imply a depreciation of Indian rupee and an appreciation of the British pound. Depreciation of a currency means that the relative value of the currency decreases. When the rupee depreciates, Indians pay more rupees for £ 1. Similarly, appreciation means that the relative value of a currency increases; if the pound appreciates, the British will have to pay less pounds for ₹ 1.

Because of the shift in demand, Indians ask for a larger amount of pounds, oq_2, which the British supply, and the balance of payments is in equilibrium.

If we start from a situation in which a country has equilibrium in its balance of payments, any change from this position will, under a system of flexible exchange rates, first influence the exchange rate. If a deficit in the country's balance of payments occurs, an excess demand for foreign currency is implied. This leads to a fall in the exchange rate so that the country will have to pay more units of its own currency for each unit of foreign currency. There can be many reasons for this deficit including an increase in imports, a fall in export, or a decrease in the inflow of foreign capital. Whatever be the reason, the effect on the exchange rate will be immediate and lead to a depreciation of the currency. The opposite happens, that is, an appreciation of the currency take place, when there is a surplus in the balance of payments.

Many economists are in favour of flexible exchange rates. But, in spite of this practical experiences of this system are quite limited. Canada had a system of flexible exchange rates from 1950 to 1961; opinions on how well the system worked is divided. It should be mentioned here that the Canadian experience may be of somewhat limited interest because the Canadian central bank kept a close watch on the fluctuations in the exchange rate and permitted it to vary only within fairly narrow limits.

The system adopted by almost all countries today, including India, is that of fixed exchange rate.[1] In this system, the government (rather the central bank) of the country fixes the exchange rate for all foreign currencies. The fixed exchange rate system may also be called the Bretton Woods System. In July 1944, in Bretton Woods in Britain forty-four countries signed an agreement establishing the International Monetary Fund (IMF). The IMF has expanded to include more than a hundred countries now.

Under the system of fixed exchange rates, although the exchange rates are in principle fixed or pegged, it is possible to change them. Any member country, in consultation with IMF, can make a change in its exchange rate up to 10 per cent. If a country wishes to make bigger changes, it has to prove to the IMF that it has 'fundamental disequilibrium' in its balance of payments.

Most countries today, therefore, belong to a system whereby they agree to keep their currencies at a fixed, pegged rate and change their value only when the economic situation forces them to do so. Exchange rates of the Indian rupee with major free currencies of the world are shown in Table 23.2.

EXCHANGE CONTROL

Exchange control means deliberate manipulation of the exchange rates in a certain direction by means of various direct and indirect methods. This is done by the government (central bank) of the country to have desired effects on the exchange rates.

1. Strictly speaking, this is only partially true. The major free currencies of the world today (currencies of the non-socialist developed countries) are floating, and not pegged. The exchange parities of these currencies are determined in the foreign exchange market on the basis of the relative strength of the currencies.

Table 23.2: Foreign Exchange Rates of Indian Rupee

Country	*Name of the Currency*	*Rupees Equivalent of One Unit of Currency*
United States	Dollar	45.14*
United Kingdom	Pound	85.65
Canada	Canadian Dollar	38.60
EU	Euro	60.07
Switzerland	Swiss Franc	39.65
Singapore	S'pore Dollar	27.67
Hong Kong	Hong Kong Dollar	5.80
South Africa	S African Rand	7.83
Japan	Yen	0.44
Denmark	Danish Kroner	8.12
Norway	Norwegian Kroner	7.45
Sweden	Swedish Kroner	6.77
UAE	Dirham	12.41
Australia	Australian Dollar	35.61
New Zealand	New Zealand Dollar	32.78

Note: The above exchange rates are those prevailing on November 30, 2004 (T.T. Selling), *The Economic Times*.

* The present rate is about 75.00 (6.10.2020)

Deliberate manipulation of the exchange rates is resorted to primarily for three reasons:

(a) it may be desired to maintain the exchange value of a currency at a level higher than would prevail otherwise, i.e. revaluation (also called over-valuation);

(b) it may be desired to maintain the exchange value of a currency at a level lower than would prevail otherwise, i.e. devaluation (also called undervaluation);

(c) it may be desired to keep the exchange value of the currency constant, i.e. maintenance of a stable exchange rate.

DEVALUATION AND REVALUATION

Devaluation is often used interchangeably with depreciation and revaluation is often taken to be synonymous with appreciation. But it may be appropriate to make some distinction between the two sets of terms. The term 'depreciation' or 'appreciation' is normally used when a currency increases or decreases in value in a free market without the authorities intervening to fix it at a particular new level. 'Devaluation' or 'revaluation', on the other hand, normally refers to the intervention of the authorities in deliberately altering the rate from one fixed parity to another.[2]

The immediate effect of devaluation is a change in relative prices. If a country devalues, for instance, by 20 per cent, it means that import prices increase by 20 per cent in terms of the home currency. An increase in import prices leads to a fall in the demand for imports. At the same time, import-competing or import-substitution industries will be in a better competitive situation. Exporters will receive 20 per cent more in home currency for every unit of foreign currency earned by them. They can, therefore, lower their prices in terms of foreign currency

2. When the floating Canadian dollar declined in value in the 1950s, it was spoken of as depreciation (there was no intervention by the Canadian Government). But the change in sterling parity from $ 2.80 to $ 2.40 in 1967 by the British Government (Bank of England) is described as devaluation.

keeping the prices in terms of home currency constant and become more competitive in the foreign markets. How much they may be able to increase their sales abroad depends primarily on foreign demand elasticities for export goods. These are immediate or short-term effects of devaluation.

The long-term effects of devaluation are, however, likely to be different. Increase in exports induced by lower-prices in foreign currencies is likely to lead to increase in production in the export industries. This will, in turn, lead to increase in demand for labour in these industries. This would tend to push up wages in the export goods industries and eventually, cost of production of export good. The chain of reactions is likely to be similar in the import-competing industries also. Because of increase in costs, exports and import-competing goods would become dearer so that the effects of devaluation on these prices would be gradually offset. And in the long-run, depending on the extent of cost increase, exports may become dearer than before devaluation, and imports may become cheaper compared to import-competing goods. So, the long-term effects of devaluation on export and import prices may just be the opposite of those in the short-run. Effects of revaluation, both in the short-run and in the long-run are in general opposite to those of devaluation. The immediate effects of revaluation are to make imports cheaper and exports dearer to foreign buyer. But the long-term effects are likely to work in opposite direction.[3]

Revaluation is commendable when the country has to make large payments abroad either due to increased volume of imports or as repayments of debts. Revaluation makes a country's exports expensive which facilitates the payments of greater amounts in foreign exchange with smaller amounts of domestic currency.

The rough rule of thumb regarding the use of the instrument of either devaluation or revaluation is: in times of war and scarcity, overvalue (revalue) your currency; in times of slump and surpluses, undervalue (devalue) your currency. But special circumstances may change this general axiom.

REVIEW QUESTIONS

1. Define 'Balance of Trade' and 'Balance of Payments' and explain the difference between the two.
2. "The Balance of Payments always Balances". Explain this with example.
3. What is 'Terms of Trade'? Discuss the 'Net Barter Terms of Trade'.
4. What is devaluation of a currency? Analyse the short-term and long-term effects of devaluation on import and export of a country.

SUGGESTED READINGS

- Bo Södersten and G. Reed, *International Economics*, Macmillan, 1994.
- C.P. Kindleberger, *International Economics*, 1973, Chapter 18.
- K.B. Kundu, *International Economics: Pure Theory*, 1979, Chapter 20.

3. Some argue that the effects of devaluation or revaluation on import and export prices will not be exactly proportional so that the terms of trade will be affected. It is said that, in case of devaluation, there will be deterioration in the terms of trade. This is likely to happen because if devaluation is to have a positive effect, a prerequisite is that export prices, quoted in foreign currency, are lowered, but import prices again quoted in foreign currency, are normally not affected to the same degree as export prices because imports generally are more diversified. This is the main reason for deterioration in terms of trade. By the same logic, revaluation is likely to lead to an improvement in the terms of trade.

APPENDIX

CONCEPTS AND MEASUREMENTS OF TERMS OF TRADE

1. Measurements which Relate to the Ratio of Exchange between Commodities

Net barter terms of trade: Discussed in the text.

Gross barter terms of trade: One shortcoming of net barter terms of trade is that those do not indicate anything about balance of payments; they do not specify whether less exports are being exchanged for the same amount of imports compared with the base period. That is, the net barter terms of trade should be corrected for unilateral transactions or exports made without compensation or imports received without counter-payment. Gross barter terms of trade does this. It measures the rate of exchange between the whole of a country's physical imports compared with the whole of its exports. In symbols,

$$G = \frac{Qm1}{Qm0} : \frac{Qx1}{Qx0} = \frac{Qm}{Qx}$$

where Qm (= Qm1/Qm0) and Qx (= Qx1/Qx0) are volume index numbers for import and exports respectively. A rise in G means a favourable change in the sense that more imports are obtained for a given volume of exports than in the base period.

The meaning of the net and gross barter terms of trade is unambiguous only when the balance of payments remains balanced. That is G = N when the value of imports is equal to the value of exports. Thus,

$$\frac{G}{N} = \left(\frac{Qm}{Qx}\right) \times \left(\frac{Pm}{Px}\right) = \frac{Qm \times Pm}{Qx \times Px} = \frac{Vm}{Vx}$$

where Vm and Vx are index numbers of values of imports and exports, respectively. If Vm = Vx, then G = N. It follows that G will diverge from N if the balance of payments includes unilateral payments.

2. Measurements which Relate to Exchange between Productive Resources

Single-factoral terms of trade: Discussed in the text.

Double-factoral terms of trade: Double-factoral terms of trade take account of changes in productivity in domestic as well as foreign export sectors. If the commodity terms of trade, N, are corrected for changes in productivity in production of import goods as well as export goods, the result is double-factoral terms of trade. Symbolically,

$$D = \frac{Px1/Px0}{Pm1/Pm0} \times \frac{Fm1/Fm0}{Fx1/Fx0} = N \times \frac{1/Zm}{1/Zx} = N \times \frac{Z}{Z}$$

where Zx and Zm are export productivity index and import productivity index, respectively. A rise in D means that one unit of a country's factors embodied in exports now commands more units of the foreign factors embodied in imports. Thus, double-factoral terms of trade show the change in the rate of exchange between a unit of domestic productive factors in exports and a unit of foreign productive factors in imports. Suppose that the exports prices fall. Then the net barter measurement would indicate a deterioration in the terms of trade. However, if productivity in export manufactures has risen more, the country is better off in real terms, and this will be reflected in an increase in the single-factoral terms of trade (S). But if productivity in imports also has risen, the double-factoral terms of trade will show a decline.

The double-factoral terms of trade, D, will be the same as commodity terms of trade, N, if constant returns to scale (constant cost conditions) prevail. But if costs vary with respect to output or time (including transport costs), the trends of the two indices will be substantially divergent. Double-factoral terms of trade will then serve as an index of international division of gain, rather than as an index of the absolute amount of gain for either country.

Again, D will diverge from S if there is a change in the factor cost of producing imports. If the commodity terms of trade and the index of export costs of a given country A remain unchanged, its single factoral terms of trade will remain the same; but its double factoral terms of trade will rise or fall according as the cost, in the other country B, of producing its exports rises or falls.

3. Measurements which Relate to Exchange of Utility

Real cost terms of trade: In terms of utility, total amount of gain from trade is measured by the excess of total utility derived from imports over total disutility involved in the surrender of exports. The amount of disutility involved in the production of exports can be obtained if the single-factoral terms of trade index, S, is multiplied by the reciprocal of an index of the amount of disutility per unit of productive resources used in producing exports. The resultant index is the real cost terms of trade index, R. In terms of symbols,

$$R = \frac{Px1/Px0}{Pm1/Pm0} \times \frac{Fx0}{Fx1} \times \frac{Rx0}{Rx1} = S \times \frac{Rx0}{Rx1}$$

where Rx0/Rx1 is the index of amount of disutility per unit of technical coefficients in exports. A rise in R indicates that the amount of imports received per unit of real cost is greater.

Utility terms of trade: The real cost terms of trade index shows the amount of foreign goods obtained per unit of real cost involved in the production of export goods. This, however, gives us only a partial idea of the amount of gains from trade. To estimate the gains from trade fully, it is also necessary to allow for changes in the relative desirability of the imports and the domestic commodities whose horny consumption is given up because of the diversion of resources to production for exports.

To take account of such changes, we must incorporate in the real cost terms of trade index, R, an index of the relative average utility per unit of imports and of foregone domestic commodities. Let us write u for average desirability of utility and a to denote the commodities whose production for domestic consumption is foregone because of the use of resources in export production. Then,

$$U = Um1/Ua1 : Um0/Ua0$$

represents the index of relative desirability of imports and foregone commodities, respectively. The resultant terms of trade index in which the index of relative desirability of imports and foregone commodities has been introduced is the utility terms of trade index. In symbols,

$$U = \frac{Px1/Px0}{Pm1/Pm0} \times \frac{Fx0}{Fx1} \times \frac{Rx0}{Rx1} \times \frac{Um1/Ua1}{Um0/Ua0} = R \times u$$

where u designates the index of relative utility of imports and foregone commodities.

Chapter 24

Economic Growth and Planning

Economists have been concerned with economic growth ever since the days of classical economics. It is, however, during the last two or three decades that the phenomenon of economic growth has been receiving increasing attention of economists. A large amount of literature has been published on the subject which contain thinking or theories of various economists belonging to different schools of thought. The major issues dealt with by some or all of these economists pertain to the definition and measurement of economic growth, stages of growth, distinction between developed and underdeveloped economies, growth models, planning for growth, etc. We shall discuss here various issues related to the nature and problems of economic growth.

This is done in two parts:

A. Economic Growth: Meaning, theories, models

B. Economic Planning

A. ECONOMIC GROWTH: MEANING, THEORIES, MODELS

WHAT IS ECONOMIC GROWTH?

Economists differ on their views about the proper definition of economic growth. In the simplest approach, and which is also the most acceptable, economic growth is defined as the increase in the real net national product or real national income (NNP at constant prices) or related aggregates like GDP or GNP. In this approach, we talk in terms of the rate of growth. If the rate of growth of NNP, GNP or GDP is high, we say that the rate of economic growth is high. Sometimes; there is a *cyclical increase* in income as happens during the upswing in business cycles. This is not to be interpreted as economic growth. Growth occurs only when there is an *increasing trend* in income, that is, increase in income is sustained. This implies that economic growth is to be understood in a long-term perspective as against purely short-term fluctuations in income.[1]

1. Some economists make a distinction between 'economic growth' and 'economic development'. In such distinction, economic growth means increase in aggregate output or national income; but economic development means not only an increase in output but also changes in the production structure and technology levels.

   It may help understanding of this distinction if we make an analogy with a human being. In the case of human beings, 'growth' refers to an increase in height (or weight), while 'development' refers to changes in a variety of factors that lead to an improvement in the overall functional capacity.

   So we can say that economic growth refers to quantitative changes in the economy while economic development refers, in addition to this, also to qualitative changes such as technical progress and structural changes in the economy.

Some economists feel that increase in national income alone cannot be a sufficient indicator of growth. It should be viewed in relation to population growth. This means more directly that economic growth should be equated not with increase in absolute income, but with increase in per capita income, that is, national income divided by total population of the country. If total income grows faster than population, then the two measures will yield similar results. If, however, the population grows at a faster rate or at the same rate as national income, the per capita income will either decrease or will remain constant. In the per capita approach, there will be no growth in these two situations, although according to the absolute income approach, there will be economic growth in both these situations.

Economic growth is sometimes equated with industrialisation. According to this approach, if the rate of industrialisation increases, economic growth takes place. There are some problems of measurement of the rate of industrialisation. One measure of increase in the rate of industrialisation, which may more suitably represent economic growth, is increase in the ratio of the working force in the non-agricultural sector to the total working force in the country. One can think of some other indicators of industrialisation.[2]

We can also think of a number of other indicators which may be associated with economic growth. One can think of indicators like per capita output of manufactured articles, amount of capital employed per worker, labour productivity, per capita food production or consumption, etc.

In conclusion, it should be mentioned that real national income is regarded as the most comprehensive indicator of economic growth. From the point of view of measurement also, since national income accounts are prepared by almost every country, estimating the rate of growth is generally not a problem.

DEVELOPED AND UNDERDEVELOPED ECONOMIES[3]

Once economic growth or development is defined it is possible to distinguish between countries at different levels of development. On the basis of the level of development countries may be broadly classified as developed and underdeveloped.

'Development' and 'underdevelopment' are relative concepts. 'Underdevelopment' implies a low level of per capita income in relation to that of developed or high-income countries. But underdevelopment also implies that there is potential for future growth. We can, therefore, define an underdeveloped country as one in which current per capita real income is low in relation to such countries as the USA, Canada and many European countries, but at the same time, one which has enough potential for significant increase in its per capita income in future.

On the basis of per capita incomes, we can classify countries into developed and economically underdeveloped. The basis for such distinction between developed and underdeveloped countries is, however, generally arbitrary. For instance, we can classify different countries of the world into

2. The most straight forward indicator of industrialisation may be the index of industrial production. But, between two periods, industrial production may increase because of higher capacity utilisation in the existing industries. This may not be generally regarded as an increase in the rate of industrialisation. Industrialisation normally indicates new and more industries.
3. In recent times, it is more customary to talk in terms of a 'less developed' or 'developing' economy than in terms of an 'underdeveloped' economy. Another similar expression used is 'undeveloped' country. All these four terms, namely 'underdeveloped', 'undeveloped', 'less developed' and 'developing' are used almost interchangeably with more or less the same meaning.

two major categories, the highly developed and the underdeveloped, and also, an intermediate group by using the following criteria:[4]

(a) Countries with per capita income of $ 765 or less are to be classified as underdeveloped countries.

(b) Countries with per capita income of $ 9,386 or more are to be classified as highly developed countries.

(c) Countries which fall within per capita income of $ 765 and $ 9,386 are to be classified as intermediate countries.

Table 24.1 shows classification of selected countries into highly developed (high income), intermediate (middle income) and underdeveloped (low income) countries. To facilitate comparison, per capita incomes of various countries have been expressed in US $ although normally per capita income of a particular country will be expressed in its national currency.

Table 24.1: Per Capita Income of Selected Countries Grouped According to the Level of Economic Development, 2000

Country	*GNP Per Capita (US$)*	*Country*	*GNP Per Capita (US$)*
High Income			
Economies			
Switzerland	40,630	Chile	4,160
Japan	39, 640	Malaysia	3,890
Denmark	29,890	Turkey	2,780
USA	26,980	Brazil	3,640
Sweden	23,750	Venezuela	3,020
France	24,990	Thailand	2,740
Netherlands	24,000	Algeria	1,600
Canada	19,380	Peru	2,310
UK	18,700	Philippines	1,050
Hong Kong	22, 990	Indonesia	980
Australia	18,720		
Spain	13,580	*Low Income*	
New Zealand	14,340	*Economies*	
Portugal	9,740	China	620
		Sri Lanka	700
Middle Income		Pakistan	460
Economies		Ghana	390
Greece	8,210	Nigeria	260
Argentina	8,030	India	340
Mexico	3,320	Kenya	280
		Nepal	200

Source: World Development Report 2002 (World Bank).

About one-fifth of the world's total population live in the highly developed countries (high income economies) whereas the majority, i.e. about two-thirds live in the underdeveloped countries

4. Intermediate countries indicate those countries which are less developed than the highly developed countries but have already developed to a considerable extent in relation to the underdeveloped countries. The criteria are given by World Bank for the year 1995 (Table 24.1).

(low income economies). The underdeveloped countries of Asia, Africa and Latin America, with about two-thirds of world population, account for only about one-eighth of world's income. Against this, the highly developed countries with only about one-fifth of total population, share about three-fifths of world income. Thus, wide differences in per capita income levels of the developed and the underdeveloped countries give rise to a highly uneven distribution of world income reflecting a high degree of economic inequality among nations.

VICIOUS CIRCLE OF POVERTY

Besides low per capita income, underdeveloped countries also have several other characteristics by which they can be more easily recognised. These characteristics can be demographic, social, economic and technological.[5] Generally, there is a high degree of correlation between low per capita income or poverty and these characteristics, and many of these characteristics are themselves interrelated.

Also, many of these characteristics are self-perpetuating or interacting with each other so that it is difficult to distinguish between the causes and the effects. Most of them can be regarded as both the causes as well as the consequences of poverty or economic underdevelopment. They typically represent circular relationships generally known as the 'vicious circle of poverty'. Figure 24.1 shows the vicious circles of economic underdevelopment. The upper half and the lower half of the figure represent the vicious circles emanating from the demand side and the supply side respectively.

Let us start with low per capita income shown in the vicious circle of the supply mechanism (lower half of the diagram). An underdeveloped economy is characterised by a low level of per capita income. The low level per capita income leads to a low rate of savings. Low rate of savings implies a low rate of capital formation. This means low growth of real capital stock and, hence, low availability of capital per worker. Low level of capital per worker leads to low output per worker. This, in turn, leads to a low level of per capita income. This completes the vicious circle from the supply side.

The vicious circle from the demand side (upper half) starts with lack of industrialisation. Lack of industrialisation in an underdeveloped country implies lack of employment opportunities in the industrial sector. This leads to high concentration of workers or population in agriculture. Overpopulation in agriculture means that more men are working on the same land. This leads to low productivity in agriculture. Low productivity in agriculture implies low agricultural output. Because, a large part of agricultural output is consumed in the agricultural sector itself for sustenance of the agricultural population, very little surplus or income is generated in this sector to create demand for industrial products. Lack of demand for industrial products leads to a low level or lack of industrialisation and the vicious circle perpetuates itself.

So, the vicious circle of poverty perpetuates. One can start with the demand circle which will lead to the supply circle or vice versa. But the process of perpetuation continues.

---

5. Some of the demographic characteristics are high birth rate, high death rate and low expectation of life at birth. Some social characteristics are high degree of illiteracy among the people, low degree of urbanisation and inequality of income and wealth. Major economic characteristics are low rate of capital formation, low productivity, low per capita consumption resulting in a subsistence level of living. The most important technological characteristic is technological backwardness reflected in traditional methods of production.

THE BIG PUSH

To move out of the vicious circle of poverty, the underdeveloped countries need a big push. This is what the theory of 'big push' states.[6] According to this theory, a big push in the form of a high initial investment is required to overcome the vicious obstacles to development in an underdeveloped economy.

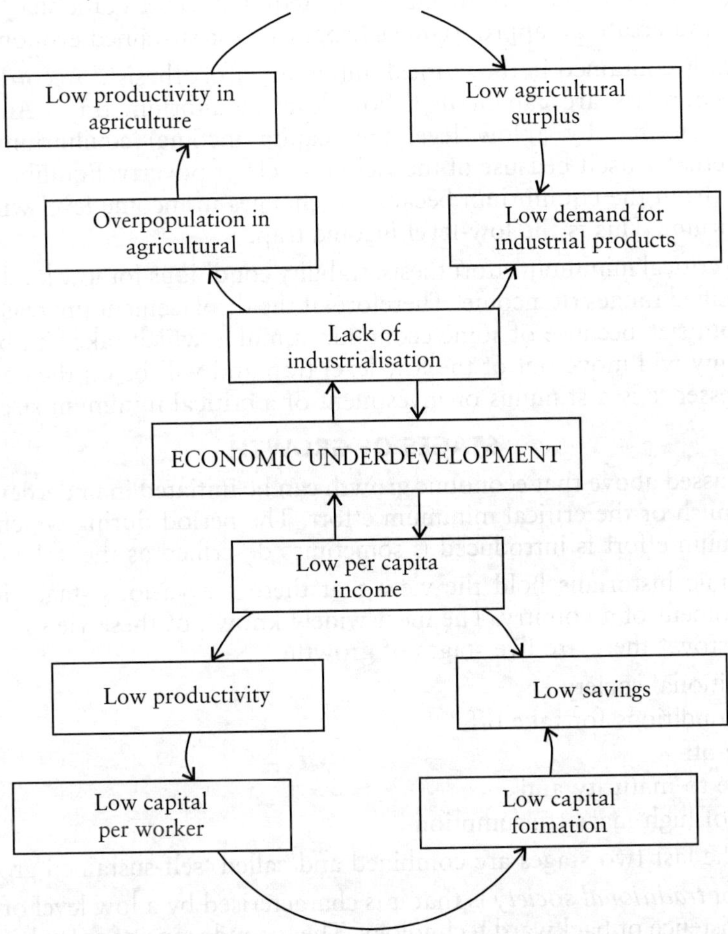

Fig. 24.1: Vicious Circle of Economic Underdevelopment

This theory is based on the hypothesis that large-scale investment gives rise to various external economies, and such economies are a prerequisite for launching economic development. The external economies arise in the form of 'social overhead capital'. 'Social overhead capital' means or comprises basic industries like power, transport, communications, etc. These industries provide the basic infrastructure for production. And, social overhead capital formation must precede other direct investments in industrial activities for the latter to be productive. So, the indivisibility of social overhead capital gives rise to external economies on the supply side.

External economies also occur on the demand side because of the indivisibility of demand, which arises from the basic complementarity of demand for industrial inputs that requires the

6. The main exponent of the theory of big push is P.N. Rosenstein Rodan.

simultaneous setting up of interdependent industries. The risk of not finding a market considerably reduces the inducement to invest especially in an underdeveloped country with small markets. Large-scale investment flowing simultaneously into several interdependent and complementary industries reduces this risk and thereby promotes new investment.

Because of the existence of these indivisibilities and the external economies, it is clear that a big push or a high dose of initial investment may be required to break the shackles of the vicious circle of poverty and create an appropriate environment for sustained economic development.

A similar idea is contained in the 'critical minimum effort thesis'.[7] According to this thesis, underdeveloped countries are caught in a 'low level equilibrium trap'. An underdeveloped economy is characterised by a low level (per capita income) equilibrium. This low-level equilibrium perpetuates itself because of the vicious circle of poverty. Equilibrium is stable, that is, any departure from the equilibrium because of changes in income level will generate forces to restore equilibrium. This is the low-level income trap.

According to critical minimum effort thesis, stability conditions for low level equilibrium hold good only in specified ranges of income. Therefore, if the displacement (increase) in income is of a certain minimum size because of some economic stimulus which takes it above the specified range, the economy will move out of the low-level trap and will be on the course to sustained growth. So, the essence is a stimulus or investment of a critical minimum size.

STAGES OF GROWTH

We have discussed above that economic growth can be initiated in underdeveloped countries through the big push or the critical minimum effort. The period during which the big push or the critical minimum effort is introduced is sometimes described as the 'take-off' stage.

Many economic historians hold the view that there are various stages in the process of economic development of a country. The most widely known of these views is that of Rostow. According to Rostow,[8] there are five stages of growth:

(a) the traditional society
(b) the preconditions for take-off
(c) the take-off
(d) the drive to maturity and
(e) the age of high mass consumption.

Sometimes, the last two stages are combined and called 'self-sustained growth'.

The essence of *traditional society* is that it is characterised by a low level of output per head because of the existence of backward technology. The second stage of growth, during which the *preconditions for take-off* develop, generally involves important economic and non-economic changes. In this stage, some fundamental economic changes take place. More important of these changes are a rise in the rate of capital accumulation above the rate of population growth, the exploitation of existing innovational opportunities as well as the creation of new ones, and the training of the labour force for specialised large-scale production. For example, increased investment and innovational activity takes place in the agricultural sector and creates a surplus that can be utilised to finance industrial expansion. Similarly, substantial investment in transportation facilities and other forms of social overhead capital is undertaken during this period.

---

7. This theory or thesis is due to Harvey Leibenstein. Refer Harvey Leibenstein, *Economic Backwardness and Economic Growth*, 1957.
8. W.W. Rostow, *The Stages of Economic Growth: A Non-communist Manifesto*, 1960.

The third stage, *the take-off*, is the crucial one. It is at this stage that the resistance to steady growth is finally overcome and growth becomes a normal condition of the economy. In the precondition stage, significant economic progress takes place, but traditional attitudes and productive techniques dominate. During the take-off period however growth becomes institutionalised in the society. The take-off is defined more precisely by Rostow as involving certain *specific* changes. First, the rate of net investment rises from 5 per cent or less to over 10 per cent of national income. Second, one or more new and rapidly growing manufacturing industries develop which can play the role of leading sectors. Third, a political, social and institutional framework emerges which is highly favourable to sustained growth. On the basis of the historical experience of such countries as the United States, Great Britain, Japan and the USSR, Rostow concludes that the take-off period lasts approximately twenty years.

Rostow has specified 'tentative, approximate take-off dates' for selected countries. These are shown below (Table 24.2).

Table 24.2: Some Tentative Take-off Periods

Country	*Take-off Period*
Great Britain	1783-1802
France	1830-1860
Belgium	1833-1860
United States	1843-1860
Germany	1850-1873
Sweden	1868-1890
Japan	1878-1900
USSR	1890-1914
Canada	1869-1914

After take-off, *the drive to maturity* starts and continues for a period of about forty years. During this period, modern technology spreads from the leading sectors to all major sectors of the economy. During this stage an economy demonstrates that it has the technological and entrepreneurial skill to produce not everything, but anything it chooses to produce.

After the drive to maturity is complete, the economy moves into *the age of high mass consumption* when the leading sectors shift towards the production of durable consumer goods and services. At this stage incomes have risen to levels where basic food, shelter and clothing are no longer the main consumption objectives of the labour force. Automobiles, TV sets, refrigerators, etc., are now the items that become the interest of the consumers. In addition, the economy, through its political process, expresses a willingness to allocate increased resources to social welfare and security. Rostow cites the United States, most countries of western Europe and Japan as countries which have reached this stage.

The theory of the stages of growth developed by Rostow is an important contribution to the theory of economic development. He rightly emphasises that there are certain distinct stages in the growth process of a country. However, his theory of the five stages of growth may not exactly hold good for many countries. One of the main criticisms against Rostow's theory is that the development patterns of various countries do not testify the exact sequencing of the five stages of growth as explained by him. Moreover, it may be extremely difficult to identify and demarcate the periods during which one stage is complete and the other stage sets in. Also, in many cases, a particular stage may not clearly exist or two or more stages may overlap to a considerable extent.

BALANCED AND UNBALANCED GROWTH

To initiate or achieve economic growth, a country has to decide about an appropriate strategy for development. In growth literature, discussion centres around two alternatives or opposite strategies, namely balanced growth and unbalanced growth. *Balanced growth*, as it indicates, means the simultaneous growth of all the major sectors of the economy. In contrast, *unbalanced growth* implies that, initially, growth should concentrate on the strategic or leading sectors which will be gradually communicated to less important sectors so that growth among the various sectors remains unbalanced. These two hypotheses represent two schools of thought on the strategy for economic development.

The balanced growth approach is based on the argument that in an underdeveloped economy, the inducement to invest is limited by the size of the market. To explain this we may use the well-known example of the shoe factory.[9] We assume that a large shoe factory is started in an underdeveloped region which provides employment to 1,000 workers. The incomes of these workers will contribute significantly to the additional income generated in the region. If the workers spend their entire income only on shoes, the shoe factory will find a ready market, generate more employment and raise income level in the economy. But it is most unlikely because shoe is not an item of daily necessity like food and workers would have many other consumption needs. In practice, the shoe factory may find it very difficult to market all its output. In that case, the shoe factory project will not be viable and the proposed investment will not be made in the economy.

For growth to take place in such a situation, the solution is 'a more or less synchronised investment on a wide range of different industries.' This would result in an overall enlargement of the market. Most industries catering for mass consumption are complementary in the sense that they provide a market for, and thus, support each other. This basic complementarity arises from the diversity of human needs. The case for balanced growth, therefore, finally rests on the need for a 'balanced diet'.[10]

The main argument of the exponents of unbalanced growth is just the opposite. According to this theory,[11] no underdeveloped country is likely to possess enough capital and resources to be able to undertake simultaneous investments in all sectors of the economy. It may, therefore, be a better development strategy to employ the available limited resources on types of investment which can induce more investment and lead to further expansion of output and employment. Growth experience of many of today's advanced countries shows that economic development has generally followed the course of unbalanced growth with growth being communicated from the leading sectors of the economy to the others. It is, therefore, appropriate to undertake large-scale investment in certain strategic industries or sectors of the economy. This, in turn, would lead to further rounds of induced investment and, thereby, keep the economy on the path of development.

This happens on account of the existence of industrial linkages. Any given investment project may have two kinds of linkages, the forward linkage and the backward linkage. Forward linkages are those effects which encourage investment in subsequent stages of production and backward linkages are those effects which encourage investment in earlier stages of production. For example, the iron and steel industry has high forward linkages and engineering industries have high backward linkages.

9. This example is from Rosenstein Rodan.
10. Ragnar Nurkse, one of the leading exponents of the balanced growth theory.
11. A leading exponent of this theory is A.O. Hirchman.

Based on estimates of forward and backward linkages of investments in different projects or industries, one can arrive at the total linkage effect of a particular investment project. The next task is to find out projects or industries with the highest total linkage.[12] Investment should be initially channelled into industries with the highest or very high total linkage. This will, in turn, induce investment in the related or linked industries.

The controversy between balanced growth and unbalanced growth developed during the late 1950s and early 1960s. But, after various criticisms, both the approaches have become highly qualified. Consequently, the controversy is not so relevant now.

In today's development context, the whole issue may be restated as follows: "while a newly developing country should aim at balance as an investment criterion, this objective will be attained only by initially following in most cases a policy of unbalanced investment. In operational terms, the crucial question has become how to determine what is the proper sequence of investment decisions...."[13]

GROWTH MODELS

Balanced growth and unbalanced growth indicate certain patterns of economic development. Various growth models have been constructed to depict different patterns of growth. These models, in addition to depicting certain patterns of growth, also specify the roles played by various economic parameters like the rate of savings, capital formation, incremental capital output ratio, etc., in the process of economic development. Many such models have been developed. One of the earliest models which is very widely known and has been used as the basis for many models formulated later is the Harrod-Domar model.

HARROD-DOMAR MODEL

We shall discuss here Harrod's version of the model.[14] It is based on two important assumptions. First, the savings assumption. This assumption states that total net saving during any time (t) is a constant proportion (s), of income of that period Y(t). Net saving means total saving minus dissaving. Also, saving refers to actual saving and not to planned saving.[15] We may, therefore, state Harrod's first assumption as

$$S(t) = sY(t)$$

where S(t) is total net saving and s, the constant saving ratio.

Harrod's second assumption relates to the acceleration principle (and may be called its variant also). The assumption states that desired investment I(t) during any time t is a constant proportion, v, of the excess of income in that period Y(t) over income of the preceding period

12. Empirical studies of inter-industry flows relating to a number of countries have revealed that the iron and steel industry has a very high, often the highest total linkage.
13. G.M. Meier, *Leading Issues in Economic Development* (Second Edition), 1970, pp. 332-33.
14. Harrod and Domar independently developed two models of growth which are very similar in approach and also based on the same assumption about savings and investment behaviour. But there is an important difference in the *formulation* of the two models. In Harrod's model, increase in income is assumed as discrete whereas in Domar's model, the increase is assumed as continuous so that Harrod's model involves solution of a first-order difference equation whereas Domar's model involves solution of a first order differential equation. Refer R.F. Harrod, *Towards a Dynamic Economics*, 1948, and, E.D. Domar, *Essays in the Theory of Economic Growth*, 1957.
15. Actual savings may differ from planned or intended savings if income of the period turns out to be more or less than was expected.

Y(t – 1), i.e. desired investment will be a constant proportion, v, of the difference Y(t) – Y(t – 1). This may be stated as

$$I(t) = v[Y(t) - Y(t-1)]$$

Since realised investment is always equal to realised or actual saving, we can state that

Realised investment (saving) = S(t) = sY(t).

Desired investment will be equal to realised investment if

$$sY(t) = v[Y(t) - Y(t-1)]$$

Dividing both sides by v, we get

or $$\frac{Y(t) - Y(t-1)}{Y(t)} = \frac{s}{v}$$

or $$G = \frac{s}{v}$$

where G is the rate of growth of income which varies directly with s and inversely with v. Therefore, the higher the rate of savings (s), the higher is the growth rate; the higher the value of the accelerator (v), the lower is the growth rate.

From Harrod's model, we can also find the pattern of growth of total income or movements in total income over time. To find this, let us start with

$$sY(t) = v[Y(t) - Y(t-1)]$$

Changing sides we get

$$vY(t) - sY(t) = vY(t-1)$$

or $$Y(t)\,(v - s) = vY(t-1)$$

Dividing both sides by (v – s), we get

$$Y(t) = \frac{v}{v-s}Y(t-1)$$

or $$Y(t) = KY(t-1) \text{ where } K = \frac{v}{v-s}$$

This is a first order difference equation and the solution to this may be written as

$$Y(t) = Y_0K^{t}*$$

where Y_0 is initial income and K as explained.

The solution shows that the growth path of income would depend on the initial value or, initial income and K, i.e. s and v, or given the initial income, the growth path of income would directly depend on K.

Depending on the values of s and v, K can be positive or negative; both the sign and the magnitude of K will determine the nature of movements in income. We shall show here the nature of income movements for only positive values of K which are more likely to happen in practice. If K is positive, there are three possibilities: K < 1, K = 1 and K > 1. Growth pattern of income, corresponding to these ranges of values of K is shown in Fig. 24.2.

---

* It is easy to derive the general solution from the equation $Y(t) = kY(t-1)$

Putting t = 1, we get $Y(1) = KY(0)$

Similarly, $Y(2) = KY(1) = K \times KY(0) = K^2Y(0)$

$Y(3) = KY(2) = K \times KY(1) = K \times KY(0) = K^3Y(0)$

Therefore, $Y(t) = K^tY(0) = Y_0K^t$

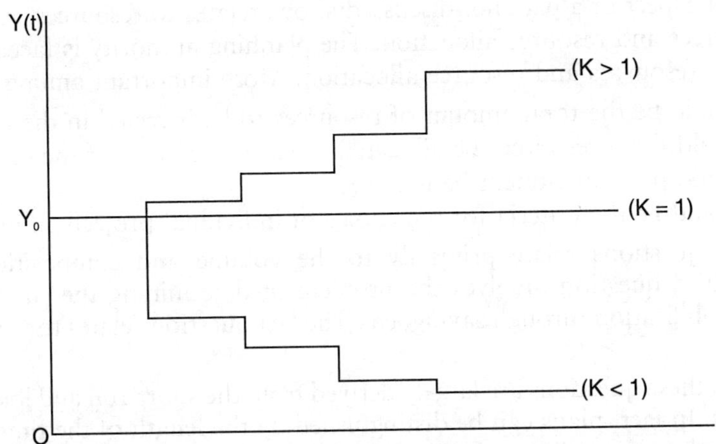

Fig. 24.2: Growth Path of Income in Harrod's Model (for positive values of K)

B. ECONOMIC PLANNING

ECONOMIC PLANNING

To achieve economic growth, planning is necessary. To attain a certain pattern or target of growth, a country has to plan for it. Economic planning plays an important role in the development process of every country.

We all have certain notions of what planning is, but it is difficult to precisely define 'economic planning'. This may be the reason why there is no consensus among economists about the definition of economic planning. We shall give a definition here which is more descriptive than definitive. An 'economic plan' may be regarded as a set of development programmes consistent among themselves, that is, implementation of one does not conflict with pursuance of any other, and the programmes lead to the attainment of certain objectives during a specified period of time in the best possible way or in the most efficient way.

The above definition or description clearly indicates that there are certain essential features of a plan or an economic plan: The first is the specification of objectives or setting up of goals or targets to be achieved. The second is the time target. Goals and objectives have to be achieved during a certain specified period of time; this defines the time horizon of planning. Third, because of a time horizon, the schemes of action should be drawn up sufficiently in advance of the period during which the schemes are to be implemented. The fourth is internal balance or consistency of the plan; the plan should take account of the interdependence and mutual repercussions of various schemes so that there is overall consistency of the development programmes. The fifth is the notion of optimisation or of attaining the objectives in the most efficient way or at the least cost in terms of time or effort or money; and, finally the sixth essential feature is that planning implies a process of coordinated and centralised decision-making; and, therefore, the existence of a central planning authority that takes the planning decisions.

One important aspect of a plan not discussed above relates to resources. All plans raise the problems of resources and resource allocation. The planning authority is faced with a number of issues related to resources and resource allocation. More important among these issues are:

(a) What should be the total amount of resources to be invested in the plan?
(b) How should these resources be allocated to various sectors of the economy?
(c) How should plan investment be financed?
(d) What should be the criteria for the choice of individual projects in different sectors?

The first two questions relate primarily to the volume and composition of aggregate investment. The third question involves the problem of determining the supply of resources, that is, resource mobilisation through saving, etc. The last question relates to various investment criteria.

The answers to these questions are largely derived from the short-run and long-run objectives set by the planners. In fact, plans can be distinguished by the length of the time horizon. There can be short-term plans extending over a period of a year or so. There can also be long-term plans covering periods of 15 to 20 years or even more. The former are generally called annual plans while the latter are known as perspective plans. Between these two, there are intermediate plans ranging from four to seven years. These types of plans, especially the five-year plans, are found to be most popular among developing countries.

ECONOMIC PLANNING IN INDIA

Economic planning in India started with the establishment of the Planning Commission in 1950.[16] Planning has been introduced into the country in the form of five-year plans. Each Five Year Plan is embodied in a plan document. The plan document is prepared and published in two stages. First, the 'Draft' Five Year Plan is published. This is followed by the 'Final Report' which is based on discussions of the Draft plan and resulting modifications, if made. During the period of implementation of the plan, mid-term appraisals are also sometimes made and published.

The First Five Year Plan (1951-52 to 1955-56) in India was, introduced in April 1951. Critics of Indian planning feel that the First Plan was modest in almost every way and did not involve, to any significant extent, serious planning effort. In terms of targets, detailed programmes, etc., a large number of commitments had already been made by the central and state governments and the job of the Planning Commission was essentially to coordinate and rationalise the various programmes of development. It is, therefore, said that the First Five Year Plan did not raise, except at a theoretical level, the manifold problems of planning. It is with the formulation and launching of the Second Five Year Plan (1956-57 to 1960-61) that the problem of planning as such began to be faced. The basic framework for this Plan was provided by the well-known Mahalanobis model. The emphasis of the model was on investment allocation among vital sectors of the economy. But the model considered only two sectors, namely capital goods and consumer goods which was later extended to four sectors. In due course, the limitations of the Mahalanobis type of model were exposed, and the need was felt for more comprehensive multi-sectoral planning models. Such models were constructed during the Third Plan (1961-62 to 1965-66) and continued to be constructed, in greater detail and sophistication, during the

16. Planning efforts in India existed even before the establishment of the Planning Commission. These efforts were made through the setting up of the National Planning Commission in 1938 and also through the 'Bombay Plan', the 'Gandhian Plan' and the 'People's Plan'. But systematic and regular plan making commenced only with the establishment of the Planning Commission.

Fourth Plan (1969-70 to 1973-74), the Fifth Plan (1974-75 to 1978-79), the Sixth Plan (1980-81 to 1984-85), the Seventh Plan (1985-86 to 1989-90) and the Eighth Plan (1992-93 to 1996-97). These models provide the basis for detailed formulation of the Indian plans.

Different plans had different priorities. The priorities depended on the major objectives. In the First Plan, the most important objectives were to rehabilitate the Indian economy devastated by the Second World War and partition of the country, and also to solve the food crisis. In the Second Plan, the principal objectives were a sizeable increase in national income and rapid industrialisation. In the Third Plan, along with increase in national income, there was equal emphasis on both agricultural and industrial development. The Fourth Plan had two basic objectives, viz. growth with stability and progressive achievement of self-reliance. In the Fifth Plan, the two major objectives were removal of poverty and attainment of self-reliance. The most important objective of the Sixth Plan was a significant step up of the rate of growth of the economy. The guiding principles of the Seventh and Eighth Plans continued to be growth with equity and social justice.

An evaluation of the Five Year Plans shows that the planning efforts in India have been only partially successful in achieving the objectives set out in various plans. But it must be admitted that persistent planning efforts since the launching of the First Five Year Plan have generated a tempo of development which is essential for sustained growth. The agricultural economy is fast transforming itself. Sufficient infrastructure for industrial development has been created. Institutional changes also have taken place in the finance and credit system and other areas which are conducive to development.

REVIEW QUESTIONS

1. Define economic growth. Mention different views or approaches to it.
2. What are the five stages of economic growth? Comment on the relative significance of the different stages.
3. What is Harrod-Domar model? Mention the assumptions and explain with equations.
4. Discuss the process of planned development in India with special reference to the five year plans.

SUGGESTED READINGS

- A.P. Thirlwall, *Growth and Development*, Macmillan, Fifth Edition, 1994.
- Y.K. Alagh, *Indian Development Planning and Policy*, Vikas Publishing House, Revised Edition, 1995, Chapter 4.
- Planning Commission (Government of India), *Five Year Plan Documents* (Draft/Final Report).

APPENDIX

FIVE YEAR PLANS IN INDIA

An account is given here of the Five Year Plans of India in terms of objectives, plan projections, outlay and investment, and plan achievements. Plan projections show the targets of growth of national income and also per capita income, savings and investment during the plan period. Outlay and investment indicate the size of the plan. Plan achievements show the actuals against projections or targets. Overall, the account gives an idea of the evolution of Indian planning.

FIRST FIVE YEAR PLAN
(April 1951–March 1956)

OBJECTIVES

1. To rehabilitate the Indian economy devastated by the effects of the Second World War and partition of the country.
2. To solve the food crisis and ease the raw material position especially in jute and cotton.
3. To check inflationary tendencies.
4. To build economic overheads such as network of roads, to renovate depreciated rolling stock in railways and also construct irrigation and hydroelectric works.
5. To formulate and execute programmes of development which would be substantial in themselves while laying the foundation for larger efforts in the corning years.
6. To initiate measures of social justice on a wide scale consistent with the directive principles of the constitution.
7. To build up administrative and other organisational needs for carrying out the programmes of development in India.

Plan Projection (Targets)

(At 1952-53 Prices)

Item	*1950-51*	*1955-56*	*% Increase*
National income (₹ crores)	9,110	10,800	18.0
Per capita income (₹)	252	281	11.0
Domestic savings as % of N.I.	5.0	7.8	–
Investment as % of N.I.	4.9	7.3	–

Outlay and Investment

(₹ Crores)

Sector	*Outlay*	*Investment*
Total	4,178	3,360
Public Sector	2,378	1,560
Private Sector	1,800	1,800

Plan Achievements

(At 1970-71 Prices)

Item	*1950-51*	*1955-56*	*% Increase*
National income (₹ crores)	17,637	21,403	21.4
Per capita income (₹)	466	508	9.0
Net domestic savings* as % of N.I.	7.0	10.0	–
Investment as % of N.I.	9.3	11.3	–

*At current prices.

SECOND FIVE YEAR PLAN
(April 1956–March 1961)

OBJECTIVES

1. A sizeable increase in national income so as to raise the level of living in the country.
2. Rapid industrialisation with emphasis on the development of basic and heavy industries.
3. A large expansion of employment opportunities.
4. Reduction of inequalities in income and wealth and a more even distribution of economic power.

Plan Projection (Targets)

(At 1952-53 Prices)

Item	*1955-56*	*1960-61*	*% Increase*
National income (₹ crores)	10,800	13,480	25.0
Per capita income (₹)	281	331	18.0
Domestic savings* as % of N.I.	8.0	9.7	0
Investment as % of N.I.	7.3	10.7	–

Outlay and Investment

(₹ Crores)

Sector	*Outlay*	*Investment*
Total	7,200	6,200
Public Sector	4,800	3,800
Private Sector	2,400	2,400

Plan Projection (Targets)

(At 1970-71 Prices)

Item	*1955-56*	*1960-61*	*% Increase*
National income (₹ crores)	21,403	25,880	20.9
Per capita income (₹)	508	559	10.0
Net domestic savings* as % of N.I.	10.9	9.3	0
Investment as % of N.I.	11.3	12.9	–

* At current prices.

THIRD FIVE YEAR PLAN
(April 1961–March 1966)

OBJECTIVES

1. To secure an increase in national income of over 5 per cent per annum, the pattern of investment being designed also to sustain this rate of growth during subsequent plan periods.
2. To achieve self-sufficiency in food grains and increase agricultural production to meet the requirements of industry and exports.
3. To expand basic industries like steel, chemical industries, fuel and power and establish machine-building capacity so that the requirements of further industrialisation can be met within a period of ten years or so mainly from the country's own resources.

4. To utilise, to the fullest possible extent, manpower resources of the country and to ensure a substantial expansion in employment opportunities.
5. To establish progressively greater equality of opportunity and to bring about reduction in disparities in income and wealth and a more even distribution of economic power.

Plan Projection (Targets)

(At 1960-61 Prices)

Item	*1960-61*	*1965-66*	*% Increase*
National income (₹ crores)	13,263	17,242	30.0
Per capita income (₹)	306	358	17.0
Domestic savings* as % of N.I.	8.5	11.5	0
Investment as % of N.I.	11.0	14.0	–

Outlay and Investment

(₹ Crores)

Sector	*Outlay*	*Investment*
Total	11,600	10,400
Public Sector	7,500	6,300
Private Sector	4,100	4,100

Plan Achievements

(At 1970-71 Prices)

Item	*1960-61*	*1965-66*	*% Increase*
National income (₹ crores)	25,880	30,003	15.9
Per capita income (₹)	559	559	0.0
Net Domestic savings* as % of N.I.	9.3	11.2	–
Investment as % of N.I.	12.9	14.8	–

*At current prices.

FOURTH FIVE YEAR PLAN
(April 1969–March 1974)

OBJECTIVES

The Plan had two basic objectives, viz., 'growth with stability' and 'progressive achievement of self-reliance'. To achieve these two objectives, the Plan aimed at the following:

1. Acceleration of the tempo of economic development.
2. Adoption of intensive agricultural development programme and building up of sizeable buffer stocks, of food grains.
3. Stabilising the general price level.
4. Achievement of self-reliance by doing away with PL 480 imports of food grains and a sustained increase of exports by 7 per cent per annum.
5. Achievement of social justice and equality by reducing the concentration of economic power.
6. Utilisation of Panchayati Raj institutions in local planning and the gradual building up of an integrated cooperative structure for establishing social and economic democracy particularly in the rural areas.

7. Reorganisation of the management of public enterprises to achieve the twin aims of a strong and well-knit public sector and the autonomous operation of the public sector.

Plan Projection (Targets)

(At 1968-69 Prices)

Item	*1968-69*	*1973-74*	*% Increase*
National income (₹ crores)	2,800	27,900	27.5
Per capita income (₹)	546	636	15.0
Domestic savings* as % of N.I.	9.0	13.2	–
Investment as % of N.I.	11.3	14.5	–

Outlay and Investment

(₹ Crores)

Sector	*Outlay*	*Investment*
Total	11,600	10,400
Public Sector	7,500	6,300
Private Sector	4,100	4,100

Plan Achievements

(At 1970-71 Prices)

Item	*1968-69*	*1973-74*	*% Increase*
National income (₹ crores)	33,544	39,691	18.3
Per capita income (₹)	589	620	5.3
Net Domestic savings* as % of N.I.	9.5	15.0	–
Investment as % of N.I.	11.3	16.6	–

*At current prices.

FIFTH FIVE YEAR PLAN
(April 1974–March 1979)

OBJECTIVES

Removal of poverty and attainment of economic self-reliance were the two major objectives of the Fifth Plan. For realisation of these objectives, the Plan aimed at the following:

1. A 5.5 per cent overall rate of growth of gross domestic product (GDP).
2. An expansion of productive employment opportunities.
3. A National Programme for Minimum Needs covering elementary education, drinking water, medical care in rural areas, nutrition, home sites for the landless labour, rural electrification and slum improvement and clearance.
4. Extended programmes of social welfare.
5. Emphasis on agriculture, key and basic industries and industries producing goods for mass consumption.
6. An adequate public procurement and distribution system for assured supply of essential consumption goods, at least to poorer sections, at reasonably stable prices.
7. Vigorous export promotion and import substitution.
8. Rigorous restraint on inessential consumption.

9. An equitable price-wages-incomes balance.
10. Institutional, fiscal and other measures for the reduction of social, economic and regional inequalities.

Plan Projection (Targets)

(At 1972-73 Prices)

Item	*1973-74*	*1978-79*	*% Increase*
National income (₹ crores)	45,050	58,875	30.6
Per capita income (₹)	775	925	19.4
Domestic savings* as % of N.I.	13.6	18.2	–
Investment as % of N.I.	15.4	18.9	–

Outlay and Investment

(₹ Crores)

Sector	*Outlay*	*Investment*
Total	53,411	47,561
Public Sector	37,250	31,400
Private Sector	26,161	16,161

Plan Achievements

(At 1970-71 Prices)

Item	*1973-74*	*1978-79*	*% Increase*
National income (₹ crores)	39,691	51,342	29.4
Per capita income (₹)	620	715	15.3
Net Domestic savings* as % of N.I.	15.0	20.0	–
Investment as % of N.I.	16.6	18.0	–

*At current prices.

SIXTH FIVE YEAR PLAN (April 1980–March 1985)

OBJECTIVES

1. A significant step up in the rate of growth of the economy, the promotion of efficiency in the use of resources and improved productivity.
2. Strengthening the impulse of modernisation for the achievement of economic and technological self-reliance.
3. A progressive reduction in the incidence of poverty and unemployment.
4. A speedy development of indigenous sources of energy with proper emphasis on conservation and efficiency in energy use.
5. Improving the quality of life of the people in general with special reference to the economically and social handicapped population, through a minimum needs programme whose coverage is so designed as to ensure that all parts of the country attain, within a prescribed period, nationally accepted standards.
6. Strengthening the distributive bias of public policies and services in favour of the poor contributing to a reduction in inequalities of income and wealth.

7. A progressive reduction in regional inequalities in the pace of development and in the diffusion of technological belie fits.
8. Promoting policies for controlling the growth of population through voluntary acceptance of the small family norm.
9. Bringing about harmony between the short- and the long-term goals of development by promoting the protection and improvement of ecological and environmental assets.
10. Promoting the active involvement of all sections of the people in the process of development through appropriate education, communication and institutional strategies.

Plan Projection (Targets)

(At 1979-80 Prices)

Item	*1979-80*	*1984-85*	*% Increase*
National income (₹ crores)	97,051	1,25,050	28.8
Per capita income (₹)	1,484	1,744	17.5
Domestic savings* as % of N.I.	21.2	24.5	–
Investment as % of N.I.	21.8	25.1	–

Outlay and Investment

(₹ Crores)

Sector	*Outlay*	*Investment*
Total	1,72,210	1,58,710
Public Sector	97,500	84,000
Private Sector	74,710	74,710

SEVENTH FIVE YEAR PLAN
(April 1985–March 1990)

OBJECTIVES

The guiding principles of the Seventh Five Year Plan should continue to be growth, equity and social justice, self-reliance, improved efficiency and productivity. Within this framework, the movement towards social justice has to be faster and there must be a sharper focus on employment and poverty alleviation. Hence, the Seventh Plan must emphasise policies and programmes which will accelerate growth in food grains production, increase employment opportunities and, what is equally important, raise productivity.

Plan Projection (Targets)

(At 1984-85 Prices)

Item	*1984-85*	*1989-90*	*% Increase*
GDP at factor cost (₹ crores)	1,93,428	2,46,881	27.6
GDP at market price (₹ crores)	2,17,762	2,81,945	29.5
Per capita GDP (₹)	2,616	3,027	15.7
Domestic savings as % of N.I.	23.3	24.5	–
Investment as % of N.I.	24.5	25.9	–

Outlay and Investment

(₹ Crores)

Sector	*Outlay*	*Investment*
Total	3,48,148	3,22,366
Public Sector	1,80,000	1,54,218
Private Sector	1,68,148	1,68,148

EIGHTH FIVE YEAR PLAN
(April 1992–March 1997)

OBJECTIVES

The guiding principles of the Eighth Five Year Plan should continue to be growth, equity and social justice, self-reliance, improved efficiency, productivity, health, education, full employment and planned growth of population. Within this framework, the movement towards social justice has to be faster and there must be a sharper focus on employment and poverty alleviation. Hence, the Eighth Plan must emphasise policies and programmes which will accelerate the growth in food grains production, increase employment opportunities and, what is equally important, raise productivity and lay emphasis on re-examination and re-orientation of role of government as well as the process of planning.

Plan Projection (Targets)

(At 1991-92 Prices)

Item	*1991-92*	*1996-97*	*% Increase*
GDP at factor cost (₹ crores)	5,19,716	6,82,473	31.32
GDP at market price (₹ crores)	5,82,356	7,64,730	31.32
Per capita GDP (₹)	6,329	8,135	28.54
Domestic savings as % of N.I.	20.7	21.6	–
Investment as % of N.I.	23.1	23.2	–

Outlay and Investment

(₹ Crores)

Sector	*Outlay*	*Investment*
Total	8,71,100	7,98,000
Public Sector	4,34,100	3,61,000
Private Sector	4,37,000	4,37,000

NINTH FIVE YEAR PLAN
(April 1997–March 2002)
OBJECTIVES

Primary objectives of the Ninth Five Year Plan can be summarised as 'Growth with Social Justice and Equity'. Specific major objectives of the Plan are as follows:

1. Priority to agriculture and rural development generating adequate employment and eradication of poverty.
2. Accelerating growth rate of the economy with stable prices.
3. Ensuring food and nutritional security for all particularly the vulnerable sections of society.
4. Providing basic minimum services of safe drinking water, primary healthcare facilities, universal primary education, shelter and connectivity to all in a time bound manner.
5. Containing the growth rate of population.
6. Empowerment of women and socially disadvantaged groups as agents of socio-economic change and development.
7. Strengthening efforts to build self-reliance.

GROWTH AND INVESTMENT TARGETS

Growth rate (GDP) of the economy during the plan period has been projected as average of 6.2 per cent per annum. Various growth targets and outlay are given below.

Growth Targets

GDP	6%-7%	Exports 14.5%
Savings	26.2%	Imports 12.2%
Investment	28.3%	

Outlay

(1996-97 Prices)

	₹ Crores	*Per cent*
Total	8,75,000	100.0
Central	4,89,361	59.3
State Plans	3,69,829	38.7
Union Territory Plans	15,800	2.0

TENTH FIVE YEAR PLAN
(April 2002–March 2007)
OBJECTIVES

The foremost objective of the Tenth Five Year Plan is to achieve an average annual growth rate of 8 per cent. In addition to this, other major objectives of the Plan are as follows:

1. High priority for human development.
2. Reduction of poverty ratio by 5 percentage points by 2007.
3. Providing gainful employment to at least the addition to the labour force during the Plan period.
4. All children to be school-going by 2003.
5. Increase in the literacy rate to 75 per cent during the Plan period.

GROWTH AND INVESTMENT TARGETS

Growth Targets

GDP Growth (Per annum)	8%	Incremental capital-output ratio (IGOR)	3.6
Saving rate (Per cent of GDP)	26.8%	Current account Deficit (Per cent of GDP)	1.6%
Investment rate (Per cent of GDP)	28.4%		

Outlay

(2001-2002 Prices)

	₹ *Crores*	*Per cent*
Total	19,68,815	100.0
Central*	7,06,000	35.9
State Plans	5,88,325	30.0
Union Territory Plans	6,74,490	34.1

* Includes Union Territories

PART–VIII

DEVELOPMENTS IN MACROECONOMICS

In this part (Chapter 25) important developments in macroeconomics have been analysed. Like most other subjects, macroeconomics is evolving and developments are taking place. These are primarily post-Keynesian developments. Some of these are a critique of Keynesian theories/thoughts; some relate to revival or revalidation of classical macroeconomics. Three significant developments have taken place in three different forms or fields: (a) Modern monetarism; (b) New classical macroeconomics; and (c) Supply side economics. These three developments and the related issues are discussed in this part (chapter).

Chapter 25

Post-Keynesian Developments in Macroeconomics

Like many other subjects, macroeconomics is also evolving and developments are taking place. These are essentially post-Keynesian developments in different aspects or areas of macroeconomics. Some of these are a critique of Keynesian theories and thoughts; some relate to revival or revalidation of classical macroeconomics in new forms. These developments, and a number of related macroeconomic issues are discussed in this chapter.

Significant developments in post-Keynesian macroeconomics have taken place in three different forms or fields:

1. Modern Monetarism
2. New Classical Macroeconomics
3. Supply Side Economics

MODERN MONETARISM

Modern monetarism owes its origin to Milton Friedman, a Nobel Laureate in economics, and, his colleagues and supporters. Friedman defended classical monetary theory and revived it through his support and vindication of the quantity theory of money developed by Fisher and the Cambridge School (discussed in Chapter 14). Classical monetarism was revived during the late 1950s and 1960s; this is known as 'modern monetarism'.

A landmark study of monetary history of the United States conducted by Friedman and Schwartz in the 1950s, revealed a strong relationship between economic fluctuations and money supply.[1] Further analysis and research by the monetarists also confirmed a strong linkage between money supply, GDP or GNP and the price level. Friedman has put it like this: "Long period changes in the quantity of money relative to output determine the secular behaviour of prices. Substantial expansions in the quantity of money over short periods have been a major proximate source for the accompanying inflation in prices."[2] Friedman also says: "Inflation is always and everywhere a monetary phenomenon in the sense that it is and can be produced only by more rapid increase in the quantity of money than in output".[3]

1. M. Friedman and K.J. Schwartz, *A Monetary History of the United States: 1867-1960*, Princeton University Press, 1963.
2. "Monetary Studies of the National Bureau" in M. Friedman, *The Optimum Quantity of Money and Other Essays*, Aldive Publication Co. Chicago, 1969.
3. P.A. Samuelson, *Economics* (Seventeenth Edn.). Tata McGraw Hill, 2002, p. 713.

Modern monetary economics contends that growth in money supply determines nominal GDP or GNP in the short-run and the price level or price movements in the long-run. This works through the quantity theory of money or the equation of exchange. Changes in the price level depend on changes in the velocity of circulation of money. Monetarists contend that the velocity of circulation of money is stable (or can even be constant). If this is so, the quantity theory or the equation of exchange proves that, if V is constant, movements in money supply (M) will affect PQ (i.e., nominal GDP) proportionally.

From this, three proportions almost follow which can be called the essence of modern monetarism:

1. Growth in money supply is the prime determinant of growth in nominal GDP.
2. Prices and wages are generally or relatively flexible.
3. Private sector is stable and fluctuations in the economy are caused more by government action.

Monetarists argue that nominal aggregate demand is primarily influenced by money supply or changes in this. Fiscal policy has no role in influencing or regulating aggregate demand. Fiscal policy has no role or impact because, if V is stable, particularly if it is constant, the only factor which can affect PQ is M. There is no way fiscal measures like taxes or government expenditure can enter or affect the system. The modern monetarists have put this more directly in an over simplified or extreme form: "only money matters".

Keynesian economics assumes wage-price rigidity; monetarists postulate general wage-price flexibility. Because wages and prices are generally flexible, changes in money supply have only insignificant impact (in the short-run) on real output. According to the monetarists, the economy operates near or at full employment (and the corresponding level of output), money supply affects mostly the price level. Fiscal policy has only negligible effect on all this.

Monetarists also have a view on the operation of the enterprise. They hold that the private enterprise is generally efficient and stable in operations. The private economy, left to itself, is not susceptible to instability. Instability comes through government action or intervention. Fluctuations in nominal GDP are caused mostly by government action (through the central bank) in regulating money supply.

Modern Monetarism is considered by many as counter revolution—counter to the Keynesian revolution in macroeconomics. Modern Monetarism received widespread support and acceptance during the 1970s and 1980s. Many developed countries adopted this as a basis for formulation of economic stabilisation policies and measures. The United States is one of the most prominent/significant among them.

MODERN MONETARISM VERSUS MODERN KEYNESIANISM

Modern Keynesians like Nicholas Kaldor and James Tobin have been very critical of the monetarist approach. In fact, they have launched a counter attack on the monetarists. They have strongly revealed the validity of the Keynesian theories. The debate—argument and counter arguments—goes on. The two views can be successfully put in two contrasting statements:

"Only money matter": Modern Monetarism

"Only money does not matter; others also matter: Modern Keynesianism[4]

4. Modern Keynesian economics can also be called mainstream macroeconomics.

Let us put these contrasting views in analytical forms. This is done through an explanation of the implications of the two thoughts/views on aggregate demand (AD) and aggregate supply (AS) curves. The contrasting AD and AS curves are presented in Fig. 25.1 and Fig. 25.2.

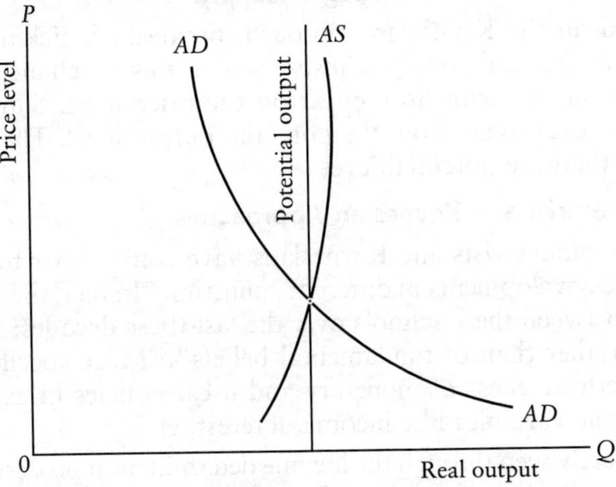

Fig. 25.1: AD and AS curves: Monetarist Approach

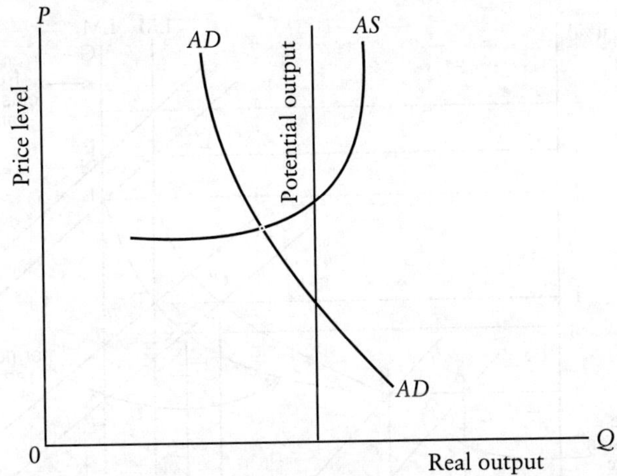

Fig. 25.2: AD and AS curves: Keynesian Approach

We explain the forms or shapes of the AD and AS curves in Fig. 25.1 and Fig. 25.2.

Let us start with the AD curves. The AD curve in Fig. 25.1 (Monetarist approach) is flatter than the AD curve in Fig. 25.2 (Keynesian approach). This is because of the assumptions of wages price flexibility and wage-price stickiness in the two approaches. The AD curve in the former is price-elastic—demand changes in response to flexible or changing price;[5] in the latter changes in demand are slow or less because of stickiness of price and relative in elasticity of demand.

5. The actual shape of the curve is rectangular hyperbola of the algebraic form ry = constant with given M and V. According to the monetarists' assumption, the AS curve is of the form PQ (=MV) = constant, a rectangular hyperbola.

Because of the same reasons, the AS curves have different shapes and slopes in the two approaches. Because of price flexibility, the supply curve adjusts itself and stays close to potential output level (Fig. 25.1). This also means that a change in aggregate demand will lead more to a change in the price level rather than aggregate supply.

On the other hand, in the Keynesian approach, because of stickiness, price movement is in a narrow or small range, and supply adjusts itself to this. A change in demand will cause a significant change in supply with little effect on the price level. Supply, however, does not increase much after it moves away from the potential output level. The equilibrium is reached at a lesser real output than the potential level.

Reconciliation of Monetarist and Keynesian Approaches

Over the years, the monetarists and Keynesians have come closer to each other because of various macroeconomic developments in different countries. "In fact, there has been considerable convergence of views between these schools over the last three decades; and, the disputes today are ones of emphasis rather than of fundamental beliefs".[6] More specifically, it boils down to the roles and relative effectiveness of monetary and fiscal policies in explaining the behaviour or variations in economic variables like income, interest, etc.

This can be more clearly seen through the income determination process with IS and LM curves (derivation of these curves was explained in Chapter 16). Determination of income and changes in income levels because of the effects of monetary and fiscal policies are shown in Fig. 25.3.

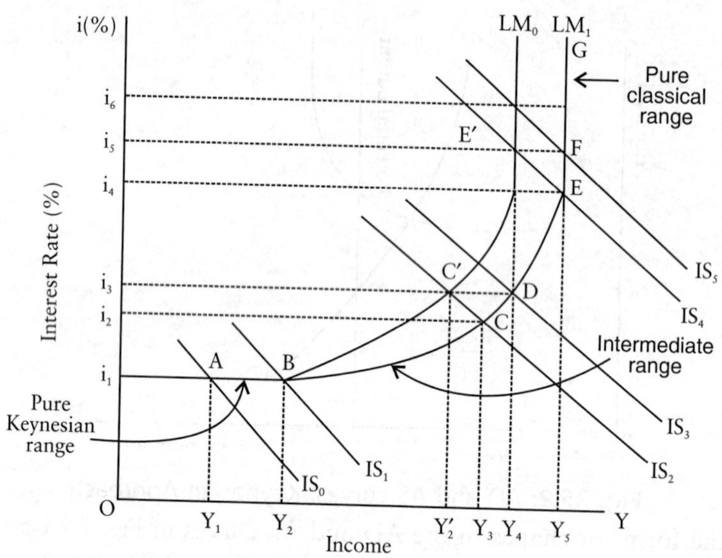

Fig. 25.3: Relative Effectiveness of Monetary and Fiscal Policies in the IS-LM Model

In Fig. 25.3, the LM curve has three ranges: pure Keynesian range (i_1 to B): intermediate range (B to E): and the pure classical range (EG). In the pure Keynesian range, the LM curve is perfectly elastic ($e = \propto$ at interest i_1); in the pure classical range, the LM curve is perfectly inelastic ($e = o$), at interest i_4 onwards: in the intermediate range, interest elasticity of the LM curve lies between o and $\propto$, i.e., $o < e < \propto$.

6. P.A. Samuelson and W.D. Nordhaus (2002), p. 716.

Relative effectiveness of monetary and fiscal policies is discussed in these three ranges.

Let us first explain the role and effectiveness of monetary and fiscal policy in Keynesian range.

In this range, money supply, or, rather, change in money supply, has no effect on the level of equilibrium income. The economy is in the Keynesian "liquidity trap". Therefore, the entire increase in money supply held as cash balance, and nothing moves to transaction balance, i.e., the circulation process. Because of this, the equilibrium rate of interest remains unchanged at i_1 investment level remain the same and the equilibrium level of income also remains unchanged at Y_1. But fiscal policy has a positive role to play in this range. A change in fiscal policy or measure, say, an increase in government expenditure through deficit financing will increase income (through expenditure approach) but, not the interest rate. The increase in income is from Y_1 to Y_2 shown through a shift in the IS schedule from IS_0 to IS_1.

In the intermediate range, both monetary and fiscal policies have positive roles to play. A change in monetary policy will change both the income level and the interest rate. If there is an increase in money supply, the LM curve shifts from LM_0 to LM_1. The LM_1 curve intersects IS_2 at point C. This means two effects: first increase in income from Y_2' to Y_3 (the original equilibrium was at point C′), and, second, decrease in interest from i_3 to i_2. An increase in money supply leads to excess liquidity in the market; part of this increase goes to the bond and security market causing a rise in bond and security prices and a fall in the interest rate; a fall in the interest rate induces additional investment, and increase in investment results in increase in income. A change in fiscal policy or measure, say, an increase in government expenditure, leads to increases in both the income level and the interest rate. Because of an increase in government expenditure, the investment schedule shifts from IS_2 to IS_3 and the equilibrium point from C to D. This means an increase in income from Y_3 to Y_4. The rate of interest increases from i_2 to i_3.

In the classical range, monetary policy is quite effective, but fiscal policy is almost ineffective. An increase in money supply shifts the LM curve from LM_0 to LM_1 and equilibrium point from E′ to E. The level of income increases from Y_4 to Y_5 and the rate of interest decreases from i_5 to i_4. The government may increase money supply by buying back bonds issued earlier at a high price; the bond holders find selling of bonds profitable. They sell bonds at high price making the interest rate to fall. People switch from bonds to other forms of investment. This results in increase in investments, and, consequently income increases. On the other hand, change in fiscal policy, say, an increase in government expenditure, causes a shift in the IS schedule from IS_4 to IS_5. This increases the interest rate from i_5 to i_6. But there is no increase in income because the LM curve is perfectly inelastic or vertical in this range.

The above analysis on relative effectiveness of monetary and fiscal policies can be concluded like this: except in the extreme ranges or situations, i.e., perfectly interest-elastic range ($e = \infty$) and perfectly interest-inelastic range ($e = o$), both monetary and fiscal policies are used together. Neither monetary policy nor fiscal policy is used in isolation. In most national economies, both the policies are used in combination-made as complementary to each other for better policy effectiveness. This implies a kind of synthesis of the monetarist approach and the Keynesian approach. Relative mix of the two approaches, i.e., relative doses of monetary and fiscal policies or measures depend on the nature and type of economic management and control required in a particular country or economy.

NEW CLASSICAL MACROECONOMICS

The origin of new classical macroeconomics can be traced to the failure of monetary and fiscal policies in controlling inflation and unemployment in many developed countries in the

1970s. Doubts were raised by a group of economists about the effectiveness of monetary and fiscal policies and instruments in successful economic management of countries. This group of economists is led by R.E. Lucas, a Nobel Laureate, T.J. Sargent and R. Barrio. The most distinctive contribution of this group or school of thought is incorporation of 'expectation' or more specifically, 'rational expectations' as a vital factor in macroeconomic analysis—economic fluctuations, inflation, unemployment, etc. Economic thought of this school is more based on the classical approach emphasising the important role of wage-price flexibility in explaining economic variables or phenomena. This is the reason why this theory or thought is called new classical macroeconomics. Because this group of economists launched a radical attack on standard Keynesian macroeconomics, they are also called 'radicalists' and their economic theory or thought is known as 'radicalism'.

RATIONAL EXPECTATIONS: FOUNDATION OF NEW CLASSICAL MACROECONOMICS

Lucas and Sargent have made the following radical observation on Keynesian macroeconomics with respect to monetary, fiscal and other policies:

"Existing Keynesian macroeconomic models cannot provide reliable guidance in the formulation of monetary, fiscal or other types of policy.... [T]here is no hope that minor or even major modification of these models will lead to significant improvement in their reliability."[7]

According to Lucas and Sargent, the solution to problems of economic management lies in incorporating rational expectation as a critical explanatory factor or variable in economic analysis.

Rational Expectations are expectations formed by efficient use of past and present information and anticipated future events. The theory of rational expectations postulates that economic decision makers at people level—individuals, families, households—use the available information intelligently and efficiently for decision making.

Keynes had recognised the significance of consumers and producers' expectations in *General Theory.*[8] He however dealt with expectations separately and did not incorporate this in mainstream macroeconomic analysis and income and employment. Till the 1980s, no serious attention was paid by economists to the role of people's expectation as a determining factor of equilibrium levels of income and employment, and their influence/impact on related/other macroeconomic variables or phenomena.

New classical macroeconomists explained the role of people's expectations in their economic decisions like this. They contend (this can be called their assumption also) that people are generally rational and well informed about the happenings or developments in the economy. Because of their rational thinking, they can interpret and analyse the possible effects of government policies—monetary, fiscal or others. They can efficiently or accurately analyse the impact of government decision—particularly monetary and fiscal policies—on their earnings, consumption, saving, investment and other economic interests and decision making. They can anticipate future course of government policies and actions, and, make prior or pre-emptive adjustments in their plans and decisions before the anticipated policies and actions are implemented. This thwart the effectiveness of particular monetary and fiscal policies.

---

7. R.E. Lucas and T.J. Sargent. "After Keynesian Macroeconomics" in *After the Phillips Curve: Perspective of High Inflation and High Unemployment*, Federal Reserve Bank of Boston, 1978.
8. Keynes had devoted two different chapters (Chapter 5 and Chapter 12) in *General Theory* to analysis of people's expectations.

Major Contentions/Conclusions of New Classical Macroeconomics

Major contentions or conclusions of new classical macroeconomics are based on two basic postulates or assumptions:

(a) Wages and prices are flexible—they adjust quickly to balance demand and supply.

(b) Economic agents—producers, consumers and labour—have access to and call the information they require to form their rational expectations and make decisions so that the government cannot "fool" them.

The radical approach of new classical macroeconomics can be applied to different areas of economics with their implications and conclusions. Two significant conclusions are:

1. Unemployment is voluntary and not involuntary;
2. There is no trade-off between inflation and unemployment.

According to the new classical economists, most unemployment is voluntary, and, not involuntary (involuntary unemployment was discussed in Chapter 11). This can be explained like this. Labour markets respond quickly, and adjust to wage changes even if those come as shocks, to rebalance demand and supply. Unemployment during economic recession increases because more people are looking for batter jobs (voluntary unemployment) and, not because they cannot find jobs (involuntary unemployment).

In this context/connection, new classical economists introduce the concept of "misperception" developed by Lucas as an additional explanatory factor for analysing unemployment during business cycles.

Misperception works like this. During recessions, high rate of unemployment occurs because workers get confused about prevailing economic conditions. They voluntarily leave their present jobs in expectation of better ones, but surprisingly land themselves in the unemployment zone. During boom or economic expansion, high output and low unemployment result when workers are 'fooled' to work harder because they misperceive or overestimate real wages. Real wages hardly change because money wages and prices increase almost proportionally.

This phenomenon is illustrated in Fig. 25.4 which shows the Phillips curve in relation to wage-push inflation (Phillips curve was explained in Chapter 13). The illustration is done through the new classical Phillips curve

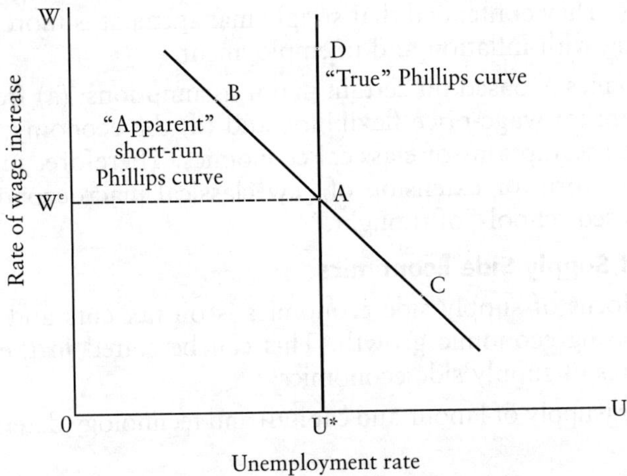

Fig. 25.4: The New Classical Phillips Curve

According to new classical macroeconomics, the true Phillips curve is vertical-AD in Fig. 25.4. The actual rate of increase in wages (W) is equal to the expected rate (W^e) and natural rate of unemployment is shown by U*. This is shown by point A. As per the true Phillips Curve, there is no trade-off between inflation and unemployment—the rate of unemployment is unaffected by wage (price) increase.

Misperception, because of sudden shocks produced in the economy gives rise to an apparent or illusory short-run downward sloping Phillips curve shown by BAC. An inflationary shock increases money wage rate above the expected level (W^e). The workers get confused. They feel their real wages have increased (this is actually neutralised by price increase); they work more and unemployment falls. This is shown by a movement from A to B along the apparent Phillips curve. Point C occurs when there is a deflationary or recessionary shock-sudden fall in wages (and prices) below the expected (W^e) level. But both points B and C (and, the short-run apparent Phillips curve) are produced by sudden shocks in the economy and misperceptions about the effects of such shocks. The vertical line is the long-run true Phillips curve; and, unemployment in an economy is mostly voluntary, and, not involuntary, and, there may not be any trade-off between inflation and unemployment.

Policy implications of new classical macroeconomics can be many. The most important of these is ineffectiveness of systematic or repetitive doses of monetary and fiscal policies and measures—say economic stimulations—to deal with cyclical fluctuations and unemployment. With flexible prices and wages and rational expectations anticipated government policies cannot be effective in regulating real output or income and controlling unemployment. This may be called the *policy ineffectiveness theorem* of new classical macroeconomics.

SUPPLY SIDE ECONOMICS

Supply side economics was discussed in Chapter 13 in connection with inflation. Here the subject is analysed in complete perceptive—origin, development, implications and review.

Supply side economics is considered to be the most recent —early 1980s—school of thought in macroeconomic analysis. The emphasis so far had been on demand side or demand management for dealing with economic fluctuations—inflation, recession, unemployment—and growth. Supply side of the market or economy and supply management had been practically overlooked. A group of economists led by A.B. Laffer, P.C. Roberts and N. Ture strongly advocated the role of supply side economics. They contended that supply management is more effective than demand management in dealing with inflation and unemployment.

Supply side economics is based on certain major assumptions: (a) free enterprise economy; (b) perfect competition; (c) wage-price flexibility, and (d) the economy is in full employment. These are actually the assumptions of classical economics. Therefore, supply side economics is also known as another form or extension of new classical macroeconomics. Some, however, call it a loosely organised school "of thought."

Major Contentions of Supply Side Economics

The central/core focus of supply side economics is on tax cuts and incentives as a means of achieving or increasing economic growth. This can be stated in the form of three policy statements or postulates of supply side economics:

(a) Factor supply (supply of labour and capital) and technology determine growth of output or income.

(b) Tax cut is the most effective incentive for saving, investment and factor supply.

(c) High tax rate reduces tax revenue and factor supply and discourages or prevents economic growth.

Supply side economists contend that both short-term and long-term growth in output or income is determined by increase in factor supply and improvement in technology. This is illustrated in Fig. 25.5.

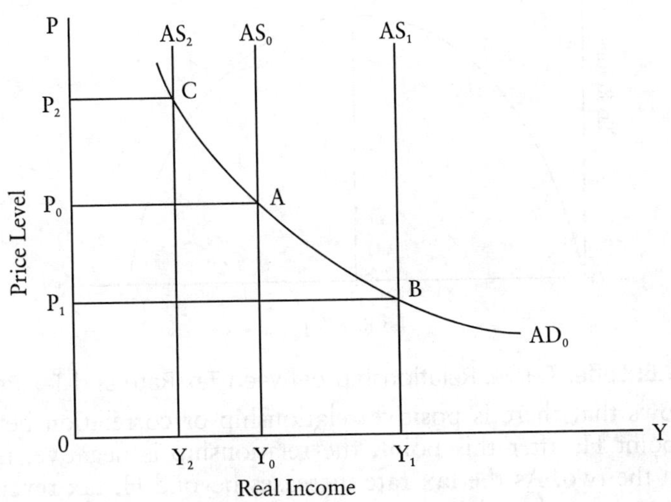

Fig. 25.5: Factor Supply and Growth in Income

Given certain factor supply and level of technology the initial or original aggregate supply curve is given by AS_0. Given the aggregate demand curve as AD_0, equilibrium is reached at point A with equilibrium levels of income and prices at Y_0 and P_0. According to the supply side economists an increase in factor supply and change or improvement in technology lead to a rightward shift in the supply curve from AS_0 to AS_1. Given the demand curve AD_0, new equilibrium is reached at point B with new income and price at Y_1 and P_1. This shows the effect of increase in factor supply and change of technology on growth of income. Income has increased from OY_0 to OY_1. The price level has fallen from P_0 to P_1. According to supply side economists, this shows that growth in income is supply-determined. This is the effect of a positive or favourable supply shock. The price effect is anti-inflationary. The opposite happens if there is negative or unfavourable or adverse supply shock because of decrease in factor supply. The aggregate supply curve shifts leftwards to AS_2 and new equilibrium is reached at point C; income decreases from OY_0 to OY_2 and price increases from P_0 to P_2. The price effect becomes inflationary.

Supply side economics postulates that a reduction in the tax rate increases post-tax return on labour and capital. This leads to increase in demand for both the factors. Given certain factor supply, increase in demand results in rise in factor prices, and, this, in turn, leads to increase in factor supply; this leads to a rightward shift in the aggregate supply curve and increase in income. The opposite process operates when there is an increase in the tax rate. This shows that a tax cut is an incentive for growth and an increase in the tax rate or a high tax rate is a disincentive for economic growth. This is how supply side economics works.

Supply side economists also postulate a relationship between tax rate and tax revenue. They argue that as the tax rate increases, tax revenue increases, but it does not increase indefinitely.

Total tax revenue increases only upto a certain level; after that, as the tax rate increases further, total tax revenue starts declining. This is illustrated through the Laffer curve developed by Arthur Laffer. The Laffer curve is presented in Fig. 25.6.

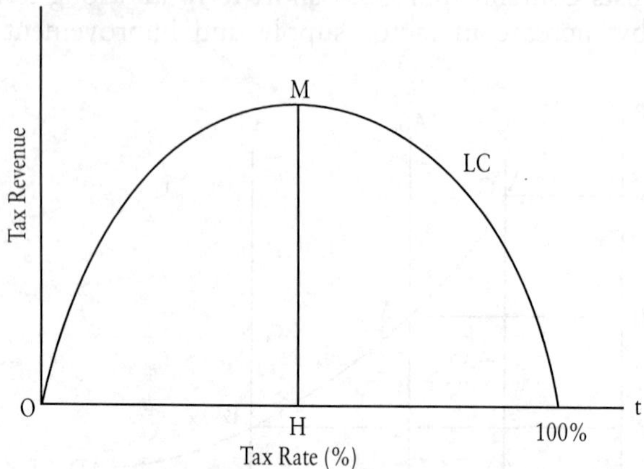

Fig. 25.6: Laffer Curve: Relationship between Tax Rate and Tax Revenue

Figure 25.6 shows that there is positive relationship or correlation between tax rate and tax revenue upto point H; after this point, the relationship is negative, i.e., there is inverse correlation between the two. As the tax rate increases beyond H, tax revenue starts declining and eventually falls to zero when the tax rate increases to 100 per cent.

The Laffer Curve and based on it, the contention of supply side economics has important policy implication. It implies that the rate of taxation should be planned in such a way that its revenue elasticity does not go down below 1. If it happens, first, it starts yielding lesser revenue; and, second, equally or more important, it acts as a disincentive for work, savings and investment, and, becomes a deterrent to growth.

In fact, supply side economics suggests a rational, or rather a radical restructuring of the existing tax system in various economies to make it growth-oriented. The proposed tax reforms/system is sometimes called "supply side tax cuts". The genesis of this approach is that economic reforms should increase incentives by lowering tax rate. The objective or goal of the economic system should be to improve productivity and increase aggregate supply rather than lay emphasis on economic management through manipulation of aggregate demand.

Review of Supply Side Economics

Supply side economics assumed great significance during the 1980s primarily because of its success in the United States. After that, questions have been raised about its effectiveness and its role has been surrounded with controversy and debate.

Critics generally agree with the basics of supply side economics and supply side programmes and tax cuts. But this school of thought is criticised for exaggerating the benefits of tax cuts and ignoring its unfavorable or negative effects. This can be explained with the example of the British economy. Unemployment in Great Britain increased from 2.6 per cent in 1970 to 3.8 per cent in 1972. The British Government adopted expansionary fiscal policy including both tax cut and increase in government spending. As a result, unemployment declined from 3.8 per cent in 1972 to 2.6 per cent in 1974. But the benefits of expansionary fiscal policy were very short-lived. Unemployment almost suddenly shot back: it increased to 5.5 per cent in 1976 and inflation increased from 7.1 per cent in 1972 to 9.2 per cent in 1973 and almost galloped to 24.3 per cent in 1975.[9]

Major criticisms against supply side economics—its policy prescriptions and their implications—can be summarised as follows:

(a) Moderate supply side effect;
(b) Effect on aggregate demand ignored;
(c) Fall in government tax revenue;
(d) Limited effect on inflation;
(e) Adverse effect on income distribution.

These are explained below.

US experience shows that tax cut leads to/results in only moderate increase in output and employment much less pronounced than advocated by the supply siders. Tax cuts need not necessarily induce or prompt people to work more; they may, instead, find it easier to maintain their consumption levels with less work. Most of the statistical evidence suggests that it is unrealistic to expect tax reduction to lead to substantial increase in either labour supply or household saving".[10] This shows the *limited effect of tax cut on supply side.*

A tax cut has significant effect on aggregate demand. A reduction in personal income tax induces individuals and households to spend more on consumption goods; similarly, a decrease in corporate tax stimulates investment spending. Both have positive impact on increase in aggregate demand; *supply side economics generally ignores this*. Supply siders, however, contend that a reduction in tax reduces government expenditure, and this means a reduction in aggregate demand. But experience of most countries shows that such simple proportional relationship does not exist; reduction in government expenditure is usually much less than the tax cut.

The genesis of supply side economics is tax cut in some form or the other. All tax cuts generally lead *to loss of revenue* and, if the loss of revenue is substantial, this may eventually result in budgetary deficit. Supply side economists like Laffer have argued that tax cut, instead of reducing revenue, actually increases tax revenue. But this has been challenged by many contemporary economists, and, is also not supported by many country experiences.

Supply side economics and its policy instruments are *not very effective in* dealing with the problem of *inflation*. The most prescribed policy measure of supply siders is tax cut; if it is in the form of reduction in personal income tax, it results in increase in personal disposable income. This encourages spending and can fuel inflationary situation. The experience of Great Britain during the mid-1970s had, in fact, proved that it creates inflationary condition, and, can even accentuate it.

Supply side economics and policies tend to increase income inequalities through adverse income redistribution. Most supply side measures like tax cut benefit the richer or higher income groups of the population much more than the poorer sections or lower income groups. This widens the gap between the disposable income of high income and low-income individuals and households. This is adverse or regressive income redistribution.

---

9. J.E. Stiglitz, *Economics*, W.W. Norton & Co., London, 2000, p. 470.
10. W.J. Baumol and A.S. Blinder, *Economics: Principles and Policies* (4th Edition), Harcourt Brace Jovanovich, New York, 1988, p. 237.

REVIEW QUESTIONS

1. What is 'modern monetarism'? Explain their basic postulates or propositions.
2. "Over the years, the monetarists and Keynesians have come closer to each other". Explain and analyse.
3. What are 'rational expectations'? Relate its role to the major contentions or conclusions of new classical macroeconomics.
4. What is the essence of supply side economics? Mention three basic postulates or policy statements of supply side economics.
5. Discuss, with your comments, major criticisms against supply side economics.

SUGGESTED READINGS

- A.B. Laffer and J.P. Seymour (Ed.). *The Economics of Tax Revolt: A Reader*, Harcourt Bruce Jovanovich, New York, 1979.
- L.S. Jerome, *Monetarists, Keynesians and New Classical Economics*, New York University Press, 1982.
- M. Feldstein, "Supply side Economics: Old Truths and New Claims", *American Economic Review*, May 1986.
- M.K. Evans, *The Truth about Supply Side Economics*, Basic Books, New York, 1983.
- P.G. Roberts, *The Supply Side Revolution*, Harvard University Press, 1983.

Macroeconomics: Knowledge Testing (QUIZ)

MACROECONOMICS: GENERAL

1. Classification of economics into macroeconomics and microeconomics is due to
   (a) Adam Smith (b) David Ricardo
   (c) J.M. Keynes (d) Ragnar Frisch
2. Macroeconomics is concerned with the study of aggregates; microeconomics is concerned with the study of individual consumers and firms; business and management are concerned with analysis of both
   (a) True (b) False
3. The term 'classical economics' was introduced by
   (a) Adam Smith (b) Karl Marx
   (c) David Ricardo (d) J.B. Malthus
4. The famous book *General Theory of Employment, Interest* and *Money* was written by
   (a) J.M. Keynes (b) Alfred Marshall
   (c) Adam Smith (d) David Ricardo
5. One of the revolutionary developments in macroeconomics took place when
   (a) Role of price expectations in aggregate supply (AS) was recognised
   (b) Theory of 'self-fulfilling prophesy' was established
   (c) Sensitiveness of the transaction demand for money to the rate of interest was proved

GDP, GNP, NATIONAL INCOME

6. Out of the following, which is the correct measure of national income of a country
   (a) GDP (b) GNP
   (c) NDP (d) NNP
7. If GDP of a country is higher than its GNP, then
   (a) 'Net factor income abroad' is negative
   (b) 'Net factor income abroad' is positive
   (c) Fiscal deficit is positive
   (d) Balance of trade is negative
8. If, in a country, consumption is ₹ 1,000, investment is ₹ 200 and exports ₹ 150, then the national income of the country is
   (a) ₹ 1,200 (b) ₹ 1,150
   (c) ₹ 1,350

9. If working hours in a country increases, then, other things being equal, the economy's GDP will
   (a) Decrease (b) Remain constant
   (c) Increase
10. Which of the following is not a component of national income?
   (a) TELCO produced ten more cars
   (b) You received ₹ 10,000 by selling shares in the market
   (c) A wholesale trader increases turnover by 5% (assuming that he makes profit)
11. If the government stops pensions and employs all pensioners for some jobs and pays them the same amount they were receiving as pensions, then India's
   (a) GDP will increase (b) GDP will decrease
   (c) There will be no effect on GDP
12. Per capita income of India in terms of purchasing power parity (PPP) is about five times higher than per capita income in nominal terms
   (a) True (b) False
   (c) The two cannot be compared
13. The country with lowest per capita income is
   (a) India (b) China
   (c) Nigeria (d) Zambia
14. The 'Hindu rate' of growth of the Indian economy is said to be
   (a) 3 per cent (b) 4 per cent
   (c) 5 per cent (d) 6 per cent

PRODUCTION, DEMAND-SUPPLY, BUSINESS CYCLES

15. Four factors of production are
   (a) Land, labour, capital and organisation
   (b) Fixed capital, circulating-capital, labour and management
   (c) Plant and equipment, raw material, labour and management
16. The input-output technique, widely used in empirical economic analysis and planning models, owes its origin to
   (a) Robert Solow (b) W.W. Leontief
   (c) P.A. Samuelson (d) None of these
17. In the input-output ratio xi/X (xi is input, i and X is total output), xi is a
   (a) Factor input
   b) Raw material input
   (c) Combination of factor input and raw material input
18. Productivity is defined/measured as
   (a) Ratio of total output to total input
   (b) Ratio of total output to labour (labour units)
   (c) Ratio of value added to labour (labour units)

19. Value added coefficient is determined as
    (a) Ratio of value added to capital
    (b) Ratio of value added to labour
    (c) Ratio of value added to output
20. Incremental capital-output ratio (ICOR) is defined/measured as
    (a) K_t/Y_t (b) I_t/Y_t
    (c) $I_t/Y_t - Y_{t-1}$
    where K is capital stock, I is investment and Y is output (income)
21. The aggregate demand (AD) curve slopes downwards partly due to the
    (a) Income effect (b) Substitution effect
    (c) Pigou effect
22. The long-run aggregate supply (AS) curve is vertical because of
    (a) Price flexibility (b) Wage flexibility
    (c) Wage-price flexibility (d) All the three
23. To stimulate or increase aggregate demand, we require
    (a) An increase in the propensity to save
    (b) A decrease in the fiscal deficit
    (c) An increase in taxation accompanied by an equal increase in government expenditure
24. Supply side economics has become important because
    (a) Monetary policy has been made relatively ineffective because of the liquidity trap
    (b) Demand management policies are not becoming very effective
    (c) Stagflation cannot be adequately checked through the fiscal-monetary policies
25. Business cycles in a country are
    (a) Normal features of the economic system
    (b) Occasional developments in the economy
    (c) Rare occurrences
26. Depression and recession in economic activity are explained as follows:
    (a) Recession indicates a mild- and short-lived setback in economic activity
    (b) Depression means stagnation of economic activity and is of longer duration than recession
    (c) Recession and depression are same
    (d) The difference between recession and depression is a matter of degree or intensity.
    Which of the above statements is not correct?
27. The innovation theory of business cycles owes its origin to
    (a) Paul A. Samuelson (b) Joseph Schumpeter
    (c) Peter Drucker (d) Michael Porter

CONSUMPTION, INVESTMENT, PRICE LEVEL

28. The relationship between the level consumption and the rate of interest was first emphasised by
    (a) Milton Friedman (b) James Duesenberry
    (c) Irving Fisher (d) Simon Kuznets
29. The multiplier works through
    (a) The marginal propensity to consume (MPC)
    (b) The marginal efficiency of capital (MEC)
    (c) Both MPC and MEC
30. The level of investment and the rate of interest are
    (a) Positively correlated (b) Negatively correlated
    (c) The relationship is not clear
31. If the rate of interest is 5 per cent, an investment project should be undertaken so long as the marginal efficiency of capital (MEC) is
    (a) Equal to 5 per cent (b) More than 5 per cent
    (c) Not less than 6 per cent
32. Foreign investment is
    (a) An intermediate variable (b) An instrument variable
    (c) A target variable (d) A policy variable
33. Inflation is correctly defined as
    (a) High price level
    (b) Rising price level
    (c) Both high price level and rising price level
34. Hyperinflation or galloping inflation occurs when the annual increase in the price level is
    (a) 50 to 60 per cent (b) 80 to 100 per cent
    (c) 100 to 200 per cent (d) 500 per cent or more
35. Stagflation is characterised by the coexistence of
    (a) Economic stability and inflation
    (b) Economic stagnation and deflation
    (c) Economic stagnation and inflation
36. Dearness allowance is determined on the basis of
    (a) Consumer price index (CPI)
    (b) Consumer price index for industrial workers (CPI-IW)
    (c) Wholesale price index (WPI)
    (d) GDP deflator

INCOME DISTRIBUTION, EQUALITY, INEQUALITY

37. In macroeconomics, income distribution means distribution of national income among
    (a) The four factors of production
    (b) Population
    (c) Both factors of production and population

38. Among the four factors, labour's share in national income is
    (a) Always the highest (b) Always the lowest
    (c) Uncertain
39. Per capita income of a country is no indicator of income equality or income inequality of the country
    (a) True (b) False
40. Relationship between economic growth and inequality has been shown in
    (a) Harrod's model (b) Phillips' curve
    (c) Kuznets' curve (d) Liquidity trap
41. Human Development Index calculated by the World Bank includes
    (a) Income inequality (b) Poverty index
    (c) Education (d) Unemployment
42. Many people have lost their jobs because of installation of computers. This has led to
    (a) Frictional unemployment
    (b) Cyclical unemployment
    (c) Structural unemployment

BUDGET, TAXATION, FISCAL POLICY, PHYSICAL POLICY

43. Which of the following is a correct indicator of the fiscal position of a country?
    (a) Primary deficit (surplus)
    (b) Revenue deficit (surplus)
    (c) Capital deficit (surplus)
    (d) Both revenue deficit (surplus) and capital deficit (surplus)
44. The built-in fiscal stabiliser is
    (a) Budget surplus (b) Government expenditure
    (c) Government revenue (d) Taxation
45. External debt to GDP ratio for India is about
    (a) 10 per cent (b) 25 per cent
    (c) 40 per cent (d) 50 per cent
46. All direct taxes are progressive and all indirect taxes are regressive
    (a) True (b) False
    (c) Difficult to say
47. Sales tax (state sales tax or central sales tax) is
    (a) Direct tax (b) Indirect tax
    (c) Can be both direct and indirect tax
48. Monopolistic and restrictive trade practices (MRTP) Act is part of
    (a) Monetary policy (b) Fiscal policy
    (c) Physical policy (d) None of these

49. Government's subsidy on fertilisers is to be considered as a
   (a) Monetary measure (b) Fiscal measure
   (c) Physical measure

MONEY, BANKING, MONETARY POLICY

50. Total money supply in a country, broadly defined, consists of
   (a) Coins and currency with the public
   (b) Coins, currency and demand deposits
   (c) Coins, currency, demand deposits and time deposits
51. Commercial banks can create money because of the
   (a) Cash reserve ratio (CRR) system
   (b) Statutory liquidity ratio (SLR)
   (c) Difference between the borrowing and lending rates of banks
   (d) None of the above
52. The cash reserve ratio (CRR) in India ranges between
   (a) 5 and 6 per cent (b) 7 and 8 per cent
   (c) 8 and 9 per cent (d) 10 and 11 per cent
53. Which of the following is not a direct instrument of monetary policy?
   (a) Open market operations
   (b) Cash reserve ratio (CRR)
   (c) Statutory liquidity ratio (SLR)
   (d) Bank rate
54. Bank rate is the rate at which
   (a) The central bank of a country provides finance to commercial banks
   (b) Commercial banks offer loans to the public
   (c) Financial institutions provide loans to business and industry
55. Effectiveness of monetary and fiscal policies in controlling business cycles is reduced by
   (a) Stagflation (b) Policy lags
   (c) Public debt (d) All the three

FOREIGN TRADE, GROWTH, PLANNING

56. Which of the following statements is correct?
   (a) Balance of trade is part of balance of payments accounts
   (b) Balance of payments is part of balance of trade accounts
   (c) Balance of trade and balance of payments are independent accounts
57. LIBOR (London inter-bank offer rate) widely used in international business transactions, ranges between
   (a) 3 and 3.5 per cent (b) 3.5 and 4 per cent
   (c) 4 and 4.5 per cent (d) 5 and 5.5 per cent

58. Which of the following statements is correct?
    (a) Devaluation of domestic currency causes exports to rise (in the short run)
    (b) Exports depend on national income
    (c) Imports do not depend on national income
59. Euro (the currency of the European Union) in terms of exchange rate, is
    (a) Weaker than US $
    (b) Stronger than US $ but weaker than Pound Sterling
    (c) Stronger than US $ and also stronger than Pound Sterling
60. Economic growth, in simple terms, is defined as increase in
    (a) NNP at constant prices (b) GNP at constant prices
    (c) GDP at constant prices (d) Any of the above
61. Economic development is preferred to economic growth because economic growth ignores
    (a) Environment (b) Population growth
    (c) Pollution (d) All the three factors
62. First Five Year Plan of India covered the period
    (a) April 1950-March 1955 (b) April 1951-March 1956
    (c) April 1955-March 1960 (d) April 1956-March 1961

ANSWERS

1. (d)	2. (a)	3. (b)	4. (a)	5. (a)	6. (d)
7. (a)	8. (a)	9. (c)	10. (b)	11. (a)	12. (a)
13. (c)	14. (b)	15. (a)	16. (b)	17. (b)	18. (c)
19. (c)	20. (c)	21. (c)	22. (c)	23. (c)	24. (c)
25. (a)	26. (c)	27. (b)	28. (c)	29. (a)	30. (b)
31. (a)	32. (a)	33. (b)	34. (d)	35. (c)	36. (b)
37. (a)	38. (a)	39. (a)	40. (c)	41. (c)	42. (c)
43. (a)	44. (d)	45. (b)	46. (a)	47. (b)	48. (c)
49. (b)	50. (c)	51. (a)	52. (d)	53. (d)	54. (a)
55. (d)	56. (a)	57. (a)	58. (a)	59. (b)	60. (d)
61. (d)	62. (b)				

Macroeconomic Database and Sources

For all those in business and managerial positions who want to keep abreast of the economic environment, it is necessary and helpful to know the sources of official statistics for various economic indicators. If one wants to know how national income of the country has grown (changed) over the years, what has been the trends in capital formation or consumption pattern, or how the price movements (indices of inflation) have taken place, or what are likely to be the future trends in growth in many sectors, one must know the sources which may be readily consulted for eliciting data or information on various sectors or macroeconomic indicators.

The objective of this section is to acquaint the management students and managers not only with the various sources of official data but also with the exact nature of the data that may be available, and their periodicity, etc. The major areas of macroeconomic database and sources discussed are:

1. National income and related aggregates
2. Agriculture and allied activities
3. Minerals and metals
4. Industry (manufacturing)
5. Small-scale industries
6. Trade, transport and services (tertiary sectors)
7. Foreign trade (import and export)
8. Prices (wholesale prices)
9. Money, currency and banking
10. Future planning

NATIONAL INCOME AND RELATED AGGREGATES

In India, estimation of national income and related aggregates is undertaken in fairly comprehensive ways by the Central Statistical Organisation (CSO), Department of Statistics, Ministry of Planning, Government of India. National income accounts are contained in the 'National Accounts Statistics', popularly or commonly known as the 'White Paper'. This is published annually by CSO.

National Accounts Statistics gives a time series of national income (NNP) and related aggregates (GDP, GNP, NDP, etc.), for a period of generally fifteen years expressed in both current and constant prices. 'Current prices' indicate the prices prevailing during the year for which the national income aggregates are estimated. These aggregates are also expressed in terms of constant prices of a particular year by using appropriate price deflators. Constant prices used in national income estimation in India at present are 1990-91 prices.

National income and related aggregates are presented in Part I of 'National Accounts Statistics' (NAS). There are five other parts of NAS which present various components and transactions related to national income aggregates. Contents of all the (six) parts of NAS are described below:

Part I Macroeconomic Aggregates

Part II Domestic Product

Part III Consumption, Saving, Capital Formation and Capital Stock

Part IV Public Sector Transactions

Part V Disaggregated Statements

Part VI Consolidated Accounts of the Nation

In Part I, NNP, NDP, GNP and GDP are estimated and reported by industry of origin. There are a total of thirteen industry groups or sectors for which national income accounts are prepared. These are agriculture, forestry and logging, fishing, mining and quarrying (primary sectors), manufacturing (registered and unregistered), construction, electricity, gas and water supply (secondary sectors), transport, storage and communications, trade, hotels and restaurants, banking and insurance, real estate, ownership of dwellings and business services, public administration and defence and other services (tertiary sectors).

AGRICULTURE AND ALLIED ACTIVITIES

The database for agriculture is also quite comprehensive. But all the data pertaining to the agricultural sector are not available from one single source as in the case of national income statistics. There are a number of publications with different periodicity which together provide the sources for agricultural statistics. All the important publications are listed below mentioning the periodicity and the nature of database contained in these sources.

Area and Production of Principal Crops in India: This is an annual publication. It gives statistics regarding area, production and productivity of all important crops of the country over different years. The estimates of area and production are released at different stages as preliminary estimates, final estimates and revised estimates.

Bulletin on Food Statistics: Published annually, it contains almost all statistics about food.

Indian Agriculture in Brief: This is an annual ready reference handbook. It provides information about all aspects of Indian agriculture in ready-to-use condensed form.

Agricultural Situation in India: This is a monthly journal. It gives information about the latest state of agriculture in India with data on rainfall pattern, progress of crops, yield rates or productivity situation, area under various crops and crop-wise production. It also contains informative articles on various aspects of Indian agriculture.

Bulletin of Agricultural Prices: This is a weekly bulletin. It contains wholesale and retail prices of various agricultural commodities in the country.

All the above publications are from the Directorate of Economics and Statistics, Ministry of Agriculture, Government of India. In addition to the above periodic publications, the Directorate also brings out two occasional publications on crop statistics. First, is the *Bulletin on Commercial Crops Statistics* which gives information on important commercial crops. This can be of particular value to trade, industry and research scholars. The second is *Indian Agricultural Statistics* (Vol. II). This is the only publication which gives agricultural statistics about each district.

Besides the above publications, a number of publications on other subjects such as agricultural wages, livestock census, cotton, wheat, jute, rice, groundnut and sugar-cane statistics add studies in the economics of farm management are also available with the Directorate.

MINERALS AND METALS

Indian Minerals Yearbook published annually by Indian Bureau of Mines (IBM), Nagpur, is the source for information and data for minerals and metals. This is almost an encyclopaedia for minerals and metals, particularly for minerals. The yearbook is divided in two parts. Part I contains data on production, consumption, prices and international trade in Indian minerals and metals; it also contains world reviews of minerals and metals. Part II of the yearbook makes mineral-wise reviews. The problem with the yearbook is that it is a lagged publication—there is a lag of about five years in its publication.

In view of this, one has to fall back upon more current publications and *Mineral Statistics of India*, also published by IBM, and published bi-annually, provides the source. This also gives a good coverage of the mineral economy of India. Besides basic statistics on production and trade in mineral and metals, it gives a time series of indices of production, trade and prices of mineral and metals. It also gives summarised data on production of states.

In addition, IBM also publishes every two months *Bulletin of Mineral Statistics and Information*. The bulletin has two parts. Part I contains mineral statistics (statistics on mineral and metal production, etc.). The statistics are given for a month, part of a year and a full year also. Part II gives mineral information (mineral legislation and policy, mining lease executed, leases granted, leases renewed, etc.).

There is also *Quick Release of Mineral Statistics of India*, published again by IBM. This is a monthly release. This publishes on a monthly basis, most of the information which appears in the bi-annual statistics, but in a less detailed form.

INDUSTRY (MANUFACTURING)

For data on capital stock, investment, installed capacity, production or gross output, value added and consumption of inputs or raw materials for the organised manufacturing sector (large and medium scale industries), the most comprehensive, and also the only source is *Annual Survey of Industries* published annually (as the title indicates) by the Central Statistical Organisation (CSO), Ministry of Planning, Government of India.

The *Annual Survey of Industries* (ASI) is published in ten volumes. Volume I contains introduction, summary tables and Annexures. Volumes II to X present the main survey, industry group-wise. The survey is presented for both the major groups (two-digit codes) and subgroups (three-digit codes) of industries. The industrial grouping followed is that of the National Standard Industrial Classification (NSIC).

The ASI provides the database for preparation of the input-output tables for the manufacturing sectors of the Indian economy and the state economies.

Besides the *Annual Survey of Industries*, CSO also publishes *Monthly Statistics of Production of Selected Industries of India* which gives information on the number of reporting units, installed capacity, production and stock. The *Monthly Statistics* follows the same industrial classifications as in ASI and gives information for the previous twelve months on the above aspects; in addition, it also gives the same information for the preceding five years.

The printed *Monthly Statistics*, just mentioned, is a lagged publication, the lag being generally of five years. To make some latest data available, CSO publishes *Monthly Production of Selected Industries of India*. As the title indicates, it gives only production data (also gives the number of units). This bulletin also gives production statistics state-wise.

For the public sector enterprises, Bureau of Public Enterprises (now called Department of Public Enterprises), Ministry of Industry, publishes annually, a report on the working of the public enterprises of the Central Government. The data for the report are collected from individual enterprises and after analysis, is presented as Public Enterprises Survey—*Annual Report on the Working of Industrial and Commercial Undertakings of the Central Government*.

The report is presented in three volumes. Volume I of the report presents an overall review of the performance of public enterprises in terms of physical, financial, economic and social objectives. Volume II depicts, commodity group-wise, the performance status of the individual undertakings highlighting the achievements during the year. Volume III presents a comparative analysis of the accounts of the undertakings.

This report covers all the undertakings falling within the purview of the Committee in Public Undertakings (COPU) of the Lok Sabha. However, it does not include the working of departmentally managed undertakings and purely financial and banking institutions.

Finally, there is *Guidelines for Industries* (*Handbook of Industrial Policy and Procedures and Annual Guidelines for Industries*) published by the Department of Industrial Development, Government of India. Part I of the Guidelines contains policies and procedures including industrial policy, industrial licencing, foreign collaboration, foreign exchange regulation, etc. Part II contains the guidelines for industries; this is given industry group-wise.

SMALL SCALE INDUSTRY

Small scale industries mostly belong to the unorganised sector and for this sector, database is always a problem. The primary source for data on small scale industries is the office of the Development Commissioner, Small Scale Industries (DCSSI), Ministry of Industry.

Handbook of Small Scale Industries, published annually by DCSSI is the only regular source for information on number of working units, production, etc., all-India and state-wise.

In 1973-74, DCSSI undertook census of small scale industrial units with reference year 1972. This was the first ever census of small scale industries undertaken in India. The census results were published in two volumes in January 1977. It is titled as *Report on Census of Small Scale Industrial Units*, Vols. I and II, Development Commissioner, Small Scale Industries. Volume I presents and analyses data by broad areas, viz. dispersal of units, inputs, i.e. materials, fuels and electricity, exports, and economic ratios. Volume II presents tables, industry-wise. This is the most comprehensive source for data on the cross-sections of the small scale industry.

Annual Survey of Industries (ASI), in its Sample Sector (in contrast to the Census Sector in which information about the large scale and medium scale industries are published), publishes the same information for the small scale industries as is done for the large and medium scale industries. The analysis for the small scale industries is done on the basis of data collected by National Sample Survey Organisation (NSSO) through Sample Surveys.

Income generated by the small scale industries (manufacturing sector) is reported in the *National Accounts Statistics* (White Paper) by CSO.

TRADE, TRANSPORT AND SERVICES (TERTIARY SECTOR)

Like the small scale industrial sector, the database for the whole of the tertiary sector (trade, transport and communications and services), which is mostly an unorganised sector, is not very strong.

Income (value-added) generated by the tertiary sectors of trade, transport and communications and services are published in the *National Accounts Statistics* (NAS). The sectors covered are railways, transport by other means, storage, communications, trade, hotels and restaurants, banking and insurance, real estate, ownership of dwellings and business services, public administration and defence and other services. (This we have already mentioned above while discussing the database for national income and related aggregates.)

Among the three tertiary sectors, viz. trade, transport and services, the database for the transport sector is much better because of the existence of two separate ministries, namely the Ministry of Railways and the Ministry of Shipping and Transport (the Ministry of Commerce is primarily concerned with foreign trade); which publish, on annual basis, various information pertaining to these two modes of transport, and also road and air transport.

Pocket Book on Transport in India, published annually by Transport Research Division, Ministry of Shipping and Transport, has a detailed coverage, and brings together in one place key statistics relating to all modes of transport, viz. road and road transport, railways, air transport, ports and shipping, inland water transport and other modes of transport including pipelines and bicycles.

Besides the *Pocket Book*, the Transport Research Division, Ministry of Shipping and Transport, also publishes annually *Basic Port Statistics of India* since 1974-75 (earlier title was *Port Transport Statistics of India*) which gives statistics on all aspects of functioning of the major ports in India.

The *Annual Report* of the Ministry of Shipping also reports on the performance and growth, including research and development, of inland water transport, road transport and shipping.

Similarly, the Ministry of Railways publishes *Report on Indian Railways* in two volumes. Volume I gives the 'Report' and volume II pertains to 'Statistics' on Indian railways.

FOREIGN TRADE (EXPORT AND IMPORT)

The only and the comprehensive source for foreign trade statistics, is *Monthly Statistics of Foreign Trade of India* published by the Directorate General of Commercial Intelligence and Statistics (DGCIS). This is published in two volumes: Volume I—Exports and Re-Exports; Volume II—Imports. Each volume publishes three tables. These are:

Table 1: India's Foreign Trade by Groups, Divisions and Sections (Exports/Imports)

Table 2: India's Foreign Trade by Countries and Economic Regions (Exports/Imports)

Table 3: India's Exports/Imports by Commodities-Countries.

Tables 1 and 2 are actually summary tables which may be or are derived from Table 3 which is the main table and constitutes the bulk of Export/Import Volume. The table presents data either for export or import for the month (in which the volume is published) and cumulative to the month from the previous April (i.e. the beginning of the year). So, the March issue of every year will give the total of annual exports/imports. Exports/imports are expressed in both quantity and value. The commodity groupings follow Indian Trade Classification Revision-2 which has been evolved on the basis of United Nation's Standard International Trade Classification (Revision-2).

In addition to the Monthly Statistics, the Directorate General of Commercial Intelligence and Statistics (DGCIS) also publishes, *Indian Trade Journal*, a monthly which gives information on price quotations, trade control, tender enquiries, etc. Part A of the journal contains information on export opportunities, trade control and price for selected products in selected Indian markets; Part B publishes reports on economic and commercial conditions of selected foreign countries which have some trade relationships with India; Part C publishes late enquiries.

On foreign trade policy, the two important and widely known publications by the Ministry of Commerce are *Import Policy* (popularly known as the 'Red Book') and *Export Policy* (popularly known as the 'Green Book'). Since 1982-83, both are published under one title: *Import and Export Policy* (Volume 1: Import and Export Promotion; Volume II: Items under Export Licensing). Both are published annually. These two policy documents embody government of India's foreign trade policy in all its ramifications. Later Import and Export Policy published was for three years (1985-88). Since 1992, five-year policy was introduced. The latest is: *Export and Import Policy* (1997-2002).

The *Handbook of Procedures* (Vol. 1 and Vol. 2) also published annually by the Department of Commerce, is a compendium of rules and procedures for imports and exports and, input-output norms.

PRICES (WHOLESALE PRICES)

For prices, both the general price level and the prices of individual commodities, the most important official source is Index Number of Wholesale prices in India (Base 1960-61 = 100) later published as *Revised Index Number of Wholesale Prices in India* (Base Year 1981-82 = 100 and now 1993-94 = 100) as a monthly bulletin by the Office of the Economic Adviser, Ministry of Industry. The bulletin publishes price data in five separate tables:

Table (I): Calendar year and financial year averages of index number of wholesale prices in India. These are indices of the general price level and give measures of inflation or inflationary trends in the country.

Table (II): Monthly index numbers of wholesale prices by major groups and groups.

Table (III): Monthly index numbers of wholesale prices of major groups, subgroups and individual commodities.

Table (IV): Weekly as well as monthly index numbers of wholesale prices by major groups, groups, subgroups and percentage changes.

Table (V): Weekly wholesale prices and index numbers of individual commodities. Individual commodities covered include the whole range of the agricultural, mineral and manufactured products.

Besides the above prices and indices, three separate index numbers are prepared which are really cost of living indices for three categories of workers or employees. These are:

1. Consumer price index numbers for industrial workers. (1982 = 100)
2. Consumer price index numbers for urban non-manual employees. (1984-85 = 100)
3. Consumer price index numbers for agricultural workers. (July 1986-June 1987 = 100)

All the above three consumer price index numbers are computed by the Labour Bureau, Ministry of Labour, and are published in their monthly publication *Indian Labour Journal* and annual publication *Indian Labour Statistics*.

MONEY, CURRENCY AND BANKING

The Reserve Bank of India, through its annual reports and monthly bulletins reports on various aspects of money, currency and banking in the country. The annual report is published as *Report on Currency and Finance*. This is published in two volumes. Volume I: Economic Review; Volume II: Statistical Statements. Both the volumes are published for the Indian financial or fiscal year (April-March).

Both the volumes are comprehensive documents (the titles, particularly of the annual report, may be rather misleading because these do not give a complete idea of the contents). As the title of Volume I of the Annual Report indicates, it presents a review of the entire economy in terms of trends and developments in all the major economic variables like national income, agricultural and industrial production, prices, etc.

Chapters V and VI of the volume are devoted to monetary and banking developments in the country. These two chapters cover various aspects of money and banking like money supply, income velocity of money, currency and coinage (monetary developments); credit policy, banking trends, selective credit control, rural credit, working of different schemes, etc. (banking developments).

Volume II of the report, as, again, the title indicates, pertains to or supports the review made in Volume I through statistical tables or statements.

The monthly *RBI Bulletin* makes financial and economic review of the country for the month of reference highlighting particularly the financial events and developments; the section on 'Current Statistics' presents statistical data for a few months (upto the month of reference) and also some annual data/statistics.

FUTURE PLANNING

Future planning for growth and development of the national economy and various sectors is done by the Planning Commission. The thinking, deliberations and recommendations of the Planning Commission are contained in the Five Year Plan documents. The most important of the documents is the Draft Five Year Plan.

Since the Fifth Five Year Plan (1974-79), the Draft is published in two volumes. Volume I starts (in Chapter 1) by presenting a long-term perspective (projections for next fifteen years) of the economy and country, including demographic perspective. In Chapter 2, it outlines the objectives and policy frame for the plan. In other chapters, it makes a review of the previous plan in terms of pattern and rates of growth, financial resources, development outlays for the Plan, etc. Volume II presents the sectoral plans. Plans are presented for a total of fourteen sectors; agriculture cooperation and community development; irrigation, command area development and flood control; power, industry and minerals; village and small industries; transport, tourism and communications; education, science and technology; health, family planning and nutrition; urban development, housing and water supply; employment, manpower and labour welfare; welfare of backward classes; backward and special areas including hill and tribal areas. Chapter 15 outlines 'other programmes' not discussed in any of the previous chapters.

Besides the Draft Five Year Plan which presents the total plan for a period of five years, plans for the individual year within the five year period are documented in the Annual Plan also published by the Planning Commission. This discusses all aspects of the plan for the year including approach, policy, financing development programmes for sectors and plan implementation. Mid-term reviews of plans are also published by the Planning Commission.

MACROECONOMIC DATABASE: CONSOLIDATED SOURCES

We have discussed above the macroeconomic database for ten major areas and the specific data sources for these areas. There are a few sources which publish consolidated data pertaining to most of these areas (except future planning). One may find one or some of the consolidated sources more handy or easily accessible. One may like to consult such a source, to start with. If more detailed information is required, the specific sources may be consulted.

The major consolidated sources for the macroeconomic data base are listed below:

1. *Statistical Abstract*—India (Yearly, Calendar Year)—Central Statistical Organisation (CSO).
2. Report on *Currency and Finance* (Vols. I and II) yearly: Financial Year, Reserve Bank of India (we have already discussed this source).
3. *Economic Survey*, Yearly; Financial Year, Ministry of Finance, Government of India.

Glossary of Economic and Business Terms

MACROECONOMICS AND MICROECONOMICS

Absolute Monopoly. If the output of a commodity or service, for which there is no substitute of any kind, were in the hands of a single producer or supplier, absolute monopoly would occur. This never occurs in actual conditions, since there are alternatives for most things.

Abstinence Theory. Also known as the Agio Theory of interest, the Abstinence Theory asserts that interest is a payment for abstaining from current consumption.

Acceleration Principle. Acceleration principle shows how an increase or decrease in consumer expenditure may cause changes in new capital formation. For example, a sufficient increase in consumer demand for a commodity may result in added facilities for producing it and conversely, a sufficient decrease in consumer expenditures may result in failure on the part of the producers to replace worn-out equipment or disinvestment. The acceleration factor, or coefficient of acceleration as it is sometimes called, is the ratio of change in investment to change in consumer expenditures. Thus, if an increase in consumer expenditures of ₹ 4,000 causes increased capital investment of ₹ 2,000 the acceleration factor or coefficient of acceleration would be 1/2. The equation is

$$\frac{1}{C} = \frac{2{,}000}{4{,}000} = \frac{1}{2}$$

Active Balance of Payments (or Trade). An alternative term for favourable balance of payments or trade.

Adverse Balance. As applied to the balance of trade or the balance of payments, it means an excess of payments over receipts, i.e. a debit balance. Such a balance is sometimes described as an unfavourable or passive balance.

Applied Economics. The branch of economics devoted to a study of practical problems with the help of the tools of analysis provided by pure or theoretical economics.

Arc Elasticity. The average degree of elasticity between the points of either a demand curve or a supply curve.

Balance of Payments. International trade and other financial dealings between countries make it necessary for them to make payments to one another. The balance of payments shows the relationships between one country's total payments to all other countries and its total receipts from them. It is thus a sort of statement of income and expenditure on international accounts. Payments and receipts on international account are of three kinds:

(i) The visible balance of trade;
(ii) Invisible items;
(iii) Capital transfers.

Balance of Trade. Known also as the visible balance, this is the relationship between a country's payments for imports of goods and its receipts from the export of goods.

Bank Rate. The minimum rate at which the central bank, acting in its capacity as 'Lender of last resort', is prepared to discount—or more accurately, rediscount—first class or bank Bill of Exchange brought by the members of the money markets. Bank rate, however, is of much greater importance than this since it is the oldest instrument of monetary policies employed by the central bank, and, rates of interest—for example, the rate charged by commercial banks on loans and overdrafts to consumers and also the rate on deposit account—move up and down with the bank rate.

Bilateral Monopoly. This occurs when there is only one buyer of commodity or service and only one seller or supplier.

Boom. A term used to describe a period when business activity is at a high level. During a boom, production expands, prices and wages rise and unemployment declines. After full employment has been reached, a boom will, unless checked, become inflationary in character.

Business Cycle. The tendency of business activity to fluctuate regularly between boom and depression. During the downswing of the cycle, there are falls in prices (including wages and production) and an increase in unemployment; during the upswing there is rise in prices (including wages) and an expansion of production and a fall in unemployment.

Capital. One of the factors of production, it has been defined as 'produced means of production'. Capital consists of machinery, tools, factory building and all kinds of industrial plants, raw-materials, partly finished goods and means of transport. Some writers regard unsold stocks of consumer goods, still in the hands of wholesalers and retailers, as capital.

Capital Formation. Also known as investment. It means increasing a country's stock of real capital. It is defined as net addition to the stock of capital.

Capital Goods. An alternative name for producers' goods, capital goods comprise goods not wanted for their own sake, but only because they assist in the production of other goods.

Capital Value. The value of an asset on its current earnings in relation to the prevailing rate of interest. For example, if the prevailing rate of interest were 5 per cent and the current annual earnings of an asset were ₹ 200, its capital value would be twenty times its earnings, i.e. ₹ 4,000.

Complementary Demand. Often known as joint demand, this occurs when two commodities are jointly demanded, one by itself giving little satisfaction. Examples of complementary or joint demand usually quoted are such pairs of things as tea and sugar, strawberries and cream, shoes and shoe laces and pens and ink.

Composite Demand. When a commodity can be used for more than one purpose, the demand for it may vary as a result of a change in demand for any one of these purposes. Raw wool is required for making cloth and carpets, steel is required in the manufacture of motor cars, for ship building, structural engineering, etc.

Constant Returns to Scale. If, without varying the proportions in which the factors of production are combined, there is an increase in output proportionate to the increase in the total quantity of factors employed, then constant returns to scale occur.

Cost Benefit Analysis. A technique for the valuation of an existing situation or project, whereby the social cost is considered in relation to the benefit it confers on the community.

Cost 'Plus' Principle. A method of fixing prices often adopted in war time and the immediate post-war years, each producer or supplier being permitted to add a prescribed percentage to what the commodity has cost him. The great drawback of this system is that the greater the cost of production of the commodity, the greater will be the profit percentage to the producer, inefficiency thus being encouraged and the more efficient firms penalised.

Cost-Push Inflation. A term used to describe an inflation (rising prices) due to increasing cost of production especially increased wages.

Cross Elasticity of Demand. When two commodities, which are close substitutes for one another, are in competition, demand and increase in the price of one will increase demand for the other. The effect of this change of price of one commodity on the quantity demanded of the other is the cross elasticity of demand.

Deficit Financing. Deliberately budgeting for a deficit. Fiscal policy through the budget is now a recognised adjunct to monetary policy. In case of a depression and serious unemployment, it has been suggested that a budget deficit should be deliberately incurred, and, tax being reduced in order to make more purchasing power available as stimulus to demand.

Deflation. A decrease in the general price level; or the converse, an increase in the value of money in terms of goods and services. Deflation may occur when the quantity of money or deposit currency in circulation is small compared with the quantity of goods and services offered, or when fear of the future or some other cost curtails consumer spending materially, thus reducing the velocity of circulation.

Deflationary Gap. Deflationary gap is defined as the amount of additional investment required to restore employment to the level of full employment.

Depreciation of Capital. In course of time, all capital wears out and has to be replaced. A certain amount of production, therefore, must be devoted every year to replacing worn out or obsolescent capital.

Depression. A term used to describe a period of heavy unemployment and stagnation of business activity. During the nineteenth century, booms and depressions succeeded one another with great regularity, the average time interval between one depression and the next being about seven years.

Derived Demand. Derived demand takes place when the demand for one commodity is not direct but is derived from the demand for another commodity. The term is particularly applicable to factors of production, since the demand for land, labour, and capital is derived from the demand for the goods for the production of which these factors are employed. The demand for capital goods is derived from the demand for the consumer goods in the production of which they assist.

Devaluation. Reducing the value of a currency in terms of the monetary metal (gold) or in terms of another currency. A country with fundamental disequilibrium in its balance of payments might devalue its currency in order to stimulate its exports (cheaper to foreign countries after devaluation) and to discourage imports (foreign goods now being dearer), and thereby restore equilibrium in its balance of payments.

Diminishing Returns. One of the laws of returns, it arises as a result of varying the proportions in which factors of production are combined. If one factor of production is fixed and increasing quantities of the other factors are combined with it, the average physical output in relation to the fixed factor will eventually diminish. Alternatively, it can be said that for each addition to the variable factor or factors, the addition to total output declines.

Disinflation. A mild form of deflation; a policy adopted to check inflation by restricting demand. The term came to be used because of the pejorative meaning the term deflation had acquired during 1930s when it came to be associated with restriction of credit and a high level of unemployment.

Disposable Income. The income of an individual or a community after all direct taxes have been deducted.

Dissaving. Dissaving occurs when an individual is living on past saving. In an inflationary period, some people, finding that with the fall in the value of money their incomes no longer provide them with the standard of living to which they have become accustomed, prefer to draw all past savings rather than suffer a reduction in their standard of living.

Dumping. Selling goods abroad at a lower price than is charged for them in the home market; it is, sometimes, an example of discriminating monopoly.

Duopoly. A form of imperfect competition where there are only two sellers of a commodity.

Duopsony. A condition in a market where there are only two buyers for a commodity or service.

Earnest Money. Also known as a token payment, it is a payment made to make binding a verbal agreement.

Economic Goods. Any commodity or service which must be paid for, directly by the individual or indirectly by the community as a whole, in money in a monetary economy or in terms of the employment of factors of production in a non-monetary economy.

Economies of Scale. This generally indicates economies of large-scale production. Economies of scale may be of two kinds—internal and external. Internal economies are those which any single firm by its own organisation and efforts can enjoy; external economies accrue because of certain factors external to the management and organisation of the firm. External economies generally accrue to all firms in the industry.

Elasticity. The degree of responsiveness of demand or supply to a change in price (income). If a small change in price results in a large change in demand or supply, the demand or supply is elastic; if, on the other hand, a large change in price has no effect whatsoever on the quantity of the commodity that is demanded or supplied; the demand or supply is perfectly inelastic; and if a change in price has an infinite effect on the quantity demanded or supplied, the supply or demand is said to be perfectly elastic.

Elasticity of Demand. The responsiveness of demand to changes in price (income). See 'Elasticity'.

Elasticity of Supply. The responsiveness of supply to a change in price (income). See 'Elasticity'.

Equilibrium. A situation in which economic forces, as they exist at the time, have no tendency to change. Equilibrium theory states that if a position of equilibrium is disturbed by some outside factors or forces, it will immediately set in motion forces to bring about a new equilibrium situation.

Ex ante. The position before some occurrence takes place. The term is used particularly with reference to savings-investment theory. Ex ante refers to what was expected before certain events took place and ex post to the actual situation which arises. Ex post saving is always equal to ex post investment, but ex post saving is not necessarily equal to ex ante saving, i.e. the amount people expected or planned to save.

Excess Demand. If the price of a commodity is below the equilibrium price, demand will exceed supply and situation of excess demand will prevail.

Factor Market. The market for factors of production. At any given period, there is a certain demand for factors of production and a certain supply available. Thus, we have the two market forces of demand and supply, and in conditions of perfect competition these two factors would determine the prices of the various factors.

Factors of Production. The resources required for production. The economists recommend only three factors of production (alternatively called agents of production or inputs)—land, labour and capital. Towards the end of the nineteenth century, a fourth factor was added, i.e. entrepreneur or organisation.

Financial Intermediaries. A term that is used to include all financial institutions engaged in some form of borrowing and lending other than commercial banks. Financial intermediaries include savings banks, building societies, hire-purchase finance companies, insurance companies, pension funds and investment trusts.

Fixed Capital. This comprises assets of a firm which are of a durable character, such as the premises, fixtures and fittings in the case of a retailer, or the factory building and equipment in the case of a manufacturing firm.

Fixed Costs. These are the costs of a firm which do not vary with every change of output. For example, once a firm has built a factory and installed the necessary machinery, the fixed costs remain same whether the firm is working at full or less than full capacity. In either case, the same amount will have to be paid in rent or rates. Depreciation will be the fixed cost and so will interest payment on existing loans. The cost of administration will vary little over a wide range of output; and so, in the short run, is also regarded as a fixed cost.

General Equilibrium. A state of equilibrium exists when there is no inducement for conditions to change. At the equilibrium price, for example, the quantity of a commodity supplied is exactly equal to the quantity demanded and while these conditions exist, there will be no tendency for the price to change. If the analysis of prices is taken for a single commodity, in isolation, the equilibrium price will be an example of particular (or partial) equilibrium as distinct from general equilibrium which takes account of the effect of a price change of one commodity on the prices of all other commodities.

GNP. Gross National Product. See 'National Income'.

Gosplan. Abbreviation for the State Planning Commission of the U.S.S.R., it was responsible for working out the plan of production for each year, the distribution of factors of production among different employments and also for long-term planning, for example, Five Year Plans.

Great Depression. The period of low economic activity and very high unemployment which characterised the greater part of the period between the World Wars and more particularly the years 1929-35, when it became worldwide is known as the period of the Great Depression.

Gross Domestic Product (*GDP*). The money value of all goods and services produced within a country excluding net income from abroad. The Gross National Product includes net income from abroad.

Gross Fixed Investment. The addition during a period of time —usually a year—to a company's or country's stock of fixed capital without making any allowances for the depreciation of the existing capital.

Hyperinflation. An alternative term for runaway or 'galloping inflation' where so great an increase takes place in the amount of money in circulation that eventually it becomes almost worthless and new currency has to be circulated.

Indivisibility. Since some units of capital are large and cannot be employed fractionally, a greater proportion of capital may have to be employed to produce a certain output than is actually required. The concept of indivisibility is important in connection with increasing returns to scale, since an expansion of production may not require additional capital but merely that existing capital be used more fully or exhaustively.

Industrial Revolution. A term used of the period covering the latter half of the eighteenth and early years of the nineteenth century (although precise dates cannot be assigned to it, it is generally recorded as the period between 1780 and 1820) when a series of inventions or innovations affecting the production of power and in the textile and iron and steel industries and transport resulted in a complete change in the character of production in the Great Britain.

Inelastic Demand. A situation in which even a considerable rise or fall in price of a commodity has little effect on the quantity demanded. Demand tends to be inelastic when there are no close substitutes for a commodity in the case of necessities of life and when demand is based on habit or when expenditure on the commodity concerned forms only a small proportion of a person's total expenditure.

Inflationary Gap. A term used for that part of government expenditure which is not covered by taxation or borrowing from the general public, and generally covered by borrowing from banks or other financial institutions, or by the government itself creating money. The inflationary gap would be expected to be large only in time of war when it is not possible to cover the enormous government expenditure by taxation.

Investment. Same as 'Capital Formation'.

Invisible Balance. The balance of payments and receipts for what are known as invisible items in a country's balance of payments. Invisible items are services and comprise shipping, banking, insurance, and other financial services, income from investment abroad, government expenditure abroad, immigrants' remittances, payments for travel, etc.

Joint Demand. When two commodities are complementary to one another, they may be jointly demanded, as for example, bread and butter, tea and sugar, etc. A change in the demand for one commodity will, therefore, bring about a similar change in demand for the other.

Joint Products. See 'Joint Demand', 'Joint Supply'.

Joint Supply. When two commodities are in joint supply, a change in the supply of one causes a similar change in the supply of the other. Examples of joint supply include wool and mutton, beef and hides, petrol and heavier oils, gas and coke, etc. In such cases, a change in the demand for one commodity will affect prices of the other through changes in its supply.

Lender of Last Resort. An essential function of a central bank is that it should be willing to lend—on its own terms of course—when the commercial banks are unwilling to do so. This is how the central bank of a country becomes lender of the last resort.

Liquidity Preference. The extent to which investors invest and institutions prefer to keep their assets liquid, that is in the form of money, rather than in some form of investment. This concept is important in Keynes's theory of money and rate of interest. According to Keynes, interest is the reward for parting with liquidity. In his theory of money, he defined the demand for money as a demand to hold money as distinct from investing it. Thus, an increase in the demand for money is the same as an increase in liquidity preference.

Macroeconomics. Macroeconomics is that branch of economics which considers the relationships between economic aggregates such as national income, consumption, employment total amount of savings and investment, etc.

Marginal Cost. The extra cost of increasing output by one more unit. Thus, if it costs one hundred rupees to produce 50 units of a commodity and ₹ 102 to produce 51 units, marginal cost is defined as ₹ 2. If marginal cost falls, production will be subject to increasing returns, whereas if marginal cost increases, production will be subject to diminishing returns and if marginal cost is constant, production will be subject to constant returns to scale.

Marginal Firm. The firm which just finds it worthwhile to continue in business. A rise in average revenue would result in its falling out of production in conditions of perfect competition. For such a firm, price = marginal cost = marginal revenue = average cost = average revenue.

Marginal Productivity Theory. The marginal productivity of a factor of production is the addition to output resulting from the employment of additional unit of the factor (land, labour or capital). According to marginal productivity theory, no factor, in conditions of perfect competition, should expect to receive as payment for its services a sum greater than the value of its marginal product, that is, its marginal revenue productivity.

Marginal Revenue. The additional revenue obtained from the sale of one more unit of output. Under perfect competition, marginal revenue = price, since in these conditions it is assumed that the demand for the product of any single firm is perfectly elastic. Under imperfect competition including monopoly, marginal revenue falls as output increases, since selling a larger quantity of a commodity necessitates a reduction in price.

Microeconomics. That branch of economics which is concerned with individuals and individual firms, their output and costs, production and pricing of single commodities, wages of individuals, etc., as distinct from macroeconomics which is concerned with aggregates—production, consumption, income, etc., of the community as a whole.

Mixed Economy. A term used to describe an economic system, such as that of India, where some planning of production is undertaken by the State, directly or through nationalised industries, and some is left to private enterprise.

Money Supply. This is generally taken to mean the total value of bank deposits, on both current account and deposit account, off the commercial banks together with the total amount of cash in bank notes and coin.

Monopolistic Competition. One of the forms of imperfect competition, it occurs when there is a large number of producers but there is differentiation of the product or services so that the product of one firm is not regarded as a perfect substitute for that of another.

Monopoly. Monopoly occurs when there is only one producer and seller of a commodity for which there is no substitute. This condition is sometimes termed also as absolute monopoly.

Monopsony. This occurs when there is only one buyer of a commodity or service.

National Debt. This is the debt owned by a government to people and institutions within its own orders (internal debts) and/or to foreign creditors (external debt).

National Income. There are two ways of looking at national income of a country. It can be regarded either as the (net) money value of the total production of goods and services, or the total of all incomes derived from economic activity during a specified period, generally one year, after allowance has been made for capital consumption.

Natural Rate of Interest. This is the equilibrium rate of interest which equates the demand for loans and the supply of loanable funds. At any given time, the actual or market rate of interest charged by banks to borrowers may be above or below the natural rate.

Net Income: The income of a business unit after the expenses of running the business have been deducted. In the case of individual income, it is the amount received after payment of income tax.

Net Investment. An amount of investment during a period after allowance has been made for the depreciation of existing capital.

Net National Product. Same as 'National Income'.

Net Profit. Gross profit less all expenses on rent, rates, taxes, wages, insurance, interest on loans (if any), and depreciation, gives net profit.

NNP. Net National Product.

Nominal Price. The estimated price of an article rather than its market price. The two might differ either because the market price has not recently been established or because supply and demand take the market price above or below the nominal price. A work of art might fall into the first category. A valuer may say that it is worth ₹ 5,000 and this would be regarded as its nominal price. However, when put up for auction it may fetch only ₹ 4,500. This would be its market price. A product in short supply might provide an example of the second category. For example, the nominal price of a new (model) car might be ₹ 2,00,000 but because the demand exceeds the supply it may not be possible to buy one below ₹ 2,50,000 because of the premium on it.

Nominal Wages. Wages in terms of money as distinct from real wages (wages in terms of the goods and services they will buy).

Normal Profit. This is the amount of profit required to keep an entrepreneur in a particular line of production. When most of the firms in an industry are earning more than normal profit, other firms will make entry into the industry; when the firms are earning less than normal profit, the industry will tend to contract. Normal profit varies between different industries according to the risk involved. Normal profit can be regarded as the minimum payment that an entrepreneur is prepared to accept. As such it constitutes some proportion of the cost of production.

Numeraire. A term sometimes used of the function of money as a measure of value.

Oligopoly. A form of imperfect competition where there are only a few sellers in contrast to perfect competition where there is a large number of sellers. Two forms of oligopoly can be distinguished perfect oligopoly where the commodity is homogeneous and imperfect oligopoly where some degree of differentiation exists between products of different firms.

Optimum Firm. This is a firm which has reached its most efficient size, at which its cost of production per unit of output will be at a minimum, so that it has no motive either to expand or reduce its scale of production.

Partial and General Equilibrium. A state of equilibrium exists when there is no inducement for a condition to change. At the equilibrium, for example, the quantity of a commodity supplied is exactly equal to the quantity demanded. And when this condition exists, there will be no tendency for the price to change. If the study of prices is taken for a single commodity in isolation, the equilibrium price will be an example of partial (or particular) equilibrium as distinct from general equilibrium which takes account of the effect of the price change of one commodity on the prices of all other commodities.

Particular Equilibrium. See 'Partial and General Equilibrium'.

Perfect Competition. A sort of theoretical market environment. The primary assumption of perfect competition is that there should be a large number of firms each of which produces only a small fraction of the total output of the commodity. The result is that no firm can influence the market price of the commodity by expanding or contracting its output so that in perfect competition firms must take the price as fixed or given. Thus, in the conditions of perfect competition, the demand for the product of an individual firm is perfectly elastic. There are a number of other characteristics which make perfect competition a unique market form.

Perfect Monopoly. An alternative term for absolute monopoly.

Phillips Curve. The curve showing that a definite relationship exists between unemployment and the rate of change of money wages, so called because Professor A.W. Phillips first introduced this relationship.

Planned Economy. Generally taken to mean State-planned economy. In its most extreme form, the State would be responsible entirely for production and distribution, and, therefore, the allocation of factors of production, including labour.

Point Elasticity. The degree of elasticity at a point on a curve, as distinct from arc elasticity, the average degree of elasticity between two points.

Price Discrimination. This means charging of different prices in different markets or for different groups of consumers for the same commodity or service. This is possible when the production of the commodity or service is in the hands of a monopolist who is able to keep the market separate from one another. Such a policy is possible only if the elasticity of demand for the commodity is not the same in each market

Purchasing Power Parity. A theory that attempts to explain the determination of the rates of exchange between currencies when exchange rates are free to fluctuate based on the relative purchasing power of the currencies in their home countries.

Pure Economics. An alternative term for Economic Theory.

Quantity Theory of Money. The steep rise in prices coupled with the large increase in the quantity of money during the seventeenth century led to the belief that there was some relationship between money supply and the price level. In its earliest and crudest form, the Quantity Theory states that an increase in the quantity of money would bring about a proportionate increase in price. In its refined form, the quantity theory is represented by the equation of exchange as MV = PT; where M represents the quantity of money—the total of bank deposits, bank notes and coins; V represents velocity of circulation, that is, the average number of times each unit of money is employed during a period; T stands for the total of all transactions that takes place for money and so is related to the volume of production; and finally, P is general price level.

Rate of Return. A method of calculating the expected profitability of a particular capital investment based on the ratio of its expected profit to its capital cost.

Recession. A temporary failing off or dullness in economic activity, not sufficient to mark a major phase of a business cycle and hence not identified as a depression. So recession implies a much milder and short-lived setback in economic activities than a depression which is a regular phase of the business cycle.

Rediscount. To discount a bill of exchange which has previously been discounted. The discount houses in the money market, unable to borrow from the commercial banks, are sometimes, compelled to rediscount at the Central Bank some of the bills they are holding and which they have previously themselves discounted on behalf of drawers.

Reflation. It is the milder sort of inflation that accompanies the upward swing, of a trade cycle and, is associated with the easing of credit restrictions to encourage an expansion of production.

Regressive Tax. A tax which falls more heavily on people with low incomes than on those with high income. Some indirect taxes, especially those imposed on foodstuffs, 'tend to' be regressive, consumption of some commodities depending more on the size of the family than on income.

Repressed Inflation. An alternative term for 'suppressed inflation'.

Slump. The period of high unemployment. In trade cycles, slumps and booms alternate with one another, the average interval between one slump and the next being about seven years, with a boom always sandwiched between them. Features of a slump are declining production, increasing unemployment and falling prices and wages.

Time Deposit. American term for a bank deposit on deposit account.

Trade Cycle. The tendency of business activity to fluctuate regularly between booms and depressions. During the downswing of the cycle, there is a fall in prices (including wages)

and production and increase in unemployment; during upswing there is a rise in prices (including wages) and expansion of production and a fall in unemployment.

Transfer Earnings. The difference between the amount a factor of production would receive in its next best employment and its current earnings is, regarded as rent or transfer earnings.

Transfer Payments. In calculating national income, interest on government stocks, old age pensions, gifts, etc., are not included because these are merely transfers from one group of people to another.

Visible Balance. An alternative term for the 'balance of trade'.

BUSINESS AND MANAGEMENT

Ad Valorem. Taxes on commodities are calculated in two ways, either according to quantity or according to value. In the case of a specific tax, the amount of the tax to be paid depends on the amount of the commodity bought. In the case of an ad valorem tax, the amount to be paid is proportionate to the value of the commodity. Many stamp duties are ad valorem.

Amalgamation. When two firms, previously independent, get together to form one new business, an amalgamation or merger takes place. When merger occurs, the old firms completely lose their identity in the new organisation. If two limited companies amalgamate, share in the old companies will be exchanged for shares in the new company at an agreed ratio.

Amortisation. The provision for the gradual liquidation of a debt. A portion of the debt may be repaid at intervals along with the interest. In the case of a wasting asset, such as a mine, a portion of income may be set aside every year to provide a fund to cover the capital which will eventually have been used up. This practice is also known as amortisation.

Annuity. A sum of money increasing annually, in one or more instalments, for a period of time. In the case of a life annuity, the payment continues till death of the person to whom it has been awarded.

Appreciation. An increase in the value of something.

(i) of stocks and shares when their prices rise on the stock exchanges;

(ii) of a currency when its value increases in terms of other currencies;

(iii) of stocks held by manufacturers and merchants during a period of rising prices. When exchange rates are free to fluctuate, an appreciation of a country's currencies occurs if the value of its exports increases relatively to the value of its imports.

Assets. When the balance sheet of a business is drawn-up, everything which it owns at the time that has a money value is listed as an asset. Its fixed assets will include such tangible things as factory buildings, machinery, plant and equipment, etc. Current assets include stock, bills receivable and cash.

Authorised Capital. When a new company is formed, its application for registration is accompanied by a statement indicating the amount of capital with which it proposes to be registered. This is known as its nominal, registered, or authorised capital. The actual amount issued may be less than this, and so, the company will be able to increase its capital at a later date up to the full amount authorised with, further application to the Registrar of Companies.

Bad Debt. A debt that is difficult or impossible to recover.

Balance Sheet. A statement showing the assets and liabilities of a business at a certain date.

Bearer Bonds. Bonds which can be transferred from one person to another. At a particular point of time, the legal owner, as that of a bank note, is the holder of the bond.

Bill of Exchange. As legally defined, a Bill of Exchange is an unconditional order in writing signed by the person giving it requiring the person to whom it is addressed to pay on demand or at a stated future date a sum of money to a person or to the order of that person or to bearer. Most bills of exchange are drawn for three months after date, except cheques, which in effect, are 'sight bills'.

Bonded Warehouse. Customs duty is payable on many commodities on their arrival at the port. If the duty is not to be paid at once, special precautions must be taken to ensure that goods are not removed without payment of duty. At the ports bonded warehouses are provided where such goods can be stored until the duty is paid, goods being transferred from the ship and released from bond only under the supervision of customs officers.

Business Enterprise. See 'Firm'.

CAD. Cash Against Documents.

Capital Market. In contrast to the money market, which is the market for very short-term loans, the capital market is the market for medium-term and long-term loans. The money market also serves the needs of the discount market whereas the capital market serves the needs of industry and consumers, governments and legal authorities. Business firms often borrow their circulating capital from the commercial banks, raise their fixed capital by an issue of shares or from their own reserves, the shares being taken up by individuals, insurance companies, investment trusts and unit trusts.

Capital Movements. A term used in connection with the movement of capital from one country to another. Such movements are of two kinds:

(i) For the purpose of investing abroad;
(ii) Speculative short-term capital movements.

When capital is exported for foreign investment it has the same effect on the balance of payments of the country it leaves as payment for imports of goods and services. The interest and dividends paid on such investments provide invisible income to the country from which the capital was exported.

Capital Transfers. See 'capital movements'.

Cartel. A monopolistic type of organisation (of German origin) established for the purpose of restricting output of member firms in order to keep up the price of their product. A central selling organisation is envisaged, the member firms, however, retaining their independence except in so far as they agree to restrict their output.

CIF. Cost Insurance and Freight.

Circulating Capital. Also known as working or fluctuating capital, circulating capital of a business firm comprises the stock, cash in hand and any debts owing to it.

COD. Cash On Delivery.

Collateral Security. Banks generally require some kind of collateral security from the people to whom they extend loan or overdraft since in the case of a loan not being repaid the security can be disposed of. The collateral security may take the form of an insurance policy or marketable securities like stocks and shares, bills of lading, warehouse warrants or bills of property.

Confirmed Letter of Credit. A letter of credit payment which has been confirmed by the paying bank.

Contango. A stock exchange term meaning carry-over. A broker, who wishes to postpone settlement of a transaction to the following month(s) may do so on payment of interest on the sum due. The term contango is also used to mean the extra payment itself.

Cost and Freight (C & F). A quotation of a price for goods on these terms mean that the charge covers the price, ex-warehouse delivery to the docks and carriage as far as the port to which the goods are to be consigned but excluding insurance and delivery from the docks to the purchaser's premises.

Cost, Insurance and Freight (*CIF*). A quotation of price for goods covering the price ex-warehouse, and including delivery to the docks carriage and insurance as far as the port to which good are to be consigned, but excluding delivery from the docks to the purchaser's premises.

Countervailing Credit. If a foreign exporter, A, sells goods through an intermediary, B, to a merchant, C, in a third country, B may obtain a countervailing credit to cover payment from C if A has obtained a confirmed credit covering the transaction.

Countervailing Duty. An import duty imposed to protect a home industry against what is regarded as unfair foreign competition.

Credit Card. A card enabling the holder to obtain goods and services on credit from specified suppliers, including travel, and hotel accommodation upto an agreed maximum amount, payment being made monthly to the issuer of the card. Cards are issued, after the applicant's credit worthiness has been considered. The main advantage of credit cards is that they economise the use of cash. They can, however, be used to obtain extended credit upto the limit assigned to the holder.

Delivery Order. A document issued by the owner of goods stored in a warehouse entitling the person whose name appears on it to collect the goods specified. In the case of goods stored in a bonded warehouse, customs duty will have to be paid before the goods can be removed.

Demurrage. A term used in connection with the charter period, it is an extra charge the charterer has to pay per day for exceeding the period of charter originally agreed upon, and detaining the vessel beyond that time.

Discounted Cash Flow. A method of assessing and comparing alternative capital projects. Comparison is made of the present values of the flow of cash that can be expected from each capital project during the course of its existence.

Earnest Money. Also known as a token payment, it is a payment made to make binding the verbal agreement.

EFTA. European Free Trade Association.

Entrepreneur. A term used to denote the organising factor in production. The entrepreneur is responsible for such economic decisions as determining what to produce and how much to produce. He must also decide what method of production to adopt and in what proportions to combine his resources of land, labour and capital. The entrepreneur is also responsible for the management of business. Many economists recognise the entrepreneur as a fourth factor of production in addition to land, labour and capital.

Equities. A popular alternative term for ordinary shares.

Eurobonds. These bonds developed out of the Eurodollar market to provide longer term loans. They are generally issued by a consortium of banks and issuing houses, usually comprising some of the London merchant banks and the French, German, and Italian commercial banks, though not the British commercial banks. Eurobonds have proved to be particularly useful to American firms wishing to establish branches or subsidiaries in Europe, especially since the U.S. government tries to restrict foreign investment by American firms.

Eurodollars. Eurodollars are claims to U.S. dollars held by banks, business firms, etc., outside the Unites States. The market in Eurodollars dates from 1957, by which time the U.S. dollars were becoming more plentiful in Europe. The decline in the use of sterling as international currency was accompanied by an increasing use of the dollars. The Eurodollars market has become one of the largest international markets for short-term funds, for in addition to U.S. dollars, it also deals in other convertible currencies.

Exchange Rate. The rate at which one currency can be exchanged for another. When two countries are on the gold standard, the exchange rate will vary only between very narrow limits. On a system of freely fluctuating exchange rates, the rate varies from day to day.

Exim Bank. Abbreviation of Export-Import Bank.

Financial Year. A term used in Great Britain for fiscal purposes. It is the period of twelve months covered by the budget and running from 6th April of one year to 5th April of the next. The financial year of a business firm can run from any date, though many allow it to coincide with the calendar year.

Financier. A term widely applied to persons/agencies having something to do with finance, such as bankers, company promoters, issuing houses, discount houses, etc. In a more restricted form, it may refer to a firm which supplies finance for some particular transaction.

Fiscal Year. A term used in the United States for the period covered by the Budget. The American fiscal year starts on first July and ends on 30th of June, the following year. In some other countries like India, the fiscal year runs from April to March. In many countries, again, like India, the fiscal year and the financial year mean the same thing as against the calendar year which runs from January to December.

Floating Capital. An alternative term for working capital.

Forward Exchange. A means of hedging against fluctuation in the rate of exchange between different currencies. It is very similar to a 'futures market' of commodities. In addition to spot rate of exchange for current exchange transactions there are also rate for dealings at some future date—one month, two months or three months ahead.

Forward Marketing. Making a bargain for the purchase of goods to be delivered at a specified future date at a price agreed at the moment. Contracts for future delivery led to the development of 'future' as a means of hedging or ensuring against serious fluctuations in price as often the case with raw materials and other primary products.

Futures. Essentially a means by which merchants or other large buyers hedge against price fluctuations of a commodity—usually a raw material in which they deal.

Futures Market. A contract for delivery of specified quantity of a certain good or commodity at an agreed price at a particular future date, the price for immediate delivery being known as the spot price.

Hard Currency. A term used for a currency which is in short supply in relation to the payment for it by other countries. The term was applied particularly to the U.S. dollar in the years following the Second World War, there was huge demand for the export of the United States during this time when the countries of western Europe found it difficult to produce and export their own goods on account of the ruinous effect of the war on their internal economies.

Hire Purchase. The features of hire purchase are that usually a tax has to be paid and the rest of the purchase price is spread over a period—six months, two years, or sometimes even longer—the article being regarded as a property of the seller until the final payment has been made.

Horizontal Amalgamation. An amalgamation of firms at the same stage of production as, for example, a group of firms engaged in dyeing or in spinning.

Horizontal Integration. With reference to the structure of an industry, it means that there is a tendency for firms to specialise in single processes instead of undertaking the entire production of the commodity from start to finish.

Import Export Bank. A U.S. institution established in 1961 to provide group insurance for American exporters. It also provides cover against political risks. Its functions are somewhat similar to those of the Export Credits Guarantee Department of the British Board of Trade. Similar banks are also being established in developing countries like India.

Infant Industry Argument. An infant industry is one that has been newly established itself permanently. Such an industry should, therefore, be protected until it is firmly established. This is the infant industry argument.

Inventory. A term of American origin, now universally used in almost all countries, for the quantity of stock (or its value) held by a business. Thus, inventory appreciation is an alternative term for stock appreciation and similarly inventory control is the equivalent of stock control.

Invoice. A document used in business giving a complete summary of a transaction involving the sale of goods.

IOU. An acknowledgement of a debt made in writing and so long as it does not include a promise to pay, not subject to stamp duty. The name of the document is an abbreviation of the phrase—'I owe you'. It is not a negotiable instrument, but merely evidence of a debt.

Issued Capital. The annual amount of capital issued by a company and allotted in shares to investors. It may be the same or less than the authorised capital.

Issuing House. A financial undertaking which specialises in making public issues of shares on behalf of the public limited companies, the issuing house generally taking up the entire issue or a large part of it. In the case of a very large issue, an issuing house will distribute part of the issue among other firms willing to act as sub-underwriters.

Joint Stock (*or Limited*) *Companies*. This type of business unit developed out of the partnership for undertakings requiring a large amount of capital. The feature of the joint stock company is the division of the capital into shares of small denominations so that investors can invest small or large sums as they please, the profit being distributed in proportion to the numbers of shares held.

Kerb Market. A street market, generally relating to the carrying on of stock exchange transactions in the street after the exchange has closed.

Lateral Integration. This occurs when a firm branches out or absorbs other business engaged in producing commodities related in some ways to its own main products as occurs in the chemical industry with its great variety of modem products.

L/C. Abbreviation of *Letter of Credit*.

Ledger. A book-keeping term. It is the book in which are posted all entries made in books of original entry. A large firm keeps the ledger in several parts, as for example, Purchasers' Ledger, Sales Ledger, etc.

Limited Company. A modern name for joint stock company.

Limited Letter of Credit. A letter of credit payable only in the towns listed on it. The issuing bank can then inform its agents or correspondents in these towns and supply them with copies of the signature of the payee who will then not require a letter of indication as would, otherwise, be necessary.

Limited Liability. The liability of shareholders in a company, public or private is limited to the amount they have paid for fully paid-up shares, or to the amount outstanding on shares purchased which were not fully paid.

Line Relationship. In any large industrial organisation, delegation of duties is essential. The term line is used to indicate the line of authority as with different ranks in the armed forces, where the line of authorities is clear. Similarly, in a workshop, there might be the works manager, foreman, charge-hands and workmen.

Liquid Assets. These are assets either in the form of money or in a form that can easily be turned into money. The liquid assets of a bank are cash (coin, notes and balances at the central bank), money at call or short notice and bills discounted.

Liquidated Damages. The amount stated in a contract as compensation to be paid for non-fulfilment of the contract.

Liquidation. The act of terminating or winding up of a company, usually because of its insolvency. Liquidation may be compulsory as a result of the court order or voluntary following a resolution of the shareholders.

Liquid Capital. Capital in the form of money.

Merger. See 'Amalgamation'.

Middleman. Any wholesaler, merchant, broker or agent who has to do with the distribution of goods between their place of production and the manufacturer (in the case of raw materials) or the retailer (in the case of foodstuffs and manufactured goods).

Mortgage. A deed showing that money has been borrowed with land or property as collateral security. Building societies assist people to buy house by lending a portion of the purchase money, the property being mortgaged with the society until the loan with interest has been repaid. The borrower is known as the mortgager and the lender as the mortgagee.

Net Working Capital. The excess of current assets over the current liabilities of a firms.

Net Worth. The excess over liabilities as shown by a firm's balance sheet, i.e. the capital owned by a business.

Ordinary Shares. Often known as Equities, these shares receive the residue to the distributed profit after commitments on preference shares and annual shares carrying priority have been made. Thus, dividend on ordinary shares vary with the profitability of the business. Holders of ordinary shares are the owners of business and show rights proportionate to their holdings.

Paid-up Shares. Shares are fully paid-up when the full amount has been paid. Most shares have to be fully paid for on their being issued. Sometime shares are only partly paid-up, the company being able to call for the balance to be paid wherever it requires this additional capital.

Prime Rate. An American term for Bank Rate.

Profit Sharing. A system of wage payments by which a firm attempts to give its employees a more direct interest in its prosperity, a portion of the profit being set aside for distribution among the employees in proportion to their wages or according to their length of service with the firm.

Redeemable Bonds (*or Stock*). Government bonds, debentures or preference shares which are repayable at par at a certain date or at some time between two stated dates.

Registered Capital. An alternative term for authorised capital.

SDR. Special Drawing Right.

Sinking Fund. A fund established for the future redemption of a debt. It was formerly customary to build-up a sinking fund by paying into it a certain sum each year from government revenue for the eventual redemption of the national debt.

Super-Tax. The original name of surtax when it was first introduced.

Terminal Market. An alternative term for a futures or forward market.

Trading Profit. An alternative term for gross profit.

UNCTAD. United Nations Conference on Trade and Development. It was established to consider how best to help development of nations.

Unfavourable Balance. A term used for a debit balance in the balance of payments or balance of trade.

Value-Added Tax. A tax levied on the value of each of the processes carried out by a business.

Vertical Combination. See 'vertical integration'.

Vertical Integration. Vertical integration means an amalgamation of firms at different stages of production.

Visible Balance. An alternative term for 'balance of trade'.

VLCC. Very large crude carrier.

Voting Shares. Shares whose owners are entitled to vote at the annual general meeting (AGM) of the company.

Wall Street. The New York Stock Exchange.

WB. World Bank.

WCO. World Customs Organisation.

WHO. World Health Organisation.

WTO. World Trade Organisation.

Z Chart. A chart with a variable (usually sales or production of an item) plotted on the vertical axis against time on the horizontal axis.

Zero-base Budgeting. A system of budgeting in which managers have to assign priority ratings to their various budget requests.

Zero-Sum Game. A situation in game theory in which one player's gain equals the joint loss of all the other players.

Index